David C. Cook
Bible Lesson
Commentary

The Essential Study Companion *for* Every Disciple

David C. Cook
Bible Lesson
Commentary

KJV

David ⓒ Cook®

transforming lives together

DAVID C. COOK KJV BIBLE LESSON COMMENTARY 2012–2013
Published by David C Cook
4050 Lee Vance View
Colorado Springs, CO 80918 U.S.A.

David C Cook Distribution Canada
55 Woodslee Avenue, Paris, Ontario, Canada N3L 3E5

David C Cook U.K., Kingsway Communications
Eastbourne, East Sussex BN23 6NT, England

The graphic circle C logo is a registered trademark of David C Cook.

Unless otherwise noted, Scripture quotations are taken from the King James Version
(Public Domain); or the New Revised Standard Version Bible, copyright 1989, Division
of Christian Education of the National Council of the Churches of Christ in the
United States of America. Used by permission. All rights reserved.

Lessons based on *International Sunday School Lessons: The International Bible Lessons for
Christian Teaching*, © 2009 by the Committee on the Uniform Series.

ISBN 978-1-4347-0270-8

© 2012 David C Cook

Written and edited by Dan Lioy, PhD
The Team: John Blase, Doug Schmidt, Renada Arens, and Karen Athen
Cover Design: Amy Konyndyk
Cover Photo: iStockphoto

Printed in the United States of America
First Edition 2012

1 2 3 4 5 6 7 8 9 10

022712

CONTENTS

SEPTEMBER, OCTOBER, NOVEMBER 2012
A LIVING FAITH

UNIT I: WHAT IS FAITH?

UNIT II: WHO UNDERSTANDS FAITH?

UNIT III: WHERE DOES FAITH TAKE US?

DECEMBER 2012, JANUARY, FEBRUARY 2013
JESUS IS LORD

UNIT I: VICTORY IN JESUS

UNIT II: EXALTING CHRIST

UNIT III: IMITATING JESUS

CONTENTS

MARCH, APRIL, MAY 2013
BEYOND THE PRESENT TIME

UNIT I: THE KINGDOM OF GOD

UNIT II: RESURRECTION HOPE

UNIT III: A CALL TO HOLY LIVING

JUNE, JULY, AUGUST 2013
GOD'S PEOPLE WORSHIP

UNIT I: THE PROPHET AND PRAISE

UNIT II: WORSHIPING IN JERUSALEM AGAIN (EZRA)

UNIT III: WORSHIPING IN JERUSALEM AGAIN (NEHEMIAH)

The 12-year-old sat polishing his saxophone a few minutes before the morning worship service. That Sunday he was playing in the wind ensemble. He could hardly wait for the opportunity to arrive.

"What a shine on that instrument!" the group's director commented.

"Thank you!" the boy replied. "My grandfather's here this morning, and he's deaf. I thought if I put on a real good shine, he could at least enjoy the glow."

Somewhere that boy had stumbled upon one of the great foundations of human relations—the ability to care about others and to anticipate their needs.

The lessons presented in this year's edition of the David C. Cook Bible Lesson Commentary are taken from selected portions of the Old and New Testaments. We will learn not only about God's power, but also about His ability to meet the humblest of needs. The Lord played His song of salvation (in a manner of speaking) to even the most tone deaf and even the most hard of heart.

Isn't that one of the gifts we bring to our service for the Lord Jesus? It's to be patient and helpful when someone misunderstands us. It's to have such love for others that we do all we can to let them know about the Savior. It's to polish our communication style so that even the most unteachable person learns.

The joy of telling others about the Messiah beckons. Let our saxophones be shiny. Let our message glow!

Your fellow learner at the feet of the Master Teacher,
Dan Lioy

USING THE *DAVID C. COOK KJV BIBLE LESSON COMMENTARY* WITH MATERIAL FROM OTHER PUBLISHERS

Sunday school materials from the following denominations and publishers follow the International Sunday School Lesson outlines (sometimes known as the Uniform Series). Because *David C. Cook's KJV Bible Lesson Commentary* (formerly *Tarbell's)* follows the same ISSL outlines, you can use the *Commentary* as an excellent teacher resource to supplement the materials from these publishing houses.

Nondenominational:
   Standard Publishing—*Adult*
   Urban Ministries—*All ages*

Denominational:
   Advent Christian General Conference—*Adult*
   American Baptist (Judson Press)—*Adult*
   Church of God in Christ (Church of God in Christ Publishing House)—*Adult*
   Church of Christ Holiness—*Adult*
   Church of God (Warner Press)—*Adult*
   Church of God by Faith—*Adult*
   National Baptist Convention of America (Boyd)—*All ages*
   National Primitive Baptist Convention—*Adult*
   Presbyterian Church (U.S.A.) (Bible Discovery Series—Presbyterian Publishing House or P.R.E.M.)—*Adult*
   Progressive National Baptist Convention—*Adult*
   Union Gospel Press—*All ages*
   United Holy Church of America—*Adult*
   United Methodist Church (Cokesbury)—*All ages*

FAITH CALLS FOR PERSEVERANCE

BACKGROUND SCRIPTURE: Hebrews 10:19-31
DEVOTIONAL READING: Romans 5:1-5

Key Verse: Let us hold fast the profession of our faith without wavering; (for he is faithful that promised). Hebrews 10:23.

KING JAMES VERSION

HEBREWS 10:19 Having therefore, brethren, boldness to enter into the holiest by the blood of Jesus, 20 By a new and living way, which he hath consecrated for us, through the veil, that is to say, his flesh; 21 And having an high priest over the house of God; 22 Let us draw near with a true heart in full assurance of faith, having our hearts sprinkled from an evil conscience, and our bodies washed with pure water. 23 Let us hold fast the profession of our faith without wavering; (for he is faithful that promised;) 24 And let us consider one another to provoke unto love and to good works: 25 Not forsaking the assembling of ourselves together, as the manner of some is; but exhorting one another: and so much the more, as ye see the day approaching. 26 For if we sin wilfully after that we have received the knowledge of the truth, there remaineth no more sacrifice for sins, 27 But a certain fearful looking for of judgment and fiery indignation, which shall devour the adversaries. 28 He that despised Moses' law died without mercy under two or three witnesses: 29 Of how much sorer punishment, suppose ye, shall he be thought worthy, who hath trodden under foot the Son of God, and hath counted the blood of the covenant, wherewith he was sanctified, an unholy thing, and hath done despite unto the Spirit of grace? 30 For we know him that hath said, Vengeance belongeth unto me, I will recompense, saith the Lord. And again, The Lord shall judge his people. 31 It is a fearful thing to fall into the hands of the living God.

NEW REVISED STANDARD VERSION

HEBREWS 10:19 Therefore, my friends, since we have confidence to enter the sanctuary by the blood of Jesus, 20 by the new and living way that he opened for us through the curtain (that is, through his flesh), 21 and since we have a great priest over the house of God, 22 let us approach with a true heart in full assurance of faith, with our hearts sprinkled clean from an evil conscience and our bodies washed with pure water. 23 Let us hold fast to the confession of our hope without wavering, for he who has promised is faithful. 24 And let us consider how to provoke one another to love and good deeds, 25 not neglecting to meet together, as is the habit of some, but encouraging one another, and all the more as you see the Day approaching.

26 For if we willfully persist in sin after having received the knowledge of the truth, there no longer remains a sacrifice for sins, 27 but a fearful prospect of judgment, and a fury of fire that will consume the adversaries. 28 Anyone who has violated the law of Moses dies without mercy "on the testimony of two or three witnesses." 29 How much worse punishment do you think will be deserved by those who have spurned the Son of God, profaned the blood of the covenant by which they were sanctified, and outraged the Spirit of grace? 30 For we know the one who said, "Vengeance is mine, I will repay." And again, "The Lord will judge his people." 31 It is a fearful thing to fall into the hands of the living God.

HOME BIBLE READINGS

BACKGROUND

The Letter to the Hebrews teaches that the Lord Jesus, as the mediator between God and humanity, has established a new and better covenant than the old one based on the Mosaic law. The new covenant is better precisely because it is established on "better promises" (8:6). If the first covenant had sufficiently met the needs of people and had adequately provided for their salvation, then there would have been no need for a new covenant to replace it (vs. 7). But the old covenant was insufficient and inadequate. It wasn't adequate in bringing people to God, and therefore a new covenant had to be established.

As Hebrews 8:10-12 and 10:15-17 reveal (see Jer. 31:33-34), the new covenant would be inward and dynamic. God's Word would have a place inside the minds and hearts of His people. The old covenant had been inscribed on tablets of stone and was external. But in regard to the new covenant, God vowed that His teachings would be internalized by His people. The new covenant would also provide a way for believers to have an intimate relationship with God. While Jeremiah echoed several Old Testament promises (see Gen. 17:7; Exod. 6:7; Lev. 26:12), the life, death, and resurrection of the Lord Jesus opened a completely new avenue for human beings to relate to their heavenly Father. Because of the salvation the Son provided, all believers could enter into God's presence.

NOTES ON THE PRINTED TEXT

Virtually every Bible interpreter divides Hebrews into two parts: 1:1–10:18 and 10:19–13:25. This division is based on a shift in the author's emphasis that begins at 10:19, where his heavy doctrinal teaching was, for the most part, concluded. Now he instructed his readers on how to apply and live out the doctrines of the Christian faith that he had taught them up to this point in his letter. Based on the Son's saving work at Calvary, the author reminded his readers that they could now enter the Father's presence. To many of the Hebrews, this may have been a bold statement. As far as they had known, only the Jewish high priest was permitted into the Most Holy Place. Yet the author issued an open invitation to all believers to confidently enter the presence of God because of the "blood of Jesus" (vs. 19).

The author explained that the access the Son inaugurated into the Father's presence was "new and living" (vs. 20). The way was fresh in that it was based on the new covenant established by Jesus' sacrifice. And it was always present because it depended on the Son Himself, our eternally living Lord. In Jesus' day, the separating curtain between the Holy Place and the Most Holy Place in the Jerusalem temple was 60 feet high by 30 feet wide and about 5 inches thick. Obviously, such a curtain could not have been torn easily, and yet when Jesus died, "the veil of the temple was rent in twain from the top to the bottom" (Matt. 27:51; see also Mark 15:38; Luke 23:45). In one sense, until that curtain was torn, access into God's presence had been limited to the Jewish high priest. But just as that curtain was torn, so Jesus' body was broken on the cross for us. As viewed symbolically by the author of Hebrews, the Son's sacrificial death was the way by which all believers were given access to the Father.

Not only do we have a spiritual sacrifice enabling us to enter the Father's presence, but we also have a great High Priest "over the house of God" (Heb. 10:21). Scripture reveals that the Son became a human being so that He could purchase our salvation through His death on the cross. Nonetheless, He still reigned supreme over all God's people. The author of the epistle had made it clear that after the Son completed His work of salvation, He returned to heaven, where He now sat at the place of highest honor, namely, the right hand of God the Father (see 1:3). From there the Son interceded for us before the Father.

In light of what Jesus had done for believers, the author urged his readers to be proactive in living for the Messiah. Because of our provisions from the Son and our position in Him, we should claim what He has promised to us. In essence, the writer said that Jesus' work of salvation should spur His people into action. Moreover, in the exhortations that followed, the author numbered himself with his readers. Indeed, three times in 10:22-25 he used the phase "let us" to introduce ways in which all believers were to respond to the Messiah's work.

The author invited his readers to draw near to God, and he encouraged them to do so with a "true heart" (vs. 22) and with the "full assurance" that "faith" brought. The author knew that it was important for God's people to be right inwardly when they entered the Father's holy presence. Therefore, the author stressed that only through faith in the Son could the redeemed be made acceptable and "draw near" to the Lord. Under the old covenant, the priests were made ritually pure by being sprinkled with blood. The writer made use of this Old Testament imagery when he said that believers were cleansed by having their "hearts sprinkled" and their "bodies washed." In this analogy, some think the author was referring to water baptism, while others say he meant an inner spiritual cleansing of the conscience from the guilt of wrongdoing. In either case, when we trust in the Son, our sins are pardoned and we are free to commune with the Father.

The author of Hebrews encouraged his readers to hold firmly to the hope in the Son they confessed (vs. 23). The writer also urged them to do so without doubt or hesitation. They could depend on God, for He was resolutely faithful to His promises. Therefore, even when believers were tempted to give up their Christian beliefs and return to their former ways of thinking and acting, they were to resist such enticements by confidently waiting for the fulfillment of God's promises. Moreover, the author of Hebrews encouraged his readers to provoke their fellow believers into loving each other toward doing good works (vs. 24). Admittedly, this would not be easy for them to do. Even so, they had plenty of incentive when they realized how much external pressure they encountered to renounce the Savior.

Outside influences were so corrosive that some of these believers were beginning to abandon their corporate times of worship. Verse 25 is often used out of context by those anxious to goad Christians into regular church attendance. Certainly, we should not give up meeting together. However, those to whom the author of Hebrews was referring were not just missing a worship service to go fishing on a nice summer Sunday. Rather, as verses 26-31 make clear, they were nonparticipants in church who were in danger of apostatizing. The latter circumstance is why the author of Hebrews exhorted his readers to get in the habit of encouraging each other. They were especially to do so as the day of Jesus' return and judgment approached.

In verse 26, the writer alluded to the sacrificial system under the old covenant, which made offerings for those who sinned unintentionally (see Num. 15:22-29; Heb. 5:2). For all that, no sacrifice was prescribed for those who sinned defiantly or blasphemously (see Num. 15:30-31). In a similar way, apostasy was a deliberate defection from the living God. Those tempted with committing apostasy were people who understood the nature of Jesus' saving work, had been active in the church, and yet rejected the Messiah. By continuing their deliberate sin of renouncing the Lord, they were left with no other "sacrifice" (Heb. 10:26) for their transgressions. In essence, they had spurned their only means of redemption, and therefore had no other person to whom they could appeal for forgiveness. The writer's words were filled with warnings of God's wrathful "judgment" (vs. 27). The author referred to the latter as a "fearful" expectation and a "fiery indignation" that would incinerate those who opposed God (see Isa. 26:11; Zeph. 1:18). In short, apostates would be punished for bearing sins for which they refused to be pardoned.

In Hebrews 10:28-29, the author used an illustration from the Old Testament to emphasize the seriousness of the apostates' situation. In particular, those who rejected the Mosaic law were executed "without mercy" (vs. 28) based on the testimony offered by "two or three witnesses" (see Deut. 17:6). The writer reasoned that since such severity existed under the old covenant, even more severity under the new covenant would fall on those who were guilty of doing the following: treating the "Son of God" (Heb. 10:29) with contempt; profaning the Messiah's blood, which He shed to purify the apostates from sin; and insulting the Spirit, who brought God's mercy to the defectors.

The author of Hebrews appealed to the Old Testament to reinforce his assertions. The first quotation in verse 30 is from Deuteronomy 32:35, in which Moses said that God's vengeance against His enemies was a divine prerogative. The second quotation was from Deuteronomy 32:36 and Psalm 135:14. The writer of Hebrews wanted to leave no doubt in his readers' minds about God's intent to punish sinners. In case his readers did not yet regard God's judgment with proper trepidation, the writer appended a final dire warning. He said it was a terrifying prospect to be judged by the "living God" (10:31). The dread, of course, was for the unbeliever. Christians looked forward to receiving God's mercy and grace. But for a hardened, incorrigible apostate, falling into the hands of the eternal Lord would indeed be a horrible experience.

SUGGESTIONS TO TEACHERS

We live today under the provisions of the new covenant. We continue to enjoy all its advantages. As you highlight these truths, you might want to contrast our present interaction with God with the less extensive level of fellowship enjoyed by those who lived under the earlier covenant. Lead your students in gratitude for God's generosity. One way we can show gratitude for God's new covenant gifts is to enjoy them to the fullest! In particular, there is . . .

1. GREATER INTIMACY WITH GOD. Through God's Spirit, all new covenant believers can know the Lord in a manner similar to and even more personally than how we know one another. In the days before Jesus came, the nation of Israel collectively could know God, but, with rare exceptions, individuals tended to know about God only through what they had heard. Under the new covenant, God has come to live not only with but also in His people.

2. GREATER KNOWLEDGE OF GOD. Through the incarnation of Jesus and the indwelling of the Holy Spirit, first-century Christians could know more about God and also know God Himself. In addition to these blessings, later generations of Christians also gained access to the complete written New Testament (which was only gradually collected and distributed). From this we see that God has given us many ways to know Him.

3. GREATER FORGIVENESS FROM HIM. God offered forgiveness to Old Testament people, but the associated ritual of animal sacrifice dreadfully complicated the process. Now through Jesus, God's people have more direct access to Him and to His grace. Not only do we receive forgiveness, but through the Spirit, we can receive assurance of that forgiveness and our resulting relationship with God.

4. GREATER CERTAINTY OF GOD'S ETERNAL FAITHFULNESS. During the period of the old covenant, the Israelites struggled to know God. As the prophets began to speak about a new day coming, their hearers might have rejoiced in what God was going to do, but generations died not seeing that new day. They might have heard God's promise of a new covenant, but they died under the old covenant. Today, we know we live in the days of God's new covenant. The covenant established through the Messiah will never change!

■ **TOPIC:** Steadfast Determination

■ **QUESTIONS:** 1. Why is it possible for believers to enter God's presence with confidence? 2. In what sense is Jesus the believers' great High Priest? 3. What are some excuses believers might give for not wanting to worship with other Christians? 4. What arguments did the writer of Hebrews use to urge His readers to remain faithful to the Savior? 5. What are some ways believers can deal with temptations they face to turn away from, rather than follow, the Lord?

■ **ILLUSTRATIONS:**

The Reason to Be Faithful. When we marry, we show that we have more than enough reasons to be faithful to our spouses. And the longer we are married, the stronger those reasons become, simply because we get to know one another better. Love is the best reason to be steadfast in our commitment.

The Letter to the Hebrews gives us a number of reasons to be resolute in our devotion to Jesus. The writer of this epistle did not tell us to grow in our love for Jesus. Instead, the author told us to consider the fact that Jesus is a "high priest over the house of God" (10:21). The more we fill our minds with Jesus' greatness, the more we will love Him and be faithful to Him.

The New Surpasses the Old. Years ago, when in I was third grade, I typed my first research paper. I recall pecking away at the keys on my mother's manual typewriter. Beginning with that ancient model, I can remember several typewriters I have known—my own first manual that helped me through college, the electric typewriter I owned that took me through graduate school, and a later model that I bought while serving as a youth pastor. That last typewriter printed by means of a ball rather than keys.

In their time, typewriters served me well. On rare occasions, when filling in hard copy forms, I still wish I owned one. But typewriters have now been surpassed. When I consider all a modern computer enables me to accomplish, do I ever think about discarding my word processor for even the best of typewriters? Not for a moment!

Throughout the Letter to the Hebrews, the writer compared Jesus with a number of Old Testament luminaries. As inspiring as these individuals and institutions once were, they paled in comparison to the glory of the Son. The author noted that Jesus is the great High Priest "over the house of God" (10:21). That is why the writer encouraged his readers to choose the eternal salvation offered by the Messiah, even if it had trials and tribulations, rather than to renounce Him for what prevailed during the Old Testament era.

The Persecution. The writer of Hebrews urged his readers to persevere in their faith (10:23) and encourage one another to be faithful in their Christian service (vs. 24).

They could remain resolute, for their hope of final redemption in the Son was "approaching" (vs. 25).

In 1979, the Marxist government in Ethiopia forced out all missionaries, giving them only a 24-hour notice. During the following 10 years, Ethiopian Christians went through a period that they simply call "The Persecution." Enemies of the faith murdered, imprisoned, or exiled Ethiopian church leaders. The pressure was so severe that a few renounced their faith. Most churches were forced to close. Trying to survive in extreme poverty under a hostile regime, and challenged even by forces of nature, most Ethiopian believers tenaciously clung to their faith in Christ.

In 1995, a small group of American Christians was able to visit Ethiopia. They found people often living in abject poverty, some communities dwelling like living fossils in the Stone Age, all subject to the ravages of curable diseases like pneumonia. The visitors also found these Christians struggling against tribal religions, powerful witch doctors, and a popular belief in demonic possession.

Despite all these handicaps, and regardless of the acute shortage of leaders (in one district, there were only 10 pastors to serve 70 congregations of 20,000 believers), the churches were filled. Children, young people, parents, and elderly members were all changed by the power of Christ and the presence of a loving church family. They witnessed to their faith in the Son, especially as they told their stories and sung their hymns of praise, accompanied by homemade flutes, drums, stringed instruments, and gourds filled with dried beans.

| **FOR YOUTH** | ■ **TOPIC:** Got Faith? |

■ **QUESTIONS:** 1. In what sense is the way Jesus opened for believers to enter God's presence "new and living" (Heb. 10:20)? 2. What are some reasons for believers to draw near to God? 3. How might the Lord use you to encourage other believers to be faithful in serving Him? 4. What attitudes did some of the early Christians have during times of persecution and suffering? Why do you think they felt this way? 5. How can believers avoid treating Jesus' redemptive work in a profane way?

■ **ILLUSTRATIONS:**

Why Have Faith? If we had to pick one reason to have faith in Christ, what would it be? Would we choose His sovereign power and glory, His upholding the universe, or His being better than the angels? Probably not. We would declare our loyalty to Him because He is our "high priest over the house of God" (Heb. 10:21).

Behind this truth is the fact that the Son died on the cross so that we could have free and full access to the Father (vs. 20). Of course, our wickedness and our desire to have things our own way were the reasons Jesus had to sacrifice Himself on Calvary. How could Jesus love us that much? The fact is that He did and therefore we do not ever want to betray Him. He paid too much for us to turn our backs on Him.

Unique Gifts Used for God. Hebrews 10:19-21 provides us a wonderful example of using the Greek language with great stylistic effect. We don't know who wrote this letter, but we do know that he must have been a highly educated person. When the author became a Christian, the Lord Jesus did not ask him to leave his education and talents behind. Instead, the Savior called him to use his thinking and writing abilities for the glory of God and the growth of the church.

Perhaps you know people who faithfully offer their skills and experience to the Redeemer for His use. For example, Joy piloted a casino boat in Baton Rouge, Louisiana, before she heard the Son's call on her life. Today Joy gives her time ministering to riverboat captains and crews. Joy knows what it's like to spend entire months away on the river. From her experience, she can minister empathetically to others who face that situation.

There's also Barb, who was a computer web-design specialist. She now gives half her time to building and maintaining a Christian website. Her site offers all kinds of information enabling believers to minister better to nearby people of other ethnic groups.

As you anticipate your future, how do you think the Lord might use your unique gifts to glorify Him and help others?

Drifting Away. Several years before my friend Brad met his wife, Kathy, she helped lead a church youth group. One youth group trip took several leaders and teens to Atlanta. While there, everyone spent an afternoon at Stone Mountain Lake. Kathy had never sailed before but decided she would take this opportunity. She pooled money with some of the kids and rented a small sailboat. The owner gave instructions he thought adequate.

Looking back, across many years, Kathy insists that the boat had problems and that the owner had no right to rent them a defective sailboat. Perhaps the problem lay with the boaters rather than the boat. We will never know for sure.

In any case, you have already figured out what happened. Out on the lake, a good breeze was blowing, but not taking Kathy in the direction she wanted. Can you imagine how the rest of the group must have laughed as they watched Kathy and her friends being towed back to shore? They had no intention of drifting away, but that's what they had done.

Hebrews 10:26-31 contains a sobering warning about allowing ourselves to move away from the faith. We discover that when we ignore our devotion to the Son, we will eventually find ourselves in spiritual peril. Thankfully, the Lord Jesus is always present to help us remain faithful to Him.

FAITH IS ASSURANCE

BACKGROUND SCRIPTURE: Hebrews 11:1-7; Psalm 46:1-11
DEVOTIONAL READING: Psalm 27:1-6

2

Key Verse: Now faith is the substance of things hoped
for, the evidence of things not seen. Hebrews 11:1.

KING JAMES VERSION

HEBREWS 11:1 Now faith is the substance of things hoped for, the evidence of things not seen. 2 For by it the elders obtained a good report. 3 Through faith we understand that the worlds were framed by the word of God, so that things which are seen were not made of things which do appear. . . . 6 But without faith it is impossible to please him: for he that cometh to God must believe that he is, and that he is a rewarder of them that diligently seek him. . . .

PSALM 46:1 God is our refuge and strength, a very present help in trouble. 2 Therefore will not we fear, though the earth be removed, and though the mountains be carried into the midst of the sea; 3 Though the waters thereof roar and be troubled, though the mountains shake with the swelling thereof. Selah. . . .

8 Come, behold the works of the LORD, what desolations he hath made in the earth. 9 He maketh wars to cease unto the end of the earth; he breaketh the bow, and cutteth the spear in sunder; he burneth the chariot in the fire. 10 Be still, and know that I am God: I will be exalted among the heathen, I will be exalted in the earth. 11 The LORD of hosts is with us; the God of Jacob is our refuge. Selah.

NEW REVISED STANDARD VERSION

HEBREWS 11:1 Now faith is the assurance of things hoped for, the conviction of things not seen. 2 Indeed, by faith our ancestors received approval. 3 By faith we understand that the worlds were prepared by the word of God, so that what is seen was made from things that are not visible. . . . 6 And without faith it is impossible to please God, for whoever would approach him must believe that he exists and that he rewards those who seek him. . . .

PSALM 46:1 God is our refuge and strength,
   a very present help in trouble.
2 Therefore we will not fear, though the earth should
      change,
   though the mountains shake in the heart of the sea;
3 though its waters roar and foam,
   though the mountains tremble with its tumult.
      Selah . . .
8 Come, behold the works of the LORD;
   see what desolations he has brought on the earth.
9 He makes wars cease to the end of the earth;
   he breaks the bow, and shatters the spear;
   he burns the shields with fire.
10 "Be still, and know that I am God!
   I am exalted among the nations,
   I am exalted in the earth."
11 The LORD of hosts is with us;
   the God of Jacob is our refuge. Selah

HOME BIBLE READINGS

Monday, September 3	Mark 10:13-16	*The Trusting Child*
Tuesday, September 4	2 Chronicles 14:2-12	*The Trust of the Weak*
Wednesday, September 5	Psalm 3	*The Prayer of Trust*
Thursday, September 6	Psalm 4	*The Security of Trust*
Friday, September 7	Psalm 27:1-6	*The Confidence of Trust*
Saturday, September 8	Psalm 27:7-14	*The Patience of Trust*
Sunday, September 9	Hebrews 11:1-3, 6;	
	Psalm 46:1-3, 8-11	*The Certain Refuge*

BACKGROUND

In this week's lesson, "faith" is a key theological term. In one sense, it refers to a person's trust in God. In another sense, it is used in the New Testament to refer to the body of truths held by followers of Christ. Belief, or faith, can be understood as having four recognizable elements. First is cognition, an awareness of the facts; second is comprehension, an understanding of the facts; third is conviction, an acceptance of the facts; and fourth is commitment, trust in a trustworthy object.

Popular opinion sees faith as irrational. It is supposedly believing in something even when your mind tells you not to. In contrast, the biblical concept of faith includes both reason and experience. Such faith, however, is not limited to what we can see. It makes unseen spiritual realities perceivable, not by willing them into existence, but by a settled conviction that what God has said about them is true.

NOTES ON THE PRINTED TEXT

In Hebrews 10:38, the writer quoted Habakkuk 2:4 to stress that the righteous person lives by faith. Based on that statement, Hebrews 11 is devoted to portraying the lives of Old Testament heroes who lived by faith. As result, chapter 11 is probably the best-loved portion in Hebrews and is often called "The Hall of Faith." It furnishes us with brief biographies of belief and encourages us to fortify our faith in God as many who have gone before us have done. The original readers of Hebrews may have wondered if it would be easier simply to fade back into their former Jewish traditions and religious practices. To them the author gave a description of biblical faith. He said that faith is a present and continuing reality. It is the confident assurance that gives substance to what we hope for (vs. 1). Faith is also the evidence for our conviction of the certainty of "things not seen."

The writer implied by his remarks that there are realities for which there is no visible evidence; and yet those realities are no less true. It is through faith that we know those realities exist, especially God's promise of salvation, which cannot be physically seen or felt. How, then, can one recognize the presence of faith in the life of a believer? The author appealed to a long list of biblical examples to answer this question. God commended them precisely because of their faith in Him (vs. 2). There are two problems some people have with the past. They either disregard it or forget it. Hebrews 11 stresses the importance of remembering the past and living by faith. We discover from the testimony of other believers who have gone before us that we can remain faithful to the Lord—despite the hardships we might be experiencing—because He will remain faithful to us.

The writer said it was the faith of the Old Testament saints that made them pleasing to God. Their trust in the Lord was well founded, for He is the Creator and Ruler of the universe (see Ps. 146:6). We perceive with the mind that the temporal ages were set in order by the spoken "word of God" (Heb. 11:3). Biblical faith also enables us to recognize and accept the truth that what is seen was made out of what cannot be seen. Despite all appearances to the contrary and despite all of the naturalistic explanations about the origin of the universe, God gave existence to the cosmos. In verse 6, the author stressed that "without faith" it is impossible to enjoy the Lord's favor. Those who approach Him must first believe that He is the true and living God. Moreover, they must accept the fact that He rewards those who "diligently seek him." Put another way, we must believe that the Lord both exists and cares for us. Here we see that faith is so foundational to the Christian life that one cannot be in a relationship with God apart from it.

Psalm 46 is one of the "Songs of Zion" (along with Pss. 48, 76, 84, 87, and 122) due to its confident affirmation of God as the faith community's source of help and strength in times of trouble. The psalm's heading reads "to the chief Musician." This suggests the piece was originally meant to be a part of the worship liturgy performed in the temple by the leader of the Levitical choir. The members of the latter included the "sons of Korah." In 46:1, "refuge" translates a Hebrew noun that denotes a place of shelter from rain, storm, or other perils. Also, "strength" renders a noun that points to what is fortified and secure. Together these words depict God as the believers' impenetrable defense.

Regardless of the adverse situation or anguishing circumstance, the Lord is always ready to help. Psalm 9:9 likewise declares that God provides safety for the oppressed and is a refuge in times of trouble. Moreover, we learn in 37:39 that the Lord protects the faithful even in the most challenging dilemmas. According to 61:3, God is comparable to a strong tower where the upright may flee when danger lurks. Even when the health of believers begins to fail and their spirit weakens, the Lord empowers them to cope with seemingly overwhelming conditions (see 71:20-23). Because He is their place of safety, they can find rest in the shadow of the Almighty (see 91:1-2) and have their eternal needs fully met (see 142:5).

Because the believers' stability is found in God, the faith community deliberately chooses to forsake fear and completely trust in Him. A series of convulsions of nature are described in Psalm 46:2-3. Some think these probably were meant to symbolize the ferocity of a war. Another option is that a doomsday scenario involving naturally occurring disasters is being portrayed. The latter included a violent series of earthquakes that cause the mountains (the epitome of all that is stable and enduring) to crumble into the sea (vs. 2). Furthermore, there's a succession of massive tsunamis that cause ocean-sized tidal waves to inundate the land. The roar and foam of the water is so intense that it even seems to cause the mountains to be shaken by the violence (vs. 3). The creation myths of many ancient Near Eastern cultures told about gods who subdued a chaotic ocean and formed the world from it. These people viewed large bodies of water as evil. While Israelite religion denied the reality of such myths, God's people nonetheless were familiar with them. Thus it was natural for the psalmists to compare encroaching evil with water that seems to engulf the land.

The imagery of upheaval introduced in verses 2-3 reappears in verse 6. This time, however, it is used with respect to nations and kingdoms of the world being locked in mortal conflict. Fallen humanity and its leaders might rage, but their dominions are doomed to one day fail. Moreover, when chaos ensues, their fiefdoms will crumble. God is the cause of this turmoil. The poet depicts His thunderous shout as the battle cry uttered by a mighty warrior that terrifies the nations and causes the kingdoms to be shaken (see Pss. 18:13; 68:33). In point of fact, at the sound of His voice, the entire planet dissolves (see Amos 9:5).

Psalm 46:7 reveals God to be full of power and grace. The verse declares that "the LORD of hosts is with us." The poet was indicating that God is like a mighty warrior-king who leads the armies of heaven into battle on behalf of His chosen people (see 24:10). The name translated "God of Jacob" (46:7) evokes the memory of one of the nation's greatest ancestors. The Lord—who graciously chose Jacob for a blessing instead of his older brother, Esau—protects the faith community (20:1). The Hebrew noun translated "refuge" (46:7; which is different from the word used in verse 1) refers to a high place or elevated stronghold. The imagery is that of a mountaintop citadel that cannot be overcome by an army of invaders (see 9:9; 18:2). Because the mighty God is on the side of the upright, they experience His gracious hand of protection.

The final portion of Psalm 46 invites us to use the eyes of our imagination to examine the aftermath of a tremendous battle. The field is strewed with the broken and smoking instruments of warfare. This is a scene of terrible destruction. But this is not just the result of one group of armed fighters overcoming another. God Himself entered the fray on the side of His people. Thus the desolation on the battlefield is His work (vs. 8). He brought peace, but He did it by carrying the battle to a decisive end. This scene cannot represent only the conclusion of a battle in Israel's history, for the psalm says God brings an end to "wars" (vs. 9) that occur throughout the planet. Likewise, God destroys whatever fighters use in combat, including bows, spears, and shields. Most likely, the scene is a preview of God's end-time victory over evil.

Psalm 46 envisions a throng of hostile nations determined to wipe out God's chosen people. The redeemed, though, have nothing to fear, for the Lord protects them. Indeed, above the din of earth's wicked people, God cries "Be still" (vs. 10), meaning "Enough! Stop!" He calls all people to recognize Him as God, and He confidently declares that He will be exalted as the supreme King throughout the entire globe (see Pss. 18:46; 99:2; 113:4; 138:6). Despite the forces of evil attempting to spread chaos in the world, the Lord of heaven's armies remains unchallenged in His rule. Understandably, the righteous consider their Creator to be like a "refuge" (46:11), that is, a lofty stronghold where they find protection (see 9:9; 18:2).

SUGGESTIONS TO TEACHERS

God spoke to the Israelites. A psalmist, centuries later, sensed the voice of God in what He had previously spoken. Much later, the writer to the Hebrews remembered these Old Testament accounts and knew that God was speaking through His ancient Word. As you have worked through portions of Hebrews 11 and Psalm 46, you have likely seen the next step: God still speaks today through the Old and New Testaments! Help your students see these steps in responding to what God says. Wise 21st-century people still . . .

1. HEAR GOD'S WORD. Jesus often referred to those who have ears to hear. He recognized that some people do not "tune" their ears to listen to the voice of God. He has spoken in the past. He continues to speak through His inspired Word. Do we take time and do we quiet ourselves so that we can hear Him speak?

2. BELIEVE GOD'S WORD. Hearing is a good step, but by itself is inadequate. Picture someone who receives a letter informing her of an unexpected inheritance. If she reads the words, but cannot believe the letter was intended for her, she may forfeit what belongs to her. Likewise we can imagine someone who sits in a church service every week, hears the Bible read, but cannot believe that the Good News applies to him or her.

3. BE FAITHFUL TO OBEY GOD'S WORD. It's hard to imagine someone who believes, but does not act on what she knows. But isn't that a good definition of procrastination? She knows that her car needs its oil changed regularly, but finds herself too busy. She then wonders why her car does not run smoothly. He knows that if he does not study for the test, he will not pass the course. But other activities distract him and he flunks out of college. God wants us to hear His Word in faith and respond by faithfully heeding what it has taught us.

4. SPEAK GOD'S WORD. God's people not only enjoy the privilege of hearing Him through His Word, but also can pass that good news along to others. Each of us can be an instrument through whom God speaks to others. They especially need to know about His all-powerful and reassuring presence. You can be the means by which others enter and mature as a part of God's family.

■ **TOPIC:** Steadfast Confidence

■ **QUESTIONS:** 1. What is the significance for you of the description of faith in Hebrews 11:1? 2. Why do you think our faith in the Son pleases the Father? 3. How has God been like a mighty warrior to you when you felt threatened by others? 4. Why is it important to look to God for hope when life feels chaotic? 5. In what ways can believers contribute to God's exaltation in the world?

■ **ILLUSTRATIONS:**

Living Faith. How much faith is enough to constitute steadfast confidence in God? Biblical insight into this matter can be found in Hebrews 11 and Psalm 46. The Old and New Testaments never describe faith as the lever to demand things from God. Rather, faith is exemplified as enduring trust in the Creator's promises, which transcend the here and now.

Faith drives us to believe that biblical values are the most important. Also, we focus our hope on the eternal city of the sovereign King. While that heavenly abode is our enduring reward, we live by faith now according to God's standards of justice and holiness.

This means that our resolute trust in the Lord moves us out from the proclamation of the Gospel to help people in need. We bring help in the here and now because our hope is firm in God's promises. Faith prompts obedience, hope, love, and hard work.

Holding on Firmly. Ann was blind from birth. Everything she knew and accomplished in life she owed to her parents' sacrifice and dedication. When her mother fell ill, Ann was distraught. She had never seen her mother. She knew only her voice and touch. For months Ann sat with her mother in a nursing home, holding her hands and talking to her. But her mother had lost her speech and could not respond. Nevertheless, Ann held on firmly every day, speaking words of comfort and hope.

In times of suffering we hold on firmly to each other and especially to God. Even when God does not seem to reply to our cries, we continue to find refuge in Him (see Ps. 46:1-3). Faith drives us to prayer and worship every day. Despite the darkness, we believe that the all-powerful Lord is with us. We also claim God's promise that nothing can separate us from His love (see Rom. 8:31-39).

Empowered by Faith. Hebrews 11:1-6 deals with the importance of faith. In particular, we are encouraged to have unwavering faith in the Savior.

Many years ago, a shoe company sent one of its salespeople to a faraway country to start a business. After a few months, the employee sent back the message: "I'm coming home. No one here wears shoes." Next, the same company sent another salesperson to the same remote area of the world to start the same business. After a few months, this individual wrote the home office the following note: "Send more order forms! No one here wears shoes."

The salesperson's attitude made all the difference in the similar situation being encountered. The first person felt that the circumstance was one insurmountable problem. In contrast, the second person regarded the situation as an opportunity to tackle.

The presence or absence of faith in the Lord is somewhat like that, too. When we lack faith in His ability to uphold us, we see our difficult situations as being impossible for us to handle. In contrast, when our faith is resting solidly on the shoulders of our Lord, He enables us to view our circumstances as opportunities waiting to be overcome.

How we feel about our issues doesn't make them go away or become less challenging. The difference is in how we see them and approach them. It's not a matter of us being strong enough, wise enough, loving enough, and so on, to succeed at what we're doing. Instead, it's us leaning on Jesus for the ability to handle the challenges we face every day.

Our Lord invites us not to be paralyzed by fear, but empowered by faith in Him. The good news is that He promises to be with us every step of the way!

FOR YOUTH

■ **TOPIC:** What Is Faith?

■ **QUESTIONS:** 1. Why does God call people to put their faith in what they cannot see? 2. Why is it important for us to believe that God exists and that He created everything? 3. What can you do to make your worship of almighty God a time of joy? 4. Why would God allow once-powerful nations to fall? 5. How can God help you cope with your greatest fears?

■ **ILLUSTRATIONS:**

Faith Alive. In his novel *A Walk to Remember*, Nicholas Sparks vividly tells how Jamie, a high school senior, brings an entirely new perspective into the life of her boyfriend. She does this, not with high-pressure religion, but by living out her own faith in God.

Eventually, not only Landon but also his family and his pals come to a new appreciation of the power of faith in the rough-and-tumble of high school life in a small town. Jamie moved them, not by her preaching, but by her living faith.

The possibilities of similar responses to faith arise almost every day. If our faith means anything (see Heb. 11:1, 6), we will put it on the line in front of our friends. We need to talk with one another about how to do this tactfully and lovingly. We need to talk about how to handle ridicule and possible loss of friends.

When our faith permeates our values and our conduct, others will see the difference.

Some will be changed, and some will not. But we are called to be faithful at all times and in all places.

An Example of Modern-Day Faith. Hebrews 11:1 tells us that biblical faith is the "substance of things hoped for" and the "evidence of things not seen." Verse 2 continues by noting that it was due to their faith that people in Old Testament times received God's commendation. Who from more recent history might be an example of modern-day faith?

Consider Stephen (not his real name), who was a wallpaper hanger in China. We would be incorrect to conclude that this occupation was the main focus of his life. He found his true meaning in his relationship with Jesus. Stephen risked his safety, especially as he pastored an illegal underground church. Stephen knew the danger well. His parents had previously spent years in prison for refusing to forsake Jesus. Stephen continued to obey God's call even when that meant leaving his wife and parents in China while he traveled to Australia to receive more Bible training.

Although Stephen had no steady source of income, he believed God would provide. And God did just that. In time, Stephen's wife and even his parents were allowed to join him. Has Stephen given up on China? By no means! He plans to return as often as he can to offer encouragement to his fellow Christians there.

The Tunnels of Life. Corrie ten Boom once said, "When a train goes through a tunnel and it gets dark, you don't throw away the ticket and jump off. You sit still and trust the engineer." Johnny was 14 years old and was en route to visit his grandparents in Switzerland. He had flown nonstop from New York to Geneva. There a travel agent had helped him transfer to a train on which he would ride to his final destination in the Oberland region of central Switzerland.

Johnny had a window seat on the train, and had enjoyed the fabulous scenery—the beautiful lakes, the towering, snow-covered Alps, and the quaint Swiss villages with their colorful flowers and chateaus. Then came the first tunnel. As the train entered the tunnel, suddenly it became pitch dark. In a moment, the train stopped. No one spoke. There was not a glimmer of light. There had been a temporary interruption in the electrical system that drove the train.

Johnny almost panicked. "Are we going to get off? How can we see how to walk? What is going to happen?" In a few moments, the lights came on in the train, the journey resumed, and it wasn't long until they emerged from the tunnel into a burst of sunlight.

Perhaps the author of Psalm 46 had a life experience that seemed at the time to be as unnerving as a dark tunnel. We, too, have experiences in life that are frightening. But there is a heavenly engineer who controls the train and who will safely bring us through.

FAITH IS ENDURANCE

BACKGROUND SCRIPTURE: Hebrews 12:1-11
DEVOTIONAL READING: James 5:7-11

Key Verses: Let us run with patience the race that is set before us,
Looking unto Jesus the author and finisher of our faith. Hebrews 12:1-2.

KING JAMES VERSION

HEBREWS 12:1 Wherefore seeing we also are compassed about with so great a cloud of witnesses, let us lay aside every weight, and the sin which doth so easily beset us, and let us run with patience the race that is set before us, 2 Looking unto Jesus the author and finisher of our faith; who for the joy that was set before him endured the cross, despising the shame, and is set down at the right hand of the throne of God. 3 For consider him that endured such contradiction of sinners against himself, lest ye be wearied and faint in your minds.

4 Ye have not yet resisted unto blood, striving against sin. 5 And ye have forgotten the exhortation which speaketh unto you as unto children, My son, despise not thou the chastening of the Lord, nor faint when thou art rebuked of him: 6 For whom the Lord loveth he chasteneth, and scourgeth every son whom he receiveth. 7 If ye endure chastening, God dealeth with you as with sons; for what son is he whom the father chasteneth not? 8 But if ye be without chastisement, whereof all are partakers, then are ye bastards, and not sons. 9 Furthermore we have had fathers of our flesh which corrected us, and we gave them reverence: shall we not much rather be in subjection unto the Father of spirits, and live? 10 For they verily for a few days chastened us after their own pleasure; but he for our profit, that we might be partakers of his holiness. 11 Now no chastening for the present seemeth to be joyous, but grievous: nevertheless afterward it yieldeth the peaceable fruit of righteousness unto them which are exercised thereby.

NEW REVISED STANDARD VERSION

HEBREWS 12:1 Therefore, since we are surrounded by so great a cloud of witnesses, let us also lay aside every weight and the sin that clings so closely, and let us run with perseverance the race that is set before us, 2 looking to Jesus the pioneer and perfecter of our faith, who for the sake of the joy that was set before him endured the cross, disregarding its shame, and has taken his seat at the right hand of the throne of God.

3 Consider him who endured such hostility against himself from sinners, so that you may not grow weary or lose heart. 4 In your struggle against sin you have not yet resisted to the point of shedding your blood. 5 And you have forgotten the exhortation that addresses you as children—

"My child, do not regard lightly the discipline of
  the Lord,
  or lose heart when you are punished by him;
6 for the Lord disciplines those whom he loves,
  and chastises every child whom he accepts."
7 Endure trials for the sake of discipline. God is treating you as children; for what child is there whom a parent does not discipline? 8 If you do not have that discipline in which all children share, then you are illegitimate and not his children. 9 Moreover, we had human parents to discipline us, and we respected them. Should we not be even more willing to be subject to the Father of spirits and live? 10 For they disciplined us for a short time as seemed best to them, but he disciplines us for our good, in order that we may share his holiness. 11 Now, discipline always seems painful rather than pleasant at the time, but later it yields the peaceful fruit of righteousness to those who have been trained by it.

HOME BIBLE READINGS

Monday, September 10	Job 5:8-18	*The Discipline of the Lord*
Tuesday, September 11	Romans 6:1-11	*The Death of Sin*
Wednesday, September 12	1 Corinthians 9:24-27	*The Race for the Prize*
Thursday, September 13	1 Timothy 4:6-10	*The Training for Godliness*
Friday, September 14	James 5:7-11	*The Endurance of the Faithful*
Saturday, September 15	1 Peter 2:18-25	*The Example of Faithfulness*
Sunday, September 16	Hebrews 12:1-11	*The Pioneer of Faith*

BACKGROUND

The Greek noun rendered "witnesses" (Heb. 12:1) is filled with significance. The Greek word is *martus* and comes from the verb *martureo*, which means "to testify" or "to bear witness." The idea is one of affirming what he or she has seen or experienced. The New Testament writers sometimes applied *martus* to those believers in Christ who were attesting to their faith while enduring persecution. Thus, in time such believers came to be known as *martyrs*, that is, those who voluntarily suffered death as the penalty for their allegiance to Christ.

The writers of the New Testament often used *martureo* to refer to believers who personally testified to Jesus' work on earth, regardless of whether suffering was present. John, in particular, noted the various witnesses who testified about Jesus. These included God the Father (John 5:31-32, 37; 8:18), the Holy Spirit (15:26), Jesus Himself (8:14, 18), Scripture (5:39), Jesus' own works (5:36), John the Baptizer (1:34), and Jesus' disciples (15:27). The concept of witness is prominent in not only the New Testament but also the Old Testament. For example, Jacob used a pile of rocks to serve as a reminder that God was a witness to the patriarch's agreement with Laban (Gen. 31:45-50). In addition, the Mosaic law required that at least two witnesses had to support a charge of wrongdoing (Num. 35:30; Deut. 17:6).

NOTES ON THE PRINTED TEXT

In Hebrews 12:1, the huge crowd of "witnesses" testifies to the life of faith. From the perspective of runners in a stadium, the spectators all around them in the stands might look something like a cloud of people. In a sense, Christians also have a cloud of people watching us: the saints in heaven. As "witnesses," they watch us and cheer us on in our race. They are also motivating examples of faithfulness.

In the ancient world, runners in a race competed without any clothing. They would strip themselves of anything that might weigh them down or entangle their arms and legs. Similarly, the Hebrew Christians were to rid themselves of every encumbrance that might prevent them from living for the Redeemer. While some of these hindrances were not inherently sinful (for example, long-standing religious traditions), others were. The latter included the fear of being persecuted, resentment toward others, and sexual immorality

(10:38-39; 12:15-16). In mentioning "the sin which doth so easily beset us" (12:1), the writer may have had in mind the danger of defection resulting from discouragement—in other words, apostasy. The presence of opposition from others tempted some first-century Christians to revert to their former way of life. In light of this, the writer urged his readers to remain steadfast in their faith even when they encountered hostile forces.

Regardless of the nature of the race, every event has a definite goal, namely, a tape to break. The wise runner is one who keeps his or her eyes on the finish line and doesn't look back. As Christians, we too have a goal—we are heading for the Savior. And so the writer of Hebrews urged, we keep our eyes fixed on Jesus (vs. 2). After all, the Redeemer is "the author and finisher of our faith." While we must persevere in our running, it is Jesus who enables us to both begin and complete the race.

One way Jesus helps us to start, continue, and finish our race is by being the ideal example. He is the champion runner of the ages. As we struggle in our race, we can know that He has already been there and has shown that the race can be won. Just as we are to focus our attention on Jesus, so He kept His eyes fixed on the joy of completing the mission the Father had given to Him. And just as we are to persevere in the race marked out for us, so Jesus "endured the cross, despising the shame."

The cross brought great suffering and disgrace, but the Son kept in mind that the glory of enduring the cross would be much greater. Despite facing the highest hurdle anybody has ever had—the cross—Jesus successfully completed His race. And instead of receiving the wreath of leaves awarded to a victorious runner in the ancient world, the Son was rewarded with supreme authority. He took His seat in the place of highest honor beside His Father's throne in heaven (see 1:3).

The writer of Hebrews, knowing that his readers would sometimes feel weary and lose heart because of opposition, urged them to reflect earnestly on what Jesus experienced (12:3). Throughout the course of His earthly ministry, the Lord had to endure terrible opposition from sinners, and yet He persevered until He won the victory. Taking inspiration from the Messiah, we can persevere in our race no matter what obstacles wicked people may place in our way. Jesus, the pioneer and perfecter of our faith, is our supreme example.

The author of Hebrews realized that his harassed and beleaguered readers were tempted to return to their former way of life. Even so, the writer urged them not to give up. He reminded them that no matter how difficult their situation had become, it had not yet led to bloodshed. Expressed differently, none of them had died for their faith (vs. 4). A schoolmaster was once asked what would be the ideal curriculum for children. He answered, "Any program of worthwhile studies, so long as all of it is hard and some of it is unpleasant." The original readers of Hebrews had been experiencing what was hard and unpleasant in their "striving against sin." Thankfully, however, none of them had so far been martyred.

Despite the fact that their struggle was not as bad as it could be, the Hebrews were being tempted to look on their suffering in the wrong way. Once more, the author referred to some Old Testament Scripture to validate his point. This time he focused on Proverbs 3:11-12, which teaches those being disciplined by the Lord to respond properly. We are not to err by making light of it. Neither are we to err by losing heart, taking the experience too seriously. Instead, we should recognize that discipline from the Lord is a sign that He loves us and considers us His spiritual children (Heb. 12:5-6). And therefore, we should accept His discipline and pay attention to what He's trying to teach us through it.

The aim of the author of Hebrews was to make his audience aware of suffering as a teaching tool used by God; in other words, discipline is pedagogical. This insight makes the writer's statement in the first part of verse 7 all the more forceful. Believers are to patiently go through divine "chastening," for the Lord is treating them as His spiritual children. When God subjects us to His hand of discipline, He shows that He cares even more for us, who are coheirs with Christ (see Rom. 8:17). Also, when the Lord corrects us, it demonstrates that we are legitimate members of His heavenly family (Heb. 12:8). Notice the way in which the writer argued from the lesser reality to the greater reality, that is, from human parents upward to the heavenly Father (vs. 9). If we respect our earthly parents when they discipline us, we should much more submit to the "Father of spirits, and live." Discipline by God should not cause us to think worse of Him, but rather to respect Him all the more. When He corrects us, His wise and loving purposes undergird His actions.

In human discipline, there is always the element of imperfection, even though our parents disciplined us as well as they knew how (vs. 10). By an upgraded contrast, divine discipline is always for our eternal benefit, in order that we might "be partakers of his holiness." God's discipline is always prudent, and we can be sure it is needed and contributes to our spiritual growth. When we submit to the Lord's hand of correction, we experience greater moral fitness. We also become increasingly conformed in every aspect of our lives to the image of Christ. The author admitted that no discipline is pleasant while it's occurring. In fact, it's downright painful. The benefit only appears later, when it yields the "peaceable fruit of righteousness" (vs. 11) by allowing ourselves to be spiritually trained in this way. The Greek verb rendered "exercised" is based on the word from which we get gymnasium. We could say discipline gives us a tough workout, but helps us get into tip-top shape.

The writer of Hebrews, perhaps returning to the running imagery, exhorted his readers to strengthen their limp hands and enfeebled knees (vs. 12). Verse 13 extends the imagery by quoting from Proverbs 4:26. The recipients of the epistle were to smooth out the racetrack (in a manner of speaking) so that even the lame could get around it without falling and hurting themselves. The idea is that, as we are running our own race, we should look out for our fellow believers and try to help them succeed in their races as well. By God's grace, the Christian life is one in which we all can eventually wear the wreath of victory—no matter what disabilities we start with.

SUGGESTIONS TO TEACHERS

The readers of Hebrews faced persecution. Many students in your class are also facing hard times of their own. The writer of the epistle used both historical facts and helpful analogies to encourage his followers toward steadfastness. Today, you can use these same images to encourage others to maintain hope and progress.

1. GOD'S PEOPLE BEFORE THEM HAD STRUGGLED AND WON. The writer opened chapter 12 by reminding his readers of the "great . . . cloud of witnesses" (12:1) that surrounded them. These witnesses were God's people from the past who had heard His promises and remained faithful to Him, despite not seeing the fulfillment of these pledges. But by the time Hebrews was written, all these witnesses had moved up into the grandstands of heaven. God's faithful people would ultimately join them in victory.

2. JESUS HIMSELF HAD STRUGGLED AND WON. "Jesus . . . endured the cross, despising the shame" (vs. 2). Because of His complete obedience to the Father, even to death, the Son has taken His seat at the "right hand of the throne of God." Contemporary believers find comfort in the fact that their Lord empathizes with their pain. God's Son faced it at its worst, and He enables Christians to be victorious today.

3. VICTORIOUS ATHLETES WILLINGLY STRUGGLE IN ORDER TO WIN. The writer used an athletic analogy to stress this point. The runners persevere in the "race that is set before" (vs. 1) them. Even when they sense themselves drooping, they forge on toward the finish line. They willingly challenge themselves. If their contest is worth all their energy and effort, how much more important it is for Christians to remain faithful to Jesus, especially as they press on toward their heavenly goal.

4. CHILDREN'S STRUGGLES WITH DISCIPLINE ENABLE THEM TO GROW. The middle portion of this week's Scripture passage employs the analogy of parents discipling their children. As loving parents allow their children to be stretched, they protect their children from anything that would truly harm them. Likewise, God always monitors our circumstances. If He chooses not to protect us from suffering, He allows only that testing that enables us to become holy as He is holy.

FOR ADULTS

■ **TOPIC:** Steadfast Fortitude

■ **QUESTIONS:** 1. In your opinion, what is the relationship between Hebrews 11 and 12? 2. What kind of weight do you think prevents believers from running their race ? 3. Why is it appropriate for God to discipline us as His spiritual children? 4. In what ways has God disciplined you? How have you responded? 5. What can you do to help other believers run their race of faith better?

■ ILLUSTRATIONS:

Trustworthy Leadership. A minister shared his experience as a small boy when he went to his first symphony orchestra concert. He marveled at the different musicians as they came onto the stage and sat down. They all seemed so different. Some were young, while others were old. Some were thin and others were big. Some had lots of hair, but others were bald. There were women and men.

One by one, the musicians picked up their instruments and began to play a few notes. It sounded like a dozen cats fighting on a hot night in the middle of the city. None of them was playing the same notes, let alone the same music. Then the boy saw a man in a long black coat walk to the center of the stage. When he raised a long, thin black stick, the noise immediately stopped. With a sweep of this man's hand, the musicians began to play again, and the sound this time was incredibly beautiful.

Jesus represents the Conductor, who gives order and meaning to our lives. He is our Leader and Guide, who watches over and provides for us so that we have the steadfast fortitude to make it through our life journey. Jesus alone is sufficiently qualified, capable, and trustworthy to do this for us. And that is why He is to be the sole focus of our faith (see Heb. 12:1-3).

Nabbed Criminal. Richard Owen of the *Times* reported that police officers in Palermo, Italy, arrested an "elusive Mafia boss" named Bernardo Provenzano, who had been "on the run" for 43 years. According to the authorities, the police came close to capturing the 73-year-old criminal on six previous occasions. But he had "always escaped after being mysteriously tipped off."

In 2006, Provenzano's situation drastically changed when he was "betrayed by laundry sent to him by his wife." The end came "in an isolated, unheated, and run-down three-room stone farmhouse barely a mile from . . . his home town." The Italian authorities estimated the Mafia boss's personal wealth at $600 million, but in recent years he lived as if he'd taken "vows of poverty." The once-powerful individual "turned out to be an elderly, pink-cheeked man with thick-lensed, metal-rimmed reading glasses."

What a contrast this legendary "boss of bosses" is to the Lord Jesus. He endured the shame of the cross so that we might be saved. And though the authorities executed Jesus as a criminal, the Father raised Him from the dead so that all who trust in Him can have eternal life. As the pioneer and perfecter of our faith, Christ alone demonstrates that He is a leader who can be trusted (see Heb. 12:1-3).

Diamond in the Rough. Years ago in a South African mine, workers dug up the Cullinan diamond. It was the largest diamond ever found, weighing one and one-half pounds. The diamond was given as a gift to Edward VII of England.

The greatest stonecutter in Amsterdam studied the Cullinan diamond for weeks. He made drawings and models to better understand the inner structure of this jewel. Then the stonecutter, after notching the diamond, struck it with his hammer, which split the diamond in two pieces. Did the stonecutter make a mistake? Not at all. By splitting the diamond in two, he enabled others to see its shape and splendor.

Sometimes, God allows us to experience stinging blows. At first, we might think God has made a mistake. But then, as we learn from this week's Scripture passage, He knows hardships will reveal the beauty of our spiritual character.

FOR YOUTH

■ **TOPIC:** Endurance to Run the Race

■ **QUESTIONS:** 1. How is the Christian life like a race? 2. In what sense is Jesus the "author and finisher" (Heb. 12:2) of our faith? 3. In what sense can one say that suffering is disciplinary? 4. What is the relationship between the discipline of God and the love of God in the lives of His children? 5. What can believers learn from the sufferings God allows them to endure?

■ **ILLUSTRATIONS:**

Supreme Commander. For decades, athletes and scientists agreed that no human being would ever run a mile in less than four minutes. And their predictions proved accurate. No one did. But one young man believed that he could go beyond that limit. On May 6, 1954, Roger Bannister broke the four-minute barrier. Now, among world-class male runners, several athletes beat Bannister's onetime record in nearly every mile race. But it took someone of Bannister's determination to be the first. He set the pattern. He became a great leader whose example others follow.

This week's Scripture text reminds us that Jesus is the best example of what it means to be a great leader. As the supreme commander of our salvation, He endured the shame of the cross. And though the authorities executed Jesus as a criminal, the Father raised Him from the dead so that all who trust in Him can have eternal life. As the pioneer and perfecter of our faith, Christ alone demonstrates that He is a leader who can be trusted.

Remaining Courageous. On July 30, 1967, 17-year-old Joni Eareckson dived into Chesapeake Bay and accidentally struck her head against a rock. That incident left her paralyzed from the neck down. At first, Joni was bewildered by what had happened to her. But then her confusion gave way to anger and despair. She tried to kill herself as a way to escape the prison of her body. However, she failed in her efforts.

Since her diving accident, Joni has become an artist, an author, a movie star in her autobiography, a spokeswoman for disabled Christians, and a gifted inspirational speaker. She has married and enjoys the company of friends and family. Despite her blessings, Joni has lived much of her life without being able to use her arms and legs.

In fact, her loved ones must bathe, dress, and feed her every day.

There are times when Joni feels discouraged about her circumstances. But despite these times, her faith in Christ remains unwavering. Joni recognizes that Jesus has enabled her to endure hardships and as a result grow in her walk with the Lord. His abiding presence has given Joni the strength to remain courageous, even in the face of overwhelming obstacles (see Heb. 12:1-3).

Personal Victory. Hebrews 12:1 tells us that there is a large crowd of believers in heaven who have successfully lived for Christ. And we can imagine them cheering us on as we run with determination the race that is ahead of us.

The runners in the first Olympic Women's Marathon were entering the stadium at the end of the race. The year was 1984 and the location was Los Angeles. On a hot day, the women had run a course through the streets of the city. For the hours they had been running, the heat had been radiating off the pavement. As they entered the Olympic Coliseum, participants needed to run a full lap around the track before crossing the finish line. An American won the race that year, but her victory is not what people remember about this particular Olympic event.

Well out of the medals, a Swiss runner, Gabriella Anderson-Schiess, came through the stadium tunnel and into view. Everyone immediately sensed that Gabriella might not make it to the end. Rather than running directly around the track, she was staggering right and left. She dragged one of her legs as if she had suffered a severe cramp. Gabriella had given her all, but was suffering from exhaustion and heatstroke.

Immediately, Gabriella's coach, accompanied by a paramedic team, rushed over to help her. The paramedics wanted to put her on a stretcher and carry her off the field. Gabriella could not speak, but could motion that she wished to be left to finish the race on her own. Had anyone offered any assistance other than a drink, she would have been disqualified from the race. She had run 26 miles; she wanted to finish the event.

The crowd rose to its feet and cheered Gabriella. They had warmly supported the American winner during her last lap, but that greeting was nothing compared to the exuberant support everyone offered Gabriella. Despite her pain and exhaustion, she pulled her body around the track and collapsed across the finish line. With perseverance, she ran her race to the very end. She won no medal, but she won the greatest of personal victories.

FAITH INSPIRES GRATITUDE

BACKGROUND SCRIPTURE: Hebrews 12:14-29
DEVOTIONAL READING: 2 Thessalonians 1:1-7

Key Verse: Wherefore we receiving a kingdom which cannot be moved, let us have grace, whereby we may serve God acceptably with reverence and godly fear. Hebrews 12:28.

4

KING JAMES VERSION

HEBREWS 12:18 For ye are not come unto the mount that might be touched, and that burned with fire, nor unto blackness, and darkness, and tempest, 19 And the sound of a trumpet, and the voice of words; which voice they that heard intreated that the word should not be spoken to them any more: 20 (For they could not endure that which was commanded, And if so much as a beast touch the mountain, it shall be stoned, or thrust through with a dart: 21 And so terrible was the sight, that Moses said, I exceedingly fear and quake:) 22 But ye are come unto mount Sion, and unto the city of the living God, the heavenly Jerusalem, and to an innumerable company of angels, 23 To the general assembly and church of the firstborn, which are written in heaven, and to God the Judge of all, and to the spirits of just men made perfect, 24 And to Jesus the mediator of the new covenant, and to the blood of sprinkling, that speaketh better things than that of Abel. 25 See that ye refuse not him that speaketh. For if they escaped not who refused him that spake on earth, much more shall not we escape, if we turn away from him that speaketh from heaven: 26 Whose voice then shook the earth: but now he hath promised, saying, Yet once more I shake not the earth only, but also heaven. 27 And this word, Yet once more, signifieth the removing of those things that are shaken, as of things that are made, that those things which cannot be shaken may remain.
28 Wherefore we receiving a kingdom which cannot be moved, let us have grace, whereby we may serve God acceptably with reverence and godly fear: 29 For our God is a consuming fire.

NEW REVISED STANDARD VERSION

HEBREWS 12:18 You have not come to something that can be touched, a blazing fire, and darkness, and gloom, and a tempest, 19 and the sound of a trumpet, and a voice whose words made the hearers beg that not another word be spoken to them. 20 (For they could not endure the order that was given, "If even an animal touches the mountain, it shall be stoned to death."
21 Indeed, so terrifying was the sight that Moses said, "I tremble with fear.") 22 But you have come to Mount Zion and to the city of the living God, the heavenly Jerusalem, and to innumerable angels in festal gathering, 23 and to the assembly of the firstborn who are enrolled in heaven, and to God the judge of all, and to the spirits of the righteous made perfect, 24 and to Jesus, the mediator of a new covenant, and to the sprinkled blood that speaks a better word than the blood of Abel.

25 See that you do not refuse the one who is speaking; for if they did not escape when they refused the one who warned them on earth, how much less will we escape if we reject the one who warns from heaven! 26 At that time his voice shook the earth; but now he has promised, "Yet once more I will shake not only the earth but also the heaven." 27 This phrase, "Yet once more," indicates the removal of what is shaken—that is, created things—so that what cannot be shaken may remain. 28 Therefore, since we are receiving a kingdom that cannot be shaken, let us give thanks, by which we offer to God an acceptable worship with reverence and awe; 29 for indeed our God is a consuming fire.

BACKGROUND

Hebrews 12:14 pulls together two threads from the preceding verses (which were studied in last week's lesson). Verse 10 mentions "holiness," while verse 11 refers to the "peaceable fruit of righteousness." Both emphases reflected strategic Hebrew ideas that, when taken together, carry the connotations of a life of spiritual wholeness. Both peace and holiness are to be goals for Christians. We are to strive to be at peace with everyone (vs. 14). That includes our fellow believers, our non-Christian neighbors, and even our enemies. We are also to seek personal purity. The author provided an incentive for seeking holiness when he said that those who are not holy will not see the Lord. God is all-holy, and He cannot tolerate moral impurity in His presence.

The twin virtues in verse 14 are the opposites of two vices mentioned in the following verses. First, the opposite of peace is the troublemaking of sinners (vs. 15). Second, the opposite of holiness is sinfulness, which includes immorality and godlessness (vss. 16-17). The author also explained some of the things involved in seeking peace and holiness. Verses 15 and 16 begin similarly: "Looking diligently lest . . ." and "Lest there be . . ." Together, these two verses show us the responsibility believers have for helping one another become the men and women God wants us to be.

NOTES ON THE PRINTED TEXT

As a way of encouraging his readers to persevere in their Christian faith, the author of Hebrews reminded them of the superiority of the new covenant over the old one. He maintained that while Mount Sinai (where the Mosaic law was given) was great, Mount Zion (representing the Messiah's kingdom) is greater still. It would be incorrect to conclude that the writer was somehow discrediting Mount Sinai, for he affirmed the central role it occupied in salvation history. By way of example, when Moses was receiving the law from God on Sinai, the mountain was burning "with fire" (12:18) and covered with "blackness, and darkness, and tempest." There were a trumpet blast and the sound of God's voice, to which the listeners could not bear to listen (vs. 19).

The sound of God's voice would not even permit animals to touch the mountain, since it had been made holy with the Lord's presence (vs. 20). The display of God's awesomeness was such that even Moses, God's prophet, was terrified (vs. 21). These historical details are confirmed in the Old Testament (see Exod. 19:12, 13, 16-19; Deut. 9:19). The term "Zion" is used over 150 times in the Old Testament. Zion is first mentioned in 2 Samuel 5:7 as a Jebusite fortress on a hill. After being captured by David, this fortress was called the City of David. Here Israel's king brought the ark of the covenant, thereby making the hill a sacred site (6:10-12).

The historical eminence of Zion eventually came to be equated with Jerusalem itself (see Isa. 40:9; Mic. 3:12). For instance, Psalm 125:1 declares that "mount Zion, . . . cannot be removed, but abideth for ever." Indeed, in biblical thought, Zion was the place where the Lord resided and presided. This explains why Hebrews 12:22 refers to Mount Zion as the "heavenly Jerusalem" and the "city of the living God" (see 11:10, 13-16; 13:14). Previously, the members of the covenant community in the Old Testament era went to Mount Sinai. In contrast, new covenant believers have journeyed to Mount Zion. Also, unlike Mount Sinai, which "might be touched" (12:18), Mount Zion is impalpable. Furthermore, Mount Sinai is a physical mountain, whereas the end-time Mount Zion is not.

The writer explained that in coming to Mount Zion, Jesus' followers had encountered several eternal blessings. The first one is "an innumerable company of angels" (vs. 22) who are in festal gathering. Second is the "church of the firstborn, which are written in heaven"(vs. 23). This worshiping community includes all Christians on earth. Because of Jesus, they will be treated like privileged heirs of heaven (see Rom. 8:17), where they already have their names enrolled. The third blessing is "God the Judge of all" (Heb. 12:23). As the end-time Judge of all creatures, the Father will not condemn but rather justify those who believe in His Son.

Fourth is "the spirits of just men made perfect." These are probably believers from the Old Testament era, such as the people mentioned in chapter 11. They have been made perfect in the sense that their souls have been cleansed from sin through the Messiah (see vs. 40).The fifth blessing is "Jesus the mediator of the new covenant" (12:24; see 8:6). Moses was the mediator of the old covenant by receiving the law from God and delivering it to the Israelites. Similarly, the Son mediated the new covenant by teaching about faith and dying so that sinners can be reconciled with the Father. Sixth is "the blood of sprinkling, that speaketh better things than that of Abel" (12:24). The "blood of sprinkling" is what Jesus shed on the cross. Whereas Abel's blood cried out for retribution (see Gen. 4:10), Jesus' blood provides forgiveness.

The writer of Hebrews urged Jesus' followers not to refuse "him that speaketh" (12:25), which is a reference to God. The author mentioned the Exodus generation as an example of what not to do. When God dwelled with the Israelites, He repeatedly warned them not to disobey Him. Despite this, they did rebel against Him, and so He punished them on several occasions. Moreover, virtually all of them died in the Sinai

Desert before the nation entered the promised land (see Num. 14:26-35). Given that this was the fate of those who refused to heed the divine message given by Moses, it is even less likely that people today will be able to escape God's judgment if they reject the Lord Jesus, who issues His warning from the throne room of heaven (Heb. 12:25). In short, the Messiah demands complete and unwavering faithfulness from His followers.

Verse 26 reveals the dire consequence of renouncing the Savior. In the time of Moses, there was a violent earthquake at Sinai (see Exod. 19:18). But at the Messiah's second coming, God promised to upturn not only the earth but also the heavens (Heb. 12:26; see Hag. 2:6). This latter episode will be much more serious than the former one. At the end of the age, all of creation will be shaken, and only what is unshakable will survive (Heb. 12:27). This refers to the Savior's kingdom, which is unshakable and will survive the coming demise. In verse 28, the writer once more stressed the enduring nature of God's kingdom, which signals the importance of this truth.

When the Bible talks about the divine kingdom, it is primarily referring to the Lord's rule over His creation. Scripture describes God's kingdom as being heavenly (2 Tim. 4:18), secure (Heb. 12:28), and eternal (2 Pet. 1:11). The Bible describes the richness of God's kingdom in a variety of ways. It is inseparably linked to righteousness, peace, and joy (Rom. 14:17). The kingdom is associated with suffering and patient endurance (Rev. 1:9), supernatural power (1 Cor. 4:20), promise (Jas. 2:5), glory (1 Thess. 2:12), and the "regeneration" (Matt. 19:28) of all things. God's kingdom is not a product of human invention (John 18:36). It is given as a gift (Luke 12:32) and humbly received (Mark 10:15). The Lord brings His people into His kingdom (Col. 1:13), makes them worthy of it (2 Thess. 1:5), and preserves them for it (2 Tim. 4:18).

Two conclusions can be drawn from the truth that believers will inherit an unshakable kingdom (Heb. 12:28). First, they should express thanks that the Father, in His grace, allows them to be saved through faith in His Son (see Eph. 2:8-9). Second, the writer of Hebrews encouraged believers to offer worship that is pleasing to God, namely, with "reverence and godly fear" (12:28). Put differently, before God's majestic presence, believers should exercise humility, especially as they offer Him praise. In support of his second conclusion, the author quoted Deuteronomy 4:24 (see Exod. 24:17; Deut. 9:3; Isa. 33:14), which says that "God is a consuming fire" (Heb. 12:29). The idea is that God tolerates no rivals, whether real or imaginary (see Jas. 4:4-5). Ultimately, people must face God either as a purifying fire or as a punishing fire, that is, to be cleansed or to be consumed.

Second Peter 3:10 reveals that when God's patience with the ungodly is finally exhausted, "the day of the Lord" will come suddenly, as a thief who strikes in the darkness. Peter used strong language typical of end-time passages to describe three events that will happen when the Messiah returns. First, the heavens will vanish with a "great noise." This renders a Greek adverb that denotes the presence of a horrific roar similar to a whirling, rushing sound. Second, the "elements" will melt away in a fiery blaze. The noun translated "elements" refers to the celestial bodies in the universe (sun, moon, and stars) as well as the chemical compounds out of which they are made (earth, air, fire, and water). Third, the planet and every deed done on it will be "burned up." The idea is that everything on earth will be obliterated. In turn, humanity will be left to stand exposed and accountable before God.

SUGGESTIONS TO TEACHERS

Jesus promised and angels confirmed that He would return bodily to the earth at a future time (see Matt. 24:30-31; Acts 1:11). The New Testament writers understood that the Messiah's return will mark the end of this age and the beginning of the kingdom of God (see 1 Thess. 4:16-17; 5:1-2; 2 Pet. 3:10; Rev. 19:11-16; 21:1-4). Moreover, the author of Hebrews confirmed that when Jesus returns, He will destroy everything temporal. Only His unshakable kingdom will remain.

1. ACKNOWLEDGING THE MESSIAH'S RETURN. Century after century, scoffers have posed many objections to the teaching that Jesus will return some day. Be that as it may, the author of Hebrews argued in favor of the return of a sovereign Lord. After all, as the writer stressed, He is the "mediator of the new covenant" (12:24) who at His second advent will bring to pass all God's kingdom promises. Emphasize to the class members that the Redeemer operates outside the confines of time and will fulfill everything He has pledged in His Word to do for them.

2. HEEDING THE LORD. Believers can look to the future with hope when they recognize their identity as the "church of the firstborn" (vs. 23). This is one reason for believers being diligent in heeding the Lord, rather than refusing to obey His Word (vs. 25). Remind the students that unwavering devotion to the Savior calls for a consciously different lifestyle from the rest of the world. Encourage them to give specific ways that this applies to them.

3. WORSHIPING GOD IN AN ACCEPTABLE MANNER. The appropriate worship of God is an important component to having a confident hope for the future. By emphasizing suitable worship in verse 28, the writer of Hebrews helps us to understand that we humans do not try to pull God into our existence through ceremonies or sacrifices. Instead, as we affirm the good news of the Son's future return, we find ourselves blessed with His abiding presence.

4. LIVING IN A HOLY MANNER. The Bible does not present theology as an intellectual exercise. There are behavioral implications for God's truth. For instance, the author of Hebrews stressed the importance of believers serving the Lord with "reverence and godly fear" (vs. 28). We do not know precisely when Jesus will return, but we can live in such a way that we affirm His return and His reign over the new heavens and earth.

■ TOPIC: Steadfast Thanks

■ QUESTIONS: 1. What contrast did the writer of Hebrews make between Mount Sinai and Mount Zion? 2. What sort of eternal future did the author say awaits believers? 3. What are some reasons you have heard the unsaved give for rejecting the Savior? 4. What will happen to the heavens and the earth at Jesus' return? 5. What are some things believers can do as they await Jesus' return?

■ ILLUSTRATIONS:

Hope in Life's Struggles. The author of Hebrews wrote to believers who were encountering challenges, frustrations, and opposition to their faith. Their decision to overcome their hardships gives us hope to remain steadfast in our faith and thankful to God for the strength He provides in the midst our difficulties.

As we overcome our afflictions, we grow stronger in our walk with Christ. These steps to maturity resemble foothills that sometimes block the view of the lofty snow-capped peaks. But because the peaks are there, we, like a mountain hiker, can push onward and upward with the Lord's help.

In Romans 8:31-34, Paul declared that regardless of our struggles, no one can stand against us, for God is for us. This being so, the question is not whether God is on our side, but whether we are on God's side. In order for us to be spiritually victorious, it is important first for us to yield ourselves fully to God. To align ourselves on God's side, our desires and ambitions must bow to God's plan.

First Things First. A traveler lost in the deserts of North Africa crawled up to the tent of a Bedouin and croaked, "Water." The Bedouin appeared and replied sympathetically, "I am sorry, sir, but I have no water. However, would you like a nice necktie?" With this, he brandished a collection of exquisite silken neckwear.

"You fool," gasped the man. "I'm dying! I need water!" "Well, sir," replied the Bedouin, "if you really need water, there is a tent about two miles south of here where you can get some, but you really should take one of these ties."

The parched traveler summoned sufficient strength to drag himself to the second tent. He collapsed at the entrance. Another Bedouin, this one dressed in a costly tuxedo, appeared at the door and inquired, "May I help you, sir?" "Water," the traveler croaked weakly. "I am very sorry, sir, but you cannot come in here without a tie!" the doorman said and promptly turned on his heel.

When Hebrews was written, there were some who thought they could spurn the Savior and still go to heaven in the end. They were wrong. Faith in the Him is a prerequisite to gain entrance to the "city of the living God" (12:22). And only by trusting in the Son can anyone become a member of the "church of the firstborn" (vs. 23).

Looking Forward. How long do you wait for a friend? That was the subject of an episode from the television comedy *Seinfeld*. Jerry and Elaine told their friend George to meet them outside their favorite restaurant at 9:00 in the morning. Jerry arrived at 8:40. Elaine arrived at 8:45.

"What's the rule for how long you're supposed to wait for a friend?" Elaine asked, already impatient. Jerry glanced quickly at his watch and said, "Five minutes. Tops." Five minutes later they gave up on George and left the place. At 8:51, George showed up, thrilled he was nine minutes early. Chances are, George wasn't going to trust his friends the next time they agreed to meet! Promises, trust, and hope go hand in hand.

Thankfully, the Christian walk is not like life on *Seinfeld*. We can put our complete trust in the fact that the Father fulfills His promises and the Son keeps His appointments. The certitude of Jesus' second coming is at the heart of the declaration in Hebrews 12:22 that we have come to "mount Sion," to the "city of the living God," and to the "heavenly Jerusalem." Verse 23 reveals that it is there we join with other members of the "church of the firstborn" (vs. 23) to offer worship to the Lord with "reverence and godly fear" (vs. 28).

The Bible confirms that Jesus will return, that believers who are dead will rise, and that Christians who are alive will join Him in the clouds (see 1 Thess. 4:13-17). No believer will be excluded. And no Christian will miss the call or be abandoned. Now that's truly a blessed hope worth waiting for!

FOR YOUTH

■ **TOPIC:** Fearful or Thankful Faith?

■ **QUESTIONS:** 1. Why were the Israelites so afraid as they stood at the base of Mount Sinai? 2. In what sense is Jesus the "mediator of the new covenant" (Heb. 12:24)? 3. As you look through the list of items associated with Mount Zion, which are you most glad to have received? 4. At the end of the age, in what way will the present heavens and earth be destroyed? 5. What emotions should characterize believers who are waiting for Jesus' return?

■ **ILLUSTRATIONS:**

A Firm Foundation of Hope. Pastor Duane Scott Willis and his wife, Janet, dearly loved the nine children God had given them. But midmorning on November 8, 1994, a fiery automobile explosion claimed the lives of their six youngest children. Eight days later, the bereaved couple explained to the media how they could make it through the sudden and horrific tragedy with unwavering hope in the Lord.

"We must tell you that we hurt and sorrow as you parents would for your children. The depth of pain is indescribable. The Bible expresses our feelings that we sorrow, but not as those without hope.

"What gives us our firm foundation for our hope is the Bible. The truth of God's

Word assures us that our children are in heaven with Jesus Christ. Our strength rests in the Word of God. The Bible is sure and gives us confidence. Everything God promises is true."

Finding the American Dream. The American dream of financial success and power used to be considered achievable. Hard work would pay off and be rewarded with wealth and position.

Today's youth, however, do not follow that formula to the American dream. In the aftermath of what is popularly known as the Great Recession, far too many young people believe the American dream is now achieved not by hard work, but by inheriting wealth from a family member or by winning a lottery! Knowing the odds against either of these events occurring, most youth seem to have no hope for the future.

The writer of Hebrews revealed that union with the Father through faith in the Son is the ultimate dream or hope for believers (see 12:22-24). This remains true regardless of whether they are young or old. Indeed, our hope resides in the Savior's eternal "kingdom" (vs. 28), not in wealth or power.

Hope in the Heavenly Savior. In the last week of March 1997, 39 people (21 women and 18 men), ranging in age from 26 to 72, committed suicide in a Rancho Santa Fe, California, mansion. The bodies were laid out on their bunk beds. Each was dressed in black pants, flowing black shirt, and new black athletic shoes. Each was covered with a purple shroud. All had identification papers. Each member believed a spaceship near the Hale-Bopp Comet was coming to collect him or her.

The 39 were members of Heaven's Gate, a group led by Marshall Herff Applewhite. The group mixed teachings opposed to Christianity and Judaism with prophecies from Revelation and a heavy dose of science fiction television shows and movies. The cultists believed that the world was coming to an end and that they had to prepare for the kingdom when all nonbelievers (or Luciferians as they were called) would be "plowed under" in the apocalypse. Only those "vessels" prepared to receive the word would be fortunate enough to escape.

In contrast, Christians place their hope not in an earthly leader, but in the Lord Jesus, the "mediator of the new covenant" (Heb. 12:24). Only He has the keys of life and death, and only He decides when He will return. Jesus' shed "blood" makes it possible for His followers to be forgiven and to remain faithful to Him, especially as they eagerly wait for His second coming.

FAITH REQUIRES LOVE

BACKGROUND SCRIPTURE: Hebrews 13:1-6; 1 Corinthians 13
DEVOTIONAL READING: John 13:31-35

Key Verse: Now abideth faith, hope, charity, these three;
but the greatest of these is charity. 1 Corinthians 13:13.

KING JAMES VERSION

HEBREWS 13:1 Let brotherly love continue. 2 Be not forgetful to entertain strangers: for thereby some have entertained angels unawares. 3 Remember them that are in bonds, as bound with them; and them which suffer adversity, as being yourselves also in the body. . . .

1 CORINTHIANS 13:1 Though I speak with the tongues of men and of angels, and have not charity, I am become as sounding brass, or a tinkling cymbal. 2 And though I have the gift of prophecy, and understand all mysteries, and all knowledge; and though I have all faith, so that I could remove mountains, and have not charity, I am nothing. 3 And though I bestow all my goods to feed the poor, and though I give my body to be burned, and have not charity, it profiteth me nothing.

4 Charity suffereth long, and is kind; charity envieth not; charity vaunteth not itself, is not puffed up, 5 Doth not behave itself unseemly, seeketh not her own, is not easily provoked, thinketh no evil; 6 Rejoiceth not in iniquity, but rejoiceth in the truth; 7 Beareth all things, believeth all things, hopeth all things, endureth all things.

8 Charity never faileth: but whether there be prophecies, they shall fail; whether there be tongues, they shall cease; whether there be knowledge, it shall vanish away. 9 For we know in part, and we prophesy in part. 10 But when that which is perfect is come, then that which is in part shall be done away. 11 When I was a child, I spake as a child, I understood as a child, I thought as a child: but when I became a man, I put away childish things. 12 For now we see through a glass, darkly; but then face to face: now I know in part; but then shall I know even as also I am known. 13 And now abideth faith, hope, charity, these three; but the greatest of these is charity.

NEW REVISED STANDARD VERSION

HEBREWS 13:1 Let mutual love continue. 2 Do not neglect to show hospitality to strangers, for by doing that some have entertained angels without knowing it. 3 Remember those who are in prison, as though you were in prison with them; those who are being tortured, as though you yourselves were being tortured. . . .

1 CORINTHIANS 13:1 If I speak in the tongues of mortals and of angels, but do not have love, I am a noisy gong or a clanging cymbal. 2 And if I have prophetic powers, and understand all mysteries and all knowledge, and if I have all faith, so as to remove mountains, but do not have love, I am nothing. 3 If I give away all my possessions, and if I hand over my body so that I may boast, but do not have love, I gain nothing.

4 Love is patient; love is kind; love is not envious or boastful or arrogant 5 or rude. It does not insist on its own way; it is not irritable or resentful; 6 it does not rejoice in wrongdoing, but rejoices in the truth. 7 It bears all things, believes all things, hopes all things, endures all things.

8 Love never ends. But as for prophecies, they will come to an end; as for tongues, they will cease; as for knowledge, it will come to an end. 9 For we know only in part, and we prophesy only in part; 10 but when the complete comes, the partial will come to an end. 11 When I was a child, I spoke like a child, I thought like a child, I reasoned like a child; when I became an adult, I put an end to childish ways. 12 For now we see in a mirror, dimly, but then we will see face to face. Now I know only in part; then I will know fully, even as I have been fully known. 13 And now faith, hope, and love abide, these three; and the greatest of these is love.

5

Monday, September 24	Psalm 18:1-6	*I Love You, O Lord*
Tuesday, September 25	Deuteronomy 7:7-11	*Faithful Love*
Wednesday, September 26	Deuteronomy 5:6-10	*Obedient Love*
Thursday, September 27	Deuteronomy 6:1-9	*Taught to Love*
Friday, September 28	John 13:31-35	*Love One Another*
Saturday, September 29	Luke 6:27-36	*Love Your Enemies*
Sunday, September 30	Hebrews 13:1-3;	
	1 Corinthians 13	*Faith, Hope, and Love*

BACKGROUND

Greek, the language of the New Testament, has four significant words for love: *eros*, *storge*, *philia*, and *agape*. The word *eros* is used primarily for physical love between the genders, but because of its debasement in pagan society, it does not occur in the New Testament. The word *storge* has special reference to love between parents and children, but could be used for the love between a ruler and his people or of a nation for its god.

The most common term for love in Greek is *philia*. This is the word of affectionate regard. It is used of love between friends, husbands and wives, parents and children (for example, Matt. 10:37; John 11:3, 36; 20:2). The term *agape* is the most common word for love in the New Testament. It is perhaps the characteristic term of Christianity. This is the love that speaks of unconditional esteem that God has for His children, and the high esteem and regard they should have for Him and their fellow human beings, especially other believers.

NOTES ON THE PRINTED TEXT

Hebrews 13:1 tells us to keep on loving one other as brothers and sisters. Often in the New Testament we read that Christians are, in effect, members of the same family, and should treat each other that way. The original recipients of Hebrews were already exercising kindness and compassion toward one another, but the writer of the letter felt a reminder would not be amiss.

Believers are not to relate only to one another, but to outsiders as well. In this regard, verse 2 urges believers to show hospitality to "strangers," which most likely refers to itinerant Christian preachers. In the first century A.D., there weren't many inns, and those that did exist often had an unsavory reputation. So travelers had to rely on householders if they were to get good accommodations during a journey. As an encouragement toward being hospitable, the writer reminded his readers that some have unwittingly hosted "angels." Verse 3 contains the directive to remember two groups: prisoners and the mistreated.

First Corinthians 13 records Paul's description of Christian love. He began his discussion by naming certain representative gifts and actions, the first of which is speaking in "tongues of men and of angels" (vs. 1). The apostle presented a hypothetical situation in which he could speak those kinds of tongues. As impressive as this may be, apart from love, Paul's speech would have been like the sound made by a noisy gong or a clanging cymbal. These were musical instruments used in pagan rituals. Put another way, his utterances would be just noise having little meaning. The absence of love would rob the gift of its value.

Paul next referred to three other spiritual gifts: prophecy, knowledge, and faith (vs. 2). Again the apostle spoke hypothetically, describing a situation in which he had these gifts in abundance. He might be able to deliver messages from God, have insight into all sorts of spiritual mysteries and truths of the divine, and have such a strong belief that he could dislodge mountains from their foundations. From a human standpoint, these gifts would be impressive. But if while Paul had these special abilities he was without love, then from the standpoint of God, the apostle would be an absolute zero. The absence of love would rob the gifted one of his value.

Paul finally referred to two impressive actions that he might perform. The first of these would be giving everything he owned to the destitute (vs. 3). Throughout the Bible we see the importance of helping those who lack what they need materially. The second action involves the apostle surrendering his body to be "burned" at the stake. This presumably refers to martyrdom by means of the flames. Other early manuscripts read, "If I . . . give over my body to hardship that I may boast." In this case, Paul may have been referring to serving others without regard for one's welfare and to boasting in the Lord in a wholesome manner about the sacrificial act. Regardless of whether burning or boasting is to be paired with helping the poor, the apostle's point in verse 3 remains the same. He taught that if he did these actions and yet was devoid of love, he would not gain anything through what he had sacrificed. The absence of love would rob service of its value.

Using both positive and negative terms, Paul described for the Corinthians what he meant by love. The apostle had previously spoken hypothetically about himself, but now he personified love for his readers. Most likely, Paul chose his words carefully to implicitly condemn errors committed by his readers. First, the apostle noted that Christlike love is known for its patience and kindness. The first of these terms is passive, while the second is active. As believers, we are to have a long fuse (so to speak) to our temper. We must not retaliate when wronged. Rather, we are to remain steadfast in spirit, consistently responding to others in a gracious and considerate manner (vs. 4).

Next, Paul described in a series of terms what love is not and does not do. Instead of envying people, love is thankful for God's blessing in their lives. Rather than arrogantly parading itself about, love is humble. Christian charity is never ill-mannered, disgraceful, or shameless to others. It does not seek its own interests or demand to get its own way, but is concerned with the welfare of others (vs. 5). Love is not easily provoked to rage or irritated. Likewise, it is not resentful. Expressed differently, love does not keep score of the transgressions others have inflicted. In addition, love never finds pleasure in the misdeeds and evil schemes of others. This last quality is paired with another. Love does not praise iniquity and injustice, but exalts in the truth of God (vs. 6). Similarly, love is overjoyed when others promote what is right in God's eyes.

Paul noted four things that Christlike love does in fullness (vs. 7). It bears all things, which means it is always supportive and helpful. This also implies that godly charity has the ability to face trials and patiently accept them. Love believes all things, meaning it searches for what is finest in people and accepts as true the very best that they have to offer. Love hopes all things, meaning it maintains confidence in God's ability to turn evil circumstances into good. Finally, love endures all things, meaning it remains faithful to God to the end of all ordeals.

Paul noted that love will never fail or come to an end. Put another way, Christian charity will last forever (vs. 8). The apostle next stressed that one day even the most spectacular of spiritual gifts will cease to be needed. For example, God will render prophecy inoperative, cause miraculous tongues to fall silent, and end the need for the gift of knowledge. Here the apostle was contrasting two periods—an earlier one in which the spiritual gifts are needed and a later one when they are not needed. Paul used several examples to illustrate the difference between the two periods. First, the distinction is like the difference between the partial and the complete, or between the imperfect and the perfect (vss. 9-10). The gifts of knowledge and prophecy, for example, put believers in touch with God only imperfectly. But in the later period, believers will be in full and perfect contact with Him.

Paul next illustrated his meaning by drawing an analogy involving childhood and adulthood. The apostle said that when he was a child, he talked, thought, and reasoned as a child. But now that Paul had become an adult, he had set aside childish ways (vs. 11). Childhood is like the first period, and childish ways are like spiritual gifts. Just as childish ways are appropriate for a child, so spiritual gifts are appropriate for people in the first period. But then (to follow the analogy further), adulthood is like the second period. It is a time in which we will put away our spiritual gifts, for they will not be appropriate any longer.

For his next illustration, Paul used an analogy involving a mirror (vs. 12). In that day, mirrors were made out of polished metal and provided a poor, distorted image of what they were reflecting. The glimpse of the Lord that we get as He is reflected in our spiritual gifts is like looking in such an imperfect mirror. In the second period, however, our vision of the Lord will not be mediated by our spiritual gifts, for we will see Him face-to-face. The apostle switched from the language of sight to that of knowledge when he noted that he, like all believers in the first period, knew God only partially. But Paul looked forward to a time when he would know God fully. Of course, the apostle was not suggesting that human beings will ever have knowledge equaling that of God. Moreover, the Lord is not limited, as people are, by conditions of the first period. He already knows all people fully, completely, and perfectly.

Verse 13 contains Paul's summation of his teaching about love. He said that Christian charity is for now and for eternity. The apostle likewise mentioned that faith and hope abide together with love, though the latter was the greatest of the trio. These three characteristics, in a sense, sum up the Christian life. As was noted in lesson 2, "faith" denotes trust in the Savior and commitment to His teachings. "Hope" refers to an unshakable confidence that the promises of the Father will ultimately be fulfilled by the Son. Thanks to Paul we have already learned what "love" denotes.

Some interpreters have suggested that the apostle meant that faith and hope, like love, are eternal, since they can be considered manifestations of love. Paul, however, more likely included faith and hope in verse 13 to remind his readers that love is for now, just as are faith and hope. When the apostle went on to say that love is the greatest virtue, he probably meant that Christian charity eclipses faith and hope because it lasts forever. But the latter two virtues, like the spiritual gifts, are for this age only. Faith is not necessary in eternity because then we will be in the very presence of God. Likewise, hope is not necessary in eternity because then our expectations will have been fulfilled.

SUGGESTIONS TO TEACHERS

Ask the class to tally some uses of the word "love" that they've heard recently. Draw upon these examples to stress how overworked is the English word "love." Next mention that "love" in 1 Corinthians 13 translates *agape*, which refers to unselfish, unconditional compassion, not sentimental feelings or erotic stirrings. Then note the following points.

1. SUPREMACY OF LOVE. Paul mentioned several gifts of the Spirit, such as speaking in tongues, profound thinking, and acts of philanthropy. Yet love surpasses them all!

2. SHAPE OF LOVE. Note the various qualities of Christian love. Then have the class members discuss times when either they or some other believers they know demonstrated the love of Christ. Remind the students that Jesus is the best example of love. Point out how consistently He exhibited a patient, unselfish compassion for others.

3. STAMINA OF LOVE. In an era of road rage and "in your face" confrontations, we may be persuaded that Christlike love is wimpy and useless. But love outlasts everything. In fact, love triumphs! The cross and resurrection pronounce God's verdict on violence and retaliation. Love proves to be more powerful than anything!

4. SUPERIORITY OF LOVE. Paul listed the top three virtues: faith, hope, and love. Each is great, and each is needed. But love is the greatest!

■ TOPIC: Steadfast Love

■ QUESTIONS: 1. Why do you think the writer of Hebrews stressed the importance of showing Christlike love? 2. How is it possible for believers to be patient and kind when others are rude to them? 3. What was Paul's main purpose in stressing that spiritual gifts are temporary, but love is permanent? 4. What can you do to become more Christlike in your love? 5. How might you encourage your fellow believers to let the love of Christ permeate their attitudes and actions?

■ ILLUSTRATIONS:

Love Comes First. Anthony Campolo tells the story of a 13-year-old hydrocephalic girl living in a Haitian missionary hospital. The girl, brain damaged and deformed, rocked nervously on her bed, day after day, year after year. The Haitian nurses, though very busy with more hopeful cases, lovingly tended this girl, feeding her, changing her diapers, and tending to her safety needs.

One day the girl accidentally rocked herself off her bed and onto the cement floor, seriously injuring herself. The nurses could have dismissed the fall as being "God's will" and cut down on her care. Instead, they chose to increase her care and to spend long hours in prayer for her.

Steadfastly loving the unlovely is a Christian's mandate and challenge (see 1 Cor. 13; Heb. 13:1-3). Will we love those we find physically and mentally repulsive? Will we care about and care for society's "hopeless"?

What Needs Love. Nobel Peace Prize winner Mother Teresa died in the fall of 1997, but her example, words, and works continue to have a lasting influence. The woman who headed a religious community that cared for the victims of disease and starvation and demonstrated unconditional and enduring love for all declared that the greatest illness in the world was not cancer or leprosy, but a lack of love. She further said that the greatest evil was indifference and intolerance.

Paul declared that the love of Christ is the greatest gift that a believer can pass on to others. In light of Mother Teresa's words and Paul's teaching, how are you going to act?

The Parable of the Pit. There's an old story called the parable of the pit. It's about a man who one day fell into a pit and could not get himself out. A subjective person saw him and said, "I feel for you down there." An objective person happened along and said, "It's logical that someone would fall down there."

A rock collector asked, "Are there any rare specimens in the pit?" A news reporter queried, "Can I have the exclusive story on your pit?" A realist happened along and said, "Now that's a pit!" An oddsmaker noted, "Chances are that anyone could fall into a pit."

A scientist saw the man and said, "I'll calculate the pressure necessary to get you out of the pit." A geologist said, "Just appreciate the rock strata in your pit." A professor gave the man a lecture on "The Elementary Principles of a Pit." A government official asked, "Are you paying taxes on your pit?" A land use inspector asked, "Did you have a permit to dig a pit?"

An evasive person talked to the man and avoided the subject of the pit altogether. A self-pitying person said, "You haven't seen anything until you've seen my pit!" An optimist said, "Things could be worse." A pessimist said, "Things will get worse!" But Jesus, seeing the man, took him by the hand and lifted him out of the pit.

Our Scripture texts for this week point to the Savior's love for us. It's an unconditional love that takes us just as we are. And His compassion inspires us to show the same sort of love to others in need around us. The question is, are we ready and willing to help?

FOR YOUTH

■ **TOPIC:** Show Some Love
■ **QUESTIONS:** 1. What does it mean to love our fellow believers as brothers and sisters in Christ? 2. Why are any of the spiritual gifts valueless apart from love? 3. What enables a believer characterized by love to bear, believe, hope, and endure all things? 4. In what sense will love last forever? 5. How does your life compare with Paul's description of love?

■ **ILLUSTRATIONS:**

Called to Love. Pastor Jeff Wallace recalled the following incident involving his daughter, Gracie, when she was a young girl. It helps us to appreciate the role that Christlike love serves among believers.

"With my daughter's hand in mine, we walked out of the convention hall where we had heard a gifted preacher convey afresh the love and grace and mercy of the Lord. I had noticed Gracie's rapt attention as the preacher spoke. I, too, was greatly moved and impressed by his message.

"I thus wasn't surprised when Gracie looked up at me and asked, 'Daddy, did you think that was a good preacher?' 'Oh, yes, sweetheart, he is a great preacher,' I responded. 'Do you think he's a better preacher than you are?' 'Oh, yes, sweetheart, he's a much better preacher than I am.' 'Not really, Daddy,' she concluded. 'The only preacher better than you is Jesus!'

"Of course, my confidence in my preaching ability was little affected by my daughter's opinion. But my heart was overjoyed by her expression of pure love and devotion. Love does that. It always affects. It always brings joy. It always builds up."

Put Away Childish Things. A radical German kindergarten program bans children from playing with toys for a three-month stretch. Originally begun in a nursery school in Penzberg (30 miles south of Munich), the program was designed to prevent children from becoming addicted to possessions. They learn to amuse themselves, develop new skills, and increase their creativity.

Paul urged his readers to put aside childish things. This means not spending all our time and energies seeking the attention and approval of others. It also means not buying the fanciest clothes or seeking to become the most popular person among our peers. Mature, loving Christians are not obsessed with the toys and trinkets of the world. Instead, they strive to serve the Lord.

Never Obsolete. Decades ago, I bought my first computer, monitor, and printer. Though certain minor problems arose with the equipment, these were repairable. And I chose to ignore such inconveniences as an aging ribbon.

But a few years later things were different when the computer broke down again. A technician said that he could not repair the equipment, for it had become obsolete. In fact, I learned that it was cheaper to scrap the computer and buy a new one than to continue having the old one repaired.

Unlike aging computer equipment, Christlike love never becomes obsolete. While even the most spectacular spiritual gifts will outlive their usefulness, this will never be true of love.

STEPHEN'S ARREST

BACKGROUND SCRIPTURE: Acts 6:8–7:53
DEVOTIONAL READING: Proverbs 8:1-11

Key Verse: Stephen, full of faith and power, did
great wonders and miracles among the people. Acts 6:8.

KING JAMES VERSION

ACTS 6:8 And Stephen, full of faith and power, did great wonders and miracles among the people. 9 Then there arose certain of the synagogue, which is called the synagogue of the Libertines, and Cyrenians, and Alexandrians, and of them of Cilicia and of Asia, disputing with Stephen. 10 And they were not able to resist the wisdom and the spirit by which he spake. 11 Then they suborned men, which said, We have heard him speak blasphemous words against Moses, and against God. 12 And they stirred up the people, and the elders, and the scribes, and came upon him, and caught him, and brought him to the council, 13 And set up false witnesses, which said, This man ceaseth not to speak blasphemous words against this holy place, and the law: 14 For we have heard him say, that this Jesus of Nazareth shall destroy this place, and shall change the customs which Moses delivered us. 15 And all that sat in the council, looking stedfastly on him, saw his face as it had been the face of an angel.

7:1 Then said the high priest, Are these things so? 2 And he said, Men, brethren, and fathers, hearken; The God of glory appeared unto our father Abraham, when he was in Mesopotamia, before he dwelt in Charran.

NEW REVISED STANDARD VERSION

ACTS 6:8 Stephen, full of grace and power, did great wonders and signs among the people. 9 Then some of those who belonged to the synagogue of the Freedmen (as it was called), Cyrenians, Alexandrians, and others of those from Cilicia and Asia, stood up and argued with Stephen. 10 But they could not withstand the wisdom and the Spirit with which he spoke. 11 Then they secretly instigated some men to say, "We have heard him speak blasphemous words against Moses and God." 12 They stirred up the people as well as the elders and the scribes; then they suddenly confronted him, seized him, and brought him before the council. 13 They set up false witnesses who said, "This man never stops saying things against this holy place and the law; 14 for we have heard him say that this Jesus of Nazareth will destroy this place and will change the customs that Moses handed on to us." 15 And all who sat in the council looked intently at him, and they saw that his face was like the face of an angel.

7:1 Then the high priest asked him, "Are these things so?" 2 And Stephen replied: "Brothers and fathers, listen to me. The God of glory appeared to our ancestor Abraham when he was in Mesopotamia, before he lived in Haran."

6

HOME BIBLE READINGS

BACKGROUND

After Jesus ascended, the church experienced explosive growth. People were entering God's kingdom by the thousands, far more than the 12 apostles could minister to. At some point, a quarrel broke out between the Jewish believers who spoke Greek and the ones who spoke Aramaic or Hebrew. The first group complained that their widows were not given their share when the food supplies were distributed each day (Acts 6:1). The Twelve responded to the crisis facing the Jerusalem church by calling a meeting of all the believers. The apostles could have assumed responsibility for overseeing the relief work. But they correctly saw this as a diversion from their main tasks of praying and preaching and teaching the Gospel. They thus decided to delegate to others the important job of administering the charitable distribution of food to the poor (vs. 2).

The apostles made it clear that those to be appointed had to be well respected and "full of the Holy Ghost and wisdom" (vs. 3). The Twelve would put them in charge of the food relief program. In turn, the apostles would have greater freedom to pray and minister God's Word (vs. 4). The apostles allowed the Greek-speaking Jewish believers to choose their own representatives (vs. 5). All seven Christians had Greek names, which suggests that they were probably Hellenists. Only one of the seven was described as a proselyte—a Greek Gentile who had become a Jew before becoming a Christian. Stephen is described as a believer full of faith and controlled by the Spirit. We can assume that the other believers chosen also met these qualifications. In fact, Stephen and Philip would later demonstrate other spiritual gifts. The primary responsibility of these seven believers, however, was one of service to the Hellenistic Jews.

NOTES ON THE PRINTED TEXT

Luke highlighted two things that the apostles did after the seven believers were chosen. First, the apostles prayed and laid hands on the seven. By following this Old Testament custom (see Num. 27:18, 23; Deut. 34:9), the apostles set apart the seven for their church duties. Second, the apostles delegated some of their church authority to Stephen and the other six believers (Acts 6:6).

The ministry of the seven believers bore fruit. The church in Jerusalem grew rapidly. Even a large number of Jewish priests became followers of the Messiah. Instead of a few people trying to do everything, other believers contributed to the well-being of the community of faith (vs. 7). According to verse 8, Stephen did more than just wait on tables. The Holy Spirit so filled him with "faith and power" that he was able to perform amazing "wonders and miracles" in the presence of others. For the first time, the ability to perform such great deeds extended beyond the apostles.

In addition to performing miracles, Stephen also proclaimed the Gospel, which disturbed the Jews who had come from different parts of the Roman Empire. One group was the "synagogue of the Libertines" (vs. 9). The synagogue was attended by Jews from Cyrene, Alexandria, Cilicia, and Asia. Both the Cyrenians and the Alexandrians had come from major cities in North Africa. Cilicia was located in the southeast corner of Asia Minor, and "Asia" was a Roman province in the western part of Asia Minor. The Hellenist Jews were constantly battling an image of being "second class" to their Hebrew brothers and sisters. Even the Talmud (a collection of Jewish writings that predates the New Testament) said these people were not to be trusted.

Since Hellenist Jews wanted to be fully accepted, they no doubt repressed any behavior that challenged Jewish traditions. Perhaps just when the Hellenist Jews seemed to be making some headway, a young Greek-speaking Jew turned Christian came on the scene, preaching repentance and belief in Jesus as the Messiah. Though the Hellenist Jews were incensed with Stephen, they were no match for his Spirit-inspired "wisdom" (vs. 10). Indeed, despite their best efforts, they failed to refute his message by debating with him.

Stephen's opponents on the sly instigated some rogues to testify that he had spoken slanderously against Moses and God (vs. 11). Naturally, what the false witnesses claimed alarmed the Jewish people and their rulers in Jerusalem. This prompted the religious elite—namely, the elders and scribes (that is, experts in the Mosaic law)—to authorize Stephen's arrest and appearance before the "council" (vs. 12). The latter was the Sanhedrin, the Jewish supreme court of the day.

The antagonists found a group of individuals who were willing to tell blatant lies. These "false witnesses" (vs. 13) claimed that Stephen spoke against the cherished institutions and laws of ancient Judaism. In particular, he was accused of claiming that "Jesus of Nazareth" (vs. 14) would demolish the temple and throw out all the "customs" Moses had given to the chosen people. These were charges similar to those that had been brought against Jesus at His trial. Some think the indictment represents a garbled version of the episode recorded in John 2:19-22.

As Stephen stood before the seated members of the high council, all of them stared at him "stedfastly" (Acts 6:15). The reason for their fixed gaze is that the face of Stephen beamed as bright as that of an "angel." This suggests that the Spirit of God was uniquely manifesting His presence in Stephen's life at that moment. Stephen's opponents had accused him of slandering Moses, the law, the Jerusalem temple, and God. The high priest in office at the time (most likely Caiaphas) asked Stephen whether he thought his accusers were telling the truth or lying about him (7:1). The high priest was the person who presided over the meetings of the Sanhedrin, or Jewish national council. This assembly was made up of 70 members: the chief priests, professional teachers of the law, and the elders. Annas had been high priest from A.D. 6 to about A.D. 15, when the Romans removed him from office. Nevertheless, the Jews still recognized him as high priest. Caiaphas, Annas's son-in-law, served as the high priest from A.D. 18 to about A.D. 36. During his tenure, he condemned Jesus to death.

Acts 7:2-53 contains the speech that Stephen gave to the Sanhedrin. It is the longest recorded public address in the book. Stephen followed Hebrew custom by surveying the history of Israel. He began by respectfully addressing his listeners as "brethren, and fathers" (vs. 2) and enjoining them to heed what he had to say. Here we see that Stephen took seriously the charges that were brought against him and grounded his defense on the teaching of the Old Testament. Unlike his detractors, Stephen was characterized by "meekness and fear" (1 Pet. 3:15) as he spoke.

Stephen directed the attention of the audience to the time when the all-glorious Lord manifested His presence to their ancestor Abraham while he lived in Mesopotamia. The religious elite of Stephen's day lauded the temple in Jerusalem as the place where God displayed His glory. Yet, when the Lord appeared to their esteemed patriarch, it was not even in Palestine, but in Mesopotamia. Stephen explained that this incident occurred before Abraham relocated with his family to Haran. This was a city in the northern part of Mesopotamia located on the Balikh River, which is a branch of the Euphrates. Terah (the father of Abraham), Nahor (Abraham's brother), and the patriarch's extended family left Ur and migrated to Haran (see Gen. 11:31). We cannot be sure why God called Abraham and not someone else. But from later events in the patriarch's life, we know he had many fine qualities. This does not mean he was perfect. In fact, Joshua 24:2 reveals that at the time Abraham was living in Ur, his family was worshiping false gods.

At first glance it might appear from Genesis 11:31 that God originally called Terah from Ur to go to Canaan. Other passages, though, make it clear that Abraham was the person whom God called to leave his homeland (see Gen. 15:7; Neh. 9:7; Acts 7:2-3). As was just noted, the patriarch began his journey to Canaan with his father, wife, and Lot, his nephew. But after traveling north along the Fertile Crescent trade route, the group arrived in Haran, where it stayed for a time, accumulating possessions and servants (see Gen. 12:5). Why did Abraham stop in Haran? Perhaps Terah, his father, was too weak to travel farther, or perhaps Terah felt at home there, since the people of Haran also worshiped the moon god. While some attribute the stay in Haran to disobedience, others suggest that the stop was just a delay necessitated by family reasons. After Terah died there (see 11:32), Abraham left and journeyed to Canaan (see Acts

7:4). In contrast, Nahor stayed behind (see Gen. 24:10). Haran is the city where Abraham's servant went to get a wife for Isaac, and later Jacob went there to find a wife (see 29:5).

SUGGESTIONS TO TEACHERS

Contrary to what some think, the Spirit is not given to make us feel warm inside. Rather, God gives us the Spirit so that we can have the power to serve the risen Lord. This week's lesson will help your students understand that the Spirit empowers them to continue the work that Jesus did.

1. EMPOWERED TO HEAL. Part of Jesus' ministry was to bring about spiritual, emotional, and physical wellness in the lives of people. According to Acts, early Christians such as Stephen continued this healing ministry. Sometimes church people shy away from any talk about God's ability to heal us from our afflictions. Why not take this opportunity to briefly discuss the issue with your students? For example, how has God dramatically changed their lives or the lives of people they know?

2. EMPOWERED TO PREACH. Preaching doesn't just mean standing up in a pulpit on Sunday morning. Every believer can—and should—be able to say something about the love of the Father through the Son. Stephen's example serves as a reminder that evangelism means heralding the Good News. Declaring the Gospel is not an optional matter, either. God wants all Jesus' followers to be involved in this great work. "But how can I say anything?" some might ask. The answer is simple and clear. The Spirit empowers every believer who asks for help.

3. EMPOWERED TO PERSEVERE. Stephen was undaunted by threats and jailing. He testified boldly about Jesus before the authorities. People could see that Stephen was serious about his faith. Are those around us able to make that kind of observation? The empowering Spirit strengthened early Christians such as Stephen to continue serving the Lord despite opposition. They refused to use the excuses we sometimes give (such as feeling overwhelmed or burned out). Furthermore, the early Christians persevered, not by claiming any human stamina or personal strength, but by relying on the Spirit. So must we!

FOR ADULTS

■ **TOPIC:** Courage to Speak

■ **QUESTIONS:** 1. What attributes of Jesus were present in Stephen's life? 2. Why did Stephen's opponents incite the false witnesses to make the particular claims they did? 3. What attitude do you think the religious elite had toward Jesus of Nazareth? 4. When you perform Christian duties, what risks might bother you the most? Why? 5. What might hinder you the most from serving in the church? What can you do to overcome this obstacle?

■ ILLUSTRATIONS:

Empowered to Witness. *Evangelism* is a word that scares many Christians. We think telling others about the Savior is the responsibility of religious experts. But this week's lesson reminds us that a relatively unknown convert named Stephen made a significant impact in witnessing for the Lord. It was possible because Stephen operated in the Messiah's life-changing power.

God gives us many opportunities to point others to Jesus. When we meet people at their deepest physical and social needs, for example, we gain opportunities to share that we serve in the name and power of the risen Lord.

Perhaps we fail to see beyond the outward appearance of many people. We think they don't need religious faith. But as we get to know them, they often admit to some glaring spiritual needs. As one woman told her friends, "The best gift I can give my family is to get my spiritual life straightened out." She has since that time come to faith in Christ!

Freedom Fighter. Stephen stands out among believers in the early church for his bold witness for Christ. Down through the centuries, there have been others who also exhibited a similar level of boldness. For instance, over 150 years ago, a brave woman named Harriet Tubman escaped from slavery. But her own freedom was not enough. She risked her life 19 more times to rescue other slaves. Harriet Tubman became the most famous conductor on the Underground Railroad, leading over 300 persons to freedom.

Harriet was born a slave in Bucktown, Maryland, around 1820. Her owners forced her to labor in the fields, and she became strong. When she was about 12, Harriet was struck on the head by an angry overseer because she refused to help tie up a runaway to be whipped. The blow caused her severe headaches the rest of her life. When she was about 29, she learned that she was to be sold and sent to a plantation farther south. She finally decided to escape.

Harriet walked 90 miles to reach Pennsylvania and continued to Canada. Her deep faith sustained her and motivated her to make daring trips back to the slave areas to guide others north to freedom. This won her the nickname "Moses of her people." Slave owners feared her so much that they put out a reward of $40,000 for her capture. But not one person she led to freedom was recaptured or killed.

Later, during the Civil War, Harriet Tubman served as a nurse, guide, cook, and soldier for the Union army. Eventually, she was able to buy a house and 26 acres in Auburn, New York. In 1903, Harriet gave the buildings and property to her church to be used as a home for the aged. This great, empowered leader passed away in 1913.

A Perseverer. The story of a man named Patrick illustrates the power of the Spirit that was present in the lives of believers such as Stephen. Patrick was born into a devout family's home in ancient Britain. When he was 16, he was carried off by marauding raiders and taken as a slave to Ireland. He was forced to tend pigs and endured cruel treatment at the hands of his pagan captors. His afflictions strengthened his faith in the Lord, and this enabled him to survive his ordeal.

Patrick escaped by walking 200 miles, and then he took a ship that carried him to Gaul. When he finally got home to his family in Britain, he announced that he sensed God was calling him to return to Ireland. His family couldn't understand why he'd risk his life and waste his time by going back to the brutal, rough pagans who had mistreated him.

Furthermore, Patrick had little formal learning. When he started classes to become a minister, he was ridiculed by the scholarly, sophisticated church leaders for his poor skills in rhetoric and classical Latin. His rustic manners and lack of education credentials caused the snobbish upper class to hesitate to ordain him. But despite opposition, he was finally ordained and commissioned to go to Ireland as a missionary.

Patrick suffered persecution by the native Irish and false charges by British church officials, showing that they continued to regard him as being unfit for ordination. Worse was Patrick's reception by Irish kings and druids. He narrowly escaped death several times, especially when he challenged the pagan king by lighting a fire celebrating the resurrection of Christ before the ruler started the flame of a heathen nature celebration. Patrick was imprisoned twice for long weeks by Irish enemies. But he persevered.

In one generation this great missionary brought the light of Christ and the torch of Western civilization to the natives on the bleak fringe of Europe. Patrick and his colleagues are credited with preserving the ancient learning that had been almost destroyed by the Vandals, Huns, and Goths in the looting, burning, and chaos that swept the continent after the fall of Rome. Society's debt to Patrick is greater than most realize!

FOR YOUTH

■ TOPIC: Speak Up!

■ QUESTIONS: 1. How do you think the people who knew Stephen best would have described him? 2. Why do you think Stephen was so bold in his witness? 3. What incorrect information about Jesus did the religious elite believe? 4. What do you believe God has called you to do in your church? How have you responded? 5. What future areas of service do you see yourself stepping into? How can you be filled with the Spirit as you begin to serve?

■ ILLUSTRATIONS:

The Power of Jesus. Many Christian young people in your class will have personally encountered some level of harassment because of their faith. Some may have heard non-Christian family members joke about their walk with God. For others, their Christian ethics may have left them feeling like outsiders at school. The point is that your students can probably relate times when they may have asked themselves whether witnessing for the Lord was worth the conflict.

This week's lesson tells us that enduring hardship for the Savior is worth it. Being harassed is nothing compared to what Jesus is doing in the lives of your class members. Like Stephen, who didn't whine when he was persecuted, your students can rejoice when the power of Jesus touches their lives and the lives of others.

Any Correlation? Dr. Richard Sloan of Columbia University published a report in the British medical journal the *Lancet* that the evidence of an association between religion and health was inconsistent and weak. He questioned whether faith boosted healing. He urged fellow physicians to be cautious when recommending faith as an aid to physical recovery.

How would Stephen have responded? With complete faith in the Savior and His presence, Stephen performed "great wonders and miracles" (Acts 6:8), including healing the infirm. God's power was unmistakable in this believer's life. The overwhelming testimony of Scripture is that the Lord Jesus can bring about spiritual, emotional, and physical wellness in the lives of people.

Taking Faith on the Road. Stephen's efforts to herald the Gospel is a testimony to the power of Christ. We discover that the Lord Jesus brings renewal to believers as well as changing those who approach Him for the first time.

A group of churchmen from Illinois chartered a bus to a two-day Christian men's conference in a nearby state. While going to the conference, the men were irritated by the driver, who couldn't locate their motel and insisted on smoking. "He had a kind of uncaring attitude and was in his own little world," said one of the leaders.

During the conference the men experienced a touch from God, and the trip home was like a rolling revival. "We sang some songs and asked for testimonies, and we had about three hours' worth," said a member of the group. "We almost asked the bus driver to slow down so we could get all the testimonies in!"

As they neared home, the men passed a hat and collected $200 for the driver. He had tears in his eyes and said, "The gift is great, but what I'm hearing from you guys is worth a lot more." Back in the church parking lot they formed a circle of prayer, and even the newly converted bus driver got involved!

STEPHEN'S MARTYRDOM

BACKGROUND SCRIPTURE: Acts 7:1–8:1a
DEVOTIONAL READING: Ephesians 6:13-20

Key Verse: They stoned Stephen, calling upon God,
and saying, Lord Jesus, receive my spirit. Acts 7:59.

KING JAMES VERSION

ACTS 7:51 Ye stiffnecked and uncircumcised in heart and ears, ye do always resist the Holy Ghost: as your fathers did, so do ye. 52 Which of the prophets have not your fathers persecuted? and they have slain them which shewed before of the coming of the Just One; of whom ye have been now the betrayers and murderers: 53 Who have received the law by the disposition of angels, and have not kept it.

54 When they heard these things, they were cut to the heart, and they gnashed on him with their teeth. 55 But he, being full of the Holy Ghost, looked up stedfastly into heaven, and saw the glory of God, and Jesus standing on the right hand of God, 56 And said, Behold, I see the heavens opened, and the Son of man standing on the right hand of God. 57 Then they cried out with a loud voice, and stopped their ears, and ran upon him with one accord, 58 And cast him out of the city, and stoned him: and the witnesses laid down their clothes at a young man's feet, whose name was Saul. 59 And they stoned Stephen, calling upon God, and saying, Lord Jesus, receive my spirit. 60 And he kneeled down, and cried with a loud voice, Lord, lay not this sin to their charge. And when he had said this, he fell asleep.

8:1 And Saul was consenting unto his death.

NEW REVISED STANDARD VERSION

ACTS 7:51 "You stiff-necked people, uncircumcised in heart and ears, you are forever opposing the Holy Spirit, just as your ancestors used to do. 52 Which of the prophets did your ancestors not persecute? They killed those who foretold the coming of the Righteous One, and now you have become his betrayers and murderers. 53 You are the ones that received the law as ordained by angels, and yet you have not kept it."

54 When they heard these things, they became enraged and ground their teeth at Stephen. 55 But filled with the Holy Spirit, he gazed into heaven and saw the glory of God and Jesus standing at the right hand of God. 56 "Look," he said, "I see the heavens opened and the Son of Man standing at the right hand of God!" 57 But they covered their ears, and with a loud shout all rushed together against him. 58 Then they dragged him out of the city and began to stone him; and the witnesses laid their coats at the feet of a young man named Saul. 59 While they were stoning Stephen, he prayed, "Lord Jesus, receive my spirit." 60 Then he knelt down and cried out in a loud voice, "Lord, do not hold this sin against them." When he had said this, he died. 8:1 And Saul approved of their killing him.

7

HOME BIBLE READINGS

Monday, October 8	Ephesians 6:13-20	*Equipped to Speak Boldly*
Tuesday, October 9	Acts 7:17-22	*The Promised Fulfillment Draws Near*
Wednesday, October 10	Acts 7:30-34	*I Have Come to Rescue Them*
Thursday, October 11	Acts 7:35-39	*The Rejection of Moses*
Friday, October 12	Acts 7:39-43	*The Rejection of God*
Saturday, October 13	Acts 7:44-50	*The Inadequacy of the Temple*
Sunday, October 14	Acts 7:51–8:1a	*You Are the Ones*

BACKGROUND

In Stephen's formal response to the Sanhedrin, he followed Hebrew custom by surveying the history of Israel. He did so to emphasize that Jesus of Nazareth was Israel's promised Messiah and Redeemer. In particular, Stephen's address sets forth a refutation of the three points of reference on which some first-century A.D. Jews placed an idolatrous emphasis: the land, the law, and the temple. Concerning the Jews' veneration of the promised land, Stephen argued that while Judah remained important, God's activities in Israel's history often took place outside of Palestine. Also, wherever God is present, that locale is considered holy (Acts 7:2-36).

Moreover, the Jews revered the law and, in turn, the one who gave them the law—Moses. But Stephen reminded his listeners that this legendary figure clearly pointed to a coming Prophet who was greater than Moses and the law. Likewise, the people rejected Moses and embraced idol worship, just as they spurned Jesus (vss. 37-43). Finally, the Jews fixated on the Jerusalem temple as a symbol of God's past workings with the nation of Israel and the source of their future hope—so much so that they ended up worshiping the shrine rather than their Creator-King. Tragically, many also seemed to confine God's work to the sanctuary alone, instead of recognizing that He transcended any edifice made by people (see Isa. 66:1-2; Acts 17:24).

NOTES ON THE PRINTED TEXT

Stephen declared the religious leaders to be as "stiffnecked" (Acts 7:51), or stubborn, as an unyielding ox or donkey. Moreover, the members of the Council were "uncircumcised" in their thoughts, emotions, and will. By this declaration, Stephen meant that the members of the Sanhedrin, though physically circumcised, were no different in their attitude and actions from the uncircumcised pagans they detested. Because the religious leaders refused to listen to God and rebelled against His Word, they were spiritually stubborn and unregenerate (see Exod. 32:9; 33:3, 5; Deut. 9:6; 10:16; 30:6; Jer. 4:4). Furthermore, instead of being genuinely devoted to the Lord, the Council was guilty of always fighting against the Holy Spirit. Stephen noted that this was the same offense their ancestors had committed.

Stephen rhetorically asked whether there ever was a spokesperson for God whom the ancestors of the Sanhedrin did not mistreat. Stephen declared that the Council's predecessors were even guilty of murdering the prophets who foretold the advent of the "Just One" (Acts 7:52), which is a reference to Jesus of Nazareth. Of course, the religious leaders rejected His claim to be the Messiah. Also, rather than heed Him as their Redeemer and Lord, they schemed with the civil authorities to have Him crucified. The irony is that the Mosaic law the Council members so highly prized contained prophecies about the coming of the Savior. Put differently, it was the members of the Sanhedrin, not Stephen, who were guilty of violating the law and desecrating all that it stood for.

Here we learn that the Mosaic law was ordained or decreed by angels. Though angels are not mentioned as being instrumental in God's issuance of the law to Moses in Exodus 20, their presence at Mount Sinai is mentioned in several other New Testament passages (see Gal. 3:19; Heb. 2:2). Mention is also made in the Septuagint version of Deuteronomy 33:2, as well as in the *Antiquities* of the first-century A.D. Jewish historian Josephus. Apparently, the involvement of angels in the mediation of the law was widely accepted by the second century B.C.

The natural reaction of the religious leaders was to be "cut to the heart" (Acts 7:54). This phrase renders a Greek verb that means to be enraged. The members of the Council also began to grind their teeth. This is an idiomatic expression to point to the presence of extreme agitation. Stephen's speech was upsetting to the religious leaders because to some extent it was a stinging indictment of a history of unbelief for the nation and its chosen people. But more specifically, in the minds of the religious leaders Stephen's claim of divinity for Jesus of Nazareth, the person whom they had schemed to be crucified, was a clear case of blasphemy. According to the Mosaic law, this offense was punishable by death (see Lev. 24:13-16).

Despite the fury of the Sanhedrin, Stephen remained under the complete control of the Holy Spirit. At Jesus' trial, He had declared to the Council that they would see the "Son of man sitting on the right hand of power" (Mark 14:62). As Stephen fixed his gaze heavenward, he had a vision of the Father's glory and the Son standing at the Lord's right hand (Acts 7:55). While the "Son of man" (vs. 56) is customarily pictured as seated at the Father's right hand, some have suggested that the Messiah had risen on this occasion to welcome the first martyr of the church. Others think Jesus was testifying on behalf of Stephen.

Stephen's words were so blasphemous to the religious leaders that they put their hands over their ears and drowned out his voice with their shouts (vs. 57). Perhaps with the fury of an uncontrollable mob, the Council rushed at Stephen, hauled him out of Jerusalem, and began to throw stones at him. Though he faced imminent death, Stephen demonstrated before his antagonists what it truly meant to honor the Lord. Stephen's desire was not to perpetuate a dead institution and its lifeless traditions.

Rather, he sought to please God, regardless of the circumstances or the cost to himself. While these things were taking place, the official witnesses took off their outer garments and laid them at the feet of a young man named "Saul" (vs. 58) of Tarsus. (He is later called Paul in 13:9.) He was a Pharisee and associated with the Sanhedrin (see Phil. 3:5). Possibly Saul was an instigator of Stephen's trial (see Acts 8:3; 9:1-2).

In ancient Israel, stoning was the most commonly prescribed form of execution for capital offenses. These offenses usually involved breaking particular Mosaic laws. Included among the crimes that carried the death penalty were child sacrifice (Lev. 20:2), involvement with the occult (20:27), working on the Sabbath (Num. 15:32-36), worshiping false gods (Deut. 13:10), rebellion against parents (21:18-21), adultery (22:21-24; Ezek. 16:38-40), and blasphemy (Lev. 24:14-16; John 10:31-33). The men of a community normally carried out the sentence of stoning (Deut. 21:21). In cases involving capital crimes, the testimony of at least two witnesses was required, and those witnesses were obligated to cast the first stones (Deut. 17:5-7; John 8:7; Acts 7:58). Execution normally occurred somewhere outside the city or camp boundaries.

The members of the Sanhedrin, not Stephen, were guilty of rebelling against God. Years earlier, during Jesus' earthly ministry, He declared that in the day of judgment, He would not be the one to accuse His opponents of sinning against the Father. Instead, it would be their esteemed lawgiver, Moses, in whom the religious authorities of the day had pinned their hopes of salvation (John 5:45). In the future time of reckoning, the critics would not be able to look to Moses as their intercessor before God (see Exod. 32:30-34; Ps. 106:23), for ultimately what Moses penned concerned the Messiah. Jesus and Moses were so intertwined that to receive or reject Moses was to receive or reject Jesus (John 5:46-47). He who is the only mediator between God and humanity is also the same person the elite spurned (see 1 Tim. 2:5). In short, to reject the Son—the Father's only provision of salvation—was to leave oneself eternally condemned (see Heb. 6:4-8; 1 Pet. 2:7-8).

While Stephen was being stoned, he made two dying requests. First, he prayed that the Messiah would receive his spirit (Acts 7:59). The comparison to our Lord's dying prayer is too striking to be overlooked (see Luke 23:46). Just as the Son had committed Himself to the Father, so Stephen cast himself upon Jesus. Thus, to Stephen's dying breath, he confirmed the deity of the Messiah. Second, while Stephen knelt on the ground, he prayed for his enemies. He asked the Lord not hold his executioners guilty for what they had done (Acts 7:60). This petition echoed Jesus' cry at His crucifixion (see Luke 23:34). Stephen, like his Master, ended his life by returning forgiveness for vengeance, and love for hatred.

Despite the terrifying prospect of death, Stephen remained calm and hopeful. Unlike his detractors, he had the assurance that God the Son—his Savior and Lord—would receive him into His glorious presence. The words "he fell asleep" (Acts 7:60) were a common euphemism for death in Scripture. The verse points to the peace with which Stephen died. His triumph was grounded in the risen Messiah. He, having conquered death, promised a future resurrection awakening for His disciples.

Earlier it was noted that a young pharisee named Saul was standing with the clothing of the executioners (see vs. 58). By doing so, Saul did not show mere passive approval of the stoning. Some have suggested that this act meant Saul was in charge of the proceedings. In any case, 8:1 shows Saul actively and wholeheartedly condoning the grizzly death of Stephen. Saul's statement about himself in 22:20 agrees with 8:1. The hatred he had of all believers before his conversion was manifested in his attitude toward Stephen. God would eventually use Saul's disdain for Jesus to lead the Pharisee to eternal life.

Acts 7:58 and 8:1 are the first mention of Saul in the book. He may have attended the synagogue where Stephen carried on his debate. Like Stephen, the Pharisee realized that Christianity was incompatible with the old religious order. Although Saul approved of Stephen's execution, Saul later was unable to forget his role in the martyr's death (see 22:20). Saul would soon find himself continuing the work Stephen and other like-minded believers had begun. Later, Saul realized he had been the worst of sinners. Because the devil had blinded his mind to the truth, only the Spirit could enlighten his understanding and convince him of his need for the Messiah. God, in His mercy, allowed this to happen so that Saul, the foremost of sinners, might be a trophy of divine grace. The former persecutor of the church thus became an ideal display of the Messiah's unlimited patience. Saul would serve as an example to others who in the future would put their trust in the Son and receive eternal life (see 1 Tim. 1:16).

SUGGESTIONS TO TEACHERS

Stephen did not court trouble, and yet he encountered opposition because many people did not understand or accept his zeal for the Savior. Unlike many, however, he did not become either overly aggressive or timid in his witness. He maintained a balance between courage and graciousness, and through this class session your students will be inspired to do the same.

1. DESIRING TO SHARE OUR FAITH. We should desire to share our faith wisely and persuasively to the unsaved so that they might be drawn to the fullness of new life in Christ. One way to do this is by being pleasant and engaging when we speak the message of the truth.

2. BEING FULL OF COMPASSION AND FORGIVENESS. Being gracious does not mean coming across as a detached, stoic person. As Stephen witnessed to the Jewish people and their leaders, he was full of compassion and forgiveness. He fearlessly spoke the truth, but his words were always undergirded by Christlike love (see Eph. 4:15).

3. GIVING ATTENTION TO HOW WE ACT. Someone once said, "Actions speak louder than words." Everyone seems to agree that the tongue is an easy instrument to play and thus its music can be either godly or ungodly. We should not just be concerned about the words we speak. We should also give attention to the way we act.

4. MAINTAINING A CONSISTENCY BETWEEN WORD AND DEED. A gracious witness is founded on consistency between our words and deeds. As believers who are characterized by love, we are convinced that our actions should reflect our renewed nature in Christ. Therefore, we owe it to God to be worthy examples of His love and mercy.

FOR ADULTS

■ TOPIC: Paying the Price

■ QUESTIONS: 1. Why were the religious leaders so calloused to the truth about Jesus? 2. In what ways were the religious leaders like their ancestors? 3. How was it possible for Stephen to remain gracious in his witness while being mistreated by the Sanhedrin? 4. Describe a time when you were courageous in speaking about the Lord. What resulted from it? 5. How would an active, consistent prayer life strengthen a believer who is facing opposition?

■ **ILLUSTRATIONS:**

Faithful Servant. Organizations in the West can be very competitive. This is evident from the sports teams that dominate athletics and the fierce rivalry that exists among businesses. Even the entertainment industry is marked by ruthless self-interest.

Individuals are also competitive. Students try to outdo their peers in terms of grades. Employees do whatever they can to climb to the top of their professions. Many people want to drive a better car and own a nicer home than their neighbors.

Being a faithful servant is a revolutionary concept to adults who are highly competitive. When you put the interests of others first, as Stephen did, you're not thinking of eliminating them to get to the top. Instead, you're cultivating relationships and showing love, even if it demands personal sacrifice. Isn't this what being a Christian is really all about?

Triumph out of Tragedy. Like Jesus, Stephen focused his thoughts on the One with whom he would spend eternity. And like Jesus, instead of hating his executioners, Stephen prayed for their forgiveness.

For hundreds of years, the Auca Indians had brutally attacked all strangers who ventured into their forests. Yet this knowledge didn't dissuade five young missionaries from penetrating the Ecuadorian jungles with the Gospel. On Sunday, January 8, 1956, Nate Saint, Jim Elliot, Pete Fleming, Roger Youderian, and Ed McCully died at the hands of the Auca Indians.

Could God have intervened to save these missionaries? Although He could have, He chose not to. Instead, God opened the way for Betty Elliot and her daughter and

Nate's sister, Rachel, to live among the very Indians who had killed their loved ones. Nate Saint's brother, Phil, later joined his sister in her efforts to evangelize the Aucan Indians. By 1972, 75 Aucas had become believers in Christ. God used the tragic deaths of five missionaries to bring about the conversion of many who otherwise would have been eternally lost.

God's Grain. Ignatius of Antioch was a devoted Christian pastor in Asia Minor near the end of the first century A.D. He was hauled to Rome because he refused to worship the Emperor Trajan as the Lord God. Ignatius steadfastly insisted that only Jesus could be given that title. Ignatius was denounced as an "atheist" and called "unpatriotic," then told to recant his views about Jesus.

Like his spiritual predecessor Stephen, Ignatius refused to back down or change his opinions. He was threatened with death, but still refused to be moved. He was then tied inside the bloody skins of freshly slaughtered animals and dragged into an arena before thousands of spectators.

Wild dogs that had not been fed for days were unleashed. Ignatius was torn apart by the ravenously hungry animals. His last words were, "I am God's grain!" The martyrdom of Ignatius, along with beautiful letters he wrote while a prisoner, spurred other believers to remain faithful servants of Christ despite the severe persecution they experienced from their enemies.

FOR YOUTH

■ **TOPIC:** Take a Stand

■ **QUESTIONS:** 1. In what ways do you think the religious leaders fought against the Holy Spirit? 2. How had the religious leaders betrayed the Savior? 3. Why were the members of the Council so enraged by Stephen's testimony? 4. What do you think would happen if you courageously witnessed for Jesus at every appropriate opportunity? 5. Why is it hard for us to remain gracious in our witness when we encounter opposition?

■ **ILLUSTRATIONS:**

Me, a Leader? There are many ideas of what constitutes effective leadership. And some of the more unsavory notions encourage using deceit and manipulation to get ahead. It should come as no surprise to the teens that the biblical view of leadership is entirely different. Consider Stephen. When threatened with the prospect of death, he did not lash out in anger. Instead, he endured the rejection and scorn.

Admittedly, these responses are some of the hardest things for believers to respond to graciously. It is natural for us to become defensive, especially when others disagree with our Christian beliefs. It also easy to feel resentful when someone belittles the truths about the Lord Jesus that we hold most dear.

Nonetheless, the Savior can help us remain patient and calm throughout our ordeal. Also, regardless of what our peers might say, He can empower us to show Christlike love. He even undergirds our boldest expressions of faith with humility and compassion to others.

Not without Opposition. Brian loved college, and it showed. He had an aptitude for almost every subject—philosophy, sociology, history, and literature. Brian loved life, too, especially since making a recommitment of his Christian faith at a campus fellowship meeting the previous semester. His testimony and love for God bubbled over wherever he went, so people were often encouraged by his spiritual and social effectiveness—but not all people.

Professor Xavier was well known for his mastery of the classics. Sadly, he was equally well known for harassing students who shared an open Christian faith. As the first week of classes began, Brian could feel a bull's-eye being painted on his chest.

The confrontation came quickly. During the Tuesday morning lecture, Professor Xavier turned to Brian and abruptly commanded him to rise and give a defense of Christianity in the light of the atrocities of the Crusades of the Middle Ages. Brian was stunned, embarrassed, and most of all, completely unprepared.

After directing Brian to be seated, the professor promptly led the classroom in a cynical "cheer" for Christian "intelligence." It was then that Brian remembered that Jesus, too, was sometimes mocked for not having an answer that pleased the religious experts of the day. And suddenly, Brian felt God's approval. As this week's lesson shows, opposition is waiting for those who stand up for the Savior and obey the Holy Spirit.

Challenged Authority. The sixth graders at a middle school in the central part of the United States had finished a unit of study about drugs when they noticed a billboard being changed outside their school. The advertisement for a hemp-based shampoo featured a huge marijuana leaf.

Trained to "Say No" to drugs, the students considered their options before writing a letter to the advertising agency. They stated that though they did not expect the firm to censor their clients' advertisements, they nevertheless objected to the placement of the billboard so near to their school. School administrators expected little to happen from the sixth graders' challenge. However, one day later the advertisement was removed!

Here was a group of 20 sixth graders who dared to object, and finally triumphed through their efforts. Like Stephen, they were willing to stand up for their convictions and challenge powerful interests.

TRYING TO BUY POWER

BACKGROUND SCRIPTURE: Acts 8:4-24
DEVOTIONAL READING: 1 Corinthians 1:18-25

Key Verse: When Simon saw that through laying on of the apostles' hands the Holy Ghost was given, he offered them money. Acts 8:18.

KING JAMES VERSION

ACTS 8:9 But there was a certain man, called Simon, which beforetime in the same city used sorcery, and bewitched the people of Samaria, giving out that himself was some great one: 10 To whom they all gave heed, from the least to the greatest, saying, This man is the great power of God. 11 And to him they had regard, because that of long time he had bewitched them with sorceries. 12 But when they believed Philip preaching the things concerning the kingdom of God, and the name of Jesus Christ, they were baptized, both men and women. 13 Then Simon himself believed also: and when he was baptized, he continued with Philip, and wondered, beholding the miracles and signs which were done.

14 Now when the apostles which were at Jerusalem heard that Samaria had received the word of God, they sent unto them Peter and John: 15 Who, when they were come down, prayed for them, that they might receive the Holy Ghost: 16 (For as yet he was fallen upon none of them: only they were baptized in the name of the Lord Jesus.) 17 Then laid they their hands on them, and they received the Holy Ghost. 18 And when Simon saw that through laying on of the apostles' hands the Holy Ghost was given, he offered them money, 19 Saying, Give me also this power, that on whomsoever I lay hands, he may receive the Holy Ghost. 20 But Peter said unto him, Thy money perish with thee, because thou hast thought that the gift of God may be purchased with money. 21 Thou hast neither part nor lot in this matter: for thy heart is not right in the sight of God. 22 Repent therefore of this thy wickedness, and pray God, if perhaps the thought of thine heart may be forgiven thee. 23 For I perceive that thou art in the gall of bitterness, and in the bond of iniquity. 24 Then answered Simon, and said, Pray ye to the LORD for me, that none of these things which ye have spoken come upon me.

NEW REVISED STANDARD VERSION

ACTS 8:9 Now a certain man named Simon had previously practiced magic in the city and amazed the people of Samaria, saying that he was someone great. 10 All of them, from the least to the greatest, listened to him eagerly, saying, "This man is the power of God that is called Great." 11 And they listened eagerly to him because for a long time he had amazed them with his magic. 12 But when they believed Philip, who was proclaiming the good news about the kingdom of God and the name of Jesus Christ, they were baptized, both men and women. 13 Even Simon himself believed. After being baptized, he stayed constantly with Philip and was amazed when he saw the signs and great miracles that took place.

14 Now when the apostles at Jerusalem heard that Samaria had accepted the word of God, they sent Peter and John to them. 15 The two went down and prayed for them that they might receive the Holy Spirit 16 (for as yet the Spirit had not come upon any of them; they had only been baptized in the name of the Lord Jesus). 17 Then Peter and John laid their hands on them, and they received the Holy Spirit. 18 Now when Simon saw that the Spirit was given through the laying on of the apostles' hands, he offered them money, 19 saying, "Give me also this power so that anyone on whom I lay my hands may receive the Holy Spirit." 20 But Peter said to him, "May your silver perish with you, because you thought you could obtain God's gift with money! 21 You have no part or share in this, for your heart is not right before God. 22 Repent therefore of this wickedness of yours, and pray to the Lord that, if possible, the intent of your heart may be forgiven you. 23 For I see that you are in the gall of bitterness and the chains of wickedness." 24 Simon answered, "Pray for me to the Lord, that nothing of what you have said may happen to me."

8

Monday, October 15	Job 26	*Who Can Understand God's Power?*
Tuesday, October 16	Acts 19:11-20	*Using the Name of the Lord*
Wednesday, October 17	1 Corinthians 1:18-25	*Christ, the Power of God*
Thursday, October 18	1 Corinthians 1:26–2:5	*Faith Resting on God's Power*
Friday, October 19	Galatians 5:16-21	*The Works of the Flesh*
Saturday, October 20	Galatians 5:22-26	*The Fruit of the Spirit*
Sunday, October 21	Acts 8:9-24	*What Money Cannot Buy*

BACKGROUND

The stoning of Stephen unleashed a firestorm of hatred against Jesus' followers. The church, being no more than a few years old at the beginning of Acts 8, faced its first real persecution. While it probably lasted only a few months, the maltreatment spearheaded by a young Jew named Saul was nevertheless severe. Saul, who was a Pharisee and perhaps a member of the Sanhedrin, was bent on stamping out this new religious movement (9:1). He sought to have the followers of Jesus imprisoned (8:3), beaten (22:19), whipped, and even executed (26:10-11).

Among the believers scattered by the persecution was Philip (8:5). He was one of the persons previously selected along with Stephen to look after the Greek-speaking widows (see 6:5). Philip, like Stephen, illustrates how a person faithful in one ministry was given a wider sphere of service. His works recorded in this chapter were only the beginning of a long, fruitful span of service (see 21:8). At some point, Philip decided to travel "down" (8:5; or downhill) from Jerusalem to the principal "city in Samaria." Samaria was a region in central Palestine first occupied by the tribe of Ephraim and part of the tribe of Manasseh.

NOTES ON THE PRINTED TEXT

When the Samaritans heard Philip's message and saw the miracles he performed, they listened intently to what he proclaimed (Acts 8:6). They knew something unusual was happening among them. They watched wide-eyed as those with evil spirits were set free and as paralytics and cripples walked (vs. 7). The record of the miracles Philip performed reads like a list of the very signs Jesus Himself had earlier done. The Savior performed many miracles during His earthly ministry, some of which are not recorded in the Gospels. His miracles were extraordinary expressions of God's power.

As Philip performed various miracles, God used these signs to give evidence of His presence and truth to a previously despised, neglected people. It is no wonder "there was great joy in that city" (vs. 8). From this information we see that supernatural power was impressive to the Samaritans. In turn, this explains why many Samaritans followed Simon, a sorcerer (vs. 9). In the ancient world, the kind of magic he practiced flourished. Luke recorded three incidents related to magic: the account of Simon (vss. 9-24), the account of Elymas (13:4-12), and the account of seven Jewish exorcists (19:13-20). Details about the magic practiced by those magicians are mostly lacking. But more generally, we know that Greco-Roman magic combined ideas from a number of sources.

The Greco-Roman magic practiced by Simon tended to be practical. On behalf of their clients, sorcerers tried to prevent or avert harm, to hurt enemies with curses, to inspire love or submission in others, and to gain revelations from the spirit world. Simon's own involvement with magic extended back a number of years. He beguiled people with his antics and claimed that he was someone important (8:9). He was able to convince the Samaritans—from the least to the most prominent—that he was the "great power of God" (vs. 10). The idea probably is that Simon either claimed to be God or alleged to be God's chief representative.

It was because of the magic Simon performed that he held such sway over the people of Samaria (vs. 11). But the arrival of Philip changed all that. He proclaimed the good news about the divine kingdom, especially as it centered on Jesus the Messiah (vs. 12). As a result of Philip's evangelistic activities, many men and women put their trust in the Messiah. They also gave evidence of their decision to believe by being baptized. We learn in Scripture that the divine kingdom embraces all who walk in fellowship with the Lord and do His will. The kingdom is governed by God's laws, which are summed up in our duty to love the Lord supremely and love others as ourselves. Moreover, this kingdom, which was announced by the prophets and introduced by Jesus, will one day displace all the kingdoms of this world, following the return of the Lord Jesus.

Simon decided to put his faith in Jesus and get baptized. Simon did so because the amazing things God did through Philip enthralled Simon. The missionary's works of power were so superior to Simon's that the former sorcerer stayed close to Philip wherever he went (vs. 13). On the one hand, Simon marveled at the miracles he saw Philip perform. On the other hand, the evangelist's intent was not to make a name for himself. Instead, his goal was to confirm the truth he proclaimed, especially Jesus' ability to rescue people from their life of sin. It was the grace of God that enabled the Samaritans and Simon to give up their sinful attitudes and believe in the Lord Jesus. Similarly, when we come to faith in the Messiah, we must surrender our old life so that we can receive a new life. Our old sinful ways of thinking, our old attitudes and prejudices, and our old habits and lifestyles must all be given up so that God can do His work in us.

In the persecution following Stephen's stoning, the apostles bravely maintained the church's presence at its original center, Jerusalem. There news of Philip's successes in evangelizing the lost of Samaria reached them. Peter and John, as representatives of the apostles, went to see for themselves what was happening in Samaria (vs. 14). Peter and John arrived at a city that had been transformed by the power of God. The two were able to build on the foundation laid by Philip. This included the apostles strengthening and developing the faith of the new believers. Thus, the first thing Peter and John did was pray that the new converts might be given the Holy Spirit (vs. 15).

Luke explained that the Spirit had not yet fallen on any of the converts. The reason is that the Samaritan believers had only undergone water baptism in Jesus' name (vs. 16). This statement raises an intriguing question. How was it possible for the Spirit not to be received by those who had believed the truth about "the kingdom of God, and the name of Jesus Christ" (vs. 12)? Bible scholars differ in their answers to this question. Problematic is the notion that Peter and John's ministry conveyed a second, separate blessing of grace—a work of the Spirit beyond His initial indwelling. Some view the apostles' work as a sort of confirmation with the goal of bringing intellectual faith up to a higher level. The most likely explanation is that this was a unique occurrence in which God used Peter and John to communicate the Spirit in such a way that the Jerusalem believers would accept the Samaritans.

Peter and John clearly expected something more to happen in the Samaritans' lives. Thus, the apostles showed their affirmation, solidarity, and support for the new converts by laying their hands on them. When the apostles did so, the Samaritan converts were given the Holy Spirit (vs. 17). The laying on of hands was a common practice among Jews for blessing people or putting them into a ministry or service. Luke did not tell what followed the praying and laying on of hands, other than to say that the Samaritan believers were granted the gift of the Spirit. Luke had earlier described in greater detail signs that accompanied fillings of the Holy Spirit (see 2:2-4; 4:31). Though we are not told exactly what happened when the Spirit came upon the Samaritans, we know that some demonstration of God's power appeared. Those who looked on recognized this manifestation as a supernatural event.

Simon, the former sorcerer, was one of the observers. (The text gives no suggestion that he was a participant.) When he saw the demonstration of God's power that came when the apostles laid their hands on the Samaritan converts and prayed, something of his former ways stirred within him. This was supernatural ability like nothing he'd ever seen, an influence and control over people far better than any scheme he'd ever used. Simon, being unable to hide his eagerness, "offered . . . money" (8:18) to Peter and John. Simon crassly reasoned that if he could manipulate the mysterious power to give others the Spirit by laying hands on them, he could then recapture his lost fame and influence (vs. 19).

Peter saw through Simon's request. The apostle told him in no uncertain terms that since he tried to use money to acquire the "gift of God" (8:20), both he and his precious silver could eternally "perish." If such language seems too harsh, it is precisely what Peter intended. In telling Simon he might languish in hell, Peter used the same word Jesus used in saying, "Broad is the way, that leadth to *destruction*" (Matt. 7:13, emphasis added). Next, Peter firmly told Simon that he could not have any "part nor lot" (Acts 8:21) in the evangelistic work, for he tried to bargain with the Lord and bribe His ambassadors. Peter urged Simon to abandon his evil plan and turn away from his sinful motives. If he did so, God could forgive him of his warped thinking (vs. 22).

Peter described Simon's spiritual condition as being consumed by envy, resentment, and greed. Moreover, the apostle said that Simon remained in bondage to wickedness (vs. 23). Even though Peter's words were blunt, they remained appropriate and effective. Verse 24 reveals that Simon displayed a change of heart. He asked that Peter would petition the Lord, so that none of what the apostle said would take place in Simon's life. After this episode, Peter and John spent a little more time solemnly proclaiming the truth of God to the local residents. Then, as the two apostles journeyed back to Jerusalem, they declared the Good News in numerous villages in Samaria (vs. 25).

SUGGESTIONS TO TEACHERS

In our lesson this week, we will explore the origins of foreign missions. Persecution is always used by God. We learn from church history that it often wakes up a congregation. That is exactly what happened in the early church as persecution drove the believers beyond their comfort zones.

1. PHILIP AND THE SAMARITAN MISSION. The early disciples knew about Jesus' kingly entrance into Jerusalem. They also knew about His death on the cross and resurrection from the dead. Moreover, they were so touched by the Spirit that they sought to tell others, regardless of their background, of the Father's love through the Son.

Often Christians today allow social differences to hinder their relationships with others. However, the command to spread the Gospel demands that we see all people as individuals for whom the Lord Jesus died. Our neighbors, our coworkers, and the people we meet every day might be waiting for us to share with them the Good News that could change their lives for eternity.

2. PETER AND SIMON THE MAGICIAN. Simon, a person who had formerly practiced sorcery and who had heard Philip preach the Gospel, believed and was baptized. The Jerusalem congregation dispatched Peter and John to Samaria, and God used them to impart the Spirit on the new converts. When Simon tried to purchase from Peter the power to impart the Spirit, the apostle rebuked him and urged him to repent of his wickedness. Through the ministry of Peter and John many more Samaritans heard the Gospel (see Acts 8:9-25). Remind your students that the Spirit cannot be manipulated for personal use. Rather, He lives in us and enables us to serve the Messiah faithfully.

3. GOD AND THE EXPANSION OF THE CHURCH. When God interrupts our plans, we must remember that if we are His spiritual children, He always has something greater for us. He is training us for greater things in His kingdom. Sometimes this involves going beyond those borders that are familiar to us. The Lord sees the total picture He has for our lives. He plans for the good and welfare of His kingdom, and He always has our good at heart.

FOR ADULTS

■ TOPIC: Power Brokers

■ QUESTIONS: 1. How did Simon the sorcerer make a name for himself in Samaria? 2. What astonished Simon the most about Philip? 3. What did Peter and John do when they arrived in the Samaritan city? 4. What is the purpose of miracles, signs, and wonders in promoting the Gospel? 5. What can we do to let go of our own ways so that God can show us His ways?

■ ILLUSTRATIONS:

Christians without Borders. In his book *Cultural Anthropology*, Paul G. Hiebert defines a social culture as an "integrated system of learned patterns of behavior, ideas and products, characteristic of a society." Our social setting usually defines who we are as a person. Most people are comfortable living and working around those with whom they are most familiar and with whom they share a social culture.

When Christ comes into our lives, He begins to replace our fear of other people with a love for them. Instead of fearing how they might harm or reject us, we are more able to think of their need for Christ, and therefore, we will want them to experience God's forgiveness and love.

We see this perspective at work in Philip's evangelistic outreach in Samaria. He could have been put off by Simon the sorcerer, who acted as if he was the great power broker of God (so to speak). Despite Simon's swagger, Philip remained committed to sharing the Gospel with him. And the Lord used Philip to bring Simon to the place where he, too, "believed and was baptized" (Acts 8:13).

Prejudicial Barriers. Christians from one ethnic group in the former Yugoslavia walked out of a service when they discovered that Christians of another group were present. Sadly, examples of such prejudicial barriers continue to be multiplied. When God's people turn the church into their exclusive club, Jesus Christ must be terribly grieved.

The ancient world was also full of cultural and ethnic barriers. Philip had the God-given task of demolishing walls of long-standing prejudice. His willingness to reach beyond intolerance to evangelize the Samaritans should cause us to reexamine our own attitudes toward others.

A Stranger on a Plane. The Spirit empowered Philip to share the Gospel with someone far different from him, Simon the sorcerer. The evangelist was willing to be used by God to bring about spiritual change in the life of someone who practiced magic.

Returning from a conference in Los Angeles, a very tired pastor from Boston wanted nothing more than a long nap on the plane ride home. But as he sat down, he noticed a young man sitting beside him who seemed terrified. Accustomed to following God's leading, the minister realized that the Lord had identified a need.

As a Hindu exchange student going to Harvard University, the young man had no faith to ease his fear of flying. The pastor shared with him that the heavenly Father loved him and that the Son had died for his sins. Before they reached Boston, the young man accepted Christ.

As Rebecca Pippert, author of *Out of the Salt Shaker*, says, "Jesus . . . wants us to see that the neighbor next door or the people sitting next to us on a plane or in a classroom are not interruptions to our schedule. They are there by divine appointment. Jesus wants us to see their needs, their loneliness, their longings, and he wants to give us the courage to reach out to them."

FOR YOUTH

■ TOPIC: Not for Sale!

■ QUESTIONS: 1. How did the people respond to Philip's evangelistic ministry? 2. What did Simon observe as he followed Philip wherever he went? 3. What job were Peter and John given to do in Samaria by the Jerusalem church? 4. How can we deal with anxieties and fears we might feel as we share the Gospel with others? 5. What should be our motives for asking God's power to be at work in our service for Him?

■ ILLUSTRATIONS:

Old Enemies—New Friends. The formation of cliques remains a prevalent phenomenon among teens. And with the existence of such groups can come the notion that people in one clique are unwelcome in another clique.

This adversarial mentality runs counter to the Gospel of Christ. He wants saved teens to share the Good News even with those they might feel are their enemies. To be sure, this can be difficult. But it's amazing how the power of Christ can break down barriers between people.

The mission field of believing young people may begin with their families, then extend into their schools or neighborhood, and finally into the larger society. Regardless of whom the Lord brings into the lives of your students, they should be alert to the opportunities to tell others how much Jesus means to them. And as Peter emphasized to Simon, God's grace is offered freely to the lost and cannot be purchased at any price.

Preaching the Word. A young seminary student was completing his graduate studies and was preparing to accept his first church. A few days before graduation, the student visited the dean of his department. He wanted the dean to share some parting words of wisdom.

"You have studied many disciplines and learned much during these past three years," the dean said. "All of this information has its importance and place." The dean continued, saying, "The best advice that I can share with you is to preach the Word! Only the Bible can make a change in the lives of those who live in this culture and other cultures. Only the heralding of Scripture can prepare individuals for eternity."

The seminary student left the dean's office with those words ringing in his ears— "Preach the Word!" He determined that, above all else, he would ground his cross-cultural ministry in the Bible. Moreover, he was following a time-honored practice. Indeed, centuries earlier an evangelist named Philip did the same sort of thing, especially as he proclaimed the Good News to people living in Samaria.

The Opportunity for a Lifetime. The Lord uses all sorts of believers to bring the lost to Christ. In this week's lesson, we learn about a Greek-speaking Jew named Philip who trusted in Christ and was persecuted (along with others) for his faith. In turn, he was instrumental in telling the people of Samaria about the Messiah and witnessing the conversion of a sorcerer named Simon.

Centuries later, the Lord also powerfully used a believer named Henry J. Heinz (1844–1919) to bring converts into the kingdom. Heinz is best known as the founder of H. J. Heinz Company, with its slogan of "57 varieties" of foods for the table. Heinz went from selling bottled horseradish to establishing a multibillion-dollar global business.

Perhaps less well known is how Heinz was a committed Christian who used his business opportunities to share the Gospel. One day after an evangelistic church meeting, the speaker said to Heinz, "I know you are a believer, but with all your energy, why aren't you up and at it for the Lord?"

Disturbed by that comment, Heinz awoke at four that morning and prayed that God would somehow use him to lead others to the Savior. Several days later, at a meeting of bank presidents, Heinz turned to the man next to him and told him about his joy in knowing Jesus. The man replied, "Because I knew you were a Christian, I wondered many times why you never spoke to me about it." He was the first of 267 people— individuals of different varieties, from all walks of life—whom Heinz introduced to Christ.

THE ETHIOPIAN EUNUCH

BACKGROUND SCRIPTURE: Acts 8:26-39
DEVOTIONAL READING: Isaiah 56:1-8

Key Verse: The eunuch said, See, here is water;
what doth hinder me to be baptized? Acts 8:36.

KING JAMES VERSION

ACTS 8:26 And the angel of the Lord spake unto Philip, saying, Arise, and go toward the south unto the way that goeth down from Jerusalem unto Gaza, which is desert. 27 And he arose and went: and, behold, a man of Ethiopia, an eunuch of great authority under Candace queen of the Ethiopians, who had the charge of all her treasure, and had come to Jerusalem for to worship, 28 Was returning, and sitting in his chariot read Esaias the prophet. 29 Then the Spirit said unto Philip, Go near, and join thyself to this chariot. 30 And Philip ran thither to him, and heard him read the prophet Esaias, and said, Understandest thou what thou readest? 31 And he said, How can I, except some man should guide me? And he desired Philip that he would come up and sit with him. 32 The place of the scripture which he read was this, He was led as a sheep to the slaughter; and like a lamb dumb before his shearer, so opened he not his mouth: 33 In his humiliation his judgment was taken away: and who shall declare his generation? for his life is taken from the earth. 34 And the eunuch answered Philip, and said, I pray thee, of whom speaketh the prophet this? of himself, or of some other man? 35 Then Philip opened his mouth, and began at the same scripture, and preached unto him Jesus. 36 And as they went on their way, they came unto a certain water: and the eunuch said, See, here is water; what doth hinder me to be baptized? 37 And Philip said, If thou believest with all thine heart, thou mayest. And he answered and said, I believe that Jesus Christ is the Son of God. 38 And he commanded the chariot to stand still: and they went down both into the water, both Philip and the eunuch; and he baptized him. 39 And when they were come up out of the water, the Spirit of the Lord caught away Philip, that the eunuch saw him no more: and he went on his way rejoicing.

NEW REVISED STANDARD VERSION

ACTS 8:26 Then an angel of the Lord said to Philip, "Get up and go toward the south to the road that goes down from Jerusalem to Gaza." (This is a wilderness road.) 27 So he got up and went. Now there was an Ethiopian eunuch, a court official of the Candace, queen of the Ethiopians, in charge of her entire treasury. He had come to Jerusalem to worship 28 and was returning home; seated in his chariot, he was reading the prophet Isaiah. 29 Then the Spirit said to Philip, "Go over to this chariot and join it." 30 So Philip ran up to it and heard him reading the prophet Isaiah. He asked, "Do you understand what you are reading?" 31 He replied, "How can I, unless someone guides me?" And he invited Philip to get in and sit beside him. 32 Now the passage of the scripture that he was reading was this:

"Like a sheep he was led to the slaughter,
 and like a lamb silent before its shearer,
  so he does not open his mouth.
33 In his humiliation justice was denied him.
 Who can describe his generation?
 For his life is taken away from the earth."

34 The eunuch asked Philip, "About whom, may I ask you, does the prophet say this, about himself or about someone else?" 35 Then Philip began to speak, and starting with this scripture, he proclaimed to him the good news about Jesus. 36 As they were going along the road, they came to some water; and the eunuch said, "Look, here is water! What is to prevent me from being baptized?" 38 He commanded the chariot to stop, and both of them, Philip and the eunuch, went down into the water, and Philip baptized him. 39 When they came up out of the water, the Spirit of the Lord snatched Philip away; the eunuch saw him no more, and went on his way rejoicing.

9

HOME BIBLE READINGS

Monday, October 22	Leviticus 21:16-24	*Blemishes That Exclude*
Tuesday, October 23	Psalm 147:1-6	*Lifting Up the Downtrodden*
Wednesday, October 24	Isaiah 56:1-8	*Gathering the Outcasts*
Thursday, October 25	Zephaniah 3:14-20	*Changing Shame into Praise*
Friday, October 26	Isaiah 16:1-5	*A Ruler Who Seeks Justice*
Saturday, October 27	Job 29:2-16	*A Champion for the Needy*
Sunday, October 28	Acts 8:26-39	*The Good News about Jesus*

BACKGROUND

In this week's lesson, we learn about the conversion of a man from Ethiopia. In ancient times, Ethiopia was located in the region of Nubia, just south of Egypt, where the first waterfall of the Nile goes into the Sudan. The modern nation of Ethiopia is located farther to the southeast. Many Bible scholars equate Ethiopia with the land of Cush (see Gen. 2:13; Isa. 11:11). Cush was an enemy of Egypt for centuries, gaining and losing independence, depending on the pharaoh who was in power. After the Assyrians conquered the Egyptians in 671 B.C., Ethiopia maintained a strong center of trade. For instance, Job saw Cush as a rich source of topaz and other minerals (see Job 28:19).

The most influential Ethiopian leader, Tirhakah, aided Hezekiah when Sennacherib invaded Judah in 701 B.C. (see 2 Kings 19:9; Isa. 37:9). The capital, Napata, was abandoned around 300 B.C. The capital of Ethiopia then moved south to Meroe, where the kingdom continued on for another 600 years. Archaeological digs in Napata and Meroe have disclosed a number of pyramid tombs, as well as temples to the Egyptian god Amun. During the New Testament era, several queens of Ethiopia bore the name Candace, which was probably a hereditary title, not a proper name. Modern Ethiopian Christians consider the eunuch of this week's text their country's first evangelist. In fact, many regard his conversion as the beginning of the fulfillment of Psalm 68:31.

NOTES ON THE PRINTED TEXT

An angel of the Lord told Philip to leave the main city of Samaria and go south to the road that led from Jerusalem to Gaza (Acts 8:26). In ancient times, Gaza was a town located about 50 miles from Jerusalem. The original city was destroyed in the first century B.C., and a new city was built near the coast. Not knowing what he would find on the desert road, Philip obeyed. Leaving behind the excitement and action among the new Samaritan converts, he traveled into the desert. God's opportunities may not always excite us. We may think we see greater potential elsewhere. Obedience like Philip's, however, opens the door for God to do things we could never have imagined.

Running through the desert south of Jerusalem was a well-traveled road, a main route toward Egypt. On the road was a "eunuch" (vs. 27) returning from Jerusalem to his native Ethiopia. By the man's chariot and servants, Philip could see he was an important government official. It's possible, though, that the Greek noun rendered "chariot" (vs. 28) was little more than an ox-drawn cart that was going only slightly faster than walking speed. Verse 27 states the eunuch was a sort of secretary of the treasury for "Candace." She was responsible for carrying out the secular duties of the reigning monarch, who was considered too sacred to perform such administrative chores.

While the Ethiopian eunuch sat in his chariot, he read aloud to himself. This was a common practice in those days for those who had reading materials. But scrolls and other reading materials, transcribed by hand, were not readily available to the average person. Only the wealthy and influential could afford literature. Even more rare was a non-Jew possessing Hebrew Scripture, as this court official did. Because the Ethiopian had managed to obtain a copy of Isaiah, and since he had traveled to worship at the temple in Jerusalem, we may conclude that he was a convert to the Jewish faith. If not, he must surely have been a "God-fearer." This was a label given to Gentiles who believed in the one true God of Israel but who had not been circumcised. In short, the Ethiopian worshiped the true God.

Philip sensed the Holy Spirit urging him closer to the chariot (vs. 29). A simple but profound lesson for us here is that in order to receive this specific divine guidance, Philip first had to obey God's general command (see vs. 26). Had the evangelist refused to go southward to this desert area, he would not have been available to receive this divine directive. Likewise, we need to make ourselves available to God by following the clear and basic principles of His Word. Philip obeyed by running up to the Ethiopian (vs. 30).

During this time, the presence of eunuchs from Africa and other places was common. Philip's conversation with the Ethiopian official, however, shows the inclusiveness of the Gospel. The Father's provision of salvation through faith in the Son is for persons of every race, kindred, and nation. In addition, Luke made it clear that the Lord had arranged for this meeting not only to expand the spread of the Gospel, but also to give salvation to someone He loved. Since the Ethiopian was reading aloud, Philip knew the Scripture verses the eunuch was contemplating. Knowing that this passage referred to the suffering Servant, Philip asked the official if he understood what he was reading.

The Ethiopian did not try to hide his ignorance. As one who wanted to comprehend God's Word, he admitted that he needed another to explain the prophet's words. Perceiving that Philip was such a person, the official invited Philip to sit next to him in his chariot (vs. 31). While it is true that the meaning of many portions of Scripture is self-evident, some passages are difficult to understand. Even Peter found portions of Paul's letters difficult to comprehend (see 2 Pet. 3:15-16). In light of this circumstance, God has provided gifted believers, who through study and the illumination of the Spirit, can expound His Word for the benefit of others.

The Ethiopian had been mulling over Isaiah 53:7-8. This passage describes a person who submitted to affliction and death without objection. He would do so to atone for humankind's sin. He was willing to die for others because He loved sinners and wanted to remove their transgressions. By oppression and unjust judgment, this person would be taken away to His death. Isaiah asked who could speak of this person's descendants. The Jews believed that to die without children was a tragedy (see 2 Sam. 18:18). The suffering Servant would have no physical descendants, for His life would be "taken from the earth" (Acts 8:33). Indeed, He would be stricken for the sins of humanity.

The eunuch asked Philip whether Isaiah was talking about himself or referring to someone else (vs. 34). What an opportunity this was to tell the Good News about the Messiah! Luke did not give the details of what Philip shared with the Ethiopian official. Nevertheless, we can assume that Philip at least expounded on Jesus as the suffering Servant, for that is what the Isaiah passage is about. In this case, the Bible prepared the eunuch's heart for the proclamation of the Gospel by creating a spiritual hunger to know about the identity of the suffering Servant. From this we see that studying God's Word often alerts people to their need for the Savior and gives them the desire to trust in Him.

Philip explained how Jesus fulfilled the prophecy, namely, how He had been condemned and crucified as the Lamb of God, and how He rose from the dead (vs. 35). This information is not the answer the Ethiopian would have received from non-Christian, first-century A.D. Jews. Most saw the passage as referring to Isaiah himself, or to the nation of Israel, not to a suffering Messiah, since that did not fit in with their idea of a conquering Savior who would deliver them from the Romans. Actually, Luke 22:37 indicates that Jesus first applied Isaiah 53 to Himself before His crucifixion, when He quoted verse 12 to the apostles at the Last Supper.

Evidently, part of the conversation between Philip and the Ethiopian included the topic of baptism. It was the government official, not Philip, who noticed water along the way and proposed that he should be baptized (Acts 8:36). Verse 37 is not in the earliest ancient manuscripts of Acts, and therefore is not printed in some contemporary versions of the Bible. Even so, the verse is consistent with the expectations the apostles had of those who put their faith in the Messiah. Specifically, trusting in the Son and being baptized go hand in hand (so to speak). Philip's statement and the official's affirmation of Jesus being the "Son of God" were indeed the fulfillment of Isaiah's prophecy.

Since the Ethiopian now trusted in the Lord Jesus, the government official ordered his chariot to be stopped. Most likely the Ethiopian was part of a caravan journeying in the same direction and moving slowly down the road. Once the chariot was no longer moving, the eunuch stepped into some nearby water and allowed Philip to baptize him (vs. 38). The baptism could have taken place at any number of locations. Tradition identifies the spot as near the town of Bethsura. The baptism, however, may have taken place nearer Gaza. Verse 39 says that once the two came out of the water, the Spirit of the Lord snatched Philip away. Some see in this description a miracle in which the evangelist was transported from the site of the baptism to Azotus. Others, however, interpret this merely as Philip's abrupt departure under the compulsion of the Spirit. The biblical text leaves no doubt that Philip carried his preaching mission farther to the north (vs. 40).

SUGGESTIONS TO TEACHERS

The conversion of the Ethiopian was yet another indication to the early believers that the Gospel was for all peoples. The occasion of the official coming to faith may have enlivened Jesus' followers to reach out to people of other cultural backgrounds. Furthermore, the Ethiopian undoubtedly shared the Good News of salvation in his home country, where more people became devoted to Jesus Christ.

1. BARRIERS TO FAITH. From a Christian perspective, a barrier to our faith is anything that hinders or blocks us from serving God and becoming an effective witness for the Messiah. Although someone might be unlike us in a number of ways, we should not allow those differences to impede us from telling that person about the Lord. Neither should we lose sight of the truth that God will be with us when we encounter barriers to faith. Through the Savior, we can overcome these barriers and share the Good News of Jesus with those who are different from us.

2. OPPORTUNITIES TO WITNESS. This week's lesson emphasizes the importance of being open to telling nonbelievers about Jesus wherever they are. Indeed, it is often outside the church building that people are converted to the Savior. Whether we are chatting with our nonbelieving grandson, our Buddhist next-door neighbor, or the woman of another ethnic group sitting next to us at a ball game, we are to be alert to the opportunities to tell people how much Jesus means to us.

3. LEARNING TO LISTEN. Philip listened to God's command and left his thriving first ministry to go to the desert. Because of the evangelist's obedience, the Ethiopian went home rejoicing to share the Gospel with others. That day, there was joy in heaven, too! Being faithful to God's Word teaches us to listen to His Spirit. He will then send us to share in situations that we never dreamed possible. Each time we follow God's leading, the Spirit can work through us with amazing results.

■ **TOPIC:** Erasing the Boundary Lines

■ **QUESTIONS:** 1. How did Philip respond to the command he received from the angel of the Lord? 2. What did Philip do to engage the official in conversation? 3. What explanation did Philip offer to the Ethiopian's question regarding Isaiah 53:7-8? 4. How might you discern a particular encounter as God's opportunity to share the Gospel? 5. Why does boldness to witness come from God?

■ ILLUSTRATIONS:

Called to Be Inclusive. Imagine how different the situation would have been had not Philip heeded the prompting of the Spirit to share the Gospel with the Ethiopian eunuch. Thankfully, Philip did not let social and cultural differences he might have had with the government official stop him from being used by God in a special way.

Many of the personal prejudices of adults have been ingrained in them since childhood. On their own, they don't have the determination and strength to overcome their deep-seated intolerances. Only God can remove those biases.

If there is any doubt about prejudice in the church, ask yourself why the statement "Sunday morning remains the most segregated time of the week" still rings true. Possibly members of your class are extremely alike. Can it be that personal prejudices have made it uncomfortable for other kinds of people to feel welcome?

This week's lesson encourages your students to seek God's help in overcoming whatever prejudices they have. This in turn will enable them to present a truly Christian witness to others.

Breaking Down Racial Barriers. Under God's direction, Philip moved twice, each time to a less likely place. He was willing to leave his comfort zone (in a manner of speaking) and reach out to others from a variety of different ethnic groups. Even today, the Lord is empowering believers to do the same.

In 1990, Bill McCartney, who was then the head football coach at the University of Colorado at Boulder, founded Promise Keepers. Throughout the years of the organization's existence, it has endeavored to unite Christian men to be a godly influence in the world.

One of the things Promise Keepers has attempted to do is break down the racial barriers that damage the church. For instance, on a Promise Keepers video, a young African American states that the organization has done something that some in America have not yet done. They have said, "I'm sorry."

Social barriers come in many other forms besides racial: economic, geographical, academic, and lifestyle. Like many people, some of your students probably come to class with biases and social barriers that they might not be aware of having.

Some of the adults in your class might even state, "It wasn't my fault, so I don't have to make the first gesture." If, however, we are to break down social barriers and proclaim the Gospel to other people, your students need to recognize their biases and be willing to change their perspective.

Encouraged to Persevere. The account of Philip's witnessing to the Ethiopian eunuch reminds us that God plans to include people in His kingdom that we might not expect. Centuries later, this again proved to be true in the life of Hudson Taylor. In the mid-1800s, he undertook what seemed to be the impossible task of bringing the Gospel to China.

Prior to going to China, though, Taylor was assigned to care for an elderly man with gangrene. Because Taylor desired to minister to the atheist's soul as well as his body, the future missionary committed his service to prayer. For a few days, Taylor only made small talk as he attended to the elderly man's wounds. After a while, a tentative discussion developed. In time during each visit, Taylor was able to speak briefly about the Savior. Rather than getting angry, as the man had with other believers, he simply turned away.

One day, Taylor walked to the door without mentioning the Savior. The patient asked why. Taylor, who had doubted whether he should continue his witnessing, tearfully bared his soul. He told the man that, more than anything, he wanted to pray for him. The man responded, "If that will be a relief to you, do."

That prayer was a turning point. Within a few days, the 80-year-old atheist put his faith in the Lord Jesus. In Taylor's autobiography, he wrote, "Oftentimes, when in my early work in China, circumstances rendered me almost hopeless of success, I have thought about this man's conversion, and have been encouraged to persevere."

FOR YOUTH	■ **TOPIC:** I Can Belong

■ **QUESTIONS:** 1. What was the Ethiopian official doing when Philip caught up with him? 2. What was perplexing to the Ethiopian as he read from Isaiah 53:7-8? 3. How can we tell that the Ethiopian was seeking truth? 4. How prepared are you to leave comfort and security to follow the Lord into new evangelistic challenges? 5. How can you use your personal testimony as you talk to others about the Savior?

■ **ILLUSTRATIONS:**

Everyone Counts. Perhaps you've heard the statement that all people are created equal, but some are more equal than others. Tragically, that's the way things often work in church youth groups. Some members seem to be more important and valuable than others. When this attitude prevails, it drives adolescents away from Jesus.

We don't know whether Philip had any initial reservations about sharing the Gospel with the Ethiopian eunuch, but if Philip did, the Spirit enabled him to overcome his biases. Likewise, there are times when the young people in your class will have to do the same, especially when new people show up at church activities. Let your students know that God plays no favorites, not even in church youth groups.

Because God wants all people to be saved, Christian youth should work hard to make everyone in their class feel accepted, welcomed, and loved. Yes, this is an act of faith on their part. Let them know they can trust the Lord to help them overcome their prejudices.

The Detrimental Effect of Prejudice. During his student days, Indian nationalist leader Mahatma Gandhi was genuinely interested in the Bible. He admitted being deeply touched by reading the Gospels and seriously considered becoming a Christian. He sensed that this religion offered a real solution to the caste system that divided the people of his country.

One Sunday, Gandhi visited a nearby church. He wanted to see the minister and ask him for instruction on how to be saved. When Gandhi entered the sanctuary, however, the ushers refused to give him a seat. They suggested that he go and worship with his own people. Gandhi left that church and never came back. He remembered saying to himself, "If Christians have caste differences also, I might as well remain a Hindu."

When we allow personal prejudices to exist in our lives, it will limit our Christian witness. With God's help we can abandon our prejudices of others who seem different from us. The Holy Spirit enabled Philip to do so, and through his witness an Ethiopian official heard the Gospel and was saved.

All Count in the Game. Though he was never credited for it, former manager and Hall of Famer Leo Durocher played a key role in Jackie Robinson's historic breaking of baseball's color line with the Brooklyn Dodgers after World War II. In 1947, the Dodgers went to Panama for several exhibition games. A number of the players were angry that Robinson, an African American, was debuting at the major league level. They drew up a petition stating that they would walk out if Robinson played.

When Durocher heard about the petition, he had all the players awakened in the middle of the night and assembled in the hotel kitchen. Without mincing words and using typical Durocher terminology, the manager told the team what he thought about their petition and their prejudices. He stated that he admired Robinson, and said he thought Robinson would make the Dodgers a better team. The petition was never mentioned again!

Durocher was one person who stood up for integrated sports. He should be respected and recognized for the courageous and unpopular stand he took. Philip, too, discovered that everyone counts when it comes to the proclamation of the Gospel and that everyone should be given an opportunity to believe in the Lord Jesus.

PAUL BEFORE AGRIPPA

BACKGROUND SCRIPTURE: Acts 25:23–26:32
DEVOTIONAL READING: Acts 23:1-11

Key Verse: [Paul] said, I am not mad, most noble Festus; but speak forth the words of truth and soberness. Acts 26:25.

KING JAMES VERSION

ACTS 26:19 Whereupon, O king Agrippa, I was not disobedient unto the heavenly vision: 20 But shewed first unto them of Damascus, and at Jerusalem, and throughout all the coasts of Judaea, and then to the Gentiles, that they should repent and turn to God, and do works meet for repentance. 21 For these causes the Jews caught me in the temple, and went about to kill me. 22 Having therefore obtained help of God, I continue unto this day, witnessing both to small and great, saying none other things than those which the prophets and Moses did say should come: 23 That Christ should suffer, and that he should be the first that should rise from the dead, and should shew light unto the people, and to the Gentiles.

24 And as he thus spake for himself, Festus said with a loud voice, Paul, thou art beside thyself; much learning doth make thee mad. 25 But he said, I am not mad, most noble Festus; but speak forth the words of truth and soberness. 26 For the king knoweth of these things, before whom also I speak freely: for I am persuaded that none of these things are hidden from him; for this thing was not done in a corner. 27 King Agrippa, believest thou the prophets? I know that thou believest. 28 Then Agrippa said unto Paul, Almost thou persuadest me to be a Christian. 29 And Paul said, I would to God, that not only thou, but also all that hear me this day, were both almost, and altogether such as I am, except these bonds. 30 And when he had thus spoken, the king rose up, and the governor, and Bernice, and they that sat with them: 31 And when they were gone aside, they talked between themselves, saying, This man doeth nothing worthy of death or of bonds. 32 Then said Agrippa unto Festus, This man might have been set at liberty, if he had not appealed unto Caesar.

NEW REVISED STANDARD VERSION

ACTS 26:19 "After that, King Agrippa, I was not disobedient to the heavenly vision, 20 but declared first to those in Damascus, then in Jerusalem and throughout the countryside of Judea, and also to the Gentiles, that they should repent and turn to God and do deeds consistent with repentance. 21 For this reason the Jews seized me in the temple and tried to kill me. 22 To this day I have had help from God, and so I stand here, testifying to both small and great, saying nothing but what the prophets and Moses said would take place: 23 that the Messiah must suffer, and that, by being the first to rise from the dead, he would proclaim light both to our people and to the Gentiles."

24 While he was making this defense, Festus exclaimed, "You are out of your mind, Paul! Too much learning is driving you insane!" 25 But Paul said, "I am not out of my mind, most excellent Festus, but I am speaking the sober truth. 26 Indeed the king knows about these things, and to him I speak freely; for I am certain that none of these things has escaped his notice, for this was not done in a corner. 27 King Agrippa, do you believe the prophets? I know that you believe." 28 Agrippa said to Paul, "Are you so quickly persuading me to become a Christian?" 29 Paul replied, "Whether quickly or not, I pray to God that not only you but also all who are listening to me today might become such as I am—except for these chains."

30 Then the king got up, and with him the governor and Bernice and those who had been seated with them; 31 and as they were leaving, they said to one another, "This man is doing nothing to deserve death or imprisonment." 32 Agrippa said to Festus, "This man could have been set free if he had not appealed to the emperor."

10

Home Bible Readings

Background

The Book of Acts presents several episodes in which Paul was able to share his background, conversion, and call to the Gentiles. One opportunity occurred before a crowd of Jews from the steps of the Fortress of Antonia outside the Jerusalem temple (21:37–22:21). A second opportunity came before the Sanhedrin (23:1-8). A third opportunity occurred before a Roman governor named Felix (24:10-23).

Caesarea was the scene for the latter episode. Paul remained imprisoned there for several years, and Felix was succeeded by Porcius Festus (vs. 27). When Paul was brought before the newly appointed governor, he requested to stand trial before Caesar's court in Rome (25:8-11). Festus approved the request (vs. 12). But in a conversation with Herod Agrippa II (who was in Caesarea at the time), Festus said he was perplexed as to how to conduct an investigation of this kind (vs. 20). Agrippa, in turn, stated his willingness to "hear the man myself" (vs. 22).

Herod Agrippa II was part of the Herod dynasty that ruled (with Roman support) areas of Judea, Galilee, and Perea during the time of Christ and the early church. Agrippa was the great-grandson of Herod the Great, who was king of Judea when Jesus was born. Herod the Great's son was Herod Agrippa I, who arrested James, the brother of John, and put him to death (see Acts 12:1-2). After the death of Herod Agrippa I in A.D. 44 (see vss. 19-23), the Romans waited 8 years before allowing Herod Agrippa II to assume power. Eventually, they permitted him to rule over the territory around and northeast of the Sea of Galilee, as well as parts of Perea. The Romans consulted with the younger Agrippa on religious matters pertaining to the Jews, a fact consistent with the desire of Festus to seek advice from Agrippa on Paul's case. Agrippa died about A.D. 100, after a reign of 50 years.

Notes on the Printed Text

A day after Festus made his request to Agrippa, a formal inquiry was held. After Agrippa and Bernice (his sister and mistress) had entered the auditorium, Festus ordered Paul to be brought in (Acts 25:23). The procurator then explained to

Agrippa that though the religious leaders wanted to see Rome execute Paul, the death sentence could not be justified (vss. 24-25). And since the accused had appealed his case to the emperor, Festus needed help in filling out the required report (vs. 26). The procurator thus asked Agrippa to assist him in deciphering the nature of the charges so that they could be clearly explained in writing to the officials in Rome (vs. 27).

When Agrippa gave Paul permission to speak, the apostle expressed his appreciation for the opportunity to address the charges the religious leaders had brought against him (26:1-2). Paul acknowledged that the dignitary had an intimate knowledge of Jewish matters (vs. 3). The apostle noted that he had been a Pharisee who meticulously observed the Mosaic law and Jewish customs (vss. 4-5). Paul declared that it was for the hope of Israel—namely, the resurrection of the dead—that he was on trial (vss. 6-8). The apostle related that at one point in his adult life he openly opposed Christianity (vs. 9). He had imprisoned many followers of Jesus (vs. 10). Paul had gone from synagogue to synagogue and city to city to find, arrest, and prosecute Christians (vs. 11).

Then one day, Paul was on such a mission to Damascus and armed with the authority and commission of the leading priests (vs. 12). At around noon, a light from heaven—far brighter than the sun in brilliance—shone down on Paul and his traveling companions (vs. 13). All of them immediately fell to the ground. But only the apostle could make sense of the voice saying to him in Aramaic, "Saul, Saul, why persecutest thou me?" (vs. 14). The heavenly voice then declared to Paul that it was hard for him to "kick against the pricks." This statement reflected an ancient Greek proverb. A young ox, when it was first yoked, usually resented the burden and tried kicking its way out. Every time the animal kicked, though, it struck some sort of sharp object (such as a goad). The point of the adage was that the ox had to learn submission the hard way. In a similar manner, Paul before his conversion was resisting God, and he found it increasingly difficult to fight against the Lord's will.

Paul wanted to know the identity of the heavenly voice. Imagine how shocked he was to learn that it was Jesus, whose disciples Paul had been persecuting (vs. 15). What he had done to these believers was the same as if he had been doing it personally to the Messiah, their Lord. Despite the severity of Paul's many sins, Jesus revealed Himself in order to forgive Paul and commission him for Christian service. Jesus ordered Paul to stand up. The risen Lord then explained that He had appeared to this former persecutor of the church to appoint him as His servant and witness. In other words, Paul would serve the Messiah as the apostle proclaimed the Good News of salvation. The content of Paul's declarations would be twofold: his present experience of seeing Christ and subsequent revelations in which Jesus conveyed important truths to the apostle (vs. 16).

The hardship Paul had inflicted on other believers would now be experienced by him as well. Despite this, Jesus pledged to protect the apostle, especially as he witnessed to both Jews and Gentiles (vs. 17). No doubt at first the thought of ministering to non-Jews must have been a psychological jolt to Paul. Nevertheless, it was the Lord's will for the apostle to take the message of grace to unsaved Gentiles, for they needed to hear the truth. Jesus was specific about Paul's goal in sharing the Gospel. God would use him to open people's spiritually blind eyes, to turn them from the darkness of sin to the light of God's holiness, and from "the power of Satan unto God" (vs. 18). By putting their faith in the Messiah, the lost would be pardoned and given a place among God's people, who were set apart because they believed. Paul declared to King Agrippa that he remained true to the vision from heaven he had experienced (vs. 19).

After the apostle's conversion, he preached in Damascus for about three years. During this period, Paul ministered in the surrounding area of Arabia, that is, before he was forced to escape in the night from the city (see Acts 9:25; Gal. 1:15-18; 2 Cor. 11:32-33). It was then that he traveled to Jerusalem to see the other apostles (see Gal. 1:18-19). Acts 26:20 records Paul's summary statement of all his evangelistic efforts during these years of sharing the truth about Jesus. It did not matter whether the apostle was in Damascus, Jerusalem, or in the rest of Judea. His emphasis remained the same. Everyone had to abandon his or her sins and turn to God in faith. Also, they were to prove the reality of their commitment by performing good "works," that is, by the upright way in which they lived. The idea is that genuine repentance is evidenced by changed behavior.

Paul explained that some antagonistic Jews arrested him in the temple courts of Jerusalem because he proclaimed the Good News about the Messiah. These enemies of the faith charged the apostle with teaching against the Mosaic law and the temple. They also falsely accused him of defiling the holy place by bringing Gentiles where they were not allowed to go (see 21:27-36). For these reasons, religious fanatics in Jerusalem attempted to murder Paul (26:21). Despite their efforts, God protected the apostle (vs. 22). Festus and other Roman officials could not quite grasp why the Jewish authorities had Paul arrested. The apostle hoped that Agrippa, who was a reputed expert in the Jewish faith, would understand how a message that gave an equal spiritual heritage to the Gentiles would enrage some Jews. Moreover, as Paul stood before Agrippa, he sought to make a connection between his calling on the road to Damascus and the reason for his subsequent arrest. The apostle's point was that his fellow Jews thought he was tearing down their faith, but they had misunderstood the reason and motivation for his obedience to his heavenly vision.

In reality, Paul was being consistent with the Jewish faith by declaring to both "small and great" alike what God had disclosed beforehand in the writings of the "prophets and Moses" about the suffering Messiah. Paul emphasized to Agrippa that the content of the apostle's message was in agreement with what was revealed in the Hebrew sacred writings. In other words, Paul taught nothing except what the Old

Testament foretold would occur. To be specific, the apostle related that Scripture prophesied the suffering, death, and resurrection of the Messiah. In fact, Jesus' rising from the dead would be like a beacon of light shining the truth and glory of God "unto the people, and to the Gentiles" (vs. 23).

During the proceedings, Festus was listening attentively. As he did so, he grew increasingly uncomfortable with the assertions Paul made about his proclamation of the Gospel to the unsaved. So, in an adroit maneuver, Festus interrupted the entire proceeding by suddenly retorting, "Paul, thou art beside thyself" (Acts 26:24). Festus also accused the apostle of becoming insane from excessive religious study. This shrewd tactic completely changed the psychological tone of the gathering by calling into question Paul's credibility as a religious leader and teacher. The apostle could have been paralyzed by fear or silenced by feelings of intimidation. Instead, he decided to remain calm and respectful as he countered that his statements were accurate and rational (vs. 25).

Even though many of the Jewish scholars of Paul's day missed it, the prophets did speak about a Messiah who would suffer, die, be raised again, and be a light to the Gentiles (see Pss. 16:8-11; 22; Isa. 53; Luke 24:44-47; Acts 2:23-33; 1 Cor. 15:3-4). Paul's statement to Agrippa presumed that he was familiar with the truths the apostle was declaring. Furthermore, Paul spoke openly with the monarch about the Savior because the apostle was certain Agrippa was well aware of the facts concerning Jesus of Nazareth. After all, none of what happened to the Messiah took place in a "corner" (Acts 26:26), that is, outside of public view. Once more, Paul tried to bring Agrippa to the point of making a decision for Christ. That's why the apostle affirmed the king's belief in the Old Testament prophets. The apostle wanted to see Agrippa put his faith in the Messiah spoken of in the Hebrew sacred writings (vs. 27).

Agrippa conveyed strong doubt that during this brief exchange, Paul would be able to talk the king into becoming a "Christian" (vs. 28). Paul wanted everyone in the chamber to become disciples of the Lord (vs. 29). At that point in the proceeding, Agrippa and the rest of the dignitaries arose and left the auditorium (vs. 30). They jointly acknowledged that Paul had not done anything to warrant capital punishment or imprisonment (vs. 31). Agrippa noted to Festus that if Paul had not appealed to the emperor, he could have been set free (vs. 32). The dignitaries did not realize, however, that God was using this series of events to bring about the apostle's proclamation of the Gospel in Rome.

SUGGESTIONS TO TEACHERS

God is pleased when we remain determined in our efforts to evangelize the lost. Despite the obstacles we encounter, there are often several ways we can overcome them. At first our options may not seem evident. In time, however, God can help us discern what course of action we should take.

1. THE REVELATION. Before his conversion, Paul had a "zeal of God, but not according to knowledge" (Rom. 10:2). Paul's persecution of the church was abruptly halted by the Lord's visitation on the road to Damascus. For many, it just isn't enough to be told that their path is headed in the wrong direction. Oftentimes, it takes a radical "wake-up" to get their attention.

2. THE INTERROGATION. Jesus got Paul's attention with the bright light, but it was the dialogue that followed that allowed Paul to understand his misdirection and the need to make changes. It's important to let those with whom we are sharing the Gospel have ample time and opportunity to ask the questions that are important to them.

3. THE TRANSFORMATION. When Paul encountered the risen Lord, he was changed forever. There is no substitute for being transformed by the power of the Lord. This is the acid test of a person's salvation and walk with God.

4. THE PROCLAMATION. While Paul was on the road leading to Damascus, Jesus got a hold on his life. But it wasn't merely to stop Paul from his relentless persecution of the church. More importantly, Paul was called to be a preacher of the Gospel. Let's never forget that it isn't enough to have a conversion experience. We must also proclaim the truth to the lost.

FOR ADULTS	■ TOPIC: Taking a Stand

■ **QUESTIONS:** 1. What was Paul focused on doing when he encountered the risen Lord? 2. What did Paul begin doing immediately after his conversion? Why? 3. How was Paul's message connected to the teachings of the Old Testament? 4. How do you think you would have handled King Agrippa's attempt to sidestep Paul's evangelistic appeal? 5. What are some ways we can creatively herald the truth about the Savior?

■ **ILLUSTRATIONS:**

Obeying the Call. What constitutes "the call" mystifies many people. God called Abraham, Moses, Samuel, Isaiah, and Paul in rather dramatic fashion. Does He still do that today? Another bothersome question is whether "the call" is reserved for people going into the ministry. When a young man told his adult sponsor that he might like to be a missionary, the sponsor replied, "Have you been called?"

In a general way, the Father calls people to faith in the Son and to lives of obedient, faithful service. This remains the case regardless of their vocation. Thus, the primary career calling of all believers is to be faithful in taking a stand for Christ while living God-honoring lives.

No believer can ever doubt what God's will is in this regard. We do not need to see a bright light in the sky, like Paul did while he was traveling on the road heading into

Damascus. We do need to study the Scriptures, pray, worship, and fellowship with other believers. In that context, God promises to make His way clear to all of us.

God Is Light. Light is the symbol of God's perfect holiness (1 John 1:5). Thus we read that God dwells in light to which no one can approach (1 Tim. 6:16). No wonder, then, that at critical junctures, the Lord has manifested His character in history through light. For instance, at Paul's conversion, God's light blazed (Acts 9:3; 26:13; 2 Cor. 4:6). Of course, the apostle's experience of seeing a bright light from heaven while traveling on the road to Damascus is only one noteworthy example.

At the dawn of time, God said, "Let there be light" (Gen. 1:3). To Israel God manifested His presence through light (Exod. 13:21; 19:16-20). Jesus' coming brought "life . . . to light through the gospel" (2 Tim. 1:10). Consequently, at Jesus' transfiguration, His essential deity flashed forth so that His clothes were "white as the light" (Matt. 17:2). In the final chapter of the Bible, we read concerning heaven: "There shall be no night there; . . . for the Lord God giveth them light" (Rev. 22:5).

Tested for the Storms. In the days when ships were built out of wood, great care was taken in selecting the piece of timber for the bow. This timber had to be exceptionally strong, for the bow, as it crashed through the waves, had to absorb the pounding of the seas and withstand the constant pressure of the water.

No ordinary tree would do. The shipwrights understood that only a hardwood that had been buffeted and bent by long exposure to harsh winds could be used. Tested and toughened, the gnarled tree was deemed suitable for the critically important part of the ship.

So it is with us. Only the believer who has learned to stand up to the tests of life is fit for the most important spiritual tasks in God's kingdom. This was certainly true in Paul's life, especially as he testified to King Agrippa (see Acts 26). Like the apostle, we should learn to accept the trials in our lives as opportunities for God to make us stronger and more suitable to carry out His program. Scripture reveals that He wants to use believers who are particularly able to withstand the storms and pressures of life.

FOR YOUTH

■ **TOPIC:** Standing by My Convictions

■ **QUESTIONS:** 1. What are some ways that Paul's life was radically changed by his conversion? 2. According to Paul's testimony, what does it mean to be called to preach the Gospel? 3. What kinds of obstacles did Paul face and overcome as he fulfilled his calling? 4. How did Agrippa respond to Paul's question? 5. What challenges do you face in proclaiming the Gospel to the lost? How can you overcome them?

■ ILLUSTRATIONS:

Life Choices in a Complex World. A young man, new in his Christian faith, wondered how to decide what to do in an important matter. He had heard about asking God for guidance, but he didn't know what to do. So he conceived a simple test. If he got a letter with a certain stamp on it, this would indicate the matter one way. If not, he would choose the other option.

Sadly, this person's method was based more on superstition than faith. Yet so often when we are deeply perplexed, we wish Jesus would appear and tell us what to do, like He did for Paul. Of course, later on Paul wrote that "we walk by faith, not by sight" (2 Cor. 5:7). We trust the Lord to direct our steps and help us to stand by our Christian convictions, even though we can't physically see Him.

Shepherding the Wild Pauls. For over 50 years, seminary professor Howard Hendricks has been recognized as one of America's foremost Christian educators and a creative communicator. Nevertheless, Hendricks indicated on a radio broadcast that as a pre-Christian teen, he had peppered every other sentence with swearwords.

Then, not long after getting saved, Hendricks forgot himself at a church meeting and unloaded a barrage of expletives. The group was horrified, and someone reprimanded him, saying, "I thought you were a Christian!"

Hendricks angrily stormed out. He might never have returned had not one wiser and gentler believer followed him out to the street corner to befriend him. This believer showed Hendricks true Christian acceptance. It mirrors the way in which the Lord Jesus used Ananias to affirm the reality of Paul's conversion experience (see Acts 9:10-19). Thank God for the Ananiases who shepherd the wild Pauls among us.

Everyone Has Seen It. In 2009, the hit movie *Avatar* outperformed all the other movies at the box office. One reason is that teenagers went to the movie over and over again.

Exit surveys showed that many of those in attendance were repeat customers. In the junior high age-group, a child who had not seen the movie was simply out of the loop, a situation that most students want to avoid. Erica and Elene, both 14, had seen the movie five times. Asked why they could see it repeatedly, they responded simply because their friends were all seeing it.

Youth want to belong to something, whether it is a club or a group that has seen a movie. Jesus has called you to be one of His disciples. Just as Paul did while traveling on the road to Damascus (see Acts 26:12-18), you too can accept Jesus' invitation and join the group. Also, get involved and make a difference by telling others about Jesus, just as Paul did when he declared the Gospel to King Agrippa (see vss. 19-29).

PAUL SAILS FOR ROME

BACKGROUND SCRIPTURE: Acts 27
DEVOTIONAL READING: Romans 1:13-17

Key Verse: So it came to pass, that they
escaped all safe to land. Acts 27:44.

KING JAMES VERSION

ACTS 27:1 And when it was determined that we should sail into Italy, they delivered Paul and certain other prisoners unto one named Julius, a centurion of Augustus' band. 2 And entering into a ship of Adramyttium, we launched, meaning to sail by the coasts of Asia; one Aristarchus, a Macedonian of Thessalonica, being with us. . . .

33 And while the day was coming on, Paul besought them all to take meat, saying, This day is the fourteenth day that ye have tarried and continued fasting, having taken nothing. 34 Wherefore I pray you to take some meat: for this is for your health: for there shall not an hair fall from the head of any of you. 35 And when he had thus spoken, he took bread, and gave thanks to God in presence of them all: and when he had broken it, he began to eat. 36 Then were they all of good cheer, and they also took some meat. 37 And we were in all in the ship two hundred threescore and sixteen souls. 38 And when they had eaten enough, they lightened the ship, and cast out the wheat into the sea. 39 And when it was day, they knew not the land: but they discovered a certain creek with a shore, into the which they were minded, if it were possible, to thrust in the ship. 40 And when they had taken up the anchors, they committed themselves unto the sea, and loosed the rudder bands, and hoised up the mainsail to the wind, and made toward shore. 41 And falling into a place where two seas met, they ran the ship aground; and the forepart stuck fast, and remained unmoveable, but the hinder part was broken with the violence of the waves. 42 And the soldiers' counsel was to kill the prisoners, lest any of them should swim out, and escape. 43 But the centurion, willing to save Paul, kept them from their purpose; and commanded that they which could swim should cast themselves first into the sea, and get to land: 44 And the rest, some on boards, and some on broken pieces of the ship. And so it came to pass, that they escaped all safe to land.

NEW REVISED STANDARD VERSION

ACTS 27:1 When it was decided that we were to sail for Italy, they transferred Paul and some other prisoners to a centurion of the Augustan Cohort, named Julius. 2 Embarking on a ship of Adramyttium that was about to set sail to the ports along the coast of Asia, we put to sea, accompanied by Aristarchus, a Macedonian from Thessalonica. . . .

33 Just before daybreak, Paul urged all of them to take some food, saying, "Today is the fourteenth day that you have been in suspense and remaining without food, having eaten nothing. 34 Therefore I urge you to take some food, for it will help you survive; for none of you will lose a hair from your heads." 35 After he had said this, he took bread; and giving thanks to God in the presence of all, he broke it and began to eat. 36 Then all of them were encouraged and took food for themselves. 37 (We were in all two hundred seventy-six persons in the ship.) 38 After they had satisfied their hunger, they lightened the ship by throwing the wheat into the sea.

39 In the morning they did not recognize the land, but they noticed a bay with a beach, on which they planned to run the ship ashore, if they could. 40 So they cast off the anchors and left them in the sea. At the same time they loosened the ropes that tied the steering-oars; then hoisting the foresail to the wind, they made for the beach. 41 But striking a reef, they ran the ship aground; the bow stuck and remained immovable, but the stern was being broken up by the force of the waves. 42 The soldiers' plan was to kill the prisoners, so that none might swim away and escape; 43 but the centurion, wishing to save Paul, kept them from carrying out their plan. He ordered those who could swim to jump overboard first and make for the land, 44 and the rest to follow, some on planks and others on pieces of the ship. And so it was that all were brought safely to land.

11

HOME BIBLE READINGS

Monday, November 5	Romans 1:1-7	*Called to Be an Apostle*
Tuesday, November 6	Romans 1:8-12	*Encouraged by Each Other's Faith*
Wednesday, November 7	Romans 1:13-17	*Eager to Proclaim the Gospel*
Thursday, November 8	Acts 27:3-12	*Paul's Journey to Rome Begins*
Friday, November 9	Acts 27:13-20	*A Fierce Storm Dashes Hope*
Saturday, November 10	Acts 27:21-32	*Keep Up Your Courage*
Sunday, November 11	Acts 27:1-2, 33-44	*Brought Safely to Land*

BACKGROUND

A centurion named Julius was placed in charge of the prisoners, including Paul (Acts 27:1). Julius was a member of the Augustan Cohort (possibly stationed in Syria-Palestine). There is considerable disagreement over the exact identity of this contingent. Some think it was an elite imperial regiment, while others maintain the troops assigned to the cohort mainly served an auxiliary function. Unlike aristocratic Romans, who aspired to higher offices, centurions like Julius usually began as regular soldiers and worked their way up through the ranks. Centurion was the highest rank that an ordinary enlisted soldier could attain and the equivalent of today's U.S. Army sergeant major.

NOTES ON THE PRINTED TEXT

From A.D. 57 to 59, Paul had been incarcerated at Caesarea (see Acts 23:33; 24:27). It was from here that the civil authorities decided to place Paul and some other prisoners on a sailing vessel bound for Italy (27:1). At this time, Paul was grouped with other prisoners. Some of them might have been convicted criminals who would eventually die as combatants before huge crowds in the games held at the Colosseum in Rome. All of them were placed on board a modest-sized, privately owned cargo ship (perhaps weighing less than 250 tons) that had originated from its home port of Adramyttium (vs. 2). This was a harbor on the west coast of Asia Minor between Troas and Pergamum. Adramyttium was also located in Mysia, a region that likewise included Assos, Pergamum, and Troas. Mysia was a crossroads for travel, trade, and conquest. Throughout the Medo-Persian and Roman periods, this region was strategic to the strength and stability of the area.

Once the vessel set sail, it was scheduled to make stops at various ports along the coast of the Roman province of Asia before finally heading to Rome. Paul was accompanied by a believer named Aristarchus, who might have functioned as the apostle's personal attendant (see Acts 19:29; 20:4; Col. 4:10; Philem. vs. 24). Aristarchus's hometown of Thessalonica was located in the Roman province of Macedonia in Greece. The writer of Acts told about some of Paul's experiences using the plural "we," which indicates that the author was with the apostle during those occasions, including his voyage to Rome (see 16:10-17; 20:5–21:18; 27:1–28:16). This clue points to Luke, who was a physician (see Col. 4:14) and a colaborer with Paul (see Philem. vs. 24).

Next, the ship sailed about 70 miles north to Sidon, and Julius was kind enough to permit Paul to visit his friends in the city (Acts 27:2-3). Once the vessel had set out to sea again, the contrary winds and choppy seas made sailing difficult. Thus the ship sailed north of Cyprus in hope that the island and the mainland of Asia Minor would break the force of the gale (vs. 4). The vessel eventually made its way to the port city of Myra in the province of Lycia, where the passengers boarded a larger Alexandrian grain ship (possibly weighing around 800 tons) heading for Italy (vss. 5-6). The prevailing winds made sailing to the port city of Cnidus difficult and slow. Though the pilot wanted to steer the vessel across the Aegean Sea to the coast of Greece, strong winds forced the vessel south. The ship sailed along the southern coast of Crete in an attempt to break the force of the gale (vs. 7). Nevertheless, the vessel still struggled to make it to a small port called Fair Havens (vs. 8).

With the passing of the Day of Atonement, the sailing season was quickly drawing to a close (vs. 9). Paul warned that continuing the journey would be dangerous (vs. 10). But the pilot and owner of the ship wanted to harbor the vessel at the larger port of Phoenix, which was about 60 miles away. This would give them a better opportunity to sell the grain on board. Julius decided to disregard Paul's admonition and continue the journey to Phoenix (vss. 11-12). When a gentle southern breeze began to blow, the crew thought it would be a good time to set sail along the shoreline of Crete (vs. 13). However, a violent northeasterly storm suddenly appeared and forced the vessel south into the open sea (vss. 14-15).

The ship headed to a small island named Clauda, which barely broke the force of the wind long enough for the crew to take aboard a small boat that was being towed by the ship and that was hindering it from steering properly in the turbulent waters (vs. 16). The crew also passed strong ropes crosswise under the hull of the vessel to prevent it from breaking apart in the storm. As the ship continued on its treacherous course, the sailors began to fear the possibility that the vessel would run aground on the sandbars of Syrtis, which were just off the northern coast of Africa. In an attempt to slow the craft down, the crew lowered the sea anchor (vs. 17). As the storm continued to violently pound the vessel, the sailors threw cargo overboard to lighten the craft (vs. 18). In a desperate attempt to save the ship, the sailors threw its rigging overboard (vs. 19). As the storm continued to rage, the passengers eventually gave up all hope of being rescued (vs. 20).

In such a raging storm, there would have been a great deal of seasickness. Also, any kind of food preparation would have been unlikely. This explains why the crew had not eaten for days. Undoubtedly, they were exhausted from the ordeal. Paul stood up and admonished them for not originally heeding his advice (vs. 21). But he tried to encourage them with the good news that not one of their lives would be lost, though the ship would be destroyed (vs. 23). The apostle related that the previous night an angel of the God whom he served revealed that Paul would make it safely to Rome to present his case to the emperor, and that none of the people on board the ship would die (vs. 24). The apostle asserted that he trusted in God's providential care, though Paul related that the vessel would run aground on some island (vss. 25-26).

After 14 days out at sea, the ship continued to be driven across the Adriatic (which extended to southern Italy). As dawn of the 15th day approached, Paul noted that for the past two weeks his fellow passengers had been watching and waiting anxiously to see how their situation might turn out. During that extended period, none of them had eaten anything (vs. 33). Now the apostle urged everyone on board the ship to eat some food and increase their chance of surviving. In fact, Paul stated that all of them would make it through the ordeal without one hair on their heads being harmed (vs. 34; for this common Hebrew expression, see 1 Sam. 14:45; 2 Sam. 14:11; 1 Kings 1:52; Luke 21:18). Then the apostle took a piece of bread, openly thanked God for the provision, broke off a portion, and ate it (Acts 27:35). His action encouraged all 276 people on board to do the same (vss. 35-37). After that, the crew threw the bags of grain (most likely wheat) overboard to further lighten the ship so that it would venture farther into shore (vs. 38).

When it was daylight, the crew spotted a coast it did not recognize. Nonetheless, they noticed a cove with a smooth, sandy beach (what is now called St. Paul's Bay). They surmised that if they could safely navigate the ship between the rocks, the sheltered bay might turn out to be a suitable spot to ground the vessel (vs. 39). With that plan in mind, the sailors cut the anchors loose and let them sink into the sea. They also untied the ropes, which were used to hold the steering oars together and the stern rudders in place. Taking this action would help the crew better pilot the ship to shore. Next, they raised the mainsail at the front of the vessel so that the wind would blow it forward to the beach (vs. 40). However, the ship encountered adverse sea conditions, struck a reef, and ran aground. While the bow of the vessel remained firmly implanted in the shoal, the stern broke apart because of the violent force of the waves (vs. 41).

As chaos and panic ensued, there was the possibility that some of the prisoners might try to escape by swimming ashore. Also, if any prisoners got away, the soldier who was supposed to be guarding them would be executed for dereliction of duty (see 12:19; 16:27). Thus to prevent this from happening, the soldiers decided to kill all the prisoners on board the ship (27:42). Evidently, however, Julius had come to respect Paul. And so, because the centurion wanted to prevent the apostle from perishing, the army officer stopped his men from doing what they had planned. Instead, Julius ordered everyone who could swim to dive first into the water and heard for shore (vs. 43). The remainder of the crew and passengers were to make it to shore by holding on to planks or other portions of the demolished ship. In this way, everyone made it to the beach unharmed (vs. 44).

SUGGESTIONS TO TEACHERS

This week's lesson helps us see that nothing good is accomplished easily. When God's people seek to serve Him, they will often run into obstacles, some of which might even be life threatening. It's in those intense moments that we can look to God for strength to do His will with an uncompromising heart.

1. NO PAIN, NO GAIN. Paul journeyed by sea on a cargo ship that seemed to be doomed from the start. Be that as it may, the dire prospects did not deter the apostle from remaining committed to the Lord and a source of encouragement to others. Most people are tempted to give up when great difficulties arise. The phrase from physical trainers seems appropriate here: "No pain, no gain." If you want the results, you have to put up with the difficulty.

2. INTEGRITY STILL COUNTS. We are surrounded by lies and distortions of every manner. And we are regularly tempted to do what everyone else seems to do—manipulate a difficult situation for our advantage. Paul shows us how to be persons of integrity and live with the consequences. No matter what our circumstances might be, integrity still counts.

3. BEING AN EFFECTIVE LEADER IS IMPORTANT. At first, we might be reluctant to take a lead role in a ministry endeavor. But there might be times—especially challenging ones—when God wants to use us in this way. Paul learned to trust in the Lord's strength and wisdom through the many trials that tested his faith. We can do the same, too, and in this way become effective leaders.

4. DO YOUR BEST AND COUNT ON GOD. Paul called on the Lord to help him be strong enough to do what was important. That reminds us to do our best—to really put out our greatest effort to accomplish our God-given goals. It also reminds us to abide in the Lord throughout the process. This means asking God to enable us to do our best for His glory.

FOR ADULTS

■ TOPIC: Weathering the Storm

■ QUESTIONS: 1. What circumstances led to Paul being taken to Italy? 2. Why had everyone on board the ship gone without food for two weeks? 3. In what ways did Paul show the traits of a natural-born leader? 4. How is it possible for believers to remain calm in life-threatening circumstances like the one Paul faced? 5. What are some noteworthy things God has done through you that He wants you to share with others?

■ ILLUSTRATIONS:

Persevering with Faith. Jonathan took the leadership of a Christian education ministry that was floundering. With boldness, wisdom, and faith he energized the work and took it to new levels of effectiveness. Then Lou Gehrig's disease struck him.

Rather than quit and spend his time complaining, Jonathan attacked his work with renewed vigor. His cheerfulness and courage inspired many.

Jonathan gave an inspiring address to the congregation, many of whom were moved to tears. Despite the life storms he faced, he did not wallow in self-pity. Instead, he challenged his fellow Christians to persevere in faith, regardless of what setbacks might come their way.

Like Paul, Jonathan knew God so deeply that he accepted his hardship with graciousness. After several years, Jonathan succumbed to the ravages of the disease. Yet as Paul did in his life, Jonathan also left a powerful mark on his church, his family, and his ministry.

In All Things Be Thankful. As Paul and others faced the prospect of being shipwrecked at sea, the apostle had the presence of mind to give thanks to God for His provision of food (see Acts 27:35). Theologian and author Leonard Sweet describes an incident that occurred during the gloomy days of 1929. There were a group of ministers in Boston, Massachusetts, who got together to plan how they should conduct their Thanksgiving Sunday services.

At this time in the nation's history, the economic situation was pretty bleak, and there seemed to be no sign of relief in sight. The bread lines were horribly long, and the stock market had lost much of its value. The phrase "Great Depression" seemed to be an appropriate description for the general mood of the country.

Out of sensitivity for the misery all around them, the ministers agreed that they should only briefly mention the subject of Thanksgiving. After all, there seemed to be little for which to express gratitude. But William L. Stiger, the pastor of a large congregation in the city, encouraged the group to approach the situation differently.

Stiger maintained that this was not the time for the ministers to give only passing mention to Thanksgiving. Instead, he thought it was an opportunity for them to help their fellow citizens put matters into perspective. For instance, the ministers could encourage others to thank God for the blessings they still enjoyed but had forgotten about because of the intense hardships everyone felt.

The Power of One, and Two and Three. Imagine how differently things would have turned out if Paul and his fellow travelers aboard the sailing vessel thought only about themselves. It's likely that many people would have perished when they experienced the shipwreck.

One day an artist decided to show on canvas the meaning of the Gospel. He began by painting a storm at sea. Dark clouds filled the sky. A flash of lightning illuminated a little boat, which could be seen disintegrating under the pounding of the ocean. People were struggling in the waters, their anguished faces crying out for help.

The only glimmer of hope appeared in the foreground of the painting, where a large rock protruded out of the water. There, clutching desperately with both hands, was one lone seaman. It was a moving scene. As one looked at the painting, one could see in the tempest a symbol of humankind's hopeless condition. And, true to the Gospel, the only hope of salvation was "the Rock of Ages," that is, Jesus, our shelter in the time of storm.

Yet as the artist reflected upon his work, he realized that the painting didn't accurately portray his subject. So he discarded the canvas and painted another. The new artwork was similar to the first. One could see the dark clouds, the flashing lightning, the angry waters, the little boat crushed by the pounding waves, and the crew vainly struggling in the water.

In the foreground, the seaman was clutching the large rock for salvation. But the artist made one key change. The survivor was holding on with only one hand, and with the other hand he was reaching down to pull up a drowning friend, who in turn, could lend a helping hand to others. The second painting is a genuine picture of the Gospel. It's about the power of one, and of two, and of three and so on, helping others. Expressed differently, the Gospel is a message of hope in which Jesus enables us, His followers, to reach out to others so that all can experience His saving grace.

FOR YOUTH

■ **TOPIC:** A Stressful Journey
■ **QUESTIONS:** 1. Why was Paul a prisoner of the Roman government? 2. How would you have felt if you were with Paul on the voyage to Rome? 3. Upon what basis did Paul tell those with him that they would survive the pending shipwreck? 4. How did Paul get and maintain the respect of the centurion? 5. Why is it important for us to rely on God when we are doing His will?

■ **ILLUSTRATIONS:**

Finishing the Job. A young man named Mike began using drugs as a way to cope with the stresses in his life. Soon he became addicted to them. Sometime after that, he went through a recovery program in an effort to get his life back on track.

Part of Mike's effort included going door-to-door, looking for odd jobs—washing windows, trimming bushes, and so on. One family asked him to spade a garden plot. This was tough work, because the 20-by-30-foot area had been lawn for many years. Mike tore into his task, but soon wearied of it because he had no idea how to use a spade. His enthusiasm did not make up for his inexperience.

The spot looked like a battlefield. Huge holes appeared everywhere. The owner came back aghast. He took Mike aside and showed him how to spade in a more orderly way. Once more, Mike tackled the plot. This time, he finished the work acceptably.

Most of us need practical help and wise counsel so that we can do God's work in His way. Growing things in God's spiritual garden is not easy. Paul was able to mature in his faith and become a discerning spiritual leader by looking to God for strength. Like the apostle, with the Lord's help, we can also join raw courage to a seasoned faith and finish our God-given responsibilities in a prudent manner.

Monsters. The story is told about a young boy named Brian. One night, after everyone had gone to bed, Brian opened the door to his parents' bedroom and quietly walked over to his mother's side of the bed and said, "Mommy, I think there's a monster under my bed!"

"What?" said Brian's mother. The child answered, "I'm afraid there's a monster under my bed. And I can't sleep with it there," he said. "Let's go see that monster," said Brian's dad. "No, I don't want to see it," said Brian.

So here's what the family decided to do. First, they turned on Brian's lights. Next, they turned on the lights in the parents' bedroom. Then, they turned on the lights in the hall. Finally, they turned on the lights in Brian's bedroom.

After that, Brian's dad went around the bed and pulled up the covers so everyone could see under the child's bed. Brian's dad stood on one side of the bed. Brian and his mother stood on the other side of the bed.

"Now," said Brian's dad, "when I count to three, we're all going to get down on the floor and look under the bed." "I don't want to," said Brian. "We can do it," said his mom. "I promise to hold your hand."

So Brian's dad counted, "One, two, three . . . ," and they all got down on the floor to look under the bed. "What do you see?" asked Brian's dad. "Nothing," said Brian. "I see you," said Brian's dad to his son.

"And I think Jesus is with us, too," said Brian's mommy. "Really?" asked Brian. "Yes, I'm sure He is," said his mother. "You were afraid that monsters were under your bed. But I believe that Jesus is with us even now. And we know that Jesus watches over us when we sleep. I even think Jesus watches under us, too." Brian had never thought about that. "Jesus watches under us" seemed like a good idea to the child.

Brian's dad said, "As long as we're here on our knees by the bed, why don't we say another prayer so we can all go back to bed." And the family did so, just like this: "Dear Jesus, we thank You for watching over us and watching under us. And the next time we're afraid there are monsters under the bed, help us to remember that You are with us and won't let any monster get near us. Amen."

From Paul's experience on the sailing vessel heading to Rome, we learn that the Lord watches over us even in the most difficult of circumstances. Jesus watches under us too—and to the left and to the right, as well as to the front and to the back. In fact, He's always with us, no matter what we're going through.

PAUL MINISTERS IN MALTA

BACKGROUND SCRIPTURE: Acts 28:1-10
DEVOTIONAL READING: Ezekiel 34:11-16

Key Verse: And it came to pass, that the father of Publius lay sick of a fever and of a bloody flux: to whom Paul entered in, and prayed, and laid his hands on him, and healed him. Acts 28:8.

KING JAMES VERSION

ACTS 28:1 And when they were escaped, then they knew that the island was called Melita. 2 And the barbarous people shewed us no little kindness: for they kindled a fire, and received us every one, because of the present rain, and because of the cold. 3 And when Paul had gathered a bundle of sticks, and laid them on the fire, there came a viper out of the heat, and fastened on his hand. 4 And when the barbarians saw the venomous beast hang on his hand, they said among themselves, No doubt this man is a murderer, whom, though he hath escaped the sea, yet vengeance suffereth not to live. 5 And he shook off the beast into the fire, and felt no harm. 6 Howbeit they looked when he should have swollen, or fallen down dead suddenly: but after they had looked a great while, and saw no harm come to him, they changed their minds, and said that he was a god. 7 In the same quarters were possessions of the chief man of the island, whose name was Publius; who received us, and lodged us three days courteously. 8 And it came to pass, that the father of Publius lay sick of a fever and of a bloody flux: to whom Paul entered in, and prayed, and laid his hands on him, and healed him. 9 So when this was done, others also, which had diseases in the island, came, and were healed: 10 Who also honoured us with many honours; and when we departed, they laded us with such things as were necessary.

NEW REVISED STANDARD VERSION

ACTS 28:1 After we had reached safety, we then learned that the island was called Malta. 2 The natives showed us unusual kindness. Since it had begun to rain and was cold, they kindled a fire and welcomed all of us around it. 3 Paul had gathered a bundle of brushwood and was putting it on the fire, when a viper, driven out by the heat, fastened itself on his hand. 4 When the natives saw the creature hanging from his hand, they said to one another, "This man must be a murderer; though he has escaped from the sea, justice has not allowed him to live." 5 He, however, shook off the creature into the fire and suffered no harm. 6 They were expecting him to swell up or drop dead, but after they had waited a long time and saw that nothing unusual had happened to him, they changed their minds and began to say that he was a god.

7 Now in the neighborhood of that place were lands belonging to the leading man of the island, named Publius, who received us and entertained us hospitably for three days. 8 It so happened that the father of Publius lay sick in bed with fever and dysentery. Paul visited him and cured him by praying and putting his hands on him. 9 After this happened, the rest of the people on the island who had diseases also came and were cured. 10 They bestowed many honors on us, and when we were about to sail, they put on board all the provisions we needed.

12

HOME BIBLE READINGS

BACKGROUND

Malta is the island on which Paul was shipwrecked (Acts 28:1). Otherwise known as *Melite* in Greek, it is located in the Mediterranean Sea between Sicily and Africa. Malta is also about 90 miles southwest of Syracuse, which then was a Greek city on the southeast coast of Sicily (see vs. 12). By 1000 B.C., Phoenicians had colonized Malta. In 218 B.C., the island was captured by Rome. This occurred at the start of the Second Punic War, which the Republic waged against Carthage (a city in North Africa). Rome granted Malta the status of *municipium*, which allowed the inhabitants a large measure of local autonomy.

Malta encompasses about 95 square miles and was a strategically located stopping point for commercial ships traveling east to west and north to south. The island's natural harbors provided shelter for oceangoing vessels from the stormy conditions of the Mediterranean Sea. A considerable portion of Malta was parched, agriculturally unproductive, and lacked any important natural resources. Be that as it may, the local residents were somewhat able to cultivate the eastern half of the island, which enabled them to produce olive oil and wool. Paul and the rest of the travelers remained on Malta for three months (vs. 11).

NOTES ON THE PRINTED TEXT

As we learned last week, Paul and other prisoners at Caesarea were turned over to a Roman centurion to be taken to the capital of the empire. They boarded a ship and stopped in several ports along the way. Because the voyage was late in the season, bad weather made progress difficult. The ship's captain ignored Paul's advice and gambled that he could reach a better harbor in which to winter. But hurricane-strength winds blew them off course. Then, after riding the storm for two weeks, the travelers were shipwrecked on the island of Malta (Acts 28:1). Paul's counsel, however, enabled all the crew and passengers to survive.

The Greek adjective translated "barbarous" (vs. 2) could also be rendered "foreigners" and refers to non-Greeks and non-Romans who were presumed to be culturally primitive. In this case, the local inhabitants of Malta were descendants of the Phoenicians, and their native language was Punic (a Phoenician dialect used by the people of Carthage). But far from being uncivilized brutes, the Maltese showed themselves to be extraordinarily kindhearted and generous to Paul and the rest of the travelers. In fact, the inhabitants of the island greeted the shipwrecked victims with a fire they had kindled. This would have been a welcome sight on a cold, rainy day, especially after a forced swim in the Mediterranean Sea.

It seems that Paul could attract attention without even trying. On this occasion, the apostle gathered an armful of sticks to add to the fire the local inhabitants had made. And as he was placing the brushwood on the flames, the heat caused a poisonous snake that was hiding in the sticks to crawl out and attach itself to his hand (vs. 3). When the people of the island saw the viper gripping Paul's hand with its fangs, they immediately concluded that he was a "murderer" (vs. 4).

The Maltese superstitiously assumed that even though the apostle had eluded the wrath of the storm, a goddess named Justice would not permit him to survive any longer. This pagan deity was believed to be the daughter of Zeus (the king of the gods in the Greek pantheon who was said to preside over the universe). Supposedly, Justice, by enacting an oracle of judgment against Paul in connection with his guilt, was carrying out the will of another goddess named Fortune or the Fates. In other words, the local residents saw the snakebite as divine retribution for the apostle's presumed crime, which the civil authorities had failed to detect or punish.

The Maltese must have been surprised when they saw Paul simply shake off the viper from his hand and drop it into the fire, where the creature died. In contrast, the apostle experienced no ill effects from the venomous bite of the snake (vs. 5). We don't know that Paul specifically prayed for God's help, but the apostle seemed quietly confident that the Lord was watching over him. Perhaps Paul recalled the Savior's visit and reassuring statement when the apostle was imprisoned in Jerusalem: "must thou bear witness . . . at Rome" (23:11). Consequently, God would not let a snakebite stand in the way of Him fulfilling His promise.

Some critics point out that no poisonous snakes are found on Malta today. The implication is that the incident recorded in 28:3-5 was not the miracle Luke made it out to be. Today's circumstances, though, on the island need not have been what prevailed almost 2,000 years ago. We can be confident that the Maltese in Paul's day knew their island and its creatures sufficiently well. They also recognized the symptoms of those who had been bitten by poisonous snakes and lizards. In this case, the local inhabitants watched with bated breath to see those symptoms overtake the apostle. Luke, too, as a physician, would have had some knowledge of snakebites and their effects on people.

The Maltese expected Paul to swell up or experience a raging fever. They also assumed the apostle would suddenly collapse and die. Yet, after they had waited a long while, they noticed that no harm came to Paul. In light of this latest development, the local residents decided to revise their theory about the apostle. Since he had twice escaped death, they jumped to a new conclusion. This time the Maltese decided he had to be a "god" (vs. 6) or perhaps one of its favored human subjects. While presuming often causes us to judge people unfairly, sometimes it causes us to inappropriately honor people. Hero worship is no better than prejudice. The apostle was neither a murderer nor divine.

A man named Publius was the chief Roman official, or local magistrate, of Malta. As such, he was responsible for maintaining peace on the island and ensuring that a sufficient amount of taxes was collected and sent to Rome. Publius occupied an estate containing fields and several buildings. Since this estate was in the general vicinity of the place where shipwrecked survivors swam ashore, it probably did not take long for him to learn about these new arrivals to Malta. The official invited the stranded crew and passengers to his spacious villa, where he provided for their needs for the next three days (vs. 7). This hospitable gesture on the part of Publius would ensure the health and safety of his guests and give them enough time to find suitable longer-term living arrangements for the winter.

At this time, the father of Publius was bedridden from a high "fever and . . . a bloody flux" (vs. 8). Evidently, the elderly man was experiencing an inflammatory disorder of the intestine, particularly the colon, which was characterized by severe abdominal pain, diarrhea, and blood loss. If left untreated, the disease could have been fatal. When Paul heard about the man's illness, the apostle was granted permission to see him. Paul first prayed to God on the behalf of the sick man. Then the apostle placed his hands on the infirm man and brought about his healing.

The startling news of what Paul had done quickly traveled over Malta (which is only 18 miles long and 8 miles wide). In a relatively short time period, infirm residents from all parts of the island came to the apostle to be healed, and he responded by curing them of their afflictions (vs. 9). Succinctly put, Paul heard about someone who was sick, and he offered to do what he could. In a sense, the apostle created his own opportunity to do good. And so out of a shipwreck came a series of healings. Moreover, from a prisoner of Rome came physical and spiritual deliverance to others. It's not difficult to imagine how grateful the Maltese felt in response to what Paul had done for their sick residents. In turn, the islanders bestowed many honors on the entire group of visitors. This included taking care of their short-term needs and outfitting them for the rest of the voyage to Rome (vs. 10).

SUGGESTIONS TO TEACHERS

This week's lesson encourages the members of your class to affirm that God has gifted His people to do His work. It does not matter, either, how difficult the circumstance might be. Even Paul continued to minister to others, despite the fact that he was a prisoner of Rome for his faith and the survivor of a shipwreck at sea.

1. CONGREGATIONS FALLING SHORT. Many people yearn for the kind of human companionship, support, and fellowship offered in Christ's body, the church. Sadly, many times they don't find it because congregations seem to be marked by disunity, cliques, and self-centeredness. That's one reason why these people look elsewhere. They join service clubs, community groups, and sports clubs, or spend a lot of time hanging out at bars.

2. BELIEVERS PARTNERING TOGETHER. Because there are congregations that fail to offer the kind of acceptance people are looking for, they do not seek the Savior in the church. This is tragic, for the church is supposed to be the one social group that transcends all our differences. As Paul did on Malta, the faith community is supposed to bear witness to people that Jesus can meet their needs. Our witness is only as valid and strong as our unified efforts to reach out to those who are hurting and struggling. Our message is heard when we sublimate our differences and work together in common purpose and love.

3. TAKING AN INVENTORY OF SPIRIT'S GIFTS. Examine with your class the different kinds of gifts bestowed by the Spirit to a congregation. Work to understand what each of these may mean for your church today. Consider who in your congregation seems to be blessed with what gifts. Are these persons encouraged to minister their gifts to others? How can the congregation give equal emphasis to all the gifts of the Spirit present within the church?

4. PUTTING SPIRITUAL GIFTS INTO PRACTICE. Many believers tend to dismiss their God-given talents, skills, and aptitudes as insignificant or unimportant in the ongoing life of the church. Nothing, though, could be further from the truth. Every spiritual gift is important and needed. And it is vital that these gifts be put into practice so that the church's ministry is complete and God is praised through them.

FOR ADULTS

■ TOPIC: Helping One Another

■ QUESTIONS: 1. How did God enable Paul and the rest of his fellow travelers to arrive safely onshore? 2. Why do you think the residents of Malta rushed to judgment concerning Paul? 3. How did Paul make the most of the situation to minister to others in the name of the Savior? 4. What are some ways you can serve others with the talents and abilities God has given you? 5. What is the greatest spiritual blessing you can imagine experiencing as a result of ministering to others for Christ?

■ ILLUSTRATIONS:

Working Together. Too often today churches get mired in arguments and division, not in spiritual unity. While the members of a congregation might embrace core theological truths, they obsess over peripheral, far less important matters. Meanwhile, the church's larger purpose and common bond in Christ get lost in the fracas.

For instance, some churches are weakened because of a false dichotomy between so-called gifted believers and the rest of the ordinary Christians. We have to make room for all believers to exercise their God-given gifts for the common good of helping one another. We cannot afford to let some Christians think they are second class because they do not have some of the more publicly recognized gifts.

While Paul was on Malta, he emphasized and demonstrated oneness, unity, and harmony. He would not tolerate disputes over the talents and abilities believers have. After all, these are intended to be used in doing God's work. When the latter remains the primary goal, it leads to a vital, loving, growing, unified congregation.

The Blessings of Service. Paul's life and ministry, including his brief stay on Malta, remind us that God spiritually blesses those who faithfully serve Him. And those blessings can reverberate from one generation of believers to the next.

For Derek, nothing was quite so enjoyable as spending an afternoon paddling out to his favorite fishing spot on a nearby lake. But on this day, there was a little snag. After digging through his worn metal tackle box, he could not find the lure he wanted. It had been his favorite—and the fish's favorite.

Now frustrated, Derek shifted lures and bobbins around and pulled out forgotten reels of fishing line. Then he found it—not the lure he had been looking for, but a lure he thought he had lost forever. It had belonged to his father, and to his grandfather. It was a family heirloom, and seeing it again reminded Derek of everything else right and good that had endured from generation to generation—including the family's faith in God.

Derek knew that God had richly blessed his grandfather and had been faithful to his father. Both of these family stalwarts had demonstrated by their lives what it means to be a godly servant and leader to others. Derek also realized that the faith his father and grandfather had in the Lord is what carried them through the hard times they experienced. As Derek spent the remainder of the afternoon on the lake, he prayed that he too would be like his forebearers. In this way, he sensed that his own children would continue to serve God and experience His spiritual blessings.

Putting Spiritual Gifts into Practice. Pastor Matthew was fatigued, frustrated, and burned out. He had pastored a little country church with less than a hundred members for six years—ever since his first week out of seminary. Wanting to do a good job in the eyes of God as well as for the congregation, he had initially set himself to his task at full speed.

Within six months, the pastor was preaching three times a week, leading an adult Bible study and three small groups, counseling five or six people a week, visiting the hospitalized and sick, and calling on prospective members. He also performed a host of administrative duties—such as printing and copying the weekly bulletin and newsletter, mailing out correspondence, meeting with the church's various committees, and leading a much-needed building renovation campaign.

Pastor Matthew decided to bare his soul over lunch to an older, neighboring minister. After listening intently and patiently to Pastor Matthew's troubles, his friend asked him, "What have you done to encourage your church members to use their spiritual gifts?"

As Pastor Matthew pondered his answer, he realized that he had assumed numerous tasks that had once been carried out by his members. It was as if every time a role came open in the church, he took it on without asking other gifted members to shoulder the task themselves. Rather than fulfill his pastoral role of equipping the saints, he had assumed too many duties himself.

God never intended the church to be a "one-man show." He provides numerous spiritual gifts throughout every congregation so that individual members of the church operate together as the body of Christ. Thus, every spiritual gift is significant and needed. As we recognize from Paul's brief time on Malta, it is vital that all these gifts be put into practice so that the church's ministry is complete and God is glorified.

■ **FOR YOUTH** ■ **TOPIC:** Somebody Is Watching You
■ **QUESTIONS:** 1. What kind of reception did the travelers from the shipwrecked vessel experience on Malta? 2. What conflicting opinions about Paul did the residents of Malta have? 3. Are there times you feel defensive when others say inaccurate things about you to others? 4. Why do you think Publius was so hospitable to Paul and his fellow travelers? 5. In what ways has God gifted you to do His work?

■ **ILLUSTRATIONS:**

Valued Team Members. Youth are introduced early to the values of working together. They work on class projects, participate in musical groups and plays, and join athletic teams. They all know that if any member slacks off, the team suffers. They also know that if any player tries to steal the show, the team is weakened. Clearly, the actions of every member are noticed and accounted for!

These are the kinds of illustrations teenagers can understand when applied to the church, which is Christ's team (in a manner of speaking). The beauty of the church is that faith in Jesus is the only requirement to be on the team. As Paul taught and displayed on the island of Malta, it doesn't depend on skill or experience. It requires only faith.

Faith is also required to accept the contributions of all other team members. Perhaps the final production will not be as professional as we would prefer, but we have to remember that the church is not only for professionals. The church is also for lifelong learners and followers of Christ. We all need to coach each other, so that our team can use its gifts to do the Lord's work.

Taming the Lion of Pride. Early on in Paul's spiritual journey as a believer, he learned that there is no place for arrogance and inflated self-importance when serving others as a follower of Jesus. Indeed, while on Malta, the apostle remained humble as he ministered to others, regardless of their status in life.

C. S. Lewis, in *Mere Christianity*, describes a great inhibitor to Christian service. He asserted that "the essential vice, the utmost evil, is pride." Lewis also noted the following: "Unchastity, anger, greed, drunkenness, and all that, are mere fleabites in comparison. It was through pride that the devil became the devil. Pride leads to every other vice. It is the complete anti-God state of mind. . . . As long as you are proud, you cannot know God. A proud person is always looking down on things and people. And, of course, as long as you are looking down, you cannot see something that is above you."

If proud people cannot truly know God, they also cannot serve Him. Moreover, when human eyes are condescendingly fixed on the faults of others, or pompously transfixed in the mirror, spiritual perspective becomes lost. In that state of mind, even works supposedly done "for the Lord" have no meaning.

Are you looking for a spiritual blessing? Better yet, do you desire to be a blessing to others? If so, first tame the lion of pride.

Gifted for God's Work. In the 1930s movie *The Citadel*, Robert Donat plays a talented, idealistic young physician who, by the film's conclusion, is on trial for assisting an unlicensed medical practitioner during an operation. His accusers claim that he forsook his oath in order to help a "quack."

The accusers don't seem to care that the operation was a success. Likewise, they are indifferent to the fact that the so-called quack clearly had a gift for medicine. For them, medical talents must fit their specific image to be valid. Otherwise, they are disregarded.

Thankfully, the Lord does not operate that way. He has gifted all sorts of believers in a variety of different ways to do His work. Some are like Paul, whom God used on Malta to bring healing to many people. Others bring aptitudes in organization, the creative arts, crisis counseling, and so on. From this we see that God accepts and works through every believer's unique spiritual gifts, regardless of how young or old he or she might be.

PAUL EVANGELIZES IN ROME

BACKGROUND SCRIPTURE: Acts 28:16-31
DEVOTIONAL READING: Deuteronomy 4:32-40

Key Verse: Be it known therefore unto you, that the salvation of God is sent unto the Gentiles, and that they will hear it. Acts 28:28.

KING JAMES VERSION

ACTS 28:23 And when they had appointed him a day, there came many to him into his lodging; to whom he expounded and testified the kingdom of God, persuading them concerning Jesus, both out of the law of Moses, and out of the prophets, from morning till evening. 24 And some believed the things which were spoken, and some believed not. 25 And when they agreed not among themselves, they departed, after that Paul had spoken one word, Well spake the Holy Ghost by Esaias the prophet unto our fathers, 26 Saying, Go unto this people, and say, Hearing ye shall hear, and shall not understand; and seeing ye shall see, and not perceive: 27 For the heart of this people is waxed gross, and their ears are dull of hearing, and their eyes have they closed; lest they should see with their eyes, and hear with their ears, and understand with their heart, and should be converted, and I should heal them. 28 Be it known therefore unto you, that the salvation of God is sent unto the Gentiles, and that they will hear it.
29 And when he had said these words, the Jews departed, and had great reasoning among themselves.

30 And Paul dwelt two whole years in his own hired house, and received all that came in unto him,
31 Preaching the kingdom of God, and teaching those things which concern the Lord Jesus Christ, with all confidence, no man forbidding him.

NEW REVISED STANDARD VERSION

ACTS 28:23 After they had set a day to meet with him, they came to him at his lodgings in great numbers. From morning until evening he explained the matter to them, testifying to the kingdom of God and trying to convince them about Jesus both from the law of Moses and from the prophets. 24 Some were convinced by what he had said, while others refused to believe. 25 So they disagreed with each other; and as they were leaving, Paul made one further statement: "The Holy Spirit was right in saying to your ancestors through the prophet Isaiah,

26 'Go to this people and say,
You will indeed listen, but never understand,
and you will indeed look, but never perceive.
27 For this people's heart has grown dull,
and their ears are hard of hearing,
and they have shut their eyes;
so that they might not look with their eyes,
and listen with their ears,
and understand with their heart and turn—
and I would heal them.'
28 Let it be known to you then that this salvation of God has been sent to the Gentiles; they will listen."

30 He lived there two whole years at his own expense and welcomed all who came to him, 31 proclaiming the kingdom of God and teaching about the Lord Jesus Christ with all boldness and without hindrance.

13

Monday, November 19	Exodus 6:6-13	*Will They Listen to Me?*
Tuesday, November 20	Deuteronomy 1:41-45	*I Told You So!*
Wednesday, November 21	Deuteronomy 4:5-14	*Charged to Teach*
Thursday, November 22	Deuteronomy 4:32-40	*The Voice of Discipline*
Friday, November 23	Deuteronomy 30:6-14	*The Word Is Very Near*
Saturday, November 24	Acts 28:16-22	*We Would Like to Hear*
Sunday, November 25	Acts 28:23-31	*Teaching Boldly and without Hindrance*

BACKGROUND

The city of Rome—where Paul was under house arrest—was located on the Tiber River on seven hills, about 15 miles inland from the Tyrrhenian Sea. In the first century A.D., Rome was one of the two largest cities in the world (the other being Xi'an, China), with a population estimated at 1 million people. Rome was a walled city of less than 25 square miles. It boasted the royal palace, ornate fountains, elaborate baths (some of which housed libraries and social clubs), the Circus Maximus (used for chariot racing and other games), and the 50,000-seat Colosseum. The Forum, where citizens engaged in political, religious, and commercial enterprises, was where Paul likely defended himself and the Christian movement. Some 82 temples were built or remodeled in Rome in the first half of the first century A.D.

During Paul's day, Rome was the political capital of an empire that extended from the Atlantic Ocean to the Persian Gulf, and from North Africa to Britain and northern Europe. As a booming metropolis, Rome was connected to other parts of the ancient world by an intricate system of highways. Also, Rome's communications system was unsurpassed at the time. In fact, during the first century A.D., the city was at the hub of trade and commerce. Because of its location and prestige, Rome was a strategic center for the spread of the Gospel. It's no wonder that people remarked concerning the city, "All roads lead to Rome."

NOTES ON THE PRINTED TEXT

Paul, Luke, and the others stayed on Malta for three months. Then in February, when the treacherous winter weather had passed, they sailed northward for Rome on an Alexandrian ship that had as a figurehead the twin gods named Castor and Pollux (Acts 28:11).

As the ship carrying Paul headed northward, it made stops at Syracuse, on Sicily's coast, and Rhegium, at the toe of Italy's boot (vs. 12). Then the travelers set out for Puteoli, which was one of Rome's main ports (vs. 13). This remained the case despite the fact that Puteoli was located 75 miles from the capital. Some believers in Puteoli invited Paul and his companions to stay for a week. They had heard about Paul and wanted to host him. They desired to hear his testimony and teaching firsthand. The Roman centurion, Julius, who seemed to be in no hurry, permitted the apostle to visit.

Next, the group headed for Rome along the Appian Way, which was one of Italy's main roads (vs. 14). The news of Paul's arrival traveled from Puteloi to Rome ahead of him. A group of believers from Rome set out to meet Paul on the way. Some stopped at the Three Taverns, a town about 35 miles south of the capital. A second group went as far as the Forum of Appius, another town 10 miles farther from Rome. Their welcome, like a red-carpet treatment for a dignitary, encouraged Paul. God used these believers to minister to the apostle and reassure him that he would not be alone in Rome. He responded by thanking God for their help (vs. 15).

After Paul's arrival in Rome, he was permitted to rent his own home, to receive visitors, and to preach the Gospel (vs. 16). Three days later, he took advantage of his freedom by trying to establish relations with the city's Jewish community. He summarized for a group of their leaders the circumstances that brought him as a prisoner to the capital of the empire. He openly acknowledged his trouble with some Jews in Jerusalem. He insisted, however, he never did anything to hurt the Jewish people. Additionally, he said he never violated the "customs of our fathers" (vs. 17).

Paul told the local Jewish leaders that the Roman government in Palestine had conducted a judicial hearing regarding the apostle's case. After cross-examining him, the officials determined that Paul had not done anything to deserve death or imprisonment (vs. 18; see 26:31). In fact, they struggled to delineate the charges being made against the accused (see 25:27). Even so, when the civil authorities sought to release the apostle, his opponents protested the decision. Moreover, when they continued to press their charges against him, Paul was forced to appeal his case to Caesar (which was his right as a Roman citizen). The apostle was careful to emphasize that he was not bringing any countercharge against his "nation" (vs. 19). He was appearing before the emperor as a defendant only. Paul's final statement demonstrated the link between Judaism and the Christian church. His ministry, which had led to his current predicament, was due to the "hope of Israel" (vs. 20).

In response to Paul, the local Jewish leaders claimed to have heard nothing negative about the apostle (vs. 21). This included the absence of any written correspondence from Judea. There weren't even verbal reports against Paul from anyone who had come from Judea. While claiming not to know anything objectionable about Paul, the Jewish leaders admitted having heard unfavorable reports about the Christian church. They called the movement a "sect" (vs. 22), which indicated that Christianity was still regarded as a splinter group of Judaism.

Despite their suspicions, the local Jewish leaders agreed to return to hear what Paul had to say about Jesus of Nazareth and the religious faction connected with Him (vs. 23). For an entire day the apostle reasoned with those who came to hear him. He testified from the Old Testament about the rule of God and the promise of the Messiah found in "the law of Moses" and "the prophets." Paul used the Jewish sacred writings to show how Jesus had fulfilled the prophecies in numerous ways. The apostle taught that the kingdom of God includes His rule in the hearts of believers. The divine kingdom was not merely limited to the nation of Israel, as the Jews had long believed.

What the Jews had long hoped for was what Paul heralded as an accomplished fact: the advent of the Messiah. This was a consistent theme in the apostle's evangelistic preaching. For instance, while at Pisidian Antioch, during Paul's first missionary journey, he told about the one in whom God had most fully revealed His grace: Jesus the Savior (13:23). Jesus was the descendant of David who had been promised in such Old Testament prophecies as Isaiah 11. Paul declared that the promises of Scripture had been fulfilled in the Messiah. The apostle quoted Psalm 2:7 in support of Jesus' divine sonship (Acts 13:33). Paul quoted Isaiah 55:3 and Psalm 16:10 to back up Jesus' resurrection (Acts 13:34-35). Those passages could not have been fulfilled ultimately in David, since the illustrious king died. But Jesus, David's descendant, was raised immortal. In Him the hopes of the prophets were fulfilled (vss. 36-37).

When Paul met with the local Jewish leaders in Rome, he convinced some in his audience, but many others remained unpersuaded (28:24). Animated debate continued among the Jews themselves, with some supporting the apostle's views and others denouncing them (vs. 25). The meeting finally broke up when Paul quoted an unflattering prophecy from the Septuagint version (an ancient Greek translation) of Isaiah 6:9-10. In doing so, the apostle declared that his listeners heard but did not understand God's truth. Likewise, they saw but did not perceive God's revelation. Their problem was that their hearts were calloused, insensitive, and unfeeling. The result was that they did not turn to God for spiritual healing (Acts 28:26-27).

In response to the local Jews' refusal to believe the Gospel, Paul declared that the Father's saving message through the Son was also being offered to the Gentiles (vs. 28). Furthermore, they would hear and heed the Good News. After the apostle had made this statement, his fellow Jews departed. As they left, they heatedly argued with one another about what Paul had said (vs. 29). Meanwhile, Paul remained in detention in his own "hired house" (vs. 30) for "two whole years." He was not assigned a place to live by the government. Rather, he paid his own living expenses. Perhaps this indicates that the apostle earned a living by tentmaking even while in custody. In any case, Paul had considerable freedom to see people. He did not hesitate to proclaim the truth about Jesus boldly and triumphantly in the heart of the empire (vs. 31).

The two-year period of house arrest is somewhat mystifying. According to one group of historians, Roman law required cases to be heard within 18 months, or they had to be dismissed. Paul's two-year wait suggests to some that his prosecutors failed to press charges within the allotted time. With bureaucratic delays, they say, Paul finally stood before Caesar for formal release after being held two years. While some see the apostle's imprisonment ending with a death sentence passed by the despotic

Nero, many others maintain that Paul took one more missionary journey before being rearrested and executed in Rome about A.D. 62–67.

Paul's final words seem to be that of a believer who was content. He affirmed that he had been faithful to do all that God had assigned to him. The apostle had no regrets, for he had surrendered his life completely to the Lord (see 2 Tim. 4:7). Paul compared his life to the offerings the Old Testament priests made (see Phil. 2:17; 2 Tim. 4:6). They poured wine or oil on a sacrifice just before it was to be burned (see Num. 15:1-12). The apostle saw this as a picture of something that was irretrievable—once the wine was spilled, it soaked into the sacrifice, the wood, and the ground around the altar. It could not be picked up. It was gone. Eventually, Paul would be gone; the last drop of his life would be poured out for the Lord. How important it is to live our lives so that at the end we will have no regrets!

SUGGESTIONS TO TEACHERS

God did not make the means of receiving His salvation complicated or difficult. Rather, He made it clear and straightforward. We are saved through faith in the Son. There is no other means of redemption. Paul made this clear to the Jewish leaders in Rome who visited him while he was under house arrest. We can imagine him using concepts found in Romans 10:9-10 to frame his Gospel presentation. As time permits, have the class members consider the following four unsophisticated and unpretentious steps one should follow in order to be justified by grace through faith.

1. CONFESS WITH YOUR LIPS. First comes the call to express what your mind has accepted. You've examined the facts, you've heard all the evidence you need to hear, you've realized your need for salvation, and you've recognized that Jesus is your only source of redemption. Thus you express that He is the Lord who rose again, the Savior of your soul, and your Messiah. Of course, confession made out loud represents a confirmation of what you have already accepted inside.

2. BELIEVE IN YOUR HEART. Second comes the belief that begins growing in your heart and never ceases to grow for the rest of your life. This belief becomes the center of your being. It is your complete trust in Jesus and in Him alone. It is your sole hope for life that never ends. It is your conviction that the Father raised the Son from the dead, and that someday He'll raise you, too, to be with Him forever.

3. EMBRACE YOUR SALVATION. Third, with confession and belief comes an assurance of salvation. You have been saved from the guilt and penalty of sin. You have been saved from the dominion of sin in your life. By embracing your salvation, you are affirming the truth of the Gospel.

4. PROCLAIM THE SAVIOR. Fourth, in return for this great gift of salvation, God asks us to love Him so much and to love others so much that we spread the Good News. Proclaim God's love for all humanity. Tell others how He has saved you—and what He has saved you from. Tell people that the Father gave His Son so that salvation could be offered as a free gift. Tell the lost how the Father yearns for all to find and accept their salvation in His Son.

FOR ADULTS	■ TOPIC: Spread the News

■ **QUESTIONS:** 1. What set of circumstances led to Paul being incarcerated in Rome? 2. Why do you think Paul asked the local Jewish leaders to meet with him? 3. What compelled Paul to request to be tried by the emperor? 4. If you were Paul, what would you have said to the Jewish representatives who met with the apostle? 5. What responses have you encountered after sharing the Gospel with others?

■ **ILLUSTRATIONS:**

Remaining Steadfast. The Bible is our best defense against evildoers, impostors, and deceivers. Therefore, just as Paul did while imprisoned in Rome, it's our duty to maintain our commitment to study, proclaim, and obey God's Word. At the same time, we must gear our families and churches for instruction in Scripture, both for salvation and for remaining steadfast in the face of various opponents of the Gospel.

Consistent with Paul's example, our Christian education programs must center on teaching salvation through faith in the Son. We dare not assume that just because people attend Sunday school and church—even those who come from Christian homes—they have necessarily come to personal faith in the Messiah.

We hope and pray that every child will respond favorably when he or she hears the Good News. Parents, teachers, and pastors committedly working together can help to bring salvation and faith to our children.

A Consistent Christian Witness. Roy held up a convenience store but was caught and sent to prison. While he was there, a chaplain shared the Gospel with him, and Roy responded by trusting in Christ for salvation. After that, Roy's life completely changed. He served the rest of his sentence in an exemplary manner, and he was released several years later. As Roy was leaving prison, the chaplain handed him a letter written by another inmate. Here's what the letter said:

> I came to this place despising both preachers and the Bible. When you told me you were saved, I said to myself, "There's another one taking the Gospel road just to get an early parole." But, Roy, I've been observing you for a couple of years, and your story has rung true. I kept track of you when you were in the yard exercising or working in the shop or eating your meals. You seldom slipped. Now I'm a Christian, too, because I've watched you! The Savior who saved you saved me!

Our Scripture text this week encourages us to live lives that are like that of Paul. From him we recognize the importance of maintaining our Christian commitment. When we do so, God can use our consistent witness to bring the lost to salvation.

Madam Sheikh. Bilquis was born and raised in a conservative Muslim family. Even before she married General Khalid Sheikh, who later became Pakistan's minister of interior, Bilquis had entertained diplomats and frequently shopped at expensive stores in Paris and London. After her husband left her, however, Bilquis retreated to her family estate in Pakistan. There, she encountered the Messiah and received Him as her Lord and Savior.

Becoming a Christian in a Muslim country came at a very high price. Bilquis lost her family, her friends, and nearly her life. Despite being shunned by her community and often being threatened, this remarkable woman did not waver in her Christian commitment. Indeed, like her spiritual predecessor Paul, while he was incarcerated in Rome, Bilquis openly acknowledged her faith in Jesus and courageously continued to tell people about the Gospel.

Finally, Bilquis had to flee from her homeland and immigrate to California. There her story has become a best-selling book, *I Dared to Call Him Father*. Not surprisingly, Bilquis Sheikh's incredible journey is a saga like Paul's, of one life forever changed by encountering the risen Lord.

FOR YOUTH

■ TOPIC: I'm Going to Tell It

■ QUESTIONS: 1. What living arrangements did the officials in Rome allow Paul to have? 2. What explanation did Paul offer the local Jewish leaders concerning his incarceration? 3. How would you have handled the stress of being incarcerated, as was Paul, for telling others about the Lord Jesus? 4. What sorts of responses did Paul experience from his Jewish peers when they met with him a second time? 5. How can you use the freedom you enjoy to proclaim the Gospel with boldness?

■ ILLUSTRATIONS:

Facing Hard Times. We only mislead people when we offer the joys and blessings of the Gospel without the hardships. In our culture, however, hardships are not so easy to define. Like Paul did in Rome, we might face some ridicule, or lose some friends, but we still have many other choices.

Perhaps we look in the wrong place for the battle to maintain our commitment to Christ. Throughout his ministry, Paul warned not just about physical but also spiritual hardships. These arise when people choose contemporary myths and reject God's Word.

In today's culture, hardships could easily consist of rejecting ungodly, unwholesome elements in entertainment, literature, and sports. After all, Satan uses music, television, radio, the Internet, books, and magazines to lure us away from God's truth. For some youths, it's a hardship to let go of these things for the sake of following Jesus. We, teachers of God's Word, can encourage them to remain committed to following the Savior—even when they face hard times—to the very end of their lives.

An Actor. The speaker at my Christian college graduation ceremony was the newly elected president of another college. He spoke eloquent words, encouraging graduates and all in attendance to work hard, to follow Christ, and to be His instruments for changing the world.

As the speaker received an honorary doctorate that day, he looked like the model of a lifelong, committed Christian leader. Unfortunately, a few years later, a board member at the other college received an anonymous tip that encouraged a study of the college president's personal history. What did that study discover? That this man had lied about his previous academic experience and that his life was a sham. He evidently held the form of godliness, but not its power.

Today, God still calls followers of His Son to mirror His life and teachings. Even while imprisoned in Rome, Paul maintained a Christlike witness and demeanor. The apostle, of course, is just one example of unwavering commitment to Christ. God also wants to work in our lives so that we, too, are living examples of unfailing devotion to the Savior and His Gospel.

A Powerful Testimony. In *Fit for Battle*, Sammy Tippit shares the story of Jerry, a foster child who had earlier suffered abuse and neglect. He also had a noticeable stutter. But Jerry had accepted the Lord and wanted to share with others the peace he had in Christ. The author notes the following about Jerry:

> When Jerry would ride the bus to school, some of the boys would make fun of him. After his experience with Christ, Jerry would say to them, "D-d-don't do that. J-J-Jesus loves you. He's in my heart." . . . It took Jerry a while to get it all out. But one by one he told all the boys about Christ. Every week Jerry would have a new friend with him in church. I baptized more people that Jerry brought to Christ than any other person in our congregation.

Jerry wasn't a great orator or theologian. He was simply a kid who was totally committed to the Savior. In fact, the most important thing Jerry shared was that he had Christ. Like Paul's own witness while imprisoned in Rome, Jerry's testimony was so clear and persuasive that he won over the hearts of many of his peers.

SPIRITUAL BLESSINGS IN CHRIST

BACKGROUND SCRIPTURE: Ephesians 1
DEVOTIONAL READING: Psalm 33:8-12

Key Verse: [God] predestinated us unto the adoption of children by Jesus Christ to himself, according to the good pleasure of his will, To the praise of the glory of his grace, wherein he hath made us accepted in the beloved. Ephesians 1:5-6.

KING JAMES VERSION

EPHESIANS 1:3 Blessed be the God and Father of our Lord Jesus Christ, who hath blessed us with all spiritual blessings in heavenly places in Christ:
4 According as he hath chosen us in him before the foundation of the world, that we should be holy and without blame before him in love: 5 Having predestinated us unto the adoption of children by Jesus Christ to himself, according to the good pleasure of his will, 6 To the praise of the glory of his grace, wherein he hath made us accepted in the beloved. 7 In whom we have redemption through his blood, the forgiveness of sins, according to the riches of his grace; 8 Wherein he hath abounded toward us in all wisdom and prudence; 9 Having made known unto us the mystery of his will, according to his good pleasure which he hath purposed in himself: 10 That in the dispensation of the fulness of times he might gather together in one all things in Christ, both which are in heaven, and which are on earth; even in him: 11 In whom also we have obtained an inheritance, being predestinated according to the purpose of him who worketh all things after the counsel of his own will: 12 That we should be to the praise of his glory, who first trusted in Christ. 13 In whom ye also trusted, after that ye heard the word of truth, the gospel of your salvation: in whom also after that ye believed, ye were sealed with that holy Spirit of promise, 14 Which is the earnest of our inheritance until the redemption of the purchased possession, unto the praise of his glory.

NEW REVISED STANDARD VERSION

EPHESIANS 1:3 Blessed be the God and Father of our Lord Jesus Christ, who has blessed us in Christ with every spiritual blessing in the heavenly places,
4 just as he chose us in Christ before the foundation of the world to be holy and blameless before him in love. 5 He destined us for adoption as his children through Jesus Christ, according to the good pleasure of his will, 6 to the praise of his glorious grace that he freely bestowed on us in the Beloved. 7 In him we have redemption through his blood, the forgiveness of our trespasses, according to the riches of his grace 8 that he lavished on us. With all wisdom and insight 9 he has made known to us the mystery of his will, according to his good pleasure that he set forth in Christ, 10 as a plan for the fullness of time, to gather up all things in him, things in heaven and things on earth. 11 In Christ we have also obtained an inheritance, having been destined according to the purpose of him who accomplishes all things according to his counsel and will, 12 so that we, who were the first to set our hope on Christ, might live for the praise of his glory. 13 In him you also, when you had heard the word of truth, the gospel of your salvation, and had believed in him, were marked with the seal of the promised Holy Spirit; 14 this is the pledge of our inheritance toward redemption as God's own people, to the praise of his glory.

HOME BIBLE READINGS

Monday, November 26	Psalm 32:1-7	*Blessed by God's Forgiveness*
Tuesday, November 27	Psalm 33:8-12	*Blessed by Being Chosen*
Wednesday, November 28	1 Corinthians 1:4-9	*Blessed by God's Gift of Grace*
Thursday, November 29	Daniel 2:17-23	*Blessed by God's Revelation*
Friday, November 30	Colossians 1:3-8	*Blessed by the Word of Truth*
Saturday, December 1	Luke 1:67-79	*Blessed by God's Redemption*
Sunday, December 2	Ephesians 1:3-14	*God Has Blessed Us*

BACKGROUND

Ephesus was located at the intersection of several major east-west trade routes and became a vital commercial, political, and educational center of the Roman Empire. The size of the city is shown by its theater, which could seat over 24,000 people. The city was perhaps best known for its magnificent temple of Diana, or Artemis, one of the seven wonders of the ancient world. (Diana was the Greek goddess of the moon, forests, wild animals, and women in childbirth.) More importantly, Ephesus figured prominently and dramatically in early church history, for Paul used the city as a center for his missionary work in that region.

The apostle evangelized Ephesus toward the end of his second missionary journey (Acts 18:18-21). When he departed, he left a Christian couple named Priscilla and Aquila to continue his work (vs. 26). When Paul wrote the Letter to the Ephesians, he was no longer an evangelist on the move. Instead, he was a prisoner in Rome. And the church he was now writing to was not opposing him and his teaching. Rather, it was basically a sound congregation that was ready to receive advanced instruction in theology and ethics. Paul began the epistle by identifying himself as an apostle. Although Paul was always ready to admit his unworthiness to receive grace, he never underrated his role as an apostle, or ambassador, for Christ since it had been given him "by the will of God" (Eph. 1:1).

NOTES ON THE PRINTED TEXT

Ordinarily in Paul's letters, he followed up his greeting to his readers with thanksgiving for them. In Ephesians, however, he delayed the thanksgiving so that he could offer extended praise to the Father (1:3-14). The apostle extolled the Father for the spiritual blessings He has given to the Son's followers (vs. 3). The first blessing Paul mentioned is that the Father "hath chosen us" (vs. 4) and "predestinated us" (vs. 5). These terms are parallel but have different shades of meaning. Just as the Father chose the Jewish nation to be His own and to receive the promised land as an inheritance, so He chose Christian believers before He made the world to be His own people and to receive the inheritance of eternal life. It can never perish, be defiled, or fade away, for it is "reserved in heaven" (1 Pet. 1:4) for us eternally.

There are at least two distinct views of what predestination means when it is discussed in Scripture. Some think that people are so debased by sin that they are unable to respond to the offer of salvation made available in the Son. It is argued that those who believe have the ability to do so only because the Father previously chose them for redemption. In other words, He gives them grace, and this enables them to believe the truth. Others think that the Father gives all people enough grace to accept the offer of salvation. This remains true even though many reject His grace. In this way, the Father predestines some for redemption in the sense that He knows beforehand those who will choose to believe the truth of their own free will.

Regardless of which view is preferred, it remains clear that the Father chose believers to "be holy and without blame before him" (Eph. 1:4). To be holy means to be distinctly different from the world so that the Father can use us for His purposes. Our holiness is the result of our having been chosen, not the reason we were chosen. To be blameless means to be free of the immoral and selfish lifestyle that marks people who are apart from God. The Father also predestined believers to "adoption" (vs. 5) as His spiritual "children." Through Jesus Christ, the Son, we become members of the Father's heavenly family. Under Roman law, adopted sons enjoyed the same standing and entitlements as natural sons. Similarly, the Father reckons believers as His true children and as recipients of all the benefits that go with that status. It's no wonder that believers give the Father praise for the wonderful grace He has poured out on them in His Son, whom the Father dearly loves (vs. 6).

Despite the magnificence of our having been chosen by the Father, this spiritual blessing is not the only one we receive. Paul also mentioned the blessing of redemption (vss. 7-8). Through redemption the Father makes His choosing effective in our lives. The Greek noun translated "redemption" (vs. 7) refers to a ransom. It was used in ancient times to describe the buying back of someone who had been sold into slavery or had become a prisoner of war. The noun also described freeing a person from the penalty of death. Because we were born with a sinful nature, the Father was not attracted to us because of any goodness He saw in us. Despite our sinful condition, He rescued us from our state of separation from His holiness. The Father did this by sending His Son to become the sacrifice for our sins. By His blood, the Messiah ransomed us from slavery to sin and from the sentence of death under which we languished.

Closely related to redemption is "forgiveness." The Greek noun Paul used had a variety of meanings, including "to send off," "to release," "to give up," "to pardon," and "to hurl." The basic idea is that when we receive the effect of the Son's redemption through faith, the Father releases us from the penalty of our sins and casts our sin debt far away from us. What the Father did for us through His Son was in harmony with the riches of the Father's grace. In addition to showering us with His unmerited favor, the Father has also lavished us with "all wisdom and prudence" (vs. 8). Before we believed, we did not have spiritual insight. But since coming to a knowledge of the truth, we can now see how things really are and can get an idea of how the Father wants us to live.

Another spiritual blessing Paul listed is our ability to know the "mystery of [God's] will" (vs. 9). The Greek noun rendered "mystery" generally denotes that which is hidden or secret. For the apostle, a "mystery" is a truth that was once hidden but has now been revealed through the Messiah. The Father's disclosure to us of His will was in accordance with His good pleasure, which He centered in His Son. Paul declared that the Father's eternal plan was to head up all things in the Son at the divinely appointed time (vs. 10). This includes everything "in heaven" and "on earth." The Greek verb translated "gather together" means to sum up. In Paul's day, when a column of figures was tallied, the total was placed at the head of the column. In a similar fashion, at the end of history all things will be seen to add up to the Son.

Earlier, in verses 4 and 5, Paul mentioned the Father's plan for believers. Now the apostle returned to that theme. He noted that the Father causes all things to happen in accordance with His single "purpose" (vs. 11). This included Jews such as Paul coming to faith in the Son. The language of Ephesians (particularly the first half) is richer and more effusive than the language in other letters Paul wrote. The apostle's style is demonstrated in this phrase: "who worketh all things after the counsel of his own will." The phrase contains inclusive terms ("all things") and several synonyms ("worketh," "counsel," and "will"). This style suits Paul's subject of the Father's grand plan for believers, the church, and the universe.

The divine purpose was that the conversion of Jews to the Son would bring the Father eternal praise (vs. 12). Similarly, according to Romans 8:28, "all things work together for good to them that love God, to them who are the called according to his purpose." The historical record is that the apostles and other Jews were the first to trust in the Son. Admittedly, the majority of Jews who were contemporaries of Paul rejected the Messiah. Nevertheless, a remnant of that generation of Jews formed the nucleus of the church. Through them, the Gospel went out to the entire world. Those early Jewish believers were walking testimonies of the Father's glory.

With Ephesians 1:13, Paul changed pronouns from "we" to "ye." He was now specifically referring to the Ephesian believers. Although Jewish Christians had been chosen for their role in starting the church, this should not make the Ephesians feel like outsiders. They, too, were included in the Son's spiritual body. Expressed differently, Jewish and Gentile believers formed one united church. Paul delineated the stages of development by which the Gentiles had become joined to Christ. It is the same process through which anyone is born again. First, the Gentiles had "heard the word of truth" when Paul or others had proclaimed the Gospel to them. Then they "believed" the truth they heard. The result was their spiritual regeneration.

Paul noted that when his readers trusted in the Son, they were marked with a "seal," which is the Holy Spirit. In other words, the Father identified believers as His own by giving them the Spirit, whom He promised long ago. By calling the Spirit a seal, Paul may have raised a number of images in the minds of his readers. At that time, seals were put on documents to vouch for their authenticity. They were also attached to goods being shipped to indicate right of possession and safeguard protection. Sometimes they represented an office in the government. Any of these uses of seals might symbolize a part of the Holy Spirit's work in the lives of those who follow the Messiah.

For Paul, the Spirit is not only a seal. He is also an "earnest" (vs. 14) or pledge. In the apostle's day, an "earnest" was an initial payment or first installment assuring a retailer that the full purchase price would be forthcoming. At the end of time, believers will receive the final installment of eternal life from the riches of the Father's grace. During the interim, the Spirit's presence in our lives assures us of coming glory. This giving of the Spirit is also to "the praise of [God's] glory" (compare vs. 12).

SUGGESTIONS TO TEACHERS

In this week's Scripture, Paul launched into a magnificent doxology, or list of praises, of what the Father has done for believers in the Son. There is nothing quite like this profile in all of Scripture. It surveys all that accrues to people the moment they commit themselves to the Lord Jesus, not just for "super" Christians, but every one of God's spiritual children.

1. APPRECIATING GOD'S BLESSINGS. Do we know what it means that we have (through no effort or merit of our own) been granted by the Father (before whom we once stood on the brink of destruction) spiritual blessings that make the fortunes of the world look like play money? If we do, we will respond, heart and soul, to the Father in unbridled praise!

2. RECOGNIZING GOD'S PROVISION OF GRACE AND PEACE. Paul noted that God the Father through His Son, the Lord Jesus, has lavished on us grace and peace. The Father bestows His grace, or unmerited favor, on sinners when they trust in the Messiah for salvation. Jesus' death on the cross also makes it possible for believers to experience peace with God.

3. DISCERNING THE PATHWAY TO HOLIN116ESS. Paul said that the Father chooses believers in His Son to be "holy and without blame" (Eph. 1:4). In other words, the Father loves us so much that He made a way for us to be morally pure and spotless in His presence. The pathway to holiness is trusting in the Lord Jesus. The Father derives great pleasure in seeing this happen!

4. ANTICIPATING THE FUTURE. The Father will bring all heavenly and earthly things under the headship of His Son. This means that every aspect of the universe will come under the Messiah's authority, probably when the Father establishes His eternal kingdom.

■ **TOPIC:** Chosen and Claimed

■ **QUESTIONS:** 1. What did Paul say that God had bestowed on the believers in Ephesus? 2. To what extent did Paul say that God has blessed us as Christians? 3. Why is it so difficult at times for us to accept God's spiritual blessings? 4. When did Paul say that the Father would bring all things under the headship of the Son? 5. What role does the Spirit serve in the life of believers?

■ **ILLUSTRATIONS:**

Appointed by God. According to folklore, General Eisenhower rebuked one of his generals for referring to a soldier as "just a private." Eisenhower reminded the general that the army could function better without its generals than it could without its foot soldiers. "If this war is won," Eisenhower said, "it will be won by privates."

In the same way, the church needs more "privates" than "generals." These are believers who have a genuine appreciation for the fact that the Father has chosen and claimed them in His Son. Moreover, the Father has identified them as His own by sealing them with the Holy Spirit (see Eph. 1:13).

Indeed, God has appointed ordinary people—including the saved adults in your class—to do the work of ministry. Meanwhile, He appoints some to be pastors and teachers to equip these "privates" so that they can win people for Christ.

What Do We Value? Millions of dollars are given away every year to winners of state lotteries. To claim their prize, people have to produce a ticket showing the winning numbers. On some occasions, officials wait for days for someone to show up with a rightful claim to the money. For many weeks no one claims the prize, because no one matches the numbers, and the jackpot is rolled over.

From the madness surrounding multimillion-dollar prizes, one would think the lottery is the biggest thing we could ever win in our lives. Meanwhile, what is really the biggest jackpot of all often goes unclaimed. It is a prize that brings lasting satisfaction and eternal life—nothing a lottery prize could ever do for us.

People fail to realize what the Father has done for us in His Son, so they don't claim the spiritual wealth that comes through faith in Him. The multitude of the Father's blessings in the Son are waiting to be claimed, and we don't need to buy a lottery ticket to win. The Father has inundated believers with every spiritual blessing. The question is, what do we value?

The Vocabulary of Praise. In Ephesians 1:3, Paul stated that the Father deserved unending praise for blessing us with "all spiritual blessings in heavenly places in Christ." This truth is the bedrock of our Christian faith and experience.

Pastor Tom Wallace relates the story of a man who had never attended his church before but listened with keen interest to the Gospel. One Sunday, at the invitation time, this person received the Son as Lord and Savior. Later, after Pastor Wallace baptized the new believer, the man clapped his hands and shouted, "Hot dog! Hot dog! Hot dog!"

Pastor Wallace said, "Our people roared with laughter. I quickly asked them for silence as I explained that this dear man had not been around the church and didn't know about such religious-sounding words as 'amen,' 'praise the Lord,' and 'hallelujah.'" Pastor Wallace explained, "This new convert's statement of praise was 'hot dog,' and he was thanking the Lord with the only vocabulary he knew."

| **FOR YOUTH** | ■ **TOPIC:** Too Blessed to Be Stressed |

■ **QUESTIONS:** 1. What are some reasons why we can offer praise to the Father? 2. For what purpose did the Father choose us in the Son? 3. What is the basis for God lavishing us with His abundant grace? 4. What is the mystery of God's will that He is making known to us? 5. What difference does it make that our future spiritual inheritance is guaranteed?

■ **ILLUSTRATIONS:**

Following God's Will. As adolescents progress through high school, the necessity of making plans for the future can cause them a lot of stress. Upon graduation, some will head off to college, while others will enter the workforce. Their common goal is to claim the best opportunities that life offers them.

One young man had his heart set on playing professional baseball. But when none of the major-league teams drafted him, his dream was smashed. What should he do? Because he was a Christian, he sought God's will. This person decided to obtain more schooling in theology and began an internship working with his church's youth. Two years later he was on his way to a foreign country to coach baseball and to introduce kids to Christ.

Most important was this young man's basic decision to follow God's will. The same is true for all of us. The Father has chosen us in the Son to be His spiritual children. Also, in Christ we have received all we will ever need for our spiritual growth and welfare. In light of these blessings (and many others), we can accept and do God's will with supreme confidence.

Working Together. James Hewett tells the story of some missionaries in the Philippines who tried to teach the Agta Negrito tribe the game of croquet. The Negritos enjoyed the game until they were told they should knock other people's balls out of the way in order to win the game. In their hunting and gathering society, the Negritos survived not by competing, but through teamwork and sharing.

Instead of trying to win the game, each native player tried to help others win, so that when the last wicket was played, the tribe shouted, "We won! We won!" That is how the spiritual family of God—which Paul described in Ephesians 1:5—should approach the Christian life together.

Cherished by God. When Marty received God's gift of salvation, he had no idea he'd hit the mother lode of spiritual blessings. At that time, Marty was quite young and really only aware that God had forgiven his sins and would one day welcome him into heaven. As far as Marty was concerned, that's all that mattered. Those two blessings alone—forgiveness and eternal life—would have been enough for him.

As Marty got older, however, and could understand more of what he was reading in Scripture, it began to dawn on him that he had far more in Christ than he'd ever imagined. Instead of being just a forgiven person, Marty came to see that the Father viewed him as holy and blameless in union with the Son.

It came as news to Marty that the Lord was not constantly frustrated with Marty's faltering steps. Quite to the contrary, God's glorious grace was poured out in Marty's life to pick him up, assure him of unconditional love, and encourage him to keep on growing in that grace. In addition, Marty was not, as he had at times imagined, some tolerated tagalong among the saints. He was an adopted, cherished member in God's great family (see Eph. 1:5).

How do people usually respond to good news? When Paul tried to describe these incredible blessings to the Ephesians, he himself got excited and burst into a pen-to-paper shout of praise. What Marty had in Christ was a fantastic life of freedom and intimacy with God to be lived in the present—right now!—along with much, much more to come. Do your students know what it means that they have been granted immense spiritual blessings by God? If they do, they will respond, heart and soul, to Him in unbridled praise.

ONE IN JESUS CHRIST

BACKGROUND SCRIPTURE: Ephesians 2–3
DEVOTIONAL READING: Ephesians 3:14-21

2

Key Verse: In whom all the building fitly framed together
groweth unto an holy temple in the Lord. Ephesians 2:21.

KING JAMES VERSION

EPHESIANS 2:11 Wherefore remember, that ye being in time past Gentiles in the flesh, who are called Uncircumcision by that which is called the Circumcision in the flesh made by hands; 12 That at that time ye were without Christ, being aliens from the commonwealth of Israel, and strangers from the covenants of promise, having no hope, and without God in the world: 13 But now in Christ Jesus ye who sometimes were far off are made nigh by the blood of Christ.

14 For he is our peace, who hath made both one, and hath broken down the middle wall of partition between us; 15 Having abolished in his flesh the enmity, even the law of commandments contained in ordinances; for to make in himself of twain one new man, so making peace; 16 And that he might reconcile both unto God in one body by the cross, having slain the enmity thereby: 17 And came and preached peace to you which were afar off, and to them that were nigh. 18 For through him we both have access by one Spirit unto the Father. 19 Now therefore ye are no more strangers and foreigners, but fellowcitizens with the saints, and of the household of God; 20 And are built upon the foundation of the apostles and prophets, Jesus Christ himself being the chief corner stone; 21 In whom all the building fitly framed together groweth unto an holy temple in the Lord: 22 In whom ye also are builded together for an habitation of God through the Spirit.

NEW REVISED STANDARD VERSION

EPHESIANS 2:11 So then, remember that at one time you Gentiles by birth, called "the uncircumcision" by those who are called "the circumcision"—a physical circumcision made in the flesh by human hands— 12 remember that you were at that time without Christ, being aliens from the commonwealth of Israel, and strangers to the covenants of promise, having no hope and without God in the world. 13 But now in Christ Jesus you who once were far off have been brought near by the blood of Christ. 14 For he is our peace; in his flesh he has made both groups into one and has broken down the dividing wall, that is, the hostility between us. 15 He has abolished the law with its commandments and ordinances, that he might create in himself one new humanity in place of the two, thus making peace, 16 and might reconcile both groups to God in one body through the cross, thus putting to death that hostility through it. 17 So he came and proclaimed peace to you who were far off and peace to those who were near; 18 for through him both of us have access in one Spirit to the Father. 19 So then you are no longer strangers and aliens, but you are citizens with the saints and also members of the household of God, 20 built upon the foundation of the apostles and prophets, with Christ Jesus himself as the cornerstone. 21 In him the whole structure is joined together and grows into a holy temple in the Lord; 22 in whom you also are built together spiritually into a dwelling place for God.

HOME BIBLE READINGS

Monday, December 3	Isaiah 57:14-19	*Reviving the Humble and Contrite*
Tuesday, December 4	1 Corinthians 3:10-16	*Building on the True Foundation*
Wednesday, December 5	Ephesians 3:1-6	*Sharing in the Promise*
Thursday, December 6	Ephesians 3:7-13	*Making Known the Wisdom of God*
Friday, December 7	Ephesians 3:14-21	*Praying for Spiritual Power*
Saturday, December 8	Ephesians 2:1-10	*Discovering the Gift of Salvation*
Sunday, December 9	Ephesians 2:11-22	*Discovering Our Oneness in Christ*

BACKGROUND

In Ephesians 2:1-3, Paul reminded his readers that they were spiritually dead before trusting in the Messiah. They had been enslaved to the world, the devil, and the flesh, and so had been objects of God's wrath. Then, in verses 4-7, Paul noted that the Father extended His mercy to the Ephesians through the Son, making them spiritually alive and giving them honor. Verses 8 and 9 reveal that when it comes to salvation, believers have no room to boast. After all, their redemption is by the Father's grace through faith in the Son.

God's grace is one of His key attributes. For instance, Exodus 34:6 reveals that the Lord is the "merciful and gracious" God. His redemption of His people from Egypt and His establishment of them in Canaan was a superlative example of His grace. He did this despite their unrighteousness (Deut. 7:7-8; 9:5-6). The Son is the supreme revelation of the Father's grace. Jesus not only appropriated divine grace but also incarnated it (Luke 2:40; John 1:14). The Son died on the cross and rose from the dead so that believing sinners might partake of the Father's grace (Titus 2:11). Even their entrance into the divine kingdom is not based on their own merit.

NOTES ON THE PRINTED TEXT

After Paul reminded the Ephesians about their former need for God to raise them from spiritual death to spiritual life by His grace (Eph. 2:1-10), the apostle went on to recount their former disadvantages in contrast with the Jews (vss. 11-13). Admittedly, some Jews considered themselves superior to Gentiles, not because of what God had done for the Jews but simply because of who they were. This prejudice carried over into the early church, as Jewish believers reckoned Gentiles to be second-class Christians unless they adopted Jewish practices. Paul had to deal with this problem often. The apostle taught that the Jews' privilege was due solely to God's grace in making a covenant with them, but many Jews identified their privilege with their circumcision, which was merely a sign of the covenant.

In Paul's day, the Jews called themselves "the Circumcision" (vs. 11) and used the insulting term "Uncircumcision" of Gentiles, such as the Ephesians. The apostle stated the use of this contemptuous term without meaning any disdain himself. In fact,

Paul affirmed that, under the Gospel, circumcision holds no spiritual significance. As he said elsewhere (see Rom. 2:29), true circumcision is of the heart. Many Jews went too far in elevating their privileges. Nevertheless, it is true that Gentiles—such as those living in Ephesus—were under some disadvantages. The apostle proceeded to describe the Ephesians' condition before they were saved.

First, Gentiles had been without the Messiah (Eph. 2:12). The promises of the coming Redeemer had been made to the Jews, and so Gentiles did not expect Him. Second, Paul's non-Jewish readers had been alienated from the citizenship of Israel and strangers to the covenants of promise. While membership in the commonwealth of Israel was not a guarantee of salvation, it was of significant value, for God had made promises of blessing to the physical descendants of Abraham and Isaac. Third, the Ephesians previously had no hope and were without God in the world. Though God had not forgotten the Gentiles, most of them knew nothing about Him. Their pagan religious practices did not put them in touch with Him, and so left them with no hope of finding peace and immortality.

Paul next turned from the dismal picture of the Ephesians' former condition of once being far away from God. Now, by means of the Son's shed blood, they had been brought near to the Father (vs. 13). The Son was the meeting point with the Father for all who believed the Gospel. So then, the Father's grace in the sacrifice of His Son was the reason for the Ephesians' change in status. When the Ephesian believers were reconciled with God, they were also brought together with Jewish believers. Of course, Jews and Gentiles were still distinct groups. But as far as the church was concerned, the Son had merged the two groups (vs. 14). Previous religious and ethnic backgrounds did not matter to their status in the church, for all were equals in the Messiah. Paul described this union as the Son tearing down the middle wall of partition, a barrier of hostility, which once separated Jews and Gentiles.

Paul was saying that in the church, Jewish believers and Gentile Christians could mingle freely. Regardless of one's religious or ethnic background, all stood in need of divine grace. Because sin entered the human race and controlled the lives of people, God in His pure righteousness could not permit human beings in His presence. Also, sin caused people to rebel against God and live without any consideration of their Creator. Because of the Son's work on the cross, the Father has dealt with sin and entered into a relationship with believers. For reconciliation to be applied individually, it is necessary that each person accept the Son's work for herself or himself.

Paul stressed that Jesus, through His atoning sacrifice, united believing Jews and Gentiles. The apostle noted in verse 15 that the Son's death nullified, or rendered inoperative, the commandments and ordinances of the law of Moses. This does not mean that the Father had cast off the moral principles of the law. Rather, the Son makes it possible for the righteous standards that people could never achieve to be attained. The Mosaic law had been given to the Jews, and because of that many felt superior to Gentiles. But Jesus, by dying on the cross, became the means of salvation for all people. Thus salvation by faith in the Messiah superseded the law.

Paul personified Jewish and Gentile believers, and said the Messiah had made one new body out of those two groups. From a spiritual perspective there were no longer Jews and Gentiles. A new body had come into existence—the church—resulting in peace. Here we see that God's grace has been poured out on all of us—no one has been left out. The Lord, in turn, wants us to imitate Him and to embrace all people with His love and acceptance. The apostle noted that the Son's death reconciled Jews and Gentiles to the Father as well as to each other (vs. 16). The Son brought an end to the hostility between sinners and the Father as well as to the hostility between Jews and Gentiles. Because the Son died on the cross, the enmity between people and the Father can die there too.

Since the Son never made Gentiles the prime focus of His earthly ministry, verse 17 must refer to the spread of the Gospel to Gentiles. The apostles and other Christians were responsible for this evangelistic effort. Thus, through the Son's early followers, He proclaimed peace through the Gospel to Gentiles (who were far away from the Father) and to Jews (who were somewhat nearer to Him). Centuries earlier, Isaiah had foretold a day when the peace of God would be proclaimed to those near and far (see Isa. 57:19).

Paul declared the fulfillment of Isaiah's prophecy through the Messiah and the proclamation of the Gospel. As the Good News was heralded, the Spirit brought Gentiles—those "afar off" (Eph. 2:17)—and Jews—those "nigh"—together before the Lord in a community of faith. Jews had been, in a sense, nearer to God than Gentiles were because they had the Old Testament revelation and because the Messiah had ministered among them. But now, both Jews and Gentiles—indeed, all people—have equal access to the Father through the same Holy Spirit because of what the Son has done at Calvary. All three persons of the Trinity make this possible (vs. 18).

After all that Paul had written about the new status of both Gentiles and Jews in Christ, the apostle next drew his conclusion. To do this, he used a construction metaphor. He said Gentiles and Jews form a single building with the Savior as the cornerstone. In ancient times, it was common practice for builders to place a stone at the corner where two walls of an edifice came together. The intent was to bind together and strengthen the intersecting walls. This practice was augmented by the fact that builders made their more permanent structures out of stone that was precisely cut and squared. Jesus, as the "chief corner stone" (vs. 20), is the foundation of the believer's faith.

Paul told the Ephesians that they were no longer outcasts. The Greek adjective rendered "strangers" (vs. 19) refers to transients who had no rights or privileges. Also, the adjective rendered "foreigners" describes residents who, by the payment of a minor tax, received protection but not full citizenship. Both terms indicate an inferior status. This was the standing of Gentiles before coming to faith in the Messiah.

Instead of being inferior, the Ephesians were now fellow citizens with the saints (that is, all of God's holy people) and members of God's household (that is, His spiritual family). In other words, like Jewish believers, saved Gentiles were now in a personal relationship with God. The Lord's household of believers is like a building that is being erected on the foundation of the New Testament apostles and prophets (see Ephesians 3:5). The Messiah is the cornerstone, or capstone, of the entire structure (2:20). This means that the church is based on the Son and the work He performed through the leaders of the church.

Like a cornerstone joining two walls together, the Messiah is the one in whom the entire structure (namely, the community of the redeemed) is united. Moreover, Jesus enables it to continuously grow into a holy temple for the Lord (vs. 21). In Paul's day, construction workers would shape and move huge blocks of stone until they fit each other perfectly. Similarly, through faith in the Son, Gentiles are joined together with Jews to form the Messiah's spiritual body. The Greek noun for "temple" that Paul used did not stand for the entire sanctuary complex, but only for the inner sanctum where God's presence dwelled. In keeping with this designation, the apostle told the Ephesians that they, as well as the Jewish believers, were part of a dwelling—the church—in which God lives by His Spirit (vs. 22).

SUGGESTIONS TO TEACHERS

In this week's lesson, we learn that the Father's grace, by the blood of His Son's sacrifice, made it possible for believing Gentiles to have a personal relationship with the triune God. Furthermore, the Son's redemptive work at Calvary broke down the barrier of prejudice and animosity between Jews and Gentiles by uniting them in faith to the Messiah.

1. NOW ALIVE. Paul stated that we were once spiritually dead, but now have been given new life in the Lord Jesus. In the truest sense, we are the new community of the redeemed. We are not among those obsessed by destruction or resigned to hopelessness. Because of the Savior's resurrection, we have the hope of one day being raised from the dead.

2. NOW ACCEPTED. Once we were separated from the Son and alienated from the Father. Formerly we were strangers to the covenants and promises of the Lord. But now through faith in the Son, we are accepted and affirmed as the Father's beloved.

3. NOW ALLIED. Have the class members consider some of the ways Paul described the new oneness they have in union with the Son: the walls of hostility dividing us have been broken; there is one new spiritual humanity instead of two; and we are members of God's household. Jesus' followers should never see each other as adversaries but as allies.

4. NOW AFFECTED. Through the Son, believers become a living temple housing the Father's holy presence. Do others in your community see the corporate life of your congregation as a manifestation of the Messiah's goodness?

| FOR ADULTS | ■ **TOPIC:** Unity, Not Uniformity |

■ **TOPIC:** Unity, Not Uniformity

■ **QUESTIONS:** 1. What was the reason for the change in status of the Ephesians? 2. What is the basis for spiritual unity between believing Jews and Gentiles in the church? 3. What is the basis for the enmity being removed from between people and God? 4. What things can you do to promote harmony and eliminate prejudice within the church and society? 5. In what sense is Jesus the cornerstone of your church?

■ **ILLUSTRATIONS:**

Heaven Knows No Such Distinctions. The Father's great expectation for the church is that regardless of race, nationality, or social background, it will be built together to become His holy dwelling. Difficult as it sometimes appears to be, God lives in the unity of His people in the church. This is why our oneness is not optional, despite our personal differences.

According to legend, the renowned church leader John Wesley once dreamed that he was at the gates of hell. He knocked and asked, "Are there any Roman Catholics here?" "Yes, many," was the reply. Wesley asked, "Any Church of England members?" "Yes, many," came the response. Wesley then said, "Any Presbyterians?" He was told, "Yes, many." Finally, the minister inquired, "Any Wesleyans here?" "Yes, many," is what he heard.

To say the least, Wesley was disappointed and dismayed, especially at the last reply! So, he turned his steps upward and found himself at the gates of paradise. Here he repeated the same questions. When he asked, "Any Wesleyans here?" he was shocked to hear someone say, "No."

Wesley responded, "Whom, then, do you have here?" A voice declared, "We do not know any of which you have named. The only name of which we know anything here is 'Christian.'"

Love, Not Prejudice. Ivan came to the United States from the Ukraine in the early 1940s. He was barely 20 years old. He wasted no time setting up his own machine repair shop, making friends, and learning the language. Unfortunately, he learned language—and ideas—better left unknown. Thirty years later, his conversation was peppered with racial slurs.

Then Pastor Martin and his family moved into the house next door. The two men hit it off immediately. They shared motor repair tips and helped with each other's home improvement projects. Ivan's wife, Delores, even babysat for the minister's children. But the Martin family did not share Ivan's prejudice.

"I knew that God could soften Ivan's heart," the minister said. "But Ivan wouldn't listen. He claimed to believe in God, but not a personal God, not a God who loved him and wanted him to have a relationship with him. And that's the way Ivan died. In many respects, he was a good man and a wonderful friend. But Ivan died with hatred in his heart."

Paul knew the trouble that carrying such toxic feelings could cause. The apostle also knew that the Father can free us of our prejudices, break down the barriers, and unite us as members of His one kingdom.

The Healthy Forest. We sometimes mistakenly imagine a great hardwood sending down roots deep into the soil. But naturalists point out that a healthy tree is one whose roots go sideways, not deep down. And the roots don't just protect that one tree, but rather are woven together with the roots of other trees in order to hold up the entire forest.

Like a healthy growth of trees in a forest, Jesus' followers do not consider merely protecting themselves. They realize that the loneliness, meaninglessness, and alienation in the world stem from the refusal of people to relate to God and to one another. Indulging in self-interest and self-preservation produces an unstable person who, like a poorly rooted tree, will be weak and easily toppled. As Paul emphasized in his teachings, all believers must be rooted together in Christ!

| **FOR YOUTH** | ■ **TOPIC:** Unity in the Community
■ **QUESTIONS:** 1. What were two ways Paul's Gentile readers had experienced alienation from the Jews? 2. What made it possible for |

believing Gentiles to be brought into spiritual union and intimacy with God? 3. What enables Jews and Gentiles to come to the Father through the Spirit? 4. What types of prejudice have you personally encountered among Christians? 5. How can you encourage other believers to embrace all people with the love and acceptance of God?

■ **ILLUSTRATIONS:**

Together in Christ. Differences among people in a community are a fact of life, and we spend most of our lives trying to accommodate them. Of course, some people never do. In extreme cases, people fight and die to keep their distinctives alive. Even when our differences do not lead to bloodshed, they cause unhappiness and despair.

Looking at how hard it is to resolve problems brought on by racial, religious, national, and economic differences, we are tempted to say there is no hope. But as Paul reveals in this week's Scripture text, the Gospel of Christ offers us the only hope we have to bring people together, despite their differences.

Our mission as believers is to help people understand who Jesus is and what He can do. Of course, we have to claim our new status as part of God's family. We have to demonstrate how we can overcome our differences in the body of Christ. We must never give up on the Father's plan to bring people together in peace and harmony under the Son's lordship.

Breaking Down Walls of Prejudice. Lian told Amy, "I'm running for class president. I'd like for you to run my election campaign." Amy was both surprised and dismayed. Lian, a Chinese student, was quiet, not well known, and had only been in the United States—and the local high school—a few months.

Lian, sensing Amy's reluctance, continued talking in slow but articulate English: "I want to do this because I want to give something to the school." "What do you think we should do first?" Amy asked. "Well, no one knows who I am. We need posters," Lian began.

With the election a week away, the two painted posters, lots of them—first by themselves and then with others. And as the group worked together, Amy realized Lian was an asset to the school. After Amy reviewed Lian's well-organized and neatly written speech, Amy knew Lian would be an excellent class president. Lian had won Amy's vote. And Lian went on to win the election!

Making superficial judgments on surface-level information—or before an evaluation should be made—is prejudice. It was a problem in the early church between saved Jews and Gentiles, and prejudice continues to be an issue in congregations today. In prayer this week, why not ask God to disclose any prejudice you might have in your heart. Then, by His Spirit, take the necessary steps to root it out.

A Sign That Divides. A group of young boys decided to build a clubhouse. They gathered together some odd pieces of lumber and built a shack in the woods. Their last act was to hand paint a sign that read, "For Boys Only!"

A few months later one of the boys wanted to widen the club's membership by admitting a girl. He argued that she played Little League baseball and seemed like a pretty good kid. After much debate, the group allowed the girl to join. The sign was taken down, and inclusion triumphed over exclusiveness.

Paul told the believers in Ephesus that Jesus came to take down the signs that divide us as people. He came to build a community of love and support. He calls us, as members of this faith community, to work to take down those signs and not erect them. Because He invites all people into fellowship with Him, He wants us to do the same.

UNITY IN CHRIST

BACKGROUND SCRIPTURE: Ephesians 4:1-16
DEVOTIONAL READING: Romans 12:3-8

Key Verse: There is one body, and one Spirit, even as ye are called in one hope of your calling; One Lord, one faith, one baptism. Ephesians 4:4-5.

3

KING JAMES VERSION

EPHESIANS 4:1 I therefore, the prisoner of the Lord, beseech you that ye walk worthy of the vocation wherewith ye are called,

2 With all lowliness and meekness, with longsuffering, forbearing one another in love; 3 Endeavouring to keep the unity of the Spirit in the bond of peace. 4 There is one body, and one Spirit, even as ye are called in one hope of your calling; 5 One Lord, one faith, one baptism, 6 One God and Father of all, who is above all, and through all, and in you all. 7 But unto every one of us is given grace according to the measure of the gift of Christ. 8 Wherefore he saith, When he ascended up on high, he led captivity captive, and gave gifts unto men. 9 (Now that he ascended, what is it but that he also descended first into the lower parts of the earth? 10 He that descended is the same also that ascended up far above all heavens, that he might fill all things.) 11 And he gave some, apostles; and some, prophets; and some, evangelists; and some, pastors and teachers; 12 For the perfecting of the saints, for the work of the ministry, for the edifying of the body of Christ: 13 Till we all come in the unity of the faith, and of the knowledge of the Son of God, unto a perfect man, unto the measure of the stature of the fulness of Christ: 14 That we henceforth be no more children, tossed to and fro, and carried about with every wind of doctrine, by the sleight of men, and cunning craftiness, whereby they lie in wait to deceive; 15 But speaking the truth in love, may grow up into him in all things, which is the head, even Christ: 16 From whom the whole body fitly joined together and compacted by that which every joint supplieth, according to the effectual working in the measure of every part, maketh increase of the body unto the edifying of itself in love.

NEW REVISED STANDARD VERSION

EPHESIANS 4:1 I therefore, the prisoner in the Lord, beg you to lead a life worthy of the calling to which you have been called, 2 with all humility and gentleness, with patience, bearing with one another in love, 3 making every effort to maintain the unity of the Spirit in the bond of peace. 4 There is one body and one Spirit, just as you were called to the one hope of your calling, 5 one Lord, one faith, one baptism, 6 one God and Father of all, who is above all and through all and in all.

7 But each of us was given grace according to the measure of Christ's gift. 8 Therefore it is said,

"When he ascended on high he made captivity itself a captive;

he gave gifts to his people."

9 (When it says, "He ascended," what does it mean but that he had also descended into the lower parts of the earth? 10 He who descended is the same one who ascended far above all the heavens, so that he might fill all things.) 11 The gifts he gave were that some would be apostles, some prophets, some evangelists, some pastors and teachers, 12 to equip the saints for the work of ministry, for building up the body of Christ, 13 until all of us come to the unity of the faith and of the knowledge of the Son of God, to maturity, to the measure of the full stature of Christ. 14 We must no longer be children, tossed to and fro and blown about by every wind of doctrine, by people's trickery, by their craftiness in deceitful scheming. 15 But speaking the truth in love, we must grow up in every way into him who is the head, into Christ, 16 from whom the whole body, joined and knit together by every ligament with which it is equipped, as each part is working properly, promotes the body's growth in building itself up in love.

HOME BIBLE READINGS

Monday, December 10	Zechariah 14:6-11	*One Lord*
Tuesday, December 11	Philippians 1:27-30	*One Faith*
Wednesday, December 12	Galatians 3:23-29	*One in Christ Jesus*
Thursday, December 13	Exodus 20:1-7	*One God*
Friday, December 14	1 Corinthians 12:4-13	*One Spirit*
Saturday, December 15	Romans 12:3-8	*One Body*
Sunday, December 16	Ephesians 4:1-16	*Building Up the Body Together*

BACKGROUND

While under his first house arrest in Rome, Paul had the time to write numerous letters. He seems to have penned epistles to the churches in Ephesus and Colosse, as well as to Philemon of Colosse, at about the same time. Paul's colleagues Tychicus and Onesimus could have dropped off one letter at Ephesus on their way to delivering the other two in Colosse (see Eph. 6:21-22; Col. 4:7-9; Philem. vss. 10-12).

Ephesians has been called "The Heavenly Epistle" and "The Alps of the New Testament." In it the apostle takes the reader from the depths of ruin to the heights of redemption. The letter contains two distinct, though related, parts. Chapters 1–3 remind the readers of their privileged status as members of Christ's body, the church, which occupies an important place in God's plan for the universe. Chapters 4–6 appeal to the readers to live in a way consistent with their godly calling rather than to conform to the ungodly society in which they lived.

NOTES ON THE PRINTED TEXT

Paul's status as an evangelist imprisoned for the cause of Christ lent weight to his appeal to the Ephesians. Since Paul had been faithful to the point of being imprisoned, they (who were under less pressure) could be faithful too. Specifically, the apostle urged his readers to live a life worthy of the calling they had received (Eph. 4:1). Having been given saving grace, they should do no less than respond to the Lord by living faithfully. This does not mean that believers were to earn their salvation by leading a worthy life. Rather, they conducted themselves uprightly as a result of their spiritual rebirth.

So that the Ephesians would know what he meant by a life worthy of their calling, Paul mentioned four virtues that ought to be theirs (and ours as Christians): lowliness, meekness, longsuffering, and forbearance (vs. 2). Each of these terms is worth considering further. The Greek noun translated "lowliness" was adapted by Christians to describe an attitude of humility. The noun rendered "meekness" refers not to weakness, but to submission to others for the sake of Christ. The noun translated "longsuffering" indicates the refusal to avenge wrongs committed against oneself. Finally, the phrase for "forbearing one another" refers to putting up with others' faults and peculiarities.

In Paul's day, Jewish and Gentile believers sometimes did not understand one another. Also, Gentile Christians from different backgrounds or with different temperaments sometimes did not get along. Paul wanted to see all believers united and harmonious. Nonetheless, unity is something we must work at. As the apostle noted in verse 3, we are to endeavor to "keep the unity of the Spirit in the bond of peace." Here we see that Christians are united through the Spirit, but our unity can be damaged if we allow our relations to become hostile rather than peaceful. That is why it is sensible to add peacemaking to the list of virtues believers ought to possess.

Next, Paul went on to show the role that unity plays in various aspects of the Christian faith. In fact, the apostle's mention of the "unity of the Spirit" prompted him to give more attention to the matter. First, Paul noted that there is one spiritual body of Christ and that its members have the same Spirit. Believers also have been called to the same glory-filled future (vs. 4). The "body" is the church. Just as a human body has many parts but is one entity, so the church has many members but is one group. Indwelling all members of the church is the Holy Spirit. As we learn from 1:14 (which we considered in lesson 1), the Spirit's presence in our lives is the guarantee of our common hope to live eternally with God in heaven. This became our hope and expectation when we accepted the call to faith.

Second, there is only "one Lord, one faith, one baptism" (4:5). All believers serve one Lord, namely, Jesus Christ. We serve this Lord because we have made the same profession of faith in Him. Also, baptism identifies us with the Messiah. The reference to baptism could be either to that of water or the Spirit (see Rom. 6:3-4; 1 Cor. 12:13). Third, there is only "one God and Father" (Eph. 4:6), who alone is sovereign over us all, in us all, and living through us all. In a culture that recognized many gods, Paul affirmed that there is only one true God, whom Christians worship and serve. He is the Father of all who believe in Him. In His relationship to His people, He is both transcendent ("above all") and immanent ("through all, and in you all"). Paul's mention of all three persons of the Trinity in verses 3-6 shows us that the Godhead harmoniously works together to bring about the unity of believers in everyday life.

Paul followed up his strong message about church unity with an equally strong message about gift diversity. The apostle noted that Jesus supplies His followers with grace, making some Christians leaders who prepare the rest for ministry so that the whole church may achieve unity and maturity. When Paul said that the Messiah gives "grace" (vs. 7), the apostle was referring to the divine blessing by which believers are equipped, or enabled, to perform ministries in the church. We do not earn grace. We are given it. Neither can we pick the kind of grace we will receive. The Son assigns it as He sees fit. We are to receive this grace thankfully and use it for the Father's glory.

To support what he had said about the Messiah's giving grace, Paul cited Psalm 68:18 in Ephesians 4:8. The picture is one of a triumphal procession in which the victor both received and distributed gifts. When applied to the Savior, this verse reveals that through His redemptive work on Calvary, He prevailed over Satan and his hosts (see Col. 2:15). Ephesians 4:8 also declares that the Messiah has given gifts to His followers ever since His ascension. Lest anyone doubt that the one who "ascended up on high" was the Lord Jesus, Paul added a parenthetical explanation in verses 9 and 10. The apostle noted that the person who ascended had previously descended to the "lower parts of the earth" (vs. 9). The main emphasis is that Jesus completely conquered sin, death, and Satan through His resurrection and ascension.

Despite the clarity of emphasis, scholars have different opinions about what Paul meant. Some think the apostle was referring to Jesus' entrance into Hades after His crucifixion (specifically, the saved portion of the underworld or realm of the dead), to take saints to heaven when He rose from the dead (see 1 Pet. 3:19-20; 4:6). Others say that the Messiah's descent refers to His death and burial in the grave. Still others claim that Paul was talking about Jesus' incarnation, in which He came to earth as a human being (see John 3:13). This person who "descended is the same also that ascended" (Eph. 4:10). Expressed differently, Jesus is not only a man who lived on earth, but also the Lord whose eternal dwelling is in heaven. Jews of the day believed there were seven heavens. But Paul said that the Son ascended "above all heavens." In fact, now He fills the entire cosmos. This means Jesus' lordship over the universe is absolute and complete because of His resurrection and ascension. He has the power and authority to be generous in bestowing gifts of grace to His followers.

All believers have at least one spiritual gift (see 1 Pet. 4:10). But in Ephesians 4:11, Paul focused on those who have received special abilities to be leaders in the churches. He mentioned apostles, prophets, evangelists, pastors, and teachers. The Greek noun rendered "apostles" is used in various ways in the New Testament. In this case, Paul was probably using the term in a restricted sense, to refer to a group of people (including himself) whom Jesus had personally chosen to found the church.

The "prophets" Paul had in mind were not Elijah, Isaiah, and the other Old Testament spokespersons. The church of Paul's day had its own prophets. These people delivered messages from God, and sometimes foretold the future. Before the New Testament books were written, about the only way God had to communicate directly to the church was through His special speakers. The other three kinds of leaders have related functions. "Evangelists" in the early church were people who conducted outreach in areas where the church had not yet been established. Put another way, they were pioneers for the faith. In the wake of the evangelists, "pastors and teachers" served already established congregations. Pastors shepherded churches, while teachers instructed them. Of course, these two roles could be combined in one person.

Despite the presence of uniquely gifted believers, they all have a common goal. The Lord wants them to equip believers to do God's work so that the church might be strengthened (vs. 12). Christians use their gifts to help one another become united in their faith and intimate in their knowledge of God's Son. The entire body benefits when each of its members is mature, fully grown in the Lord, and measuring up to the full stature of Christ (vs. 13). As long as believers remain immature, they will be like a ship tossed on a stormy sea. As the winds of opinion blow in one direction, some Christians are easily swayed by it. Then as another gust of ideas blasts across their bow, they change their mind about what they believe. According to verse 14, Jesus' followers are not to be characterized by spiritual immaturity and ignorance. Paul's frequent sea voyages, including his harrowing trip to Rome (see Acts 27:1–28:14), may have prompted the seafaring metaphor he used in Ephesians 4:14.

Paul did not want God's people to be fooled by the cleverly worded lies of religious impostors. Instead, the apostle urged believers to hold to the truth in love (vs. 15). Expressed differently, honesty, veracity, and compassion should characterize all that believers say and do. Believers are also to become more like the Savior in every area of their lives. This is as it should be, for He is the head of the church. Under His direction, this spiritual body is fitted together perfectly.

By calling Jesus "the head," Paul was revisiting the analogy between the church and the body. Believers make up the members of Christ's body, with Him as our Head. Paul liked this analogy because it indicates the organic connection between Jesus and His followers. As each part does its own unique and special work, it helps the other parts to grow (vs. 16). Each member of the Messiah's spiritual body is to work together in harmony to promote the growth and vitality of the church. As a result, the entire body becomes healthy, mature, and full of love. Every believer should operate with one another so that all might mature and come to know the Son more fully.

SUGGESTIONS TO TEACHERS

Every gifted church member is like a ligament in the body. The body grows because all parts work together. The same is true of the church. The church is weakened when members fail to serve one another. But when love motivates and permeates our service, everything fits and everyone grows. Moreover, our Lord is honored and praised.

1. LIVING IN UNITY AND PEACE. Paul stressed that part of our calling is to live in unity and peace with one another in the church. Admittedly, if we are humble, gentle, patient, and forgiving, unity and peace will be easier to achieve. Believers will not fight for their own rights, criticize others, and lose their tempers.

2. WORKING HARD TO MAINTAIN OUR ONENESS. Achieving unity and peace requires hard work. That said, our task is not to put on an outward appearance of unity. Instead, it is to keep the unity we already have in the Holy Spirit. Our task is to live at peace with one another so that we will not undermine our spiritual unity. Since we are one in Christ, we must live together in light of that fact.

3. FOSTERING SPIRITUAL MATURITY. Paul's description of spiritual maturity explodes our usual attitude toward ministry in the church. We are not playing church. We are moving toward the "fulness of Christ" (Eph. 4:13). That's why using our spiritual gifts is so important. If we don't use them, we lose and the entire church suffers. We also fail to reach all that Jesus wants to do for us.

4. PROMOTING GROWTH, NOT DESTRUCTION. The answer to false teaching is the truth of the Gospel and the apostles' doctrine. God's Word is our strong defense. But we are not supposed to be rough with spiritual infants. Instead, we are to handle them carefully so they will grow. Using our spiritual gifts means teaching with love, patience, and understanding. Our purpose is promoting growth, not destruction.

| **FOR ADULTS** | ■ **TOPIC:** Living Together |
| | ■ **QUESTIONS:** 1. What connection is there between humility, gentle- |

ness, and patience? Why must all three virtues be present in the believer's life? 2. In what way are believers joined together in the body of Christ? 3. How do evangelists, pastors, and teachers fit into the divine plan? 4. What enabling grace has the Savior given you to share with others? 5. In what way is the body of Christ to be built up? Why is this important?

■ **ILLUSTRATIONS:**

Building Others Up. An officer parachuting off a plane was so intent on leaping out at the right coordinates that he ordered silence to the lower-ranking soldier beside him. "But, Lieutenant—" continued the private. "Not another word!" snapped the officer. As the lieutenant made ready to jump, the private pulled him to the floor. "Like I've been trying to tell you, your chute's torn!" shouted the soldier to his now-grateful superior.

Although this story is fictional, it isn't too far-fetched. In real life, words heard and heeded can and do make tremendous differences in our being able to live together within the body of Christ (see Eph. 4:2-3). Have you ministered beneath or beside someone who, because he or she "knew it all," would not listen to others? Worse, have you exhibited that kind of behavior yourself?

Building others up in love requires us to graciously listen to them. God wants our work with fellow believers to edify, not diminish, the body of Christ (see vss. 15-16).

Evangelizing for the Future. In July 1865, William Booth established the Christian Mission in London's East End. His goal was to combat poverty and religious indifference. But Booth's ministry was unique. His model was the British military, and his congregation lived in some of London's most forsaken neighborhoods.

By the time Booth's organization established a branch in the United States in 1880, it was called the Salvation Army. Ministers, known as officers, worked to reach the social classes that had been previously overlooked or ignored by the larger, more traditional denominations. However, the organization's methods and practices were first ridiculed and criticized by other Christians in America, that is, until President Grover Cleveland officially endorsed the Salvation Army in 1886.

The Salvation Army was a successful evangelistic voice for many who felt utterly unlovable. But they did not stop with salvation. Today, Salvation Army churches minister to congregations in 82 countries worldwide, in a diverse variety of socioeconomic settings, equipping believers to continue to evangelize for the future.

Paul was well aware of how dissimilar people can be on the outside. The human tendency is to focus on those differences. But when the apostle wrote Ephesians, he urged a different path. He directed believers to focus on their common inheritance in God's grace, and in our unity help one another to grow in humility, patience, and love (see 4:2-3, 14-16).

An Inclusive Church. Paul said that believers were united in body, in Spirit, in hope, in the Lord Jesus, in baptism, and in God the Father (see Eph. 4:4-6). Therefore, believers were to be diligent to preserve their oneness in Christ (see vs. 3).

When Henry Coffin became pastor of the Madison Avenue Presbyterian Church in New York City in 1905, he was chagrined to find two separate congregations under one roof. There was a small chapel for use by lower-class families for worship. These were denied access to the main sanctuary, a common practice in the city at that time.

Coffin got the church officers to combine all families into one worshiping congregation and stopped the long-standing practice of pew rents. He saw to it that the doors of the church were no longer locked between Sundays. He welcomed health and welfare groups to meet at the Madison Avenue Church. Other congregations took their cue from Henry Coffin, and unlocked their doors to the community. And Madison Avenue Church's membership grew from about 500 members in 1905 to over 2,200 by the time Coffin left.

FOR YOUTH

■ TOPIC: We Are One
■ QUESTIONS: 1. What did Paul urge believers to do? 2. Which godly virtues did Paul want to see characterize the lives of believers? 3. What can you do to help keep unity in your church? 4. Why are the spiritual gifts Paul mentioned given to the church? 5. How can you encourage other believers to grow in spiritual maturity?

■ ILLUSTRATIONS:

All Together Now. "All for one and one for all" is a great rallying cry for French musketeers, political movements, and football teams. It sounds so wonderful. It assumes that each individual will lay aside his or her own preferences for the sake of others.

But when we allow Jesus to break down barriers, we do much more than paper over our differences. We have to confess and acknowledge that hostility does exist. We also have to admit that unless we allow Jesus to change us from within, we won't be able to achieve oneness in human relationships.

Because Jesus gives each of us a new heart and new motivation, we can seek His help and power to get along with everyone, regardless of our differences. We accept people as they are, and see them as objects of God's love in the Gospel. We also show humility and love—demonstrating Christlikeness to people who are very different from ourselves—so that we can all become one family in Christ (see Eph. 4:2-6).

A Spiritual Gift in Action. In Ephesians 4:7, Paul stated that Jesus' gifts to believers are personal and individual. Moreover, He has assigned grace-gifts to every believer. Our task is to use our spiritual gifts in unique ways according to our personalities, skills, qualifications, education, and experience.

One Sunday morning in 1856, a congregation of well-dressed people had been ushered to their rented space in Chicago's Plymouth Congregation Church. Suddenly, there was a commotion near the door. Many turned and looked. Something occurred that had never before been seen by the elite congregation.

In walked a 19-year-old salesman. Following him was a motley group of tramps, slum people, and alcoholics. The young man led his visitors to four pews he had personally rented for them. The Spirit empowered him to continue doing this important work each Sunday until God called him into a worldwide ministry. The young man was Dwight L. Moody.

Elitism. On July 19, 1998, owners of several of Europe's top soccer clubs met in London to form their own super league in the 2000–2001 season. The meeting of powerhouse teams was so secret that the clubs would not admit that a meeting ever took place.

The clubs, which were the richest at the time, were also unhappy with the Premier League. This was the group that oversaw the 20-club league prevalent in that era. The elitist clubs preferred to play only each other on a regular basis rather than other teams. These groups wanted to exclude others from playing because they supposedly were not as good at the game.

The same feelings of elitism existed in the early church, too. And it took the Spirit of God to break such prejudice. The Lord's ultimate goal was to get believers to come together in the oneness of their "faith" (Eph. 4:13) and in the "knowledge of the Son of God."

LIVE IN THE LIGHT

BACKGROUND SCRIPTURE: John 1:1-14; Ephesians 4:17–5:20
DEVOTIONAL READING: Psalm 97

Key Verse: Be ye therefore followers of
God, as dear children. Ephesians 5:1.

4

KING JAMES VERSION

JOHN 1:1 In the beginning was the Word, and the Word was with God, and the Word was God. 2 The same was in the beginning with God. 3 All things were made by him; and without him was not any thing made that was made. 4 In him was life; and the life was the light of men. 5 And the light shineth in darkness; and the darkness comprehended it not. . . .

EPHESIANS 5:1 Be ye therefore followers of God, as dear children; 2 And walk in love, as Christ also hath loved us, and hath given himself for us an offering and a sacrifice to God for a sweetsmelling savour. . . .

6 Let no man deceive you with vain words: for because of these things cometh the wrath of God upon the children of disobedience. 7 Be not ye therefore partakers with them. 8 For ye were sometimes darkness, but now are ye light in the Lord: walk as children of light: 9 (For the fruit of the Spirit is in all goodness and righteousness and truth;) 10 Proving what is acceptable unto the Lord. 11 And have no fellowship with the unfruitful works of darkness, but rather reprove them. 12 For it is a shame even to speak of those things which are done of them in secret. 13 But all things that are reproved are made manifest by the light: for whatsoever doth make manifest is light. 14 Wherefore he saith, Awake thou that sleepest, and arise from the dead, and Christ shall give thee light.

NEW REVISED STANDARD VERSION

JOHN 1:1 In the beginning was the Word, and the Word was with God, and the Word was God. 2 He was in the beginning with God. 3 All things came into being through him, and without him not one thing came into being. What has come into being 4 in him was life, and the life was the light of all people. 5 The light shines in the darkness, and the darkness did not overcome it. . . .

EPHESIANS 5:1 Therefore be imitators of God, as beloved children, 2 and live in love, as Christ loved us and gave himself up for us, a fragrant offering and sacrifice to God. . . .

6 Let no one deceive you with empty words, for because of these things the wrath of God comes on those who are disobedient. 7 Therefore do not be associated with them. 8 For once you were darkness, but now in the Lord you are light. Live as children of light— 9 for the fruit of the light is found in all that is good and right and true. 10 Try to find out what is pleasing to the Lord. 11 Take no part in the unfruitful works of darkness, but instead expose them. 12 For it is shameful even to mention what such people do secretly; 13 but everything exposed by the light becomes visible, 14 for everything that becomes visible is light. Therefore it says,

"Sleeper, awake!
  Rise from the dead,
and Christ will shine on you."

Monday, December 17	Psalm 97	*Light Dawns for the Righteous*
Tuesday, December 18	Ephesians 4:17-24	*The Way of Darkness*
Wednesday, December 19	Ephesians 4:25-32	*Putting Away the Old Ways*
Thursday, December 20	Ephesians 5:15-20	*Be Careful How You Live*
Friday, December 21	Matthew 2:1-11	*We Have Seen His Star*
Saturday, December 22	John 1:6-14	*We Have Seen His Glory*
Sunday, December 23	John 1:1-5;	
	Ephesians 5:1-2, 6-14	*Light Shines in the Darkness*

BACKGROUND

Christian tradition has consistently affirmed the apostle John as the author of the Gospel that bears his name. Clearly, this Gospel was written by an eyewitness of the events he described. The Gospel's details about the topography of Palestine and the towns that relate to Jesus are all accurate. The author's familiarity with Jewish customs and religious practices is also dramatically evident in this Gospel. Most importantly, however, the fourth Gospel provides us with unparalleled insights into the Lord Jesus. It is only in this account that we learn about the marriage feast at Cana (2:1-11), the Lord's discussion with Nicodemus (3:1-21), the raising of Lazarus (11:1-44), the washing of His disciples' feet (13:1-17), and the great "I am" declarations (6:35; 8:12, 58; 9:5; 10:7, 9, 11; 11:25; 14:6; 15:5). John also gave memorable glimpses of Thomas (11:16; 14:5; 20:24-29), Andrew (1:40-41; 6:8-9; 12:22), and Philip (6:5-7; 14:8-9).

John clearly stated his purpose for this Gospel in 20:31. The apostle affirmed that Jesus is the Messiah and the Son of God. According to John, Jesus was not merely a human being, a man possessed with a type of Christ spirit, or a spirit being who merely appeared human. Jesus is God who came in the flesh and now rules in heaven. Throughout this Gospel, John constantly showed Jesus to be the Son of God. John's presentation of Jesus' miracles, teachings, and experiences all point to Him as the Messiah. John's Gospel was intended to convince people to place their trust in the Lord Jesus as the Son of God, who died for their sins and will one day come again.

NOTES ON THE PRINTED TEXT

John 1:1 declares that since "the Word" existed "in the beginning," He could not be a created being. In reality, "the Word was God" and "with God" at the same time. Though distinct persons, God the Father and God the Son share the same divine nature (along with God the Holy Spirit). In short, the one whom we call Jesus was with the Father from the very beginning (vs. 2). Verse 3 reveals that the Father brought all things into existence through the Son. Likewise, Colossians 1:16 affirms that all things in heaven and on earth were created by the Son. This includes whatever is visible or invisible, along with all principalities and powers. Similarly, Hebrews 1:2 adds that even the temporal ages owe their existence to the Son, the One through whom the Father has spoken in "these last days."

The Son's provision of life—both physical and spiritual—is another major theme in John's Gospel. The apostle tied life in the Son to the metaphor of "light" (1:4). John often contrasted the darkness of sinful humanity with the light of the Messiah—not only in his Gospel but also in his first letter (see 1 John 1:5; 2:8). The Son dispels the darkness and reveals the Father's truths by the light of His Word (John 1:5). For this reason, darkness is hostile to the light. In Scripture, light symbolizes all that is wholesome and genuine, while darkness portrays the opposing qualities of error and evil. Both the Old Testament and the New Testament equate light with the truth of the Word. For instance, Psalm 119:105 says that God's Word of Truth is a lamp to the believers' feet and a light for their path. Also, in 2 Corinthians 4:4, Paul said that the devil had blinded the eyes of unbelievers so that they could not see "the light of the glorious gospel of Christ."

When people encounter the Son revealed in John 1:1-5, it should bring about a profound change in the way they think and act, especially in comparison to the unsaved. This includes emulating the Son in their attitudes and priorities. We find this emphasis in the Letter to the Ephesians, where Paul urged his readers to put off their old sinful selves and put on new righteous selves (4:17-24). To illustrate what he meant, the apostle explained in verses 25-28 that the Christian's life should be marked by speaking truth instead of falsehood, avoiding sins associated with anger, and laboring honestly instead of stealing. Verses 29-32 deal with some of the issues involved in replacing the old self with the new self: unwholesome talk versus edifying talk, and malice versus love. Next, in 5:1, we read about how we ought to imitate God. Paul's injunction is more than just in the matter of forgiveness. Christians are to reflect the holiness of God in all aspects of their lives. As children try to copy their parents, so we should try to copy our heavenly Father. And to imitate God means to walk in the way of "love" (vs. 2).

Paul referred to the example of the Son to illustrate how we should love. Jesus showed us His love by giving Himself up as a sacrifice for our sins. Just as Old Testament sacrifices of animals sent up a pleasing aroma to the Lord (see Exod. 29:18), the Messiah's death was a fragrant offering. It was an acceptable sacrifice to the Father because of the Son's perfection of love. In brief, His love is unselfish, pure, and active. Evidently, Paul expected some people in the Ephesian church to say that his standards of morality were higher than necessary. The apostle called the arguments employed by such individuals "vain words" (Eph. 5:6). The moral standards Paul taught were not his own but God's, and the Lord does indeed judge those who disobey His standards. Thus the Ephesians were not to be deceived by people with low moral standards or be "partakers with them" (vs. 7) by joining in their sin.

Paul once more called upon his readers to remember their past without the Son. The apostle told the Ephesians that before putting their faith in the Messiah, they had not only lived in moral and spiritual "darkness" (vs. 8), but also had *been* darkness. Now, after becoming followers of the Savior, they not only lived in moral and spiritual "light," but also *were* light. Since the Ephesians had been enlightened and were themselves Christ-reflecting lights, Paul made two demands on them. Both of these requests amount roughly to the same thing: the Ephesians were to shun evil and do good.

First, the apostle's readers were to live as "children of light." Presumably, this means they were to follow the light of the Son and consequently do what the Father approves. They were to consistently show by their attitudes and actions to which kingdom they belonged—the Savior's kingdom of light, not Satan's kingdom of darkness. Paul added a parenthetical statement to provide examples of the conduct of those who live in God's light. The apostle said that the "fruit" (vs. 9), or product, of this light is "all goodness and righteousness and truth." The Greek noun rendered "goodness" refers to kindness, generosity of spirit, and moral excellence. The noun translated "righteousness" describes justice and fairness. The noun rendered "truth" stands for genuineness and honesty. As for Paul's second demand, he told the Ephesians to try to learn what is pleasing to the Lord (vs. 10). In every situation that comes up, and every time we have a decision to make, we should seek the Father's will. Once we have discerned what God desires, we should determine to follow His leading.

In verse 11, Paul directed his readers not to be participants in the "unfruitful works of darkness." Instead, followers of the Messiah were to "reprove" the deplorable nature of these sordid acts. On the one hand, believers were not to commit sins. On the other hand, they were to unmask iniquity for what it truly is, namely, disobedience to almighty God. Unlike light, which produces wholesome spiritual fruit such as goodness, righteousness, and truth, darkness is barren and leads to nothing good, whether temporal or eternal.

What the reprobate did "in secret" (vs. 12) was so disgraceful that Paul thought some of its shamefulness putrefied believers who spoke unnecessarily about these degenerate activities. Be that as it may, the apostle's statement did not conflict with what he said in verse 11 about believers exposing the true nature of wickedness. Specifically, it is God working through us who unmasks sin. The apostle compared the process to "light" (vs. 13) shining into the darkness and making "manifest" what was previously concealed. It is God's Word operating in the lives of Jesus' followers that discloses evil deeds so that their true character can be seen by everyone (vs. 14).

Exposure by the light of Christ is just what the unsaved require, especially if they are to be convinced of their need for change. To support his point, Paul quoted a fragment of poetry, which appears to have been based on Isaiah 9:2 and 60:1. The immediate source of the quote is not known. It might have been from a chorus addressed to

Christian converts during their baptismal service. Whatever its source, the poetry urges the unregenerate to wake up from their sleep by putting their faith in the Messiah. As a result, they would be regenerated. The image is that of a corpse being given new life and rising from its casket. The poetry emphasizes that the Messiah shines His light so that sinners can see a way out of the darkness.

SUGGESTIONS TO TEACHERS

Imagine the scenario: you and a group of people are confined for a time in a place where no copy of the Bible is available. Let's assume that your group is in a detention camp, where you have access to paper and pencils. If your fellow prisoners asked you to write something about God, something that could be passed around in the camp, what would you state about Jesus? Use this hypothetical situation as a lesson starter. Then have your students compare what they would write to the compositions of John and Paul. They both were emphatic about letting their readers know about Jesus.

1. JESUS, OUR ETERNAL CREATOR. The eternal God and complete creation are encompassed in the opening verses of John's Gospel. What a vast view of the cosmos! Those in the class who may be science buffs or science fiction readers should become aware that the apostle's words placed Jesus into the history of the universe. Imaginary tales about spaceships, intergalactic travel, and time warps turn into puny fantasies when contrasted with John's breathtaking statements about Jesus as the Word of God existing from the very beginning.

2. JESUS, OUR LIGHT. Have the members of your class take note of the word "light." It appears throughout John's writings (see John 1:4-5). Light is an essential term to describe the meaning of the Messiah. Let your imagination roam as you picture what existence without light was like. Darkness brings gloomy thinking as well as gloomy living. Light, as characterized by the presence of Jesus in our lives, brings hope and even life itself.

3. JESUS, OUR SHINING EXAMPLE. In Ephesians 5:1-2, Paul urged believers to show kindness to one another, just as the Father has showered them with the love of His Son. The apostle also exhorted Christians to be as generous in giving of themselves to one another, just as the Son offered Himself on their behalf. Moreover, Paul stressed that believers are to be unconditional in the compassion they demonstrate, for the love the Father has shown them through the Son was absolute and limitless.

4. JESUS, OUR MOTIVATION TO CHANGE. In verses 6-14, Paul contrasted two different approaches to life. One is characterized by iniquity and debauchery, while the other is known for its virtue and integrity. The apostle emphasized that the upright example set by Jesus motivates His followers to shun the spiritual darkness associated with sin and embrace the light of new life in Him. Also, as part of this change, believers are to seek the Lord's will and to expose sin.

■ **TOPIC:** Living by Example

■ **QUESTIONS:** 1. According to the apostle John, who is Jesus? 2. What aspects of God's character are we to imitate? 3. What are some definite steps believers can take to be more loving toward others? 4. What does it mean for us to walk as "children of light" (Eph. 5:8)? 5. What are some ways that believers can "reprove" (vs. 11) wicked deeds?

■ **ILLUSTRATIONS:**

A Perfect Imitation. When Animal Kingdom, Walt Disney World's newest Orlando, Florida, attraction, was under construction throughout most of the 1990s, park developers struggled with some unique problems. One was dealing with the intelligence of their new residents.

Although nearly all of the other animals would be free to roam vast spaces during the day, at night they were all brought into their pens for safekeeping. Despite being well cared for, these animals yearned to be free. And they realized that one way to attain that freedom was to imitate the actions of their human caretakers with the intent of exploiting any weaknesses they could find in their captors' behavior.

In Ephesians 5, Paul indicated that believers should also have a strong desire to be truly free from all forms of immorality. Unless we wish to remain captive to the evil that surrounds us, we need to emulate the Savior in every aspect of our lives (see vss. 1-2).

An Event Worth Celebrating. On Monday night, January 19, 1953, stores and theaters were practically empty. City streets weren't as busy as usual. For half an hour, telephones stopped ringing. The reason: Lucy Ricardo (the character played by Lucille Ball on the hit television show *I Love Lucy)* was having a baby. It seemed as if everyone in the United States with a television set was watching and celebrating along with the mother.

Other people's babies do that to us, even fictional newborns or babies of the rich and famous. These are children and parents we'll probably never have the chance to meet. For a moment, babies pull us out of daily life and give us a warm, drooling reminder of innocence, simple pleasures, and life's great possibilities.

The celebration of Jesus' birth brings all those emotions and more. In addition to the feelings we would have for any new birth, we bring the knowledge that the Creator of the universe (see John 1:3) came to earth as a vulnerable infant. We recall the thousands of years of waiting and watching for God's promised deliverer. And then Jesus came, just a little baby, just like us.

Lucy, Desi, and Little Ricky now exist only in reruns, and several generations have been born that have no firsthand memory of that highly rated episode. Thankfully, the account of Jesus' birth will never fade from the public eye. The truth about the divine

Word (see vss. 1-2) being born as a human is as real and powerful as when it first occurred. And that's an event worth celebrating!

Like Father, Like Son. History was made in organized baseball in 1989. For the first time, a father and son played simultaneously in the major leagues. Ken Griffey Jr., the 19-year-old son of Ken Sr., started for the Seattle Mariners while his 39-year-old father played for the Cincinnati Reds. The physical skills of the father were evident in the son.

How often that occurs! A son resembles his father, or a daughter resembles her mother. But something far more significant is true in the life of Jesus. The very nature of His Father is shown in the Son (see John 1:1). Just as so many of the characteristics of Ken Griffey Sr. were evident in his son, so we see the characteristics of God when we look at Jesus.

Our loving heavenly Father, through His Son, Jesus, wanted to show us what real compassion is like (see Eph. 5:2). This may be one of the reasons why Christianity grew so rapidly in its earliest years. Believers today are to be witnesses for the One who was revealed in human form.

FOR YOUTH ■ **TOPIC:** Go Light!
■ **QUESTIONS:** 1. What role did Jesus have in creating the world?
2. Why is it important for us to walk in the way of love? 3. What are some ways we can discern what pleases the Lord? 4. How can we avoid getting involved in the "unfruitful works of darkness" (Eph. 5:11)? 5. Which character traits mentioned by Paul do you most need to work on improving in your life?

■ **ILLUSTRATIONS:**

Meaningful Celebration. Christmas recalls the birth of Jesus, the Light of the world (see John 1:4-5). The season reminds us that He first loved us by coming to earth as a human being. In turn, we have the privilege of knowing and loving the Savior. What better opportunity is there than this holiday to create a meaningful celebration to honor Him?

So, how can we celebrate? We can call some of our friends together to have a simple time of commemorative worship. Or we can be alone and, in a creative way, let Jesus know how glad we are that He chose to be among us. In doing these sorts of things, we can draw near to the Messiah. Furthermore, through meaningful celebration, we can deepen our relationship with Him.

The True Joy of Christmas. In *Our Daily Bread,* David McCasland writes about a visit he made one December to New York City's Metropolitan Museum of Art. As he paused to admire the magnificent Christmas tree, he saw that it was covered with angels and surrounded at its base by an elaborate 18th-century nativity scene. McCasland also spotted nearly 200 figures, including shepherds, the Magi, and a crowd of townspeople. All of them looked in anticipation toward the manger or gazed up in awe at the angels.

But McCasland noticed that there was one other figure that appeared different from the rest. He saw a barefoot man who was carrying a heavy load on his back and looking at the ground. McCasland realized that this person, like many young people today, was so weighed down that he couldn't look up to see the Messiah.

Perhaps some of us can relate to how dejected this man probably felt. We know from personal experience that Christmas can be a difficult time, especially as we try to carry the heavy burdens that fill our lives. The good news is that Jesus, the Light of the world (see John 1:4-5), came to remind us of God's love and abiding presence. With Jesus at our side, we do not have to go through the holiday season alone.

Even as we begin our journey into the new year, we are reminded that Jesus is always with us. He remains our source of strength, peace, and joy in the most difficult times in our life.

A Copycat! In February 2002, the *BBC News* service reported that researchers in Texas had successfully cloned a domestic cat. The resulting kitten was appropriately named CopyCat. The work was described in the scientific journal *Nature*, which noted that this was the first time anyone had cloned a pet. According to one of the researchers, the cloned cat appeared healthy and energetic.

Jesus is no clone. He is God the Son, the Word of God enfleshed (see John 1:1-2). In the Incarnation, God is the Creator, not a genetic engineer.

CHRIST'S LOVE FOR THE CHURCH

BACKGROUND SCRIPTURE: Ephesians 5:21–6:4
DEVOTIONAL READING: John 3:16-21

Key Verse: Submitting yourselves one to
another in the fear of God. Ephesians 5:21.

KING JAMES VERSION

EPHESIANS 5:21 Submitting yourselves one to another in the fear of God. 22 Wives, submit yourselves unto your own husbands, as unto the Lord. 23 For the husband is the head of the wife, even as Christ is the head of the church: and he is the saviour of the body. 24 Therefore as the church is subject unto Christ, so let the wives be to their own husbands in every thing. 25 Husbands, love your wives, even as Christ also loved the church, and gave himself for it; 26 That he might sanctify and cleanse it with the washing of water by the word, 27 That he might present it to himself a glorious church, not having spot, or wrinkle, or any such thing; but that it should be holy and without blemish. 28 So ought men to love their wives as their own bodies. He that loveth his wife loveth himself. 29 For no man ever yet hated his own flesh; but nourisheth and cherisheth it, even as the Lord the church: 30 For we are members of his body, of his flesh, and of his bones. 31 For this cause shall a man leave his father and mother, and shall be joined unto his wife, and they two shall be one flesh. 32 This is a great mystery: but I speak concerning Christ and the church. 33 Nevertheless let every one of you in particular so love his wife even as himself; and the wife see that she reverence her husband.

6:1 Children, obey your parents in the Lord: for this is right. 2 Honour thy father and mother; which is the first commandment with promise; 3 That it may be well with thee, and thou mayest live long on the earth. 4 And, ye fathers, provoke not your children to wrath: but bring them up in the nurture and admonition of the Lord.

NEW REVISED STANDARD VERSION

EPHESIANS 5:21 Be subject to one another out of reverence for Christ.

22 Wives, be subject to your husbands as you are to the Lord. 23 For the husband is the head of the wife just as Christ is the head of the church, the body of which he is the Savior. 24 Just as the church is subject to Christ, so also wives ought to be, in everything, to their husbands.

25 Husbands, love your wives, just as Christ loved the church and gave himself up for her, 26 in order to make her holy by cleansing her with the washing of water by the word, 27 so as to present the church to himself in splendor, without a spot or wrinkle or anything of the kind—yes, so that she may be holy and without blemish. 28 In the same way, husbands should love their wives as they do their own bodies. He who loves his wife loves himself. 29 For no one ever hates his own body, but he nourishes and tenderly cares for it, just as Christ does for the church, 30 because we are members of his body. 31 "For this reason a man will leave his father and mother and be joined to his wife, and the two will become one flesh." 32 This is a great mystery, and I am applying it to Christ and the church. 33 Each of you, however, should love his wife as himself, and a wife should respect her husband.

6:1 Children, obey your parents in the Lord, for this is right. 2 "Honor your father and mother"—this is the first commandment with a promise: 3 "so that it may be well with you and you may live long on the earth."

4 And, fathers, do not provoke your children to anger, but bring them up in the discipline and instruction of the Lord.

Monday, December 24	1 John 4:7-12	*God Is Love*
Tuesday, December 25	John 3:16-21	*God's Gift of Love*
Wednesday, December 26	Romans 5:6-11	*The Proof of God's Love*
Thursday, December 27	John 13:1-9	*The Example of Jesus' Love*
Friday, December 28	John 15:9-17	*Abiding in Christ's Love*
Saturday, December 29	1 John 3:18-24	*Following the Commands of Christ*
Sunday, December 30	Ephesians 5:21–6:4	*Following the Example of Christ*

BACKGROUND

Ephesians 5:21 urges believers to be subject to one another out of reverence for God. The Greek verb rendered "submitting" was used in literature outside of the Bible in the sense of soldiers subordinating themselves to their superiors, or of slaves yielding to their masters. Here, the verb does not mean a forced submission, but rather voluntarily giving up one's rights and will.

Because of our selfish human nature, we do not naturally want to yield or adapt to anyone. But since we love and respect the Savior, and since He asks us to submit to one another, we must do so. Paul developed what he meant about submission by discussing three sets of household relationships—those between wives and husbands (vss. 22-33), between children and parents (6:1-4), and between slaves and masters (vss. 5-9).

NOTES ON THE PRINTED TEXT

Paul directed all believers to submit to one another because of their fear of the Lord (Eph. 5:21). In verse 22, Paul stated that wives are to submit to their husbands. It is helpful to consider what Paul did not mean by his statement. He was not saying that women are inferior to men or that all women must submit to all men. And even though the apostle said wives should submit "in every thing" (vs. 24), the teaching of Scripture as a whole indicates that a wife should not submit when her husband wants her to act in a way that is clearly contrary to God's will (compare Acts 5:29).

Paul made a comparison in Ephesians 5:23-24 by noting that a wife is to submit to her husband just as she—indeed, just as all the church—submits to the Savior. That's because a husband is the head of his wife just as the Messiah is the head of the church. This comparison helps us only if we understand what Paul meant by the Son being the head of the church. New Testament scholars have taken different positions on this. According to one group of experts, Jesus is the head of the church in the sense that He is the church's source and origin. On the basis of this interpretation, these scholars conclude that a wife must honor and love her husband, but the two may share decision making equally. According to another group of experts, the Messiah is the head of the church in the sense that He is its leader and authority. Based on this interpretation, these scholars suggest that a wife should honor and love her husband, but he should oversee family decisions.

The wife is not the only partner in a marriage who has a duty to the other. While she is to submit to her husband, he must love her sacrificially and unconditionally (vs. 25). In a male-dominated Roman society, the news that husbands owe their wives any duty must have sounded revolutionary. Once again, Paul put husbands in the place of the Savior and wives in the place of the church to help clarify his meaning. A husband is to love his wife even as Jesus loves the church.

Verses 25-31 contain the apostle's description of how the Son loves the church and how husbands should love their wives. The Greek verb translated "love" in these verses is *agape*. Generally speaking, the term refers to an unselfish and active concern for another. This is the appropriate word, since Jesus' love for us motivated Him to give up His life for us (vs. 25). Throughout this passage, Paul used wedding and marriage terms to picture the Savior's love for the church. Before a wedding ceremony in ancient times, the bride would carefully wash herself and put on clean clothes. Similarly, the Messiah cleanses His bride, the church, by the "washing of water by the word" (vs. 26). (Some think this statement is part of a reference to early baptismal practices.) After this washing, the bride of Christ is "glorious . . . not having spot, or wrinkle, or any such thing" (vs. 27). Expressed differently, the redemption the Son won on the cross cleanses members of the church of sins, making us "holy and without blemish" in the Father's sight.

In modern wedding ceremonies, it is traditional for the bride's father to present the bride to the groom. But in ancient weddings, ordinarily a friend of the groom would present the bride to the groom. According to Paul's description, neither the modern tradition nor the ancient tradition will be followed in the Messiah's wedding ceremony with the church, which will take place at the end of time. Jesus will act as both the presenter and the groom, since He will present the church to Himself.

Why does the Savior love the church so much that He gave Himself up for it, washes it, and will present it to Himself? It's because the church is His spiritual body (vs. 30). A person naturally loves his or her own physical body, and shows that love by taking care of it (vs. 29). Similarly, a husband should love his wife as much as he loves himself. Indeed, by loving his wife in this unselfish manner, a husband "loveth himself" (vs. 28).

In verse 31, Paul quoted Genesis 2:24 to show how a married couple are joined. Adam realized that Eve was, quite literally, bone of his bones and flesh of his flesh. Eve had been made from Adam. This illustrates that the bond of marriage is strong. In fact, the Greek verb translated "joined" (Eph. 5:31) literally means "to glue upon." Paul's implication was that a man must love the woman to whom he is joined (in a manner of speaking) by marriage.

Genesis 2:24 has a dual implication. People have always known that it refers to the relationship between husbands and wives. But only after the Savior's coming to earth did some realize that it also refers to the relationship between Jesus and the church. That's what Paul meant when he called it a "great mystery" (Eph. 5:32). As noted in lesson 1, the apostle was referring to a deep secret that had been disclosed through the Redeemer. In verse 33, Paul summarized his instructions to husbands and wives. Husbands are to love their wives as they love themselves, and wives are to respect their husbands. The lordship and example of the Son are the basis for such a mutually loving and submissive relationship.

Next, Paul addressed the relationship between children and their parents. We may not often think of children reading the apostle's letters (or listening as they were read aloud) along with adults in the churches. But 6:1-3 is one place where the apostle addressed children directly. He told them plainly that it is proper for children to obey their parents (vs. 1). This obedience by children is to take place "in the Lord." Paul imagined a family in which both parents and children believe in the Savior. Neither mother nor father but Jesus is the family's ultimate authority. Therefore, the parents make rules consistent with Christian principles, and the children obey their parents as they would obey Jesus.

How can the fifth commandment be the "first" (vs. 2) with a promise if the second commandment also seems to have one (Exod. 20:5-6; Deut. 5:9-10)? The fifth may have been "first" in the sense that it was the initial (and primary) one taught to children. Or the fifth is at least one of the first divine injunctions in importance. Perhaps to make the requirement of child obedience sound less like a duty and more like an opportunity, Paul drew attention to the promise attached to the fifth commandment: "That it may be well with thee, and thou mayest live long on the earth" (Eph. 6:3). The promise does not give absolute assurance that those who are obedient to their parents will have a long and easy life on earth. But generally, the promise indicates that God blesses those who honor their parents.

After telling the children to be obedient, Paul turned his attention to the fathers (vs. 4). Here Paul's teaching was truly countercultural. According to the Roman law of *patria potestas* (Latin for "power of a father"), the male head of a family exercised nearly absolute authority over his children, the extended descendants in the male line (regardless of their age), and those adopted and reared in the family. Only the male head was entitled to any rights in private law, and even property acquired by other family members was owned by the father. He could murder an unwanted newborn, make his children work in the fields wearing chains, sell his children into slavery, or impose capital punishment on a family member.

Far from advocating such parental tyranny, Paul told fathers—and by implication, mothers—they didn't have absolute power over their children. The apostle taught that while parents have the right to require obedience from their children, parents should not make such severe demands on their children that the latter become exasperated. Provoking children to anger creates discouragement and resentment, and often leads to outright rebellion. Instead of frustrating, enraging, or ridiculing their children, parents should adopt rules and policies that are objective, fair, and sensible.

SUGGESTIONS TO TEACHERS

The KJV of Ephesians 5:21 says that believers should submit to one another "in the fear of God." The NRSV reads "out of reverence for Christ." In either version, the idea is that no believer is inherently superior to any other Christian. All of God's people should relate to each other in an attitude of humility and submissiveness.

1. VOLUNTARY SUBORDINATION. In thinking about personal relationships, the one between husbands and wives naturally comes to mind. It is to be characterized by mutual respect and submission to one another out of reverence for Jesus' example of humble submission. Paul did not imply that either the wife or the husband should be a doormat for the other. Rather, the apostle's emphasis was following the example of the Savior. Jesus submitted to the will of His Father, and believing spouses should do the same. Because Jesus is their Lord, they voluntarily subordinate their rights for the good of the other family members.

2. MUTUAL CARING. Paul said the husband should be willing to sacrifice everything for his wife. Also, he should make her welfare of foremost importance. Furthermore, the husband should care for his wife as he would care for his own body. The presence of these virtues in a marriage is honoring to the wife and pleasing to God.

3. NURTURING CHILDREN. Parents should be loving and even tempered with their children. They should not impose such harsh expectations on their children that they become frustrated and consequently loathe the authority of their parents. To bring up their children "in the nurture and admonition of the Lord" (6:4), parents should use a variety of appropriate methods. In this way, parents teach their children about God and encourage them to live uprightly.

4. HONORING PARENTS. Paul's instruction to children looks back on one of the Ten Commandments, which instructs young people to honor their parents. Obedience honors parents and brings blessings to children, including the promise of a long, enjoyable life.

■ **TOPIC:** Family Matters

■ **QUESTIONS:** 1. What is the motivation for us submitting to one another? 2. What did Paul mean when he said that wives should submit to their husbands? 3. In what sense is Jesus the head of the church? 4. What was

Paul illustrating by his comments regarding Jesus' love for the church? 5. How should we who are parents treat our children?

■ ILLUSTRATIONS:

Our Supreme Desire. When it comes to claiming our family responsibilities as believers, not understanding what they are isn't the problem. The Savior's commands are clear and straightforward. Our difficulties arise when, knowing what we are supposed to do, we lack the courage, faith, and will to act.

We have not genuinely understood the nature of spiritual warfare and how important basic spiritual training is for us. We have not invested sufficient time and energy in growing our faith, studying God's Word, praying, and being filled with the Spirit.

We can read Paul's guidelines for happy marriages and family life. Yet, for these guidelines to help us, we need to maintain a vital faith in the Savior. We can't abide by our responsibilities if we have a weak faith. Jesus must be Lord of everything in our lives. Our supreme desire must be to please Him.

What Kind of Commitment? *Public Perspective* is a journal produced by the Roper Center for Public Opinion Research at the University of Connecticut. In this publication, the center shows the results of careful polls carried out by George Gallup.

One survey indicated what Gallup called "gaps" in religious affairs by Americans. For instance, "the ethics gap" showed disturbing differences between what people said and what they did. Gallup also identified what he labeled "the knowledge gap." He pointed out a huge difference between what persons in this country claim to believe and their appalling lack of the most basic knowledge about their faith.

The third was "the church gap." Gallup found that Americans view their faith mostly as a matter between themselves and the Lord, not tied to or affected by any congregation or religious institution. They were not influenced by the church or any form of organized religion, and saw no need to be committed to any faith community.

Gallup summed up his report by suggesting that Americans want the fruits of faith but few of its obligations. Of the list of 19 social values tested in the polls, "following God's will" ranked low on the list, coming after "happiness, satisfaction, and a sense of accomplishment."

God's design for marriage and family is based on the mutual commitment of husbands and wives. In order for these divine institutions to survive and thrive, spouses need to remain unwavering in their love for each other. Toward this end, in Ephesians 5:31, Paul quoted Genesis 2:24, where oneness rests on the woman being taken out of man. Here, Paul argued for oneness based on common membership in the Savior's body (Eph. 5:30), and on the far higher sanction of the oneness of Christ and the church (vs. 32).

Daily Preparedness. Annie Sherwood Hawks was born in Hoosick, New York, which is a tiny upstate village. She was only 14 when she began writing poems for newspapers.

Annie became a member of the Hanson Place Baptist Church in Brooklyn, New York, when she married and moved there in 1859. Dr. Robert Lowry, the pastor, was the person responsible for Annie's career of hymn writing, and he wrote music for several of her hymns, including "I Need Thee Every Hour." Her hymns were published in various popular hymnbooks.

Annie wrote this hymn while completing her routine family tasks. The song expressed her great joy in the constant companionship of the Master. Annie was surprised at how well received the hymn was in churches. It was only when Annie experienced the loss of her husband that she realized how comforting the hymn could be in times of sorrow.

Like Annie Hawks, it is imperative that we develop strong spiritual lives during peaceful times. Then, when difficulties come, we are more likely to remain committed to our church and individual families. And in this way, we demonstrate our reverence for the Lord (see Eph. 5:21).

FOR YOUTH

■ **TOPIC:** It's Not about You!

■ **QUESTIONS:** 1. What does it mean for believers to submit to one another? 2. Why should wives submit to their husbands? 3. In what manner should husbands love their wives? 4. How much does mutual love and respect characterize your relationship with your family and friends? 5. Why should you choose to obey your parents?

■ **ILLUSTRATIONS:**

A Place for Everyone. Sociologists tell us we have yet to see the fruit of family breakdown in the United States. But anyone in touch with children and teenagers knows very well how bitter that fruit is in their lives. They begin to doubt their personal worth and self-identity, and question whether there remains any safe and secure place for them.

What we used to call the traditional family barely survives. Many adolescents live with single parents, or as part of "blended" families. They are trying to make some sense out of separation and divorce and where they fit in.

Against this stark backdrop, Paul's picture of marriage and family life reads like a fairy tale. We need to take a lot of time, in groups and one-on-one, to try to rebuild these shattered lives and dreams. Above all, we need to offer teenagers the good news that there is a place for them—and everyone—in the family of God.

We do not abandon God's Word just because so many today have violated His design for the family. Instead, we continue to love, serve, teach, and train. We do so, not only by words, but also by the integrity of our own commitment to the Savior and His will.

Bringing Beauty and Harmony. Fred Rogers, the beloved creator of the outstanding *Mister Rogers' Neighborhood,* and his great pianist, Johnny Costa, were asked to visit a Christmas party at Children's Hospital in Pittsburgh. The children were ecstatic. One little boy suffering from cerebral palsy wanted to sing a carol to honor the guests. The child's disease made his speech halting and uncertain.

When the little fellow began to sing "Silent Night," the sound was wavering. He not only had difficulty in framing the words for the carol but shifted key frequently. The first bar of the familiar carol was rendered so poorly that nearly everyone present involuntarily shuddered. Everyone, that is, except Fred Rogers and Johnny Costa.

Costa was at the portable organ when he began quietly to provide background music for the boy's attempted solo. As the youngster struggled on slowly and changed key frequently, Johnny wove lovely chords with each change in each line. The effect was such that the youngster's rendition took on a quality of rare beauty and harmony. Then others began to join the child. Costa seemed to anticipate where the next croak on the scale would be in the boy's singing, and worked each note into a performance of "Silent Night" in which everyone participated and enjoyed themselves.

In the same way, the Holy Spirit gives believers wisdom and helps them build unity within the church family and individual families. Husbands and wives are empowered to submit to one another mutually (see Eph. 5:21). And children receive divine grace to obey their parents (see 6:1). When the Spirit is allowed to lead, the faltering efforts of God's spiritual children are woven into a harmonious masterpiece of beauty for the Lord.

Becoming More Like the Original. A Greek writing tablet that predates the Christian era is on display in the British Museum. It is the classical equivalent of a child's notebook for learning the alphabet. The initial line has been written by the instructor. The student has traced the second as best he can by looking at the first. Every succeeding line, however, is a reproduction, not of the first line of writing, but of the last, so each successive line shows a wider divergence from the original than the one before.

As saved teens pursue holiness, especially in an attempt to fortify their biological and spiritual families, it is best for them to keep their eye on the original—the Lord Jesus—not on flawed substitutes. After all, He loved the church family so much that He gave His life for it (see Eph. 5:25). In turn, Christian adolescents honor the Savior by obeying their parents (see 6:1). When saved teens do so, they show that they are becoming more like the original, the Messiah.

PROCLAIMING CHRIST

BACKGROUND SCRIPTURE: Philippians 1:12-30
DEVOTIONAL READING: Psalm 119:169-176

Key Verse: What then? notwithstanding, every way, whether in pretence, or in truth, Christ is preached; and I therein do rejoice, yea, and will rejoice. Philippians 1:18.

KING JAMES VERSION

PHILIPPIANS 1:15 Some indeed preach Christ even of envy and strife; and some also of good will: 16 The one preach Christ of contention, not sincerely, supposing to add affliction to my bonds: 17 But the other of love, knowing that I am set for the defence of the gospel. 18 What then? notwithstanding, every way, whether in pretence, or in truth, Christ is preached; and I therein do rejoice, yea, and will rejoice. 19 For I know that this shall turn to my salvation through your prayer, and the supply of the Spirit of Jesus Christ, 20 According to my earnest expectation and my hope, that in nothing I shall be ashamed, but that with all boldness, as always, so now also Christ shall be magnified in my body, whether it be by life, or by death.

21 For to me to live is Christ, and to die is gain. 22 But if I live in the flesh, this is the fruit of my labour: yet what I shall choose I wot not. 23 For I am in a strait betwixt two, having a desire to depart, and to be with Christ; which is far better: 24 Nevertheless to abide in the flesh is more needful for you. 25 And having this confidence, I know that I shall abide and continue with you all for your furtherance and joy of faith; 26 That your rejoicing may be more abundant in Jesus Christ for me by my coming to you again.

NEW REVISED STANDARD VERSION

PHILIPPIANS 1:15 Some proclaim Christ from envy and rivalry, but others from goodwill. 16 These proclaim Christ out of love, knowing that I have been put here for the defense of the gospel; 17 the others proclaim Christ out of selfish ambition, not sincerely but intending to increase my suffering in my imprisonment. 18 What does it matter? Just this, that Christ is proclaimed in every way, whether out of false motives or true; and in that I rejoice.

Yes, and I will continue to rejoice, 19 for I know that through your prayers and the help of the Spirit of Jesus Christ this will turn out for my deliverance. 20 It is my eager expectation and hope that I will not be put to shame in any way, but that by my speaking with all boldness, Christ will be exalted now as always in my body, whether by life or by death. 21 For to me, living is Christ and dying is gain. 22 If I am to live in the flesh, that means fruitful labor for me; and I do not know which I prefer. 23 I am hard pressed between the two: my desire is to depart and be with Christ, for that is far better; 24 but to remain in the flesh is more necessary for you. 25 Since I am convinced of this, I know that I will remain and continue with all of you for your progress and joy in faith, 26 so that I may share abundantly in your boasting in Christ Jesus when I come to you again.

6

153

HOME BIBLE READINGS

BACKGROUND

The Philippian believers knew that Paul was awaiting his trial before Caesar. It was possible that he could be sentenced either to death or to a long, harsh imprisonment for sedition against Rome. His friends in Philippi probably prayed fervently that God would comfort and deliver him from his unpleasant and precarious situation. Aware of their concern for his welfare and safety, the apostle wanted to assure them in this letter that God was not only caring for him but also bringing unexpected and marvelous fruit to his ongoing ministry (Phil. 1:12).

Paul was especially excited about the Lord's work among the emperor's guards, for everyone there knew that the apostle was under arrest because of his courageous defense of the Gospel. Some of them had received the Son as their Lord and Savior. It was clear to everyone that the apostle was not under house arrest because he had violated a civil law or because he was a political agitator. The sentries who were responsible for guarding Paul probably observed how he lived out his faith in the Messiah. Some may have listened to the apostle's teachings about the Savior and shared what they learned with other palace guards, noting that Paul's characteristics were nothing like those of most other criminals they guarded. Moreover, the Gospel was advanced not only among these guards but to many other people as well (vs. 13).

NOTES ON THE PRINTED TEXT

Paul attributed the proclamation of the Gospel by other Christians in Rome to the apostle's "bonds in Christ" (Phil. 1:13). Whether Paul was describing an actual condition in which he was chained to a guard or was referring to his imprisonment and sufferings in general is not clear. In any case, he was elated that his example encouraged other Christians to be brave and bold in declaring the Word of God (vs. 14). There was the possibility that all of Paul's believing readers might also come under the iron fist of the Roman authorities. If the Lord could still bring fabulous fruit to the apostle's ministry while he was under house arrest, they too could be fruitful for the Lord whether in or out of prison.

Although believers were courageously proclaiming the Gospel in Rome, Paul was not ignorant of the rationale behind their preaching and teaching. Some were doing it for the right reasons, which he praised, but others were doing it for the wrong reasons. They were not preaching the Savior to nonbelievers out of "good will" (vs. 15), but out of "envy and strife." Yet why would believers be impelled in these ungodly ways? They were certainly members of the Christian community. Most of these were probably jealous of the prestige Paul had earned within the Christian community and competed for the same authority he held among them.

Unlike Paul's rivals, his friends in Rome preached the Good News about the Messiah with unimpeachable motives. Their evangelism sprang from the love they had in the Savior—a love that empowered them to tell nonbelievers about the compassion Jesus has for the lost. In addition, they understood why Paul was under house arrest—not because he was an outlaw, but because he stood up for the Gospel of Christ. Knowing this also instilled in these believers the courage to boldly stand up for the Lord Jesus as well (vs. 16).

Evidently, Paul's rivals were not content just to operate apart from the apostle's ministry. They were also motivated by the desire to intensify his dilemma while he was under Roman custody. They may have figured that their preaching would place Paul into further jeopardy with the civil authorities, perhaps even contributing to his conviction. With the apostle out of the way, they could enhance their standing within the Christian movement in Rome. Thus it was clear to Paul that these preachers were insincere in proclaiming the Gospel and that selfish ambition was their underlying motive (vs. 17).

Despite the malevolent intentions of the apostle's rivals, he didn't care about their ill will toward him as long as the Gospel was preached. If nonbelievers were hearing the Good News about Jesus Christ and receiving Him as their Lord and Savior, that was all that counted to Paul. He didn't care what happened to him as long as people were coming into the kingdom. Therefore, he was not concerned about the motives behind the preaching of selfish competitors. The apostle only wanted to be sure that people were receiving the right message about the Savior. Evidently they were, for Paul was overjoyed at knowing that Christians were advancing the Gospel even within the capital of the Roman Empire (vs. 18).

Paul was confident that he was securely in God's hands. The apostle believed that whatever befell him would bring glory and honor to the Father because He was in control of Paul's life and the circumstances that affected his existence. Therefore, though the apostle was under house arrest in Rome, he could rejoice and keep on rejoicing, for the Lord was with him and sustaining him. Also, Paul knew that his Philippian friends were praying for him. A unique intimacy had developed between the apostle and the Christians in Philippi, and Paul naturally cherished their deep concern for him.

What is more, the apostle coveted the prayers of other Christians, for he appreciated the distinctive power that believers' prayers had in enlisting God's aid (vs. 19). Paul likewise valued the strengthening he received from the Spirit of Christ, which supplied him with the courage, determination, and hope to persevere joyfully under his current circumstances. Most certainly the apostle depended on the Lord's Spirit to deliver him from any situation that brought hardship to him. Whatever the Roman authorities decided to do with Paul, God Himself would vindicate the apostle.

As Paul awaited his trial, his major concern was not whether the Father would save his life, but whether the apostle would present himself in such a way that the Son would be exalted. In fact, Paul was both eager and hoping to bring glory and not shame to the Lord. The Greek noun rendered "earnest expectation" (vs. 20) provides a vivid picture of one who cranes his or her neck to catch a glimpse of what lies ahead. The apostle was letting his readers know that, while ignoring all other interests, he keenly anticipated honoring the Lord during his trial.

Paul realized that the verdict could mean life or death for him physically. That is why he referred to "my body" in verse 20. Throughout the long ministry in which he preached the Gospel, whether to friendly crowds or hostile ones, the apostle always sought to exalt the Messiah in his body. Now, whether the Romans released or executed Paul, he desired above all else that his Lord still be exalted in him. In a few words the apostle beautifully summed up the no-lose situation of belonging to Jesus: "For to me to live is Christ, and to die is gain" (vs. 21). This immortal affirmation expresses a believer's faith and hope. To Paul the gain meant much more than the eternal benefit of heaven. The profit was that the Gospel of Christ would be further advanced if the apostle was martyred for his faith and hope in the Son.

Paul was confident that he would continue to be fruitful in his ministry if the Romans did not execute him. In fact, even if he was forced to serve more time in prison, he would continue to proclaim the Gospel. He remained certain that nonbelievers would turn to faith in the Messiah because of the apostle's preaching. Indeed, due to Paul's strategic position in Rome, he would have additional opportunities to be God's instrument in bringing more people into the kingdom (vs. 22).

Nonetheless, to be with the Son in heaven was also appealing to the apostle. In fact, if he were given a choice to continue to minister God's Word or be in the presence of Christ, Paul confessed that the decision would be difficult to make. Yet he stated that he would choose to be with the Savior, for the apostle would have a much deeper intimacy with Jesus in heaven, though Paul already enjoyed a close relationship with the Son here on earth (vs. 23). Despite the apostle's own inclination to depart, he believed it was more important for him to remain. In fact, his whole reason for staying was for the sake of tending to other people's spiritual welfare, specifically for the pastoral care of his friends in the church at Philippi (vs. 24).

With bold confidence, Paul told the Philippians that he was certain he would live in order to fulfill his duties in bringing them to spiritual maturity. Perhaps the great responsibility he had in caring for so many young believers throughout the Mediterranean world convinced him that it was too soon for him to die. Evidently, the

Lord gave the apostle a premonition or an assurance that he would not be executed. Maybe word was passed to him that the Roman authorities looking at his case were favorable to him. Whatever the reason, Paul was now unmistakably upbeat (vs. 25).

Moreover, the apostle thought that the Romans would not only spare his life but also give him his freedom, for he promised the Philippians that he would visit with them once again (vs. 26). We do not know whether this joyous meeting ever occurred. If it did, the Philippian Christians would have been thrilled to see their friend and mentor. They would have listened carefully to his stirring account of how the Lord was glorified through the apostle's harrowing yet rewarding experiences in Rome.

SUGGESTIONS TO TEACHERS

We may look at our lives and see nothing but clutter and chaos, and conclude that there is no evidence of a pattern or purpose at all. We may only see how disorganized we are, how boring our existence is, or how chaotic our activities have become. Jesus, on the other hand, wants to beautify and arrange each of our lives according to His purposes.

1. DEALING WITH THE IMPURE MOTIVES OF OTHERS. Paul noted that one group of believers spread the Gospel for selfish reasons, like politicians seeking to advance their own causes. The apostle, however, was not dispirited by this circumstance, for the Savior gave to Paul's life meaning and purpose. Have your students consider how the apostle's attitude encouraged others to proclaim the Savior to their friends and neighbors.

2. FACING DEATH WITH COURAGE. Paul could be courageous about the possibility of martyrdom because he knew that death would be a "gain" (Phil. 1:21). Expressed differently, the prospect of execution meant that he would be with the Savior. In turn, the apostle would experience unending joy in the presence of the Lord. Encourage the members of your class to look at their life circumstances in the way Paul regarded his. How might doing so transform their attitude toward living?

3. SERVING OTHERS. While the prospect of being with the Redeemer appealed to Paul, he also desired to go on serving churches, such as the one at Philippi. Let the adult learners know that the apostle recognized the benefits of—as well as the need for—continuing ministry to the congregations he had founded. If the class members were faced with this option, how willing would they be to undertake it for the glory of the Savior and the betterment of His followers?

4. BEING TRANSFORMED BY JESUS' GLORY. Jesus has the wisdom, knowledge, and power to turn our dark hallways, dust-filled corners, and cluttered rooms into something bright, clean, and inviting. Paul saw this pattern and purpose even as he was imprisoned in Rome. He discovered, and your students can too, that the darkest prisons can become beautiful when they are decorated with Jesus' glory.

■ **TOPIC:** Motives and Messages

■ **QUESTIONS:** 1. What were some of the impure motives some had for proclaiming the Gospel? 2. How was it possible for Paul to continue to rejoice while under house arrest in Rome? 3. What did Paul recognize as the advantage to being set free at his trial? 4. How strongly do you believe that God is involved in your current circumstances? 5. Why is it important for us, as Jesus' disciples, to remain calm when we are harassed for our faith in Christ?

■ **ILLUSTRATIONS:**

Living Is Christ. One day a Christian writer asked a graduate student what was his motive for living. The student said he wanted to finish school and get a good job. "Then what?" the writer asked. Well, the student said he would get married and raise a family. "Then what?" the writer asked a second time. The student said he would like to have a successful career and make enough money to take care of his family and retire comfortably.

"Then what?" the writer asked a third time. "What do you mean?" the student asked, bewildered. The writer challenged the student. "Is that all there is to life? And what about the life to come after you die? Then what?" Like many people, the student had never thought about a higher purpose in life, or about his eternal future.

Christians, too, must check their reasons for living, since it is easy for them to follow the world's values and goals. If we really believe the message that "to live is Christ" (Phil. 1:21), we will devote ourselves to more than successful careers, money, and retirement. Jesus will determine our interests and how we spend our time, energy, and money.

Refusing to Give Up. A woman asked a pastor to visit her father in the hospital. He had suffered a heart attack after a flood had wiped out his business.

The woman thought her father would be open to spiritual counsel and turn to Jesus in faith. Perhaps the former business owner would take the flood as God's warning for him to repent. Sadly, however, the older man was angry with God for the flood. If it was God's final warning, the heart attack victim paid no attention to the Lord.

Paul never allowed this sort of response to undermine his boldness in sharing Jesus with the unsaved. Regardless of where the apostle ministered—whether in the city of Philippi or chained to a guard under house arrest in Rome—he wanted to be sure that everyone he encountered was saved.

When the members of your class adopt this way of thinking, they will be better able to overcome impediments they encounter in witnessing for Jesus. He will enable them to work together to encourage even the most hard-hearted of unbelievers to trust in Him for salvation. Even when some refuse, the class members can remain resolute in proclaiming the Gospel to others.

A Thankful Heart. While Paul confidently anticipated his release from Roman imprisonment, he acknowledged that it might be God's will for him to die in Rome. The apostle did not avoid that prospect, but faced it realistically with "earnest expectation" (Phil. 1:20). For Paul, the prime issue was not whether he lived or died, but honoring the Savior.

In July 1941, the Nazis selected nine prisoners at Auschwitz to starve to death as punishment for the escape of an inmate. One of the nine randomly chosen was a Polish citizen who had a wife and two sons. Before the nine were placed in starvation bunkers, a Franciscan monk named Maximilian Kolbe volunteered to take the place of Franciszek Gajowniczek.

Kolbe survived more than 14 days without food or any water. In August 1941, the Nazis decided to end his life with a lethal injection. Gajowniczek spent five years, five months, and nine days in Auschwitz. Prisoner number 5659 was tattooed on his left forearm. Kolbe's personal sacrifice was pivotal in Gajowniczek making it through the horror of Auschwitz.

After Gajowniczek was freed from the death camp, he determined to live the rest of his life for the betterment of others. In this way, he hoped to bring some good out of the tragic death of Kolbe. Gajowniczek traveled extensively in Europe and the United States, telling his story and laying church cornerstones in memory of his benefactor.

Gajowniczek died on March 13, 1995, at the age of 94. He had spent 50 years witnessing to the courage and love of the monk who died a torturous death in his place. Should not we Christians thankfully tell of our Savior's self-sacrifice on our behalf?

FOR YOUTH

■ TOPIC: Truth Is Truth

■ QUESTIONS: 1. Why were some believers motivated by love to tell others about Jesus? 2. What basis did Paul have for anticipating that he might be set free from his Roman imprisonment? 3. Where do you think Paul found the courage to remain bold in telling others about the Savior? 4. What can you do to further develop a single-minded purpose of living for Jesus? 5. How might you encourage other believers to find joy and purpose in their circumstances?

■ ILLUSTRATIONS:

Hope during Hardship. During a high school wrestling match, Caleb "the underdog" appeared on the verge of losing. The state champion was about to pin him. But suddenly, in what seemed like a miracle, Caleb threw off his opponent and defeated him. How? Because Caleb never gave up hope in the midst of hardship.

Wrestling is a picture of the Christian life. Paul reminded his readers of the truth that they wrestled with powerful spiritual opponents. He himself demonstrated what it was like. The apostle never quit, despite physical beatings, abuse, and imprisonment. Rather than succumb to defeat and despair, he came up rejoicing. He refused to be pinned.

The same spiritual principles can work for saved teens. As they pray for one another and the Holy Spirit helps them, eternal good can come out of their most difficult moments (see Phil. 1:19).

Renewing Our Trust. In *Basic Principles of Biblical Counseling*, Larry Crabb writes that all people have two fundamental needs: significance (*I do matter!*) and security (*I need someone to trust*). Society threatens each person's significance by reducing his or her identity from a name to a number, a tiny pebble on the information highway of computer technology.

Because our world is in a state of constant flux, change also threatens our security. Depending on human love or financial riches for security is often like putting our weight on a broken ladder. In this confused world, renewing our trust in the Lord can become the basis for our overcoming all threats (whether real or imagined) to our significance and security.

As we learn from Paul's statement in Philippians 1:21, we find our significance in life through faith in the Savior. And because He is the object of our trust, we need not feel alarmed by the circumstances that overtake us. Moreover, our testimony of trust in the Savior will tell people, "You can depend on the Lord. He never changes!"

Competing Loyalties. Nine-year-old Jason's bike broke. Because it could not be repaired, he asked his stepfather to buy him a new one. Several days later, at the bike shop, Jason looked over the rows of shiny new bikes and made his selection. When he showed it to his stepfather, he was told that he was in the wrong section and that he did not need a new bike. A used one would be fine.

When Jason protested, his stepfather took him outside and showed him the family car, which was purchased a few months earlier. "Do you know what year's model this is?" his stepfather asked. Jason learned that even though his parents could have bought a new car, they chose not to, so that some of their income could be used in charitable ways. Their loyalty was in helping others, not in merely gratifying their own desires. Jason's stepfather was trying to teach him the same lesson about the choices he made.

Like Jason and his family, you need to decide where you want your loyalties to be. Will they reside with you, or will you offer your loyalty to Jesus and His followers? Paul gave us the pattern to follow when he made serving the Lord and others his highest priority (see Phil. 1:20). Likewise, we exalt the Savior by living in fellowship with Him and giving Him first place in whatever we decide to do.

JESUS' HUMILITY AND EXALTATION

BACKGROUND SCRIPTURE: Philippians 2:1-13
DEVOTIONAL READING: James 3:13-18

Key Verse: Let this mind be in you, which
was also in Christ Jesus. Philippians 2:5.

KING JAMES VERSION

PHILIPPIANS 2:5 Let this mind be in you, which was also in Christ Jesus: 6 Who, being in the form of God, thought it not robbery to be equal with God: 7 But made himself of no reputation, and took upon him the form of a servant, and was made in the likeness of men: 8 And being found in fashion as a man, he humbled himself, and became obedient unto death, even the death of the cross. 9 Wherefore God also hath highly exalted him, and given him a name which is above every name: 10 That at the name of Jesus every knee should bow, of things in heaven, and things in earth, and things under the earth; 11 And that every tongue should confess that Jesus Christ is Lord, to the glory of God the Father.

NEW REVISED STANDARD VERSION

PHILIPPIANS 2:5 Let the same mind be in you that was in Christ Jesus,
  6 who, though he was in the form of God,
    did not regard equality with God
    as something to be exploited,
  7 but emptied himself,
    taking the form of a slave,
    being born in human likeness.
And being found in human form,
  8 he humbled himself
    and became obedient to the point of death—
    even death on a cross.
  9 Therefore God also highly exalted him
    and gave him the name
    that is above every name,
  10 so that at the name of Jesus
    every knee should bend,
    in heaven and on earth and under the earth,
  11 and every tongue should confess
    that Jesus Christ is Lord,
    to the glory of God the Father.

7

BACKGROUND

Philippians 2:3 urges believers to be characterized by "lowliness of mind," in which they "esteem" each other better than themselves. In ancient times, the Greeks disdained the quality of humility Paul described, for they regarded it as shameful. It was something to be avoided and overcome with positive thoughts and actions. Believers, however, operated differently. God wanted them to recognize their true sinful condition and need for His grace. This is in keeping with the biblical concept of humility, which means to think rightly about one's position in life. Here we see that humility is a continual appreciation of our need for the Savior and of our need to always depend on Him. This was the opposite of the Greek concept of freedom, which called for a person to not be subject to anyone or anything, including God.

For the Son, "lowliness of mind" meant a recognition of His role as a servant in becoming human. Since He was sinless, recognition of His true condition did not involve the presence of iniquity. He did, however, demonstrate the need to depend daily on the Father for strength. In light of what has been said, how can we demonstrate such Christlike humility? Paul advised that believers should look to the interests of other Christians, not just address their own concerns (vs. 4). Without ignoring what is important to us, we can daily show others that we value and appreciate what is important to them.

NOTES ON THE PRINTED TEXT

In Philippians 2:1-4, Paul emphasized the importance of his readers displaying humility toward one another. In this regard, the supreme example of humility was the attitude that Jesus had when He rescued us from sin. If we truly are to be in the Messiah, then we should also have this attitude of loving humility in relationship with others and self-sacrificing obedience to God. This was the attitude that Paul wanted the Philippians to embrace (vs. 5).

In verse 6, we discover that prior to the Son's incarnation, He eternally existed as God with the Father and the Spirit. One of the key doctrines of the Christian faith is that Jesus is, always was, and always will be God. In fact, Paul declared in Colossians

2:9 that in the Lord Jesus all the fullness of the Godhead dwelled in bodily form. Philippians 2:6 reveals that even though Jesus is God, He decided not to use His privileges as God to seize His share of divine glory and honor. Instead, He chose the path of lowly obedience.

The Son acted upon His decision to be obedient to the Father by emptying Himself. This is the literal meaning of the Greek phrase that the KJV translates as "made himself of no reputation" (vs. 7). In this selfless act, Jesus did not give up His divinity, but laid aside His kingly privileges as God to become a human being. He also did not choose to be an earthly monarch, a wealthy merchant, a powerful military leader, an idolized athlete or entertainer, or even a renowned philosopher. Jesus became a servant. Once Jesus became fully human through His incarnation, people who knew Him could see that He possessed the full nature of a human being—except that He was without sin. He hungered as any human would. He felt the discomfort of hot and cold weather as any person would. He became tired after a long walk in the same way His fellow travelers became exhausted.

In verse 7, Paul described three steps in Jesus' mission. He "made himself of no reputation"; He "took upon him the form of a servant"; and He was born "in the likeness of men." From birth to death, Jesus lived in humility. He was born in a stable. His parents were refugees in Egypt. Jesus grew up in obedience to His parents. He worked at a humble trade, that is, as a carpenter. Jesus cried with those who grieved. He washed the feet of His disciples. Paul summarized the Messiah's self-emptying this way: "Though he was rich, yet for your sakes he became poor, that ye through his poverty might be rich" (2 Cor. 8:9). Because of Jesus' sinlessness, however, He could choose whether to die. All individuals are subject to physical death unless the Father decrees differently. But the Son could conceivably have rejected this final conclusion to His earthly life. Jesus, however, chose to die—not to just leave this life peacefully like Enoch, but to perish on the cross in anguish and humiliation so that we might live in renewed and eternal communion with the Father (Phil. 2:8).

The Son lived completely obedient to His Father. This included the Son voluntarily permitting Himself to die like a common criminal for our sins. The enormous pain of Jesus' humiliation was described by the Old Testament prophets, the psalmists, and the writers of the four Gospels. To the Jews of Jesus' day, crucifixion was the epitome of shame. This gruesome form of execution showed that the victim was languishing in disgrace outside the blessing of God's covenant (see Deut. 21:23; Gal. 3:13). To the Romans, crucifixion was repulsive and reserved for foreigners and slaves. Believers today tend to know little, if anything, about this kind of humiliation. In Philippians, Paul did not dwell on the details of Jesus' unjust trials, and the way He was mocked, beaten, and nailed to the cross. Rather, the apostle emphasized the stigma of being executed in this way. His provision of this key information enables us to grasp the horror connected with Jesus' atoning sacrifice.

Admittedly, when Jesus' executioners dragged Him to the cross, He could have called down legions of angels (see Matt. 26:53). Yet Jesus did not do this. Against the backdrop of His humility, how do we attain the high ambition Paul had for Christ's spiritual body, the church? One way is for us to lay aside our personal rights for the sake of ministering to others. Another way is for us to practice looking at our lives and circumstances—as well as the lives of our fellow believers—from the perspective of Jesus. We do this because we are one through faith in the Messiah. Here we discover that Jesus is not an abstract philosophical example. Instead, He is a living person who, through the Holy Spirit, dwells in us and empowers us to live according to this high standard. Consequently, it is possible for believers to foster the same humble disposition modeled by the Savior. We look to Him for our inspiration and example. In short, genuine humility comes from allowing the fullness of the Son to be expressed in our daily lives.

Paul could not end his extended illustration with the Messiah on the cross. The place of honor that Jesus willingly forsook was given back to Him with the added glory of His triumph over sin and death. In response to the Son's humility and obedience, the Father supremely exalted Jesus to a place where His triumph will eventually be recognized by all living creatures (Phil. 2:9). The apostle emphatically tells us that every person who has ever lived will someday recognize the Son for who He is, namely, the supreme Lord revealed in the Old Testament as Yahweh (see Acts 2:33-36). The "name of Jesus" (Phil. 2:10) signifies the majestic office or position the Father bestowed on the Son, not His proper name. By bowing their knees, every human being and angel will acknowledge Jesus' deity and sovereignty. Also, everyone will confess that Jesus is Lord—some with joyful faith, others with hopeless regret and anguish (vs. 11). Centuries earlier, the prophet Isaiah had announced the words of the Messiah: "Unto me every knee shall bow, every tongue shall swear" (Isa. 45:23; see Rom. 14:11; Rev. 5:13). Philippians 2:6-11 affirms that this universal acknowledgment of Jesus' lordship will ultimately come to pass.

Immediately following Paul's description of the supreme humility and obedience of Jesus' servanthood, the apostle charged his friends in Philippi to be as obedient as the Messiah was. When Paul labored among them, they obeyed his instructions. Moreover, they had followed the apostle's teachings after he had left. Now Paul told them to maintain their diligence in submitting themselves to God's Word. This was not so that they might earn their salvation, but that they would express their salvation in such a way that the spiritual health of their Christian community would grow in unity. The apostle characterized how he expected them to act by adding the phrase "with fear and trembling" (vs. 12). He was not saying they should comply strictly out of fear of what God would do to them if they weren't obedient, but that they should strive to be Christlike while having utmost reverence for the Lord. In fact, it is only God who gives us the desire and power necessary to do His will (vs. 13).

Our great comfort in the Christian life is that God continually works His good and perfect will in us. We always live in tension between laboring for God and His kingdom as faithfully and diligently as we can, and allowing God to inspire and train us to do what He desires. We are not alone in the spiritual battle. After all, the Lord is present in our lives to build our confidence and give us the hope we need to fulfill His purposes for us and for His church. This is why we must be completely dependent upon God, especially if we are to be faithful to Paul's charge. While salvation is entirely a work of God and a free gift of His grace, it does require a response of obedient faith on our part. Also, while God deserves all the glory for our deliverance from sin, we are not totally passive in how the inner change affects our daily activities. Paul set a high standard for Christian humility, love, and unity. And the apostle knew that the Lord works in us, His spiritual children, to reach that standard successfully.

SUGGESTIONS TO TEACHERS

In the world, aggression is considered a strength, while humility connotes weakness. Occasionally, a servant—such as a devoted minister of the Gospel—is honored. But for every one of these individuals, there are hundreds of arrogant athletes, politicians, actors, and others who count ego and pride as virtues. Few among them would be willing to tie on the apron of a servant (so to speak).

1. CHOOSING TO BE DIFFERENT. Being clothed with the humility of Christ means seeing ourselves as God sees us and respecting others by loving them unconditionally. Jesus did far more for us by leaving the glories of heaven to become a human being and eventually dying on the cross for our sins. Out of gratitude for Him, we should treat one another with kindness, sensitivity, and compassion.

2. TAKING THE LEAD TO BE DIFFERENT. Christian leaders are the role models for other believers. First, they must lead by example, as our Lord did. He did not call believers to do anything He Himself had not done or was not willing to do. He lived His life as a servant, died for the unrighteous, and loves the unlovely without limits.

3. BEING OTHERS FOCUSED. In this way of thinking and acting, Christian leaders become role models of humility by submitting to Jesus, rather than advocating a personal agenda. These leaders also acknowledge the need for resources beyond themselves. Any church leader's burden will be lightened by casting his or her cares on the Lord.

4. AFFIRMING THE VALUE OF OTHERS. A godly leader respects every person in the congregation. If that happens, each member in turn will see others as people of value who are appreciated for what they contribute to the church. The world's theme song is "I Did It My Way!" In contrast, every member of the body of Christ should say, "I will do this the Lord's way, for the benefit of others."

■ **TOPIC:** Attitude Counts

■ **QUESTIONS:** 1. What effects does Jesus' humiliation have on the Christian's outlook on life? On the life of the church? 2. Why is it hard to live by the principle that exaltation follows humiliation? 3. Which is easier—to be humble before God or before other people? 4. How do we develop humility and dispose of selfish ambition? 5. How might your church's business meetings be different if Philippians 2:6-11 was read thoughtfully before the meeting started?

■ **ILLUSTRATIONS:**

Genuine Humility. Paul wanted the believers in the Philippian church to radically change their attitude. The apostle did not call for a conference on management. Instead, he called for a fresh look at the suffering Savior. Until His followers took Him seriously, they would not discover genuine and joyful humility.

A Christian pastor said, "A person who profoundly changed my life was not a preacher or the leader of a big organization. She was a cheerful office worker at the local bus company. She never married. She used her home and her slim resources to develop Christian maturity among college students. Many of them—including myself—went into the ministry at home and abroad."

Few of us recognize the power of humble, exuberant Christian service. But when the books are revealed, we may be surprised to learn that the major influences in God's kingdom come from believers whose attitude was unselfish and compassionate. Our own lives and our churches are immeasurably enriched when we follow the mind of Christ.

The Answer Is on the Ceiling. In our relationships with others, the Father wants us to imitate His Son's humility (see Phil. 2:5). When we obediently respond to God's Word, the Lord works through us, giving us the will and the energy to obey Him (see vs. 13). God wants us to be active in serving Him, and to do so in a way that is thoughtful and discerning. This includes humbly recognizing that we cannot do everything that we know needs to be done in our congregation.

A dedicated church member named Stacy was intently looking at the ceiling in her hospital room when her pastor walked in. "Finding any answers up there, Stacy?" he asked jokingly. "In a strange way, I am," Stacy said. "You see that ceiling?" They both looked up. "It does just what a ceiling is supposed to do. It doesn't try to be the door, the window, or the floor."

Stacy continued, "Pastor, I thought being a sweet, humble Christian meant never saying 'no' to anybody for anything. And since I've retired, I've worked harder around the church and in the community than I did on my job." To this the pastor nodded in agreement.

Then Stacy admitted, "But I'm in the hospital because of a stomach ulcer. I've been trying to be everything to everybody. Yet what I really need to do is find my specific purpose in life and do that. Just that. And say 'no' to everything else."

Extending a Humble Helping Hand. It was the most cluttered that David's 300-acre farm had ever looked. Fifteen combines, 24 grain trucks, and about 50 friends had converged on his land. By the end of the day, 60,000 bushels of corn would be harvested, then transported to a nearby grain elevator.

The oil company David had used for years had provided the fuel. His local bank had provided a catered lunch. Family and friends had provided the labor—and kind words of remembrance. This is how the farm community in a Midwest town mourned the unexpected death of one of its own. For a day, everyone's usual priorities had been shelved. David's widow had needed a humble helping hand—in fact, many hands!

When was the last time any of us dropped everything to help someone for a day? Right now, is there someone who needs us to put his or her needs ahead of our own? When we do so, we heed what Paul urged in Philippians 2:5, namely, to imitate Jesus' self-sacrificing humility in our relationships with others.

<table>
<tr><td>

FOR YOUTH

</td><td>

■ **TOPIC:** Similar Minds

■ **QUESTIONS:** 1. How was it possible for Jesus, who is fully God, to become fully human? 2. Why did the Father highly exalt the Son?

</td></tr>
</table>

3. Why is it often challenging for us, as believers, to model the humble attitude of the Lord Jesus? 4. What place does Christlike humility have in your daily relationships? 5. How is it possible for us, as Jesus' followers, to be humble without becoming a human doormat?

■ **ILLUSTRATIONS:**

What Me, Serve? Imagine trying to herd a barn full of stray cats. No matter how hard we strive, these independent-minded animals will not be corralled. It often seems just as impossible to get adolescent church members to adopt a similar mind-set when it comes to serving one another in their congregation.

Paul reminded us in Philippians 2:5-11 that the Lord Jesus and His priorities are supposed to be number one in the lives of believers and in the church. This remains true regardless of whether we are ministers, deacons, trustees, Sunday school teachers, or other church officers. This knowledge calls for humble servanthood in Jesus' name.

Often, however, we are like the woman in a certain congregation who was asked to prepare a snack for her children and others in her church youth group for one evening. She retorted in a scalding tone, "You mean you are asking me to come up to the church and do the work of a servant?" Exactly!

Keeping the Balance. *The Apprentice* is a nighttime television series in which a diverse group of candidates—many of them young, talented, and ambitious—pit their wits and skills against one another to win the prize of being hired by the Trump Organization and earning a hefty six-figure salary. During one season, those with "book smarts" go up against those with "street smarts." Then during another season, it's song and movie entertainers pitted against sports legends. Regardless of the venue, the competitive atmosphere remains the same. And in the end, it's not about being nice or polite. It's about remaining on top at any cost.

If believers aren't careful, they can find themselves getting sucked into this cut-throat way of living in which ambition and conceit trample sensitivity and kindness. On the one hand, the Lord does not call His people to be human doormats. On the other hand, the humble example of Jesus reminds us that considering the needs of others is just as important as ensuring our own desires are satisfied (see Phil. 2:5-11).

Setting Aside Privileges. Jim, a Christian who started out his career as a sports reporter, thoroughly enjoyed the privileges that came with the job—passes to sports events, access to players, and things like that. Later on, he had to make a big career decision.

Should Jim stay in the newspaper business, or should he enter Christian service? If he chose the latter, he knew he was saying good-bye to his last free pass. Nevertheless, Jim set aside those privileges and says, "I have never regretted the decision. God more than made up for any passes I relinquished. He gave me the most satisfying work I could do in editing, writing, teaching, and preaching."

Sometimes it's hard to choose what we know to be God's will. Sometimes we're afraid God will cheat us out of something good. Do you ever consider what Jesus thought when the Father asked Him to set aside His privileges in heaven, to come to earth and take on human limitations, and to die a criminal's death for our sins (see Phil. 2:6-8)? The Son's humiliation and exaltation prove that the Father will never let us down. We can trust Him completely to do the very best for us.

GAINING IN JESUS CHRIST

BACKGROUND SCRIPTURE: Philippians 3:1-11
DEVOTIONAL READING: Matthew 13:44-46

Key Verse: What things were gain to me, those
I counted loss for Christ. Philippians 3:7.

KING JAMES VERSION

PHILIPPIANS 3:7 But what things were gain to me, those I counted loss for Christ. 8 Yea doubtless, and I count all things but loss for the excellency of the knowledge of Christ Jesus my Lord: for whom I have suffered the loss of all things, and do count them but dung, that I may win Christ,

9 And be found in him, not having mine own righteousness, which is of the law, but that which is through the faith of Christ, the righteousness which is of God by faith: 10 That I may know him, and the power of his resurrection, and the fellowship of his sufferings, being made conformable unto his death; 11 If by any means I might attain unto the resurrection of the dead.

NEW REVISED STANDARD VERSION

PHILIPPIANS 3:7 Yet whatever gains I had, these I have come to regard as loss because of Christ. 8 More than that, I regard everything as loss because of the surpassing value of knowing Christ Jesus my Lord. For his sake I have suffered the loss of all things, and I regard them as rubbish, in order that I may gain Christ 9 and be found in him, not having a righteousness of my own that comes from the law, but one that comes through faith in Christ, the righteousness from God based on faith. 10 I want to know Christ and the power of his resurrection and the sharing of his sufferings by becoming like him in his death, 11 if somehow I may attain the resurrection from the dead.

Monday, January 14	Matthew 18:10-14	*The Value of Each One*
Tuesday, January 15	Matthew 10:26-30	*You Are of More Value*
Wednesday, January 16	Romans 2:17-29	*The Value of the Spiritual*
Thursday, January 17	Matthew 13:44-53	*The Value of the Kingdom*
Friday, January 18	Luke 9:23-27	*The True Value in Following Jesus*
Saturday, January 19	Philippians 3:1-6	*No Value in Earthly Achievements*
Sunday, January 20	Philippians 3:7-11	*The Surpassing Value of Knowing Christ*

BACKGROUND

Throughout Paul's evangelistic ministry, he encountered religious legalists who challenged his apostolic authority and claimed that their accomplishments were more impressive anything than he had done. In response, Paul indicated that he had plenty of reasons to put confidence in his personal ancestry and professional achievements, especially based on the legalist's standard of righteousness. As a matter of fact, no one was a more zealous defender of the Jewish laws and customs than had been the apostle.

Moreover, whatever credentials the legalists claimed they had, Paul contended that he was far more qualified than any of them to speak as a Jew on matters of observing the Torah (Phil. 3:4). For instance, Paul noted that he was circumcised on the eighth day after his birth (v. 5). The implication is that his parents were devout Jews, who faithfully followed the Mosaic laws (see Gen. 17:12; 21:4; Lev. 12:3) and trained their son in his religious duties from the time he was an infant. How many of the apostle's detractors could say the same?

Next, Paul stressed his birthright as a Jew. Not only was he a member of God's chosen people by birth (see Rom. 9:3-4; 11:1), but he was also from the tribe of Benjamin. Jacob was the son of Isaac and the grandson of Abraham, and together these three men were the patriarchs of the nation of Israel. Jacob had twelve sons, two by his beloved wife Rachel. The older was Joseph, and the younger was Benjamin (see Gen. 35:18, 24; 46:19; 1 Chron. 1:28; 2:1–2; Matt. 1:2; Luke 3:33–34). One of the 12 tribes of Israel was descended from Benjamin. Israel's first king was Saul, a Benjamite (see 1 Sam. 9:1-2; 10:20-21; Acts 13:21). When Israel divided into the northern kingdom of Israel and the southern kingdom of Judah, the tribe of Benjamin remained loyal to the tribe of Judah (see 1 Kings 12:20-24). Furthermore, Jerusalem and the temple in the holy city were located within the district of Benjamin (see Josh. 18:15-16).

Paul's was a "Hebrew of the Hebrews" (Phil. 3:5). This meant, in part, that he was the Hebrew son of Hebrew parents (rather than merely a proselyte to the faith). In more contemporary parlance, one might say that Paul was a true or pure-blooded Hebrew—if one could ever be found. He was part of an elite group that had been taught Hebrew (or Aramaic), the ethnic language of the Jewish people, and schooled in the Jewish traditions (see Acts 22:2-3; Gal. 1:14). To his birth and training as a Jew, Paul added three personal achievements. Foremost, he was a Pharisee. Within the Jewish community, no group of people was more highly esteemed as strict observers of the law of Moses. In fact, Gamaliel, one of the most respected rabbis in the Pharisee party of the day, was Paul's mentor (see Acts 22:3; 23:6; 26:5).

Additionally, the former Pharisee demonstrated his fervor for the law by zealously persecuting Christians, whom he once believed were God's enemies (see 1 Cor. 15:9). The zealot not only denounced the followers of Jesus, but also actively hunted them down in order to imprison and execute them (Phil. 3:6). As a matter of fact, before Paul's conversion, he would settle for nothing less than the total destruction of the church (see Acts 8:3; Gal. 1:13). In a way, Paul was even more blind to the truth of the Gospel than were the Judaizers. Finally, he said he was "blameless" (Phil. 3:6) according to the righteousness stipulated in the law. Put another way, if the law could produce righteousness in a person, then Paul would qualify, for by any human measure he was faultless in his observance of the Jewish commands and rituals.

NOTES ON THE PRINTED TEXT

Paul's credentials as a religious zealot were impeccable. Yet, despite this fact, he rejected as inconsequential everything he had accomplished as an upstanding Jew before his dramatic encounter with Jesus the Messiah on the road to Damascus. In light of the Savior's work in the apostle's life, Paul considered his birth as a Benjamite Jew, his high standing in the party of the Pharisees, and even his scrupulous adherence to the Mosaic law to be ineffectual in securing his redemption. All that had been a "gain" (Phil. 3:7) to Paul (and which the legalists prized), he counted as a "loss" because of his devotion to the Messiah. Expressed differently, what the apostle once regarded as sterling personal assets he now regarded as grave liabilities.

Paul candidly admitted that every single thing about which he once boasted as a Jew he now considered to be a "loss" (vs. 8). This was especially so when compared to the far greater value of knowing the Messiah as "Lord." Likewise, the apostle welcomed, rather than resented, suffering the loss of "all things." Indeed, he regarded them as "dung." The underlying Greek noun was used in the vernacular of the day for fecal matter—that is, detestable excrement or worthless manure meant to be discarded in a sewer (see Isa. 64:6).

In Philippians 3:8, the Greek noun that Paul chose for "knowledge" expresses the idea of understanding and perceiving an object in an intelligent manner. The word implies personal acquaintance, experience, and familiarity. Thus, when Paul spoke about knowing Jesus, the apostle was not just referring to gathering theological facts about the Son. More importantly, Paul had in mind experientially knowing the Messiah. In other words, the apostle desired to know Jesus in an ever-deepening personal union on a day-to-day basis. Furthermore, Paul wanted to have an ongoing relationship through his encounter with the Redeemer, especially as He worked in the apostle's life (see Jer. 31:34; Hos. 6:3; 8:2; John 10:27; 17:3; 2 Cor 4:6; 1 John 5:20).

Paul was now ready to press his point home. As righteous as he might have appeared in his relentless zeal to obey the Mosaic law, he now realized that true righteousness can come only through faith in Christ (Phil. 3:9). The latter refers to trusting in the Messiah for salvation. A less likely option is to translate the original as "through the faithfulness of Christ," which emphasizes the steadfast obedience of the Savior (see 2:6-11).

The Judaizers had demanded that believers be ritually purified through circumcision. Paul's argument was that he was circumcised and did far more in his efforts to be justified under the Mosaic law. And yet none of that was of any value to God. The upshot is that no one can attain righteousness. Only God can offer it, and it is received when people believe in the Lord Jesus. The implication is that the merit arising from Jesus' atoning sacrifice is the basis of salvation. Moreover, faith is the means by which believers are joined to the Son and His merit. These truths were at the heart of Paul's teaching, and he wanted his Philippian friends to permanently establish them as the doctrinal cornerstone of their church.

Amazingly, Paul wanted to know more about both Jesus' sufferings and His resurrection power. While many believers want more of His power, few would seem to crave the "fellowship of his sufferings" (3:10). Paul, however, regarded suffering for Christ as a sought-after privilege (see Rom 8:17; 2 Cor. 12:10). The apostle understood that the power of Jesus' resurrection was rooted in His self-denial, which led to the cross. The Son taught that His followers would have to take up their own crosses (see Matt. 16:24; Mark 8:34; Luke 9:23). Paul realized there was spiritual power in participating in Jesus' sufferings. This was the reason the apostle willingly faced incredible hardships for the sake of the Gospel.

There were two realms, then, in which Paul wanted to grow in his knowledge of the Savior. The first included a personal awareness of the power that raised Jesus from the dead. To be specific, the apostle wanted to experience that power daily working in his life in order to bring about Jesus' righteousness in Paul (see Rom. 6:1-14; Eph. 1:18-23; 2 Cor. 12:1-10). Second, the apostle wanted to have fellowship with Jesus in His sufferings. The idea is that through Paul's own sharing in the adversity and anguish that came with being a committed believer, he would understand more fully the anguish Jesus endured on the cross. In the process, the Father would transform the apostle into the image of His Son (see Col. 1:24; 1 Thess. 1:6; Heb. 10:34; Jas. 1:2; 1 Pet. 4:12-16).

In all this, Paul wanted to conform to Jesus' death. The latter consisted of the apostle divesting himself of personal gains and regarding them as complete losses (see Phil. 3:7-8). Being conformed to the Savior also involved crucifying the "flesh with the affections and lusts" (Gal. 5:24). Paul's ultimate goal was not to languish moribund in a state of lifelessness. Rather, it was to be raised from the dead along with other believers on the day appointed by God (Phil. 3:11). At the Messiah's second advent, Paul would completely know Jesus as supreme Ruler and Redeemer.

On the one hand, the apostle was uncertain about the outcome of his current situation as a prisoner in Rome and how boldly he would witness for Christ in the face of impending execution. On the other hand, Paul had no doubt that he (and all believers) would be raised from death to life at the end of the age (see Dan. 12:2; John 5:29; Acts 24:15; Rom. 8:30-31; 1 Cor. 15:20-23; 1 Thess. 4:13-17; 2 Tim. 1:12; Rev. 20:4-15). In short, the apostle's confession of faith in the Messiah made it clear that salvation totally and without question depended on the atoning work of the Lord Jesus.

SUGGESTIONS TO TEACHERS

This week's lesson considers the faith journey of Paul as it is recorded in Philippians 3:1-11. Verses 1-6 reveal that in the past, before he put his faith in Christ, Paul trusted in his human attainments. According to verses 7-11, after Paul encountered the risen Lord on the road to Damascus, the apostle made growing in the knowledge of Christ the central focus of his existence in the here and now.

1. SEEING TEMPORAL GAINS AS LOSSES. Paul regarded his former accomplishments and elevated position in the Jewish community as a disadvantage to his current Christian walk. The apostle used such words as "loss" (vs. 8) and "dung" to describe his former prestige and way of life. Emphasize to the students that if we let them, the things from our past as unbelievers can keep us from getting to truly know the Lord Jesus.

2. RECOGNIZING THE GIFT OF RIGHTEOUSNESS. Paul's radical reevaluation of his life led him to the conclusion that knowing the Messiah and receiving righteousness as a gift by faith were worth more than anything else. Likewise, the students must individually decide whether the value of gaining Christ is worth considering all their religious works as nothing more than garbage.

3. APPRECIATING OUR RELATIONSHIP WITH JESUS. Paul revealed that the righteousness that comes from worldly success, even if it is religious in nature, is utterly useless. Take time to explain that in order to be saved, everyone must possess the righteousness of the Father. Also, note that He makes this available to every believer because of his or her relationship with the Messiah.

4. EXPERIENCING JESUS FULLY IN OUR LIVES. Paul wanted to know Jesus more by experiencing fully His resurrection power. But Paul also wanted to "fellowship" (vs. 10), or share, in Jesus' sufferings. Emphasize that knowing Jesus means far more than memorizing biblical facts about Him. The goal of all believers is to have an ongoing relationship with the Savior through which they can experience Him working in their lives. This includes times of anguish and loss.

■ TOPIC: Gain and Loss

■ QUESTIONS: 1. Which aspects of Paul's former life as a Pharisee would he have once considered to be an advantage? 2. How would you compare personal losses to gains that have resulted from your decision to follow Jesus? 3. Why did Paul supremely value knowing the Messiah as Lord? 4. What type of righteousness does a person need to possess in order to be saved? 5. What motivates you to serve Jesus and His followers?

■ **ILLUSTRATIONS:**

A Point of Contact. Where do we meet the Lord today? Some people claim they can encounter Him in nature or experience Him by taking drugs (among various options). Gaining access to God is somehow thought to be a mystical experience reserved for a few privileged people who are into religion. Supposedly, all others are at a loss when it comes to knowing the Lord.

However, when we examine God's Word, we discover that the Savior wants all people to be in a personal relationship with Him. That's why the Father sent the Son to earth almost 2,000 years ago. Jesus loved us, died for us, and rose from the dead for us. In doing so, He made it possible for us each to experience Him fully in our lives (see Phil. 3:8, 10). This is no religious secret reserved for an elite class of individuals. It is plainly made known in the Bible.

In turn, our task is to help others come to know Jesus as their personal Savior. We can encourage them to put their trust in the Son and receive eternal life. When they do so, they will be given the righteousness that freely comes from God on the basis of faith (see vs. 9).

New Life Now. Phillips Brooks was one of the greatest preachers in America in the 1800s. He's also the author of the popular Christmas carol "O Little Town of Bethlehem."

In his preaching, Brooks noted the following: "The great Easter truth is not that we are to live newly after death. That is not the great thing. It is that we are to be new here and now by the power of the Resurrection."

Centuries earlier, Paul made a similar point when he declared his intense desire in his daily life to know Christ and the "power of his resurrection" (Phil. 3:10). Paul also wanted to share in Jesus' "sufferings" and become like Him "unto his death." Moreover, the apostle looked forward to the hope of being raised from death to life as a result of what Jesus had done for him at Calvary (vs. 11).

Going the Right Way. In the movie *Planes, Trains and Automobiles*, John Candy and Steve Martin play two hapless travelers who constantly bump into each other as they try to get home to Chicago for Thanksgiving. At one point, the two are driving in a rental car late at night and going down the wrong side of a stretch of highway.

Another driver (traveling in the lane the two are supposed to be in) shouts, "You're going the wrong way!" However, the two men are so certain that this other individual doesn't know what he's talking about, that they scoff, "How would he know which way we want to go?"

Before Paul trusted in the Messiah, the apostle thought he was spiritually heading in the right direction. But then, Paul encountered the risen Lord on the road heading to Damascus. The apostle learned he wasn't going the right way. From then on, Paul regarded all his worldly "gain" (Phil. 3:7) to be "loss" for Christ's sake.

Likewise, regardless of what our personal and professional accomplishments might be, they cannot gain us entrance into heaven. The right way of thinking is for us to "count all things but loss" (vs. 8) for the sake of what is infinitely more valuable, namely, the "knowledge of Christ Jesus," our Lord.

FOR YOUTH

■ **TOPIC:** Win or Lose?

■ **QUESTIONS:** 1. Why did Paul consider his former accomplishments as a Pharisee to be a "loss" (Phil. 3:7)? 2. Why is it so hard for believers to consider their religious deeds as so much garbage? 3. How can you tell when spiritual pride is in your heart? What can you do to get rid of it? 4. What does it mean to know Jesus as Lord? 5. Why would Paul want to share in Jesus' "sufferings" (vs. 10)?

■ **ILLUSTRATIONS:**

What Are the Limits? The only restrictions on youth used to be the age of driving, drinking, and voting. Today, the situation is different. The rules now extend to what adolescents can't wear to school, the weapons and drugs they can't carry into the building, the hours they can't keep, and the portable media devices they aren't allowed to use.

It seems as if teens have lost more privileges than they have won. Of course, it's no use arguing that the reason for some of these rules is to ensure the safety and well-being of young people. It's common knowledge that if some youths had not started to carry the habits of adult lawbreakers into high school, the rules would not be necessary.

Despite this seemingly restrictive situation, there's good news for Christian youth (as well as all other believers). Whatever they feel they've lost up to this point in their lives is more than offset by the eternal gains belonging to them as Jesus' followers. In fact, nothing this world has to offer or threatens to take away can compare with the treasure of personally knowing the Messiah as Lord.

The Joy of Being Forgiven. Jackie is a youth Sunday school teacher and a clerical worker. She has two children: a 12-year-old and a 2-year-old. The mother is moving to a new home soon.

Looking at Jackie and her smiling kids, one might never suspect the heartache of her past. Jackie is a compliant person who "sought love in all the wrong places" (as she puts it). She now recognizes that having her self-worth dependent on how others felt about her was disastrous for her life. It led her to hop from relationship to relationship, then become addicted to alcohol and crack cocaine.

Jackie's bad habits had a price. She neglected her firstborn son and herself. Eventually, they lived out of her car. Then she came to the "faith of Christ" (Phil. 3:9) and began to experience the joy of being forgiven. At first, Jackie's life did not completely right itself. She fell into old patterns. But after her second child was born out of wedlock, she realized she must give up her old sinful ways so that she might "win Christ" (vs. 8).

When we trust in Jesus for salvation, we become new creations. Although all our actions are not perfect, in the eyes of the Lord we are forgiven. We can thank Jesus for the new life He gives us when we receive Him by faith. We can also place at His feet any part of our lives that needs to be surrendered.

Finding True Freedom. It was a beautiful day for a wedding. Phil was a young evangelical minister, and Jenna was a young Jewish psychiatrist who had been converted to the Messiah five years before she met Phil. Though Jenna's family remained unconverted, they loved Jenna with a deep affection. They loved Phil, too.

Prior to the wedding, Phil and Jenna would often pray for Jenna's family. They particularly prayed that through the symbolism of the wedding ceremony, this lovely Jewish family would somehow understand the hope of the "resurrection of the dead" (Phil. 3:11) for all who put their trust in the Messiah.

The wedding ceremony began with a mixture of Jewish and Christian traditions. The Messianic rabbi spoke about the one new spiritual person who is created as Jew and Gentile came together. As the bride and groom prepared to say their vows, a cantor sang a traditional wedding blessing.

Altogether, it was a beautiful mixed-tradition wedding. But it wasn't until the wedding reception that the new couple received their wish. At the toast, a box was opened, and hundreds of monarch butterflies slowly rose to fill the reception gardens. It was then that Jenna's mother said, "Now I see that Yeshua [Jesus] comes to release us all, to make us free as the butterfly." Soon, the rest of Jenna's family would come to know the Messiah personally by faith (see vs. 10).

STAND FIRM

BACKGROUND SCRIPTURE: Philippians 3:12–4:1
DEVOTIONAL READING: Matthew 25:14-29

Key Verse: Whereto we have already attained, let us walk by the same rule, let us mind the same thing. Philippians 3:16.

KING JAMES VERSION

PHILIPPIANS 3:12 Not as though I had already attained, either were already perfect: but I follow after, if that I may apprehend that for which also I am apprehended of Christ Jesus. 13 Brethren, I count not myself to have apprehended: but this one thing I do, forgetting those things which are behind, and reaching forth unto those things which are before, 14 I press toward the mark for the prize of the high calling of God in Christ Jesus.

15 Let us therefore, as many as be perfect, be thus minded: and if in any thing ye be otherwise minded, God shall reveal even this unto you. 16 Nevertheless, whereto we have already attained, let us walk by the same rule, let us mind the same thing.

NEW REVISED STANDARD VERSION

PHILIPPIANS 3:12 Not that I have already obtained this or have already reached the goal; but I press on to make it my own, because Christ Jesus has made me his own. 13 Beloved, I do not consider that I have made it my own; but this one thing I do: forgetting what lies behind and straining forward to what lies ahead, 14 I press on toward the goal for the prize of the heavenly call of God in Christ Jesus. 15 Let those of us then who are mature be of the same mind; and if you think differently about anything, this too God will reveal to you. 16 Only let us hold fast to what we have attained.

9

HOME BIBLE READINGS

BACKGROUND

In Philippians 3:12, Paul stated that he strove to lay hold of the goal of becoming more Christlike. It's clarifying to note that the apostle used the metaphor of a race to illustrate what it means to wholeheartedly follow the Messiah. Both the Greeks and the Romans were avid fans of sporting contests. Sometimes the Roman games were violent and cruel, but often combatants merely engaged in feats of strength, endurance, and speed.

Running was one of the more popular sports. When runners won their races, they might win prizes of wealth. Of far more value to most of them, however, was the honored recognition they received. After each contest, a herald proclaimed the victor and his hometown, and a judge presented the athlete with a palm branch. At the conclusion of the games, each victor received a wreath made of olive or laurel leaves (see 3:14; 4:1). According to Greek tradition, an oracle in the city of Delphi had established this custom.

NOTES ON THE PRINTED TEXT

In Philippians 3:7-11, Paul described the kind of knowledge about the Messiah the apostle desired to experience. Paul also wanted to correct any misconceptions the Philippians might have had about what he had previously said. He noted that he had not yet acquired a perfect knowledge concerning the Savior, nor was the apostle insinuating that he had reached a state of spiritual flawlessness. Instead, Paul was pursuing the redemption that the Son had attained for him—the redemption that the apostle would fully possess when the Father raises believers from the dead. On the one hand, the Messiah had already redeemed Paul. On the other hand, he recognized the need to press on to the goal of reaching the level of Christlike maturity the Son had set for all His followers (vs. 12).

Paul repeated his statement that he had not yet attained the spiritual perfection that comes only with the final resurrection. Moreover, the apostle emphasized to his "brethren" (Phil. 3:13) in Christ that human credentials were powerless in meriting God's favor. Assuredly, if Paul did not claim to be spiritually complete, then the Christians in Philippi (as well as the legalists) could not make such a boast. The latter notwithstanding, there still remained two initiatives that Paul and all other believers could undertake, especially as they strove with single-minded determination for the lofty goal of Christlike maturity held out before them.

First, believers could put their past behind them. For Paul this included his abandoned career as a Jewish zealot and all his successes up to that point. Despite his outward attainments and dedication to the Mosaic law, he had failed to acquire God's favor or personal righteousness. Paul was not talking about obliterating the memories of his former life. Instead, he did not want to recall his bygone achievements with the intention of noting how they had contributed to his spiritual progress. Nor did the apostle want to dwell on his past sins (which may have included the execution of Christians), for God no longer held these transgressions against him.

Second, Paul and his fellow Christians in Philippi could strive for the future prize that awaited them, namely, the culmination or consummation of their salvation. The apostle used specific Greek words to draw a picture in the minds of his readers of an athlete who is participating in a running contest. Just as sprinters exert all of their efforts to push forward and reach the finish line, so Paul used every effort to drive himself forward in becoming more conformed to Christ's glorious image (see Rom. 8:29; 2 Thess. 2:14; 1 John 3:2). The great difference between races in a sporting event and the race Christians are running in is that a sporting event has only one winner. In the case of the Christian life, all who finish the race win (see 1 Cor 9:24-27; 1 Tim. 6:12; Heb. 12:1).

Paul's utmost effort to win the prize was not to run faster or longer than all other Christians, but to reach a common objective of being conformed to the glorious image of the Son. Expressed differently, the apostle was not trying to excel above all other believers, but to win a prize that Jesus will award to all who run for Him (Phil. 3:14). Paul did not say exactly what the prize would be, but he did indicate that he would receive it in heaven in the presence of his Lord and Savior, Jesus Christ. Moreover, God was the one who called Paul to press on toward this objective (see Rom. 8:30; Gal. 1:15), which especially included becoming more Christlike. Furthermore, it was God who enabled the apostle to run the race (Phil. 1:6; 2:12-13). Thus, Paul fully participated in the race of the Christian life for the glory and honor of God.

Here we see that Paul's concept of the Christian life was that of a mountain climber who continually worked his way to the summit. He was not content to stop at a lower level of spiritual maturity. Moreover, the apostle regarded salvation, not as an entry pass into a life of ease, but as the beginning of a lifelong pursuit to achieve the Lord's will. Such a view transforms a dull, static concept of Christian living. We routinely ask ourselves whether we are becoming what Jesus wants us to be, and achieving what He wants us to do. Behind these concerns is the reason why Jesus saves us and makes us righteous. It's not for our self-fulfillment, but for the accomplishment of His purposes. Jesus takes hold of every believer for a specific, lifelong objective. And when we discern and fulfill that multifaceted aim, we enjoy the God-given blessing of ultimate satisfaction.

Paul had plumbed new depths of spiritual insight and maturity, perhaps too deep for some of his fellow Christians to follow. Could everyone be as intense as he was in his pursuit of becoming more like the Savior and achieving His will? Possibly not. But those who had reached some degree of spiritual maturity could accept the apostle's testimony and teachings. Apparently, he was aware of some Philippian Christians who believed they had arrived spiritually. They may have looked down upon those who did not share their belief about themselves. In the apostle's subtle manner of rebuking this group, his statement about maturity was his way of regarding them as spiritually immature (Phil. 3:15). Paul was convinced that if a Christian was sincere in his or her desire to faithfully serve the Son, in time the Father would show that believer that everything the apostle said was true. In fact, he was so confident about the biblical basis for his teaching that he called upon God to correct those who disagreed with him.

Undoubtedly, most of the Philippians agreed with Paul's primary teaching on the importance of pursuing Christlike maturity. But some might have questioned, or could not understand, the secondary points of what he had written. Again, the apostle felt that those who truly seek God's truth will be rewarded with the full measure of understanding. Paul recognized that God had imparted varying levels of spiritual insight to the members of the Philippian church. His instruction was that they put into practice the truths they had already learned (vs. 16). In other words, he admonished them to walk according to what the Lord had taught them.

Neither the apostle nor anyone else can expect more from a Christian. In fact, to demand more is to overstep what the Holy Spirit is doing in that believer's life. This truth notwithstanding, Paul was confident that in time the Father would graciously help His spiritual children advance in their comprehension of what it means to know and serve the Son. This included all believers pressing on to spiritual maturity in light of what they already understood. The apostle's main point is that we must not quit. Neither should we give up our pursuit of conforming to the Son's glorious image. In short, the race goes on, one Spirit-empowered step at a time. As we live in obedient faith, the Son makes clear to us the full scope of why He has called us to Himself.

Paul trusted in God's sovereignty. For instance, the apostle believed God was in control of not only his life, but also the lives of the Christians in Philippi. Though some of the Philippians might have disagreed with Paul, he was confident that God would enlighten them to the truths he declared and change their behavior accordingly. Nevertheless, Paul's strong belief in God's sovereignty did not silence him. Put another way, the apostle did not think the best solution was to stand back and let the misunderstanding somehow resolve itself. Instead, since Paul knew that he had the gift of communicating God's truth, he voiced his views so these Christians would have the tools to advance in their walk with the Lord. Admittedly, whether they used these tools was up to them.

Paul's plan was to humbly provide direction for God's flock in Philippi, while trusting that the Lord would use the apostle's efforts to bear fruit for the kingdom. For those who might think they had arrived at spiritual perfection, Paul pointed to his example as someone who had room to grow. Undoubtedly, the apostle had set an excellent example in these areas during the time he had spent laboring in the church in Philippi. So the Philippians clearly understood what he meant when he told them to consider him as a godly role model (vs. 17). Of course, they saw much more of him than is recorded in the Book of Acts. Nevertheless, Luke did provide us with an invaluable account of Paul's activities in Philippi, which the believers there could recall and imitate.

SUGGESTIONS TO TEACHERS

At one time Paul had persecuted Jesus' followers. In this week's Scripture passage, however, we learn that the apostle focused on the future the Lord called him to, not his past. We are also called to rid ourselves of every weight that slows us down, especially the sin that so easily causes us to stumble. Moreover, our Savior wants us to run with determination the race that God has set before us (see Heb. 12:1). Doing this ensures our spiritual growth.

1. REFUSING TO BE PREOCCUPIED WITH THE PAST. Paul could have allowed himself to wallow in self-pity for the horrible ways he once treated other believers. Thankfully, the apostle recognized the full extent of what it means for believing sinners to be forgiven. Have the class members consider those things in their past life that would keep them from getting to know the Lord, especially if they were to obsess on them.

2. GETTING ON WITH THE PRESENT. Paul urged believers not to be satisfied with their current maturity in Christ, for there is always room for spiritual growth. Let the students know that thinking we have arrived at full maturity is already a step backward. Paul would urge them, as he did the Philippians, to take a goal-oriented approach to life. This includes getting on with the present aim of striving to become more Christlike.

3. MAINTAINING A FUTURE FOCUS. Paul encouraged his readers to follow his example and not be either legalistic or worldly in their Christian lives. He also challenged them to focus on their heavenly citizenship. Your students, too, can benefit from maintaining a future focus, particularly looking forward to Jesus' return and the glorious transformation of their bodies. Let them know that as they look forward to being with the Lord in heaven, they will seek to live in a way that pleases Him.

FOR ADULTS

■ **TOPIC:** Gaining the Prize

■ **QUESTIONS:** 1. Why would it have been inappropriate for Paul to claim he had achieved full spiritual maturity? 2. What are some ways that believers can press on to spiritual maturity? 3. Why is it important for believers to put their past behind them, especially as they become more Christlike? 4. What was the nature of the heavenly "prize" (Phil. 3:14) that Paul strove to receive? 5. How would you summarize the biblical point Paul was making to his readers in verse 15?

■ **ILLUSTRATIONS:**

Striving to Be Christlike. Sadly, when people talk about "church," they often focus on programs, staff, buildings, and denominational differences. There's more than enough criticism to go around, which means outsiders are frequently turned off by what they see and hear.

However, the essence of the Christian life is none of these. Indeed, the previously mentioned concerns often get in the way of genuine, saving faith. The reality of the latter is demonstrated by trusting in Jesus and focusing one's life on obeying His will. In the case of Paul, he had to jettison a lot of religious baggage that kept him from knowing and serving the Lord. Saved adults have to do the same.

Striving to be Christlike is more important than anything else. If we find something in our lives that distracts us from anticipating the prize of spending eternity with the Savior, we have to discard it. This may mean radical changes for some people who have been in church for years. Regardless of the adjustments that need to be made, it is well worth it in order to become more conformed to Christ's glorious image.

Progressing Forward. Some churches that have a "new building" plan or some other program of giving will put a huge thermometer painted on a sign in the foyer. At the top is the financial goal, perhaps hundreds of thousands or even millions of dollars. Hopefully, each week the red line goes a little higher. And every Sunday people are reminded of how far the congregation has to go to reach the top.

What if we had the same kind of device to measure the future-oriented focus of our walk with Christ, especially our zeal to grow in spiritual maturity? Perhaps the red line would vary from week to week. But we hope that gradually the line would head upward, particularly as believers progress forward in their knowledge of and obedience to the Savior.

However, to be honest, in some cases it's easier to get excited about reaching a financial goal than a spiritual one. Why are we so reluctant to take our spiritual temperature? Surely, we can confess that our relationship with the Lord should be our first concern. Too easily we have allowed our minds to focus on earthly things. And too easily we have let the supreme value of Jesus slip away from us. Now is the time for us to press ahead in becoming more Christlike!

Using the Cruise Control. Years ago, when I was in college, I made several cross-country drives. My truck did not have cruise control, and my own efforts to keep my speed under control were unsuccessful.

For instance, I would get in a hurry and unknowingly press on the gas pedal too hard. Or, after hours of driving across flat, marker-free terrain, my sense of speed would become numbed and I would slow down. After college, I sold my truck and bought a car with cruise control. What a relief it was to be able to surrender control of the gas pedal just by pressing a little button on my steering wheel.

Allowing the Lord Jesus to control the present and future focus of our lives is similar to my surrendering control of my gas pedal to the cruise feature on my car. When we are in control of our spiritual lives, our efforts are inconsistent, and we often fail to do what's right. However, when the Savior is allowed to be in charge, He faithfully leads us in the right direction, heading toward spiritual maturity.

FOR YOUTH

■ TOPIC: Press On!

■ QUESTIONS: 1. What motivated Paul to strive so hard to press on to spiritual maturity? 2. What do you think it means to wholeheartedly follow the Messiah? 3. What is the advantage of believers maintaining a future focus, especially as they seek to become spiritually mature? 4. What are some ways you can motivate your Christian peers to grow in their walk with the Lord? 5. Why should believers put into practice the biblical truths they have learned?

■ ILLUSTRATIONS:

Moving Ahead. One of the favorite ways to prove that a diet works is to show before and after pictures. Typically, the photo on the left shows an obese person weighing 350 pounds, but the photo on the right shows the same individual weighing 150 pounds. The ad reminds potential customers that this outcome could be true for them, that is, if they stick to their diet.

Paul's story is something like that. He told us what he was like before his encounter with the risen Lord, and then the apostle told us the remarkable changes that occurred after his conversion. We can read about the dramatic changes in Philippians 3.

Of course, the key to weight loss is sticking to the diet, not just for a few weeks, but for a lifetime. The same was true for Paul. He kept on pressing ahead toward his goal of spiritual maturity and Christlikeness. In short, the apostle maintained a future focus.

Paul never said he had arrived at the place where he could relax. In contrast, many teens start the Christian walk, but fail to keep at it. They do not pursue the present and future goal of Christlikeness as doggedly as they should. Paul's example can motivate them to keep shedding the weight of sin and remain spiritually trim in order to win their race of faith in the Lord Jesus.

Undaunted Devotion. According to Bill Shaikin of the *Los Angeles Times*, U.S. Speed skater Joey Cheek made Olympic history on February 13, 2006, when he won the men's 500-meter race in Turin, Italy. But even more amazing than this athletic feat was Cheek's announcement minutes after his victory that he would donate his $25,000 gold medal award from the U.S. Olympic Committee. It would go to refugees from the Darfur region of western Sudan so that "children in African refugee camps might have a chance to play sports." He also urged "Olympic sponsors to support the same relief effort."

Cheek's decision is one filled with courage, commitment, and compassion. These are the same sorts of virtues that Paul said should be part of the lives of all believers. In fact, the apostle used the analogy of a sports race to urge believers to remain focused, single-minded, and undaunted in their devotion to the Savior and His followers. Like an Olympic speed skater, they were to strain to reach the end of the race and receive the eternal, heavenly prize promised to them in the Savior.

Acquiring Knowledge. In 1997, IBM showcased a supercomputer called Deep Blue. This machine was so advanced that it beat the reigning chess champion, Garry Kasparov, in a six-game match. Then, in 2011, IBM presented another supercomputer named Watson. Because of its sophisticated artificial intelligence, the machine was able to beat two of the best human contestants on the game show *Jeopardy*.

Today's society puts a premium on mastering vasts amounts of knowledge. Indeed, futurists state that we are relentlessly pressing on from an industrial society to a paperless, information one. The image of this age is no longer the foundry or the assembly line, but the microprocessor chip. Silicon, not steel, is the new king.

However, the question to this age is not "How do we process information now that computers have made it so plentiful and so easy?" but "How do we acquire knowledge? How do we learn?" Christians have always believed in sharing knowledge. In fact, it's known as witnessing. Paul, through his testimony, shared with the Philippians his knowledge of the Messiah. Saved teens can also share what they know with their peers by pointing the way to Jesus.

THE SUPREMACY OF CHRIST

BACKGROUND SCRIPTURE: Colossians 1:15-20
DEVOTIONAL READING: Ephesians 1:17-23

Key Verse: For it pleased the Father that in him should all fulness dwell. Colossians 1:19.

KING JAMES VERSION

COLOSSIANS 1:15 Who is the image of the invisible God, the firstborn of every creature: 16 For by him were all things created, that are in heaven, and that are in earth, visible and invisible, whether they be thrones, or dominions, or principalities, or powers: all things were created by him, and for him: 17 And he is before all things, and by him all things consist. 18 And he is the head of the body, the church: who is the beginning, the firstborn from the dead; that in all things he might have the preeminence. 19 For it pleased the Father that in him should all fulness dwell; 20 And, having made peace through the blood of his cross, by him to reconcile all things unto himself; by him, I say, whether they be things in earth, or things in heaven.

NEW REVISED STANDARD VERSION

COLOSSIANS 1:15 He is the image of the invisible God, the firstborn of all creation; 16 for in him all things in heaven and on earth were created, things visible and invisible, whether thrones or dominions or rulers or powers—all things have been created through him and for him. 17 He himself is before all things, and in him all things hold together. 18 He is the head of the body, the church; he is the beginning, the firstborn from the dead, so that he might come to have first place in everything. 19 For in him all the fullness of God was pleased to dwell, 20 and through him God was pleased to reconcile to himself all things, whether on earth or in heaven, by making peace through the blood of his cross.

10

HOME BIBLE READINGS

Monday, January 28	Ephesians 1:17-23	*Christ, the Head of the Church*
Tuesday, January 29	Revelation 1:1-6	*Christ, the Firstborn of the Dead*
Wednesday, January 30	John 17:20-26	*Christ, One with the Father*
Thursday, January 31	2 Corinthians 5:16-21	*Christ, the Reconciler to God*
Friday, February 1	Romans 5:15-21	*Christ, the Channel of God's Grace*
Saturday, February 2	Matthew 4:18-25	*The Compelling Call of Christ*
Sunday, February 3	Colossians 1:15-20	*The Person and Work of Christ*

BACKGROUND

Paul wrote Colossians while under house arrest in Rome. The apostle began this letter with thanksgiving for what the Father had done in raising up the church at Colosse (1:3-8). Paul reminded the believers in the city about their priceless spiritual heritage. Then he penned a magnificent prayer for them (vss. 9-14). He concluded his prayer with thanksgiving for the Father's deliverance of believers from the power of darkness, as well as for redeeming and forgiving them in the Son. This majestic spiritual reality led the apostle to comment on the supremacy of the Messiah over all creation (vss. 15-28).

Paul's teaching about the person and work of the Son was needed at Colosse because the church was plagued by religious frauds. They tried to convince believers to venerate a cadre of inferior created beings and angelic mediators, rather than the Savior (see 2:8, 18). The apostle reminded his readers that the Son is the full and final revelation of the Father, and that all human ideas must be brought into subjection to the Son. In brief, the only adequate response to heretical teaching is a correct understanding of, and commitment to, Jesus as the supreme Creator and Redeemer (see Eph. 1:20-23; Phil. 2:6-11).

NOTES ON THE PRINTED TEXT

Some experts think Colossians 1:15-20 was originally part of an ancient Christian hymn or poem. If so, it may have been used as a creedal confession during worship. Paul may have expanded certain parts of the hymn to clarify the truth about the Messiah that the counterfeit teachers in Colosse were disputing. There is considerable debate as to how many stanzas there are in this hymn and how the lines should be broken down. The following arrangement has been suggested by several Bible scholars. Stanza one (vss. 15-16) praises Jesus Christ as the one who brought the universe into existence. He is the Lord over all things. Stanza two (vss. 17-18a) professes Jesus Christ as the one who unifies the universe. He is the head of the church. Stanza three (vss. 18b-20) proclaims Jesus Christ as the one who reconciles the universe through the sacrifice of His life on the cross. He is our Redeemer.

In verse 15, Paul declared the personhood of the Messiah, namely, that He is the "image of the invisible God." The Son is not merely a reflection or copy of the Father, whom no one can see with physical eyes. Nor does the Son simply represent the Father. The Greek noun rendered "image" means "likeness" or "manifestation of," and indicates that the Son is the perfect embodiment of the Father's character and nature. In contrast, human beings are made in the image of God (see Gen. 1:26-27; 5:1; 9:6). In this sense, we reflect the Father's character in finite ways. For example, God is all-powerful, but we have some power; God is all-knowing, while our knowledge is limited; and God is everywhere, yet we can only be in one place at one time. While Jesus' human nature is characterized by these sorts of limitations, His divine nature has no such limitations. This is the difference between people being made in the image of God and Jesus being the visible image of the unseen God.

Moreover, the Son is "the firstborn of every creature" (Col. 1:15). In some contexts, the Greek adjective rendered "firstborn" denoted what was first in order of time. By way of example, in Paul's day the term was used to refer to a firstborn child. In other contexts, the term referred to someone who was preeminent in rank. For instance, when Isaiah spoke about "the firstborn of the poor" (Isa. 14:30), he used a Hebrew noun that refers to the poorest among the impoverished. The second usage best fits the context of Colossians 1:15, in which Paul emphasized the priority of the Son's rank over creation. So, when the apostle referred to the Messiah as the "firstborn" over all creation, Paul did not mean that the Son was the first creature the Father brought into being, but rather that the Son reigns supreme over all that exists.

Nothing that has been brought into existence—whether it dwells in heaven or inhabits the earth, whether we can see it or it is imperceptible to our eyes—has come into being without the Son's involvement. Moreover, the apostle stressed the Son's preeminence over the angelic realm. As noted earlier, within the Colossian heresy was the worship of angels. By listing the perceived hierarchy of angels ("thrones, or dominions, or principalities, or powers," vs. 16), Paul attacked the systematic division of the angelic realm. Since the apostle referred to the visible as well as invisible, this hierarchy probably includes human institutions. Paul exposed as foolish any homage to human or angelic authorities because, in fact, Jesus is Lord over them all. Indeed, the Father formed the creation not only through His Son but also for His Son. Thus, the ultimate purpose of creation is the Messiah Himself. According to God's redemptive plan, He designed the world in such a way that it can have real meaning only in the Son.

Paul noted two more traits about the Son's divine nature in relationship to creation. First, He eternally preexisted before the Father made all things (vs. 17). Several times in this hymn the apostle used the phrase "all things" or words to that effect (see vss. 15, 16, 17, 18, 20). Paul was repeatedly stressing that the Messiah is supreme over whatever exists, and in this instance the Son was forever with the Father and the Spirit prior to the creation event.

Second, the apostle affirmed the Son as the sustainer of all creation (vs. 17). The writer of Hebrews also elaborated on this theme when he noted that the Son is the outshining of the Father's glory, perfectly represents His essence, and upholds the cosmos by His "word of his power" (Heb. 1:3). Deists believe that God created the world and then left it alone, allowing it to run on its own. In direct contradiction to this belief, Scripture makes it clear that the Son maintains His creation and bears it along to its divinely appointed destiny. If He were to abandon it, utter chaos would result and the world would simply stop existing.

Next in Paul's hymn, the apostle praised the Son for His character and redemptive work. The false teachers in Colosse denied the supreme importance of the Messiah. The apostle may have expanded on the original poem to spotlight the Messiah's preeminent position as the ruler over God's people and the Son's incomparable work as the reconciler of all creation. By doing this, Paul assured his readers that their faith in the Lord Jesus was not in vain, despite the clever yet deceptive doctrines of the Colossian heretics. Paul noted that the Son marks a new beginning for humanity. In a sense, Jesus was like Reuben, who was the patriarch Jacob's "firstborn" (Gen. 49:3). As Reuben was the beginning of Jacob's children, so the Son is the beginning of a new generation of redeemed people.

In Romans 8:29, Paul noted that those whom the Father foreknew He additionally decided from the outset to become like His Son, so that He would be the first among a cohort of spiritual brothers and sisters. Furthermore, the apostle noted in Colossians 1:18 that the Son was the first to be raised from the dead. In fact, He will never die again. Because of the resurrection of Jesus' body, those who trust in the Messiah for salvation will also be raised from the dead. This corresponds to what Paul declared in 1 Corinthians 15:20. We learn that the risen Lord is "the firstfruits of them that slept." Moreover, the Son reigns supreme because He conquered all of the Father's enemies, the last being death (vss. 25-27). In short, the Messiah holds first place in all things (Col. 1:18).

Paul next articulated another key doctrine, that is, the deity of the Son. The apostle reaffirmed this central truth of the Christian faith later in this letter (see 2:9). When Paul said the Father was pleased to have all the fullness of the Godhead dwell in the Son, the apostle implied that Jesus of Nazareth completely and permanently possesses all the attributes of God. Expressed differently, the Redeemer is God. Yet, in 1:19, Paul was not merely stating a Christian creed, but deepening its theological meaning. The apostle noted the Father's pleasure in having His full divine nature reside in His Son, the Lord Jesus.

Furthermore, Paul praised the Messiah not only as divine ruler but also as supreme reconciler (vs. 20). What the Messiah accomplished is equally important as who He is. It is only through the Son that the Father reconciled everything to Himself. No imagined deity, no mythical angel, and no celebrated human being could have achieved what the Savior did. This statement was a reminder to the Colossians to rebuke any self-stylized expert who taught otherwise. In this ancient hymn, Paul declared that the Lord Jesus is the reconciler of all things. The apostle probably added the phrase "whether they be things in earth, or things in heaven" to this Christian song. It is a further defining of "all things" just mentioned, and Paul's way of affirming that the Messiah's reconciling work affects everything. In short, nothing is beyond the reaches of the Son's redemptive work.

Some modern interpreters of the Bible understand verse 20 to mean that Jesus has saved everyone who has and ever will be born. In fact, they use this verse to support their doctrine of universalism—namely, the teaching that the Messiah will redeem every human being and even all angels, including those who have fallen. Paul, however, was not speaking about everlasting redemption, but of the subjugation of all human and heavenly beings to their rightful position as God's subjects. Thus, the Son has rendered all the Father's enemies powerless—both those people whose fellowship with God is renewed and those people and demons who remain His eternal foes. And where does this event take place? It occurs at the cross, where the Son shed His blood and gave His life so that we might have peace with the Father. Indeed, Jesus accomplished two goals on the cross. First, He cleansed us of our sins in order to bring us into His kingdom. Second, He defeated all our enemies so that nothing can stand between us and the Father (see Rom. 8:38-39).

SUGGESTIONS TO TEACHERS

The Lord Jesus dominates the landscape of Colossians 1:15-20. In these verses, Paul declared that the Messiah is God and emphasized His divine attributes. One attribute that the apostle stressed was Jesus' Sonship, especially in connection with His atoning work on the Cross.

1. THE MESSIAH'S IDENTITY. Paul taught that Jesus is the visible image of the unseen God and that the Son eternally existed before the creation of the world. The Messiah is not only sovereign over all creation but also the one through whom the Father brought all things into existence. This includes all the angelic beings and human authorities. The entire universe owes its continuing existence to the Son. For these reasons He deserves our worship and service.

2. THE MESSIAH'S SOVEREIGNTY. The supremacy of the Son in our lives begins when we invite Him to become our Lord and Savior. After all, He said that He came to give us life to the full (see John 10:10). No one else can give us eternal life. And we need it because we are spiritually dead in sin. There is no true life available to us other than in the Redeemer.

3. THE MESSIAH'S AUTHORITY. Many people today worship false gods. In contrast, the one true God has revealed Himself in His Son, the Lord Jesus. As His followers, we live under His authority. Admittedly, there are times when our faith will be tested by those who ridicule us and say they don't believe in God. Yet by prayer and Scripture study, we can be better witnesses to the authority of the Son.

4. THE IMPORTANCE OF MAKING THE RIGHT CHOICE. All of us have options in life, even when it comes to the things of God. Because our eternal future is on the line, it is important that we make the right choice—indeed, the only real choice from the Lord's perspective. Encourage your students not only to receive Jesus by faith, but also to live for Him all the days of their lives.

<table>
<tr><td>**FOR ADULTS**</td><td>■ **TOPIC:** Awed by Greatness
■ **QUESTIONS:** 1. In what sense is Jesus the visible "image" (Col. 1:15) of the unseen God?</td></tr>
</table>

2. Why is it important for believers to emphasize that Jesus created all things? 3. How can Jesus' followers draw comfort from the truth that He is the head of the church? 4. How does reconciliation between the Father and His spiritual children occur? 5. What sort of "peace" (vs. 20) did Jesus' shed blood establish?

■ **ILLUSTRATIONS:**

Focusing on the Son. Tony had a business associate who wanted to discuss religion in general. Tony, though, gently refused. Instead, he faithfully talked about his awe for the greatness of Jesus, whom Paul revealed is the "firstborn of every creature" (Col. 1:15).

During one conversation, Tony left his peer with the question, "Do you have eternal life?" Tony explained that the issue is new life through faith in the Creator, not religion (see vs. 16). One day several months later, the same individual came to Tony and exclaimed, "I've got life!" He meant he had trusted in Jesus for salvation.

The supremacy of the Son in our lives begins when we put our faith in Him as our Lord and Savior. After all, no other person could have died for our sins and reconciled us to the Father (see vs. 20). Because Jesus is God the Son, the Father accepted nothing less than the sacrifice of His Son. Therefore, only through Jesus can we become members of God's spiritual family.

A Terrible Rift. "Maybe 10 years ago, I heard a rumor about our pastor that could have threatened the life of the church, if it had gone unaddressed," says Rick, a former member of his congregation's board of elders. "I heard it from a friend, who had heard it from her boss. My friend said she'd get in trouble if her boss found out she'd told me. So I promised her I'd keep her identity a secret."

Rick continued, "When the elders next met, I told them the rumor, believing we would develop a response, and that would be that." Instead, the pastor asked Rick where he heard the rumor. Rick recalls, "The pastor wanted to speak to the source directly. I agonized over my promise of confidentiality and the duty I owed the church.

In the end, I decided that the only way healing could occur in our congregation would be for me to give the pastor my friend's name. Later, I phoned her and told her what I'd done."

Rick thought an apology would set things right. But he was incorrect. He noted that "nothing was right after that. It seems I'd done the unforgivable. It would have taken a miracle from God for us to be reconciled again."

In Colossians 1, Paul drew a similar conclusion about the terrible rift between humanity and God that was caused by sin. Nothing we can do is able to set things right and restore our broken relationship with the Father. It would take a miracle from God. The good news is that the Father agrees, and He sent His Son, the Lord Jesus, to make "peace" (vs. 20) through His "blood," which He shed on the "cross."

Seeking Reconciliation. In 1997, *The Peacemaker* hit the movie theaters. It's an action thriller about an American army colonel and his female civilian supervisor. They work together to track down stolen Russian nuclear weapons before they're used by terrorists. The film is filled with car chases, off-color humor, and foul language.

The Hollywood version of achieving peace is a far cry from what is revealed in Scripture. For example, in this week's lesson we learn that a restored relationship with the Father is only possible through faith in the Son (see Col. 1:20). Jesus gave Himself as an atoning sacrifice so that we might be at peace with God. This is the good news of reconciliation that we are called to embrace and proclaim to others!

FOR YOUTH

■ TOPIC: Eternal Ruler

■ QUESTIONS: 1. What did Paul mean when he said that Jesus is the "firstborn of every creature" (Col. 1:15)? 2. In what sense do "all things consist" (vs. 17) in the Son? 3. How does Jesus' resurrection from the dead give hope to believers? 4. What does it mean for believers to be reconciled to the Father through faith in the Son? 5. What difference has your faith in the Messiah made in your life?

■ ILLUSTRATIONS:

The Image of God. One day a disciple of Jesus named Philip said, "Lord, show us the Father, and it sufficeth us" (John 14:8). Many young people are asking for the same sort of thing. They want to see authentic Christianity lived by those who claim to be followers of the eternal Creator and Ruler (see Col. 1:16). They are not directly demanding to see the "invisible God" (vs. 15), but they rightly expect to see Him in the lives of those who say they are believers.

The Son is the only one who perfectly bore the Father's glorious "image." Even so, Paul revealed that in union with the Messiah, we likewise can be regarded as God's holy children. As others see the presence of the Son in us, they get a taste of what it means to see the Father's image.

Jesus said that He would unveil Himself to others by living in us. He promised to show Himself when we love and obey Him. The implication is that younger and older believers alike stand in the gap between God and an unbelieving world.

Double Agent. In 1994, former Central Intelligence Agency operative Aldrich Ames was imprisoned for being a double agent. In what is regarded as one of the most damaging spy cases in U.S. history, Ames admitted he sold secrets to the Soviet Union and then Russia. The prosecution maintained that his actions led to the deaths of at least 10 American agents in the former Soviet Union. Accordingly, a court in Arlington, Virginia, sentenced Ames to life imprisonment without parole.

What a contrast this double agent is to the Lord Jesus. He is the Creator of the universe and the Lord of the church (see Col. 1:16). And it is in this dual role that He is able to reconcile us to the Father (see vs. 20). The Savior can even take the broken lives of young people and turn them around for temporal and eternal good. That is the wonderful news of redemption!

Bridging the Gap. I once heard the story of a little girl whose parents were experiencing great difficulties in their marriage. All they seemed to have in common was their tremendous affection for their daughter, Sally. One day, Sally wandered into the street to play and was knocked down by a bus. While she was in a coma, she was rushed to the hospital, where physicians determined her injuries were too great to save her. Her parents hurried to the hospital, then stood helpless, watching her from either side of her bed.

Abruptly, Sally's eyes opened, and she tried to smile. Then she took one arm from under the bedsheet and held it out toward her father. "Daddy," she said, "give me your hand." Turning toward her mother, Sally extended her other arm, and her mother grasped her other hand. With the daughter's last bit of strength, she drew those hands together as she died, trying one final time to bridge the gap between the two people she loved so much.

That story is a picture of the bridge of reconciliation the Son built at Calvary, as He extended the loving hand of the Father to the hand of sinful humanity (see Col. 1:20). Calvary's bridge was costly to build, but without it the great gulf between us and God would never have been bridged.

FULL LIFE IN CHRIST

BACKGROUND SCRIPTURE: Colossians 2:6-15
DEVOTIONAL READING: Romans 8:31-39

Key Verse: Ye are complete in him, which is the
head of all principality and power. Colossians 2:10.

KING JAMES VERSION

COLOSSIANS 2:6 As ye have therefore received
Christ Jesus the Lord, so walk ye in him: 7 Rooted and
built up in him, and stablished in the faith, as ye have
been taught, abounding therein with thanksgiving.
8 Beware lest any man spoil you through philosophy
and vain deceit, after the tradition of men, after the
rudiments of the world, and not after Christ. 9 For in
him dwelleth all the fulness of the Godhead bodily.
10 And ye are complete in him, which is the head of all
principality and power: 11 In whom also ye are circumcised with the circumcision made without hands, in
putting off the body of the sins of the flesh by the circumcision of Christ: 12 Buried with him in baptism,
wherein also ye are risen with him through the faith of
the operation of God, who hath raised him from the
dead.
13 And you, being dead in your sins and the uncircumcision of your flesh, hath he quickened together
with him, having forgiven you all trespasses;
14 Blotting out the handwriting of ordinances that was
against us, which was contrary to us, and took it out of
the way, nailing it to his cross; 15 And having spoiled
principalities and powers, he made a shew of them
openly, triumphing over them in it.

NEW REVISED STANDARD VERSION

COLOSSIANS 2:6 As you therefore have received
Christ Jesus the Lord, continue to live your lives in
him, 7 rooted and built up in him and established in
the faith, just as you were taught, abounding in thanksgiving.
8 See to it that no one takes you captive through philosophy and empty deceit, according to human tradition, according to the elemental spirits of the universe,
and not according to Christ. 9 For in him the whole
fullness of deity dwells bodily, 10 and you have come
to fullness in him, who is the head of every ruler and
authority. 11 In him also you were circumcised with a
spiritual circumcision, by putting off the body of the
flesh in the circumcision of Christ; 12 when you were
buried with him in baptism, you were also raised with
him through faith in the power of God, who raised him
from the dead. 13 And when you were dead in trespasses and the uncircumcision of your flesh, God made you
alive together with him, when he forgave us all our
trespasses, 14 erasing the record that stood against us
with its legal demands. He set this aside, nailing it to
the cross. 15 He disarmed the rulers and authorities and
made a public example of them, triumphing over them
in it.

11

HOME BIBLE READINGS

BACKGROUND

In Colossians 2, Paul emphasized three ways to live spiritually in the Son. First, we are to be "rooted and built up" (vs. 7) in the Redeemer. This phrase brings two pictures to mind. One is of a plant rooted in the ground. The other is of a structure being built above ground. This mixed metaphor actually combines two important features of the growth of one's Christian faith. At the same time we are growing upward in the Savior, our roots in the faith should also be deepening. Second, we are to be "stablished in the faith." Specifically, Paul was exhorting us to stay committed to the truth of the Gospel, which empowers us to live in harmony with the Father's will.

Third, we are to be "abounding" with gratitude. This includes being thankful that Jesus died for our sins and now lives in us. For these and other reasons, we should show our appreciation to God in all that we do. Paul's objective in giving this much emphasis to the Messiah was so that people would come to know Him and devote their lives to Him. With respect to the Colossian believers, the apostle wanted them to understand who Jesus truly is and what He had done for them. This knowledge would protect them from doctrinal error and invigorate their faith. This type of knowledge can do the same for us who are rooted and grounded in Christ.

NOTES ON THE PRINTED TEXT

Paul urged the believers in Colosse to draw upon deeper spiritual resources as they continued to anchor their lives in the Son (Col. 2:6). In a manner of speaking, they were to sink their roots deep in the Messiah, build their lives on Him, and in this way become stronger in their faith. All the while, they were to give praise to God at all times (vs. 7).

Paul warned his readers not to be fooled into believing the deceitful doctrines of the false teachers who had slipped in among them. Quite possibly, these heretics were present when the apostle's letter was read to the church members and were livid at hearing his censure of them. Nevertheless, Paul was not one who made any effort to spare the feelings of those who tried to lead believers into doctrinal or moral error. The apostle's language in verse 8 vividly portrays the consequence of being misled by a philosophy that is empty of any value and deceptive in its intent. Those who were captivated by it are like people who are kidnapped or captured during a war. In short, the false teachers were spiritual enemies who treacherously preyed upon Jesus' followers.

Paul went on to characterize this evil philosophy as being manmade. God had not revealed this doctrine. Rather, it was the product of corrupted human minds. Moreover, this philosophy was based on the strictly human ideas found in the world. They consisted of instructions on acquiring secret knowledge and codes, angel worship, eating and drinking practices, and religious rituals. Yet very little of it reflected the well-known public teachings of the Savior.

The precise meaning of the Greek noun translated "rudiments" (Col. 2:8) is debated among scholars. One option is that it refers to the rudimentary teachings of fallen humanity. A second option is that the focus is on how elemental spiritual forces operated in and controlled the world (under the permission and authority of God). It would be incorrect to conclude that Paul was arguing against the study of philosophy as an academic discipline. Instead, the apostle was warning against adopting any point of view or teaching that was contrary to the Gospel (see Gal. 1:6-9).

At this point in his letter, Paul sensed the importance of affirming the deity of the Son. Previously, in Colossians 1:19, the apostle declared that the Father was "pleased" to have His full divine nature reside in the Son. As was noted in lesson 10, this is a permanent dwelling, not a temporary one. Again, in 2:9, the apostle stated that the inner essence of the Godhead in its entirety resided in the Messiah—even in His human body. This statement unequivocally rejects the view that the Son did not have a bodily form and that the human body is evil. More importantly, this verse affirmed both the divine and human natures of the Savior. He is God who has lived as a human being.

Paul declared in verse 10 that believers have been brought to fullness in the Son. By this the apostle meant they were complete through their spiritual union with Him. Paul dismissed the claim of the false teachers who said believers are deficient and therefore need further spiritual enlightenment. The apostle also rejected the idea that believers must practice additional religious rituals in order to reach spiritual perfection. The Son, who is Lord over all the powers and forces in the supernatural and the natural realms, has already provided everything we need for salvation and spiritual growth. Jesus is not one of many spirit beings or angels, but the supreme commander over every power and authority.

Before the advent of the Messiah, the Israelites were members of a special covenant with God (see Rom. 9:4-5). Their males affirmed this covenant by being physically circumcised. Now, following the coming of the Savior, there is a new sign that indicates those who are God's people. It is no longer a physical mark but a spiritual one that the Savior has performed, and not just for men, but also for all people who put their faith in Him. That sign is a circumcision of the heart in which the whole self ruled by the flesh is cut away and discarded (see Deut. 10:16; Jer. 4:4; Rom. 2:28-29; Phi. 3:3). In turn, believers are freed from the power of the sinful nature. Indeed, the apostle said, it is "circumcision of Christ" (Col. 2:11), and it is by this that we enter into a covenant of grace with God—both Jew or Gentile (see Eph. 2:11-19; 1 Pet. 2:10).

Next, Paul associated baptism with circumcision (Col. 2:12). The apostle vividly paralleled the act of baptism with the dramatic events at the end of Jesus' earthly ministry. After the Son died on the cross, His friends buried His body. But then the Father raised Him from the dead, never to die again. In baptism, we are symbolically buried and raised from the dead, never to experience spiritual death. In truth, Jesus has washed away our sins with the blood He shed on the cross. As a result of our identification with Him by faith, our old sinful selves, along with their passions and desires, were nailed to the cross (see Rom. 6:6; Gal. 5:24). We can now be in a right relationship with the Father because the Son's redemptive work at Calvary atoned for our sins completely.

Paul continued to pile up more facts about the complete nature of the victory we have in union with the Messiah. The apostle noted that before our conversion, we were spiritually lifeless because of our transgressions and the unregenerate condition (or "uncircumcision," Col. 2:13) of our flesh. At this point, we stood judged and condemned by God. Then, when we trusted in the Son for our salvation, the Father spiritually regenerated us and pardoned us of all our trespasses. This inner re-creation of our fallen human nature is known as the new birth. We experience passing from spiritual death to new life, for Jesus took the judgment due us because of our sins. In the Messiah's resurrection, He conquered the death penalty, which enabled us to receive forgiveness of our transgressions.

Because we were born in a state of sin and committed innumerable iniquities, the Mosaic law declared us to be guilty and demanded our punishment. It was as if there was a certificate listing the divine decrees we had violated and tallying up the full extent of our indebtedness to God. In a manner of speaking, the Father wiped out the unfavorable record of our debts. Another way of putting it is that He took that long list of charges against us and nailed every last one of them to the Cross (vs. 14). The Father could do this because the Son's atoning sacrifice fully satisfied the law's demands. At Calvary, Jesus took our judgment on Himself. Now that we are united to the Messiah by faith, the law's power to condemn us is taken away.

The Cross signifies the Son's complete and lasting victory over all spiritual "principalities and powers" (vs. 15) arrayed against the Father. As a result of what Jesus did at Calvary, He disarmed every evil entity, both in heaven and on earth. He also disgraced and humiliated them publicly. The image is that of an ancient post-battle victory procession in which spectators witness the return home of a conqueror. Trailing behind him are his defeated enemies, now stripped and in chains. Because of our union with the Son by faith, we can join His victory procession and offer praises to Him as or conquering King (see 2 Cor. 2:14). From a theological perspective, even the worst f human and satanic wickedness is no match for the love of the Father and the resurrection power of the Son. In order for the Father to bring about this amazing triumph over evil, the Son had to experience the horror of crucifixion. In turn, Satan's eternal doom was sealed when the Father raised His Son from the dead.

SUGGESTIONS TO TEACHERS

Even in the early days of the church, Paul had to deal with people who were slithering into congregations and trying to distort the Gospel message. Consequently, the apostle reminded believers in Colosse and elsewhere to keep their focus on the Son and not on idle notions that diverted them from the Lord. Let this information form a historical backdrop as you discuss the following points with the students.

1. DEFENDING THE GOSPEL. Today, religious charlatans are spreading false teachings about the Messiah. For this reason alone, it is important for the class members to prepare themselves to defend the Gospel. To do so, they should study the Bible regularly and be ready to tell everyone who asks them who Jesus is and what He is doing in their lives.

2. COMBATING HERESY. Paul warned the Colossians not to turn away from the Savior and be taken in by the false doctrines of the world. Similarly, your students need to know that spiritual frauds continue to pose a threat to the body of Christ. The best way to combat heresy is by knowing and teaching the truth of God's Word.

3. EMPHASIZING JESUS. Paul disclosed to his readers that the false teachers had an incorrect view of the Messiah. That is why the apostle declared the Son to be God. Paul also stressed that in Him is the power to cleanse people of their sins and raise them from the dead into everlasting fellowship with the Father. Encourage the class members to live by these important biblical doctrines.

4. EXPERIENCING JESUS' SUFFICIENCY. The religious charlatans plaguing the believers in Colosse made it sound as if it was not possible to enjoy a full life in the Son. Paul countered this incorrect notion with the truth of Jesus' sufficiency for the believer. The apostle revealed that Jesus triumphed over evil when He willingly gave Himself up on the cross. Remind the students that His victory is the basis for them overcoming sin in their lives.

FOR ADULTS

■ **TOPIC:** It's a Wonderful Life!

■ **QUESTIONS:** 1. Why is it important for us not only to believe in Jesus but also to live in union with Him? 2. What real danger is there in allowing Christians to be misled by spiritual frauds? 3. How can we tell if supposedly "new" teaching is in agreement with the Gospel, or is of purely human origin? 4. How is it possible for the Messiah to be divine and human at the same time? 5. What has the Father done for those who put their faith in the Son?

■ ILLUSTRATIONS:

The Fullness of Life. A young father of two children lost his wife when their second child was born. One night as the grieving father was praying for strength, God directed him to Colossians 2:10. The Lord reminded him through this verse that he was spiritually complete in the Savior, despite the death of his wife.

The Holy Spirit touched this struggling believer. He confessed that he did not need anything more than he had in Jesus—not even a wife and mother for his children. God comforted the young father with the wonderful fullness of life he already had through faith in the Son. The believer's heart and mind came to rest and peace.

Too often, it seems, we come to God with complaining spirits. We wish we had something more. Supposedly then we would be satisfied. But no matter how much religious frauds say we need of what the world has to offer, we can find true satisfaction only in the Lord Jesus. He has given us fully of Himself. And He wants us to enjoy the riches of our faith relationship with Him.

That's why we need to bolster our minds with the truths of God's Word about our spiritual resources. Sometimes the Father has to strip us spiritually bare (as it were) before we come to grips with the fact that the Son is more than sufficient to meet all of our needs.

When More Is Less. In Colossians 2:12-13, Paul taught that the Father brought believers back to spiritual life in much the same way that He resurrected His Son. And because believers have been made alive in the Son, they have all they need for life and godliness. Nothing else has to be added, for the Messiah is all-sufficient.

Several years ago, an acquaintance named Bob met me at the appointed time, well dressed, Bible in hand. On the exterior, he could have fit in at any of the Bible-believing churches in our college town. As we sat together over a cup of tea in the student union, his mood was upbeat. Although we had only met the day before, Bob jumped into a comfortable conversation with me, pointing out Scripture and sharing his life story. I listened, genuinely interested.

Then Bob came to his conversion experience. He had come to believe a "faith plus works Gospel"—with a strong emphasis on works. Although highly-educated and well versed in Scripture, he didn't understand that people couldn't enter the kingdom of God on their own merits. When we add to the good news about the all-sufficiency of Jesus, we distort the truth, deceive ourselves, and mislead others. In this case, more is less.

It's Free! Why are people so often itchy to misrepresent the truth of the Gospel by trying to add something to it? Why do they feel compelled to pay for their salvation, when God has declared that doing so is impossible? Well, like a gift that seems too expensive, like an award we know we really didn't deserve, salvation is, in a sense, embarrassing to receive. After all, we messed up beyond repair, and Jesus came and owned the consequences for our poor character and appalling behavior (see Col. 2:14).

And it gets worse. If we'll let Jesus pay for our failure by trusting in His atoning sacrifice, we get off "scot-free" (see vs. 13). In our hearts, we wish we could do something. We trick ourselves into thinking that we need to do our part in making things right. But this is where we must get rid of our pride or lose out on the best offer ever.

| **FOR YOUTH** | ■ **TOPIC:** 360° of Living |

■ **QUESTIONS:** 1. Why is it important for us to be filled with gratitude for the new life we have in the Son? 2. On a day-to-day basis, what difference does it really make for us to be rooted and grounded in Jesus? 3. How can we avoid being deceived by the erroneous teachings of religious charlatans? 4. What difference does it make to our lives that we have been spiritually raised with Jesus from the dead? 5. How does Christian baptism compare with Jewish circumcision?

■ **ILLUSTRATIONS:**

Only One Gospel. Both inside and outside the church the presence of commitment is seriously lacking. People shun obligation because they think it will prevent them from doing what they want in order to enjoy a whole or complete life. This attitude is extremely harmful among adolescent Christians who profess to believe in the vital doctrines of the faith.

For instance, a hesitancy to stand firmly on the truth of the Gospel can lead to spiritual confusion. It is only when we, as believers, preserve the integrity of the Good News, that the doctrinal foundation of the church will withstand the attacks of spiritual frauds.

That is why Paul warned the Colossians not to turn away from the Savior and be taken in by the false teachings of the world. The apostle declared that the Son is God. In Him is the power to cleanse people of their sins and raise them from the dead into everlasting fellowship with the Father. Moreover, Jesus triumphed over evil when He willingly gave Himself up on the cross.

A Full Life in Christ. Enjoying a full spiritual life in the Son is something like enjoying a full tank of gas. What a thrill it is to joyride around town, or spin around the countryside, knowing that our tank is full. But the laws of physics soon catch up with us. No matter how sporty or powerful our car might be, it won't run on empty.

When we confess our faith in the Son, He gives us all the fuel we need (in a manner of speaking) for time and eternity. The full tank is there all the time, whenever we need it. But occasionally we try to run on "foreign" fuel. We think we've outgrown our need of Jesus. Or we'd like to try some alternatives to Him.

Sooner or later, that false gas will let us down. Perhaps for a while, we try to run on empty, because we refuse to turn on the fuel that is Jesus. He spiritually lives in us, but sometimes because of our sin and neglect, we cannot tap into it. Our lives rust away like an abandoned car in a vacant field.

Paul reminded us that we have to drive our roots of faith deeply into Jesus. We cannot afford to lose vital connection with Him. Therefore, every spiritual discipline we find in our church and among our Christian friends must be welcomed. This includes worship, Bible study, prayer, and Christian service. When we engage our minds and hearts in serving Jesus, our joyride with Him will go on forever!

Not All Traditions Are Good. The frauds plaguing the believers in Colosse wanted them to embrace the practice of legalistic traditions as a necessary requirement for being saved. This is a case where rites and rituals threatened to undermine the faith of a thriving community of believers. It should come as no surprise that even today not all traditions are good. They can hurt others and us as well.

I'm reminded of my dog, who has certain traditions. In the last couple of months, he's even picked up a new one. I now have two dogs: Bonhoeffer, my wise and thoughtful four-year-old collie, and Oreo, my wild and crazy one-year-old mutt. Bonhoeffer has always been very good about letting me know when he wants to go outside. He will casually walk up to the door that leads to the side yard and scratch the door three times. Whenever I open the door, Oreo shoots outside like a flying flash—way ahead of Bonhoeffer, who casually walks down the steps and out into the yard.

For the sake of this story, you also need to know that sometimes Oreo drives Bonhoeffer absolutely nuts! Oreo nips at Bonhoeffer's heels and jumps up on his head and bites his ears and steals his chew bone and steps on his tail and wakes him up while he's trying to take a nap. I'm amazed that Bonhoeffer hasn't killed that little puppy. It says a lot about the patience of that dog just by mentioning the fact that he's never even hurt Oreo.

But back to Bonhoeffer's new tradition. There are times when Bonheoffer has taken all that he can from Oreo. (In the words of Popeye, "I've stands all I can stands and I can't stands no more!") Now when Bonhoeffer reaches the limit of his patience, he walks over to the door and scratches it three times. While Bonhoeffer stands at the door waiting to go out, I open the door. Out shoots Oreo like a flying flash. Then Bonhoeffer looks up in my eyes, breathes a sigh of relief that Oreo is outside, and walks over to the couch and lies down! He's achieved his goal of getting rid of his pest, and now he can get some rest for just a little while!

CLOTHED WITH CHRIST

BACKGROUND SCRIPTURE: Colossians 3:1-17
DEVOTIONAL READING: Psalm 107:1-9

Key Verse: Above all these things put on charity,
which is the bond of perfectness. Colossians 3:14.

KING JAMES VERSION

COLOSSIANS 3:5 Mortify therefore your members which are upon the earth; fornication, uncleanness, inordinate affection, evil concupiscence, and covetousness, which is idolatry: 6 For which things' sake the wrath of God cometh on the children of disobedience: 7 In the which ye also walked some time, when ye lived in them.

8 But now ye also put off all these; anger, wrath, malice, blasphemy, filthy communication out of your mouth. 9 Lie not one to another, seeing that ye have put off the old man with his deeds; 10 And have put on the new man, which is renewed in knowledge after the image of him that created him: 11 Where there is neither Greek nor Jew, circumcision nor uncircumcision, Barbarian, Scythian, bond nor free: but Christ is all, and in all.

12 Put on therefore, as the elect of God, holy and beloved, bowels of mercies, kindness, humbleness of mind, meekness, longsuffering; 13 Forbearing one another, and forgiving one another, if any man have a quarrel against any: even as Christ forgave you, so also do ye. 14 And above all these things put on charity, which is the bond of perfectness. 15 And let the peace of God rule in your hearts, to the which also ye are called in one body; and be ye thankful. 16 Let the word of Christ dwell in you richly in all wisdom; teaching and admonishing one another in psalms and hymns and spiritual songs, singing with grace in your hearts to the Lord. 17 And whatsoever ye do in word or deed, do all in the name of the Lord Jesus, giving thanks to God and the Father by him.

NEW REVISED STANDARD VERSION

COLOSSIANS 3:5 Put to death, therefore, whatever in you is earthly: fornication, impurity, passion, evil desire, and greed (which is idolatry). 6 On account of these the wrath of God is coming on those who are disobedient. 7 These are the ways you also once followed, when you were living that life. 8 But now you must get rid of all such things—anger, wrath, malice, slander, and abusive language from your mouth. 9 Do not lie to one another, seeing that you have stripped off the old self with its practices 10 and have clothed yourselves with the new self, which is being renewed in knowledge according to the image of its creator. 11 In that renewal there is no longer Greek and Jew, circumcised and uncircumcised, barbarian, Scythian, slave and free; but Christ is all and in all!

12 As God's chosen ones, holy and beloved, clothe yourselves with compassion, kindness, humility, meekness, and patience. 13 Bear with one another and, if anyone has a complaint against another, forgive each other; just as the Lord has forgiven you, so you also must forgive. 14 Above all, clothe yourselves with love, which binds everything together in perfect harmony. 15 And let the peace of Christ rule in your hearts, to which indeed you were called in the one body. And be thankful. 16 Let the word of Christ dwell in you richly; teach and admonish one another in all wisdom; and with gratitude in your hearts sing psalms, hymns, and spiritual songs to God. 17 And whatever you do, in word or deed, do everything in the name of the Lord Jesus, giving thanks to God the Father through him.

12

201

Home Bible Readings

Background

In Colossians 3:16, Paul encouraged his readers to minister to one another in singing "psalms and hymns and spiritual songs." The "psalms" were probably the canticles found in the Old Testament Psalter. "Hymns" most likely were lyrics composed by Christians to honor God. "Songs" may have been called "spiritual" either to distinguish them from similar compositions by non-Christians or because they referred to spontaneous singing in the Spirit.

The idea is that the words in our worship songs are meant to express the compassion and truth of the Savior. These hymns can either be taken from the Old Testament psalms or be newly written lyrics of praise. Whatever the type of music, it is clear that the Spirit should guide the words, the music, and the singer. Furthermore, we are to praise the Father and the Son in song not just with our lips, but more importantly with all our heart—that is, our whole being.

Notes on the Printed Text

In Colossians 3:5, Paul urged believers to discontinue sinning and being enslaved to evil. Figuratively speaking, they are to "mortify" whatever earthly desires lurk within them. The apostle listed five vices that are indicative of the old fallen nature. These included "fornication," or illicit sexual relations; " uncleanness," or moral impurity; "inordinate affection," or carnal cravings; "evil concupiscence," or depraved desires; and "coveteousness," or the insatiable hunger for material possessions—which is idolatry. Paul followed his admonition with a stern warning. The Father will not ignore unrepented sins. Instead, He will show His displeasure with these vices on the day of judgment when the Son returns. Divine retribution will fall on those who have sold themselves out to such wickedness (vs. 6).

Evidently, most of Paul's readers were Gentiles from pagan backgrounds. They had probably indulged in the sins he just described. Now, however, Jesus had forgiven and renewed them and given them a new way in which to live. Therefore, they were not to be characterized by their former pagan existence (vs. 7). After all, this old way of life was buried in the past for the true follower of the Messiah. To reinforce the apostle's point, he listed a second catalog of vices that have more to do with verbal offenses (vs.

8). Paul commanded his readers to get rid of "anger," or outbursts of temper; "wrath," or the violent expression of hatred; "malice," or vindictive spite; "blasphemy," or destructive gossip; and "filthy communication," or vulgar speech.

Paul urged believers to discontinue lying to one another (vs. 9). The apostle may have been noting actual spiritual maladies within the congregation at Colosse. The problem could have been a source of mistrust and conflict that was beginning to flare up in the church. Paul presented a vivid picture of what it means to turn away from a life of sin and walk in newness of life in the Savior. It is like taking off old, dirty clothes and putting on new, clean garments. Expressed differently, we are to strip off all the disgusting habits we had when we were nonbelievers and clothe ourselves with godly behavior that reflects the character of the Son. This is only possible as the Holy Spirit empowers us to do so.

As a result of putting on a new self in the Messiah, believers are "renewed in knowledge" (vs. 10). In turn, they come to understand their Creator better and conduct themselves in a manner that is pleasing to Him. For the remainder of the believers' sojourn on earth, the Son renews their minds and transforms their thinking, with the result that they choose to do the Father's perfect will (see Rom. 12:2). In this new way of living, there are no distinctions between any of us who belong to the Son. To reinforce this truth, Paul gave examples from his day of social barriers that separated groups of people (Col. 3:11).

Paul did not just tell his readers to abandon all forms of sin. He also exhorted them to demonstrate and cultivate Christlike virtues. The motivation for doing so was their status as "the elect of God" (vs. 12). Put another way, they were God's chosen people. As such, the Lord considered them to be His "holy and beloved" spiritual children. By putting to death the vices of the old self and putting on Christian love, they demonstrated the reality of the new life they had in the Son. They also promoted harmony within their fellowship.

To further encourage a holy way of life, Paul listed five virtues that should spiritually clothe believers. He first urged the Colossians to array themselves with "bowels of mercies." This refers to an affectionate sympathy for others, especially for those in need. Second, the apostle affirmed the value of "kindness." His readers were to have a generous and helpful regard in their dealings with others. "Humbleness of mind" was third on Paul's list. He certainly was not advocating self-mortification as the false teachers had done, but was speaking about meekness in behavior and attitude that is respectful and not haughty or pretentious. Fourth, the apostle wanted the believers in Colosse to exhibit "meekness." By this he meant showing congenial consideration toward others. Finally, Paul stressed the importance of "longsuffering." He wanted his readers to have a tolerant and forgiving spirit toward those who wronged them.

Paul's next admonition pertained to forgiveness. Even within the church, believers often rub each other the wrong way, and it's easy to harbor a grudge against a

Christian brother or sister. The apostle, however, instructed the Colossians to resist such a temptation and instead be forbearing and forgiving when they felt they had been mistreated (vs. 13). Furthermore, making allowance for the faults of others and being willing to overlook an offense were the means by which believers clothed themselves with the Christian virtues listed in verse 12. Paul then recalled how the Lord forgave us (vs. 13). The implication is that if Jesus could pardon us, who have wronged Him infinitely more than we have been mistreated, how much easier it should be for us to forgive those who have frustrated us.

Of course, Paul knew that forgiving is not easy to do. Yet the apostle also believed that the Son empowers us to be like Him, especially as the Holy Spirit conforms us to the Savior's image. This gives us the ability to be patient with one another no matter how great a loss someone has caused in our lives. Most of all, Paul asked the Colossians to clothe themselves with "charity" (vs. 14), or love. Metaphorically speaking, Christlike compassion is like an overcoat that rests on top of all the other virtues. When Jesus' followers are dressed in this manner, they will enjoy perfect unity. The Messiah will have knit us all together in a single, multicolored, multipatterned tapestry by His transforming love.

After Paul described the kind of conduct the Colossian believers should maintain, especially within their fellowship, he explained how it was possible for them to obey his instructions. In essence, he said they must live day-by-day totally under the lordship of the Savior. This involved letting the peace that He supplied control their thoughts, emotions, and actions. The Greek noun rendered "peace" (vs. 15) denoted the presence of harmony and tranquility. Unlike worldly forms of concord, this peace was a special, personal gift from the Savior (see John 14:27). Moreover, this peace is the embodiment of the Messiah, "for he is our peace" (Eph. 2:14).

Since the biblical writers thought of the heart as the center of a person's being, Paul, in effect, was calling upon believers to submit their entire being to the control of the Son's peace. The reason for doing so is that the Father has called us to peace (Col. 3:15). Moreover, the Father wants His spiritual children to live in harmony, not as separate individuals, but as a unified community of believers. Since we are all members of one spiritual body, of which Jesus is the appointed head (see 1:18; 2:19), we must not let our selfishness disrupt the health of His body. Paul also directed us to be thankful. He didn't ask us to just express gratitude to the Father, but to have a constant attitude of thankfulness for being a redeemed member of the Son's spiritual body. The apostle wanted believers to be a grateful people who appreciated what the Savior was doing within them.

Living as the Father's grateful children includes letting the message about the Son, in all its richness, completely fill our lives (3:16). This admonition means more than just a simple reading and rote memorization of the Bible. It is allowing the Word of God to affect every aspect of our existence. For instance, we allow Scripture to shape our decisions and determine our thinking patterns. We also seek to live by it on a daily basis. As Jesus' message dwells in us richly, we are better able to instruct and exhort one another in a prudent and discerning manner. Moreover, the Spirit enables us to draw upon all the wisdom provided by the Savior as we go about our daily lives. Indeed, God's Word is the basis for us "singing" with gratitude.

Paul concluded this part of his instructions with an admonition that the believers in Colosse were to do everything in Jesus' name (vs. 17). Put differently, they were to think, behave, and minister in light of the Messiah's supreme authority and character. Since the Lord has claimed us with His atoning blood, we belong to and are dependent on Him. Accordingly, His name should be stamped on all that we do and say as His representatives to the unsaved. This includes us expressing gratitude through the Son to the Father.

SUGGESTIONS TO TEACHERS

Holy living does not mean that we must just avoid negative behaviors, but that we practice positive behaviors as well. Use the class session to encourage your students to take off degrading conduct and put on new, Christlike virtues.

1. CULTIVATING HOLY LIVING. Begin by explaining that Paul used the metaphor of undressing and dressing to describe how we should live in a manner that is characterized by holiness. The idea is to get rid of our sinful lifestyles and replace them with new, godly ones.

2. ACTING AS GOD'S CHOSEN PEOPLE. Next, emphasize that God's choosing us as His people is the motivation to change from a worldly to a holy life. Through faith in the Son we become a community of believers who express Christlike virtues. These include compassion, kindness, forgiveness, and love.

3. BEING RULED BY GOD'S PEACE. Be sure to note that Christians are to be full of the peace and joy supplied by God. Expressed differently, His peace is to rule over the members of Jesus' spiritual body. In this approach to life, the peace of God decides our arguments much as an umpire would.

4. USING MUSIC TO TEACH. Finally, encourage the students to use musical forms of praise to teach the Savior's message to one another. Regardless of the form and style in which we convey Jesus' teachings, all of it should be wrapped in a garment of gratitude. Indeed, everything we say and do must be characterized by an attitude of thankfulness for what the Father has done for us in the Son.

■ **TOPIC:** Breaking Bad Habits
■ **QUESTIONS:** 1. Why is it important for believers to put to death the cravings of their earthly nature? 2. How can believers develop spiritu-

al goals that keep Jesus at the center? 3. How can believers keep their families unsullied from sexual defilement found in print and electronic media? 4. What are some ways the "word of Christ" (Col. 3:16) lives in the hearts of believers? 5. How does "giving thanks to God" (vs. 17) regulate the kinds of things believers do?

■ ILLUSTRATIONS:

A Healthy Diet of Christian Virtues. If you've been in a supermarket recently, you might have noticed the numerous shelves of natural food supplements. In recent years, these products have become big business. People pay soaring prices because they put a high priority on their physical health.

In contrast, you find the purveyors of so-called junk food are also doing quite well. They cater to people who have the bad habit of eating and drinking anything, as long as it's filling and tastes good to them. They spend money, too, but not according to the rules of good nutrition. They go for whatever appeals to them, no matter if it is bad for them. Their priority is satisfying their taste buds.

In the supermarket of life, we have to make wise spiritual choices that enable the "word of Christ" (Col. 3:16) to abide in and among us. Some people place a higher priority on godly living than others do. Paul made it clear what our choices must be if we profess to be Jesus' followers (see vss. 5-14). We can't go on consuming a diet of sin that will ruin us. The Bible tells us what those poisons are, as well as the overwhelming benefits of the healthy diet of Christian virtues.

Leading Holy Lives. "You know, pastor, not everyone's cut out to be a Father Damien," Gil told his minister after the Sunday sermon. That morning's message had included the account of a Belgian missionary named Father Damien. In the late 1800s, he volunteered to oversee a leper colony on the Hawaiian island of Molokai.

Damien, whose given name was Joseph de Veuster, ministered to the lepers' spiritual needs. But he also became their physician, for few medically trained professionals would come to the island. Damien also worked with the Hawaiian government to improve the water supply, dwellings, and food supply for the settlement. After five years, Damien's actions motivated numerous others to devote themselves to the colony. But eventually, Damien himself contracted leprosy and died on the island in 1889.

To Gil, it all sounded pretty incredible. "I'm no martyr," he told his pastor. "You don't have to be," Gil's minister responded. "God doesn't call everyone to go to a remote island and die for His sake. But He does call all of us to lead holy lives—wherever we are." Or, as Colossians 3:17 states, regardless of what we say or do, it should be accomplished in the "name of the Lord Jesus."

Hope to Hold On. Imagine what it would be like to be a prisoner in a foreign land, or under a tyrant ruler. Many Christian families were split apart in the early centuries as fathers were taken from their homes and cast into darkened dungeons. And it was not only the heads of households who suffered these imprisonments, tortures, and death. History records many accounts of Christian children and teenage boys and girls being carried away as well.

From accounts such as *Foxe's Book of Martyrs* and others, we see that it was the inward hope of being the "elect of God" (Col. 3:12) and becoming "holy and beloved" members of His spiritual family that was shining like a radiant light in these prisoners. Though their bodies were tortured and imprisoned, in their hearts they were free and filled with divine "peace" (vs. 15). They held on to the hope of being with the Lord forever in the life after death. In light of their testimonies, shouldn't we be able to rest in the hope of Christ's resurrection and strength in our present circumstances? After all, He has chosen us to be part of His spiritual body called the church.

FOR YOUTH

■ **TOPIC:** Clothed with Love

■ **QUESTIONS:** 1. What does it take for believers to put to death the sins Paul listed in Colossians 3:5? 2. What aims and ambitions are acceptable for believers? 3. How can believers clothe themselves with the qualities of righteousness? 4. Why are forgiveness and love so important to holy living? 5. Why is it important for the "peace of God" (vs. 15) to reign in the hearts of believers?

■ **ILLUSTRATIONS:**

Life on a Higher Level. A missionary wrote to a friend about her son. "Isaac, at 6'3" and 180 lbs., is looking forward to Duke basketball camp and hopes to get on his high school team this year. He just returned from a church mission trip to Jamaica. He'll be in the 11th grade next year and hopes to maintain his straight-A record."

Isaac illustrates life on a higher level. What makes the difference? For one thing, his values and choices have been solidly anchored in the Lord Jesus. Does this mean Isaac has been spared problems and hardships? Not at all. He recently has been through some very rough patches.

Colossians 3:9 and 10 clearly explain what we have to do to achieve life on a higher level. There are vices we need to discard like an old, filthy garment, and some new virtues (such as Christlike love) we need to clothe over our regenerate selves. If we are serious about following Jesus, we have to study these truths and ask the Holy Spirit to lead us in paths of obedience.

Someone to Look Up To. When Sevda came from Romania two years ago, she became a part of an American family to begin her new life. As a middle-school child, she learned a new language and adapted to a new culture. She did both well.

Now Sevda is sharing what she has learned. Two boys, also from Romania, recently have been adopted into Sevda's family. She has gladly welcomed them. She even has taken on the role of teacher by helping her younger siblings to "know the ways of their parents' household."

Sevda and her two brothers share in both the love and the generosity of their adoptive parents. And out of love for their parents, they strive to obey and please them. To know how, the brothers look to their older sister.

Perhaps there is a younger person in your life who looks up to you. As a follower of the Lord Jesus, you can be a role model to these preteens of someone who has "put on the new man" (Col. 3:10). When they look at you, they can see what it means to be a chosen member of God's family and how to live in an upright, loving, and virtuous manner (see vs. 14).

Heirs to the Family Fortune. More billionaires have been created in the last decade of world history than all other decades put together. With the momentum of technology, those who are one day sitting in a college dorm room pooling change to pay the pizza delivery person are the next day sitting in corporate board rooms. Story after story could be told describing the pauper-to-prince testimony of countless new millionaires.

But it wasn't always this way. One only has to travel a bit to see the effects of the old style of getting rich—accumulating wealth from one generation to the next. Travel to Asheville and see the giant Vanderbilt estate; take note of the Walton fortune when you shop Wal-Mart next time out; and consider the Rockefeller story when you see the gas tank of a car being filled.

The preceding observations notwithstanding, there are no larger inheritances, nor are there any greater number of heirs, than in God's spiritual family. They are His chosen people (see Col. 3:12) from all walks of life (see vs. 11), whom He has invited to be citizens of His kingdom. Indeed, it is only in the divine kingdom that we are allowed to take our eternal inheritance with us when we die.

SPIRITUAL DISCIPLINES

BACKGROUND SCRIPTURE: Colossians 4:2-17
DEVOTIONAL READING: 1 Corinthians 9:19-27

Key Verse: Say to Archippus, Take heed to the ministry which
thou hast received in the Lord, that thou fulfil it. Colossians 4:17.

KING JAMES VERSION

COLOSSIANS 4:2 Continue in prayer, and watch in the same with thanksgiving; 3 Withal praying also for us, that God would open unto us a door of utterance, to speak the mystery of Christ, for which I am also in bonds: 4 That I may make it manifest, as I ought to speak.

5 Walk in wisdom toward them that are without, redeeming the time. 6 Let your speech be alway with grace, seasoned with salt, that ye may know how ye ought to answer every man.

NEW REVISED STANDARD VERSION

COLOSSIANS 4:2 Devote yourselves to prayer, keeping alert in it with thanksgiving. 3 At the same time pray for us as well that God will open to us a door for the word, that we may declare the mystery of Christ, for which I am in prison, 4 so that I may reveal it clearly, as I should.

5 Conduct yourselves wisely toward outsiders, making the most of the time. 6 Let your speech always be gracious, seasoned with salt, so that you may know how you ought to answer everyone.

13

HOME BIBLE READINGS

BACKGROUND

Colossians 3:18–4:1 records Paul's instructions to Christian households. These exhortations parallel what the apostle wrote in Ephesians 5:21–6:9. There he directed married couples to be kind and considerate to one another (5:21). In Colossians 3, Paul specified that wives were to understand and affirm their husbands (vs. 18). In turn, the apostle urged husbands to be loving, rather than resentful, toward their wives (vs. 19). In regard to children, Paul said they would please the Lord by obeying their parents (vs. 20). Also, parents were not to exasperate their children and cause them to lose heart (vs. 21).

Slavery was a stark reality in the ancient world. At least one-third of the population in the Roman Empire was in bondage, and some historians put the percentage at over one-half. Most slaves labored in private homes. God never ordained slavery as He sanctioned marriage and the family. Eventually, Christian influence helped remove the blight of slavery from human society. But the day when that would be possible came long after Paul's time. And so, since slavery existed, the apostle tried to counsel believers who were involved in it. Specifically, the apostle instructed Christian slaves to be obedient and respectful to their human masters. Slaves were to do so wholeheartedly because of their reverent fear of the Lord (vs. 22).

In many instances, slaves did their work grudgingly and out of compulsion. They cared little if their efforts made their masters more prosperous or increasingly comfortable. Slaves did just enough work to keep from being beaten or otherwise mistreated. Paul urged Christian slaves to adopt a different attitude. Regardless of the work they performed, they were to do so with enthusiasm. The apostle also advised genuine submission to human masters, not because the latter deserved it, but because the slaves were actually serving a heavenly Master (vs. 23). He was none other than the Lord Jesus. Paul promised that when the Messiah returned, He would bestow on Christian slaves (as well as all believers) an eternal inheritance as their reward (vs. 24). Moreover, the apostle assured his fellow, enslaved Christians that those who acted unjustly or wickedly would receive the consequences of their wrongdoing, and there would be no exceptions (vs. 25).

In the early Christian church, slaves probably outnumbered masters, but obviously there were some in the latter category. For example, Philemon of Colosse (to whom

Paul wrote one of the New Testament letters) certainly was a slaveholder. The apostle did not tell the Christian masters to free their slaves. Instead, he directed them to treat their slaves in a just and fair manner, for slaveholders likewise were accountable to their "Master in heaven" (4:1). Put another way, the masters were not independent rulers over their slaves. Paul's admonition constituted a major break from the usual superior attitude of masters to slaves. Perhaps in this way, the apostle helped pave the way for an end to slavery.

NOTES ON THE PRINTED TEXT

It would be incorrect to assume that maintaining Christlike relationships is just a simple process of following specific rules and regulations. While human initiative and effort are involved, all of it must be bathed in prayer (Col. 4:2). The Greek verb rendered "continue" means "to persevere in" or "to be steadfastly attentive to," and indicates that prayer is to be a consistent part of every believer's life. Furthermore, being vigilant in prayer requires earnestness, readiness, and determination. Paul directed his readers both to pray diligently and to maintain an attitude of thankfulness and praise. This is the opposite of being filled with anxiety, irritation, or smugness.

Paul wanted his readers to do more than pray for themselves. He also wanted them to remember to offer prayer to God on behalf of the apostle and his colleagues in ministry. In particular, the believers in Colosse were to petition God to give the evangelistic team new and increased opportunities to herald His message to the lost. This was the good news about the "mystery of Christ" (Col. 4:3). The latter phrase referred to the truth that the Father intended for salvation through faith in His Son to be made available to Jews and Gentiles alike (see 2:2).

In Ephesians 3:2-6, Paul explained more fully what he meant by the Greek noun rendered "mystery." (See also the comments made on this term in lessons 1 and 5.) We learn that the apostle regarded himself as a steward whom God appointed to serve as a missionary to the lost (vs. 2). By preaching the Gospel to the Gentiles, Paul had become a means by which God extended the message of grace to people who previously had been without hope for salvation. The apostle himself had told the early converts of Ephesus about his role. Later converts would have heard about him from others. The Lord disclosed His will to Paul "by revelation" (vs. 3). This refers to Paul's meeting with the risen Messiah on the road to Damascus. At that time, the Savior charged Paul with taking the Gospel to the Gentiles (see Acts 9:15; 26:16-18).

One aspect of the divine secret is God's plan to bring all things under the Messiah's authority, including the entire cosmos (see Eph. 1:9-10). A second aspect is that God's grace includes Gentiles as well as Jews (3:6). According to the Father's redemptive plan, the time had arrived to disclose His compassion toward those Gentiles who became devoted followers of the Son. Indeed, all the blessings enjoyed by saved Jews have also been bestowed upon believing Gentiles. The Messiah dwells in them as assuredly as He lives in Jewish believers, and both possess the same "hope of glory" (Col. 1:27).

Previously in Ephesians, Paul had written about God's grace for the Gentiles (see 2:11-22, which was covered in lesson 2). As the Ephesians reread those earlier parts of the letter, they could understand Paul's insight into the "mystery" (3:4). The apostle wanted his readers to appreciate his knowledge and understanding of the divine plan regarding the Messiah, not so that they would admire Paul, but so that they would accept his teachings. He explained that what God had not disclosed about His redemptive plan to former generations, the Holy Spirit "revealed unto [God's] holy apostles and prophets" (vs. 5) of the early church so that everyone might hear about it.

Paul explained that by means of the Gospel, Gentiles were now "fellowheirs" (vs. 6) with Israel. In other words, Gentile and Jewish believers alike could inherit the kingdom of God. Also, by believing the Good News, Gentiles become members together of the "same body." That is, Gentile and Jewish believers were part of one united body with the Messiah as its Head. Moreover, the Gospel has given Gentiles a share in the "promise in Christ." This meant both Gentile and Jewish believers could enjoy the covenant blessings.

To us, it may seem obvious that Gentiles needn't convert to Judaism to be acceptable in God's sight, but that's because we live long after Paul. For the early Jewish Christians, who were raised with the idea that only Jews could have a serious relationship with God, this was a radical concept. Still, God had intended Gentile inclusion all along. Perhaps no one in the early church understood the change that had occurred in the Son as thoroughly as did Paul. Now that Gentile believers are a major part of the church, we may find it easy to forget our spiritual heritage is Jewish. But if we consider how Jews would have perceived a Gentile's eternal status before the divine secret was revealed, we should be all the more grateful for God's abundant grace.

As Paul and his colleagues freely shared the Gospel with Jews and Gentiles alike, the missionaries encountered stiff opposition from those who were antagonistic to their message. This is one reason why, as the apostle wrote to the believers in Colosse, he did so while imprisoned in Rome and awaiting trial (Col. 4:3). Despite his sobering circumstance, Paul refused to shirk his God-given responsibility to tell others about the Savior. Even so, the apostle did not operate in his own strength. Instead, he made the truth plainly and clearly known in the power of the Holy Spirit. This is one reason why Paul asked his readers to keep him in prayer as he shared the Good News with whomever would listen (vs. 4).

Paul encouraged his readers to conduct themselves with "wisdom" (vs. 5) toward outsiders, namely, those who were unbelievers. The Greek noun rendered "wisdom" denoted the presence of skill in managing a broad range of responsibilities, as well as displaying prudence in one's interpersonal relationships. So instead of the believers in Colosse wasting their time and energy on frivolous pursuits, the apostle urged them to make good use of every moment the Lord gave them to share the Gospel (for example, while at work, at civic forums, and at the marketplace).

Paul instructed his readers to ensure their conversation was always gracious. By this the apostle meant their "speech" (vs. 6) was to be characterized by compassion and kindness. This is possibly one reason why, in Ephesians 5:4, the apostle said believers are to have nothing to do with obscenity, foolish talk, and coarse joking (compare 4:29). These kinds of speech are sinful because they harm both those who speak them and those who hear them. In place of improper speech, believers are to give thanks to God. Expressing gratitude is beneficial to all who speak and hear it. Moreover, the speech of Jesus' followers is to be "seasoned with salt" (Col. 4:6). In other words, they needed to have a wholesomeness about them that enabled them, through the words they spoke, to be a blessing and a moral preservative in the world.

SUGGESTIONS TO TEACHERS

Paul encouraged believers to live faithfully and responsibly for the Lord. This included being devoted to prayer and remembering to pray for others. It also involved acting wisely among unbelievers and maintaining a gracious disposition in all one's interactions with the unsaved.

1. BEING DILIGENT IN PRAYER. In Colossians 4:2, Paul stressed the importance of being earnest in prayer. Take a few moments to explore with the students what prayer means to them. Of course, an entire series of lessons could well be devoted to this topic. Nonetheless, allow ample time to discuss why persistence in prayer is important (see Eph. 6:18).

2. BEING EFFECTIVE IN PRAYER. Let the class members know that they can find strength in the Lord through prayer (see Jas. 5:16). Note that spiritual battles are lost and Christians retreat when they fail to pray. More specifically, they quit the faith race, drop out of worship and service, and lose their love for the Savior when they do not pray.

3. BEING WISE. Paul taught that believers should conduct themselves in "wisdom" (Col. 4:5) among the unsaved. Explain that this includes loving, not despising, the lost. It also includes blessing those who are unkind to the students, doing good to those who dislike them, and praying for those who are mean-spirited to them (see Matt. 5:44).

4. BEING SALTY. Paul stated that the conversation of believers needed to be "seasoned with salt" (Col. 4:6). In a figurative sense, we need to have a wholesomeness about us that enables us to be a source of spiritual truth in the world. Otherwise, if we become too much like the world, we become morally insipid.

■ **TOPIC:** Support through Mentoring

■ **QUESTIONS:** 1. Why do you think it is sometimes a challenge for believers to be persistent in prayer? 2. Who are some devoted Christian ministers the Lord might want you to keep in prayer? 3. What reason did Paul give for being imprisoned in Rome? 4. Why did Paul think it was important for him to "speak the mystery of Christ" (Col. 4:3)? 5. Why would it be detrimental for believers to act foolishly around the unsaved?

■ **ILLUSTRATIONS:**

Leadership, Cooperation, and Survival. Paul urged the believers in Colosse to be known to others for their godly deeds and words (see Col. 4:5-6). This included behaving wisely and being gracious in how they treated others. At first, their role model was Paul's beloved coworker Epaphras, who told them about the Lord Jesus (see 1:7). Later, there were other godly mentors who encouraged them to remain faithful in their Christian commitment (see 4:7-9).

In 2004, Peter Lane Taylor, a correspondent for *National Geographic Adventure Magazine*, did a story on how a small group of Ukrainian Jews avoided "being captured by Nazis." It was 1942, and the Stermer family faced a grim outcome at the hands of the Germans advancing on the small village of Korolówka.

To stay alive, the matriarch of the family, Esther Stermer, told one of her sons to "find a place" where all of them could safely "hide in the forest." The adolescent succeeded in discovering a labyrinth of local caves "about five miles to the north." Next, as a result of Esther's leadership and mentorship, 38 people decided to cooperate with one another. This decision proved crucial to their survival.

The cave dwellers huddled together in "what is know as the Priest's Grotto." There they learned to eat, sleep, and survive in near-total darkness. The horrors of the Holocaust continued right over their heads. Entrances to the cave were sealed time and again, and food was brought in from rare forays aboveground.

Finally, the signal came: a message inside a bottle lowered down a chimney-like entrance to the grotto by their connection to the outside world. The Germans had left and Russian troops were entering their village. The Stermers' unity of spirit and collective determination enabled them, as a group, to survive.

Depending on God. In the movies, fighting evil is simply a matter of having the right equipment. But in real life, spiritual warfare involves a far more powerful weapon—completely depending on God for help. Anything less, and it is like waving a plastic wand over an empty top hat and expecting "magic" to happen. There's no power in the plastic. It's a mere prop. Only the trained illusionist can take that empty hat and amazingly fill it with a living rabbit.

When it comes to combating evil and sin in our world, the real power is in the sovereign Lord of all creation. Thus, to be victorious, we must put ourselves in God's hands. We do this by devoting ourselves to prayer (see Col. 4:2). This includes interceding on behalf of others (see vs. 3). When we are persistent in prayer, God is faithful to give us the spiritual tools we need to stand our ground when the day of evil comes.

What Is Prayer? Colossians 4:2-4 is only one of many places in Scripture in which the importance of prayer is emphasized. The basic concept is straightforward enough. Prayer is simply talking to God, in which we bring Him our requests and offer Him our thanks. Still, it's appropriate for us to dwell a little further on the basic dynamic of prayer.

Let's consider the following analogy. Praying is like plugging a lamp cord into an electrical outlet. Plugging the cord into the outlet does not create the electrical power. It simply makes contact with it. It enables electrical power to flow from the outlet, through the cord, and into the lamp. It is the same with praying. Praying does not create divine power. It simply makes contact with it. It enables divine power to flow from God, through us, and into the lives of other people for His glory.

FOR YOUTH

■ **TOPIC:** Get Spiritually Fit
■ **QUESTIONS:** 1. What is prayer, and why do you think it is important? 2. What are some ways you can encourage other believers to be diligent to pray? 3. Why did Paul want the believers in Colosse to remember him in prayer? 4. How does the Lord want His followers to act toward unbelievers? 5. What does it mean to have speech that is "seasoned with salt" (Col. 4:6)?

■ **ILLUSTRATIONS:**

Godfather of Fitness. Until his death in 2011, Jack LaLanne was known as the "Godfather of fitness" because of his expertise in exercise and nutrition. But it wasn't always that way for him. As a young adolescent, he recalled being addicted to sugar and junk foods.

Then, when LaLanne was 15, he heard a pioneer in America's wellness movement, Paul Bragg, give a lecture on health and nutrition. That speech motivated LaLanne to radically change his lifestyle. He began to eat properly and exercise regularly. In time, he became physically fit. He also gained recognition as a weight lifter and bodybuilder. He devoted the rest of his life to encouraging people to better themselves through exercise and fitness.

For saved teens, even more important than physical wellness is their spiritual fitness (see 1 Tim. 4:8). And one of the ways they can become spiritually healthier and more robust is by means of prayer. This includes devoting themselves to praying regularly, and remaining alert and thankful as they petition God on behalf of themselves and others (see Col. 4:2-4).

Standing Firm. Remember playing king of the mountain at recess or with friends in your neighborhood? If there was ever a time to stand firm, that was it. Later on, the football scrimmage line represented the place to stand firm, especially if you were playing defense.

The most important place for us to stand firm is in our walk with the Lord. These days, though, we see teenagers dropping like flies all around us. This is somewhat due to their inability to resist the allure of drugs, illicit sex, and unwholesome electronic media. Part of the reason they spiritually fall is the lack of teaching and encouragement in the faith from Christian mentors.

Our great responsibility is to uphold younger believers in prayer on a regular basis (see Col. 4:2-4). We can petition the Lord to keep saved adolescents from spiritually stumbling. We can also ask the Lord to give believing teens the wisdom and patience to resist the temptations all around them to morally compromise in their faith.

Lesson from the Math Class. Can you imagine a high school teacher in a mathematics class saying to some students, "Oh, you don't have to concern yourself with learning to add and subtract numbers. The most important issue in solving calculus problems is whether you're really tall!" Being a tall person has nothing to do with solving calculus problems. But knowing the fundamental rules of addition and subtraction is imperative to this and other areas of mathematics.

The same principle is true in terms of living faithfully and responsibly for God. Whether we're tall or short doesn't matter. But knowing the Savior by faith and relying upon the power of the Holy Spirit for victory over sin is crucial, especially if we want to be effective in all we do for the Lord.

This is where continuing earnestly in prayer becomes a high priority for us (see Col. 4:2). When we spend time in prayer, the Spirit can prompt us to be more alert to our needs, as well as to those of others. Also, through prayer, the Spirit can enable us to be more attentive to opportunities to serve that the Lord opens up to us (see vss. 3-4). Finally, as we spend time with God in prayer, He can clarify for us prudent ways in which to act and respond to our unsaved peers (see vss. 5-6).

DANIEL'S VISION OF CHANGE

BACKGROUND SCRIPTURE: Daniel 7
DEVOTIONAL READING: Daniel 6:25-28

Key Verse: His dominion is an everlasting dominion, which shall not pass away, and his kingdom that which shall not be destroyed. Daniel 7:14.

KING JAMES VERSION

DANIEL 7:9 I beheld till the thrones were cast down, and the Ancient of days did sit, whose garment was white as snow, and the hair of his head like the pure wool: his throne was like the fiery flame, and his wheels as burning fire. 10 A fiery stream issued and came forth from before him: thousand thousands ministered unto him, and ten thousand times ten thousand stood before him: the judgment was set, and the books were opened. 11 I beheld then because of the voice of the great words which the horn spake: I beheld even till the beast was slain, and his body destroyed, and given to the burning flame. 12 As concerning the rest of the beasts, they had their dominion taken away: yet their lives were prolonged for a season and time. 13 I saw in the night visions, and, behold, one like the Son of man came with the clouds of heaven, and came to the Ancient of days, and they brought him near before him. 14 And there was given him dominion, and glory, and a kingdom, that all people, nations, and languages, should serve him: his dominion is an everlasting dominion, which shall not pass away, and his kingdom that which shall not be destroyed.

NEW REVISED STANDARD VERSION

DANIEL 7:9 As I watched,
thrones were set in place,
    and an Ancient One took his throne,
his clothing was white as snow,
    and the hair of his head like pure wool;
his throne was fiery flames,
    and its wheels were burning fire.
10 A stream of fire issued
    and flowed out from his presence.
A thousand thousands served him,
    and ten thousand times ten thousand stood attending
        him.
The court sat in judgment,
    and the books were opened.

11 I watched then because of the noise of the arrogant words that the horn was speaking. And as I watched, the beast was put to death, and its body destroyed and given over to be burned with fire. 12 As for the rest of the beasts, their dominion was taken away, but their lives were prolonged for a season and a time. 13 As I watched in the night visions,
I saw one like a human being
    coming with the clouds of heaven.
And he came to the Ancient One
    and was presented before him.
14 To him was given dominion
    and glory and kingship,
that all peoples, nations, and languages
    should serve him.
His dominion is an everlasting dominion
    that shall not pass away,
and his kingship is one
    that shall never be destroyed.

HOME BIBLE READINGS

BACKGROUND

In Daniel 1, we learn that, as new arrivals in Babylon, Daniel and his companions passed a test involving what they ate and learned. After refusing the king's food for 10 days, they appeared healthier than the young men who had eaten the royal food (see vss. 8-16). Moreover, verse 17 states that God gave the four Hebrew youths extraordinary "knowledge and skill in all learning and wisdom." Later on, however, three of them were cast into a fiery furnace for refusing to worship Nebuchadnezzar's golden image; but God preserved them (chap. 3). Many years later, jealous officials charged Daniel himself with praying to his God, despite King Darius's decree against doing so. For this infraction, Daniel was thrown into a den of lions; but God protected Daniel from any harm (chap. 6).

These historical accounts are what most of us remember about Daniel. In one sense, they are incidental to his prophecies, though they do spotlight the faith and character of the Hebrew captives. We discover that God has been, and is, in the business of using human institutions (for example, empires, nations, companies, and cities) to accomplish His will. Chapter 7 of the book is a case in point. It concerns Daniel's dream involving four beasts. The "first year of Belshazzar" (vs. 1) would be about 553 B.C. when Daniel saw in his vision a "lion" (vs. 4), a "bear" (vs. 5), a "leopard" (vs. 6), and a hideous, exceedingly strong creature (vs. 7). These beasts were graphic depictions of four successive empires, namely, Babylonia, Medo-Persia, Greece, and Rome (see 7:17; 11:30).

NOTES ON THE PRINTED TEXT

In the vision recorded in Daniel 7, it was the fourth beast that seemed to capture the elder statesman's attention the most (see vs. 19). Daniel was riveted by the huge iron teeth this brute used to consume its prey (see vs. 23). We learn from ancient history that the legions of Rome used their superior military might to overrun and assimilate other nations, including the remnants of the once powerful but later divided kingdom of Greece. The "ten horns" (vs. 20) Daniel saw in his dream represent the vast sweep of the beast's authority, which was manifested either in ten monarchs or kingdoms arising from the Roman Empire (see vs. 24). It is debated whether these entities existed at the same time as Rome or came after its demise. For instance, one common view is that the horns symbolize a second phase of the fourth kingdom, namely, a revived Roman Empire that will materialize in the last days. This view notwithstanding, there is no direct evidence in the biblical text to support such a distinction.

In verse 8, Daniel noted that while he was contemplating the ten horns, a smaller horn suddenly appeared. In turn, three of the earlier horns were plucked up by their roots to make room for the formidable newcomer (see vss. 20, 24). One view is that this entity symbolizes the rise of the Antichrist (see vs. 21). This individual not only deceives the earth, but also seeks to control it through the military, economic, and religious systems of the world (see 2 Thess. 2:1-10; 1 John 2:18, 22; 4:1-4; 2 John 7; Rev. 19:19). Another view is that the smaller horn represents an evil world system that embodies the Antichrist's wicked characteristics. Ancient Rome would be one example of a human government that endorsed the persecution of believers, the spread of immorality, and the proliferation of heretical ideas.

Regardless of which option is preferred, the despicable nature of the smaller horn is unmistakable. Daniel 7:8 says this entity had humanlike eyes that could never be satiated and a mouth that spouted arrogant claims. Verses 21 and 25 reveal that the imposing horn was allowed to wage war for a set time period against God's holy people, as well as oppress and defeat them. Verses 9 and 10 record Daniel's vision of a heavenly courtroom scene, the immediate backdrop of which is God's plan for judging the wicked and vindicating the upright (see vss. 22, 26). The broader literary context of these verses is the elder statesman's dream concerning the four world empires of Babylon, Medo-Persia, Greece, and Rome.

It's worth noting that verses 9 and 10 are characterized by symmetry and balance, which is consistent with the beauty and order that distinguish the supreme Judge of the cosmos. This situation contrasts sharply with the churning of the sea and its beasts, which represents the agitation found in the tyrannical waters of human rebellion (see vss. 2-8). Despite the pompous claims and defiant actions of the anti-God forces in the world, none of them can withstand the judgment of the Lord (see vs. 27). From this truth redeemed humanity learns that all would-be antagonists are completely muzzled and condemned by the God of glory.

In his vision, Daniel saw thrones being set up, followed by "the Ancient of days" (vs. 9) taking His place to administer justice. In this verse, God is portrayed in human form as a revered, prudent, and authoritative judge. Paul referred to Him as the "King of kings, and Lord of lords" (1 Tim. 6:15), the One who alone possesses immortality, who dwells in unapproachable light (vs. 16), and upon whom no human is able to look directly. Daniel noticed that the attire of the eternal God was white as snow, and His hair was white like pure lamb's wool. The chariot-like throne on which the Ancient One sat was ablaze and mounted on fiery wheels (see Pss. 50:3; 68:4; 97:3; 104:3-4;

Isa. 6:1-4; 19:1; 66:15; Ezek. 1:27; Nah. 1:3). A "fiery stream" (Dan. 7:10) emerged from the all-glorious throne. It was as if flames emanated like solar flares from all around Him. The heavenly host who attended to the Creator-King and served Him were countless in number. This was the awe-inspiring backdrop for convening the divine tribunal (see Pss. 82:1; 94:2; 96:13).

As Daniel's dream continued to unfold, he was captivated by the arrogant remarks mouthed by the small horn. As he watched, he noticed that the small-horned beast was eventually put to death. Next, its corpse was cremated in an intense fire (Dan. 7:11). The elder statesman noted that the Lord had already removed the authority belonging to the rest of the beasts Daniel described earlier. Be that as it may, God permitted them to go on living for a "season and time" (vs. 12). It's unclear why the Lord allowed the preceding kingdoms to continue for an indefinite span, along with their inhabitants and customs. What is certain is that God will one day judge all evil. Likewise, no matter how dark things may appear, believers have the assurance that the Lord will watch over them and bring them through their trials.

Verse 13 spotlights the coronation of the "Son of man." The preceding phrase emphasizes that this person was a representative of the people of God. In contrast to the grotesque and arrogant small horn, the individual Daniel saw was characterized by divine power and holiness. To the elder statesman it appeared as if the "Son of man" was being carried along by the clouds of the sky, just as a triumphant monarch might ride in his chariot to vanquish his foes. A procession of angels escorted the "Son of man" into the presence of the Ancient One.

The New Testament identifies the "Son of man" as Jesus of Nazareth. During the His trial before the Sanhedrin, the high priest demanded to know whether Jesus claimed to be the Messiah, the "Son of God" (Matt. 26:63). In response, He affirmed His identity. Moreover, Jesus declared that a future day was coming in which everyone would see the divine Savior seated in the place of power at the Father's right hand. The onlookers would also see the "Son of man" (vs. 64) arriving on the "clouds of heaven" (see Ps. 110:1; Mark 14:62; Luke 22:69).

Daniel 7:14 says that to the Son of God was conferred ruling authority, along with honor and royal sovereignty, so that all people of every race, nation, and language would worship and serve Him. Unlike earthly rulers and empires, the "dominion" of the Messiah is eternal, His authority will never cease, and His "kingdom" will never be "destroyed." In Revelation 5:11-14, we find similar truths being emphasized. John recounted hearing the singing of countless numbers of angels around God's throne, along with the voices of the living creatures and of the elders (vs. 11). The heavenly choir praised the Lamb for His worthiness. It was fitting for Him to receive glory, power, and praise for who He is and what He has done. In particular, He is the Son of God, the One who died on the cross so that those who trust in Him might become His servants in His kingdom (Rev. 5:12).

John next heard every creature in heaven, on earth, under the earth, and in the sea sing hymns in adoration to the Father and the Son. The idea in verse 13 is that every creature in the universe united their voices to give unending praise to God and His Son, the Messiah. The four living creatures affirmed their praise by declaring "Amen" (vs. 14), and the 24 elders responded appropriately by prostrating themselves in worship before the throne. We live in uncertain times, and there are days when the future seems bleak. We should not lose hope, however, for the Savior was worthy to take the scroll (mentioned in vss. 1-9) and open its seals. This means God allowed Him to carry out His plan for the world. The future is not in doubt, for the Son will bring to pass all that the Father has planned for His people.

SUGGESTIONS TO TEACHERS

The rulers of Daniel's day may not have gotten the point (but we should) that all earthly kingdoms are fragile and temporary compared to the eternal kingdom of God. The dream that Daniel experienced should encourage us to put our primary allegiance in the kingdom of God and not in any worldly connection.

1. GOD KNOWS ALL THINGS. There are many unanswered questions about what God has planned for the future. And at times, we might want to know more than what He has revealed in His Word about His eternal kingdom and the reign of His Son. The Father doesn't often disclose hidden knowledge to His people, but He certainly can when He wants to.

2. ALL POWER DESCENDS FROM HEAVEN. This truth is evident in the heavenly scene Daniel saw of the "Ancient of days" (Dan. 7:9) taking His seat on His royal throne. Romans 13:1 reminds us that the "powers that be are ordained by God." When we look at any world leader—and even a lower authority, like our boss—we should remember that they have their authority from God.

3. EVERY NATION IS TEMPORARY. Some nations last a long time, but history is filled with the accounts of once-invincible nations succumbing to the power of other nations. While we can rejoice when God grants peace to our nation, we must put our trust in Him alone and not in our "national security."

4. THE KINGDOM OF GOD IS THE GREATEST. From a heavenly perspective, the realm where God reigns is superior beyond comparison to the earthly kingdoms that come and go. Are you a citizen of that greatest kingdom? If not, then for you everything depends on your becoming such a citizen through faith in the King, Jesus Christ.

5. WHAT GOD SAYS CAN BE TRUSTED. Daniel's dream is just one part of the prophetic message of the Bible. We can believe every part of that message because it comes from the all-knowing God. Looking for certainty in an uncertain world? Here it is!

■ **TOPIC:** Better Days Ahead

■ **QUESTIONS:** 1. How do you think Daniel felt when he saw the "Ancient of days" (Dan. 7:9) take His seat on the throne? 2. In what way are believers called to offer the sort of praise given by the multitude of attendants before God's throne? 3. What are some reasons for identifying the "Son of man" (vs. 13) with Jesus of Nazareth? 4. How is your attitude toward life affected by the prospect of the Son's future return? 5. What are some indications of the Son's eternal reign that you can see in the present?

■ **ILLUSTRATIONS:**

Certainty in an Uncertain World. On March 11, 2011, a 9.0-magnitude undersea earthquake occurred off the coast of Japan. This event triggered a massive tsunami. Within minutes, waves as high as 124 feet crashed into the Japanese coast and in some areas seawater traveled up to six miles inland. Along with causing hundreds of billions of dollars in property damage, the horrific natural disaster claimed the lives of tens of thousands of victims.

News such as this is enough to convince most people that we live in uncertain times. And as we get older, we are eventually touched (either directly or indirectly) by disease and loss of loved ones. Other personal hardships we may encounter include financial loss, marital upheaval, and deep psychological turmoil.

What are we to do in a world filled with so much uncertainty? To whom should we turn for help and the hope of better days ahead? The Book of Daniel (which is the focus of this week's lesson) urges us to put our hope in the "Ancient of days" (7:9), who alone is all-powerful. Even in our moments of crisis, we can draw strength and encouragement, guidance and help from the Creator and Lord of the universe. When we rest our confidence in Him, we will never be disappointed.

The Coming Storm. On September 21, 1938, a hurricane of monstrous proportions struck the East Coast of the United States. William Manchester, in his book *The Glory and the Dream*, writes that "the great wall of brine struck the beach between Babylon and Patchogue (Long Island, New York) at 2:30 P.M. So mighty was the power of that first storm wave that its impact registered on a seismograph in Sitka, Alaska, while the spray, carried northward at well over a hundred miles an hour, whitened windows in Montpelier, Vermont. As the torrential 40-foot wave approached, some Long Islanders jumped into cars and raced inland. No one knows precisely how many lost that race for their lives, but the survivors later estimated that they had to keep the speedometer over 50 miles per hour all the way."

For some reason the meteorologists—who should have known what was coming and should have warned the public—seemed strangely blind to the impending disaster. They either ignored their instruments or simply couldn't believe them. And, of course, if the forecasters were blind, the public was too.

"Among the striking stories which later came to light," writes Manchester, "was the experience of a Long Islander who had bought a barometer a few days earlier in a New York store. It arrived in the morning post September 21, and to his annoyance the needle pointed below 29, where the dial read, 'Hurricanes and Tornadoes.' He shook it and banged it against the wall; the needle wouldn't budge. Indignant, he repacked it, drove to the post office, and mailed it back. While he was gone, his house blew away."

At times, that's the way we can be in our spiritual walk with the Lord. He summons us to recognize His sovereignty as the "Ancient of days" (Dan. 7:9) and the One who deserves from us the same sort of praise offered by the countless numbers of attendants in heaven (vs. 10). Instead, if we can't cope with His spiritual "forecast," we blame the "barometer" (for example His Word), or ignore it and throw it away!

Lasting Kingdoms. Daniel 7:14 reveals that to the Messiah belongs an "everlasting dominion." Likewise, His "kingdom" will never be "destroyed."

While serving as a missionary in Laos, John Hess-Yoder discovered an illustration of the kingdom of God: "Before the colonialists imposed national boundaries, the kings of Laos and Vietnam reached an agreement on taxation in the border areas. Those who ate short-grain rice, built their houses on stilts, and decorated them with Indian-style serpents were considered Laotians. On the other hand, those who ate long-grain rice, built their houses on the ground, and decorated them with Chinese-style dragons were considered Vietnamese. The exact location of a person's home was not what determined his or her nationality. Instead, each person belonged to the kingdom whose cultural values he or she exhibited."

So it is with us. On the one hand, we live in the world. On the other hand, as members of the Messiah's eternal kingdom, we are to live according to His ethical standards and spiritual values.

FOR YOUTH

■ **TOPIC:** The Future Is Sure

■ **QUESTIONS:** 1. How do you think you would have responded if you had gone through the visionary episode experienced by Daniel? 2. In what sense is Daniel 7:9-10 describing a courtroom scene? 3. Who was the "horn" (vs. 11) spewing arrogant remarks? 4. What can you do to ensure that the "Son of man" (vs. 13) is Lord of every aspect of your life? 5. How does the truth of the Messiah's eternal reign give you hope to endure hardship?

■ **ILLUSTRATIONS:**

It Keeps On Going and Going and Going. There's a certain company that markets its product by claiming that it can keep battery-operated devices going, and going, and going. This self-assured optimism is reflected throughout society in the West. It doesn't seem to matter whether we're talking about young people, middle-aged people, or people heading into retirement. Individuals from each age-group seem to have this durable confidence that their future is guaranteed to turn out right. And so they can do whatever they want, however they want, and whenever they want.

A study of the Book of Daniel exposes the folly of such thinking. Even young people are not the captains of their own destiny (in a manner of speaking), though they might like to think they are. Ultimately, the future course of our lives falls under the rule of God. He determines when we are born and when we will die. Even such things as the shape of our hands and the size of our feet are controlled by Him. Isn't it time we begin to acknowledge this in the way we live?

The Eternal Kingdom of the Messiah. Daniel 7:11-12 reveals that all human kingdoms eventually come to an end and their rulers are destined to die. In contrast, verse 14 discloses that the kingdom of the Messiah is eternal and His authority is unending.

The once-mighty Napoleon is reported to have made this statement: "Alexander, Caesar, Charlemagne, and myself founded empires. But on what foundation did we rest the creatures of our genius? Upon force. But Jesus Christ founded an empire upon love. And at this hour, millions of persons would die for Him. I die before my time, and my body will be given back to the earth to become food for the worms. Such is the destiny of him who has been called the 'great Napoleon.' What an abyss between my deep misery and the eternal kingdom of Christ, which is proclaimed, loved, adored, and is still existing over the whole earth."

Technical Knowledge. A teenage boy was deeply interested in scientific subjects, especially astronomy. So his father bought him an expensive telescope.

Since the boy had studied the principles of optics, he found the instrument to be most intriguing. He took it apart, examined the lenses, and made detailed calculations on the distance of its point of focus. The boy became so absorbed in gaining a technical knowledge of the telescope itself that he never got around to looking at the stars. He knew a lot about that fine instrument, but he missed seeing the wonders of heaven.

To know all the facts and figures contained in the Bible is not the end for which the "Ancient of days" (Dan. 7:9) has given us His Book. One purpose is that we might recognize His awe-inspiring splendor. Another goal is that we might draw spiritual strength from the ruling authority and sovereignty of His Son (vs. 14).

DANIEL'S PRAYER

BACKGROUND SCRIPTURE: Daniel 9:3-19
DEVOTIONAL READING: James 5:13-18

Key Verse: To the Lord our God belong mercies and forgivenesses, though we have rebelled against him. Daniel 9:9.

KING JAMES VERSION

DANIEL 9:4 And I prayed unto the LORD my God, and made my confession, and said, O Lord, the great and dreadful God, keeping the covenant and mercy to them that love him, and to them that keep his commandments; 5 We have sinned, and have committed iniquity, and have done wickedly, and have rebelled, even by departing from thy precepts and from thy judgments: 6 Neither have we hearkened unto thy servants the prophets, which spake in thy name to our kings, our princes, and our fathers, and to all the people of the land. 7 O LORD, righteousness belongeth unto thee, but unto us confusion of faces, as at this day; to the men of Judah, and to the inhabitants of Jerusalem, and unto all Israel, that are near, and that are far off, through all the countries whither thou hast driven them, because of their trespass that they have trespassed against thee. 8 O Lord, to us belongeth confusion of face, to our kings, to our princes, and to our fathers, because we have sinned against thee. 9 To the Lord our God belong mercies and forgivenesses, though we have rebelled against him; 10 Neither have we obeyed the voice of the LORD our God, to walk in his laws, which he set before us by his servants the prophets. 11 Yea, all Israel have transgressed thy law, even by departing, that they might not obey thy voice; therefore the curse is poured upon us, and the oath that is written in the law of Moses the servant of God, because we have sinned against him. 12 And he hath confirmed his words, which he spake against us, and against our judges that judged us, by bringing upon us a great evil: for under the whole heaven hath not been done as hath been done upon Jerusalem. 13 As it is written in the law of Moses, all this evil is come upon us: yet made we not our prayer before the LORD our God, that we might turn from our iniquities, and understand thy truth. 14 Therefore hath the LORD watched upon the evil, and brought it upon us: for the LORD our God is righteous in all his works which he doeth: for we obeyed not his voice.

NEW REVISED STANDARD VERSION

DANIEL 9:4 I prayed to the LORD my God and made confession, saying,

"Ah, Lord, great and awesome God, keeping covenant and steadfast love with those who love you and keep your commandments, 5 we have sinned and done wrong, acted wickedly and rebelled, turning aside from your commandments and ordinances. 6 We have not listened to your servants the prophets, who spoke in your name to our kings, our princes, and our ancestors, and to all the people of the land.

7 "Righteousness is on your side, O Lord, but open shame, as at this day, falls on us, the people of Judah, the inhabitants of Jerusalem, and all Israel, those who are near and those who are far away, in all the lands to which you have driven them, because of the treachery that they have committed against you. 8 Open shame, O LORD, falls on us, our kings, our officials, and our ancestors, because we have sinned against you. 9 To the Lord our God belong mercy and forgiveness, for we have rebelled against him, 10 and have not obeyed the voice of the LORD our God by following his laws, which he set before us by his servants the prophets.

11 "All Israel has transgressed your law and turned aside, refusing to obey your voice. So the curse and the oath written in the law of Moses, the servant of God, have been poured out upon us, because we have sinned against you. 12 He has confirmed his words, which he spoke against us and against our rulers, by bringing upon us a calamity so great that what has been done against Jerusalem has never before been done under the whole heaven. 13 Just as it is written in the law of Moses, all this calamity has come upon us. We did not entreat the favor of the LORD our God, turning from our iniquities and reflecting on his fidelity. 14 So the LORD kept watch over this calamity until he brought it upon us. Indeed, the LORD our God is right in all that he has done; for we have disobeyed his voice.

HOME BIBLE READINGS

Monday, March 4	Daniel 1:8-15	*Daniel's Resolve*
Tuesday, March 5	Daniel 1:16-21	*Daniel's Recognition*
Wednesday, March 6	Daniel 2:1-11	*The King's Challenge*
Thursday, March 7	Daniel 2:12-16	*Daniel's Intervention*
Friday, March 8	Daniel 2:36-49	*Daniel's Success*
Saturday, March 9	Daniel 9:15-19	*Daniel's Prayer of Supplication*
Sunday, March 10	Daniel 9:4b-14	*Daniel's Prayer of Confession*

BACKGROUND

The events of Daniel 9 took place during the first year of the reign of Darius the Mede (Dan. 9:1). That began in 539 B.C., the year Babylon was conquered by the Medo-Persians. Daniel had been in captivity for 66 years, since 605 B.C. At this time, he would have been about 82 years old. The last date recorded in the Book of Daniel is 536 B.C., "the third year of Cyrus king of Persia" (see 10:1). Media was a region northeast of Babylon (which is today part of northwest Iran). Almost nothing is known about the origins of the ancient Indo-European people known as the Medes, and only a few words of their language have survived. Persia, modern Iran, was located south of Media.

While the kings of Persia and Media had made joint military campaigns into southwest Asia in 559 B.C., 20 years later Darius overthrew Belshazzar to gain control of the Babylonian Empire. Belshazzar knew about his own fall in advance because of a handwritten message inscribed on his palace wall (see Dan. 5). The rise of the Medo-Persians was a providential act of God. Daniel apparently knew that the rise of Darius paved the way for the return of the Israelites to their homeland. Daniel understood from Jeremiah's prophecies (which the elder statesman regarded as being verbally inspired) that the 70-year exile begun by the "desolations of Jerusalem" (9:2) was nearing its end (see Jer. 25:11-12; 29:10).

NOTES ON THE PRINTED TEXT

Daniel's expectation for his people drove him to his knees in prayer. Two distinct terms appear in Daniel 9:3. The first, simply rendered "prayer," was a general word often used in intercessory entreaties. The second word, translated "supplication," denoted a petition for mercy and compassion. On behalf of his people, Daniel pleaded with God for mercy. Daniel also cried out to the Lord first in confession, and then in petition.

In describing how he prayed, Daniel said that he turned his face to the Lord. This could mean Daniel set aside his normal routine and devoted himself entirely to prayer. It may also allude to the practice of praying in the direction of Jerusalem. Earlier in this book, we read how Daniel prayed in his upstairs room, where the latticed windows opened toward Jerusalem (6:10). Daniel approached the throne of grace with fasting, adorned in sackcloth (a rough material similar to burlap) and ashes. All three of these were signs of deep repentance or personal grief and loss (Dan. 9:3; see Ezek. 27:29-31).

Daniel recognized that the exile in Babylon was God's judgment for Israel's sin. The prophet also understood what God's covenant with His people required if they were to receive forgiveness, restoration, and divine blessing. The people of the nation had to confess their sin and obey the commands of God (Dan. 9:4-5). In this knowledge, Daniel confessed the sins of the people, not once but four times (vss. 5, 8, 11, 15). He included himself as if he were personally involved in Israel's wickedness, rebellion, and disobedience. Even though God had graciously sent the prophets to turn His people back, the nation as a whole had ignored their message. According to Daniel, all Israel was guilty before God (vss. 6, 8-11). The elder statesman began his prayer by affirming that the sovereign Lord is both "great and dreadful" (vs. 4). Additionally, God was faithful to fulfill His covenant promises with those who loved and obeyed Him. These truths formed the theological foundation of Daniel's confession.

Daniel did not hesitate to affirm the Lord's faithfulness to the Mosaic covenant. As it happened, God remained more loyal in His devotion to His chosen people than they had been to Him. In verse 5, the elder statesman acknowledged that the faith community had sinned against its Creator and Redeemer in every imaginable way. They were guilty of committing iniquity and participating in wicked acts. They also rebelled by scorning His commands and dodging His teachings. Moreover, the chosen people refused to heed the Lord's prophets, who humbly served Him. The latter spoke as His representatives in the authority of His name to a wide audience of people, including monarchs and princes who ruled the inhabitants of the Promised Land (vs. 6).

Daniel affirmed the righteousness of the Lord in His person and actions. Expressed differently, God was characterized by equity, justice, and truthfulness in His dealings with the faith community. His chosen people, though, suffered public disgrace as a result of their disloyalty to God. The shame was carried by the leaders of Judah, the citizens of Jerusalem, and all the rest of the inhabitants of Israel. Because they transgressed God's ways, He was in the right to scatter them far and wide (vs. 7). All the chosen people experienced the humiliation of being dragged away to foreign lands because of their extensive and repeated acts of sin against the Lord (vs. 8).

If it had been any lesser ruler, that monarch would have immediately punished his subjects for a single act of insurrection. Yet despite the faith community's ongoing rebellion, the sovereign Lord remained merciful and forgiving (vs. 9). His compassion was evident when He gave the Mosaic law. Also, despite the chosen people's violations of God's edicts, He freely pardoned them. Sadly, the recipients of His favor refused to heed His stipulations and listen to His teachings, as set before them through His prophets (vs. 10).

Prior to the destruction of Jerusalem by the Babylonians, many people of Judah did not believe that God would destroy His own temple and His holy city until it actually happened. They continued in their worship of other gods. The prophets repeatedly pointed out that the people's unfaithfulness would bring judgment, and it did, namely, their 70-year exile in Babylon. The people's rejection of the prophets proved the unfaithfulness of those whom God had chosen. Although the Lord's representatives occasionally foretold future events, their primary responsibility was calling the nation to obey God in the present. They spoke to Israel's leaders and, through them, to all the people.

Tragically, the entire nation was guilty of violating God's injunctions and stubbornly refusing to follow His will (vs. 11). Because the Lord is just in everything He does (see vs. 7), He had no other option but to pour out on His wayward people the judgment solemnly threatened in the Mosaic law (see Deut. 28:15-68). God had given His people a very straightforward choice—either obey Him and be blessed or disobey Him and suffer terrible curses. Because Israel had chosen the latter course, the Lord kept His word by doing exactly what He had forewarned. The calamity referred to in Daniel 9:12 is the destruction of Jerusalem and the exile of the chosen people to Babylon. As far as the faith community was concerned, no other disaster on record seemed as horrendous as the tragedy the inhabitants of Judah experienced at the hands of their enemies in 586 B.C.

Centuries earlier, the Mosaic law forewarned the chosen people about the unimaginable horrors they would endure if they rebelled against the Lord. These alarming calamities were meant to bring God's people back to Him, but they refused to entreat the Lord's favor (vs. 13). Moreover, despite the unparalleled "evil" (that is, calamity) brought upon the nation, the people were still not turning away from their sin and submitting themselves to God's well-founded moral standards recorded in the law. Because the sovereign Lord of Israel is characterized by justice and rectitude, He intentionally allowed His wayward people to experience catastrophe at the hands of their foes (vs. 14).

Daniel's petition for divine favor was grounded in an awareness of how God had faithfully acted throughout the course of Israel's history. The premier example of this was the Lord's deliverance of His people out of the land of Egypt with great power. Because of that mighty act, God brought lasting honor to His name. But this did not prevent His chosen people from sinning and behaving wickedly (vs. 15). As a consequence of this sobering truth, the only thing Daniel could do was appeal to the Lord on the basis of His justice.

In view of all of God's faithfulness and mercy in connection with His covenant promises, the elder statesman humbly asked the Lord to turn His raging anger away from Jerusalem. It was the chosen city built on His holy mountain (vs. 16) and thus the place where God decided to dwell and reign (see Pss. 43:3; 68:16; Isa. 24:23). As such, it was intended to be the sacred site where the people could enjoy a transcendent encounter with God, in addition to finding refuge, peace, and joy in His presence (see Isa. 2:1-5; Mic. 4:1-5).

In short, Daniel was entreating the Lord to end Jerusalem's condition as an object of scorn among the surrounding nations. Suggested here is the idea that the fortunes of a country, whether good or bad, were an indicator of its deity's power and might. A positive outcome for Judah would require God to forgive the sins of the current generation of Jews and the iniquities committed by their ancestors (Dan. 9:16). With humility and courage, Daniel petitioned God to "hear" (vs. 17) the prayer of His servant. Expressed differently, the prophet asked the Lord to graciously accept his request to show favor on His devastated sanctuary. Daniel was convinced that God would bring honor to His name by smiling once again (in a manner of speaking) on His temple. Though it lay in ruins, the Lord could enable His people to rebuild it.

SUGGESTIONS TO TEACHERS

Daniel recognized that Judah's sin brought condemnation and guilt on the nation. Moreover, the transgressions of God's chosen people alienated them from Him and prevented them from experiencing His abundant blessings in the Promised Land. The Lord used Daniel to acknowledge the sins of his predecessors and pray that God would inundate them with His mercy.

1. ACKNOWLEDGING OUR SINS. Quite often God uses circumstances and other people to get our attention and draw us back to Him. In difficult times, we should be especially sensitive to how God may want to speak to us through them. Tragically, though, when trouble comes, it is all too easy for us to point the finger of blame and guilt toward others while excusing ourselves. It is difficult to imagine anyone among the Israelites more righteous and blameless than Daniel. Yet he was the one on his knees begging God's forgiveness for his sin and that of his people. If we want renewal and revival in our churches, the first step is for us to look into a mirror and ask the Lord to begin with the one we see.

2. RECOGNIZING GOD'S MERCY. We see from Daniel's prayer that the path toward restoration with God includes recognizing His mercy. We learn from the New Testament that the Father loved the world so much that in His mercy, He gave His Son to atone for the sins of the lost (see John 3:16). The Father did not require any religious acts or works of righteousness on our part before He sent us His Son. Moreover, He did not limit His salvation to only certain kinds of people or to those with correct behavior. God opened the door of His mercy to every sinner.

3. CLEARING THE WAY FOR OUR PETITIONS. The wonderful truth arising from this week's lesson is that God still answers the prayers of His children today. But there is a condition. He expects us to be walking in obedience to His will when we come to Him with our requests (see John 15:7). If there is unconfessed sin in our lives, the first prayer the Lord wants to hear from us is one of confession and repentance.

Then the way is clear for prayers of petition. Indeed, that was Daniel's practice when he approached the throne of grace, and God responded favorably to him. The same can also be our experience, if we so desire.

FOR ADULTS

■ **TOPIC:** Have Mercy!

■ **QUESTIONS:** 1. In what ways had the Lord remained faithful to His covenant? 2. What role did God's prophets serve in the life of the faith community? 3. In what sense were the chosen people of Daniel's day experiencing humiliation? 4. What usually moves you to pray? 5. How willing are you to identify in prayer with the sins of other believers?

■ **ILLUSTRATIONS:**

Mercy from God. None of us is immune from disobeying the Lord. Spiritual waywardness is something all believers struggle with at some point in their journey of faith (see 1 John 1:8-10).

Even when we go through the painful process of repentance, we must never forget that God shows mercy and graciously bestows blessings upon us because it pleases Him to do so, not because we deserve it. Many people, believers and unbelievers alike, act as if God is somehow obligated to grant any and all requests made of Him. But since sin placed all humanity under a death sentence, it would be unwise indeed to demand that a just and holy God give us what we deserve.

Daniel was well aware of God's righteousness (see Dan. 9:7, 14). Moreover, the elder statesman affirmed the faithfulness and compassion of the Lord (see vss. 4, 9). This week's study of Daniel's prayer on behalf of the chosen people can become an opportunity for your students to seek the Lord's forgiveness for transgressions in their lives. When they do, they will discover that He is ready and willing to lavish them with His mercy and grace.

The Power of Intercessory Prayer. Daniel set a powerful example when it comes to intercessory prayer. He was not put off by identifying with the transgressions committed by God's chosen people. Indeed, Daniel fervently embraced the opportunity to petition the Lord on behalf of the faith community.

Because Mork Eiwuley from Ghana had no visa, he would not be able to attend the leadership school for Christian publishers in Colorado Springs, Colorado. Then, to his surprise, he met a woman who was able to pull strings and get his visa at the eleventh hour.

"That," Mork said, "never happens." It wasn't until Mork arrived at the institute that he found out the story behind his story. Patti, an employee of Cook Communication's U.S. ministry, along with most of her 250 colleagues, had agreed to pray for one of the publishers scheduled to attend. Her publisher was Mork. On the very day she started praying for him, he received his visa. "What never happens, happened," Mork smiled. "People at Cook were praying for me. That's how I got my visa."

The Advocate. Nancy Grace is an anchorwoman for *CNN Headline News* and *Court TV*. In *Guideposts*, she explained why she is so tough on crime and criminals. In the summer of 1981, her fiancé, Keith, was at a "convenience store to buy sodas" when a mugger "shot him five times in the neck and head." Nancy relates that from that day on, the sheltered life she knew as a child growing up "on the outskirts of Macon, Georgia," had ended.

It would take months for Nancy to process the horrific murder of Keith and to figure out what to do next. Nancy sensed that God wanted her to study law at Mercer University. After graduating, she began working as an attorney. Eventually, she was "walking into courtrooms, staring down criminals, and badgering judges into meting out tough sentences." Nancy realized that as a result of Keith's death, God gave her a mission she could have never imagined on her own. Nancy had become an advocate for the innocent and vulnerable members of society, "their voice in a world that, though essentially good, is embattled by evil."

Daniel had a similar concern for those around him. He was so inundated by grief over the devastation of Jerusalem and exile of his people, that he made intercession and confession on their behalf for their sin against God. From the New Testament we learn that Jesus is the believer's Advocate. His intercession on their behalf before the throne of God enables them to experience divine mercy, grace, and forgiveness.

FOR YOUTH

■ **TOPIC:** Prayer of Confession

■ **QUESTIONS:** 1. In what ways had the chosen people sinned against the Lord? 2. Why do you think Daniel made such an effort to identify with the transgression of the faith community? 3. What would people say about the Lord just by observing you as one of His followers? 4. Why would the Lord, who is compassionate and forgiving, allow His people to be exiled? 5. What are some ways you can be truly contrite before the Lord when you ask for His forgiveness?

■ **ILLUSTRATIONS:**

Confess! Daniel knew how to pray. Unreserved confession of sin opened his heart to the Lord. Complete submission to God's will also prepared the prophet for divine direction. Like Daniel, we should first go to the Lord in confession, then listen with an attitude of submission and openness to hear what He wants to say to us.

At first, the idea of admitting personal sins might be difficult for some believing teens to accept. Most likely, they have not seen this humble attitude in their peers. And perhaps many of the adults in their life are more inclined to blame others for their misdeeds.

In situations such as this, you can remind your students of the example Daniel set. He was not told to identify with the sins of God's people. Yet Daniel humbly did so. Likewise, he did not hesitate to confess his own transgressions to the Lord. Like him, when saved adolescents do so, they will experience the blessing of God's forgiveness.

As Contrite as We Should Be? A Christian friend once declared to me that he had no fear of God because Scripture teaches that the perfect love of God expels all fear (see 1 John 4:18). Sadly, because my friend misunderstood this verse, his sins rarely disturbed him. Since he felt that God loved him so much, he also felt God would naturally and promptly forgive him whenever he sinned.

Thankfully, most of us do not share my friend's attitude. But can we truly say we are as contrite as we should be when we ask for God's forgiveness? If not, then we need to learn from Daniel to be much more sincere and humble when we repent before our Lord.

From Dream to Reality. Daniel set a godly example of how believers can intercede for one another in prayer to God. In 2006, the Association of Baptists for World Evangelism (ABWE) reported that in Luís Eduardo Magalhães, Brazil, the intercessory prayers of believers turned a dream into a reality. The town is an agricultural-industrial center on "Bahia state's western frontier." At first, its residents doubted whether a new church building could be erected in four weeks. But according to ABWE, the people saw "God's hand and some of His choice volunteers at work" to bring about what seemed impossible.

In response to the petitions of many Christians, God provided for Emmanuel Baptist Church in Bahia "four one-week building teams from the Construction for World Evangelization ministry in Tampa, Florida." First came bricklayers, who got the work started. They were followed by carpenters, who covered the structure. Plumbers and electricians made the building functional, while painters and finishers brought the project to completion. At the end of the four-week period, the congregation moved from the "garage behind the missionaries' house to its new, permanent home." This was to "God's glory and the doubters' amazement!"

GABRIEL'S INTERPRETATION

BACKGROUND SCRIPTURE: Daniel 8
DEVOTIONAL READING: Psalm 91:1-12

Key Verse: The vision of the evening and
the morning which was told is true. Daniel 8:26.

3

KING JAMES VERSION

DANIEL 8:19 And he said, Behold, I will make thee know what shall be in the last end of the indignation: for at the time appointed the end shall be. 20 The ram which thou sawest having two horns are the kings of Media and Persia. 21 And the rough goat is the king of Grecia: and the great horn that is between his eyes is the first king. 22 Now that being broken, whereas four stood up for it, four kingdoms shall stand up out of the nation, but not in his power. 23 And in the latter time of their kingdom, when the transgressors are come to the full, a king of fierce countenance, and understanding dark sentences, shall stand up. 24 And his power shall be mighty, but not by his own power: and he shall destroy wonderfully, and shall prosper, and practise, and shall destroy the mighty and the holy people.
25 And through his policy also he shall cause craft to prosper in his hand; and he shall magnify himself in his heart, and by peace shall destroy many: he shall also stand up against the Prince of princes; but he shall be broken without hand. 26 And the vision of the evening and the morning which was told is true: wherefore shut thou up the vision; for it shall be for many days.

NEW REVISED STANDARD VERSION

DANIEL 8:19 He said, "Listen, and I will tell you what will take place later in the period of wrath; for it refers to the appointed time of the end. 20 As for the ram that you saw with the two horns, these are the kings of Media and Persia. 21 The male goat is the king of Greece, and the great horn between its eyes is the first king. 22 As for the horn that was broken, in place of which four others arose, four kingdoms shall arise from his nation, but not with his power.
23 At the end of their rule,
  when the transgressions have reached their full measure,
  a king of bold countenance shall arise,
  skilled in intrigue.
24 He shall grow strong in power,
  shall cause fearful destruction,
  and shall succeed in what he does.
  He shall destroy the powerful
  and the people of the holy ones.
25 By his cunning
  he shall make deceit prosper under his hand,
  and in his own mind he shall be great.
  Without warning he shall destroy many
  and shall even rise up against the Prince of princes.
  But he shall be broken, and not by human hands.
26 The vision of the evenings and the mornings that has been told is true. As for you, seal up the vision, for it refers to many days from now."

HOME BIBLE READINGS

BACKGROUND

The episode recorded in this week's lesson occurred in 551 B.C., which was two years after the dream recorded in chapter 7. In 8:1, Daniel said he experienced a vision. According to verse 2, he saw himself in the walled city of Susa at the Ulai Canal. Daniel remembered lifting his eyes and seeing a ram standing on the bank of the canal. This unusual animal had two long horns. One of them was longer than the other, even though the longer one began to grow later than the shorter one (vs. 3). Daniel noticed the creature butting westward, northward, and southward, and no other beast was able to stop it or help its victims. The ram did whatever it wanted and acted arrogantly (vs. 4).

While Daniel pondered the meaning of what he had seen, suddenly a male goat with a conspicuous horn between its eyes appeared. It was moving so fast out of the west that its feet did not even seem to touch the ground (vs. 5). The goat attacked the ram with savage force (vs. 6). In fact, the goat was so enraged that when it smashed into the ram, the goat broke off the ram's two horns and the latter was powerless to resist the attack. The goat threw the ram to the ground and trampled on it, and no one could deliver the ram from being overpowered (vs. 7). For a while, the goat acted even more arrogantly. But when its horn was at the height of its power, it was broken off. In its place arose four other conspicuous horns, with each one extending in the four directions of the earth (vs. 8).

Out of these four prominent horns Daniel saw a small horn emerge. Soon, however, it became exceedingly large, with its enormous power extending toward the south, the east, and the "pleasant land" (vs. 9). The latter is a reference to Israel (see 11:16, 41). Eventually, the horn grew strong enough to attack the "host of the heavens" (8:10). In this context, the reference most likely is to God's faithful remnant, who valiantly try to resist their wicked foe (see Gen. 15:5; Exod. 12:41; Dan. 12:3). Moreover, the horn challenged the "prince" (Dan. 8:11) of the chosen people by profaning the Jerusalem temple. This included stopping the regular burnt offering and then pillaging and desecrating the entire shrine. In the course of the horn's sinful rebellion against God, the horn was able to commit barbarous acts against His chosen people. The horn even succeed in trampling on God's truth by authorizing the destruction of copies of the Mosaic law. It seemed as if the horn succeeded in whatever it did (vs. 12).

At this point, Daniel heard one angel ask another angel how long the events in the vision would last (vs. 13). Daniel learned that it would literally be "two thousand three hundred evenings and mornings" (vs. 14) before the temple was restored (see vs. 26). Some consider this to be a reference to the evening sacrifice and the morning sacrifice (see Exod. 29:38-42; Num. 28:3-5; Dan. 9:21). In this case, the elapsed time would be 1,150 days (or 3 years and 55 days). Others consider the phrase in Daniel 8:14 to be reminiscent of the creation account in Genesis 1. In this case, the reference to evening and morning would be equivalent to an entire day. Hence, the expression denotes 2,300 days (or 6 years and 111 days). In either case, it is difficult to pinpoint a specific event within ancient Jewish history that marked the outset of this horrific period. In contrast, the cleansing and rededicating of the Jerusalem temple (following the sacrilegious acts committed by Antiochus IV Epiphanes) signaled the end of this period. The latter occurred on December 14, 165 B.C., when Judas Maccabaeus led a group of his fellow Jews to liberate the sanctuary. This victory is commemorated each year by the observance of the Jewish holiday of Hanukkah.

NOTES ON THE PRINTED TEXT

As Daniel watched the vision unfold, he struggled to make sense of it. Just then, he saw a humanlike creature standing in front of him (Dan. 8:15). The elder statesman remembered hearing a voice calling out from the Ulai Canal. The voice referred to the supernatural messenger in Daniel's presence as "Gabriel" (vs. 16) and directed him to explain to Daniel what he had seen in the vision. Gabriel explained that the double-horned ram Daniel noticed symbolized the rulers of the Medes and Persians (vs. 20; see vss. 3-4). Next, Gabriel stated that the male goat represented the future "king of Grecia" (vs. 21; see vs. 5).

The huge horn between the male goat's eyes symbolized Alexander the Great (356–323 B.C.). The goat's swift movement (see 7:6) depicted the meteoric rise of the Greek Empire under Alexander's leadership. In fact, in three major battles spanning just three years (334–330 B.C.), he was able to defeat the once powerful Persian empire (see 8:6-7). The first engagement, which took place in 334 B.C. at the Granicus River, opened Asia Minor to Alexander. The second battle, which occurred in 333 B.C. at Issus, enabled him to take control of Syria, Canaan, and Egypt. The third battle, which took place in 331 B.C. at Arbela, resulted in the routing of the remaining Persian army.

From there, Alexander and his forces made their push toward what is today territory belonging to Afghanistan, Pakistan, and India. At this point, the extent of his control exceeded that of the Persian Empire. Be that as it may, Alexander's troops were exhausted and they refused to advance farther eastward. He then decided to return to Babylon, where he suffered an untimely death at the age of 33 (see vs. 8). As a result, the empire founded by Alexander divided into four parts under the control of his regional commanders (see vs. 22): (1) Macedonia and Greece under Antipater and Cassender; (2) Thrace and Asia Minor under Lysimachus; (3) Syria under Seleucus I; and (4) Egypt under Ptolemy I. Historical records indicate that these four kingdoms were not as strong as the empire established by Alexander, in terms of both the territory they controlled and the military power they wielded.

Verse 23 skips ahead about 150 years to a time when rebellious acts had run their course. This verse points to the emergence of a wicked ruler from one of the four Greek kingdoms (see vs. 9). The king whose beginning was seemingly lackluster is Antiochus IV Epiphanes, who ruled the Seleucid Empire from 175 to 164 B.C. Initially, his kingdom lacked cohesion, being politically fragmented and financially weak. Antiochus addressed this issue by aggressively implementing a program of Hellenization. The latter refers to the spread of ancient Greek culture and language. Antiochus also sponsored the worship of Zeus. This was the god of the sky and thunder in Greek mythology and the chief deity of the Greek pantheon. Throughout much of his reign, the relationship between Antiochus and the Jewish inhabitants of Palestine was terse and violent. He ended up trying unsuccessfully to wipe out the Jewish people and their religious faith. Verse 23 describes him as of "fierce countenance," which points to someone who was insolent and rash. Antiochus was also deceitful and adept in devising sinister schemes.

Antiochus was not the lawful successor to the Seleucid throne. That is why, as verse 24 predicted, he used underhanded techniques to obtain control of the empire. His tumultuous reign resulted in extraordinary amounts of death and destruction. In fact, he ended up slaughtering many who were oblivious to his ploys. Verse 25 adds that Antiochus was characterized by arrogance, and he tried to advance his agenda by means of treachery and deceit. For instance, he took the name Epiphanes (which literally means "God manifest") because he mistakenly considered himself to be the human embodiment of Zeus. Some think the description of Antiochus prefigures the Antichrist, who will arise in the end times to oppose God and persecute His chosen people (see 2 Thess. 2:3-4; 1 John 4:3).

Daniel 8:10 draws attention to the armed conflict Antiochus waged against the Jewish inhabitants of Palestine. Historical records indicate that Antiochus unceasingly persecuted the Jewish people. This included banning their right to practice long-standing ceremonial practices connected with their worship of the Lord in the Jerusalem temple. Antiochus was also guilty of entering the Most Holy Place of the sanctuary and ransacking the silver and gold vessels. Furthermore, in the temple court, he built an altar to Zeus on top of the bronze altar to the Lord and had swine slaughtered there (see 8:11-12; 11:31). These profane acts against the Jewish people (especially their warriors and priests) amounted to an attack against the God of Israel, the "Prince of princes" (8:25). The demise of Antiochus did not occur by any human agency. For instance, he did not perish in battle, and he was not assassinated by any of his foes. Instead, Antiochus died in 164 B.C. in Tabae in Persia as a result of a sudden psychological or physical malady.

Gabriel affirmed that the "vision" (vs. 26) concerning the 2,300 evenings and mornings was correct (see vs. 14). Moreover, what this celestial messenger declared about the distant future (at least from Daniel's perspective) proved to be historically accurate. For the time being, though, Daniel was directed to "shut up the vision" (vs. 26) he had written on a scroll. Gabriel explained that the vision Daniel recorded needed to remain a secret, for it concerned a series of events occurring centuries after his lifetime. Understandably, the elder statesman was emotionally and physically exhausted from his visionary experience (vs. 27). Indeed, he felt sick for several days after that astonishing episode. Nevertheless, once Daniel felt better, he resumed his official duties in service to the king.

SUGGESTIONS TO TEACHERS

Sometimes it can feel scary to think about the future. And so, we might be tempted to ignore passages like Daniel 8:19-26. But they are in the Bible for our benefit and can teach us many valuable life lessons.

1. **THE NEAR AND FAR VIEW.** Some of what Daniel saw in his vision in 551 B.C. concerned events that would occur within his lifetime. For instance, the rise of the Medes and Persians included the overthrow of Babylon 12 years later in 539 B.C. Other aspects of Daniel's vision concerned people and episodes that occurred centuries after his death. And it might be that some of what Daniel saw prefigured what would take place toward the end of the age.

2. **A TIME OF GREAT SUFFERING.** Part of Daniel's vision included the prediction that a future ruler would cause intense suffering for the chosen people. Sometimes individuals are inclined to think that the world will continue on forever much as it has in the past. But thanks to Daniel and other saints of antiquity, we know better. There is a dramatic wrap-up of history coming in the future, and it's in our own best interests to ally ourselves with the ultimate winner of that contest: the Lord Jesus.

3. **GOD IS MERCIFUL TO HIS OWN.** Daniel's vision reveals that God would not allow His chosen people to be persecuted indefinitely. He eventually brought about the demise of their nemesis. Similarly, we may have to pass through some dark days in our lives. But God still cares for us and continues to bring about His good plan. From the perspective of heaven, our suffering will look insignificant compared with the glory we will then enjoy.

4. **WE SHOULD APPROACH PROPHECY HUMBLY.** God included prophecy in His Word so that we would have some idea about the sweep of history and the certainty of His ultimate victory over evil. Therefore, we can seek to understand prophe-

cy in Scripture as much as we want—as long as we maintain a humble attitude that recognizes biblical prophecy doesn't tell us everything and we may not even understand all that it does tell us.

<table>
<tr><td>**FOR ADULTS**</td><td>■ **TOPIC:** Dreams for a Better Tomorrow
■ **QUESTIONS:** 1. What is the appointed time of the end referred to in Daniel 8:19? 2. What was distinctive about the double-horned ram</td></tr>
</table>

Daniel saw? 3. What will characterize the ruler of "fierce countenance" mentioned in verse 23? 4. In addition to fortune-tellers and psychics, what other individuals might try to mislead believers about the future? Why is it unwise for believers to trust what these frauds claim to "predict"? 5. Why must the Bible be the lens through which we look at the future?

■ **ILLUSTRATIONS:**

Sit Up and Take Notice! A U.S. Army officer told about the contrast in his pupils during two different eras of teaching at the artillery training school at Fort Sill, Oklahoma. In 1958–60, the attitude was so lax that the instructors had a problem getting the men to stay awake to listen. During the 1965–67 classes, however, the men, hearing the same basic lectures, were alert and took copious notes. The reason? These men knew that in less that six weeks they would be facing the enemy in Vietnam.

The vision Daniel saw of a ram and a goat was not one he would have ignored or taken lightly. After all, it concerned the future of God's chosen people. Both during and after the experience, Daniel pondered the meaning and significance of the vision (see Dan. 8:5, 15, 27).

When we approach the prophetic portions of God's Word, what is our typical response? Is it one of ambivalence or intense interest? Hopefully, it will be the latter. After all, the Bible's predictions about the future concern us. This is one reason why the class members are wise to sit up and take notice as you guide them through this week's lesson.

Justice Is Done. In Daniel's vision of a ram and a goat, he learned about the future emergence of a wicked individual who would be "mighty" (Dan. 8:24), "destroy wonderfully," and "prosper." He would succeed in destroying the "holy people," "magnify himself in his heart" (vs. 25), and "stand up against the Prince of princes." Eventually, though, justice would be served when God allowed this despot to be destroyed apart from any human means.

By any measure, Osama bin Laden was also a wicked individual. The founder of the terrorist organization al-Qaeda was responsible for the planning and execution of a number of mass-casualty attacks against military and civilian targets. The most notorious of these was the assault that took place in the United States on September 11, 2001, in which thousands of innocent people were killed.

For over nine years after that dreadful event, bin Laden avoided being apprehended by the U.S. government. During this time, he was able to hide out in Pakistan. Then, on May 2, 2011, a dramatic turn of events occurred. A small team of U.S. special forces raided a heavily fortified compound in Abbottabad, Pakistan, where bin Laden was staying.

In the ensuing firefight, the elite unit killed bin Laden. Next, they transported his corpse to the aircraft carrier *USS Carl Vinson* for burial in the north Arabian Sea. Not long after that, President Barack Obama fittingly stated in a speech to the nation that "justice has been done" and that the "world is a better place."

Living with Hope, Even in the Midst of Adversity. During his lifetime, Daniel had experienced moments of adversity. Likewise, during his experience of the vision concerning a ram and a goat (Dan. 8), he learned about future hardships awaiting the chosen people. Be that as it may, Daniel also carried the assurance that the "Prince of princes" (vs. 25) would prevail over the enemy of the righteous remnant.

Václav Havel was a Czech poet, playwright, essayist, politician, and dissident. He served as the tenth and last president of Czechoslovakia (1989–1992) and the first president of the Czech Republic (1993–2003). Havel spoke these words from his years of suffering oppression and persecution: "I am not an optimist, because I am not sure that everything ends well. Nor am I a pessimist, because I am not sure everything ends badly. I just carry hope in my heart. . . . Life without hope is an empty, boring, and useless life. I cannot imagine that I could strive for something if I did not carry hope in me. I am thankful to God for this gift. It is as big a gift as life itself."

FOR YOUTH	■ **TOPIC:** A Curious Dream ■ **QUESTIONS:** 1. Who is it that explained to Daniel the meaning of the vision he experienced? 2. What kingdom did the "rough goat" (Dan.

8:21) symbolize? 3. What horrendous acts would the ruler who understood "dark sentences" (vs. 23) be guilty of committing? 4. If you were Daniel, do you think you would have "fainted" (vs. 27) after experiencing his vision? Explain. 5. Why is it possible for us to entrust our future to the Lord?

■ **ILLUSTRATIONS:**

Preparation for the Future. In 2010, the movie thriller *A Nightmare on Elm Street* hit the theaters. In this remake of a 1984 film having the same title, a serial killer named Freddy Kruger murders people in their dreams. This results in their actual death in real life.

What a contrast the above is to the vision recorded in Daniel 8! The prophet's dream was about the future of God's chosen people. While it was a disturbing experience for the elder statesman, he not only successfully woke up from the dream, but also lived to record what he had seen and heard.

Scripture contains a number of prophecies such as Daniel's about the future. The Bible records these not to shock us, but to encourage us to live faithfully for the Lord. Saved teens need to know that they can use the truths they glean from this week's lesson to prepare them for the many spiritual battles they will face from the forces of darkness.

Building for the Future. The vision appearing in Daniel 8 concerned the future of God's chosen people. The clear message was that their welfare and destiny rested in His hands.

Each summer thousands of young persons join together to repair and rebuild houses for people who cannot afford to pay for the repairs. The program that brings these youth together is called "World Changers." Through instructions and on-the-job training, participants learn how to repair roofs, paint houses, and rebuild crumbling porches.

The physical work is coupled with daily devotions. Almost every young person who participates talks about the joy he or she receives from being able to help someone else. They point out how much they learn about the love of God and helping Him to build for a better future by driving nails and painting wood. Giving really is more fun than receiving.

Never Discouraged! A Little League baseball game was being played one Saturday when a visitor stopped to watch. Walking up along the first baseline, he asked the boy playing nearby whether he knew the score.

"We're behind thirteen to nothing," the boy replied. "Thirteen to nothing!" the visitor bellowed with a jolt. "Hey, you don't seem very discouraged about it." "Naw," answered the youngster. "Why should I? We haven't been up to bat yet!"

That kind of attitude is the outlook Christians should have as they follow the Lord each and every day. Even in moments of great difficulty, believers can obtain encouragement from the truth that the "Prince of princes" (Dan. 8:25) will enable them to prevail for time and eternity.

THE LORD'S SUPPER

BACKGROUND SCRIPTURE: Luke 22:14-30
DEVOTIONAL READING: 1 Corinthians 10:14-22

Key Verse: He that is greatest among you, let him be as the younger; and he that is chief, as he that doth serve. Luke 22:26.

KING JAMES VERSION

LUKE 22:14 And when the hour was come, he sat down, and the twelve apostles with him. 15 And he said unto them, With desire I have desired to eat this passover with you before I suffer: 16 For I say unto you, I will not any more eat thereof, until it be fulfilled in the kingdom of God. 17 And he took the cup, and gave thanks, and said, Take this, and divide it among yourselves: 18 For I say unto you, I will not drink of the fruit of the vine, until the kingdom of God shall come. 19 And he took bread, and gave thanks, and brake it, and gave unto them, saying, This is my body which is given for you: this do in remembrance of me. 20 Likewise also the cup after supper, saying, This cup is the new testament in my blood, which is shed for you.

21 But, behold, the hand of him that betrayeth me is with me on the table. 22 And truly the Son of man goeth, as it was determined: but woe unto that man by whom he is betrayed! 23 And they began to enquire among themselves, which of them it was that should do this thing. 24 And there was also a strife among them, which of them should be accounted the greatest.

25 And he said unto them, The kings of the Gentiles exercise lordship over them; and they that exercise authority upon them are called benefactors. 26 But ye shall not be so: but he that is greatest among you, let him be as the younger; and he that is chief, as he that doth serve. 27 For whether is greater, he that sitteth at meat, or he that serveth? is not he that sitteth at meat? but I am among you as he that serveth. 28 Ye are they which have continued with me in my temptations. 29 And I appoint unto you a kingdom, as my Father hath appointed unto me; 30 That ye may eat and drink at my table in my kingdom, and sit on thrones judging the twelve tribes of Israel.

NEW REVISED STANDARD VERSION

LUKE 22:14 When the hour came, he took his place at the table, and the apostles with him. 15 He said to them, "I have eagerly desired to eat this Passover with you before I suffer; 16 for I tell you, I will not eat it until it is fulfilled in the kingdom of God." 17 Then he took a cup, and after giving thanks he said, "Take this and divide it among yourselves; 18 for I tell you that from now on I will not drink of the fruit of the vine until the kingdom of God comes." 19 Then he took a loaf of bread, and when he had given thanks, he broke it and gave it to them, saying, "This is my body, which is given for you. Do this in remembrance of me." 20 And he did the same with the cup after supper, saying, "This cup that is poured out for you is the new covenant in my blood. 21 But see, the one who betrays me is with me, and his hand is on the table. 22 For the Son of Man is going as it has been determined, but woe to that one by whom he is betrayed!" 23 Then they began to ask one another, which one of them it could be who would do this.

24 A dispute also arose among them as to which one of them was to be regarded as the greatest. 25 But he said to them, "The kings of the Gentiles lord it over them; and those in authority over them are called benefactors. 26 But not so with you; rather the greatest among you must become like the youngest, and the leader like one who serves. 27 For who is greater, the one who is at the table or the one who serves? Is it not the one at the table? But I am among you as one who serves.

28 "You are those who have stood by me in my trials; 29 and I confer on you, just as my Father has conferred on me, a kingdom, 30 so that you may eat and drink at my table in my kingdom, and you will sit on thrones judging the twelve tribes of Israel."

HOME BIBLE READINGS

BACKGROUND

The Passover that Jesus ate with His disciples followed a well-established Jewish pattern for celebrating this feast. A Jewish family normally purchased a lamb several days before the festival. They then took the animal to the temple to be sacrificed by the priests. The family would next take the lamb home, where they roasted it in the afternoon. Passover began at sunset on that day, and the Passover meal was eaten sometime that evening. Before the actual meal was eaten, all the participants washed their hands.

During an opening prayer, the first of four cups of diluted wine was blessed and passed around. Each person reclining at the table then took herbs and dipped them in salt water. (The diners would lean on their left elbow, facing the table with their feet away from it, and eat with their right hand.) Next, the host took one of three flat cakes of unleavened bread, broke it, and laid some of it aside. Thanksgiving was made to God, and more of the bread was broken apart. The host dipped bread in a sauce usually made of stewed fruit, and then distributed a portion to each person gathered at the table. Finally, the time for the main meal arrived. Eating a roasted lamb was the high point of the evening.

NOTES ON THE PRINTED TEXT

As the time drew near, Jesus sent Peter and John ahead into Jerusalem to prepare the Passover meal (Luke 22:8). They were to look for a man carrying a water pitcher and follow him (vss. 9-10). Since women in ancient Jewish culture usually carried these jars, it would have been no problem for Peter and John to recognize the man Jesus was referring to. The owner of the house to which Peter and John were led was evidently expecting them. Upon their inquiry (vs. 11), he showed them a second-floor room complete with furniture (vs. 12).

Next, the disciples—who probably gained access to the upper room by stairs on the outside of the house—prepared the Passover meal (vs. 13). Perhaps Jesus used the question recorded in verse 11 to keep the exact location of the meal a secret from His numerous enemies. Some think Jesus prearranged the meeting as a way for one of His Jerusalem followers to encounter Peter and John at the city gate. Others, however, think the meeting demonstrates Jesus' supernatural knowledge. In any case, at the time designated by Jesus, He gathered with the Twelve to eat the Passover meal (vs. 14). He told them how much He wanted to share the celebration with them before His time of suffering (vs. 15). The Redeemer explained that this would be the last time He would eat the Passover until it was "fulfilled in the kingdom of God" (vs. 16).

It was after Jesus and His disciples had eaten the Passover meal that He instituted the Lord's Supper. Jesus took the third cup (which was known as the "cup of blessing") and uttered a prayer of thanks to God. He then instructed each of His disciples to take the cup and share its contents among themselves (vs. 17). Jesus emphasized the solemnity of the occasion by stating that He would not "drink of the fruit of the vine, until the kingdom of God shall come" (vs. 18).

The Savior next took a flat cake of unleavened bread, broke it, and passed it around so that each of His disciples could eat a portion of it. Perhaps while this was still occurring, He noted that the bread represented His body, which He was offering on their behalf (vs. 19). Jesus then took the fourth cup and said that its contents represented His blood, which He was pouring out through His atoning death on the cross. Jesus' sacrifice of Himself made it possible for God to establish a new covenant in which forgiveness and knowledge of Him would be possible for all who believed (vs. 20; see Jer. 31:31-34).

The various elements used in the Lord's Supper are visible reminders of Jesus' saving work. For instance, the bread symbolizes His body and the cup represents His blood (see 1 Cor. 10:16; 11:23-26). The acts of eating and drinking the elements in the supper (which are also two of the most basic acts of life) point to our dependence upon the Son. Just as we are reliant on food and drink for physical life, we are dependent upon Jesus' death and resurrection for eternal life.

Jesus declared that one of the Twelve would betray Him. In fact, His betrayer was reclining at the table with the group (Luke 22:21). No one but Jesus knew that Judas Iscariot was the turncoat, and so they all began to suspect each other. They found it hard to believe that they had a traitor in their midst (vs. 23). Jesus' upcoming crucifixion had been decreed by God (see Rev. 13:8). This truth, however, did not erase the guilt that rested on Judas for betraying the Messiah. Judas willingly cut a deal with the religious leaders, and he would justly suffer the eternal consequences of his crime (Luke 22:22).

The disciples' discussion about who would betray Jesus may have turned into a debate about who among them was the most loyal. If so, this degenerated into an argument about who was the best, or greatest, disciple (vs. 24). Of course, the betrayer was the worst. But who among the others was acting sensibly? More importantly, why would they even argue over the issue? Peter, James, and John composed the inner circle of disciples. Did that make them the best? Or was it those who had healed the most, or who garnered the largest number of followers for Jesus? The disciples looked at greatness the way we usually do, that is, in terms of supposedly grand accomplishments for God's kingdom, not in terms of humble and sacrificial service.

Jesus had dealt with the oversized egos of His disciples before. Now as He faced the cross, He again had to stop their arguing. John wrote that at some point in the evening, Jesus wrapped a towel around His waist and washed the feet of the Twelve, taking on the role of a lowly servant (see John 13:1-17). Perhaps initially, none of the disciples dared to ask Jesus why He had chosen to wash their feet. Despite all His teaching on servanthood, He may have felt the need to do this task because the Twelve still did not understand the concept of being a servant. Although Jesus knew He was in His last hours before His death on the cross, He remained calm, reflective, and serious. He took the time to show His followers how much He loved them and how much they were to love others.

During the farewell meal, the Savior noted that the kings of the world ordered their subjects around, even though these rulers loved to be called "benefactors" (Luke 22:25). The intent was to portray the rulers as champions of their people. But the title had a condescending ring to it, especially since so many "benefactors" were ruthless tyrants who measured greatness by the nations they conquered and the people they enslaved. In contrast, Jesus told His followers they were to treat one another differently. He urged them to "be as the younger" (vs. 26), namely, the ones to whom the least favorable duties were often assigned. The Messiah also stated that normally the master sits at the table and is served by his underlings. But Jesus had humbly served His followers. This was to remind them that their greatness would be equal to the services they rendered unconditionally and unselfishly to others (vs. 27).

In the Old Testament, servanthood is a common concept. In many places, Scripture mentions hired laborers and slaves. But more important are the references to servants of God. People who were in covenant with the Lord considered Him their master. For example, Elijah declared to God, "I am thy servant" (1 Kings 18:36). And when God spoke, He sometimes called one of His followers "my servant" (for instance, see 2 Kings 21:8). This servant-master relationship between a person and God is also in the New Testament. Believers are servants of the Son, who is Himself the servant of His Father. But in the New Testament, a related idea occurs. Believers are not only servants of God, but also servants of one another (see Mark 10:43; 2 Cor. 4:5).

If any of Jesus' followers thought they were too good to stoop to any menial task of serving others, they did so only by placing themselves above their Lord. He was the suffering Servant, who had come to minister to others and give His life as a ransom for the sins of the world (see Mark 10:45). Jesus solemnly assured the Twelve (and all who trust in Him for eternal life) that slaves are not greater than their master. Likewise, messengers are not greater than the person who sends them (see John 13:16). Jesus' use of the word "sent" reminded His disciples that He had been sent to them by the Father. In turn, Jesus was sending His followers out to serve others, beginning with the proclamation of the Gospel (see 20:21-23).

The Lord Jesus, by example as well as by precept, introduced His followers to this principle of servanthood toward one another. Therefore, He is the believers' model of unselfish service. Those who willingly, consistently, and wholeheartedly follow His example are promised blessings (see John 13:17). Thus, the only way for believers to be truly fulfilled and satisfied in their relationship with the Savior is for them to be willing to accept and perform the role of a servant.

Jesus had commanded His disciples to serve one another rather than seek individual greatness. This did not mean, however, they would go unnoticed. Jesus made it clear that He knew how they had stood with Him in His various trials (Luke 22:28), which included temptations (see 4:1-13), hardships (see 9:58), sorrows (see 19:41), and rejection (see John 1:11). The Messiah promised His followers future blessings and authority at the end of the age. The image is one of a victory banquet in which Jesus' followers would rejoice in His triumph (see Rev. 19:9). They also would be given the right to rule at His return (see Matt. 19:28; 2 Tim. 2:12). In fact, the authority that the Son would bestow on them was like the authority that the Father had bestowed on Him (see Luke 22:29-30).

SUGGESTIONS TO TEACHERS

So much material is packed into this week's lesson that you may find it difficult to cover all of it, especially if your students get sidetracked in discussing relatively insignificant matters. Be sure to keep the main goal of the lesson in focus, namely, that there is eternal joy in serving others unconditionally and unselfishly.

1. AUTHORITIES' SCHEMING. It's ironic that the chief priests and scribes conspired to silence Jesus (see Luke 22:2). From this we see that even religious people sometimes stoop to do ungodly things. We must guard ourselves against the proud attitude that leads us to think we can impose our will on others in the church and claim that it is God's will.

2. JUDAS'S SELLOUT. Stick to the facts presented in Scripture (see vs. 3), and don't let the class members drift into unproductive psychologizing and theorizing about Judas. Be sure to point out that the sinful motives and acts of Judas can be found in all of us. For instance, have not each of us betrayed our Lord at various times?

3. JESUS' SUPPER. This portion of the lesson is an opportunity for your students to think about the meaning of the Lord's Supper. Let them know that it enables believers to bring to remembrance—in a visibly dynamic and dramatic way—the Messiah's past sacrifice for our sins, His present sustaining of our life, and His future return. The Lord's Supper serves as a message to both the saved and the unsaved that Jesus' atoning sacrifice is for all who are lost.

4. DISCIPLES' SERVANTHOOD. People are often confused about the way to achieve true greatness. Ask your students, "What does popular culture tell us about who is great?" Then note that Jesus' teaching runs counter to society's notions by stressing that true greatness is found in humbly serving others. End the teaching time by talking about the joy of serving others unconditionally and unselfishly.

| FOR ADULTS | ■ **TOPIC:** The Privilege of Serving
■ **QUESTIONS:** 1. Why was Jesus so eager to eat the Passover meal with the Twelve? 2. How did Jesus respond when the disciples argued |

about who was the greatest among them? 3. What promise to the disciples did Jesus make about the future kingdom? 4. Why is it important for us to serve others unconditionally and unselfishly? 5. Why do we sometimes struggle to serve in this way?

■ **ILLUSTRATIONS:**

Service—The Way to Greatness. Military heroes stand out in our history as great people, and many of them were. Yet, in every conflict there are examples of greatness among those who never rose to leadership. For example, during World War II, four chaplains found greatness, not in leading, but in setting an example; not in being served, but in serving; and not in being first, but in being last.

These chaplains—George Fox, Alexander Goode, Clark Poling, and John Washington—were on a troopship headed for Europe when the vessel was torpedoed. Rather than use their life jackets themselves, the four chaplains handed them to others. They went down with the ship, for they had caught the spirit of what Jesus taught concerning greatness.

Though we may not aspire to be president, commanding officer, or even mayor, we are still tempted to shun what Jesus said about greatness. We would rather spend lots of time and energy advancing our personal fortunes. This is pointless, however, for unselfish, humble service is the only path to true and lasting greatness in God's kingdom (see Mark 10:43).

True Greatness? Ty Cobb was undoubtedly one of the great players of baseball. During his 24 seasons, 22 with the Detroit Tigers (1905–26) and 2 with the Philadelphia Athletics (1927–1928), he all but wrote baseball's record books. He finished his career with a lifetime batting average of .367, still highest in the history of the game. In 1936, he was the first man to be elected to the Baseball Hall of Fame.

Cobb was also noted for his fierce competitive spirit. He reportedly had a violent temper and an abusive personality that endeared him to almost no one. He was described as "ruthless and mean-spirited" and had a "no-holds-barred" style of play.

Cobb and his wife, Charlie, had five children. But his focus on baseball took its toll on the family. Off the field, Cobb's family had to deal with his turbulent disposition and sarcastic manner. Charlie finally divorced Ty in 1947, charging extreme cruelty throughout their marriage. Cobb remarried again in 1949, but it also failed, ending in divorce seven years later.

On the field, Casey Stengel said in 1975, "no one even came close to Ty as the greatest all-time ballplayer. That guy was superhuman, amazing." But off the field, Cobb was pathetic. While obviously a remarkably talented ballplayer, he wrestled with an extremely combative nature. And though he was a success in baseball, Cobb failed in other, more important areas of life, perhaps because he didn't understand the meaning of true greatness as Jesus defined it (see Luke 22:26-27).

Paragliding Evangelizing. A preacher thought he could serve the Lord by trying a dramatic stunt. One day, in December 1998, he went up in a motored paraglider over a town in southern England and soared over a crowd of spectators. Bellowing through a bullhorn, he preached a hellfire sermon. Police arrested the man, and the court fined him about $1,700. The preacher defended his sensationalism by saying, "I thought that maybe if they heard this voice booming out from the sky, they would think it was God!"

The preacher failed to understand that God doesn't work that way. Rather than shout at us from the sky, the Lord came among us as One who serves. And He calls us to serve one another humbly. Thus service, not shouting, is the way to greatness in the divine kingdom.

 FOR YOUTH

■ **TOPIC:** A Lesson in Service

■ **QUESTIONS:** 1. What did Jesus say was the significance of the bread and cup? 2. Why was Jesus' promise about the future kingdom important to His disciples? 3. How does understanding the Passover meal help you more fully appreciate the significance of Communion? 4. What criteria do you use to determine greatness? 5. What forms of serving others bring you the greatest satisfaction? Why?

■ **ILLUSTRATIONS:**

Who Is the Greatest? Youth often wonder who among them is the greatest, and they answer that question in several different ways. Some consider intelligence, while others think about athletic ability. There are adolescents who define greatness either in terms of what they have, who they know, or how they look.

In the hustle and bustle of making a name for themselves, youth can become mean and selfish. It's no wonder, then, that Christian young people struggle with Jesus' concept of true greatness. He taught that thinking of others counts the most. Also, our desire for worldly greatness must be supplanted by the higher goal of growing in Christlikeness (see 2 Pet. 3:18).

The young people in your church should be encouraged to let their attitude of greatness mirror that of the Savior. They can do so knowing that He loves and accepts them just as they are. And if we also treat them that way, they will see true greatness in action.

Understanding Artist. Flemish artist Dieric Bouts (1415–1475) was contracted by a church in Belgium to paint a large mural measuring 6 feet by 5 feet. Aided by consultants, Bouts painted in the traditional Northern Renaissance style.

Jesus sits at the center of a rectangular table covered by a white tablecloth. His disciples sit upright, eyes riveted on the Savior, with their hands folded in reverential prayer. Pewter plates, a pewter chalice, and glasses sit prominently on the table. A candelabra hangs above Jesus, whose right hand points upward as He instructs His disciples. Meanwhile, His left hand holds a thin wafer.

What is interesting is that behind Jesus, Bouts has added members of the church to the interior of the Flemish room. They peer at Jesus through a kitchen window and stand behind the table's seated participants, acting as servants.

Bouts understood that God has called us to be His servants. He also wants us to serve one another. According to Jesus, this is the path to true greatness.

Ultimate Mark of Greatness. By now the newest class to the Pro Football Hall of Fame will have been announced. Each of those elected in this group will be enshrined, along with the other greats of the game, at Canton, Ohio's Pro Football Hall of Fame. Perhaps you have read about their achievements on the field—games played, touchdowns achieved, yardage run, passes caught or completed, and so on.

It's a great honor to be considered one of football's greatest players. But Jesus said that an even higher level of greatness existed among those who humbly serve others. To be a servant of the King is the ultimate mark of greatness.

THE LORD HAS RISEN!

BACKGROUND SCRIPTURE: Luke 24:1-35
DEVOTIONAL READING: Luke 24:22-26

Key Verse: And their eyes were opened, and they knew
him; and he vanished out of their sight. Luke 24:31.

KING JAMES VERSION

LUKE 24:13 And, behold, two of them went that
same day to a village called Emmaus, which was from
Jerusalem about threescore furlongs. 14 And they
talked together of all these things which had happened.
15 And it came to pass, that, while they communed
together and reasoned, Jesus himself drew near, and
went with them. 16 But their eyes were holden that
they should not know him. 17 And he said unto them,
What manner of communications are these that ye have
one to another, as ye walk, and are sad? 18 And the one
of them, whose name was Cleopas, answering said unto
him, Art thou only a stranger in Jerusalem, and hast not
known the things which are come to pass there in these
days? 19 And he said unto them, What things? And
they said unto him, Concerning Jesus of Nazareth,
which was a prophet mighty in deed and word before
God and all the people: 20 And how the chief priests
and our rulers delivered him to be condemned to death,
and have crucified him. 21 But we trusted that it had
been he which should have redeemed Israel: and beside
all this, to day is the third day since these things were
done. . . . 28 And they drew nigh unto the village,
whither they went: and he made as though he would
have gone further. 29 But they constrained him, saying,
Abide with us: for it is toward evening, and the day is
far spent. And he went in to tarry with them. 30 And it
came to pass, as he sat at meat with them, he took
bread, and blessed it, and brake, and gave to them.
31 And their eyes were opened, and they knew him;
and he vanished out of their sight. 32 And they said one
to another, Did not our heart burn within us, while he
talked with us by the way, and while he opened to us
the scriptures? 33 And they rose up the same hour, and
returned to Jerusalem, and found the eleven gathered
together, and them that were with them, 34 Saying, The
Lord is risen indeed, and hath appeared to Simon.
35 And they told what things were done in the way, and
how he was known of them in breaking of bread.

NEW REVISED STANDARD VERSION

LUKE 24:13 Now on that same day two of them were
going to a village called Emmaus, about seven miles
from Jerusalem, 14 and talking with each other about
all these things that had happened. 15 While they were
talking and discussing, Jesus himself came near and
went with them, 16 but their eyes were kept from recognizing him. 17 And he said to them, "What are you
discussing with each other while you walk along?"
They stood still, looking sad. 18 Then one of them,
whose name was Cleopas, answered him, "Are you the
only stranger in Jerusalem who does not know the
things that have taken place there in these days?" 19 He
asked them, "What things?" They replied, "The things
about Jesus of Nazareth, who was a prophet mighty in
deed and word before God and all the people, 20 and
how our chief priests and leaders handed him over to
be condemned to death and crucified him. 21 But we
had hoped that he was the one to redeem Israel. Yes,
and besides all this, it is now the third day since these
things took place. . . ."

28 As they came near the village to which they were
going, he walked ahead as if he were going on. 29 But
they urged him strongly, saying, "Stay with us, because
it is almost evening and the day is now nearly over." So
he went in to stay with them. 30 When he was at the
table with them, he took bread, blessed and broke it,
and gave it to them. 31 Then their eyes were opened,
and they recognized him; and he vanished from their
sight. 32 They said to each other, "Were not our hearts
burning within us while he was talking to us on the
road, while he was opening the scriptures to us?"
33 That same hour they got up and returned to
Jerusalem; and they found the eleven and their companions gathered together. 34 They were saying, "The Lord
has risen indeed, and he has appeared to Simon!"
35 Then they told what had happened on the road, and
how he had been made known to them in the breaking
of the bread.

5

Monday, March 25	Luke 23:13-25	*The Trial before Pilate*
Tuesday, March 26	Luke 23:32-38	*The Crucifixion of Jesus*
Wednesday, March 27	Luke 23:44-49	*The Death of Jesus*
Thursday, March 28	Luke 23:50-56	*The Burial of Jesus*
Friday, March 29	Isaiah 53:3-9	*The Messiah's Suffering*
Saturday, March 30	Luke 24:1-12	*Discovery of the Empty Tomb*
Sunday, March 31	Luke 24:13-21, 28-35	*The Lord Has Risen Indeed!*

BACKGROUND

The Resurrection is the central fact of human history. The church has persisted through the centuries in spite of persecution because it is built on the reality of the Resurrection. The Resurrection provides us with proof that Jesus is indeed who He claimed to be: the Son of God, the Savior, and our returning King.

After Jesus died on the cross, Joseph of Arimathea and Nicodemus had prepared the Savior's body in the traditional way (see John 19:39-40). But some of Jesus' followers—women from Galilee—wanted to honor Him in a more personal way. After the Sabbath (which ended Saturday at sunset), they bought spices to anoint Jesus' body (see Mark 16:1). Then early Sunday morning, the women headed for the tomb (Luke 24:1). They knew where to go because they had watched Jesus' burial (see 23:55).

Because the four Gospels have some differing details about the morning of Jesus' resurrection, some critics have dismissed the event as an untrue or embellished story. However, a close look at the four accounts shows that the differences give each one the flavor of eyewitness testimony, and all of them agree that Jesus rose from the dead. One point of difference is which women went to the tomb that Sunday morning. Luke 24:10 mentions Mary Magdalene, Joanna, and Mary the mother of James. Matthew 28:1 mentions the two Marys, while Mark 16:1 omits Joanna and adds Salome. John 20:1 only identifies Mary Magdalene as going to the tomb.

One likely explanation for the differences is that several women went to the sepulchre, in different groups and at different times. John, for example, reports at least two visits of Mary Magdalene to the tomb (John 20:1, 10). Her first visit seems to have been with the other women, for she told Peter and John, "They have taken away the Lord out of the sepulchre, and we know not where they have laid him" (vs. 2). Peter and John then went back with Mary to the tomb to look for themselves. John's Gospel also focuses on Mary Magdalene's account of the events because she seems to be the spokesperson for the group of women. Matthew, Mark, and Luke all refer to her first in their reports of who was there that morning.

Those who doubt the Resurrection today should consider that skeptics in the first century A.D. were able to check out the facts with eyewitnesses. For instance, the disciples were at first doubters. Despite the women's excitement, the Eleven did not accept what the women reported. Even the women's enthusiasm seemed like pure nonsense to the Eleven, that is, like the crazy babbling of someone hallucinating with a fever (Luke 24:11). Verse 12 reveals that Peter was the first to respond by running to the tomb to check it out for himself. Next, John outran Peter and reached the tomb first, but he waited for Peter before entering the sepulchre (see John 20:3-6). Peter saw the empty graveclothes, but still could not bring himself to believe (Luke 24:12).

NOTES ON THE PRINTED TEXT

In all, the Bible records 11 appearances of the resurrected Messiah, but there may have been other instances (see Acts 1:3). The first episode Luke wrote about was the risen Lord's encounter with two disciples walking from Jerusalem to Emmaus (Luke 24:13). The latter town has not been positively located, but in Jesus' time, it was about seven miles (possibly northwest) from Jerusalem. One of the disciples Jesus encountered on the road to Emmaus was named Cleopas (see vs. 18). All attempts to identify him further have been unsuccessful. He apparently was a faithful follower of Jesus, for he was present with the disciples in the upper room when the women reported on their trip to the empty tomb (see vs. 23). We have no information at all on the other disciple. Possibly this person was the wife of Cleopas, since it appears they lived at the same place (see vss. 28-29). But it's also possible that the traveling companion of Cleopas was his son, his brother, or his friend.

These two disciples were talking about what had recently happened to Jesus (Luke 24:14). No doubt, the two disciples were disappointed and depressed. Suddenly, their conversation was interrupted by a wonderful turn of events. Jesus came up and joined in their discussion (vs. 15). But amazingly, they were "kept from recognizing" (vs. 16) the Savior. One possibility is that the two never really got a good look at Jesus as they walked toward the west, perhaps as the sun was setting on the horizon (see vs. 29). A second option is that the two failed to recognize Jesus because they weren't really expecting to see Him. A third option is that Jesus intentionally prevented the two from identifying Him so that He could first explain the meaning of the Scriptures to them.

The stranger asked the two disciples what matters they were deliberating so intently as they made their way to Emmaus. The pair, whose faces were disheartened, paused for a moment in their walking (vs. 17). Both were astounded that this stranger was unaware of the momentous events that had recently taken place in Jerusalem (vs. 18). When the stranger asked for more information, the two explained that Jesus of Nazareth was recognized by many as being a "prophet" (vs. 19), that is, an anointed spokesperson for God to others. This is evident by the "mighty" deeds He performed and the message He proclaimed.

The pair further noted that the religious leaders delivered Jesus to the civil authorities to be condemned to death and crucified (vs. 20). The two, along with many others, previously held onto the hope that Jesus was the Messiah, that is, the person who would redeem "Israel" (vs. 21). That aspiration, though, seemed to be shattered when Jesus died on the cross. And now it was the third day since that tragic event had occurred. The Jewish desire for the nation's redemption came from a misconception about the Messiah taken from selected Hebrew prophecies. Most first-century A.D. Jews looked for the Messiah to come as a political hero who would deliver their nation from Roman rule and reestablish the throne of David. They knew about the glory, but they didn't recognize the suffering of the Messiah.

The two disciples continued their story. Just that morning they heard startling news (vs. 22). Some women returned from the tomb and claimed that Jesus' body was gone and the sepulchre was empty. The women also said they saw a "vision of angels" (vs. 23), who announced that Jesus was not dead but alive. Moreover, the two disciples told Jesus about the visit made by Peter and John to the empty tomb. But they had not yet personally seen the risen Lord (vs. 24). Just then, Jesus rebuked the two disciples for being so foolish in failing to believe the prophecies recorded in the Old Testament about the promised Messiah (vs. 25). In essence, their understanding was incomplete, for they knew only one side of what the prophets had foretold.

Next, Jesus declared that it was the Father's will for His Son first to "suffer" the crucifixion and death before being raised to "glory" (vs. 26). Then, Jesus guided the two disciples through the Scriptures by explaining how the events of the past few days had been foretold and fulfilled (vs. 27). By this point the group was nearing the outskirts of Emmaus. Perhaps Jesus signaled by His body language that He intended to continue His journey down the road (vs. 28). The two, however, implored Jesus to accept their hospitality to lodge with them for the night at their residence. They explained that it was early evening and the darkness of nighttime, with all its potential dangers, was fast approaching. In turn, Jesus decided to accept their offer (vs. 29).

After the travelers reached the home of the two disciples, the latter most likely prepared a simple but adequate meal for themselves and their guest. While they reclined at the table, the stranger took some bread, blessed and broke it, and started to give the two disciples some of the bread (Luke 24:30). Instantly, they were enabled to recognize that the risen Lord was in their presence. As soon as the pair knew who Jesus was, He vanished out of their sight (vs. 31). As the two began to process this encounter with Jesus, they admitted they felt as though their hearts were on fire with new life. This was especially so while they walked on the road and listened to Jesus explain to them the messianic passages of the Old Testament (vs. 32).

The two disciples couldn't wait to tell Jesus' other followers back in Jerusalem what had happened. So they hurried out into the night, prepared to hike the seven miles through darkness (vs. 33). When the pair arrived in Jerusalem, the others were talking about another appearance of the risen Savior to Peter (vs. 34). Undoubtedly, the group was thrilled to learn that the disciple who previously had denied the Lord was one of the first Jesus wanted to see again. At this point, the two Emmaus disciples described their encounter with Jesus while they were walking on the road. They also told how they finally realized His identity when He broke the "bread" (vs. 35) during the meal the two had prepared.

SUGGESTIONS TO TEACHERS

State it boldly! If the Father had not raised the Son from the dead, your class would not be gathering to study this week's lesson. In fact, there would be no church building, no congregation, and no hope of heaven. Notable scholars maintain that without the resurrection of Jesus, the shape and direction of all subsequent history would have been different. The news of the Savior's resurrection is the pivotal event not only for us as His followers but also for all humankind, namely, that there is eternal joy in serving others unconditionally and unselfishly.

1. REAPPEARANCE TO THE UNSUSPECTING. Be sure to stress that the two Emmaus disciples were not expecting to see Jesus alive from the dead. This fact rules out any rumors that His resurrection was a story concocted by the early church. Those who may be skeptical of the statement that the Father raised the Son from the dead should carefully examine Luke 24.

2. REMINDER OF SCRIPTURE'S PROMISE. Have your students spend some time considering Jesus' encounter with the two Emmaus disciples. Note that as Jesus walked with them, He explained how the events of the past few days had been prophesied in the Old Testament. Likewise, stress that because the two disciples opened their hearts to the Son, He in turn opened their understanding. This can also be true for your students, especially when they read their Bibles in light of Jesus' resurrection.

3. REVELATION AT THE TABLE. When Jesus and the two disciples sat together to eat the evening meal, Jesus broke the bread and gave thanks for it. In that moment, their "eyes were opened, and they knew him" (vs. 31). We can only guess what triggered their recognition. Was it the way Jesus prayed for the meal? Did they suddenly recall how He had broken bread for over 5,000? Did they see the nail scars in His hands? Give the class an opportunity to discuss this further.

4. RESOLVE OF JOYFUL DISCIPLES. In each of the appearances of the risen Lord, His followers were filled with joy. In the case of His appearance among the disciples gathered in Jerusalem, they welcomed His command to herald the good news of His resurrection far and wide. The Lord also wants the believers in your class to tell others about the risen Lord. They don't do this in their own power. Rather, the Spirit abides in all Christians and enables them to be potent witnesses for Jesus.

FOR ADULTS

■ **TOPIC:** Hope Restored

■ **QUESTIONS:** 1. How do you think the two Emmaus disciples were feeling as they walked along the road? 2. How did Jesus get the two disciples to share their thoughts? 3. What fueled the excitement of the two disciples as they hurried back to Jerusalem? 4. What does it mean to be a witness to the reality of the risen Messiah? 5. What role does the Spirit serve in the witness believers bear concerning Jesus?

■ ILLUSTRATIONS:

Seeing Is Believing. Each of the Gospels tells many engaging accounts about people who met Jesus. But after His death and resurrection, the nature and focus of the disciples' encounters with Him changed dramatically. He both calmed their fears and removed their doubts about His resurrection,

There are times when believers feel confused or doubtful about whether Jesus is truly alive. In those moments of uncertainty, He restores their hope with His reassuring presence. He helps them to see that He is no longer in the grave, but has risen from the dead. This gives them the confidence to believe the truth and to affirm it to others, even skeptical family members and friends.

When believers encounter obstacles to faith, we can encourage them to look afresh at the evidence surrounding Jesus' resurrection. They need to know that believing in Him is of eternal importance. They can also be told that Jesus will never reject them, for He is full of grace, truth, and love. When they believe in Him, they receive new life, forgiveness, hope, and peace.

Easter in the Cemetery. A visitor to Paris decided to attend an Easter celebration. The worship started in a small chapel with a beautiful service at midnight. The following day, on Sunday, the faithful gathered again. This time they assembled in the main sanctuary. Then, while being led by the pastor, the worshipers walked out to a nearby cemetery.

The pastor waited until the participants gathered nearby, then announced dramatically, "Christos voskres!" (which means "Christ is risen!"). While the group stood among the graves of deceased loved ones, they responded enthusiastically, "Voistennu voskres!" (which means "Yes, He is risen!"). Despite the fact that beloved family members and friends had died, these Christians faithfully and joyously affirmed the truth of Jesus' resurrection and the hope of eternal life that it holds for all believers.

What a Ruse! A rich Englishman died and left most of his estate to a London hospital. He had sat on the board of directors of the hospital for many years. In his will, the deceased attached a strange condition to his generous bequest. He stipulated that he had to be in attendance at each monthly meeting of the board of directors!

The board of the hospital thus arranged to have the Englishman's body embalmed and preserved in a suitable storage place in the hospital. Every month for over 100 years, at meetings of the hospital's board of directors, attendants routinely bring in the mummified form and carefully place the man's remains at the head of the table. In this way the minutes of the meetings are able to report that the Englishman is "present." What a ruse!

The Gospels present a drastically different account of Jesus. His corpse was not propped up so that gullible followers could be fooled into thinking He was somehow with them. Rather, many saw Jesus alive from the dead. Of this there is no doubt! Though we can't see, hear, or touch Jesus physically now, we can draw near to Him through the Holy Spirit, who abides in all Christians.

| **FOR YOUTH** | ■ **TOPIC:** A Mystery Guest
■ **QUESTIONS:** 1. What were the probable summary points that the two Emmaus disciples were discussing as they made their journey? |

2. What do you think prevented the pair from initially recognizing Jesus? 3. How did the two disciples feel when they were with Jesus that first Easter Sunday? 4. Why do others need to know that Jesus has risen from the dead? 5. Who are some believers you know whose lives have been changed after receiving Jesus as Savior?

■ **ILLUSTRATIONS:**

You Are a Witness! To many young people the idea of a person rising from the dead seems either mysterious or far fetched. This is why it is important for saved adolescents to be reliable witnesses for Christ to their peers. One need not possess an advanced degree in theology to be a spokesperson for the risen Lord. The only qualification is knowing Him by faith.

These days, young people face so many conflicting claims made by members of different world religions that they are often turned off by invitations to come to church. Thankfully, there are times when they are willing to listen to believers give a clear and simple presentation of the Gospel. The issue is not joining a religion, but rather coming to know the risen Lord in a personal way.

These same people are also willing to study the Bible in small groups. They respond favorably when asked, "Have you ever read about Jesus and His resurrection from the dead?" Such an inquiry may open the door to a group discussion about the Savior's life and teachings. When the Lord makes this opportunity available, Christian teens are wise to take full advantage of it!

The Evidence. A father was explaining to his five-year-old son how Jesus died and then revisited His followers after rising from the dead. "That's what we believe," the father said. "That's how we know Jesus is the Son of God, because He came back from the dead just as He said He would." "Do you mean like Elvis?" the boy observed.

We have no evidence that Elvis ever came back from the dead, but there is a great deal of evidence for Jesus' resurrection. Perhaps some of the greatest evidence is the fact that Jesus lives in the hearts of believers today. For Christians, the resurrection of Jesus is at the core of their faith and the focus of their witness to others.

Without the Resurrection, every word of Jesus is transformed into a lie, every belief we hold is undermined, and everything the church has accomplished for almost 2,000 years is pointless. But of course Jesus did rise from the dead. Our preaching, believing, and hoping have not been in vain. That's why on Easter, throngs of people crowd the church. They know that Easter is the most glorious day of the year, and they know why that is true. It's Resurrection Day!

Surprise! A two-year-old girl could hardly wait for Easter to come. She had a new dress to wear and new shoes to go with it, but her father wondered whether she knew the true meaning of the holiday.

"Kara," he asked, "do you know what Easter means?" "Yes, I do," she smiled. "What does it mean then?" With a smile on her face and her arms raised, she cried, "Surprise!" What better word could there be to describe Easter?

No one expected a crucified person to rise from the dead. Even the religious leaders, who put a guard on the tomb, did not do so because they expected a resurrection. The women came that morning to anoint a body, not find an empty grave. No one expected Jesus to be alive, but He was—and He still is! Surprise!

THE LORD APPEARS

BACKGROUND SCRIPTURE: Luke 24:36-53
DEVOTIONAL READING: 1 Corinthians 15:1-8

Key Verse: These are the words which I spake unto you, while I was yet with you, that all things must be fulfilled, which were written in the law of Moses, and in the prophets, and in the psalms, concerning me. Luke 24:44.

KING JAMES VERSION

LUKE 24:36 And as they thus spake, Jesus himself stood in the midst of them, and saith unto them, Peace be unto you. 37 But they were terrified and affrighted, and supposed that they had seen a spirit. 38 And he said unto them, Why are ye troubled? and why do thoughts arise in your hearts? 39 Behold my hands and my feet, that it is I myself: handle me, and see; for a spirit hath not flesh and bones, as ye see me have.
40 And when he had thus spoken, he shewed them his hands and his feet. 41 And while they yet believed not for joy, and wondered, he said unto them, Have ye here any meat? 42 And they gave him a piece of a broiled fish, and of an honeycomb. 43 And he took it, and did eat before them. 44 And he said unto them, These are the words which I spake unto you, while I was yet with you, that all things must be fulfilled, which were written in the law of Moses, and in the prophets, and in the psalms, concerning me. 45 Then opened he their understanding, that they might understand the scriptures, 46 And said unto them, Thus it is written, and thus it behooved Christ to suffer, and to rise from the dead the third day: 47 And that repentance and remission of sins should be preached in his name among all nations, beginning at Jerusalem. 48 And ye are witnesses of these things. 49 And, behold, I send the promise of my Father upon you: but tarry ye in the city of Jerusalem, until ye be endued with power from on high.
50 And he led them out as far as to Bethany, and he lifted up his hands, and blessed them. 51 And it came to pass, while he blessed them, he was parted from them, and carried up into heaven. 52 And they worshipped him, and returned to Jerusalem with great joy: 53 And were continually in the temple, praising and blessing God. Amen.

NEW REVISED STANDARD VERSION

LUKE 24:36 While they were talking about this, Jesus himself stood among them and said to them, "Peace be with you." 37 They were startled and terrified, and thought that they were seeing a ghost. 38 He said to them, "Why are you frightened, and why do doubts arise in your hearts? 39 Look at my hands and my feet; see that it is I myself. Touch me and see; for a ghost does not have flesh and bones as you see that I have." 40 And when he had said this, he showed them his hands and his feet. 41 While in their joy they were disbelieving and still wondering, he said to them, "Have you anything here to eat?" 42 They gave him a piece of broiled fish, 43 and he took it and ate in their presence.

44 Then he said to them, "These are my words that I spoke to you while I was still with you—that everything written about me in the law of Moses, the prophets, and the psalms must be fulfilled." 45 Then he opened their minds to understand the scriptures, 46 and he said to them, "Thus it is written, that the Messiah is to suffer and to rise from the dead on the third day, 47 and that repentance and forgiveness of sins is to be proclaimed in his name to all nations, beginning from Jerusalem. 48 You are witnesses of these things. 49 And see, I am sending upon you what my Father promised; so stay here in the city until you have been clothed with power from on high."
50 Then he led them out as far as Bethany, and, lifting up his hands, he blessed them. 51 While he was blessing them, he withdrew from them and was carried up into heaven. 52 And they worshiped him, and returned to Jerusalem with great joy; 53 and they were continually in the temple blessing God.

6

HOME BIBLE READINGS

Monday, April 1	1 Corinthians 15:1-8	*Appearances of the Risen Lord*
Tuesday, April 2	John 20:11-18	*The Appearance to Mary Magdalene*
Wednesday, April 3	John 20:24-29	*The Appearance to Thomas*
Thursday, April 4	John 21:1-8	*The Appearance to Seven Disciples*
Friday, April 5	John 21:9-14	*Breakfast with the Disciples*
Saturday, April 6	John 21:15-19	*Simon Peter Called to Follow*
Sunday, April 7	Luke 24:36-53	*You Are Witnesses of These Things*

BACKGROUND

The Greek noun translated "witnesses" (*martus*; Luke 24:48; Acts 1:8) is the origin of the English word *martyr* and means to testify to something on the basis of what one has seen or heard. After Jesus' ascension, the Eleven plus other disciples gathered to choose someone to replace Judas as an apostle. Peter said that this person should be a "witness" (Acts 1:22) to the Resurrection and someone who had been with Jesus since His baptism.

In one sense, then, a witness was someone who actually saw the risen Lord and could testify, as in a courtroom, to the reality of the Resurrection. Nonetheless, the writer of Hebrews also called anyone who perseveres for the faith a witness, and says all believers are surrounded by "so great a cloud of witnesses" (Heb. 12:1). These witnesses include those who have testified to the reality of the Gospel, and their witness encourages us to testify today.

NOTES ON THE PRINTED TEXT

At this time, Jesus' followers were gathered behind locked doors because they feared what the religious authorities might do to them (see John 20:19). They had legitimate concerns in light of what had happened to Jesus. Despite the locked doors, though, Jesus had no problem entering the room and standing in the midst of His disciples. Jesus' resurrection body, while real and tangible, nonetheless possessed certain properties that indicate it was glorified, or altered in some unknown way. Not only could Jesus appear and disappear bodily, but also He could pass through solid objects. He greeted His disciples by saying, "Peace be unto you" (Luke 24:36). In light of His resurrection, this statement took on new significance. Through faith in Him, peace with God was possible (see Rom. 5:1). The Savior's greeting also complemented His statement recorded in John 19:30 ("It is finished"), for His work on the cross was the basis of peace between God and believers (see Eph. 2:14-17).

The disciples were terrified, troubled, and perplexed by Jesus' sudden appearance. In fact, they thought they were seeing a ghost (Luke 24:37). We can easily understand why they were so alarmed, for they had not expected to see Jesus in bodily form. Jesus didn't berate His disciples for their lack of faith. Instead, He gently confronted their fears and doubts by asking them two simple and direct questions (vs. 38). This prompted them to think more objectively about the situation. The Savior wasted no time targeting the doubts of His followers. His goal was to replace their uncertainty with faith. This was important, since faith was the basis for being in a saving relationship with Him (see 2 Cor. 5:7).

Perhaps someone else would have scolded the disciples for their confusion, fear, and doubt. Thankfully, Jesus took a different approach. He pointed to His body as factual evidence that He had physically risen from the dead (Luke 24:39). The disciples knew that disembodied spirits could not be touched. Jesus could, and that's why He invited them to look at His hands and feet, which carried the scars of His crucifixion. They could see that Jesus was no hallucination or figment of their imagination (vs. 40). Here was indisputable proof that Jesus had conquered death. Despite this, some critics still speak of a so-called spiritual resurrection, for they deny the bodily resurrection of the Son. Their assertions, however, do not square with the evidence.

After examining Jesus' body, the disciples were overcome with joy and amazement. Though the proof of His resurrection was clear, they still remained baffled. They could not deny that Jesus was standing before them, but His resurrection did not fit their preconceptions (vs. 41). Rather than get annoyed and impatient, Jesus remained calm with His disciples. The Savior asked for something to eat (vs. 42). After being given a piece of fish, He ate it, thereby proving that He was not a ghost (vs. 43). Through this and other appearances, Jesus thoroughly convinced His disciples that He had indeed risen from the dead. John 20:20 adds that once the disciples recognized their Lord, they were "glad."

Jesus reminded His followers that while He was previously with them, He told them how the messianic promises recorded in the Old Testament were ordained by God to be fulfilled. The Law, the Prophets, and the Psalms—the three major sections of the Hebrew Scriptures—reveal truths about the Redeemer that had to occur. Luke 24:44 affirms that there is a strong interrelationship between the Old and New Testaments. Succinctly put, the triune God brought the universe into existence; human beings sinned, bringing moral and spiritual corruption to themselves and their world; and now the Godhead has made redemption possible through the atoning work of the Son. The divine plan of redemption began at Calvary, continues even now, and will one day be complete when God creates a new heaven and new earth.

At this point, Jesus opened the minds of the disciples to comprehend the Scriptures (vs. 45). While the specific texts are not listed in this verse, it's possible they included the many Old Testament passages appearing elsewhere in the Gospel of Luke and the Book of Acts. The threefold thrust of those prophecies was that the Messiah had to die on the cross (see Pss. 22, 31, 69, 118, Isa. 53), rise from the dead (see Pss. 16:10; 110:1), and have the good news of salvation heralded to the lost (Luke 24:46; see Matt. 28:19; Mark 13:10).

Part of the Gospel proclamation included an emphasis on repentance for the forgiveness of sins (Luke 24:47). This Hebrew concept included the idea of turning from wrongdoing as a prelude to experiencing the Father's offer of pardon through faith in the Son. Beginning at Jerusalem (the initial center and focus of the Gospel), the followers of the Savior were to announce the Good News to the nations of the world (see Isa. 49:6; Luke 2:32; Acts 13:47). Acts 2 records how this began on the day of Pentecost.

The disciples must have been surprised at Jesus' words. Generally, Jews believed that Gentiles were outside the favor of God, or that if Gentiles were to receive God's favor, they first had to become Jews. But here was Jesus telling His disciples to disperse into the world and make disciples of people from all nations (see Matt. 28:19). The Father had opened His arms wide to graciously receive all people who love and believe in His Son.

Jesus declared to His followers that they were witnesses of all that had occurred (Luke 24:48). The idea of proclaiming everything that happened in connection with the Savior is a key concept in the Book of Acts (see 1:22; 2:32; 3:15; 5:32; 10:39, 41; 13:31; 22:15, 21; 26:16). In 1:8, for instance, the risen Lord told His disciples that they and future believers would testify about Him in Jerusalem, in all Judea and Samaria, and to the farthest regions of the earth. They would not do this alone and in their own strength. Instead, the Holy Spirit would empower them for effective Christian service.

In Luke 24:49, Jesus referred to the Spirit as the One whom the Son was sending and whom the Father had previously promised to His people. This divine pledge is rooted in Old Testament passages such as Jeremiah 31:31 and Ezekiel 36:26-27. Also, when John prepared the way for the advent of the Messiah, the messenger declared that Jesus would baptize people with the Holy Spirit (Luke 3:16). As the disciples heralded the Good News, they helped to fulfill what God had promised to do. Moreover, Jesus pledged to clothe His followers with "power from on high" (24:49). This is a reference to the Holy Spirit, who would enable them to bear much fruit by leading many lost people to put their trust in the Redeemer for salvation.

The ascension of Jesus took place 40 days after His first postresurrection appearance to His disciples (see Acts 1:3, 12). In Acts, Luke gave us a fuller account of the event and described Jesus' activities during the 40 days. Luke 24:50 states that when Jesus ascended, the disciples were with Him at Bethany. This was a small village located two miles southeast of Jerusalem on the road to Jericho. The town was on the eastern slope of the Mount of Olives. Bethany was the home of Mary, Martha, and Lazarus, and it was there that Jesus raised Lazarus from the dead (see John 11:17-44). In the house of Simon the leper, a resident of Bethany, a woman anointed Jesus with an expensive jar of perfume (see Mark 14:3-9). At the time of Jesus' ascension, He blessed His disciples. Then, they watched spellbound as Jesus rose upward until they could no longer see Him (Luke 24:51).

After Jesus ascended to heaven, His disciples worshiped their glorified Lord and returned to Jerusalem full of joy (vs. 52). As the years went by and the disciples recalled the sight of His departure, they must have been thrilled to realize He would be returning in the same way (see Acts 1:11).We know from verse 13 that in the days following the Ascension, Jesus' disciples were staying in the upper room. So when Luke says they stayed "continually in the temple" (Luke 24:53), he meant they went to the Jerusalem sanctuary at the regular times for prayer (see Acts 3:1).

Why did Jesus leave the earth in such a dramatic fashion? We may never know for sure, but one view is that it was important for His earthly ministry to come to a definite conclusion. Put another way, the disciples needed to experience a specific point in time when Jesus returned to heaven. Also, by leaving this earth, Jesus was in a position to dispatch the Holy Spirit to minister through all believers everywhere (see John 16:7). The Lord Jesus is now seated at the right hand of His Father (see Eph. 1:20). He is our "advocate" (1 John 2:1), who speaks to the Father in our defense. Also, Jesus is our great High Priest (see Heb. 7:26), who is preparing a place for us to join Him someday (see John 14:2-3).

SUGGESTIONS TO TEACHERS

Jesus' disciples saw an amazing prophecy come to pass. It was the fulfillment of the Father's best promise, namely, the resurrection of His Son from the dead. In connection with this truth, be sure to emphasize the following points during the teaching time:

1. THE REALITY OF JESUS' RESURRECTION. The earliest followers of the Messiah faithfully declared that the Father had raised the Son from the dead. We are not witnesses to the Resurrection in the same sense as Mary Magdalene, Peter, and the other disciples. Expressed another way, we are not eyewitnesses of the risen Lord. But we have firsthand accounts recorded in the New Testament of those who saw Jesus alive from the dead. By comparing these reports, we can see why it's much more reasonable to conclude that Jesus did indeed rise than that He did not.

2. THE SIGNIFICANCE OF JESUS' RESURRECTION. Over the centuries, many skeptics have tried to disprove the truth of the Resurrection. Some, such as Josh McDowell and Lee Strobel, concluded that the evidence for the Resurrection is far stronger than the evidence against it. And perhaps most conclusive of all is the reality of Jesus manifesting His resurrection life through us. There is no better news than the Resurrection. It means victory over death. It signifies new life that begins now and goes on for eternity.

3. THE POWER OF JESUS' RESURRECTION. The question for us is the following: What are we doing with this great news? We wouldn't keep the news of the birth of a new child or grandchild to ourselves. Neither would we fail to mention that we'd been promoted at work. Are we telling others of the even greater news that Jesus lives? After all, we have the Holy Spirit empowering us for faithful and effective Christian service. He will enable us to witness to the reality of the Resurrection with genuine fervor.

FOR ADULTS	■ **TOPIC:** Promises Kept

■ **QUESTIONS:** 1. Why was it necessary for the Old Testament prophecies concerning the Messiah to be fulfilled? 2. What specific things did the Old Testament reveal would happen to the Messiah? 3. What relationship is there between repentance and forgiveness of sins? 4. How would you convince an unbeliever that Jesus literally rose from the dead? 5. Why is it important to rely on the power of the Spirit when telling others about the risen Savior?

■ **ILLUSTRATIONS:**

Promises Made and Fulfilled. Promises have fallen on hard times. Once, a person's word was as certain a guarantee as you could get. Then spoken words became suspect, and the written contract was born. Now we've spurned even that symbol of trust. Today, it seems there is no contract that can't be broken in the name of money, better business deals, or more pressing priorities.

How different the situation is with the promises recorded in Scripture. Long ago, the Father spoke through the Old Testament prophets about the advent of His Son. These promises were literally fulfilled, including the truth that Jesus would suffer, die, and be raised from the dead.

Even today, God is faithful to fulfill His promises in the lives of His spiritual children. As the students in your class live in the hope of that truth, God will again bring about His pledges to them. Though they might not always understand His ways, they will discover that He remains true to His Word concerning them.

A Lost Gospel? Matthew, Mark, Luke, and John compose the four accepted Gospels of the New Testament. But in a book titled *The Lost Gospel*, Herb Krosney chronicles how another (nonbiblical) version of the life of Jesus was found. It's called the Gospel of Judas, and there's been an international effort to authenticate, conserve, and translate this ancient papyrus document dating to the second century A.D. It is a Coptic copy of an original Greek manuscript.

In the four Gospels of the New Testament, Judas Iscariot is portrayed as the disciple who betrayed Jesus to the Romans for 30 pieces of silver. But in this 66-page codex, a very different Judas emerges. He is shown to be the Messiah's best friend and favorite disciple, the one whom Jesus asks to betray His identity. Supposedly, doing this will bring about the fulfillment of prophecy, the liberation of Jesus' soul from the body that entraps Him, and the soul's ascension to heaven. This revisionist view of

Judas depicts him as enabling all of us to find an inner spark within ourselves that will empower us to attain eternity and immortality.

In A.D. 180, an early church leader named Irenaeus (who lived in the city that is now Lyon, France) wrote a condemnation of the Gospel of Judas. Irenaeus knew from the canonical Gospels that the Lord Jesus, not Judas Iscariot, made the ultimate sacrifice for the sins of humankind. And the Messiah alone fulfills the Old Testament promises of salvation (see Luke 24:44).

Good News Is for Sharing. Sometimes people fail to grasp what really matters. For example, on November 7, 1917, the Bolsheviks stormed the Winter Palace in Moscow, Russia, setting off the Russian Revolution, which is now accepted as one of the top history-making events of the twentieth century. That same day, however, the lead story in the *New York Times* dealt with Tamany Hall's victory in local elections.

Similarly, when Tacitus wrote his authoritative chronicle of Rome around A.D. 100, he made only a passing reference to Christians. He dismissed everything about the Messiah and His followers with a brief reference to them as minor troublemakers during the reign of Nero.

Today, of course, Nero gets only a passing reference, and the Roman Empire has long ago disappeared. But Jesus' resurrection continues to be good news worth sharing. Nothing can eclipse that event!

 FOR YOUTH ■ TOPIC: From Fear to Faith

■ QUESTIONS: 1. What is the relationship between the Messiah and the Old Testament? 2. What happened to enable the disciples to understand how Jesus fulfilled the biblical prophecies concerning the Messiah? 3. Why did the Lord want the message of repentance to be proclaimed to all nations? 4. What are the top reasons why you believe in Jesus' resurrection? 5. What are some effective, inoffensive ways you could raise the issue of Jesus' resurrection with unbelievers?

■ ILLUSTRATIONS:
Power from on High. Does heaven exist? A young man asked the pastor of his church that question after a funeral service had been given for the young man's mother. It is also a question that Americans were asked in a telephone survey by *TIME/CNN*. Eighty-one percent of Americans said that they believed in heaven, while 66 percent claimed that they believed a person has both a body and a soul in heaven.

Perhaps the more important question concerns the reality of the Resurrection. Luke's Gospel leaves no doubt. Jesus rose from the dead, and it is the reason His first disciples went from being fearful to filled with faith. Jesus' resurrection is also the basis for the believer's hope of eternal life. Because the Son has conquered sin and death, His followers can also have victory over them. And Jesus has given believers the wonderful privilege of sharing this good news with the entire world!

Afraid of God. The picture some people have of God is similar to the view that the German subjects had of their emperor Frederick William. Legend has it that he was once out walking in a town when he was seen by one of the residents. To his surprise, the man tried to slip quickly inside a doorway in order not to be seen. The emperor roared, "Where are you going?" The man, realizing that he had been spotted, timidly said that he was going into the house. "Your house?" demanded the ruler. Quaking, the man said it wasn't. "Then why are you trying to enter it? You're a burglar, aren't you?"

The man feared that he would be seized and jailed. Deciding that his only hope was to tell the truth, he stammered, "I was trying to avoid you, your majesty." The emperor bristled. "Avoid me. Why?" "Because I fear you, Your Majesty," replied the now-shaken man. Frederick then grabbed his heavy stick and struck the citizen on the chest, shouting, "You are not supposed to fear me. You are supposed to love me! Now love me, you swine. Love me!"

Thankfully, this isn't God's way. In fulfillment of the Old Testament messianic prophecies, Jesus rose from the dead to provide salvation for those who are alienated and separated from Him because of sin.

A New Beginning. Radical turnarounds command attention. When people known for profanity and immorality, for example, suddenly act differently, others want to know why. Consider the young man who was addicted to drugs. When his friends found out he had successfully stopped his addictive behavior, they wanted to know how it was possible. This gave him an opportunity to tell them how Jesus' resurrection had made a profound difference in his life.

The first-century Christians also experienced a new beginning. Jesus' disciples had forsaken Him when He was arrested and crucified. But after Jesus' resurrection, they publicly proclaimed Him as Lord and told people to repent. Jesus can also transform the lives of the students in your class. He can give them the courage to tell their families and friends that He has risen from the dead, just as God promised.

THE HOLY SPIRIT COMES

BACKGROUND SCRIPTURE: Acts 2:1-36
DEVOTIONAL READING: John 15:1-7

Key Verse: They were all filled with the Holy Ghost, and began to speak with other tongues, as the Spirit gave them utterance. Acts 2:4.

KING JAMES VERSION

ACTS 2:1 And when the day of Pentecost was fully come, they were all with one accord in one place.
2 And suddenly there came a sound from heaven as of a rushing mighty wind, and it filled all the house where they were sitting. 3 And there appeared unto them cloven tongues like as of fire, and it sat upon each of them. 4 And they were all filled with the Holy Ghost, and began to speak with other tongues, as the Spirit gave them utterance.

5 And there were dwelling at Jerusalem Jews, devout men, out of every nation under heaven. 6 Now when this was noised abroad, the multitude came together, and were confounded, because that every man heard them speak in his own language. 7 And they were all amazed and marvelled, saying one to another, Behold, are not all these which speak Galilaeans? 8 And how hear we every man in our own tongue, wherein we were born? 9 Parthians, and Medes, and Elamites, and the dwellers in Mesopotamia, and in Judaea, and Cappadocia, in Pontus, and Asia, 10 Phrygia, and Pamphylia, in Egypt, and in the parts of Libya about Cyrene, and strangers of Rome, Jews and proselytes, 11 Cretes and Arabians, we do hear them speak in our tongues the wonderful works of God. 12 And they were all amazed, and were in doubt, saying one to another, What meaneth this? 13 Others mocking said, These men are full of new wine.

NEW REVISED STANDARD VERSION

ACTS 2:1 When the day of Pentecost had come, they were all together in one place. 2 And suddenly from heaven there came a sound like the rush of a violent wind, and it filled the entire house where they were sitting. 3 Divided tongues, as of fire, appeared among them, and a tongue rested on each of them. 4 All of them were filled with the Holy Spirit and began to speak in other languages, as the Spirit gave them ability.

5 Now there were devout Jews from every nation under heaven living in Jerusalem. 6 And at this sound the crowd gathered and was bewildered, because each one heard them speaking in the native language of each. 7 Amazed and astonished, they asked, "Are not all these who are speaking Galileans? 8 And how is it that we hear, each of us, in our own native language? 9 Parthians, Medes, Elamites, and residents of Mesopotamia, Judea and Cappadocia, Pontus and Asia, 10 Phrygia and Pamphylia, Egypt and the parts of Libya belonging to Cyrene, and visitors from Rome, both Jews and proselytes, 11 Cretans and Arabs—in our own languages we hear them speaking about God's deeds of power." 12 All were amazed and perplexed, saying to one another, "What does this mean?" 13 But others sneered and said, "They are filled with new wine."

7

HOME BIBLE READINGS

Monday, April 8	John 14:18-24	*I Will Not Leave You Orphaned*
Tuesday, April 9	John 15:1-7	*Abide in Me*
Wednesday, April 10	John 16:1-11	*The Coming of the Advocate*
Thursday, April 11	Acts 2:22-28	*Raised Up and Freed from Death*
Friday, April 12	Acts 2:14-21	*The Promise of the Spirit*
Saturday, April 13	Acts 2:29-36	*The Promise Received*
Sunday, April 14	Acts 2:1-13	*The Day of Pentecost*

BACKGROUND

Last week we learned that the Lord's teaching during the 40-day period before His ascension included a command that the apostles were to wait in Jerusalem until they had received the gift of the Holy Spirit (see Luke 24:49; Acts 1:4-5). With the Spirit's power, they would become witnesses of Jesus' work and message of forgiveness. The Spirit would enable the disciples to perform mighty deeds and work in the hearts of their listeners to convince them of the truth of the Gospel.

Jesus described expanding zones of influence, beginning at Jerusalem, spreading throughout Judea and Samaria, and eventually reaching to the "ends of the earth" (Acts 1:8). Interestingly, the literary movement of Acts follows this general pattern of expansion. The events recorded in chapters 1 through 7 occurred in Jerusalem; those of chapters 8 and 9 took place in Judea and Samaria; and the action of chapters 10 through 28 progressed from Caesarea to Rome.

NOTES ON THE PRINTED TEXT

Acts 2:1 reveals that the Spirit came upon the disciples while they were assembled in one place. In addition to the fact that they gathered together in a single location, this verse implies that the disciples were in agreement in their thinking and purpose on Pentecost. This Jewish festival, which means "fiftieth," was the second of three main yearly feasts. Passover and Tabernacles were the other two annual festivals requiring the presence of all Jewish males. Pentecost was also known as the Feast of Weeks, the Day of Firstfruits, and the Feast of Harvest. The festival was always on a Sabbath day. The feast was celebrated 50 days after the Passover (Lev. 23:15-16). Some have seen a connection between Pentecost and the giving of the law on Mount Sinai, which may have occurred on the fiftieth day after the Exodus.

Pentecost was basically a celebration of the grain harvest, a period that lasted about seven weeks. Barley and wheat were the primary harvest foods. The poor and strangers were especially welcome during this festival. During Pentecost, the people would bring their offerings of firstfruits to the Lord. A special sacrifice was presented in the temple during this time. A wave offering of new bread made from the recently harvested wheat was presented before the Lord, along with sin and peace offerings. No celebrating was to occur until after this ceremony. Every male Israelite was to appear in the sanctuary. Jews from all over the known world would come to Jerusalem to celebrate this feast of thanksgiving.

All at once and unexpectedly, the disciples heard a sound from heaven that was similar to that of a turbulent "wind" (Acts 2:2). The noise filled the entire house where they were meeting. In the context of this incident, the wind was a physical indication of the presence of the Spirit. In Scripture, wind and breath are common symbols of God's Spirit (see Ezek. 37:9, 14; John 3:8).

The sight of "tongues like as of fire" (Acts 2:3) was even more unusual than the sound of the wind, perhaps being reminiscent of the thunder and lightning that accompanied God's giving of the law to Moses on Mount Sinai (see Exod. 19:16-19). The tongue-shaped flames appeared to stand over each disciple's head (Acts 2:3). This incident was significant, for it indicated that God's presence was among Jesus' followers in a more powerful and personal way than they had ever experienced before. The disciples could sense the Spirit's coming audibly (through wind) and visibly (through fire). Moreover, they were filled with the Holy Spirit (vs. 4). As evidence of His presence, the Spirit enabled them to speak in other tongues. Apparently these were actual languages or dialects being voiced by the disciples to the visitors from many countries in Jerusalem. The Spirit had come to empower Jesus' followers to reach out to the lost with the saving message of the Gospel.

Some think Jesus' followers were at that moment in one of the courts of the Jerusalem temple (Luke 24:52-53). In a few instances, Luke uses the Greek word for "house" in Acts to refer to the temple, and Luke's Gospel closes with the statement that the disciples "were continually in the temple, praising and blessing God" (24:53). Those who hold this view also suggest that the disciples had the best chance of attracting a large crowd in the temple precincts than in the upper room. Those who think the Spirit came upon the disciples in the upper room of a house argue that "one place" (Acts 2:1) more naturally refers back to the space mentioned in 1:13. They also point out that Luke more often uses the common Greek word for temple rather than the word for house. With the entire city of Jerusalem filled with pilgrims, the disciples could have attracted a large crowd by coming down to the street after the Holy Spirit had come upon them.

The disciples, being enthusiastic in their baptism of power, spilled out into the streets of Jerusalem. As was noted earlier, the population of Jerusalem swelled with pilgrims attending the festival of Pentecost (Acts 2:5). This event proved to be a strategic time for the Father and Son to send the Holy Spirit. Visitors who heard God being miraculously praised in their own languages—and were perhaps among that day's 3,000 converts (see vs. 41)—could take the good news of salvation in the Messiah back with them to their homelands.

While the Spirit operates quietly, God sometimes sends visible and audible signs of His work. The wind, fire, and inspired speech all have their roots in Jewish tradition as signs of God's presence. This did not escape the notice of the foreign Jews who heard the sound of tongues. They were amazed that locals could fluently speak languages from around the Roman Empire (vs. 6). With their curiosity aroused, crowds of people quickly gathered together to discuss what could be behind all the commotion. They could tell by the distinctive accent of Jesus' followers that they were mainly from Galilee (vs. 7). In general, the Jews living in Jerusalem looked down upon those from Galilee because it was so far away from the religious center of the nation (see John 7:52).

Evidently, the throng operated under the assumption that the disciples spoke only one or two languages. Consequently, they were perplexed that these simple, uneducated Galileans could speak fluently in so many different native dialects, which in turn could be understood by the diverse group of pilgrims (Acts 2:8-11). In this amazing turn of events, the Lord began to reverse the confusion that occurred at the tower of Babel thousands of years earlier (see Gen. 11:1-9). Whereas then God scattered the human race over all the earth, on the day of Pentecost He brought all sorts of different people back together to hear the message of salvation.

Both ethnic Jews and converts to Judaism heard the Messiah's disciples using the crowds' own languages to declare to them the wonderful things God had done. These visitors came from all across the Roman Empire (Acts 2:9-11). At the time when the New Testament was written, the entire civilized world (with the exception of the little-known kingdoms of the Far East) was under the domination of Rome. From the Atlantic Ocean on the west to the Euphrates River and the Red Sea on the east, from the Rhone, the Danube, the Black Sea, and the Caucasus Mountains on the north, and to the Sahara on the south, stretched one vast empire under the headship and virtual dictatorship of the emperor.

"Parthians" (vs. 9) lived in the region that constitutes what is today modern Iran. As was noted in lesson 2, "Medes" refers to the ancient Indo-European inhabitants in what is today part of northwest Iran. "Elamites" denotes those living in the region located north of the Persian Gulf, with the Tigris River forming its western boundary. "Mesopotamia" (modern-day Iraq) is the region located between the Tigris and the Euphrates. "Judea" is the Greco-Roman name for the land of Judah. "Cappadocia" was a large region in Asia Minor bordered on the north by the Kingdom of Polemon, in the south by Cilicia and Syria, in the west by Galatia and Lycaonia, and in the east by Armenia and Syria. "Pontus," located along the southern shore of the Black Sea, was bordered on the west by Bithynia and on the southeast by Galatia. "Asia" refers to a Roman province located in western Asia Minor.

"Phrygia" (vs. 10) was a tract of land centered on the great Anatolian plateau of Asia Minor. "Pamphylia," located on the southern coast of Asia Minor, was bordered on the west by Lycia and on the east by Cilicia Tracheia. The kingdom of "Egypt," located in northeastern Africa, extended south about 550 miles from the Mediterranean Sea. "Libya" was the stretch of territory encompassing north Africa west of Egypt. Most of the Jews who lived there resided in "Cyrene," which was the capital of a region called Cyrenaica. "Rome" was located about 15 miles from the mouth of the Tiber River on the Italian Peninsula. The city was a sprawling metropolis of about one million people and the imperial capital of the empire. "Cretes" (vs. 11) were residents of an oblong-shaped island located 60 miles southeast of the mainland of Greece. "Arabians" were residents of Arabia, which was located between the Red Sea and the Euphrates River.

The pilgrims were excited but confused by the episode of speaking in tongues unfolding before them. The crowds kept asking one another what its significance might be (vs. 12). Regrettably, some in the throng took a less charitable view. They crassly joked that Jesus' disciples were drunk from having ingested too much wine (vs. 13). The Savior would use the bewilderment of the pilgrims as an opportunity to shine the light of the Gospel into their sin-filled lives.

SUGGESTIONS TO TEACHERS

A study of Acts makes it clear that the Spirit is relevant to the church. Also, every believer needs Him to live for the Savior. This week's lesson about the coming of the Spirit on the day of Pentecost will open up to your students a new and deeper understanding of how God wants to work in their lives. It should also encourage them to be more faithful and obedient to the Savior.

1. THE GODLY CONFLAGRATION. The disciples on the day of Pentecost vividly remembered the Spirit's presence and power in their midst. He was among them like wind and fire! The Spirit's presence came upon them in such force that they were changed forever. The Spirit kindled a burning awareness of Jesus' nearness and love. Be sure to discuss how the promise of the Spirit applies to Jesus' followers today. Are the members of your class fervent in their devotion to the Savior?

2. THE CRITICAL COMMENTS. Some bystanders sneered at the way the Spirit-filled disciples expressed what happened. These critics claimed that the disciples were drunk (see 2:13). The disciples, however, didn't allow the put-downs and criticism to stop them from proclaiming the Gospel. Christians today also encounter critics. Let the students know that the Spirit can enable them to continue witnessing for Jesus despite opposition from unbelievers.

3. THE CONFIDENT COMMUNICATOR. Note that Peter was boldly preaching to the crowd. This was the same person who had previously denied being a follower of Jesus. What prompted Peter and his associates to risk their lives by telling people in Jerusalem about the Messiah and His resurrection? It was the power of the Spirit! The same Spirit empowers every believer today to share his or her faith with others.

4. THE CONSTANT COMPANION. Some today whimper that God seems absent or that He has deserted them. But this isn't true of those who have been touched by the Spirit! Those rejoicing in the Spirit know they're never alone. When we're saved, the Spirit abides in us and helps us live for the Savior. When we yield control of our lives to the Spirit, He helps us overcome our selfish impulses. And when God's Spirit is in control of our lives, we consider other people's needs above our own wants and desires.

| **FOR ADULTS** | ■ **TOPIC:** Power to Change |

■ **QUESTIONS:** 1. Why were the disciples gathered together on the day of Pentecost? 2. What did Jesus' followers do when they became filled with the Holy Spirit? 3. What utterly amazed the pilgrims about the tongues episode? 4. How can you promote unity among believers you know who are from a different background or tradition than you? 5. What are some specific ministries the Holy Spirit has empowered you to perform?

■ **ILLUSTRATIONS:**

United by the Spirit. People are usually skeptical if they cannot see evidence of a claim. The unoficial motto of the state of Missouri (the "Show-Me State") reflects the attitude of many adults. If we claim that God's Spirit is dwelling in us, then we need to give evidence of His presence. One way to show we have had a genuine and lasting encounter with the Spirit is by the powerful changes in behavior He has made in us (for example, by our trusting in the Savior, shunning sin, and remaining united with our fellow believers).

This was the central thrust of Peter's message on the day of Pentecost. Adults need to know that Peter's promise of forgiveness and the indwelling Holy Spirit extended beyond his current audience to future generations and to those living in other lands. Although Peter may not have realized it at the time, his words included the Gentiles as well.

Essential Common Ground. When people are suddenly thrown together by unexpected circumstances, unusual events often result. Whether they are prisoners of a terrorist group, or survivors of an airplane crash, people have a way of connecting when it becomes necessary for survival. When survivors sleep each night in a shivering, huddled mass on a dark mountainside, questions of who drives a compact car versus who drives a luxury automobile are not pondered.

Unexpected circumstances can throw us into a new "community." We find ourselves trying to adjust to the new culture and economy of that life. And we quickly discover that there is much more that we have in common than we have as differences with one another. Only after we become completely saturated in this new community do we begin to feel the luxury of picking at the differences that we sometimes arbitrarily identify.

We are members of a new kingdom founded on the day of Pentecost by the Lord Jesus. As such, we should become aware of all that we share in common with the other constituents in this community. The differences we see—whether they be in lesser doctrines or styles of worship—should never keep us from identifying together as part of the body of Christ.

Difficulty of Waiting. Retired television host Hugh Downs and his wife were once in Washington, D.C., preparing to return to New York. A call came telling them that their flight had been canceled. Downs quickly checked on train schedules and discovered a train that was leaving for New York in 45 minutes.

Mrs. Downs was in the shower, so Hugh decided to speed up their departure by packing their bags. He hurriedly threw their clothing and belongings into suitcases, called the bellhop, and had their luggage sent to Union Station. A few minutes later, Mrs. Downs emerged from the bathroom, wrapped in a towel. Calling to her husband, she asked if he would bring her green dress.

Sometimes, as Hugh Downs discovered, we take matters into our own hands too hastily. Jesus' disciples may have wanted to do that before the day of Pentecost by doing the Lord's will impulsively in their own strength. But Jesus told them to wait patiently until they were "baptized with the Holy Ghost" (Acts 1:5). Being willing to wait for the Lord is not easy, but absolutely necessary!

FOR YOUTH	■ TOPIC: Hope for Power

■ **QUESTIONS:** 1. What was significant about the visible ways in which the Spirit of God manifested His presence to the disciples? 2. What sorts of people heard the disciples proclaim the wonderful things God was doing? 3. What crass remark did some in the crowds make regarding what they heard and saw among Jesus' disciples? 4. What is the essential common ground that all believers in Christ share with one another? 5. Why is it important to approach tasks and ministries in the power of the Holy Spirit?

■ **ILLUSTRATIONS:**

The Power of the Faithful. Some of the most interesting conversion stories I have heard involve people studying to be ministers. The standard assumption is that these people are already saved. Occasionally, this isn't the case.

There are many reasons why individuals want to train for church leadership. Even teens are known to wrestle with this issue. Often, though, the desire—whether it is to help others, exercise abilities in teaching and counseling, enjoy a position of respect and influence, and so on—is void of God's presence and power.

As we learn in this week's lesson, an individual claiming to be a Christian, regardless of his or her age, is spiritually powerless when not connected with the Savior and operating in the Spirit. What a dynamic change occurs when a young person stops trying to live for God in his or her own strength and starts faithfully serving Him with the limitless resources of the Spirit!

Power to Do God's Work. Twenty years ago, when Jeremy was fresh out of high school, he had no idea that he would be standing where he was now. Back then, all he knew for sure was that he was beginning the life that he had dreamed of since he was 12. Jeremy was now a senior communications specialist aboard the *USS Nimitz*, one of the largest nuclear-powered aircraft carriers in the world.

As Jeremy stood at attention in full dress "whites," he received his citations for effective service, and at the ripe old age of 38, he was now officially retired. For Jeremy, retirement was just a change of direction, not a slowing of pace. In six weeks, he would begin a new career. His job would be to link together computer networks of Christian missionary agencies through state-of-the-art communication technologies. Jeremy barely could comprehend how the Lord had so perfectly prepared him for this new job. The Spirit gave Jeremy such specific skill training so many years before that now it seemed too good to be true.

Believers who are continually dedicating their future needs and direction to God experience this same principle that worked in Jeremy's life. It is one of the most common miracles of all. Specifically, as He did with the believers on the day of Pentecost, the Spirit uses circumstances in our lives to prepare us for ongoing Christian service. The Spirit also prepares and provides for needs and opportunities that we have not yet encountered. We discover that the Spirit is always present to empower us for His work.

Effects of Power. At Pittsburgh's Carnegie Science Center, the lecturer was discussing electrical energy and needed someone to touch the Van de Graff Generator. A fourth grader volunteered to go forward and place her right hand on the large shiny silver ball. As she touched the device, her long blonde hair rose up on her head. While no one in the audience could see the electrical charge, the effects were quite obvious.

On the day of Pentecost, no one could actually see the Spirit. However, His presence was powerfully evident to Jesus' followers. The Spirit enabled them to be bold in their witness and sensitive to the needs of their fellow believers.

LIVING WITH HOPE

BACKGROUND SCRIPTURE: 1 Thessalonians 4:13–5:11
DEVOTIONAL READING: Psalm 38:9-15

Key Verse: God hath not appointed us to wrath, but to obtain salvation by our Lord Jesus Christ. 1 Thessalonians 5:9.

KING JAMES VERSION

1 THESSALONIANS 4:13 But I would not have you to be ignorant, brethren, concerning them which are asleep, that ye sorrow not, even as others which have no hope. 14 For if we believe that Jesus died and rose again, even so them also which sleep in Jesus will God bring with him. 15 For this we say unto you by the word of the Lord, that we which are alive and remain unto the coming of the Lord shall not prevent them which are asleep. 16 For the Lord himself shall descend from heaven with a shout, with the voice of the archangel, and with the trump of God: and the dead in Christ shall rise first: 17 Then we which are alive and remain shall be caught up together with them in the clouds, to meet the Lord in the air: and so shall we ever be with the Lord. 18 Wherefore comfort one another with these words.

5:1 But of the times and the seasons, brethren, ye have no need that I write unto you. 2 For yourselves know perfectly that the day of the Lord so cometh as a thief in the night. 3 For when they shall say, Peace and safety; then sudden destruction cometh upon them, as travail upon a woman with child; and they shall not escape. 4 But ye, brethren, are not in darkness, that that day should overtake you as a thief. 5 Ye are all the children of light, and the children of the day: we are not of the night, nor of darkness.

6 Therefore let us not sleep, as do others; but let us watch and be sober. 7 For they that sleep sleep in the night; and they that be drunken are drunken in the night. 8 But let us, who are of the day, be sober, putting on the breastplate of faith and love; and for an helmet, the hope of salvation. 9 For God hath not appointed us to wrath, but to obtain salvation by our Lord Jesus Christ, 10 Who died for us, that, whether we wake or sleep, we should live together with him.

11 Wherefore comfort yourselves together, and edify one another, even as also ye do.

NEW REVISED STANDARD VERSION

1 THESSALONIANS 4:13 But we do not want you to be uninformed, brothers and sisters, about those who have died, so that you may not grieve as others do who have no hope. 14 For since we believe that Jesus died and rose again, even so, through Jesus, God will bring with him those who have died. 15 For this we declare to you by the word of the Lord, that we who are alive, who are left until the coming of the Lord, will by no means precede those who have died. 16 For the Lord himself, with a cry of command, with the archangel's call and with the sound of God's trumpet, will descend from heaven, and the dead in Christ will rise first. 17 Then we who are alive, who are left, will be caught up in the clouds together with them to meet the Lord in the air; and so we will be with the Lord forever. 18 Therefore encourage one another with these words.

5:1 Now concerning the times and the seasons, brothers and sisters, you do not need to have anything written to you. 2 For you yourselves know very well that the day of the Lord will come like a thief in the night. 3 When they say, "There is peace and security," then sudden destruction will come upon them, as labor pains come upon a pregnant woman, and there will be no escape! 4 But you, beloved, are not in darkness, for that day to surprise you like a thief; 5 for you are all children of light and children of the day; we are not of the night or of darkness. 6 So then let us not fall asleep as others do, but let us keep awake and be sober; 7 for those who sleep sleep at night, and those who are drunk get drunk at night. 8 But since we belong to the day, let us be sober, and put on the breastplate of faith and love, and for a helmet the hope of salvation. 9 For God has destined us not for wrath but for obtaining salvation through our Lord Jesus Christ, 10 who died for us, so that whether we are awake or asleep we may live with him. 11 Therefore encourage one another and build up each other, as indeed you are doing.

Monday, April 15	Isaiah 59:9-15a	*The Hopeless Human Situation*
Tuesday, April 16	Isaiah 59:15b-21	*The Source of Hope*
Wednesday, April 17	Psalm 38:9-15	*Waiting in Hope*
Thursday, April 18	Romans 4:16-25	*Hoping against Hope*
Friday, April 19	Hebrews 6:13-20	*Seizing the Hope Set before Us*
Saturday, April 20	Romans 15:7-13	*The God of Hope*
Sunday, April 21	1 Thessalonians 4:13–5:11	*Encourage One Another with Hope*

BACKGROUND

First Thessalonians 4:17 reveals that a time is coming when a whole generation of believers in Christ will be privileged to miss out on death. At Jesus' return, all believers living on the earth will be caught up in the air to meet the Lord. And the bodies of Jesus' followers will be instantaneously glorified, so that they will be like the resurrected believers. The believers who are caught up will have a double reunion. They will be reunited with the Savior as well as with their deceased loved ones in the faith. The joy of this gathering is probably beyond our imagination.

The main purpose of the rapture is to meet the Lord. When a dignitary paid a visit to a Greek city in ancient times, leading citizens went out to meet him and to escort him on the final stage of the journey. Paul similarly pictured Jesus as being escorted by His own people, those newly raised from the dead and those who will have remained alive. Having met the Lord in a glorified existence, they will never have to leave Him again.

NOTES ON THE PRINTED TEXT

Previously, during Paul's short stay in Thessalonica, he declared that Jesus will come again. The apostle also taught about the resurrection of the dead. But Paul evidently had not described how the dead will participate in the events surrounding the Lord's second coming. The apostle knew that if he cleared up the Thessalonians' confusion about death, he would in the process reassure them. Believers, Paul said, need not grieve "even as others which have no hope" (1 Thess. 4:13). Of course, the "others" are unbelievers. Historians attest to the truth of Paul's words about pagan despair in the face of death. The best philosophers and teachers of the ancient world had no real hope to offer their followers. Literature of the time is filled with pictures of hopelessness at death. Inscriptions on tombs reflect the same dread. Ancient myths describe scenes of the utter darkness of the afterlife.

Paul argued in verse 14 that, since Jesus rose from the dead, believers can be certain they, too, will be resurrected. Moreover, Jesus will bring with Him all the believing dead, in their resurrected form, when He returns as He promised. Because the

Messiah survived death, the survival of believers beyond death was as equally certain. Some Bible commentators have suggested that early on in his career, Paul expected to be among those who are still alive at the time of the Lord Jesus' coming. They base this view, first of all, on passages in early letters written by the apostle where he used the word "we," seeming to include himself with those who will be alive (for example, vss. 15, 17).

Yet passages in letters written later in Paul's career seem to indicate that the apostle expected to be among those who would die and be resurrected (for instance, 2 Cor. 4:14). Some commentators who favor this view suggest that the primary incident that changed Paul's mind was his close brush with death in the Roman province of Asia (see 1:8-10). Other commentators believe we cannot know whether the apostle expected to survive until the Savior's return. They point out that Paul regularly identified himself with his readers by saying "we." Therefore, nothing can be proved by his use of that pronoun.

The Thessalonian believers were evidently concerned that their dead loved ones would be at a disadvantage when Jesus returned. But that would not be the case. In fact, Paul stated on the authority of the exalted Messiah that the righteous dead will be the first to join the Savior in a resurrection existence (1 Thess. 4:15). The apostle did not try to specify when the Lord's coming will happen. But Paul did say that when it occurs, three signs will accompany it: (1) a loud "shout" (vs. 16), (2) "the voice of the archangel," and (3) "the trump of God." The three signs mean the same thing: an announcement of Jesus' coming.

At that time, deceased believers will be the first to be resurrected from the dead in an immortal and glorified form. Then they, along with Christians alive at the time, "shall be caught up . . . in the clouds" (vs. 17). The order of events suggests that at Jesus' return, deceased believers will "rise first" (vs. 16) before the events of verse 17 take place. The Greek verb translated "caught up" can also be rendered "snatched away." This verb carries the ideas of irresistible strength and total surprise.

The Thessalonians had two questions related to the Lord Jesus' return. First, they wondered whether believers who die before the Messiah's second advent will miss out on the blessings of that time. Verses 13-18 contain Paul's assurance that not only will the dead in Christ participate in those blessings, but also they will join the Savior in a resurrected existence prior to Christians who are alive at the Second Coming. The apostle's readers also wanted to know how and when all the events connected with Jesus' return will happen (5:1). Paul reminded them of what he had told them before, namely, that the timing of that future day is unknown. Paul went on to tell his readers that they ought to keep looking forward to the day of the Lord with confidence.

Evidently, the Thessalonians were engaging in speculation about "the times and the seasons" of Jesus' return. Paul gently chided his readers for their useless endeavor. He really should not have had to write to them on this subject, because they knew that the day of the Lord's return will come suddenly and unexpectedly, like a "thief in the night" (vs. 2). People will be lulled into false security right up until the day of the Lord. They will be talking about "peace and safety" (vs. 3) when destruction suddenly strikes. Paul made reference to a pregnant woman's going into labor. The apostle's main focus was not on the intense pain of labor, but rather on the rapid and unexpected way in which the experience starts. The unsaved, being surprised by the commencement of the day of the Lord, will not escape this future time of unprecedented travail.

The history of human life on the earth is filled with more scenes of destruction than any of us care to contemplate. But in verse 3, commentators believe Paul was referring to a future time of unprecedented difficulties, usually called the Great Tribulation period. This passage does not necessarily mean that all people will die during the future time of harrowing distress, only that the destruction will be terrible and there will be no avoiding it. The apostle referred to the immediate arrival of a pregnant woman's labor pains to emphasize how quickly God's wrath will strike the wicked. The use of childbirth to illustrate spiritual truth is seen both in the prophets and in the teachings of Jesus (see Isa. 13:6-8; Jer. 4:31; Mark 13:8). In rabbinic writings, the sufferings preceding the establishment of the messianic age are often called labor pains. Sometimes, the point is the intense pain of labor, but in 1 Thessalonians 5:3, Paul's emphasis is on the sudden onset of labor pains.

Paul's readers were not to be taken by surprise by the day of the Lord. While they could not predict its timing, they knew with certainty that it was coming, and they could expect it to happen (vs. 4). After all, they were "children of light" (vs. 5) and "children of the day." Moral purity and truth characterized them. In contrast, unbelievers belonged to the "night" and were at home in the "darkness." Impurity and falsehood characterized them.

In verses 6-8, Paul further compared the saved and unsaved. Like people who sleep, unbelievers are spiritually insensitive and unaware of the coming of the day of the Lord. Their drunkenness represents their lack of proper self-control. In contrast, believers live in the brightness of spiritual awareness and keep themselves alert and sober. We often think about sobriety in terms of avoiding some form of sin. But in verse 8, Paul had in mind self-control's positive virtues. It means to put on the breastplate of faith and love and to don as a "helmet" the "hope of salvation."

Paul previously mentioned the trio of faith, hope, and love in 1:3. Faith is the means by which we enter the Christian life, and day by day we trust in the Lord for our care. The love that exists between God and us prompts us to be compassionate and kind to one another. The hope of salvation means that, while divine wrath awaits unbelievers, we who are Christians will abide forever with the Lord. The day of the Lord will indeed bring "sudden destruction" (5:3), but this "wrath" (vs. 9) is not meant for Jesus' followers. Believers, of course, along with everyone else, deserve God's wrath because of our sin. But instead of receiving judgment for our misdeeds, we will receive salvation because of what Jesus has done for us.

In the end, it does not really matter whether we pass away before Jesus comes, for He died (and rose again from the dead) so that we can abide with Him forever. Moreover, whether we are living or deceased, our eternal future will be the same: "We should live together with him" (vs. 10). The everlasting joy we are promised in union with the Son is not a dry biblical truth, but rather a wonderful source of encouragement and edification. Thus, believers are to "comfort" (vs. 11) one another and "edify" each other in their faith. In fact, this is to continue until Jesus returns.

SUGGESTIONS TO TEACHERS

Some Christians believe we are living in the "last days," and there is considerable false teaching about this topic. Therefore, Paul's message to the Thessalonians is one we need to hear clearly today. We do not need to speculate concerning "the times and the seasons" (1 Thess. 5:1) of Jesus' return, but we certainly need to "watch and be sober" (vs. 6), that is, be ready at all times for His coming, whenever it may be. How can we be ready? Some of the same things we do to get ready for a trip apply to being ready for Jesus' return.

1. BE FISCALLY READY. We look at our finances before a trip to be certain we have the money we need and have made the proper financial arrangements. In a similar way, we are to give to God that which is His to support His work here until Jesus comes. Jesus said that where our treasure is, that's where our heart will be too (see Matt. 6:21).

2. BE PHYSICALLY READY. For a trip there is usually the physical preparation of packing. While we cannot "pack" for our trip to heaven, physically we should always be aware of who we are with and what we are doing in light of Jesus' return. In other words, if Jesus came today, would there be things we do now we wouldn't want Him to find us doing? Are we being His witnesses to those around us, or would they never guess we are Christians by our words and actions?

3. BE EMOTIONALLY READY. Trips can be emotional experiences, something you are either up for or not. As a Christian, would your emotions at this time say, "This world is not my home," or "I am both in the world and of the world. I'm too tied to things here to even think about leaving"?

4. BE SPIRITUALLY READY. You may pray before a trip, asking God to watch over your travels. Of course, you first need "salvation by our Lord Jesus Christ" (vs. 9) for your final, heavenly trip. But beyond that, like the Thessalonians, is your life characterized right now by faith, love, and hope? Paul finished chapter 5 with a virtual checklist of "spiritual" things we should all be doing every day as we wait for Jesus to return. That should be our checklist as well.

■ TOPIC: Great Expectations

■ QUESTIONS: 1. What did Paul want the Thessalonians to be informed about? 2. What will happen to Christians who have already died when Jesus comes again? 3. What will happen to Christians who are still alive when Jesus returns? 4. How should we act as we wait for the Savior's return? 5. As you anticipate the day of the Lord, what are some ways you can encourage others to exhibit self-control by living a life of faith, love, and hope?

■ ILLUSTRATIONS:

Getting Ready. The newly married couple set up housekeeping in a ground-floor apartment in an old house located on a traditional street with lawns and flowers. For some time they ignored how their place looked. But one day they got word that visitors were coming: the husband's parents, who kept their place clean and sharp inside and out.

The couple sprang into action: cleaning rooms, pulling weeds, and cutting grass. It was almost like the coming of the Lord. In the nick of time they made their place sparkle, and it passed inspection.

What would we do differently today if we knew that Jesus would knock on our door tomorrow? It's so easy to dismiss the coming of the Lord, because we get so deeply involved in our own concerns. Our agenda becomes more important than His.

Since we do not get advance word about Jesus' coming, we can take steps to be ready to meet Him. Thinking about that prospect helps us shape our program more like His and less like ours.

Wait and Watch. The Lord has given special commendation to those who not only *wait* for His return, but also earnestly *watch* for Him. The difference between these terms can be illustrated by the story of a fishing vessel returning home after many days at sea. As they neared the shore, the sailors eagerly watched the dock where a group of their loved ones had gathered. The skipper looked through his binoculars and identified some of the wives he saw waiting there.

One man became concerned because his wife was not on the dock. Later, he left the boat sadly and trudged up the hill to his home. As he opened the door, his wife ran to meet him, saying, "I have been waiting for you!" Quietly, he replied, "Yes, but the other men's wives were watching for them." While this man's wife obviously loved him, she had not been actively watching for his homecoming as he had hoped.

In the same way, sometimes I am so anxious for my spouse to return home from work, I find myself walking to the front door several times to check and see if she has turned up the street toward home. Other times I am surprised by her suddenly walking in the door. Though I knew she would be coming, I had gotten preoccupied with other things—which at the time I thought were important. That is what happens when we fail to be ready for Jesus to return at any time. This is not a good time to be surprised.

Now Instead of Later. President John F. Kennedy once said, "The time to repair the roof is when the sun is shining." My grandfather said somewhat the same thing when he told me, "The time to shut the barn door is not after the cow is already gone." The time to get ready for Jesus to come is not when He has returned. Now is the time to get ready for Jesus.

We all need to be doing things every day to help us prepare to meet Him, whether that meeting is at the Second Coming or when we die. Don't put off reading your Bible, or saying your prayers, or talking to someone who is lonely, or sharing the Gospel with someone who is lost. Every day we can be getting ready to meet Jesus, in small and big ways.

| **FOR YOUTH** | ■ **TOPIC:** Hope for Resurrection |

■ **TOPIC:** Hope for Resurrection
■ **QUESTIONS:** 1. Who will Jesus bring with Him when He returns? 2. How will we know that it is Jesus when He returns? 3. First Thessalonians 5:2 says that Jesus will come like a thief in the night. What does that mean? 4. What is one thing you are currently doing that tells others you are ready for Jesus to come back? 5. What can you do to avoid both ignoring the day of the Lord and becoming excessively preoccupied with it?

■ **ILLUSTRATIONS:**

It's Your Life! Psychologists tell us that many teenagers have little sense of their own mortality. They take crazy risks because they think they are immortal. They make career choices based on the best offers, looking for satisfaction in the future based on positions and money.

However, when accidents take the lives of their friends, adolescents are forced to think about life and their future. Christians step up at times like these and offer a totally different perspective on life and its meaning.

Because Jesus died, rose from the grave, and is coming again, we can fit our goals and fears into His good and perfect will. We do not have to be nervous about our future because we know it is with Jesus. Thus, knowing Jesus makes life worthwhile.

Ready or Not. The wreckage of the luxury liner *Titanic*, thought to have been "unsinkable," now rests 13,120 feet down on the Atlantic Ocean floor. In its day, the *Titanic* was the world's largest ship, weighing over 46 tons, being 882 feet long, and rising 11 stories high. The vessel employed a crew and staff of almost 1,000 and could carry nearly 2,500 passengers. The ship was ready for its passengers with a complete gymnasium, heated pool, squash court, and the first miniature golf course.

Even for all the elegant and luxurious extras this ship had, it still lacked some basic equipment needed for survival if something "unthinkable" happened. It was short the needed number of lifeboats for all of its passengers and crew, and on its first voyage it was short a simple pair of binoculars needed for the lookouts to spot icebergs. On its first trip, the ship received at least seven warnings about dangerous icebergs in its path. However, the captain and others were more concerned with getting to America in record time instead of watching out for the safety of the ship and its passengers.

The night of April 14, 1912, the unthinkable happened to the unsinkable. Near midnight, the great *Titanic* struck an iceberg, ripping a 300-foot hole through 5 of its 16 watertight compartments. It sank in 2 1/2 hours, killing 1,513 people.

Sometimes we act as if Jesus is never coming back, despite the knowledge that He is. The *Titanic* supplies a lesson for us all. If the people in charge had been more watchful and more diligent in doing the right things, many lives would have been saved, and possibly the entire ship would have made it to its destination on time. Jesus wants us to be ready and expectantly waiting for what He will bring us today or tomorrow.

Fish for Life. A young boy stood idly on a bridge, watching some fishermen. Seeing one of them with a basket full of fish, he said, "If I had a catch like that, I'd be happy." "I'll give you that many fish if you do a small favor for me," said the fisherman. "I need you to tend this line awhile. I've got some business down the street."

The young boy gladly accepted the offer. After the man left, the trout and bass continued snapping greedily at the baited hook. Soon the boy forgot everything else, and was excitedly pulling in a large number of fish. When the fisherman returned, he said to the young boy, "I'll keep my promise to you by giving you everything you've caught. And I hope you've learned a lesson. You mustn't waste time daydreaming and merely wishing for things. Instead, get busy and cast in a line for yourself."

This young boy made the most of his time, not realizing that he was really going to benefit the most from the amount of energy he put into catching the fish. He could have just as easily put out only enough effort to catch one or two fish. It's your life. What you get out of it depends greatly on what you put into it. As you think about being prepared for the Second Coming of Christ, "fish" as if your heavenly reward depends on it.

HOPE FROM GOD'S GRACE

BACKGROUND SCRIPTURE: 2 Thessalonians 2
DEVOTIONAL READING: Titus 3:1-7

Key Verse: Now our Lord Jesus Christ himself, and God, even our Father, which hath loved us, and hath given us everlasting consolation and good hope through grace, Comfort your hearts, and stablish you in every good word and work. 2 Thessalonians 2:16-17.

KING JAMES VERSION

2 THESSALONIANS 2:1 Now we beseech you, brethren, by the coming of our Lord Jesus Christ, and by our gathering together unto him, 2 That ye be not soon shaken in mind, or be troubled, neither by spirit, nor by word, nor by letter as from us, as that the day of Christ is at hand.

3 Let no man deceive you by any means: for that day shall not come, except there come a falling away first, and that man of sin be revealed, the son of perdition. . . . 9 Even him, whose coming is after the working of Satan with all power and signs and lying wonders, 10 And with all deceivableness of unrighteousness in them that perish; because they received not the love of the truth, that they might be saved. 11 And for this cause God shall send them strong delusion, that they should believe a lie: 12 That they all might be damned who believed not the truth, but had pleasure in unrighteousness.

13 But we are bound to give thanks alway to God for you, brethren beloved of the Lord, because God hath from the beginning chosen you to salvation through sanctification of the Spirit and belief of the truth:
14 Whereunto he called you by our gospel, to the obtaining of the glory of our Lord Jesus Christ.
15 Therefore, brethren, stand fast, and hold the traditions which ye have been taught, whether by word, or our epistle.

16 Now our Lord Jesus Christ himself, and God, even our Father, which hath loved us, and hath given us everlasting consolation and good hope through grace, 17 Comfort your hearts, and stablish you in every good word and work.

NEW REVISED STANDARD VERSION

2 THESSALONIANS 2:1 As to the coming of our Lord Jesus Christ and our being gathered together to him, we beg you, brothers and sisters, 2 not to be quickly shaken in mind or alarmed, either by spirit or by word or by letter, as though from us, to the effect that the day of the Lord is already here. 3 Let no one deceive you in any way; for that day will not come unless the rebellion comes first and the lawless one is revealed, the one destined for destruction. . . . 9 The coming of the lawless one is apparent in the working of Satan, who uses all power, signs, lying wonders, 10 and every kind of wicked deception for those who are perishing, because they refused to love the truth and so be saved. 11 For this reason God sends them a powerful delusion, leading them to believe what is false, 12 so that all who have not believed the truth but took pleasure in unrighteousness will be condemned.

13 But we must always give thanks to God for you, brothers and sisters beloved by the Lord, because God chose you as the first fruits for salvation through sanctification by the Spirit and through belief in the truth.
14 For this purpose he called you through our proclamation of the good news, so that you may obtain the glory of our Lord Jesus Christ. 15 So then, brothers and sisters, stand firm and hold fast to the traditions that you were taught by us, either by word of mouth or by our letter.

16 Now may our Lord Jesus Christ himself and God our Father, who loved us and through grace gave us eternal comfort and good hope, 17 comfort your hearts and strengthen them in every good work and word.

9

Monday, April 22	Psalm 75	*An Appointed Time*
Tuesday, April 23	Malachi 4	*The Day Is Coming*
Wednesday, April 24	Psalm 84	*No Good Thing Withheld*
Thursday, April 25	Psalm 121	*My Help Comes from the Lord*
Friday, April 26	Titus 3:1-7	*The Hope of Eternal Life*
Saturday, April 27	1 Thessalonians 5:23-28	*Kept Sound and Blameless*
Sunday, April 28	2 Thessalonians 2:1-3, 9-17	*Eternal Comfort and Good Hope*

BACKGROUND

In 2 Thessalonians 2:13, Paul called his spiritual children those who were "loved of the Lord." God had demonstrated His love for them by choosing them for salvation. This shows that God's love is not a vague, emotion-charged slogan. Put another way, His love is not the basis of some blind hope for a silver lining in the clouds. The Father's love has been verified in history by what He has done for the church. To be specific, He sent His beloved Son as the atoning sacrifice for the sins of the entire world (see 1 John 2:2).

After Paul described the future, when the Messiah will judge lawless people, the apostle turned his attention to the distant past. He noted that from the very "beginning" (2 Thess. 2:13) God chose the believers in Thessalonica to "salvation." Paul made similar claims in other letters (for example, see Eph. 1:4). These passages are understood in different ways by Christians. Some think that God long ago predestined some individuals (but not others) for receiving His salvation. Others say that God formed His plan of salvation long ago, but that the matter of who receives salvation is determined by the exercise of free human will.

NOTES ON THE PRINTED TEXT

In 2 Thessalonians 2:1, Paul returned to one of the subjects he had discussed in 1 Thessalonians 4:13-18, namely, the second coming of the Savior. At the same time, the apostle expanded on the subject of the coming judgment of God (see 2 Thess. 1:7-9). Paul was seriously alarmed by a report—supposedly from him—that was upsetting the church at Thessalonica. He told the people there to recognize that what others told them was false (2:1-2), to know what must happen before Jesus' return (vss. 3-4), to learn about the restrainer of evil (vss. 5-7), to be aware of spiritual counterfeits (vss. 8-10), and to accept the truth of God's judgment (vss. 11-12).

Why were Paul's readers in such turmoil? He blamed it on a message purported to have come from him. Allegedly, the second advent of the Messiah had already occurred, and the Thessalonians had missed it. Paul categorically denounced the interpretation in a disturbing prediction, report, or "letter" (vs. 2) that certain false prophets had made. The apostle firmly declared that nothing he had ever said or written could be correctly interpreted to mean that the Second Coming had already occurred. The Thessalonians, rather than being shaken, troubled, and excited, could hold onto what the apostle had taught them. He had clearly said that they would not miss the return of Christ (see 1 Thess. 4:17).

To help his readers stand firm, Paul declared something of what will happen in the end times. First, there will be a rebellion against God. Of course, people have always rebelled against God, but this will be worse than anything that has happened before. The apostle stressed the climactic nature of this apostasy by calling it the "falling away" (2 Thess. 2:3), in other words, an insurrection that will far exceed anything else like it in human history (see also Matt. 24:10-12; 2 Tim. 3:1-9; 2 Tim. 4:1). Second, "the man of sin" (2 Thess. 2:3) will be revealed. This title is appropriate, for he will break God's injunctions. Presumably, this person will be the leader of the rebellion. He will defy everything considered to be holy or sacred and even claim that he himself is God (vs. 4; see Isa. 14:13-14; Ezek. 28:2-9; Dan. 11:36). Despite his bombastic assertions, this person is destined for "perdition" (2 Thess. 2:3).

Regardless of how deplorable the situation becomes, the triumph of the Savior, the vindication of the saints, and the demise of the wicked are ensured (vs. 8). In the meantime, the devil's agent of lawlessness will use whatever tactics and schemes are at his disposal to persecute believers and undermine the will of God. Paul provided a graphic description of the wicked one's powers. This self-glorifying individual will be under Satan's control. Indeed, the devil will give his henchman unusual abilities to perform miracles, signs, and wonders. Satan's work will be seen in the most audacious deceptions (vs. 9).

The tragic outcome will be destruction for people who allow themselves to be duped by this Satan-inspired miracle worker. People usually flock after an unusual phenomenon, but a miracle in and of itself proves nothing. Works of power will be used to deceive people into worshiping the lawless one. People will fall into this snare because they find no place in their hearts for the truth of the Gospel, the acceptance of which leads to salvation (vs. 10). The Good News must not only be acknowledged, but also upheld. The latter is demonstrated when converts allow God's Word to rule their lives. In contrast, to reject the Gospel is to spurn the divine offer of salvation.

Because the unsaved reject the Good News, the Lord eventually sends on them a deluding influence so that they embrace what is wrong (vs. 11). Put differently, God will use their sin as a punishment against them. He will let them continue in their profane ways so that they are fooled into believing an assortment of lies. The world is filled with deceivers and falsehoods, all of which are inspired by Satan, the "father" (John 8:44) of lies. But the specific deception Paul was talking about in 2 Thessalonians 2:11 is the counterfeit claim made by the devil's operation.

The lawless one deludes unregenerate humanity to believe that he is divine and worthy of veneration (vs. 4). Those taken in by this deceit not only reject the Gospel, but also delight in evil. It's no wonder that God condemns them (vs. 12). This presumably refers to eternal punishment in hell. Here we see that more than intellect is involved in accepting the Gospel. In Scripture, belief always includes the will and the emotions. Paul emphasized the connection between the two. Moreover, refusing to believe the truth and delighting in wickedness are interrelated.

On the one hand, Paul foresaw a time when the Messiah will judge the lawless one, along with all who will follow this satanic deceiver (vss. 8-12). But the apostle hastened to assure his readers that they would not be among those judged. They were destined for blessing by God (vss. 13-14). This is why Paul thanked God for the Thessalonian believers—not so much because of who they were in themselves, but because of who they had become through God's grace to them.

The salvation of the Thessalonians (and that of all believers) came through the work of the Spirit. He enables the lost to believe the Good News and grow increasingly holy in their lives. Paul emphasized both the Spirit's sanctifying work and the individual's "belief of the truth" (vs. 13). With respect to the apostle's readers, God the Spirit had made unholy people holy, and the people themselves had put their faith in the truth about the Messiah. At this point, we should note the contrast between the Thessalonian believers and the future followers of the lawless one. Those whom God will judge "believed not the truth" (vs. 12), while the Thessalonians were saved through "belief of the truth" (vs. 13).

On a practical and historical level, Paul's proclamation of the Gospel had been the means by which God called the Thessalonians to salvation. No doubt, the apostle was pleased and overjoyed to be used by the Lord in this important way. One reason God called the Thessalonians to salvation was so that they might share in the "glory" (vs. 14) of Jesus. This was a far different destiny than that awaiting the followers of Satan's wicked confederates. They would be eternally condemned.

In light of the Thessalonians' decision to trust in the Lord Jesus for salvation, Paul urged them to remain steadfast in their faith. This included standing firm on the solid ground of the apostolic teaching they had received from the missionaries. Also, rather than be misled by spiritual frauds, they were to maintain a strong grip on the biblical truths Paul and his colleagues had imparted to them. It did not matter whether it took place directly in person or indirectly by means of letters (vs. 15). Either way, the proclamation of the Gospel had effectively contributed to the salvation of the Thessalonians. Therefore, it was only logical for them to continue to heed what the missionaries had taught them.

Given the challenges the believers in Thessalonica faced, it would not be easy for them to hold fast to biblical truth. Indeed, they would need help—divine assistance. So at this point in his letter, Paul prayed that God would encourage and strengthen them. In the apostle's prayer, he invoked both the Lord Jesus Christ—God the Son—and God the Father (vs. 16). The Lord "loved" His spiritual children and by means of His "grace" bestowed on them "everlasting consolation" and a "good hope." When speaking of the love of the Father for believers, the apostle may have had in mind the sacrifice of the Son for sinners. Surely no greater evidence of the Father's love could be imagined. Most likely, then, "everlasting consolation" refers to the effects of salvation. Because the Thessalonians had been redeemed, they had received a permanent change of attitude. For similar reasons, the "good hope" was their confident assurance of receiving future kingdom blessings. Put another way, they had every reason to expect kindness from the Lord Jesus at His second coming.

The love, encouragement, and hope believers receive from the Father through faith in the Son are the basis for Paul's specific prayer request for the Thessalonians. He wanted God to encourage their hearts and strengthen them in every good thing they did and said (vs. 17). Given their situation, these are the areas in which the apostle thought they needed God's assistance the most. Because of persecution and false teaching in Thessalonica, and perhaps for other reasons as well, Paul's readers needed encouragement. God could give them the spiritual uplift they required. He could also refresh their hearts and give them the grit they needed to go on believing and obeying the truth.

SUGGESTIONS TO TEACHERS

Saint Teresa of Avila, who experienced hardship as a servant of Christ, once remarked in exasperation in a prayer, "Lord, if this is how You treat Your friends, no wonder You have so few of them!" Even believers have their moments of feeling dejected.

1. HARDSHIPS IN MINISTRY. Let the members of your class know that being a Christian isn't easy. Shallow preaching sometimes leads people to think that becoming a Christian is always going to be fun, pleasant, and rewarding. But following Jesus means experiencing hardships. Invite your students to discuss what trials they encounter as servants of the Lord.

2. TRUTH IN THE SAVIOR, NOT ONE'S SELF. Our spiritual power and guidance come from the Savior. The world, in contrast, advocates a counterfeit message of self-reliance and advertises ways to enhance one's ego. The popular notion is that with enough know-how and drive, people can accomplish whatever they want. Point out to the students the folly of such arrogance. It is only with the Lord's help that we can rise above the trials that sometimes overtake us.

3. VICTORY IN THE SON. Yes, believers suffer. And, yes, they often are subjected to hardships. But God has the final word. Through the risen, living Lord, we can look beyond the present moment of hardship and heartache and live in confidence of ultimate victory! With this truth in mind, ask the members of your class to consider the ramifications of 2 Thessalonians 2:14 for their daily lives.

4. COMMITMENT TO BIBLICAL TEACHING. Paul encouraged the Thessalonians to "stand fast, and hold the traditions which ye have been taught" (vs.

15). Since the New Testament had not yet been written, it was very important for the early church to remember what the apostles said. Another word for traditions could be "teachings." These apostolic truths are worth embracing during the storms of persecution.

FOR ADULTS	■ **TOPIC:** Sure Source of Hope

■ **QUESTIONS:** 1. In what ways did God show His love to the believers in Thessalonica? 2. How does the Holy Spirit use the proclamation of the Gospel to bring about the salvation of the lost? 3. Why is it important for us, as Jesus' followers, to stand firm in the faith? 4. In what ways has the truth of salvation in Christ provided you with "good hope" (2 Thess. 2:16)? 5. What are some specific ways you can serve the Lord in "every good deed and work" (vs. 17)?

■ **ILLUSTRATIONS:**

Standing Firm. We run the risk of skepticism when we read about the physical obstacles the believers in Thessalonica faced and overcame with the help of the Lord. We wonder if we would have responded with the same level of hope to the challenges they endured. Regardless of whether God calls us to go through similar circumstances, the importance of standing firm in the faith remains unchanged.

Jesus' earliest followers succeeded because of their complete commitment to the Savior. They loved Him so much, and they wanted to obey Him so completely, that they persevered and grew in spiritual wisdom and understanding. Through the sanctifying work of the Spirit and belief in the truth of the Gospel, they were able to finish the race of life successfully.

There is no other way for believers today. Despite many popular but false "secrets" on the market, we are challenged to turn to Jesus as our sure source of hope and stand firm in the provision of His grace. When we love and serve Him above everything else, He enables us to rise above our difficulties and setbacks.

The Zero-Moment Point. Seafaring people have an expression to describe the position from which a ship in distress cannot recover. It's called the "zero-moment point." This results when the wind and waves become so severe that the vessel is unable to right itself and begins to founder.

Undoubtedly, there were times when the believers in Thessalonica came to a "zero-moment point" in their lives. While we don't know all the details, we can assume that it probably involved some terrible beating and imprisonment, or acute disappointment over the attacks and rejection by others in their community, or a combination of any of these, or some other unnamed severe affliction.

Despite hardship that would have devastated most of us, many of the early followers of Jesus did not founder. Why? It's because they stood firm in their commitment to the Lord. Indeed, they would attribute their recovery from their "zero-moment points" to the gracious intervention of the Savior.

When such times arise in our lives and we see no hope for ourselves, we can depend on Jesus to always remain with us. With Him at our side, we can be confident of eventual triumph!

Persecuted for Jesus' Sake. In Cairo, Egypt, a teenage Coptic Christian girl was kidnapped by Muslim extremists. During her nine-month captivity, she was forced to fast, pray, and memorize the Koran. She was physically and sexually abused. Sulfuric acid was poured on her wrist to obliterate a tattoo of the cross, and her captors threatened to pour it on her face if she dared to remove the Islamic veil that they had forced her to wear. Terrorized, she signed papers of conversion to Islam in order to escape. She is now being sheltered and treated by a group of concerned Christians.

This poor girl is only one of an estimated 200 to 250 million Christians whose lives are at risk. Nina Shea, director of the Puebla Program on Religious Freedom, notes that persecution, torture, enslavement, imprisonment, and the forcible separation of children from parents are only some of the trials that believers face in Islamic countries and in China.

As Paul noted in 2 Thessalonians 2, being a follower of the Lord Jesus is not easy. Elsewhere, Paul wrote that believers could expect to be persecuted (see 2 Tim. 3:12). If you have not suffered for your faith, then give God thanks. And if you have endured affliction, then look to the Father for strength to stand firm for the Son.

FOR YOUTH

■ **TOPIC:** Hope Grounded in God's Grace

■ **QUESTIONS:** 1. What role did the Spirit have in the salvation of the Thessalonians? 2. In what sense will believers one day share in the glory of the Lord Jesus? 3. How is it possible for us, as believers, to hold fast to biblical teaching when we are harassed for our faith? 4. In what ways have you recently experienced "everlasting consolation" (2 Thess. 2:16) from God? 5. How might you rely upon the Spirit to give you the strength you need to serve the Lord effectively?

■ **ILLUSTRATIONS:**

Committed to Stand Firm. Power from weakness is an oxymoron in today's culture. Smart people tell us to use power to get ahead and make something of ourselves. The importance of power is the unwritten message that undergirds the media's assault on our minds. We are sold power cars, power computers and other digital devices, and power cosmetics.

However, we learn from the Gospel that in our own power, we are dead. So teenagers are forced to choose between society's power and Jesus' power. He was dismissed by the crowds because He refused to use His power to overthrow the Romans, who had conquered, subjugated, and persecuted the Jews.

Instead, Jesus showed that real, eternal power comes only through His cross. In today's culture, to remain firmly committed to Him requires enormous courage and faith. But Paul convincingly showed that by Jesus' power, believers could not only endure hardships, but also live with grace, hope, and purpose. The Gospel's power really is better, and it lasts forever.

Praying for God's Help. Paul taught in 2 Thessalonians 2 that God doesn't require us to rely on our own limited resources to serve Him and others. Instead, He promises that He'll supply all the grace we need to remain committed to Him, if we'll come to Him and ask for help.

Consider the example set by a youth pastor named Steve. He understands his limitations and doesn't try to be self-sufficient. He knows that he would quickly become overwhelmed in his work with teens, especially if he didn't spend time in personal prayer, asking for God's strength and guidance to stand firm in his faith.

Steve doesn't stop there, however. He surrounds himself with prayer support from believers with whom he works. He also has developed accountability relationships in which he tells one or two close Christian friends about his struggles and needs so they can encourage him and pray for him.

Scriptural and Social Holiness. The Methodist movement began as a meeting seeking to bring renewed commitment and spiritual holiness within the Church of England. John and Charles Wesley, the founders of Methodism, met with a small group derisively called the "Holy Club" on the campus of Oxford University. Their goal was to engage in a disciplined pattern of worship, prayer, and Bible study. In this way they sought to stand firmly in their faith.

The group practiced scriptural and social holiness. In point of fact, genuine Christianity for the Wesleys involved both word and deed in promoting the kingdom of God on earth. They exemplified the truth recorded in 2 Thessalonians 2:13, which says that "God hath from the beginning chosen you to salvation through sanctification of the Spirit and belief of the truth." Similarly, our personal relationship with the Lord Jesus must be translated into acts of love and service toward others.

A LIVING HOPE

BACKGROUND SCRIPTURE: 1 Peter 1:1-12
DEVOTIONAL READING: Lamentations 3:19-24

Key Verse: Blessed be the God and Father of our Lord Jesus Christ, which according to his abundant mercy hath begotten us again unto a lively hope by the resurrection of Jesus Christ from the dead. 1 Peter 1:3.

KING JAMES VERSION

1 PETER 1:1 Peter, an apostle of Jesus Christ, to the strangers scattered throughout Pontus, Galatia, Cappadocia, Asia, and Bithynia, 2 Elect according to the foreknowledge of God the Father, through sanctification of the Spirit, unto obedience and sprinkling of the blood of Jesus Christ: Grace unto you, and peace, be multiplied.

3 Blessed be the God and Father of our Lord Jesus Christ, which according to his abundant mercy hath begotten us again unto a lively hope by the resurrection of Jesus Christ from the dead, 4 To an inheritance incorruptible, and undefiled, and that fadeth not away, reserved in heaven for you, 5 Who are kept by the power of God through faith unto salvation ready to be revealed in the last time.

6 Wherein ye greatly rejoice, though now for a season, if need be, ye are in heaviness through manifold temptations: 7 That the trial of your faith, being much more precious than of gold that perisheth, though it be tried with fire, might be found unto praise and honour and glory at the appearing of Jesus Christ: 8 Whom having not seen, ye love; in whom, though now ye see him not, yet believing, ye rejoice with joy unspeakable and full of glory: 9 Receiving the end of your faith, even the salvation of your souls.

10 Of which salvation the prophets have enquired and searched diligently, who prophesied of the grace that should come unto you: 11 Searching what, or what manner of time the Spirit of Christ which was in them did signify, when it testified beforehand the sufferings of Christ, and the glory that should follow. 12 Unto whom it was revealed, that not unto themselves, but unto us they did minister the things, which are now reported unto you by them that have preached the gospel unto you with the Holy Ghost sent down from heaven; which things the angels desire to look into.

NEW REVISED STANDARD VERSION

1 PETER 1:1 Peter, an apostle of Jesus Christ,

To the exiles of the Dispersion in Pontus, Galatia, Cappadocia, Asia, and Bithynia, 2 who have been chosen and destined by God the Father and sanctified by the Spirit to be obedient to Jesus Christ and to be sprinkled with his blood:

May grace and peace be yours in abundance.

3 Blessed be the God and Father of our Lord Jesus Christ! By his great mercy he has given us a new birth into a living hope through the resurrection of Jesus Christ from the dead, 4 and into an inheritance that is imperishable, undefiled, and unfading, kept in heaven for you, 5 who are being protected by the power of God through faith for a salvation ready to be revealed in the last time. 6 In this you rejoice, even if now for a little while you have had to suffer various trials, 7 so that the genuineness of your faith—being more precious than gold that, though perishable, is tested by fire—may be found to result in praise and glory and honor when Jesus Christ is revealed. 8 Although you have not seen him, you love him; and even though you do not see him now, you believe in him and rejoice with an indescribable and glorious joy, 9 for you are receiving the outcome of your faith, the salvation of your souls.

10 Concerning this salvation, the prophets who prophesied of the grace that was to be yours made careful search and inquiry, 11 inquiring about the person or time that the Spirit of Christ within them indicated when it testified in advance to the sufferings destined for Christ and the subsequent glory. 12 It was revealed to them that they were serving not themselves but you, in regard to the things that have now been announced to you through those who brought you good news by the Holy Spirit sent from heaven—things into which angels long to look!

10

HOME BIBLE READINGS

Monday, April 29	Job 6:8-13	*I Have No Help in Me*
Tuesday, April 30	Job 7:1-6	*Days without Hope*
Wednesday, May 1	Job 14:7-17	*Will Mortals Live Again?*
Thursday, May 2	Psalm 31:9-16	*My Times Are in Your Hands*
Friday, May 3	Psalm 31:19-24	*The Lord Preserves the Faithful*
Saturday, May 4	Lamentations 3:19-24	*Hope in God's Faithfulness*
Sunday, May 5	1 Peter 1:3-12	*New Birth into a Living Hope*

BACKGROUND

A fisherman by trade, Peter was known for his impulsiveness and tendency to speak before thinking. The Lord in part used Peter's mistakes to shape him into a humble but powerful leader for the church. The two letters of Peter represent part of the apostle's effort to fulfill that expectation. He began his first epistle by referring to himself as an "apostle of Jesus Christ" (1 Pet. 1:1). In the New Testament, the term "apostle" is used to refer to God's special envoys who helped lay the foundation for Christian churches. After Jesus' death and resurrection, the term was applied to someone to whom Jesus had appeared and who had received a divine call to preach the Gospel.

Apostolic teaching was to be the norm for the doctrine and fellowship of the church. The apostles' common witness was the yardstick against which all Christian teaching was measured. Some Bible interpreters believe apostleship was restricted to those disciples who had seen Jesus with their own eyes. Other interpreters think the term did not always have such a restricted meaning. Those whom the New Testament calls or assumes to be apostles include the Twelve (Luke 6:13), Paul (Rom. 1:1), James (Gal. 1:19), Barnabas (Acts 14:14), Silas and Timothy (1 Thess. 1:1; 2:6b), and Andronicus and Junias (Rom. 16:7).

NOTES ON THE PRINTED TEXT

L et's imagine for a moment that we're holding a beautifully cut diamond up to the light. Each of its sides sparkles as we slowly turn and examine the precious stone. This suggests how beautiful and multifaceted is God's salvation. Peter said in his first letter that he was filled with gratitude as he thought about what it meant to be redeemed through faith in the Messiah. The apostle's outburst of praise following his greeting is distinctively Jewish and Christian in content (see 1 Pet. 1:1-2). Giving thanks to God was a typical feature of Jewish prayer. The blessing in verse 3, however, has a richer conception of God than one would find in traditional writings. The one Peter praised was not just God, but God the Father as revealed by His unique and precious Son.

Peter referred to the Savior in three different ways. As "Lord," His power is absolute and unchallengeable. "Jesus" is the Greek form of Joshua, which means "the Lord saves." "Christ" literally means "Anointed One" and is used to refer to the Messiah promised by God in the Old Testament. In verse 3, Peter praised the Father for His tremendous display of mercy in providing salvation from sin through His Son. Next, the apostle referred to the new-birth experience. When people trust in the Lord Jesus, the Spirit does a work upon their fallen human nature. He completely transforms their inner being so that they want to live for God rather than themselves. As they renounce the ways of the world, their lives manifest the changes made by the Spirit.

Peter noted that Christians not only are born again but also are heirs of God. He will give them an eternal, heavenly inheritance that can never be destroyed by time, the elements of nature, or the powers of darkness. God also protects this inheritance from thieves. He preserves it safely in heaven for His people (vs. 4). Great corporations, worth millions and billions of dollars, often go bankrupt. Devious people misappropriate funds, causing huge financial empires to crash. But such will never happen to the inheritance God has set aside for His children.

God also watches over those who trust in His Son. The Greek verb rendered "kept" (vs. 5) conveys the idea of vigilantly defending a fortress. Believers can count on God's protection regardless of the hardships they might encounter. The salvation Peter mentioned in this verse refers to the believer's complete deliverance from sin in the future. When Jesus returns, He will raise His people from the dead and give them glorified bodies. Then they will fully enjoy the eternal riches of heaven.

The original readers of Peter's first letter could rejoice in all that God would do for them. The Greek verb rendered "greatly rejoice" (vs. 6) refers to a jubilant expression of gratitude. The recipients of the apostle's epistle were to maintain a confident expectation of the future. In turn, this forward-looking attitude would sustain them, especially as they endured all sorts of trials that caused them grief. No doubt some of the persecutions were physical, but more likely Peter had in mind social stigma, ridicule, the loss of status, and even the loss of their livelihood. The believers were paying a heavy price for their faithfulness to the Messiah.

Admittedly, no persecution is easy to take. But Peter tried to get his readers to view their troubles from an eternal perspective. These hardships were "for a season." One day God would bring their suffering to an end and eternally reward them for their faithfulness. In short, a Christian's attitude toward suffering makes all the difference on its effect in that person's life. On the one hand, if hardship and difficult circumstances are constantly viewed as unfair and undeserved, then a root of bitterness can spring up in the heart of the believer that hinders his or her spiritual growth. On the other hand, if a Christian views suffering as normal for the committed follower of the Lord Jesus, then hardship and difficult circumstances become an expected part of life. Also, these afflictions are often viewed as a special time for growth and opportunities to become more like the Messiah in His humility and perseverance.

Peter explained that God allowed the recipients of his letter to experience persecution to refine and verify the genuineness of their faith in the Son (vs. 7). As people used fire to refine precious metals, such as gold, so God used trials to distinguish true faith from superficial profession. At the same time, He used suffering to strengthen faith. Gold is a metal that most societies highly value. Despite this, gold will one day cease to have value. The faith of Christians, however, is enduring. When the Savior is disclosed at His second coming, the believers' trust will result in praise, glory, and honor. The Greek noun translated "appearing" stresses the unveiling of Jesus' glory and greatness.

Peter reminded his readers that God had saved them so that they too might share in the glory of Jesus when He is once again manifested. In this present age, the Father has veiled the presence of the Son. Although the original recipients of Peter's letter had never personally seen the exalted and risen Savior, their love for Him was unquestionable. Despite the fact that they could not visibly see the Messiah, they continued to trust in Him for redemption (vs. 8). The original readers of Peter's first letter were not depressed about their vexing situation. They were overflowing with a joy that cannot be explained, a joy that was sustained by the hope of future glory. They could be this way because they realized that salvation in the Messiah was the goal or consummation of their faith (vs. 9). Although they already enjoyed certain aspects of salvation, their full possession of it awaited the return of the Son.

Peter had just been speaking about the salvation Jesus provides to all who believe. Now the apostle noted that numerous Old Testament prophets had spoken about this grace of God, which He would make available to Gentiles as well as Jews (vs. 10). Generally speaking, prophets were God's authorized and accredited representatives. They proclaimed His message of hope and judgment under specific circumstances.

Sometimes God disclosed mysteries through Scripture that were beyond the comprehension of those who recorded them (see Dan. 12:8-9). In this case, the prophets did not completely understand what the Spirit inspired them to write. But in due time, He revealed the meaning to those for whom the information was intended. First Peter 1:10 adds that while these spokespersons for God could see some details of the Lord's redemptive plan, there were many specific facts that eluded their grasp. Be that as it may, these prophets still diligently searched Scripture to learn about God's provision of salvation (see Luke 10:24).

The "Spirit of Christ" (1 Pet. 1:11) refers to the Holy Spirit, whom Jesus sent (see John 16:7). The Spirit revealed to the Old Testament prophets that the Messiah would suffer and be glorified (see Ps. 22; Isa. 53; Luke 24:25-27). However, they did not comprehend the whole of the Lord's plan to save Gentiles by means of a suffering Messiah. For instance, the prophets failed to understand that the Redeemer would die during His first coming and that He would return in glory at His second coming.

The Spirit had revealed to the Old Testament prophets that they were ultimately serving future generations of believers (1 Pet. 1:12). The prophets ministered to New

Testament believers when they foretold the Messiah's sufferings and glories. The messengers of the Gospel related these same truths to the church after Jesus' resurrection and ascension. Looking back, we can see how God was working through these Old Testament prophets, even though they were not fully aware of how God was using them.

Those who proclaimed the Good News did so in the power of the Holy Spirit, whom the Lord had sent from heaven (see John 14:16, 26; Acts 2:33). The same Spirit who inspired the prophets also directed the Gospel messengers. Peter's point seems to be that there is a united message proclaimed in the Old and New Testaments concerning the Messiah and His salvation. The apostle noted that even angels have a strong desire to know the truths of the Gospel. The keen interest angels have in redemption is highlighted by the Greek verb rendered "to look into" (1 Pet. 1:12). It means "to stoop over to inspect intently." First-century Jews believed angels knew more than humans about divine matters, but in this case those who have accepted the Gospel understand far more than even the angels. In short, God ultimately uses the church to make His plan known to angels (see Eph. 3:10).

On the basis of God's wonderful gift of grace, those who have benefited from it should show evidence of their new relationship with God in certain specific ways. That is why Peter exhorted his readers to "gird up the loins of your mind" (1 Pet. 1:13). Expressed differently, they were to ready their minds for action. In Bible times, when people who dressed in loose clothing wished to move about quickly or perform tasks requiring significant freedom of movement, they would prepare themselves by tucking the folds of their robe under their belt. Drawing upon this vivid imagery, Peter admonished his readers to be disciplined in their thinking and prepare themselves for vigorous and sustained spiritual exertion.

SUGGESTIONS TO TEACHERS

Peter called on his readers to praise the Father and Son for a redemption that was planned in eternity past, was anticipated by Israel's prophets, and climaxed with the redemptive work of Jesus and His resurrection. He is the guarantee of our hope for an eternal inheritance in heaven.

1. A LIVING HOPE. As a result of trusting in the Son, a Christian receives a living hope and an imperishable, eternal inheritance (1 Pet. 1:3-4). The Father also protects believers so they can claim their everlasting inheritance at the Son's return (vs. 5).

2. A PRICELESS, ETERNAL REALITY. Neither gold nor anything it can buy will last forever. It all eventually perishes. In contrast, faith in the Lord Jesus connects believers with eternal realities and heaven's greatest treasures (vs. 7).

3. A JOY-FILLED FAITH. Faith is a matter of believing in the Lord Jesus, even though we don't see Him. Likewise, we love Him, even though He is not visible to us. That faith brings us joy, especially as we celebrate our salvation (vs. 8).

4. A FULFILLMENT OF WHAT WAS FORETOLD. The Old Testament prophets understood they weren't just speaking for themselves and their time, but also for those who would know about Jesus' suffering and triumph. Believers today also benefit from the prophets' service, for Christians can recognize how the ancient prophecies were fulfilled in the Messiah (vss. 10-12).

FOR ADULTS	■ **TOPIC:** Hopeful Living

■ **QUESTIONS:** 1. What do believers receive when they trust in the Messiah? 2. In what way is faith described in 1 Peter 1:8? 3. For whom were the prophets speaking and writing when they spoke about the coming salvation? 4. Do you sometimes find it hard to maintain your focus on the Son as you serve Him and His people? If so, why? 5. What can you do to proclaim God's mighty acts to the unsaved?

■ **ILLUSTRATIONS:**

Endurance in God's Strength. A woman fell under an oncoming commuter train and became trapped by the first car. Paramedics came to her rescue, but were frustrated because they could not ease her from under the train. They told the engineer not to move the train. Then they inserted an inflatable airlift bag under the 50-ton car and slowly raised it six inches to release her.

God's strength comes to our rescue like that time and again. We feel crushed under our heavy burdens and no one seems to be able to help us. But when we cry out to God, He lifts the burden and releases us to find joy, hope, and peace for daily living (see 1 Pet. 1:3). Beyond our immediate release, God also guarantees us a crown of life. We are the firstfruits of His creation and He will not allow us to go under (see vss. 4-5).

Growing in Christlikeness. The cocoon of the emperor moth is flask-like in shape. To develop into a perfect insect, it must force its way through the neck of the cocoon by hours of intense struggle. Entomologists explain that this pressure to which the moth is subjected is nature's way of forcing a life-giving substance into its wings.

Feeling sorry for the moth, an observer said, "I'll lessen the pain and struggles of this helpless creature!" With small scissors he snipped the restraining threads to make the moth's emergence painless and effortless. But the creature never developed wings. For a brief time before its death it simply crawled instead of flying through the air on rainbow-colored wings!

Sorrow, suffering, trials, and tribulations are wisely designed to grow us into Christlikeness. The refining and developing processes are oftentimes slow, but through grace, we emerge triumphant. Peter was aware of this as he reminded the early believers of their living hope in the Son. We also need tangible ways to remind ourselves. Sometimes we do this by repeating a favorite saying, performing a certain activity, or singing a song we sang as a child.

Living in Hope. It's wonderful to hear laughter at a memorial service for a dearly loved friend. And it was terrific to hear it at Sue Bielat's service.

Sue died of cancer at the age of 64—too soon, according to those gathered at the service. They mourned the sudden loss of their friend, coworker, wife, mother, and grandmother. They choked back tears as they sang hymns. But most important, they laughed as they remembered the joy she brought to her life. And they laughed because she still lived.

With God, Sue was more alive than she had ever been before. There was no doubt that now she was in the Lord's presence, echoing the apostle's proclamation found in 1 Peter 1:3. It is a promise that gives every believer the reason to mix his or her tears of grief with the sound of joyful, hopeful laughter.

FOR YOUTH

■ **TOPIC:** A Clean Slate

■ **QUESTIONS:** 1. What is the living hope to which believers have been called? 2. Why did Peter say that faith is more valuable than gold? 3. What did the prophets know about the Messiah, and what did they continue to search carefully to find out? 4. What can you do to keep alive a sharp interest in the salvation Jesus has given you? 5. What good works has God prepared for you to do in the coming week?

■ **ILLUSTRATIONS:**

A Living Hope. Years after the end of World War II, a few Japanese soldiers still hid on remote Pacific islands, awaiting the next battle. They had lost touch with the world and assumed that hostilities were still going on. Yet their war had already been lost. What a picture of "dead hope."

But what would a "lively hope" (1 Pet. 1:3) look like? We might simply turn the gaze of our faith to the cross, where a battle has already been won on our behalf. When we trust in the Son, who rose from the dead, He wipes clean the slate of sin in our lives. Now we hopefully await His victory's full manifestation at His return, when He will finally be "revealed" (vs. 5).

Walking by Faith. A wise Christian once told a student who was worried about his doubts that he should consider the ocean surf. The waves rise and fall. The troughs are times of doubt, while the crests are times of vital faith. But all the time the waves march inexorably toward the shore. The troughs do not prevent the water from moving ahead.

In Peter's first letter, he reminds us that walking by faith, in the midst of trials and doubts, is like the preceding scenario. We have to trust the unseen hand that drives the waves to drive us also to our crown of life. The Lord Jesus knows when we are in the pits and when we are on the mountaintops. Wherever we are, and whatever our circumstances, we keep on trusting Him. The Savior is a generous giver of all good gifts. By faith we take His gifts and march through the storms triumphantly.

My Inheritance in Heaven. The children gathered in front of the sanctuary for the children's sermon. The pastor sat on the platform steps, which placed him near eye level with his youngest parishoners. He talked earnestly in simple language to the children about being good and going to heaven.

At the end of his talk, the pastor asked, "Where do you want to go?"

The little voices chorused, "HEAVEN!"

"And what must you be to get to heaven?" the pastor asked.

"DEAD!" the boys and girls yelled.

The children missed their pastor's point. But they were correct that the full inheritance of the Christian will be realized in the life to come (see 1 Pet. 1:3-4).

EQUIPPED WITH HOPE

BACKGROUND SCRIPTURE: 2 Peter 1
DEVOTIONAL READING: Psalm 130

Key Verse: According as his divine power hath given unto us all things that pertain unto life and godliness, through the knowledge of him that hath called us to glory and virtue. 2 Peter 1:3.

KING JAMES VERSION

2 PETER 1:4 Whereby are given unto us exceeding great and precious promises: that by these ye might be partakers of the divine nature, having escaped the corruption that is in the world through lust.

5 And beside this, giving all diligence, add to your faith virtue; and to virtue knowledge; 6 And to knowledge temperance; and to temperance patience; and to patience godliness; 7 And to godliness brotherly kindness; and to brotherly kindness charity. 8 For if these things be in you, and abound, they make you that ye shall neither be barren nor unfruitful in the knowledge of our Lord Jesus Christ. 9 But he that lacketh these things is blind, and cannot see afar off, and hath forgotten that he was purged from his old sins. 10 Wherefore the rather, brethren, give diligence to make your calling and election sure: for if ye do these things, ye shall never fall: 11 For so an entrance shall be ministered unto you abundantly into the everlasting kingdom of our Lord and Saviour Jesus Christ.

12 Wherefore I will not be negligent to put you always in remembrance of these things, though ye know them, and be established in the present truth. 13 Yea, I think it meet, as long as I am in this tabernacle, to stir you up by putting you in remembrance; 14 Knowing that shortly I must put off this my tabernacle, even as our Lord Jesus Christ hath shewed me.

NEW REVISED STANDARD VERSION

2 PETER 1:4 Thus he has given us, through these things, his precious and very great promises, so that through them you may escape from the corruption that is in the world because of lust, and may become participants of the divine nature. 5 For this very reason, you must make every effort to support your faith with goodness, and goodness with knowledge, 6 and knowledge with self-control, and self-control with endurance, and endurance with godliness, 7 and godliness with mutual affection, and mutual affection with love. 8 For if these things are yours and are increasing among you, they keep you from being ineffective and unfruitful in the knowledge of our Lord Jesus Christ. 9 For anyone who lacks these things is nearsighted and blind, and is forgetful of the cleansing of past sins. 10 Therefore, brothers and sisters, be all the more eager to confirm your call and election, for if you do this, you will never stumble. 11 For in this way, entry into the eternal kingdom of our Lord and Savior Jesus Christ will be richly provided for you.

12 Therefore I intend to keep on reminding you of these things, though you know them already and are established in the truth that has come to you. 13 I think it right, as long as I am in this body, to refresh your memory, 14 since I know that my death will come soon, as indeed our Lord Jesus Christ has made clear to me.

11

Monday, May 6	Romans 15:14-21	*Full of Goodness and Knowledge*
Tuesday, May 7	Proverbs 1:2-7	*The Beginning of Knowledge*
Wednesday, May 8	Titus 1:5-9	*An Example in Self-Control*
Thursday, May 9	Matthew 24:9-14	*Enduring to the End*
Friday, May 10	1 Timothy 2:1-7	*A Life of Godliness and Dignity*
Saturday, May 11	1 Peter 3:8-12	*Love for One Another*
Sunday, May 12	2 Peter 1:4-14	*Standing on God's Precious Promises*

BACKGROUND

The call to holiness that is so evident in 1 Peter also resonates strongly in 2 Peter. In 1:2, the apostle stressed getting to know the Father and Son more and more. Then, in verse 3, Peter noted that, through our increased knowledge of the Lord, we become more responsive to His "divine power." The emphasis here is on living in a godly way. The apostle explained that our knowledge of the Son and His provision of the Father's own power make it possible for us to pursue "life and godliness." Further incentive can be found in the truth that the Lord has invited us to share in His own "glory and virtue."

There is also an emphasis on having "all things" we need to be godly. A heretical group known as the Gnostics was telling Christians that they did not have everything necessary to live in a reverent manner. Supposedly, they also needed to be enlightened by a secret, mystic knowledge. Many cults today claim to lay hold of an exclusive saving knowledge that can be obtained only through various levels of teaching. In contrast, the revelation that God has provided is sufficient, not only for our salvation, but for an abundant life as well.

NOTES ON THE PRINTED TEXT

Ultimately, our focus is not on acquiring the world's fame and fortune, for these are fleeting. Instead, it is to live in a manner that pleases God. The Lord has made this possible by bestowing on us "exceeding great and precious promises" (2 Pet. 1:4). The Greek noun that is rendered "promise" had a special meaning in ancient Hellenic culture. It was used in connection with public announcements of events that concerned everyone, as in the notification of public games and sacrifices to gods. The word implied some type of emphatic, state-sponsored proclamation.

The implication is that here were promises that were made decidedly and openly for the benefit of all believers (not covertly to an elite few). It was a pledge given voluntarily, without coercion. Perhaps the most profound promise is that we will "be partakers of the divine nature." The idea here is not that we will gradually become divine, but that we grow in a host of Christian virtues. The more we pursue holiness, the more we will shun our evil desires and the "corruption" of the world that they spawn.

When Peter said that Christians can "be partakers of the divine nature," he took a risk by using the language of his opponents to express an eternal truth. The Gnostics believed a person could become divine through secret knowledge and enlightened thinking. The truth is that though we will never become little gods (so to speak), we can participate fully in the spiritual life offered by the one true God (see Rom. 8:9; Gal. 2:20; Col. 1:27; 1 Pet. 2:2-3; 1 John 5:1). This is especially so as we worship Him in all His glory (while looking forward to our own glorification) and imitate His goodness.

In light of all the provisions we have in the Redeemer, we can be faithful and fruitful in our lives. We start by "giving all diligence" (2 Pet. 1:5) to appropriate our God-given blessings. Sanctification is the work of the Lord (see 1 Thess. 5:23). Nonetheless, the Bible contains many exhortations for believers to do their part in becoming more holy (see Phil. 2:12-13). "Faith" (2 Pet. 1:5) is the starting point, and to it believers are to add "virtue" (or "goodness"). This is one of several moral excellencies that Peter mentioned. The idea is that, with unwavering trust in the Savior as their foundation, believers press on in a disciplined way to cultivate integrity and rectitude in their lives. Peter next mentioned "knowledge." While an objective understanding of revealed truth is included, the apostle also had in mind a practical application of that truth.

When Jesus' followers heed the teachings of Scripture, it will lead to "temperance" (vs. 6). Peter was referring to a mastering of one's carnal desires. Because believers know God and are empowered by Him, they are able to control their fleshly passions. In turn, they become more patient. They are less likely to be discouraged and succumb to temptation, and more likely to persevere in doing what is right. This ability to endure allows "godliness" to flourish. Christians become more reverent and devoted to the Lord, and less preoccupied with themselves.

A heightened loyalty to God results in believers having increased "brotherly kindness" (vs. 7). This mutual affection is displayed in serving one another, sharing with one another, and praying for one another. These activities, in turn, foster genuine "charity" (or "love"). This form of compassion is not flustered by the personal cost of reaching out to others in need. This sincere love seeks the highest good of others for the glory of the Savior.

Peter urged believers to continue growing in their life of godliness. Indeed, he wanted to see the various qualities he listed earlier present and developing in their lives. "Abound" (2 Pet. 1:8) renders a Greek verb that can also be translated "increasingly grow in measure" or "superabound." The tense of the verb indicates that the situation the apostle described is to be an active and ongoing experience for believers.

It would be erroneous to think that the virtues mentioned in verses 5 through 7 can be added in a mathematically precise, sequential fashion. Instead, they are developed together and evidenced gradually over many years of walking with the Lord. The goal, of course, is that these moral excellencies will be present in us without limit (vs. 8). Their abundance indicates spiritual health in Christians. Peter noted that if believers continue to grow in this way, they will become increasingly productive and fruitful, rather than "barren" and "unfruitful," in their knowledge of the Savior.

Once again, we see that knowing God is more than an intellectual exercise. This truth stands, regardless of what religious frauds might otherwise assert. Knowing more and more about the Lord Jesus is intended to foster spiritual vitality. The other alternative is to fail to develop the graces Peter mentioned, which results in spiritual loss. The apostle declared that those opting for this are blind and shortsighted, for they have failed to fully appreciate the cleansing and forgiveness from "old sins" (vs. 9) secured by the Messiah. "Purged" translates a Greek verb that refers to Christians being cleansed from the guilt associated with their transgressions through the atoning sacrifice of the Son.

Peter was discussing two different mind-sets. One is obsessed with the concerns of this present life, while the other is sensitive to eternal, spiritual realities. Though we live in the world, the things of God should be our supreme focus. Thus, we are to make every effort to confirm our "calling and election" (vs. 10). In his first letter, Peter pointed out that God's election of His people to salvation was because of His foreknowledge (see 1 Pet. 1:2). So, the apostle urged believers to seize the opportunity to increase their assurance of salvation by cultivating the virtues listed in 2 Peter 1:5-7.

Peter was not saying that Christians can make their salvation more secure by their works. Good deeds are never to be considered spiritual "fire insurance" (in a manner of speaking). The tense of the Greek verb, which is rendered "make" (vs. 10), can also be translated "to make for oneself." This means that the increasing assurance of salvation is a benefit of consistent obedience to God. With this kind of assurance, God's people can expect a joyous welcome into His eternal kingdom (vs. 11). Here we see that there is more to heaven than just getting through the proverbial pearly gates. Scripture is full of promises of everlasting reward to those who are faithful. The greeting believers will receive when they enter God's presence will be rich because of the blessings the Father has lavished upon those who belong to Him through the redemptive work of His Son.

By remaining loyal to the Father and ministering to our fellow believers, we show that we truly are "partakers of the divine nature" (vs. 4), that we fully appreciate the atoning sacrifice of the Son, and that we value His "exceeding great and precious promises" to us. Such a consistent life orientation indicates we will not succumb to doubt or despair concerning our spiritual status. Rather than spiritually stumble and "fall" (vs. 10), we will be assured of our salvation. This assurance also includes our eventual entrance into the "everlasting kingdom" (vs. 11) of the Messiah. The Lord, in turn, will honor our life of faithful service with more abundant privileges in heaven.

At times, even mature believers can wane in their diligence to grow in the Lord. This is especially true in moments of hardship. Peter was determined to remind his readers about the truths he had previously shared. The apostle's decision did not mean that his readers were ignorant of the truth or had failed to stand firm in it. Peter's intention was to ensure they remained firmly "established" (vs. 12) in the faith and diligent in applying it to their lives. The Greek verb that is rendered "established" can also be translated "to make stable" or "to fix securely in place."

In some way, Peter had become increasingly aware of the short time he had left in the "tabernacle" (vs. 13) of his body. John 21:18-19 records a statement Jesus made concerning the way in which Peter would die. Perhaps the apostle had this in mind as he approached the end of his life. The Greek noun that is rendered "tabernacle" (2 Pet. 1:13) can also be translated "tent." This is a metaphorical reference to one's body being laid aside like a temporary shelter. It is clarifying to note that Paul literally referred to the physical body we live in as an "earthly house" (2 Cor. 5:1) and "tabernacle," which we inhabit for a time while we wait to put on our new, heavenly bodies (vs. 4).

Peter said he knew that his upcoming death was near. He metaphorically referred to the event as a removal of his earthly tabernacle. The Greek verb that is translated "knowing" (2 Pet. 1:14) refers to a definite awareness of the facts. In the apostle's case, the Messiah previously revealed to him what would eventually happen to him (see John 21:18-19). This impression is reinforced by the past tense of the verb that is rendered "hath shewed" (2 Pet. 1:14).

SUGGESTIONS TO TEACHERS

This week's lesson text offers Peter's summary of the Christian life. It abounds with references to knowledge and knowing, truth, and memory or recollection. Peter looked at the knowledge of the triune Godhead as more than an intellectual claim. To know the Father, Son, and Holy Spirit was to believe in them and live for them with all one's heart, mind, and strength.

1. BASIS OF FAITH. Knowing God means getting acquainted with the glory of His character and the excellence of His deeds among humanity. God's "glory and virtue" (2 Pet. 1:3) form the basis for faith in His "exceeding great and precious promises" (vs. 4) in the Bible. Those assurances form the basis for the confidence that a life of corruption can be exchanged for a life reflecting the divine nature.

2. PATH OF FAITH. Peter linked several virtues leading from initial faith to ultimate love. They may be logically sequential, but in practice they develop simultaneously. You don't necessarily master one before attempting the next. We are not to be timid but bold in our confidence that the Savior will reproduce His character in us.

3. GOAL OF FAITH. The Father has called His spiritual children to be effective and fruitful in living out their knowledge of the Son. Faith clearly sees that goal and the path to it. We must not shut our eyes or turn them myopically to the things of the world near at hand. Otherwise, we will stumble into ineffective and fruitless living. The goal is to live effectively and fruitfully for the Savior.

4. REMINDER TO HAVE FAITH. Peter knew that established Christians don't need new truth as much as they need motivation to put foundational truth into action. He committed the rest of his life to reminding his first-century readers—and Christians ever since and into the future—to hold on to the basis of faith, to walk the path of faith, and to pursue the goal of faith.

| FOR ADULTS | ■ **TOPIC:** Life Worth Living
■ **QUESTIONS:** 1. What does the Lord's divine power provide for believers? 2. What is the basis for growing in the Christian virtues that |

Peter listed? 3. Why did Peter want to continue reminding his readers of their hope in the Savior? 4. What can believers do to ensure they are spiritually maturing? 5. How can believers fight the tendency to forget the truths of the faith?

■ **ILLUSTRATIONS:**

Pursuing Virtue. The young woman flew off to see her family in South America. She was meticulous about her preparations. She thought she had everything she needed. But when she arrived, she found that she had forgotten to pack one of her prescription medicines. She called home, and her husband took care of the matter.

Our pride tells us that we have everything we need to pursue virtue on our own. But Peter would say that such an attitude is counterproductive. An attitude of pride prevents us from grasping all that the Father has done for us in the Son. As believers, we participate in Jesus' divine nature and His promises. So, we can claim His power and wisdom and be bold about our faith and godliness.

We have everything we need in the Savior to live for Him. The Lord, in turn, has commissioned us to use His resources to grow in His grace for His glory.

Free Virtue Download. Over the years, as mobile devices have become increasingly powerful, so have the types of operating systems (or OS) they use. The latter is a software program that enables a variety of portable electronic gadgets to run the applications stored on them. Without an OS, such handheld marvels as smartphones and tablet computers would be useless. Perhaps that is why programmers are constantly trying to improve and update these complex systems.

Imagine that the Maker of all human beings is recalling all units manufactured—regardless of make, year, or OS—because of a serious defect in the primary component of the heart. A malfunction occurred in the code of the original prototype units (named Adam and Eve), resulting in the reproduction of the same defect in all subsequent units. This defect is technically termed "Substantial Internal Non-morality," or more commonly SIN, and is primarily symptomized by loss of moral judgment.

The manufacturer, who is neither liable nor at fault for this defect, is providing factory-authorized repair and service, free of charge, to correct this pernicious flaw. The number for the recall station in your area is: P-R-A-Y-E-R. Once connected, please upload your burden of SIN by pressing REPENTANCE. Next, download J-E-S-U-S into the heart drive. No matter how big or small the SIN defect is, the JESUS repair will replace it with (1) faith, (2) goodness, (3) knowledge, (4) self-control, (5) endurance, (6) godliness, (7) mutual affection, and (8) love (see 2 Pet. 1:5-7).

Please consult the operating manual, the HOLY BIBLE, for further details on the use of these fixes.

Know Thyself. Years ago, an antiquated steam engine chugged slowly through the countryside on its unimportant branch line. The only passenger in one car was a nervous salesman who was new to his territory and the train. More or less suddenly, the train lurched to a halt. The salesman called to the conductor, who explained that there was a cow on the track.

Five minutes later, the train puffed into motion and creaked a few more miles down the track before wheezing once more to stop. "Just a temporary delay," the conductor said before the salesman could complain. "We'll be on our way in a moment." Not to be robbed of his chance to gripe, the salesman asked, "What is it now? Did we catch up with that cow again?"

How many of Peter's virtues did the salesman fail to display to the conductor? How many should we cultivate in our walk with the Savior?

FOR YOUTH

■ **TOPIC:** A Sure Escape Route
■ **QUESTIONS:** 1. What are some of the precious promises God has given to us in Scripture? 2. How can believers avoid becoming spiritually nearsighted? 3. Why is it important for believers to affirm the truth of Jesus' second coming? 4. How can believers strive to maintain self-control in their lives? 5. What can you do to encourage your unsaved peers to put their faith in Jesus for salvation?

■ **ILLUSTRATIONS:**

Got What It Takes? A church was built more than 100 years ago in an affluent Midwestern suburb. It flourished and grew to some 900 members. Facilities were added to accommodate people and programs. But somewhere along the way the congregation stopped growing. Its numbers dwindled to less than 100.

Such stories are not unusual. They testify to the fact that churches don't always have what it takes to remain vibrant. Indeed, it's possible for entire congregations to stop growing, shrink in numbers, and die. We can point to many reasons for this phenomenon, including the possibility that individual members lost their vision for what God had called them to do.

All Christians—regardless of their age, gender, and social or economic status—must keep growing in faith. There's no escaping this truth. That's why Peter's concrete reminders are so important. We can easily become sidetracked. Personality clashes sap our energies. We must keep adding qualities of spiritual power to ourselves and our churches.

Brand-Name Spirituality. Legend has it that Alexander the Great was once called to discipline a foot soldier whose behavior in battle bordered on cowardice. His commander wanted to know how severely to punish him.

Alexander the Great walked up to the accused soldier, stood toe to toe with him, and glared at him with piercing eyes. "What is your name, boy?" intoned the general. "Alexander," the young soldier almost whispered.

The general stood a long time, struggling to master his rage. With ice and steel in his voice, Alexander the Great said quietly, "You change your conduct in battle or you change your name. Do I make myself clear?" The soldier squeaked, "Yes, sir!" Alexander the Great turned on his heel and strode away.

We bear the name of the Lord Jesus (see 2 Pet. 1:8). So, we need to live up to that name in all that we think, say, and do (see vss. 5-7).

Being a Person of Distinction. A prosperous young Wall Street broker of a century ago met and fell in love with a rising young actress of gentility and dignity. He frequently escorted her about town and wanted to marry her. Being a cautious man, he decided that, before proposing marriage, he should have a private investigating agency check her background and present activities. After all, he thought to himself, I have both a growing fortune and my reputation to protect against a marital misadventure.

As a further precaution against notoriety, the young man requested that the agency not reveal his identity to the investigator making the report on the actress. In due time the investigator's report arrived. It said the actress had an unblemished past, a spotless reputation, and her friends and associates were of the best repute. The report concluded, "The only shadow in this sunny picture is that she is often seen around town in the company of a young broker of dubious business practices and principles."

According to 2 Peter, being a person of distinction isn't about outward signs of success. For instance, having a gigantic home, a spacious corner office, the latest model car, or designer clothes is not the Lord's goal for us. Instead, it's to embrace His "exceeding great and precious promises" (1:4) to us and in this way become "partakers of the divine nature."

HOPE THROUGH STEWARDSHIP

BACKGROUND SCRIPTURE: 1 Peter 4
DEVOTIONAL READING: Luke 16:10-13

Key Verse: As every man hath received the gift, even so minister the same one to another, as good stewards of the manifold grace of God. 1 Peter 4:10.

KING JAMES VERSION

1 PETER 4:1 Forasmuch then as Christ hath suffered for us in the flesh, arm yourselves likewise with the same mind: for he that hath suffered in the flesh hath ceased from sin; 2 That he no longer should live the rest of his time in the flesh to the lusts of men, but to the will of God. 3 For the time past of our life may suffice us to have wrought the will of the Gentiles, when we walked in lasciviousness, lusts, excess of wine, revellings, banquetings, and abominable idolatries:

4 Wherein they think it strange that ye run not with them to the same excess of riot, speaking evil of you: 5 Who shall give account to him that is ready to judge the quick and the dead. 6 For for this cause was the gospel preached also to them that are dead, that they might be judged according to men in the flesh, but live according to God in the spirit.

7 But the end of all things is at hand: be ye therefore sober, and watch unto prayer. 8 And above all things have fervent charity among yourselves: for charity shall cover the multitude of sins. 9 Use hospitality one to another without grudging. 10 As every man hath received the gift, even so minister the same one to another, as good stewards of the manifold grace of God. 11 If any man speak, let him speak as the oracles of God; if any man minister, let him do it as of the ability which God giveth: that God in all things may be glorified through Jesus Christ, to whom be praise and dominion for ever and ever. Amen.

NEW REVISED STANDARD VERSION

1 PETER 4:1 Since therefore Christ suffered in the flesh, arm yourselves also with the same intention (for whoever has suffered in the flesh has finished with sin), 2 so as to live for the rest of your earthly life no longer by human desires but by the will of God. 3 You have already spent enough time in doing what the Gentiles like to do, living in licentiousness, passions, drunkenness, revels, carousing, and lawless idolatry. 4 They are surprised that you no longer join them in the same excesses of dissipation, and so they blaspheme. 5 But they will have to give an accounting to him who stands ready to judge the living and the dead. 6 For this is the reason the gospel was proclaimed even to the dead, so that, though they had been judged in the flesh as everyone is judged, they might live in the spirit as God does.

7 The end of all things is near; therefore be serious and discipline yourselves for the sake of your prayers. 8 Above all, maintain constant love for one another, for love covers a multitude of sins. 9 Be hospitable to one another without complaining. 10 Like good stewards of the manifold grace of God, serve one another with whatever gift each of you has received. 11 Whoever speaks must do so as one speaking the very words of God; whoever serves must do so with the strength that God supplies, so that God may be glorified in all things through Jesus Christ. To him belong the glory and the power forever and ever. Amen.

12

BACKGROUND

It would have been hard for the believers of northwest Asia Minor, to whom Peter wrote, to consider the possibility of enduring further mistreatment as followers of the Messiah. Although the prospect was unpleasant, there were spiritual benefits to suffering unjustly. Foremost in Peter's mind was the truth that the Christian "hath ceased from sin" (1 Pet. 4:1).

There are two primary ways of understanding what the apostle meant. According to one view, he was referring to the character-building effects of suffering. As enemies of the church persecuted God's people, they were forced to decide what was most important in life. Consequently, the things of the world become less attractive. According to a second view, Peter was thinking about the spiritual union of believers with the Messiah in His suffering and death. This identification is symbolized by baptism, which the apostle had talked about in 3:21. The Redeemer died to sin in the sense that, after His death and resurrection, He was no longer subject to the power of sin and death. Similarly, believers were dead to the power of sin and alive to the Father through their identification with the Son (see Rom. 6:11).

NOTES ON THE PRINTED TEXT

In 1 Peter 3:18, the apostle stressed that Jesus, who was innocent, died for the guilty so that they might have the opportunity to be saved. After a brief digression in verses 19-22, Peter returned to the theme of unjust suffering in 4:1. When Peter said that Jesus "suffered for us in the flesh," the apostle was referring to the Savior's crucifixion and death. The Messiah did not value His physical life so much that He refused to die on the cross, and His followers were to adopt this same attitude. They were to accept the fact that living and dying for the cause of Christ were more important than preserving their earthly existence.

Due to the experience of unjust suffering, the recipients of Peter's letter were more likely to spend their time on earth doing what God wanted, not doing the evil things that people wanted (vs. 2). The apostle said his friends had already spent enough time in the past living like pagans, that is, people who did not know the Lord (vs. 3). At one time the Christians followed their evil desires. They participated in lewd activities, got drunk, indulged in orgies, and caroused with others. They even worshiped idols.

The readers of Peter's letter were grateful that they no longer lived immorally. Of course, their unsaved acquaintances did not understand why they chose to abandon sin. Those who opposed the faith were shocked that God's people refused to do the wasteful things they did. That is why the former friends of the Asia Minor Christians maligned them for their virtuous behavior (vs. 4). Peter knew that it was difficult for his fellow believers to endure such persecution. He explained that one day God would require their enemies to explain their reprehensible actions. The unsaved would stand condemned before the One who will judge the living and the dead (vs. 5).

In verse 6, the apostle explained that Jesus' disciples had proclaimed the Gospel to people who were now dead. Some think Jesus, between His death and resurrection, preached and offered salvation to all the dead who had lived in pre-Christian times. Others connect this preaching with 3:19 and 20 and say the dead were the people of Noah's day. A third group says Jesus preached salvation to the righteous of Old Testament times. Each of these views gives the impression that the preaching took place after the people had died. Yet the Bible teaches that once people pass away, there will be no second chance to get saved (see Heb. 9:27). Most likely, then, Peter was referring to people who had died after becoming followers of Christ. In other words, they heard the Good News while they were still alive and then subsequently died.

These believers had experienced the same judgment that eventually falls on all people, namely, death (see Rom. 5:12). When the Father raised His Son from the dead, He triumphed over death (see 6:9). However, the full extent of that victory is not yet manifested in the lives of God's people. Of course, they enjoy new life through union with Christ. And they have the assurance of knowing that one day the Savior's victory over death will extend to their physical bodies (see Rom. 8:11; 1 Cor. 15:25-26).

There are two other ways of understanding the reference to judgment in 1 Peter 4:6. Possibly the apostle was talking about either God's discipline or eternal condemnation (see 1 Cor. 11:30; Rev. 20:11-15). Or the judgment was the unfair way the wicked judged Christians. In that case, their evaluation was based on human, not divine, standards of behavior. Whichever view is preferred, Peter's emphasis remains the same. Those who hear the Gospel preached and who trust in the Messiah are saved from divine wrath. They also enjoy new life with God. The Spirit gives them eternal life, and neither persecution nor death can take it away from the true followers of Christ.

First Peter 4:7-11 contains a series of practical, everyday principles the apostle laid down for his readers to understand and follow. Peter began by saying that the culmination of the present age was at hand (vs. 7). Some claim this statement is a veiled reference to the destruction of Jerusalem in A.D. 70. A more likely view, however, is that Jesus had ushered in the messianic era. Peter implied that the entire period between the first and second comings of the Son made up the "last times" (1:20; compare Heb. 1:1-2 and 1 John 2:18).

In light of the fact that Jesus would one day return, the apostle urged his readers to be "sober" (1 Pet. 4:7), that is, alert and levelheaded in their thinking. The Christians were to know why they existed, make sensible decisions, and act in a reasonable manner. Peter also encouraged his friends to "watch," that is, be self-controlled and sober in spirit. They were to maintain mental and moral balance in a sinful and self-indulgent world. A serious and sensible disposition would help the believers do a better job of praying. Scripture teaches that we are always to keep in touch with God through prayer and receive power and strength from Him. Prayer is a vital link with God that strengthens our relationship not only with Him, but also with our fellow Christians.

Verse 8 might contain the most all-embracing of the commands in this section, for it tells the readers to maintain earnest, sincere "love" for one another. The apostle's readers were already exercising Christlike love, but Peter discerned that a reminder would not be amiss. The apostle could give his readers such a command, for godly love is not just an emotion, but also a decision that leads to action. This kind of love makes it possible for one to genuinely care for others regardless of how he or she feels about them. In times of persecution when believers are feeling stressed, there is a greater chance for them to say or do something that is offensive to others. Love becomes a key factor in maintaining unity, for it does not keep track of wrongs. Instead, it continually extends forgiveness to others (see Prov. 10:12; Matt. 18:21-22; 1 Cor. 13:4-7).

As the Christians faced hardship, it would be easy for them to forget the needs of others. Peter reminded his readers to do what they could to extend "hospitality" (1 Pet. 4:9) to their fellow believers without complaining or grumbling. In those days, there weren't many inns, and the lodges that did exist often had an unsavory reputation. So travelers had to rely on households if they were to get good accommodations during a journey. By welcoming people into their home and meeting their needs, the readers of the apostle's letter would show God's love in tangible ways.

Peter next mentioned that the Lord had given the Christians of Asia Minor spiritual gifts and that they were to use these to serve others (vs. 10). The Greek noun translated "gift" is *charisma*. The plural form of this word is *charismata*—"gifts." Both words are related to the word *charis*, which means "grace" or "favor." Thus *charisma* is a gift of grace. The Holy Spirit bestows on Christians special abilities to accomplish the will of God. They do not own the gifts. Instead, they are stewards of what God has graciously provided for them. These gifts of grace take various forms, and they are to be faithfully used wherever and whenever possible.

The spiritual gifts that Peter mentioned in verse 11 represent only a few of the many that God had given His people in Asia Minor. The apostle noted that some had a special ability to declare the truths of Scripture. This included all forms of speaking (for example, preaching, teaching, prophesying, and speaking in tongues). Peter reminded his readers that they were proclaiming the message of God (as opposed to a mere human message). Others had a unique ability to serve others. Peter exhorted them to minister to people in God's strength, not their own.

As the believers diligently help one another and rely on the Father for enabling, they bring Him honor through His Son, the Lord Jesus. For instance, others will see believers ministering in the name of the Son and praise the Father for it. The thought of God being honored moved Peter to write a doxology of praise at the end of verse 11. Glory and power belonged to the Lord for ever and ever. Peter then affirmed this truth with an "Amen," which might be paraphrased "So be it!"

SUGGESTIONS TO TEACHERS

This week's lesson encourages the members of your class to ponder the importance of the gifts of the Spirit to everyone in the congregation. The lesson should also remind them that every ability given by the Spirit is equally valued and important to the proper functioning of the church.

1. VALIDITY OF SPIRITUAL GIFTS. First Peter 4:10 presumes that every believer has at least one spiritual gift, if not more than one. In brief, the presence and practicality of spiritual gifts are a theologically valid truth to affirm to the students.

2. VARIETIES OF THE SPIRIT'S GIFTS. Examine with your class the different kinds of gifts bestowed by the Spirit to a congregation. Work to understand what each of these may mean for your church today. Consider who in your church seems to be blessed with what gifts. Are these persons encouraged to minister their gifts to others? How can the congregation give equal emphasis to all the gifts of the Spirit present within the church?

3. VALUE OF INDIVIDUAL GIFTS. Invite the students to share how they might be a blessing to others through the exercise of their spiritual gifts. To get the discussion started, you might consider sharing a few personal thoughts about how the Spirit has equipped you to serve the church.

4. VITALITY OF THE BODY. End the class session by discussing the ways in which the church is similar to a human body. Be sure to stress that every member of the congregation—even the believers who seem the least significant—are needed to help the church remain healthy, growing, and productive.

FOR ADULTS

■ **TOPIC:** Serving One Another

■ **QUESTIONS:** 1. What attitude did Jesus display when He suffered and died on the cross? 2. Why is it sometimes hard to reject enticements to sin and follow the will of God? 3. What can believers do to remain spiritually alert and sober at all times? 4. In what ways can the presence of Christlike love "cover the multitude of sins" (1 Pet. 4:8)? 5. What are some creative ways you could use your home to minister to others?

■ ILLUSTRATIONS:

Work Together. Too often today a discussion about spiritual gifts ends up in arguments and division, not in spiritual unity. We don't have to agree on the precise meaning of the special abilities mentioned in 1 Peter 4:10-11 to find common ground in a larger purpose. But many times, our larger purpose and our common bond in Christ get lost in our heated debates.

Meanwhile, some churches are weakened because of a false dichotomy between so-called gifted believers and the rest of ordinary Christians. We have to make room for all believers to exercise their gifts for the common good. We cannot afford to let some Christians think they are second class just because they might not have some of the more publicly recognized gifts.

Thankfully, Peter emphasized oneness, unity, and harmony. He did not glorify the gifts. He would not tolerate fighting over any special ability, all of which are intended to build Christ's body. The whole point of Peter's admonition was to produce a vital, loving, growing, and unified fellowship, not one shattered by arguments and bickering.

Lesson from the Hive. Tommy decided that he would capture a honeybee, care for it, and eventually collect some honey. He carefully lowered a large jar over a flower on which a bee had settled to gather nectar. He snipped off the stem, capped the jar, and jubilantly carried the trapped bee to the little one-bee hive that he had painstakingly prepared.

The new home for Tommy's lone bee had plenty of water, plenty of clover for food, plenty of warmth, and plenty of fresh air. Tommy was certain that he had provided all the necessary ingredients to care for his bee. But to his dismay, the bee was dead three days later. Only when he talked to an experienced beekeeper did Tommy learn that a bee cannot survive in isolation. Individual bees are kept alive by living in community with one another.

The same lesson might be applied to us as a community of faith. We need each other to survive as Christians. In isolation, we would find it impossible to remain faithful. But as we work together through the unstinting exercise of our spiritual gifts, we can encourage one another (see 1 Pet. 4:10-11). Clearly, our unity as fellow believers is a great source of spiritual strength!

The Need for Diversity. Imagine that the main hospital in your community is staffed only by heart specialists. They are all world-famous experts who can deal with the unique needs of heart patients. In fact, these physicians can utilize the best and latest medical technology in their field. But how effective is the hospital in meeting the diverse medical needs of your community?

In this fictional situation, there is no one to suture lacerations and set broken bones. There's also no one to care for the trauma victims and cancer patients. Furthermore, no one has any desire to treat patients who have problems of the stomach, liver, gall-bladder, intestines, brain, or urinary tract.

A hospital cannot survive long with just heart specialists. Similarly, a church is ineffective if it only has believers with one spiritual gift. The congregation needs a whole spectrum of believers with a wide variety of special abilities to meet the needs of their fellow Christians (see 1 Pet. 4:10-11).

FOR YOUTH

■ **TOPIC:** A Changed Life
■ **QUESTIONS:** 1. How can the experience of hardship discourage believers from engaging in sin? 2. Why are the unsaved often surprised when believers refuse to participate in immoral activities? 3. How has the knowledge of God's judgment affected your efforts to spread the Gospel? 4. What are some ways believers can show the compassion of Christ to one another? 5. What are some spiritual gifts the Lord has given you to use for the benefit of others?

■ **ILLUSTRATIONS:**

Members of the Same Team. Youth today are introduced early to the values of working together. They work on class projects, participate in musical groups and plays, and join athletic teams. They all know that if any member slacks off, the team suffers. They also realize that if any player tries to steal the whole show, the team is weakened.

These are the kinds of illustrations adolescents can understand when applied to the church, which is Christ's spiritually gifted team (see 1 Pet. 4:10-11). When teens put their faith in Him, He brings about a profound change in their lives. They now have the Spirit empowering them to serve one another in a loving and sacrificial manner. The beauty of the church is that faith in Jesus is the only requirement to be on His team. It doesn't depend on skill or experience.

Faith in Jesus is also required to accept the contributions of all other team members. Perhaps the final production will not be as stellar as we would prefer it to be. But we have to remember that the church is not just for professionals. It is also for life-long learners and followers of the Savior. In this regard, we need to coach each other, so that our team can become as strong as possible.

Mitten Theology. In *The Secret Place*, Charlotte Burkholder tells us that fingers in a mitten are in contact with one another, and that each contributes body heat. Therefore, these fingers keep warmer than those in a glove, where each finger is wrapped separately.

These observations are a reminder that believers must spiritually keep together and allow each other to contribute to the common good of the church. This is done when every believer uses his or her God-given spiritual gifts without hesitation (see 1 Pet. 4:10-11). In short, we are most useful to the Lord and to one another as the body of Christ when we are practicing a "mitten" faith together instead of "glove" living.

Code Talkers. In early February 1998, Carl Gorman died. The 90-year-old was a Navajo artist who taught at the University of California. He was also the father of celebrated artist R. C. Gorman.

Carl, though, gained fame as the original and oldest of 400 Navajo Code Talkers. During World War II, the Japanese broke the army, navy, and air corps codes. However, the marines used the native Navajo tongue and turned the language into a secret weapon. Navajo is a language without an alphabet and with an irregular syntax. In 1942, only about 50,000 Navajo actually spoke the language, having resisted all the efforts by the U.S. government to Americanize them. (Gorman's teachers at a mission school had chained him one whole week to an iron pipe in an effort to force him not to use his native tongue!)

Gorman and his colleagues worked out words for military terms and used a two-tier code where English terms were represented by Navajo words. (For instance, a hummingbird was a fighter, and a swallow became a torpedo plane.) The code was so secure that it was never broken by the Japanese. And the code was so valuable that it remained top secret until it was finally declassified in 1968, when secure high-speed electronic coding was developed. Thirty-four years later, in 2002, the Code Talkers were awarded the Congressional Medal of Honor.

Gorman's gift was simple and plain. However, without his gift and those few others who also had this special ability, the war effort in the Pacific might have gone differently. From this we can see that every believer's spiritual gifts, no matter how seemingly insignificant, are important to the body of Christ (see 1 Pet. 4:10-11).

Sadly, many believers tend to dismiss their God-given talents, skills, and aptitudes—even their spiritual gifts—as trivial or unimportant in the ongoing life of the church. Nothing could be further from the truth! Every spiritual gift is important and needed. It is vital that these gifts be put into practice so that the church's ministry is complete and God is praised through them.

THE DAY OF THE LORD

BACKGROUND SCRIPTURE: 2 Peter 3
DEVOTIONAL READING: John 14:1-7

Key Verse: The Lord is not slack concerning his promise, as some men count slackness; but is longsuffering to us-ward, not willing that any should perish, but that all should come to repentance. 2 Peter 3:9.

KING JAMES VERSION

2 PETER 3:1 This second epistle, beloved, I now write unto you; in both which I stir up your pure minds by way of remembrance: 2 That ye may be mindful of the words which were spoken before by the holy prophets, and of the commandment of us the apostles of the Lord and Saviour:

3 Knowing this first, that there shall come in the last days scoffers, walking after their own lusts, 4 And saying, Where is the promise of his coming? for since the fathers fell asleep, all things continue as they were from the beginning of the creation. 5 For this they willingly are ignorant of, that by the word of God the heavens were of old, and the earth standing out of the water and in the water: 6 Whereby the world that then was, being overflowed with water, perished: 7 But the heavens and the earth, which are now, by the same word are kept in store, reserved unto fire against the day of judgment and perdition of ungodly men.

8 But, beloved, be not ignorant of this one thing, that one day is with the Lord as a thousand years, and a thousand years as one day. 9 The Lord is not slack concerning his promise, as some men count slackness; but is longsuffering to us-ward, not willing that any should perish, but that all should come to repentance. 10 But the day of the Lord will come as a thief in the night; in the which the heavens shall pass away with a great noise, and the elements shall melt with fervent heat, the earth also and the works that are therein shall be burned up.

11 Seeing then that all these things shall be dissolved, what manner of persons ought ye to be in all holy conversation and godliness, 12 Looking for and hasting unto the coming of the day of God, wherein the heavens being on fire shall be dissolved, and the elements shall melt with fervent heat? 13 Nevertheless we, according to his promise, look for new heavens and a new earth, wherein dwelleth righteousness. 14 Wherefore, beloved, seeing that ye look for such things, be diligent that ye may be found of him in peace, without spot, and blameless. 15 And account that the longsuffering of our Lord is salvation.

NEW REVISED STANDARD VERSION

2 PETER 3:1 This is now, beloved, the second letter I am writing to you; in them I am trying to arouse your sincere intention by reminding you 2 that you should remember the words spoken in the past by the holy prophets, and the commandment of the Lord and Savior spoken through your apostles. 3 First of all you must understand this, that in the last days scoffers will come, scoffing and indulging their own lusts 4 and saying, "Where is the promise of his coming? For ever since our ancestors died, all things continue as they were from the beginning of creation!" 5 They deliberately ignore this fact, that by the word of God heavens existed long ago and an earth was formed out of water and by means of water, 6 through which the world of that time was deluged with water and perished. 7 But by the same word the present heavens and earth have been reserved for fire, being kept until the day of judgment and destruction of the godless.

8 But do not ignore this one fact, beloved, that with the Lord one day is like a thousand years, and a thousand years are like one day. 9 The Lord is not slow about his promise, as some think of slowness, but is patient with you, not wanting any to perish, but all to come to repentance. 10 But the day of the Lord will come like a thief, and then the heavens will pass away with a loud noise, and the elements will be dissolved with fire, and the earth and everything that is done on it will be disclosed.

11 Since all these things are to be dissolved in this way, what sort of persons ought you to be in leading lives of holiness and godliness, 12 waiting for and hastening the coming of the day of God, because of which the heavens will be set ablaze and dissolved, and the elements will melt with fire? 13 But, in accordance with his promise, we wait for new heavens and a new earth, where righteousness is at home.

14 Therefore, beloved, while you are waiting for these things, strive to be found by him at peace, without spot or blemish; 15 and regard the patience of our Lord as salvation.

13

313

Monday, May 20	2 Timothy 3:1-9	*Distressing Times Will Come*
Tuesday, May 21	Jeremiah 23:23-32	*Warnings for False Prophets*
Wednesday, May 22	James 5:1-6	*Warnings for Rich Oppressors*
Thursday, May 23	Hosea 14:1-7	*Return to the Lord*
Friday, May 24	Micah 4:1-5	*Teaching the Ways of God*
Saturday, May 25	John 14:1-7	*I Will Come Again*
Sunday, May 26	2 Peter 3:3-15a	*The Promise of the Lord's Coming*

BACKGROUND

The phrase the "last days" (2 Pet. 3:3) is sometimes used in the Old Testament to refer generally to events that would take place in the future, both near and distant. When the New Testament speaks of the "last days," it refers to events connected with Jesus' return. The phrase also includes the period from the Savior's first advent to His second advent.

Peter used this same phrase in his first letter to describe the age in which his readers were already living (1 Pet. 1:20). He also used it in his sermon on the day of Pentecost, when he pointed to the giving of the Holy Spirit as fulfillment of events that the prophet Joel had foretold would take place in the "last days" (Acts 2:17). Paul used the phrase in his prediction of the general decline in conditions that were to occur prior to Jesus' return (2 Tim. 3:1). Both Peter and Paul recognized that the "last days" had already arrived.

NOTES ON THE PRINTED TEXT

Peter concluded his second epistle with words of endearment used four times between this point and the end of the epistle (2 Pet. 3:1). The apostle wrote several times to the Christians living in Asia Minor to warn them about the false teaching of spiritual frauds and remind them of important apostolic truths. The goal was to "stir up [their] pure minds."

Moreover, Peter wanted to refresh the memory of his readers and thereby encourage them to do some honest consideration of what they had been taught (vs. 2). That included all that God's "holy prophets" had spoken long ago. Their oracles are recorded in the Old Testament, which initially was the primary collection of sacred writings used by believers in the first century. Peter also wanted the Christians in Asia Minor to recall what he and the other apostles taught. This especially concerned what their Lord and Savior, Jesus Christ, had commanded them to do—namely, to be morally vigilant, especially as they awaited His return in glory.

In the Greek text, Peter literally noted that as the end of the age drew near, "scoffers in their scoffing" (vs. 3) would arise. The Greek noun that is translated "scoffers" refers to the fraudulent prophets and teachers mentioned in 2:1. They already had infiltrated the faith community in Asia Minor, and they would continue to plague the body of Christ until His return (see Matt. 24:3-5, 11, 23-26; 2 Tim. 3:1-5; Jude 18). The charlatans were guilty of deriding God's Word and being propelled by their "own lusts" (2 Pet. 3:3; see 2:13-22).

Peter focused with the greatest intensity on the Christian belief attacked by these scoffers, namely, the Messiah's promise of His second advent (see Matt. 10:23; 16:28; 24:3, 32-36; Mark 9:1; Acts 1:11). Regrettably, the false teachers mocked the believers' hope, reminding them that nothing had changed since the "beginning of the creation" (2 Pet. 3:4). The "fathers" might refer to the patriarchs (Abraham, Isaac, and Jacob; see Acts 3:13; Rom. 9:5; Heb. 1:1), or perhaps even to the first Christian martyrs such as James and Stephen (see Heb. 13:7). In any case, the religious frauds' implicit argument was that if Jesus had not yet returned, He would never do so.

Peter noted that the spiritual frauds intentionally suppressed some key biblical facts. One truth is that at the dawn of time, God used His powerful utterance to command the heavens and the earth into existence (2 Pet. 3:5; see Pss. 33:6; 148:5). The Lord not only had the power to create the earth with the use of water, but He also had the right to destroy the same planet by means of water (2 Pet. 3:6). The apostle was referring to the flood that inundated and wiped out all who inhabited the world in Noah's day (that is, except for Noah and his family, who were all safe in the ark).

The conclusion Peter drew was that the same God who in the past destroyed the earth with water will one day destroy both the existing "heavens" (vs. 7) and "earth" with fire. Peter noted that just as the wicked were destroyed in the Flood, so will it be at the end of the age, when the entire universe is destroyed by fire. It will be a time of "judgment and perdition" reserved specifically for the "ungodly." The account of the Flood proved the inevitability of divine judgment and testified to God's patience. Even more importantly, the biblical record was evidence of the reliability of Scripture. Thankfully, just as God preserved Noah and his family from the Flood, so He will deliver those who have trusted in the Messiah for salvation.

The religious charlatans had insisted that the delay in the promised coming of the Messiah proved that it was never going to happen. To counter this pernicious error, Peter sought to clarify for his readers how God viewed time. Again the apostle used words of endearment as he encouraged these believers not to let an important fact escape their notice (vs. 8). Evidently, he summarized the words of Moses recorded in Psalm 90:4. Peter noted that just because the Son had not yet returned did not mean that the Father was "slack concerning his promise" (2 Pet. 3:9). Despite what the false teachers alleged, Peter considered the apparent delay of Jesus' return, not as a doubt-producing dilemma, but as a means of God's grace. The verb that is rendered "long-suffering" literally means "to be long-spirited" and refers to a forbearing disposition. The Lord was lengthening the period of time in which people could repent and be delivered from eternal destruction.

When God's patience is finally exhausted, the "day of the Lord" (vs. 10) will come suddenly, as a thief who strikes in the darkness (see 1 Thess. 5:2; Rev. 3:3; 16:15). Jesus also taught that His second advent would be unexpected, like the unwelcome intrusion of a burglar (see Matt. 24:42-44; Luke 12:39-40). But unlike the housebreaker, Jesus will have every right to take whatever He wishes, for there is no power, position, or possession that does not already belong to Him.

Peter used strong language typical of end-time passages to describe three events that will happen when the Messiah returns. First, the heavens will vanish with a "great noise" (2 Pet. 3:10; see Isa. 13:10-13; 34:4; Rev. 6:14). The latter renders a Greek adverb that denotes the presence of a horrific roar similar to a whirling, rushing sound. Second, the "elements" (2 Pet. 3:10) will melt away in a fiery blaze. The noun that is translated "elements" refers to the celestial bodies in the universe (sun, moon, and stars) as well as the chemical compounds out of which they are made (earth, air, fire, and water).

Third, the planet and every deed done on it will be "burned up." This renders a Greek verb that can also mean to "be consumed by fire." In this case, the idea is that everything on earth will be obliterated. In turn, humanity will be left to stand exposed and accountable before God. Another textual reading uses a different verb that can be translated "laid bare." This reading points to the truth that one day every human creation will be entirely exposed and perfectly judged by God. Since eventually all earthly things will be completely destroyed, believers should desire all the more to live in a manner that is pleasing to God. Specifically, they are to be holy and godly in their conduct (vs. 11). Moreover, because death for any of us is but a heartbeat away, and because the Son could come soon, we should feel an urgency to glorify the Father in our daily living.

A difference of opinion exists concerning the phrase "hasting unto the coming" (vs. 12) in regard to the "day of God" (which is another way of referring to day of the Lord). Some think the phrase is merely a description of the eagerness with which believers anticipate the Messiah's return. Others, however, relate Peter's statement to the belief that Christians can do things to speed up the Lord's advent. A recorded prayer of the early Christians, "Maranatha! Come, Lord Jesus" (see 1 Cor. 16:22; Rev. 22:20), corresponds with this perspective.

Peter repeated his earlier declaration that the heavens will be burned up and dissolve, and the celestial bodies will melt in a blaze (2 Pet. 3:12). The apostle quickly reassured Christians that, though the fire would destroy creation, God promised to provide a "new heavens" (vs. 13) and a "new earth." The latter anticipates John's statement in Revelation 21:1. Both of these verses likely have their roots in the words of Isaiah 65:17 and 66:22. At the end of the age, the cleansing fire of God's holiness will make everything new, renovating, renewing, and purifying the heavens and the earth. In turn, the new creation will be a place in which one finds "righteousness" (2 Pet.

3:12). This "righteousness" is a Greek noun that points to the presence of such virtues as integrity, purity, and rectitude.

Once more Peter encouraged his readers to accept the glorious anticipation of a new heaven and earth as a challenge to live righteously before God. This is accomplished by following the ethical example of the Savior, who was "without blemish and without spot" (1 Pet. 1:19). In turn, believers are to ensure that their lives are morally "without spot, and blameless" (2 Pet. 3:14). A virtuous person is more likely to be a peaceful one. To emphasize this point, Peter referred again to the meaning of God's patience as an invitation to "salvation" (vs. 15).

In this the apostle was repeating what he knew Paul had already written to his readers. Indeed, this was a common theme in his letters (vss. 15-16). While Peter wanted his readers to note the similarity and harmony between his teachings and those of Paul, Peter admitted that some of the statements Paul wrote were "hard to be understood." Untaught and irresponsible people tried to twist and misrepresent these obscure texts (for example, 1 Cor. 5:5; 7:29; 15:29; Col. 1:24; 1 Tim. 2:15). Yet Peter placed Paul's writings on the same level as the Old Testament Scriptures. In this way, Peter showed his high regard for the God-given wisdom and authority of his fellow apostle in the Lord.

SUGGESTIONS TO TEACHERS

Jesus promised and angels confirmed that He would return bodily to the earth at a future time (see Matt. 24:30-31; Acts 1:11). The New Testament writers understood that the Messiah's return will mark the end of this age and the full realization of the kingdom of God (see 1 Thess. 4:16-17; 5:1-2; 2 Pet. 3:10; Rev. 19:11-16; 21:1-4). Peter addressed the promised return of Jesus because false teachers were challenging its truthfulness.

1. THE CHALLENGE TO THE PROMISE. Century after century, scoffers have posed the same objections to the teaching that Jesus will return some day. Generations have come and gone, they assert, and Jesus hasn't returned. Therefore, He isn't coming. Everything is as it has always been from the beginning of time, they claim. So Jesus' return isn't going to break the pattern. Doubters want Christians to feel self-conscious or presumptuous for imagining that Jesus might do something in their time that He hasn't done for past generations.

2. THE PROOF OF THE PROMISE. Peter demonstrated several fallacies in the reasoning of the scoffers who deny that Jesus will return bodily. Peter argued in favor of the return of a sovereign Lord, for He operated outside the confines of time. Also, He did so with the best interests of His creatures in mind. Furthermore, He remained committed to deal with the effects of the Fall on creation and humankind.

3. THE IMPLICATIONS OF THE PROMISE. The Bible does not present theology as an intellectual exercise. There are behavioral implications for God's truth.

Peter presented compelling arguments for holiness and godliness from the fact that the day of the Lord Jesus will come as suddenly and quickly as a thief would in the night. We cannot know when Jesus will return, but we can live in such a way that we affirm His return and His reign over the new heavens and earth.

4. THE RESPONSE TO THE PROMISE. While believers wait for the Lord, we should strive to imitate Jesus in peace, purity, and patience. We should seek to build lasting stability in our lives by growing in grace and the knowledge of the Son. Second Peter ends as it began with an emphasis on the transforming knowledge of the Father and His Son (1:2-3, 5, 8; 3:18).

FOR ADULTS	■ TOPIC: Ready and Waiting

■ **QUESTIONS:** 1. Why did Peter write his second letter? 2. What lessons did Noah's flood offer for those who were troubled by the apparent delay in Jesus' return? 3. If the Father is faithful to His promise, why has the Son not yet returned? 4. If you had only two hours to live before Jesus' return, how would you spend that time? 5. What can you do to keep believers from being fooled by false teaching?

■ **ILLUSTRATIONS:**

The Best Is Yet to Come. Every believer encounters challenges, frustrations, and opposition. These steps to maturity in the Savior are like foothills that sometimes block the view of the lofty, snowcapped peaks. But because the peaks are there, Christians, like mountain hikers, can push onward and upward.

What is the highest peak of biblical hope? It is the return of Jesus and eternal life in His presence (see 2 Pet. 3:14-15). That hope should lighten every step and quicken the heart of all believers. Most importantly, they realize that the best part of God's plan for them is yet to come. Because the Lord is the "God of hope" (Rom. 15:13), He is able to "fill you with all joy and peace in believing, that ye may abound in hope, through the power of the Holy Ghost."

An Eternal Perspective. This week's lesson focuses on the call to live a life that clearly reflects the eternal perspective of our Savior. In brief, the reality of our relationship with Jesus shows in our lives.

Teacher LouAnn MacQueen had just buried her father when a car crash killed one of her high school students. The boy's death shocked classmates and staff. "I cried so much at his funeral," LouAnn said. "It was so empty. Neither the boy nor his family had any religious beliefs."

LouAnn was recruited to help counsel grieving students. Although she was still hurting, she knew her faith in the Savior was strong enough to bring her through. She also wanted to share her eternal hope with those she counseled.

A coworker noticed the care LouAnn took with each student and asked, "You're a Christian, aren't you? I could tell by the way you talked about death." Others had encouraged students to voice their questions. LouAnn pointed the students to the One with the answers. By sharing the everlasting truths found in the Gospel, LouAnn touched many lives at a crucial time of need.

Scoffers, Beware! Friday at quitting time, Jim said, "Boss, have you got any extra work I can do tonight?" "Sure," Jim's boss replied, "but I can't pay you overtime." "That's okay," Jim answered. "I just don't want to go home."

"Why not?" Jim's boss asked. "Well," Jim admitted, "I've been in the doghouse since last night." "Uh-oh," his boss interjected. "What did you do to deserve that?" "I honestly don't know." Jim shrugged. "It must be one of those woman things. I was minding my own business, relaxing in front of the TV. My wife comes in and asks, 'What's on the TV?' I swear all I said was, 'Dust!' She's been mad ever since!"

Jim's wife failed to see any humor in her husband's dig at her housekeeping. God gets more than a little miffed at teachers in the church who go by His Son's name and scoff at the teachings of the Bible (see 2 Pet. 3:3-4).

FOR YOUTH	■ TOPIC: Hope Motivates Holy Living

■ **QUESTIONS:** 1. Why did Peter sense the need to stimulate his readers to wholesome thinking? 2. What did Peter declare will occur in the last days? 3. What important biblical truth did the false teachers try to suppress? 4. How strong is your anticipation of Jesus' return? 5. How is the way you live now affected by the inevitability of Jesus' return?

■ **ILLUSTRATIONS:**

Got Hope? The story is told of how villagers incorrectly thought a vagrant passing through their town was the government inspector. They not only treated him as royalty, but also quickly set into motion a plan to cover up years of fraud. Their mistaking the man for someone else cost them dearly.

This fable is a reminder of how important it is to search for hope in the right place—namely, the Messiah of the Bible—not some figment of our imagination. Jesus is no longer a newborn baby in a manger. Nor is He merely a wise and loving person. He is the Lord of life, the King of kings, and the Savior of the world.

Down through the centuries, people of faith recognized these truths about Jesus. The returning Savior was for them light, hope, and salvation (see 2 Pet. 3:14-15). In fact, all who receive Jesus by faith can partake of the forgiveness and grace He now offers.

Let Sleeping Dogs Lie. Upon entering a little country store, a stranger noticed a sign reading, "Danger! Beware of Dog!" posted on the glass door. Inside, he noticed a harmless old hound dog asleep on the floor beside the cash register.

The stranger asked the store manager, "Is that the dog folks are supposed to beware of?" "Yep, that's him," the store manager replied. The stranger couldn't help but be amused. "That certainly doesn't look like a dangerous dog to me. Why in the world would you post that sign?" "Because," the owner replied, "before I posted that sign, people kept tripping over him."

You may not think that cults and off-the-wall teachings look dangerous. They may seem harmless enough. But leave them alone. They may not eat you alive, but they can make you stumble morally and spiritually (see 2 Pet. 3:3-4, 16-17).

Time Is Relative. Mary was so excited that John had asked her out on a date, she was ready 20 minutes early. It disappointed her that he wasn't on time. By the time he was 30 minutes late, she was angry with John.

After an hour, Mary was angry with herself for caring in the first place. She took off her makeup, put on her pajamas, gathered all the junk food in the pantry, and sat down to watch television with the dog. As her favorite show was coming on, the door-bell rang. It was John. He stared at her wide eyed. "I'm two hours late, and you're still not ready?"

John is without excuse, and Mary is blameless unless she sics the dog on him. However, don't let Jesus' return sneak up on you. He didn't name a day or hour. Be ready all the time (see 2 Pet. 3:10, 14).

HOLY, HOLY, HOLY

BACKGROUND SCRIPTURE: Isaiah 6:1-12
DEVOTIONAL READING: Joshua 24:14-24

Key Verse: Holy, holy, holy, is the LORD of hosts:
the whole earth is full of his glory. Isaiah 6:3.

KING JAMES VERSION

ISAIAH 6:1 In the year that king Uzziah died I saw also the Lord sitting upon a throne, high and lifted up, and his train filled the temple. 2 Above it stood the seraphims: each one had six wings; with twain he covered his face, and with twain he covered his feet, and with twain he did fly. 3 And one cried unto another, and said, Holy, holy, holy, is the LORD of hosts: the whole earth is full of his glory. 4 And the posts of the door moved at the voice of him that cried, and the house was filled with smoke.

5 Then said I, Woe is me! for I am undone; because I am a man of unclean lips, and I dwell in the midst of a people of unclean lips: for mine eyes have seen the King, the LORD of hosts. 6 Then flew one of the seraphims unto me, having a live coal in his hand, which he had taken with the tongs from off the altar: 7 And he laid it upon my mouth, and said, Lo, this hath touched thy lips; and thine iniquity is taken away, and thy sin purged. 8 Also I heard the voice of the Lord, saying, Whom shall I send, and who will go for us? Then said I, Here am I; send me.

9 And he said, Go, and tell this people, Hear ye indeed, but understand not; and see ye indeed, but perceive not. 10 Make the heart of this people fat, and make their ears heavy, and shut their eyes; lest they see with their eyes, and hear with their ears, and understand with their heart, and convert, and be healed. 11 Then said I, Lord, how long? And he answered, Until the cities be wasted without inhabitant, and the houses without man, and the land be utterly desolate, 12 And the LORD have removed men far away, and there be a great forsaking in the midst of the land.

NEW REVISED STANDARD VERSION

ISAIAH 6:1 In the year that King Uzziah died, I saw the Lord sitting on a throne, high and lofty; and the hem of his robe filled the temple. 2 Seraphs were in attendance above him; each had six wings: with two they covered their faces, and with two they covered their feet, and with two they flew. 3 And one called to another and said:
"Holy, holy, holy is the LORD of hosts;
the whole earth is full of his glory."
4 The pivots on the thresholds shook at the voices of those who called, and the house filled with smoke. 5 And I said: "Woe is me! I am lost, for I am a man of unclean lips, and I live among a people of unclean lips; yet my eyes have seen the King, the LORD of hosts!"

6 Then one of the seraphs flew to me, holding a live coal that had been taken from the altar with a pair of tongs. 7 The seraph touched my mouth with it and said: "Now that this has touched your lips, your guilt has departed and your sin is blotted out." 8 Then I heard the voice of the Lord saying, "Whom shall I send, and who will go for us?" And I said, "Here am I; send me!"
9 And he said, "Go and say to this people:
'Keep listening, but do not comprehend;
keep looking, but do not understand.'
10 Make the mind of this people dull,
and stop their ears,
and shut their eyes,
so that they may not look with their eyes,
and listen with their ears,
and comprehend with their minds,
and turn and be healed."
11 Then I said, "How long, O Lord?" And he said:
"Until cities lie waste
without inhabitant,
and houses without people,
and the land is utterly desolate;
12 until the LORD sends everyone far away,
and vast is the emptiness in the midst of the land."

HOME BIBLE READINGS

Monday, May 27	2 Chronicles 26:1-5	*Setting Yourself to Seek God*
Tuesday, May 28	2 Chronicles 26:16-21	*From Success to Pride to Destruction*
Wednesday, May 29	2 Kings 15:32-38	*Following a Father's Example*
Thursday, May 30	Isaiah 6:9-13	*People Dulled to God's Presence*
Friday, May 31	Joshua 24:14-24	*Choosing to Serve a Holy God*
Saturday, June 1	Psalm 24	*Seeking the Face of God*
Sunday, June 2	Isaiah 6:1-8	*Encountering the Holy God*

BACKGROUND

About the same time that Amos, Hosea, and Micah lived, another prophet, named Isaiah, came upon the scene in Judah. The messages recorded in Isaiah were addressed to God's people as they approached a great turning point in their history. Eighteen years after the prophet began his ministry, Assyria would conquer and exile the northern kingdom of Israel (722 B.C.). And 136 years later, Babylon would defeat and deport the southern kingdom of Judah (586 B.C.). Throughout Isaiah's long ministry, he preached about the Lord's righteousness, warned about judgment for sin, and proclaimed God's love and forgiveness. Isaiah also prophesied the glory that awaits those who remain faithful to God.

Isaiah 6 is the prophet's record of how he heard and responded to God's call. At first, it may seem odd that Isaiah's commission to prophesy does not come until after five chapters of prophecies. (These chapters deal with such themes as judgment, discipline, exile, restoration, and blessing.) But probably Isaiah placed his commissioning account here to demonstrate he had the credentials to deliver the opening series of oracles against Judah. Isaiah 6 is highly relevant, for God is still calling people to be His spiritual children and to serve Him unreservedly. He is still looking for people who, like Isaiah, will respond in obedience and dedication. Personal commitment like the prophet's is rare in any age.

NOTES ON THE PRINTED TEXT

God dramatically called Isaiah to his prophetic ministry "in the year that King Uzziah died" (Isa. 6:1), namely, 740 B.C. Uzziah was a monarch of Judah, and he helped restore the nation to some of its former glory. Isaiah said he "saw also the Lord." The prophet did not physically see God's innermost nature. Rather, Isaiah was able to perceive the Lord in appearance seated upon a heavenly throne with the hem, or fringe, of His robe filling the celestial temple. This description expresses the overwhelming presence of God as both King and Judge over all creation. Isaiah's lofty view of God gives us a sense of the Lord's greatness, mystery, and power. The Lord used Isaiah's vision to commission him as God's messenger to His people. Isaiah was given a difficult assignment. He had to tell people who believed they were blessed by God that the Lord was going to destroy them instead because of their disobedience.

Accompanying the Lord were "seraphims" (vs. 2), that is, spiritual beings who served as God's attendants. The literal meaning of "seraphims" is "burning ones," which suggests they had a fiery appearance. Evidently, they were bright creatures, even though they had to hide their faces before God's brighter light. Nowhere else are they spoken of in the Old Testament. The seraphims Isaiah saw had six wings, two of which covered their faces in reverence and awe before the Lord. Because they had no glory to compare with God's, they could not look on Him directly. Two of the seraphims' wings covered their feet, which suggests humbleness. They remained humble before the Lord, even though they engaged in divine service. The seraphims' final two wings were used to fly, which signifies that they existed to do God's bidding.

Drawn against the backdrop of Judah's sin and Isaiah's personal needs, God's holiness came through powerfully in the prophet's vision. God Himself was the focus of this heavenly scene. The angels lauded God with the thunderous chorus, "Holy, holy, holy, is the LORD of hosts" (vs. 3). The threefold repetition was the strongest way in the Hebrew language to stress nothing is as holy as God. The basic meaning of "holy" is to be set apart from that which is commonplace. The word also refers to what is special or unique. That the entire earth is filled with God's glory emphasizes the cosmic perspective of Isaiah's prophecies. He would proclaim that the Lord reigns supreme over all creation and that His salvation and judgment encompass all nations. God's regal position is the basis for His moral authority as the transcendent and sovereign Judge. Also, His holy character establishes the ethical standard for upright conduct and gives Him the right to decree to human beings how they should behave. Moreover, His infinite holiness is the basis for people worshiping Him. Indeed, God's holiness is the theme of worship in heaven (see Rev. 4:8).

Often in the Old Testament, phenomena such as earthquakes, smoke, fire, and lightning accompany a manifestation of God. Isaiah noted that the thunderous chorus of the seraphims shook the doorframes of the celestial temple (Isa. 6:4). Also, smoke filled the entire heavenly sanctuary. The Hebrew word rendered "smoke" possibly reflects the cloud of God's glory that filled the tabernacle, which Moses had built in the wilderness (Exod. 40:34). Both the shaking and the smoke that Isaiah described were manifestations of God's holiness, especially as it related to judgment.

Isaiah's encounter with the Lord proved to be a life-changing experience for him. First, God's presence made him realize the depth of his sinfulness. Second, seeing even the seraphims humbly covering themselves before the Lord must have reminded the prophet of his moral imperfection. These emphases are reflected in the Hebrew term rendered "woe" (Isa. 6:5), which conveys a feeling of great sorrow or distress. When the prophet exclaimed, "I am undone," he made it seem as if his destruction had already occurred. Isaiah could have made excuses, pleaded for mercy, or fallen back on his good deeds. But he did none of these things. Instead, he fully accepted God's judgment. Isaiah knew that what he had seen and heard had left him totally helpless before the Lord.

Isaiah confessed that he and his people were guilty of "unclean lips." While this admission possibly included uttering vulgar language, most likely Isaiah had something else in mind. The people's lips were instruments of religious hypocrisy and of false professions of faith in God. Other Old Testament prophets and Jesus consistently charged God's people with worshiping with their lips, while their hearts were far from the Lord. Similarly, though the people of Judah claimed to believe in God, they violated His laws and worshiped idols. Isaiah was careful to include himself in this indictment. And though he did not have to confess the sins of his people, he did. The prophet realized his need for the Lord to cleanse and purge him of his wrongdoings. In addition, he needed his lips purified so that he could praise the Lord with the seraphims and declare God's message to the people.

Isaiah reported seeing "the King, the LORD of hosts." The depiction is one of a divine warrior who commanded the hosts of heaven and earth. Upon Isaiah's confession of his sinfulness, a seraph flew over him with a hot coal, which had been taken from the celestial altar (vs. 6). This coal symbolized the redeeming power of God to purge and forgive sins. When the angel touched the prophet's lips with the coal, both his iniquity and his guilt were removed. Also, his sin was forgiven (vs. 7). Of course, the coal did not atone for Isaiah's transgressions. Rather, God did through the offering of a sacrifice, namely, the atoning work of the Messiah on the cross (see Rom. 4:25-26). With Isaiah's cleansing over, God moved directly to the business for which He had called Isaiah into His presence. God had seen that the people of Judah were not following His ways, so He wanted someone to tell them of their need for change and to warn them of what to expect. He chose Isaiah for this job.

God did not come right out and tell Isaiah the job He had for him. Instead, God wanted Isaiah to volunteer for the assignment. So the Lord asked, "Whom shall I send?" (vs. 8). Though previously, Isaiah felt unfit to serve God as a prophet, now Isaiah was eager. Before, he had said, "Woe is me" (vs. 5). But now he said, "Here am I; send me" (vs. 8). Now God proceeded to give Isaiah the core of the message he was to deliver to the people. Surprisingly, Isaiah was to tell them that they would hear the truth without understanding it and would see the truth without perceiving it (vs. 9). The Lord informed Isaiah that his ministry would have little positive spiritual impact. In fact, the people's hearts would become even more hardened against God. Isaiah's prophecy would lead to the further callousing of their hearts, dulling of their spiritual hearing, and clouding of their spiritual vision (vs. 10).

Isaiah did not object to the commission God had given him. Before knowing his commission, Isaiah had accepted it, and now he would not shrink from it. But understandably, he was curious how long God would want him to minister to people of calloused hearts. So the prophet asked, "Lord, how long?" (vs. 11). God's reply was that

Isaiah should continue preaching until the land of Judah was devastated and abandoned, its inhabitants having been taken into exile (vs. 12). Since the Babylonian captivity did not occur for another century and a half, Isaiah would have to keep up his poorly received message for the remainder of his life.

The news of coming exile must have shaken Isaiah. But God gave him good news with the bad. A remnant of the nation—a "tenth" (vs. 13)—would survive the future exile. This refers to the portion of Jews who returned from Babylon. The remnant of the nation would be further reduced by invasion and warfare. But as terebinth and oak trees, when cut down, leave stumps from which shoots may sprout, so the survivors among the remnant would be a stump from which the nation again would grow. The nation might reach a point at which it would look as good as dead, but where God is, there is life.

SUGGESTIONS TO TEACHERS

Undoubtedly, your students have heard of someone claiming to be "called" by God. Perhaps some of the adults feel a bit uncomfortable with this term. Or perhaps they might have serious questions about what it means to experience a call from the Lord. Some might even feel slightly resentful, especially since there are times when those who supposedly experienced a divine "call" were considered spiritually superior by others. This week's lesson should help clarify the matter of God's calling a person.

1. AWE BEFORE THE CREATOR. While in the presence of the Lord, Isaiah caught a glimpse of God's majesty and power. Such an extraordinary experience required a reverent response. The talk that we sometimes hear these days of God being some sort of "buddy in the sky" is irreverent. It should not take place among those truly called by the Lord.

2. AWARENESS OF FAILURE. Isaiah immediately realized how undeserving he was of God's favor. Isaiah's sense of personal inadequacy and national failure was overwhelming. A genuine call means an awareness of how great God is and how unmerited we are of His grace.

3. ACCEPTANCE BY GOD. The keynote in a true call of God is knowing His love. Isaiah realized that he had been forgiven. Similarly, divine grace floods the consciousness of those who have actually experienced God's call.

4. ANSWER TO GOD'S CALL. Those who are truly called by God have a keen awareness of His nearness and goodness. Such an awareness demands an appropriate response. Isaiah's "Here am I; send me" (Isa. 6:8) is at the heart of every undisputed call.

5. ACCOUNTABILITY BEORE GOD. A real call from God always entails a task. It also includes the responsibility to fulfill that task. In the case of your students, this means them leading a consistently obedient life of service to others. Emphasize that everyone who believes in the Lord Jesus has been divinely summoned to minister to others in His name.

FOR ADULTS

■ TOPIC: Beyond Description

■ QUESTIONS: 1. How did Isaiah feel at the sight of the Lord seated on His celestial throne? 2. When was there a time when you experienced the majesty of God? How did you feel? 3. Why did the seraphims use their wings to cover themselves in the Lord's presence? 4. How did Isaiah react to what he heard and saw in his vision? 5. In what ways has God recently made known His greatness and holiness to you?

■ ILLUSTRATIONS:

A Commitment to Change. The church is a voluntary organization. No one is compelled to join it. Every believer is a volunteer. Thus, we cannot force members to accept duties. Of course, we can ask them to do certain things and pray that they would say yes, and God honors these efforts.

Perhaps that seems like a risky way to run an organization. Yet it's God's way for His church, which is really a spiritual body, not merely a business. Our desire is that believers will be so overwhelmed by the grandeur of God's holiness, love, and mercy, as Isaiah was, that they will gladly volunteer for service at home and abroad. It is a commitment to be changed by God and to be one of His agents of change in a sin-cursed world.

We have to resist the pressure to program believers into slots. Instead, we should encourage them to be sensitive to God's leading and to worship Him in a genuine manner. When they approach Him in this way, they will be spiritually transformed, and the church will grow in God's grace.

Hardened Hearts. Most people are familiar with cholesterol. This is the glistening, white, soapy substance that attaches itself to the inside of blood vessels. As it thickens and builds up, it causes heart attacks, hardening of the arteries, or blockages in blood vessels.

God called Isaiah to his prophetic ministry because the hearts of the people were hardened toward the Lord. Tragically, the Israelites' years of indifference toward God had blocked their awareness of His love. God ordered Isaiah to tell the people how serious their condition was.

The Lord wanted the prophet to know that He would strengthen him and be with him throughout his long and difficult ministry. Knowing this would help Isaiah avoid becoming discouraged or frustrated. Remember Isaiah when you feel frustrated at not being heard by others.

Truth-Speaking Martyr. Isaiah experienced the call of God in a dramatic way. There are times, though, when God's call comes through the needs that surround us. Likewise, God's call is always a summons to serve. And usually the call to meet a need means not only serving, but also sacrificing.

Some refer to Harry T. Moore as America's first civil rights martyr. Moore felt called to campaign for justice and equality for African Americans in obscure towns in Florida before and immediately after World War II. At that time, Florida was third in the nation in lynchings. The Ku Klux Klan had infested the ranks of the local politicians, businesspeople, and police officers. Florida State officials were not sympathetic to civil rights complaints. In such a toxic climate during the late 1930s and '40s, Moore quickly acquired the reputation of being a "troublemaker."

This brave man petitioned to get equal pay for African American teachers, started voter registration drives, and fired off letters to the governors about the latest atrocity against African Americans. Unlike later civil rights leaders, Moore had no national media to publicize his cause. And he did not have the support of people from the north to finance him. Nevertheless, because Moore believed fervently in equality and democracy, he spoke the truth, even in the presence of threats.

Like many other spokespersons of truth, Harry Moore paid with his life. He was killed in a bombing attack on Christmas Day, 1951. Moore's death, however, was not in vain. Because of his courageous efforts, Florida's African American voter registration was years ahead of that in other southern states.

FOR YOUTH

■ **TOPIC:** Awed beyond Words
■ **QUESTIONS:** 1. What do you think the scene was like for Isaiah as he gazed upon God's heavenly sanctuary? 2. What were the seraphims doing around the throne of God? 3. How have you responded to the presence and power of God in your life? 4. What is the significance of the seraphims repeatedly declaring the holiness of the Lord? 5. In what ways has your relationship with God inspired you to worship Him through service?

■ **ILLUSTRATIONS:**

Sacrifices for Going Deeper. The young man was quite an athlete, but he had to spend time on the bench before he was allowed to play in the game. Though he often volunteered to play, other athletes sometimes got the nod from the coach. Later on, when war broke out, the young man was drafted into the army. But in that setting, he never volunteered for frontline duty with the infantry. Instead, he tried to get an easy desk job in headquarters.

Our churches give us nice, comfortable places to worship, pray, and study the Bible. But our devotion to God calls for us to make a deeper, longer-lasting sacrifice.

In brief, God wants us to go out into the world with the good news of salvation so that the lost might be saved. God also wants all of us to be ready for action on the front lines of spiritual warfare.

Isaiah felt awed beyond words in the presence of the holy Lord. And in response to God's call, the prophet stepped forward. He didn't know exactly what challenges he would face, but he knew God, and that was enough for him.

Courage to Stand. The Lord not only called Isaiah to perform a difficult task, but also gave him the strength to remain faithful to his calling throughout the rest of his life. It all started when Isaiah courageously declared, "Here am I; send me" (Isa. 6:8).

In 1521, Martin Luther appeared before the Diet of Worms, presided over by Charles V, Holy Roman emperor. Luther's life was clearly in danger. He acknowledged that the books considered heretical were his own, but he refused to repudiate them unless convicted that he had strayed from the Scriptures.

One tradition has held that Luther's concluding words in his heroic declaration were "Here I stand. I cannot do otherwise." A solitary person, filled with courage from his fresh reading of Scripture, dared to challenge the might of the church and state in his day. In so doing, he helped to set in motion the Protestant Reformation.

Standing Up for What Is Right. Like Isaiah, those who are truly called by God recognize the importance of living in a morally virtuous manner. Consider Lakita Garth, a former Miss Black California and second runner-up in the Miss Black America Pageant. Garth is the founder of Sex Education Character Support, a public school program that encourages abstinence. Also, she has been featured in numerous publications and on television shows.

Garth, having learned the art of self-control from her mother, admits that she was the only child in her family to escape drugs, gangs, and the consequences of unchaste behavior. Today, she courageously encourages young people to stand up for what is right. It takes courage to advocate curfews and boundaries. It also takes true grit to promote self-control and self-discipline. Like Isaiah, Garth speaks the truth, and so should you!

GIVE THANKS

BACKGROUND SCRIPTURE: Isaiah 12
DEVOTIONAL READING: Psalm 92:1-8

Key Verse: In that day shall ye say, Praise the LORD, call upon his name, declare his doings among the people, make mention that his name is exalted. Isaiah 12:4.

KING JAMES VERSION

ISAIAH 12:1 And in that day thou shalt say, O LORD, I will praise thee: though thou wast angry with me, thine anger is turned away, and thou comfortedst me. 2 Behold, God is my salvation; I will trust, and not be afraid: for the LORD JEHOVAH is my strength and my song; he also is become my salvation. 3 Therefore with joy shall ye draw water out of the wells of salvation.

4 And in that day shall ye say, Praise the LORD, call upon his name, declare his doings among the people, make mention that his name is exalted. 5 Sing unto the LORD; for he hath done excellent things: this is known in all the earth. 6 Cry out and shout, thou inhabitant of Zion: for great is the Holy One of Israel in the midst of thee.

NEW REVISED STANDARD VERSION

ISAIAH 12:1 You will say in that day:
I will give thanks to you, O LORD,
    for though you were angry with me,
your anger turned away,
    and you comforted me.
2 Surely God is my salvation;
    I will trust, and will not be afraid,
for the LORD GOD is my strength and my might;
    he has become my salvation.
3 With joy you will draw water from the wells of salvation. 4 And you will say in that day:
Give thanks to the LORD,
    call on his name;
make known his deeds among the nations;
    proclaim that his name is exalted.
5 Sing praises to the LORD, for he has done
        gloriously;
    let this be known in all the earth.
6 Shout aloud and sing for joy, O royal Zion,
    for great in your midst is the Holy One of Israel.

Monday, June 3	Psalm 92:1-8	*Giving Thanks Is Good*
Tuesday, June 4	Psalm 95:1-7	*Coming into God's Presence with Thanksgiving*
Wednesday, June 5	1 Chronicles 16:8-13	*Remembering God's Wonderful Works*
Thursday, June 6	1 Chronicles 29:10-18	*Giving Thanks and Praise to God*
Friday, June 7	1 Timothy 4:1-5	*Receiving God's Goodness with Thanksgiving*
Saturday, June 8	Luke 17:11-19	*Where Are the Other Nine?*
Sunday, June 9	Isaiah 12	*Giving Thanks to the Lord*

BACKGROUND

Isaiah 12:3 metaphorically refers to God's future act of deliverance as the "wells of salvation" from which the chosen people would "draw" life-giving and life-preserving "water." The latter might also be a historical allusion to the Israelites' time of wandering in the Sinai Desert. For example, Exodus 15:22-25 records an incident at Marah in which the people challenged Moses' leadership. When the Israelites arrived at this locale, they found they could not drink the water because it was bitter. So they began to complain, thinking they would soon die of thirst. Moses cried out to the Lord. And in response to Moses' plea, God instructed Moses to toss a particular piece of wood into the water. When he did so, the water became drinkable.

While the Israelites were encamped at Marah, God issued a decree for them. It was a law that would test them at that moment as well as into the future. The Israelites had just demonstrated their true nature. Instead of trusting God to provide for their needs (such as drinking water), they had manifested their lack of belief by grumbling. The point of the decree was that the Israelites were to rely completely on God. As they did so, He pledged to watch over them, protect them, and meet their most basic needs (vs. 26). An immediate example of God's provision would be the time the Israelites spent encamped at Elim. This was a desert oasis with 12 springs and 70 palm trees (vs. 27). The Hebrew word transliterated *Elim* means "great trees," but earlier it might have meant "gods." Accordingly, some scholars think that Elim could have been a sacred site for nomads who dwelled in that area. In any case, it was here that the Israelites spent some time and were refreshed by the readily available water God provided.

Additional passages of Scripture refer to God in ways that parallel Isaiah 12:3. For example, Psalm 36:9 describes the Lord as the "fountain of life," and Jeremiah 2:13 calls Him the "fountain of living waters." These are the sorts of truths that Isaiah 12 says are one reason for giving thanks to God. Both Old and New Testament Scriptures point out that believers should offer praise to God for His perfections, for His mighty works, and for His gracious benefits. While giving thanks to the Lord is viewed as a mark of His people (see Eph. 1:13-14; Phil. 1:11; 1 Pet. 2:9), one of the marks of unbelievers is their refusal to offer praise and express gratitude to God for His many temporal blessings (see Rom. 1:21; Rev. 16:9).

NOTES ON THE PRINTED TEXT

Isaiah foretold a future time of hope that would be a "day" (Isa. 12:1) of victory and joy, especially as the Lord defeated Israel's foes and restored the chosen people to the Promised Land. Isaiah, in using the personal pronoun rendered "I," spoke as a representative for all the faithful remnant. Centuries earlier, Moses followed a similar approach as he and the Israelites stood on the shoreline of the Red Sea (see Exod. 15:1). For them, it was a moment to celebrate the Lord's vanquishing of Pharaoh and his army. For a future generation of Israelites, the occasion for praise would be God freeing them from such oppressors as Assyria and Babylon.

The chosen people acknowledged that they did not deserve to experience deliverance from the Lord. After all, for many years they refused to heed His commands, as recorded in the Mosaic law (see Isa. 1:4). Understandably, God was "angry" (12:1) with His people and allowed them to be overrun by foreign powers (see 5:25; 9:12). Eventually, the northern kingdom of Israel fell to the Assyrians in 722 B.C. Then, in 586 B.C., the southern kingdom of Judah ended at the hands of the Babylonians. Amazingly, though, the Lord "turned away" (12:1) from His "anger" and once again comforted the faithful remnant (see 40:1-2). God's consolation and compassion were the basis for His people giving Him thanks.

Isaiah 12:2 reveals that one day the covenant community would together proclaim that the God of Israel was its deliverer. Because He alone was the true source of their "salvation," they could have faith in Him and not fear any negative repercussions. Indeed, the sovereign Lord was the fountainhead of His people's "strength" and the basis for their joyous "song." A similar refrain is found in Psalm 118:14, in which the king and the nation joined to express their heartfelt gratitude for the victory the Lord had given them over their enemies. Assuredly, with Him as their defender and protector, they could look to the future with renewed hope.

The latter part of Isaiah 12:2 echoes Exodus 15:2. Here, Moses and his fellow Israelites praised God, whose strength and power had been clear in His overthrow of the Egyptians. Verse 3 aptly refers to the Lord as a "man of war," for He deserved the credit for defeating the forces of Egypt. The chosen people also proclaimed that the "LORD is his name." It's possible this statement was a final taunt to Pharaoh, who had asked earlier, "Who is the LORD, that I should obey his voice to let Israel go?" (5:2). The song of Moses then turned to some of the details of God's victory in the Israelites' behalf. For instance, the people sang about Pharaoh and his army being inundated by the waters of the sea (15:4-7). The faithful remnant also recalled how the Egyptians drowned: "they sank into the bottom as a stone." Moreover, the upright recounted how the Lord, who is "glorious in power," "dashed in pieces" and "hast overthrown" and "consumed . . . as stubble" the Egyptians.

In the future day of promised deliverance, the members of the covenant community would summon one another to express gratitude and offer "praise" (Isa. 12:4) to the Lord. The underlying Hebrew verb means "to declare aloud in public" or "to give open acknowledgment." Moreover, the faithful remnant were directed to "call upon his name." This phrase means to invoke God's name, especially when petitioning Him for help. The motivation for doing so can be found in Exodus 3. For instance, in verse 14, God revealed Himself as "I AM THAT I AM." This phrase signified that God is pure being, and that He is the self-existent One. Verse 15 reveals that the ever-living Lord is also the God of Abraham, Isaac, and Jacob. These patriarchal names would have captured the attention of the Israelites. Assuredly, it was to these individuals that God had first revealed His covenant. So, from one generation to the next, God would be known as the Lord who was faithful to the covenant promises He made to the people of Israel.

The righteous remnant were not just to ask God for help. They were also to declare to the "people" (Isa. 12:4) the Lord's mighty acts and announce that His "name is exalted" (see Pss. 105:1; 148:13). Once more, Moses' song uttered at the Red Sea is brought to mind, in which the faithful remnant chorused that the highly exalted Lord had "triumphed gloriously" (Exod. 15:1). Isaiah 12:5 directs the faithful remnant to "sing" praises to God. The reason calls to mind the statement made in verse 4 about God's mighty acts. In verse 5, they are referred to as "excellent things." Put another way, the Lord had acted marvelously in delivering His beleaguered people from their foes. While the covenant community was to encourage one another with this truth, they were not to keep it to themselves. Instead, they were to publicize God's tremendous deeds to "all the earth." In other words, even Gentiles needed to know what the Lord had done so that they too could come to saving faith in Him. The implication is that the benefits of God's plan of redemption went beyond Israel to include all the inhabitants of the earth (see 11:10).

In 12:6, God's people are referred as citizens of "Zion." The latter is first mentioned in 2 Samuel 5:7 as a Jebusite fortress on a hill. After being captured by David, this fortress was called the City of David. Here Israel's king brought the ark of the covenant, thereby making the hill a sacred site (see 6:10-12). In the Old Testament, Zion is also called "the city of God" (Ps. 46:4), God's place of "rest" (132:14), God's "holy hill" (2:6), the "holy city" (Isa. 48:2), and the "glorious holy mountain" (Dan. 11:45). Eventually, Zion came to stand for the entire city of Jerusalem. Moreover, in early Christian thought, Zion represented the "city of the living God, the heavenly Jerusalem" (Heb. 12:22).

Isaiah 12:6 instructed the covenant community to "cry out and shout" for joy. The reason is that the "Holy One of Israel" was in their midst and acted mightily among them, particularly by setting them free. As 40:1 makes clear, the news of Israel's deliverance was to be a source of comfort to His chosen people. Verse 9 describes it as "good tidings" that was to be proclaimed to "Zion" and "Jerusalem." In view of what the Lord planned to do on behalf of the covenant community, verse 25 asked to whom could anyone "liken" Him. Likewise, who could be His "equal"? The obvious answer is that there was no one like the Lord. After all, He alone was the "Holy One." As such, He ruled unchallenged over the faithful remnant and exercised supreme authority over all the earth. Consequently, there was no power in the entire cosmos that could prevent the Lord from fulfilling His promises of deliverance to His people.

SUGGESTIONS TO TEACHERS

Some of your students may have had great disappointment in their lives. Frustration, resentment, and bitterness may have kept them from developing a close relationship with God. The two songs of praise recorded in Isaiah 12 provide an opportunity to help them enter a new and rewarding relationship with God.

1. REMEMBERING THE PAST. God's people recalled the former days when the Lord was angry with them because of their sin. They also drew comfort from the realization that He had pardoned them (see vs. 1). Likewise, it is appropriate for the class members to take stock of their past misdeeds. But then it is just as important for them to affirm the truth of God's forgiveness and allow themselves to be consoled by His lavish grace.

2. BEING FILLED WITH JOY. Even though the faithful remnant had been dominated by foreign powers, the Lord pledged to set them free. Indeed, this promise was the abundant "wells of salvation" (vs. 3) from which they would obtain real and lasting "joy." God is just as capable of doing "excellent things" (vs. 5) in the lives of the students, beginning with salvation through faith in Christ. In turn, the redeeming presence of God can become the basis for being filled with joy.

3. PRAISING THE LORD. Feeling joyful need not be an entirely inward experience. Consider the Israelites, whom Isaiah instructed to "cry out and shout" (vs. 6) for the great and glorious acts of God they experienced in their lives. Similarly, believers today have the tremendous privilege and responsibility of openly and expressively giving thanks to the Lord. Encourage the adults to regularly offer praise to God and celebrate the gracious ways in which He deals with people and situations.

FOR ADULTS	■ **TOPIC:** Sing and Shout! ■ **QUESTIONS:** 1. What are some specific ways believers can give thanks to the Lord? 2. What are a couple of reasons given in Isaiah 12

for offering praise to God? 3. Why was the Lord initially angry with His people? 4. Why did God eventually turn away from His anger? 5. How can proclaiming that God has "done excellent things" (vs. 5) benefit believers spiritually?

■ ILLUSTRATIONS:

Praising God for Deliverance. For seven long years (1985–1991), friends, colleagues, and loved ones brought their petitions to God to deliver Terry Anderson from his captors. Anderson, an Associated Press employee, was one of several Americans whom Muslims kidnapped in Lebanon and held hostage.

In his book, *Den of Lions,* Anderson says that despite the beatings and deprivation he suffered, his faith in the Lord remained strong. When he was finally released and asked about his feelings toward his abductors, Anderson said, "I am a Christian. I am required to forgive."

Clearly, God had answered the petitions of those who prayed for Anderson, as well as Anderson's own prayers for release. In the aftermath, the former hostage offered "praise" (Isa. 12:1) to the Lord. Whether in churches, on television, or in print, Anderson declared God to be his source of "salvation" (vs. 2).

The Light of Hope. The image can be almost too familiar, even cliché: "Light in the midst of darkness." Nevertheless, this important theme shines throughout Scripture—from creation, with God's "Let there be light" (Gen. 1:3), to the concluding future promise of a new Jerusalem with no need of lamp or sun, for the "Lord God giveth them light" (Rev. 22:5).

So why is it that believers can be so slow to look for God's light of "salvation" (Isa. 12:2) in the midst of darkness? Why do they often resemble foolish mariners, thinking they've become familiar enough with the sea that they should be able to navigate their tiny ships of faith through life's stormy waters themselves?

"Who needs a lighthouse?" some believers boast. "I know where I'm headed!" others retort. But what is their tune when those dark clouds of despair and driving storms of personal tragedy start tossing them around like pieces of paper on the turbulent waves of life? Think about it: How would we react if we saw a lighthouse's brilliant shaft slice through such darkness? Most of us would rightly expect estatic relief and joy. If ever there was a case of the proverbial "light at the end of the tunnel," this would be it!

So, what is it that we're looking for? The believers' final destination is eternal glory with God. And the guiding light is the promise of salvation found in His Word (see Isa. 12:2-3). Mature spiritual vision has to be developed in order to be consistently joyful in difficulties. But it begins with a first glance from the mayhem around us and up to the horizon, especially toward the shores of God's new world. There's no doubt that Isaiah saw such "excellent things" (vs. 5) and urged God's people to proclaim them in "all the earth."

Deep Joy. How do you define deep "joy" (Isa. 12:3)? How is it different from the happiness we feel at a family party, or the excitement at a football game? Does the divine promise of "wells of salvation" really open a new dimension of experience that surpasses everything else?

Sometimes the good news that the Lord is our "salvation" (vs. 2) is rejected as a crutch for weak people. Some individuals think that if you're strong, you don't need a Redeemer. But as we consider the testimony of other believers, it does not appear that their faith is a crutch. Instead, they exude remarkable strength under stress.

The promises of God's Word offer answers to our deepest longings for joy, security, and freedom from worry. The truths of Scripture are not a psychological formula. Instead, they point to a person—the Lord Jesus. For believers, He is their source of eternal deliverance and unmerited pardon.

Ultimately, only Jesus brings deep, satisfying joy that's not dependent on circumstances. Only He gives an inner gladness that sustains us in our darkest hours. It is our privilege to know Him better each day and to make Him "known in all the earth" (vs. 5).

 FOR YOUTH

■ **TOPIC:** Wow! Thanks!

■ **QUESTIONS:** 1. What does it mean to offer praise to the Lord? 2. What are some reasons you can think of to give thanks to God? 3. Why is it important for believers to look to the Lord as their refuge and defense? 4. What are some "excellent things" (Isa. 12:5) God has done for you? 5. In what ways has the "Holy One" (vs. 6) demonstrated His greatness to you?

■ **ILLUSTRATIONS:**

Reasons for Giving Thanks. Derek has been a Christian since he was a child. Though he had his rebellious teenage years, as an adult, he has more faithfully loved and served the Lord. If you asked Derek today what was the greatest source of his personal joy in Christ, he would tell you it was found in his praise for the "excellent things" (Isa. 12:5) the Lord has done.

In Derek's early 20s, he read A. W. Tozer's *The Knowledge of the Holy,* on the attributes of God (see the reference in vs. 6 to the "Holy One of Israel"). As Derek read about the various and unique attributes that God possessed, Derek was continually amazed by the Lord's greatness. When Derek's father died at an early age, and when Derek overcame his own personal challenges and health issues, he found himself praising God, from whom the "wells of salvation" (vs. 3) came.

For Derek, it always seemed right to give thanks and praise to God, regardless of life's circumstances. Derek also believes that praise is the most important gift that a person can give to the Lord. For Derek, it is the obvious expression of one who has seen the greatness of God in some small way.

A Heart of Worship. Bill had memorized the verse when he was a teen in Sunday school years ago: "With joy shall ye draw out of the wells of salvation" (Isa. 12:3). Bill had probably recited that verse dozens of times when he was in high school.

But this Sunday morning, as the young man left for church, the words of that familiar verse were bothering him, especially that word "joy." Despite his salvation in Christ, was Bill truly glad to be going to church this morning, or even most mornings? For some reason, he had developed almost a belligerent attitude toward the Lord and church.

Bill often thought something like the following: "God, I showed up today. Let's see what You can do for me. Can you make the Sunday school lesson interesting? Can You liven up the sermon? Can we sing songs that I know? Can I leave church feeling good this morning?"

Throughout the morning, the Scripture verse continued to bother Bill. The class lesson was about preparing one's heart to "praise the LORD" (vs. 4). And the teacher quoted someone named Richard Foster, who said, "If worship does not change us, it has not been worship. To stand before the 'Holy One' (vs. 6) of eternity is to change. Worship begins in holy expectancy and ends in holy obedience."

As Bill left class to attend the coming worship service, he was already feeling changed. Surprisingly, he was glad to be in church that morning. Moreover, Bill was ready to "sing unto the LORD" (vs. 5) with all his heart.

Finding Joy in the Lord. One of America's great distance runners was Gil Dodds. He was a Christian, and when he signed his autograph, he added "Phil. 4:13." People thought he had run the mile in Philadelphia in four minutes and thirteen seconds, which was hardly a great accomplishment. They did not know that "Phil. 4:13" was a reference to Paul's claim that he could do everything through the Lord Jesus. Gil Dodds tried to give credit to the Savior for his athletic achievements.

However we do it, we must show people that the Lord makes a difference. Ultimately, He is our "salvation" (Isa. 12:2), the One in whom we "trust," and the reason we are not "afraid." His abiding presence is the source of our spiritual "strength" and the motivation for our "song." We are able to express "joy" (vs. 3), for He is the wellspring of our "salvation."

Admittedly, unbelievers are quick to size up Christians when they appear to be under a lot of pressure. That's why it's so important to find joy in the Lord, and to point people to Him for whatever He has enabled us to do. Yes, this is a tough assignment. Yet with Jesus at our side, we can make His name "known in all the earth" (vs. 5).

MEANINGLESS WORSHIP

BACKGROUND SCRIPTURE: Isaiah 29
DEVOTIONAL READING: Luke 8:9-14

Key Verse: This people draw near me with their mouth, and with their lips do honour me, but have removed their heart far from me, and their fear toward me is taught by the precept of men. Isaiah 29:13.

KING JAMES VERSION

ISAIAH 29:9 Stay yourselves, and wonder; cry ye out, and cry: they are drunken, but not with wine; they stagger, but not with strong drink. 10 For the LORD hath poured out upon you the spirit of deep sleep, and hath closed your eyes: the prophets and your rulers, the seers hath he covered. 11 And the vision of all is become unto you as the words of a book that is sealed, which men deliver to one that is learned, saying, Read this, I pray thee: and he saith, I cannot; for it is sealed: 12 And the book is delivered to him that is not learned, saying, Read this, I pray thee: and he saith, I am not learned. 13 Wherefore the Lord said, Forasmuch as this people draw near me with their mouth, and with their lips do honour me, but have removed their heart far from me, and their fear toward me is taught by the precept of men: 14 Therefore, behold, I will proceed to do a marvellous work among this people, even a marvellous work and a wonder: for the wisdom of their wise men shall perish, and the understanding of their prudent men shall be hid. 15 Woe unto them that seek deep to hide their counsel from the LORD, and their works are in the dark, and they say, Who seeth us? and who knoweth us? 16 Surely your turning of things upside down shall be esteemed as the potter's clay: for shall the work say of him that made it, He made me not? or shall the thing framed say of him that framed it, He had no understanding?

NEW REVISED STANDARD VERSION

ISAIAH 29:9 Stupefy yourselves and be in a stupor,
    blind yourselves and be blind!
Be drunk, but not from wine;
    stagger, but not from strong drink!
10 For the LORD has poured out upon you
    a spirit of deep sleep;
he has closed your eyes, you prophets,
    and covered your heads, you seers.
11 The vision of all this has become for you like the words of a sealed document. If it is given to those who can read, with the command, "Read this," they say, "We cannot, for it is sealed." 12 And if it is given to those who cannot read, saying, "Read this," they say, "We cannot read."
13 The Lord said:
Because these people draw near with their mouths
    and honor me with their lips,
    while their hearts are far from me,
and their worship of me is a human commandment
    learned by rote;
14 so I will again do
    amazing things with this people,
    shocking and amazing.
The wisdom of their wise shall perish,
    and the discernment of the discerning shall be
    hidden.
15 Ha! You who hide a plan too deep for the LORD,
    whose deeds are in the dark,
    and who say, "Who sees us? Who knows us?"
16 You turn things upside down!
    Shall the potter be regarded as the clay?
Shall the thing made say of its maker,
    "He did not make me";
or the thing formed say of the one who formed it,
    "He has no understanding"?

Monday, June 10	Isaiah 1:10-17	*Fruitless Worship*
Tuesday, June 11	Isaiah 2:5-17	*Worshiping Our Own Achievements*
Wednesday, June 12	Isaiah 58:1-7	*Lives Untouched by Religious Observances*
Thursday, June 13	Jeremiah 13:1-11	*Refusing to Listen*
Friday, June 14	Zechariah 7:8-14	*Tuning Out God*
Saturday, June 15	Luke 8:9-15	*Receiving the Word*
Sunday, June 16	Isaiah 29:9-16	*Hearts Far from God*

BACKGROUND

In Isaiah 29:5-8, the Lord's spokesperson foretold God's gracious deliverance of Jerusalem. As history shows, in 701 B.C., the Assyrians destroyed dozens of towns in Judah and seemed bound to finish the job of demolishing Jerusalem. Undoubtedly, the invaders then would have dissolved the nation. But the Lord did not want the Assyrians to go that far. While they were camped around Jerusalem, God miraculously destroyed a large part of the army in one night (see 2 Kings 19:35-36; 2 Chron. 32:21; Isa. 37:36-37). Isaiah prophesied that before this event, at the very moment the invaders were about to destroy Jerusalem, God would suddenly move against them in judgment, and the city would be saved.

Isaiah 29:5 says the enemies would become "like small dust." Verse 6 uses dramatic imagery to depict the all-powerful Lord's judgment as being accompanied by thunder, an earthquake, a loud noise, a windstorm, and consuming flames of fire (see Exod. 19:16-19; Ps. 18:7-15; Hab. 3:3-7). The prophet aptly compared Jerusalem's deliverance from the attacking "multitude" (Isa. 29:7) to a person waking up from a nightmare. In contrast, when the invaders figuratively "awaketh" (vs. 8) from the siege, they would feel as though they had dreamed of eating and drinking, but were still hungry and thirsty. Put another way, even though the aggressors were determined to overrun "mount Zion" (or Jerusalem), they would leave without achieving their goal. In short, they would feel dissatisfied.

NOTES ON THE PRINTED TEXT

After describing the siege and deliverance of Jerusalem, Isaiah again began discussing the deplorable spiritual condition of the city's inhabitants. This was necessary, for it was their sin that would lead God to use the Assyrians to judge His people. Isaiah exhorted the wayward residents to be astounded concerning the judgment the Lord would bring on them (Isa. 29:9). After all, from a divine perspective, they were completely blind, drunk, and staggering. Expressed differently, the chosen people were in a spiritual stupor when it came to heeding the Lord's directives and being sensitive to His will.

Verse 10 compares sleep to a liquid that the Lord poured out on His wayward people. The consequence of this divine action was spiritual dullness among Jerusalem's residents. Furthermore, He closed the eyes of the prophets and covered the heads of the seers. The parallel way in which the second half of the verse is arranged indicates that all of the city's acclaimed visionaries were spiritually blind. The indictment is that even the most esteemed religious leaders failed to pay attention to what God repeatedly tried to tell them.

The preceding verse is cited in Romans 11:8. In verse 7, Paul explained that the majority of the Israelites had tried to obtain righteousness by keeping God's law. Yet, because no one could be justified by human effort, the chosen people failed to obtain reconciliation with God. In turn, these individuals became "blinded." To illustrate the dire nature of this condition, Paul quoted from Deuteronomy 29:4 and Isaiah 29:10. These verses indicate that Israel's condition resulted from spiritual drowsiness, judicial blindness, and deafness to the things of God (Rom. 11:8). Consequently, the people became impervious to spiritual truth. Futhermore, this hardening had continued "unto this day" (that is, from Isaiah's time to Paul's day). To make clear the results of divine hardening, Paul appealed to Psalm 69:22-23 (Rom. 11:9-10). The apostle maintained that because the Israelites did not respond to God's truth in repentance, their eyes were darkened and their backs were bent under the heavy weight of their own guilt and punishment.

"Vision" (Isa. 29:11) denotes the prophetic revelation God had given to Isaiah. "Book" refers to documents made from sheets of leather, papyrus, or parchment that people joined together in long rolls (typically from 10 to 12 inches wide and as much as 35 feet long). The ends of these scrolls were then attached to two wooden cylinders and rolled up from left to right. Isaiah declared that his own messages were like a sealed document to the rebellious inhabitants of Jerusalem and Judah.

Isaiah imagined a situation in which a scroll containing his prophetic oracles was handed over to a person who could read (for example, a religious leader). Then, when he was politely asked to disclose the document's contents, he would respond that he was unable to do so because he found the scroll to be "sealed." A variant of this scenario involved giving the document to someone else who could not read (for instance, a common person). And when this individual was asked to do so, he would state that he was illiterate (vs. 12). These two imaginary episodes illustrated the refusal of all the Judahites to pay attention to the divine oracles Isaiah declared. The prophet must have found it frustrating to lay out warnings and instructions that the people needed to know, and then to have them spurn him.

Though the residents of Jerusalem and the inhabitants of Judah rejected Isaiah's prophecies, they did maintain their religion. The Lord acknowledged that His people declared with their "mouth" (vs. 13) that they were devoted to Him. And "with their lips" they said all sorts of reverent things about Him. But God declared that the people's ritual honoring of Him was a sham. In particular, they were disloyal in their hearts (that is, the fountain of their thoughts, emotions, aspirations, and endeavors). Moreover, their displays of worship consisted of humanly devised rituals. Just as the people had spurned Isaiah's oracles, they also refused to turn to the Lord in heartfelt obedience (see Isa. 58:2-5; Hos. 7:14; 8:1-2; 10:1-2; Mic. 3:11).

Centuries later, Jesus applied Isaiah 29:13 to the Pharisees (see Matt. 15:7-9; Mark 7:6-8). The Savior correctly sized up the religious leaders as being "hypocrites." The underlying Greek term originally referred to actors who wore masks on stage as they played different characters. When applied to the Pharisees and scribes, the term meant they were not genuinely religious. They were merely playing a part for all to watch (see Jas. 1:26-27). Jesus, in quoting Isaiah 29:13, declared that even though the Pharisees venerated God with their words, they showed contempt for Him by their thoughts and actions. They made their worship of God a farce by replacing divine commands with humanly constructed injunctions. Jesus was making it clear that it was wrong to ignore the Lord's specific laws and substitute one's own self-generated traditions.

In 1446 B.C., the chosen people witnessed the awesome wonders of God as He delivered them from Egypt. Now the residents of Jerusalem and the inhabitants of Judah would again be astounded with amazing wonders. There is a bit of irony in Isaiah 29:14, for the marvelous work of God would involve the judgment, not the deliverance, of the Judahites. In short, the Lord would use His awesome power to deal firmly with their rebellion. In this way, He would disprove the alleged prudence of the "wise" and discredit the supposed insight of the "prudent." The immediate historical context seems to be counsel given by advisers in Judah's royal court advocating that illicit alliances be made with the nation's powerful, pagan neighbors.

In 1 Corinthians 1:19, Paul cited Isaiah 29:14. Previously, in 1 Corinthians 1:18, the apostle stated that the message he proclaimed centered on the Cross. Paul also revealed that though the good news about the Messiah has the power to save lives eternally, to unbelievers it is sheer folly. Moreover, as long as unbelievers reject the Gospel as being foolish, they are doomed to perish (vs. 18). But to those who are saved through their faith in God, the message of the cross is a demonstration of God's power. Then, in verse 19, Paul quoted from Isaiah 29:14 to point out that the Father used the good news about His Son to destroy the wisdom of the worldly wise and to annihilate the understanding of those who imagined themselves clever.

Isaiah interjected a "woe" (Isa. 29:15). This time the declaration of doom was upon those corrupt leaders and people who in their skewed thinking actually believed they could second-guess the Lord and hide their misdeeds from Him. They falsely imagined that by performing their iniquities in secret, they would remain immune from detection and prosecution (see Pss. 10:11; 64:5-6). Isaiah represented the folly of questioning God in the personification of a pot doubting the potter (Isa.

29:16; see 45:9). The point is that God knew all that the wicked were doing and would judge them for their pride and rebellion.

As before, judgment is couched in the context of God's grace. Isaiah 29:17-24 reminds us to look beyond the dark days of Assyria to a time of future restoration for the faithful remnant of Israel. In the future kingdom of the Messiah, the once devastated land would become fertile. Moreover, the wicked would be banished from the Lord's presence. Also, He would elevate His chosen people and their nation to a place of unparalleled prominence.

In Romans 9:20, Paul cited Isaiah 29:16. Previously, in Romans 9:19, the apostle anticipated a question that might surface in his readers' minds. If God hardens whomever He wishes to harden, then how can He hold individuals responsible for their actions? Also, if God's will is irresistible, then such blame appears misplaced. Paul responded in verse 20 by rebuking the arrogant attitude with which these sorts of questions were asked. The apostle did not condemn honest inquiry. Instead, he reprimanded those who sought to escape personal responsibility by placing the blame for their sin upon God. This type of blame shifting is common among people who refuse to acknowledge their transgressions. To illustrate his point, Paul drew an analogy between God and a potter. The apostle argued in verse 21 that the potter has the right to make out of one lump of clay some pottery for noble purposes and some for common use. Just as the potter is "sovereign" over clay, so God, the Creator, is sovereign over all created beings.

SUGGESTIONS TO TEACHERS

Your first task in teaching this week's lesson is to help your students understand the conflict between Isaiah and the religious elite of his day. More importantly, you will want to help class members see the implications of this disagreement for their own lives. In what ways today do we still imitate the hypocritical attitudes and practices of spiritual frauds? How can we reverse those habits so that we can live as Jesus' true disciples?

1. A COMPROMISED COMMITMENT. The Judahites' failure to be loyal to the Lord led them to engage in evil practices. Moreover, they were in such a spiritual stupor that it was as if they had become drunk, though without wine, and staggered, yet not due to taking in a drop of alcohol (see Isa. 29:9).

2. SPIRITUAL BLINDNESS. The twisted thinking and perverted ways of the leaders and people of Judah eroded their sense of living uprightly before the Lord. In short, they had become spiritually blinded to God's commands (see vs. 10). What about us? How conscious are we of living in a virtuous way in God's sight?

3. AN EXCESSIVE FOCUS ON EXTERNALS. The religious leaders of Judah followed the tradition they had received, and they passed it on to their contemporaries (see vs. 13). Some of today's leaders and peers loudly repeat the same sort of message: "Make sure you look good. Appearance is all-important."

4. A DIRE OUTCOME. Because the people's ritual honoring of God was a sham, He would astound the hypocrites with the awesome power of His judgment (see vs. 14). Our commitment to the Lord must be exhibited in the way we live. Faith is what we do, not merely what we believe (Jas. 2:18).

FOR ADULTS	■ TOPIC: More Than Words

■ **QUESTIONS:** 1. What would cause God's people to be astounded (see Isa. 29:9)? 2. Why did Judah's religious leaders fail to pay attention to what God repeatedly tried to tell them? 3. In what sense were Isaiah's messages like a closed book to the rebellious inhabitants of Jerusalem and Judah? 4. How can believers avoid elevating humanly devised traditions over God's Word? 5. What sources of spiritual insight from God can you use to grow stronger in your devotion to Him?

■ **ILLUSTRATIONS:**

Experiencing Sin's Consequences. Most of us probably remember the first time we ran afoul of one of the laws of the universe. Perhaps we touched a hot stove and got burned. Or maybe we fell off a bicycle and got some scraped knees and elbows. Or possibly we fell out of a tree and broke an arm.

The result of our pain was discovering how things work in the world. We learned about the qualities of heat and gravity. However, sometimes it takes us awhile to realize that the universe also has moral laws, and that we suffer when we break them.

Biblical history confirms what we learn by experience—we cannot escape God's moral laws. Consider the people of Judah. Though they claimed to worship the Lord, they violated God's commands and thought there would be no consequences (see Isa. 29:13). Civil leaders, religious officials, and common people alike indulged in sin. Then, the Judge of the universe decided to act, and Judah suffered the consequences (see vs. 14).

God's character has not changed. No amount of wishful thinking can remove His holiness and justice. Judah's eventual exile should send us a powerful message to confess and repent before it is too late.

A Matter of the Heart. Roger remembered how impressed he was after only a few encounters. It was the first church that had asked him to serve as senior pastor, and Jack was one of the congregational leaders.

Roger, who grew up in a pastor's home, recalled the people with whom his parents worked. Roger had seen every kind of church leader one could imagine. Some were wonderful, and some were scoundrels. Some served with God's heart, while others merely paid Him lip service (see Isa. 29:13).

Roger admits that he was a bit skeptical when he accepted the invitation to lead a small congregation in an idyllic farming community of fruit orchards. Would these leaders be like some who served with Roger's father? Would they be people whose actions looked righteous, but who replaced divine commands with humanly constructed injunctions?

Many years before the two met, Jack was a leader who had received a deep understanding of the ways of God. Jack ended up serving with Roger for more than a decade, and Roger never grew tired of watching the grace Jack shared with those who were struggling through the issues of their lives and faith.

There were countless examples Roger could recall of Jack's genuine devotion working with actions. He ended up being instrumental in modeling to a small flock of believers that pure faith was truly a matter of the heart.

Difficult Discovery. A White House correspondent for a television station made a grueling trip to Germany to cover the president's visit there. The reporter came back with a case of laryngitis. But he dismissed his hoarseness, declaring that throat problems were an occupational hazard. The correspondent had dealt with a husky voice and throat maladies many times before, and made light of his laryngitis. But the hoarseness persisted.

Instead of taking it easy, the reporter gave several speeches around the country and tried to maintain his busy broadcasting schedule. But when the throat problem continued, he finally went to a specialist, who discovered two nodes behind his vocal cords. Thankfully, the nodes proved to be benign and not cancerous. The physician said the nodes might disappear on their own if the correspondent would remain silent for five weeks. But the reporter was not enthusiastic about this prescription. "If I don't talk, I don't eat," he groused.

This reporter experienced the results of refusing to obey simple health rules in caring for his voice. Similarly, the people of Judah experienced the consequences of refusing to obey the moral requirements of God (see Isa. 29:14). Disobedience always brings disappointment and sometimes disaster.

 FOR YOUTH

■ TOPIC: Are You for Real?

■ QUESTIONS: 1. Why would God's people be characterized by drunkenness and staggering? 2. What was the cause of the spiritual dullness among Jerusalem's residents? 3. In what sense were the Judahites guilty of paying lip service to God? 4. How is it possible for believers to go through the motions of worshiping God and yet be guilty of disobeying Him? 5. If our lives are inconsistent with our faith, how does that impact our influence among the unsaved?

■ ILLUSTRATIONS:

Here Come the Consequences! A gang of kids sullenly scuffed along the platform at the train station. The train they wanted to board had just pulled away, and they fell into griping and accusing one another. They suffered the consequences of being late.

Like the people of Judah in Isaiah's day, we'll eternally suffer if we fail to realize the importance of obeying God. Serving Him is more than paying lip service (see Isa. 29:13). The Lord wants us to be sincere in the way we honor Him.

When we're young, it's easy to think we'll pay attention to God when we get older. However, if we neglect Him now, there is a strong possibility that we may never turn our hearts to Him in faith. Thankfully, God's grace is always available when we reach out to Him in faith. But we must do so now, for we do not know when a time of reckoning will come.

Acting Like a Believer. As a young woman, Sharon knew how to act like a believer. She taught Sunday school, tithed regularly, and even attended prayer meetings every week. In short, she claimed to worship God, but her heart was far from Him (see Isa. 29:13).

So how did Sharon, in the later years of her life, end up so distant from God's ways? If you were to talk with her, she'd tell you: "Oh sure, I used to do all that stuff just to fit in—to look good around all the other believers. But my heart was never in any of it. I just decided I wasn't going to live that lie anymore. Hey, at least I'm living authentically now."

Sadly, instead of bringing her heart in line with her faith-like actions, Sharon simply let her actions fall in line with her faithless heart. She had the right idea about living authentically, but she chose the wrong direction.

Living a lie is never a good idea. But God longs to transform our hearts so we can live joyfully, freely, and willingly within His righteous ways.

Lacking a Suitable Reference Point. Several years ago, the Pennsylvania Department of Transportation set out to replace a bridge. After demolishing the old structure, workers began building a new one, laboring from each side of the river.

Everything seemed to be proceeding nicely until it was discovered that the two spans arching out from the opposite banks were not in line with each other. In fact, by the time the two sides came closer, one was wide of the other by 13 feet! Investigators finally discovered that the supervisors of the work crews on the two sides of the river had each been using their own reference point.

In life, people and nations alike must rely on an external moral reference point (namely, God and His Word). The people of Judah and their civil and religious leaders refused to acknowledge this truth and suffered accordingly.

THE GLORIOUS NEW CREATION

BACKGROUND SCRIPTURE: Isaiah 65
DEVOTIONAL READING: Isaiah 42:1-9

Key Verse: I create new heavens and a new earth: and the former shall not be remembered, nor come into mind. But be ye glad and rejoice for ever in that which I create. Isaiah 65:17-18.

KING JAMES VERSION

ISAIAH 65:17 For, behold, I create new heavens and a new earth: and the former shall not be remembered, nor come into mind. 18 But be ye glad and rejoice for ever in that which I create: for, behold, I create Jerusalem a rejoicing, and her people a joy. 19 And I will rejoice in Jerusalem, and joy in my people: and the voice of weeping shall be no more heard in her, nor the voice of crying. 20 There shall be no more thence an infant of days, nor an old man that hath not filled his days: for the child shall die an hundred years old; but the sinner being an hundred years old shall be accursed. 21 And they shall build houses, and inhabit them; and they shall plant vineyards, and eat the fruit of them. . . . 23 They shall not labour in vain, nor bring forth for trouble; for they are the seed of the blessed of the LORD, and their offspring with them. 24 And it shall come to pass, that before they call, I will answer; and while they are yet speaking, I will hear. 25 The wolf and the lamb shall feed together, and the lion shall eat straw like the bullock: and dust shall be the serpent's meat. They shall not hurt nor destroy in all my holy mountain, saith the LORD.

NEW REVISED STANDARD VERSION

ISAIAH 65:17 For I am about to create new heavens
and a new earth;
the former things shall not be remembered
or come to mind.
18 But be glad and rejoice forever
in what I am creating;
for I am about to create Jerusalem as a joy,
and its people as a delight.
19 I will rejoice in Jerusalem,
and delight in my people;
no more shall the sound of weeping be heard in it,
or the cry of distress.
20 No more shall there be in it
an infant that lives but a few days,
or an old person who does not live out a lifetime;
for one who dies at a hundred years will be
considered a youth,
and one who falls short of a hundred will be
considered accursed.
21 They shall build houses and inhabit them;
they shall plant vineyards and eat their fruit. . . .
23 They shall not labor in vain,
or bear children for calamity;
for they shall be offspring blessed by the LORD—
and their descendants as well.
24 Before they call I will answer,
while they are yet speaking I will hear.
25 The wolf and the lamb shall feed together,
the lion shall eat straw like the ox;
but the serpent—its food shall be dust!
They shall not hurt or destroy
on all my holy mountain,
says the LORD.

4

BACKGROUND

The Book of Isaiah reveals that God's chosen people had rebelled against Him. Yet the prophet still prayed that God would not be angry with them forever (64:8-9). Isaiah petitioned the Lord to take pity on His people, their nation, and their temple. Isaiah implored God to glorify Himself by allowing the faithful remnant to return to Judah and rebuild their devastated nation (vss. 10-12). In the remaining two chapters of Isaiah the Lord gave His answer to the prayer of His spokesperson. Israel failed to stay close to the Lord, though they sought Him in a superficial way. So in response to Isaiah's prayer, the Lord declared that He would reveal Himself to the people who had not even sought Him (namely, the Gentiles; 65:1).

God had repeatedly reached out with love to His stubborn and sinful people. Yet they rebelled against Him by offering sacrifices and burning incense to idols (vs. 3). They sat in burial graves to consult the spirits of the dead, and they devoured ceremonially unclean meat (vs. 4). Despite the people's claims of being pious, they were an irritation to the Lord (vs. 5). Yet, in answer to Isaiah's rhetorical question (64:12), God promised not to remain silent. He would punish His people for their rebellion and idolatry, but He would not destroy the entire nation. Just as there might be a few good grapes in a cluster, so there would be a faithful remnant in Israel (65:6-8).

God assured Isaiah that His chosen people would be blessed with many descendants, they would be restored to their homeland (vs. 9), and the entire region would be transformed (vs. 10). Ironically, those who worshiped (as the NRSV relates) the pagan gods of "Fortune" (vs. 11) and "Destiny" would meet theirs, dying by the sword, for they spurned God's love and rejected His commandments (vs. 12). In this chapter, the contrasting fates of those who follow God and those who don't is apparent: The all-powerful Lord would bless the upright with joy, abundance, and life. However, He would bring emptiness, anguish, and death to the wicked (vss. 13-16).

NOTES ON THE PRINTED TEXT

Isaiah's final prophecies most likely applied in part to the exiles returned from Babylon. But his language clearly goes beyond any fulfillment in ancient history. For instance, notice that earlier, while prophesying about end-time judgments,

Isaiah had said, "The heavens shall vanish away like smoke, and the earth shall wax old like a garment" (51:6). Now the prophet recorded God's declaration that in place of the old heavens and earth He would create "new heavens and a new earth" (65:17). So glorious would the new creation be that God said "the former things shall not be remembered, nor come into mind." Those former things, such as weeping and crying, would give way to new things, including gladness, rejoicing, and delight.

Isaiah 65:17 reminds us of Revelation 21:1, where the apostle John declared that he saw "a new heaven and a new earth." These are total replacements for their old counterparts, which God had destroyed. He evidently did this to eliminate any corrupting presence or influence of sin (see 2 Pet. 3:7, 10-13, which was covered in lesson 13 from last quarter). But John was not thinking merely of a world free of sin and hardness of heart. More importantly, the apostle's vision was of a creation new in all its qualities.

The Lord commanded His people to "be ye glad and rejoice for ever" (Isa. 65:18). They were to express joy over what God would create. He pledged to create the new Jerusalem as a place of happiness, and the people inhabiting it would be a source of joy for the community of the redeemed. God, too, would find joy in the new creation. He would "rejoice in Jerusalem, and joy in [His] people" (vs. 19).

What a contrast this is with God's previous dismay over His chosen nation. In the holy city, no one would ever again hear the "voice of weeping" and of "crying." In the New Testament, John revealed that in the eternal state, God will permanently dwell, or tabernacle, among the redeemed of all ages. They will be His people, and He will be their God. Also, five scourges of human existence will not exist in the eternal state—tears, death, sorrow, crying, and pain. The new order of things will eliminate all these forms of sadness (Rev. 21:3-4).

In Isaiah 65:20-25, the prophet described what the new creation would be like for God's people. Expositors differ over whether these verses refer to the heavenly state (the metaphorical view) or to a future period in which Christ will rule on earth (the literal view). Regardless of whether one takes the passage metaphorically or literally, it contains four promises of blessing. Those who would live in the newly created Jerusalem (1) would have long lives, (2) would not labor in vain, (3) would be speedily answered by God when they pray, and (4) would live in an environment without hostility.

Seen together, these blessings apparently indicate that the effects of the Fall would be reversed in the new heavens and new earth and new Jerusalem. The first blessing is longevity (vs. 20). The Old Testament reports that lives stretching to hundreds of years were the rule in early human history. Similarly, in the new creation, infant mortality would drop to zero; all would live to adulthood. Moreover, a tombstone recording a life span of 100 years would not be remarkable for denoting a long life, as in our day, but for denoting a short life.

The second blessing in the new creation is profitable toil (Isa. 65:21-23). The people of Isaiah's time lived and died with the vagaries of agricultural life. Droughts and pestilence caused great damage. The pagans prayed to fertility and weather gods and goddesses. But the Lord's chosen people were supposed to trust Him to supply all their needs.

After the Fall, God's curse on humanity included the declaration that labor to earn food would be difficult (see Gen. 3:17-19). In the new creation, people would continue to work, but they would have no worries about not receiving the fruits of their labor. Others (perhaps unscrupulous rich people or invaders) would never take what they have earned with their own hands. Generation after generation, the people of God would be blessed.

Isaiah related these truths in terms that people living in his day could understand. For instance, God's people would live in the houses they built and eat the fruit of their vineyards (Isa. 65:21). The Lord would prevent invaders from taking these from them. In fact, God would enable His people to live a long life and enjoy the "work of their hands" (vs. 22). The labor of the redeemed community would not be in vain, and their children would not be doomed to calamity (vs. 23). After all, the Lord would bless them and their children with safety, health, and prosperity. Such blessings would be both physical and spiritual in nature.

The third blessing in the new creation is answered prayer (vs. 24). In the Garden of Eden, Adam and Eve enjoyed the immediate presence and conversation of the Lord. Similarly, while people in the new creation are praying, even before they make the request, God would answer them. This describes a close fellowship between God and people. Such is echoed in Revelation 22:3-4. The apostle John noted that in the new creation the Father and the Son will be seated on their thrones, and the redeemed will worship and serve them continually. God will establish unbroken communion with His people, and He will claim them as His own.

Of noteworthy mention is the fourth blessing in the new creation, namely, peace (Isa. 65:25). The Fall introduced hostility into the world, and murder was committed by the next generation. But in the new creation even the animals would stop preying on one another. Perfect harmony would reign. We see this expectation for wellness and wholeness repeated in the New Testament. God promised to give water from the life-giving fountain to everyone who was thirsty (Rev. 21:6). This pledge is a vivid reminder of the refreshment and satisfaction believers would enjoy in heaven. In the eternal state, God would satisfy the yearnings of the soul. This assurance was grounded in the Lord's own nature. Those who overcame in this life would receive an eternal inheritance and an eternal relationship. They would be the eternal children of the eternal God (vs. 7).

In the new Jerusalem, God would be worshiped face-to-face. The city would be a cosmopolitan place, where redeemed humanity in all its cultural diversity would live together in peace. God would vindicate the faith of the redeemed by not permitting anything immoral or wicked to enter the holy city (vss. 22-27). In previous chapters of Isaiah, the prophet had foretold both the demise of Judah and the exile of the nation's inhabitants to Babylon. But he also foresaw their return to Judah. Beyond that, Isaiah saw the glorious future awaiting all the redeemed, namely, intimacy and unbroken communion with the Lord.

It's no wonder Paul declared, "I reckon that the sufferings of this present time are not worthy to be compared with the glory which shall be revealed in us" (Rom. 8:18). Currently, we see the world as it is—physically decaying and spiritually infected with sin. But Christians do not need to be pessimistic, for they have hope for future glory. They look forward to the new heavens and new earth that God has promised, and they wait for God's new order that pledges to free the world of sin, sickness, and evil.

SUGGESTIONS TO TEACHERS

Though God's people may have been at their lowest ebb emotionally during their exile in Babylon, they had from Isaiah a message of tremendous hope. The Lord told them about a new creation, setting the stage for His people to remain optimistic because He would ultimately be victorious. He would eventually rescue and save all those who persevered in their faith, hope, and trust in Him. Believers today can draw the following from this prophecy of hope.

1. THINGS WILL GET BETTER FOR US. Whatever pain or sorrow or hurts that we're facing right now are merely tests of our endurance and perseverance. Our sole task is to keep our eyes on the Lord and listen to Him through His Word as He provides direction and protection for our individual lives. If we endure and persevere in our faith, we have the sure and certain hope of being rewarded—of being the recipients of God's ultimate and fantastic promises.

2. THINGS WILL GET BETTER FOR OUR CHILDREN. Past generations of people have been quite concerned about making things better for future generations. Much of this concern has been directed toward efforts at making future generations better physically, mentally, emotionally, and (especially) financially. God puts back in the hearts of His people the desire for their children to be better off spiritually. And if this is a concern of our present generation, God promises that future generations of our children will be blessed by Him with eternal peace.

3. THINGS WILL GET BETTER FOR GOD'S PEOPLE. The supreme hope for the culmination of the future kingdom of God is that His people will be better off because the effects of sin will be eliminated. God's grace will overrule all wickedness, and His goodness and righteousness will create an atmosphere of peace and prosperity, where all the spiritual members of His family will be blessed.

■ TOPIC: Nothing's Going to Be the Same

■ QUESTIONS: 1. What do you think will happen to this present creation when God brings the new heavens and new earth into existence? 2. What sort of emotions will prevail among the inhabitants of the new Jerusalem? 3. How will the lives of the redeemed be different in the future time of glory? 4. In light of these truths, how might the believers' idea of God sometimes be too small? 5. How can the hope for a new heavens and a new earth become a purifying factor in your life as a Christian?

■ ILLUSTRATIONS:

A New Creation. On May 22, 2011, an extremely powerful tornado struck Joplin, Missouri. The twister leveled nearly a third of the city, killed scores of people, and injured hundreds of others. Amid the tangled remains of large buildings, residental homes, and cars, an elderly man looked at his ruined house and exclaimed, "This was all I had. Now it's gone!"

For many people life is limited to their possessions. They have no life beyond their homes, furniture, and cars. As Christians, we believe there is more to life than mere possessions, but it's hard to define what we mean. Paul got it right when he noted that, through faith in Christ, we become "a new creature" (2 Cor. 5:17). "Old things are passed away; behold, all things are become new."

This truth explains why we look at everything in life from a new perspective. It's also what Isaiah urged God's people to do. Through the prophet, God gave His promise to create new heavens and a new earth, and a new Jerusalem. In fact, those in the new Jerusalem would have long life, profitable work, answers to their prayers, and peace.

Enduring Hope in God's Promise. Victor Hugo, in his story "Ninety-Three," tells of a ship caught in a dangerous storm on the high seas. At the height of the storm, the frightened sailors heard a terrible crashing noise below the deck. They knew at once that this new noise came from a cannon, part of the ship's cargo, that had broken loose.

The cannon was moving back and forth with the swaying of the ship, crashing into the side of the ship with terrible impact. Knowing that it could cause the ship to sink, two brave sailors volunteered to make the dangerous attempt to retie the loose cannon. They knew the danger of a shipwreck from the cannon was greater than the fury of the storm.

That is like human life. Storms of life may blow about us, but it is not these exterior storms that pose the gravest danger. It is the terrible corruption that can exist within us that can overwhelm us. The furious storm outside may be overwhelming, but what is going on inside can pose the greater threat to our lives. Our only hope lies in conquering that wild enemy. Trusting God and believing His promise of a new heavens and a new earth (see Isa. 65:17) is our only hope of stilling the tempest that can harm our souls and cripple our lives.

No More Weeping. "God, where were you in Paris?" asked a church leader named Josef Homeyer, his voice quavering with emotion as he addressed 350 people at a worship service in Hanover, Germany, after a Concorde airliner burst into flames and crashed outside Paris on July 25, 2000, killing 113 people, most of them German tourists, Reuters reported. "Why have you deserted us? Our hearts are heavy."

Homeyer then reminded the mourners of the hope of a "new heavens and a new earth" (Isa. 65:17). After him, a church leader named Horst Hirschler reminded the audience of a similar tragic incident two years earlier, when a high-speed train crashed near Hanover, taking the lives of more than 100 people. One minute vacationers were happily looking forward to the time of their lives, and the next minute they were faced with death, the pastor said. "What a tragic transformation."

The only real consolation is that even the Son of God had asked His Father in heaven, "Why hast thou forsaken me?" before He died on the cross, Hirschler said. The minister assured his audience that Jesus Christ is with those who are feeling desperate and who mourn over the loss of their loved ones. "You will never fall deeper than into God's hand."

FOR YOUTH

■ **TOPIC:** In with the New!

■ **QUESTIONS:** 1. In your opinion, what are the best promises that God made to His people in Isaiah 65:17-25? 2. What feelings or emotions do you think this prophecy was meant to stir up among God's people? 3. Once God creates the new heavens and new earth, what do you think life will be like for us as believers? 4. In what ways does this prophecy call to mind the Genesis account of creation and the Fall? 5. What does Isaiah's vision of the future mean for us?

■ **ILLUSTRATIONS:**

Perfect World. A radical change takes place when adolescents trust in Christ. They experience new life. This means the Spirit graciously replaces their fallen human nature with a new one. Their relationship with God is restored, obedience to and dependence on the Lord supplant their rebelliousness and unbelief, and their hatred is exchanged for unconditional love.

For some youth the idea of being given new life sounds bizarre. For others, the advantages of being born again appear too good to be true. Finally, there are individuals who feel smugly comfortable in their life of sin and do not want to change.

The world might scoff at the idea of receiving new life in Christ and the promise of a "new heavens and a new earth" (Isa. 65:17). However, saved teens know from God's

Word that it is a reality. They also need to know that inner renewal cannot be purchased with money or earned by doing good deeds. The lost must put their faith in Christ in order to experience the new birth.

Former Things Shall Not Be Remembered. Several years ago, Pastor Jeff discovered a tragedy at the parsonage that left his daughter, Gracie, in tears. The minister had left a little lavender-colored ceramic planter out on the deck. But this little planter was special. It had "Baby" molded into the side, and when it was wound up, a music box inside played a lullaby.

This planter had been given to Pastor Jeff's family 11 years before by some dear friends just after Gracie was born. The minister surmised that it must have been the rising and falling of the temperatures over several seasons that somehow shattered that little treasure into multiple pieces. His daughter glared at the pieces in her hands, tears streaming from her eyes at her sense of the loss.

We all feel saddened when an earthly treasure is taken from us. But the hope of future glory in heaven can go a long way toward helping us through a trying situation. The hope of being restored to their homeland along with the hope for "new heavens and a new earth" (Isa. 65:17) would help the exiled Jews to endure their disastrous circumstances in Babylon.

A Glorious Future. Charlie Brown looks worried. But Lucy, who is sitting at her psychiatrist stand, explains that worrying is a waste of time. "You can't worry about the future, Charlie Brown," Lucy says. "You can't worry about next year or next month or next week or even tomorrow, for that matter."

As Charlie Brown listens attentively, Lucy continues, "And you certainly shouldn't worry about the past. What's done is done. If you have to worry, you should worry about this very moment." "This very moment?" Charlie Brown asks. "Why this moment?" Suddenly, a soccer ball slams into his head, sending him flying through the air.

Charlie Brown's dilemma has been plaguing humankind since the Fall: Life contains a good deal of cause for concern. Even saved adolescents find plenty to worry about, be it only for the moment. For the Jews who would be returning from Babylonian exile, the problems that lay ahead would be formidable. They would struggle with poverty and oppressions from within and from without.

For believing teens (along with all other Christians), no worry or problem will deny them their ultimate victory. Isaiah's conclusion to his amazing book is a perfect wrap-up for what God has been communicating all along to His people. The Lord assures the upright that a glorious future awaits them. The shame and sorrow of the past will be replaced by unending joy and prosperity. How could any concern help but pale in comparison to that great hope?

JOYFUL WORSHIP RESTORED

BACKGROUND SCRIPTURE: Ezra 1:1–3:7
DEVOTIONAL READING: Matthew 23:29-39

Key Verse: They kept also the feast of tabernacles, as it is written, and offered the daily burnt offerings by number. Ezra 3:4.

KING JAMES VERSION

EZRA 3:1 And when the seventh month was come, and the children of Israel were in the cities, the people gathered themselves together as one man to Jerusalem. 2 Then stood up Jeshua the son of Jozadak, and his brethren the priests, and Zerubbabel the son of Shealtiel, and his brethren, and builded the altar of the God of Israel, to offer burnt offerings thereon, as it is written in the law of Moses the man of God. 3 And they set the altar upon his bases; for fear was upon them because of the people of those countries: and they offered burnt offerings thereon unto the LORD, even burnt offerings morning and evening. 4 They kept also the feast of tabernacles, as it is written, and offered the daily burnt offerings by number, according to the custom, as the duty of every day required; 5 And afterward offered the continual burnt offering, both of the new moons, and of all the set feasts of the LORD that were consecrated, and of every one that willingly offered a freewill offering unto the LORD. 6 From the first day of the seventh month began they to offer burnt offerings unto the LORD. But the foundation of the temple of the LORD was not yet laid. 7 They gave money also unto the masons, and to the carpenters; and meat, and drink, and oil, unto them of Zidon, and to them of Tyre, to bring cedar trees from Lebanon to the sea of Joppa, according to the grant that they had of Cyrus king of Persia.

NEW REVISED STANDARD VERSION

EZRA 3:1 When the seventh month came, and the Israelites were in the towns, the people gathered together in Jerusalem. 2 Then Jeshua son of Jozadak, with his fellow priests, and Zerubbabel son of Shealtiel with his kin set out to build the altar of the God of Israel, to offer burnt offerings on it, as prescribed in the law of Moses the man of God. 3 They set up the altar on its foundation, because they were in dread of the neighboring peoples, and they offered burnt offerings upon it to the LORD, morning and evening. 4 And they kept the festival of booths, as prescribed, and offered the daily burnt offerings by number according to the ordinance, as required for each day, 5 and after that the regular burnt offerings, the offerings at the new moon and at all the sacred festivals of the LORD, and the offerings of everyone who made a freewill offering to the LORD. 6 From the first day of the seventh month they began to offer burnt offerings to the LORD. But the foundation of the temple of the LORD was not yet laid. 7 So they gave money to the masons and the carpenters, and food, drink, and oil to the Sidonians and the Tyrians to bring cedar trees from Lebanon to the sea, to Joppa, according to the grant that they had from King Cyrus of Persia.

5

HOME BIBLE READINGS

Monday, June 24	Matthew 23:29-39	*Jesus' Lament over Jerusalem*
Tuesday, June 25	Jeremiah 7:30–8:3	*The Coming Judgment*
Wednesday, June 26	2 Kings 24:1-12	*Jerusalem Falls to the Babylonians*
Thursday, June 27	2 Chronicles 36:15-21	*The Destruction of Jerusalem*
Friday, June 28	Ezra 1:1-8	*Rebuild a House for God*
Saturday, June 29	Ezra 2:64-70	*The People Respond*
Sunday, June 30	Ezra 3:1-7	*Restoring the Worship of God*

BACKGROUND

Ezra and Nehemiah were originally placed together as one book. In the Hebrew Bible, this document preceded Chronicles, which was the last of the historical books. Esther was grouped with Song of Songs, Ruth, Lamentations, and Ecclesiastes—five small books that are read annually on Jewish holidays. The Song of Songs belongs to the Passover observance, Ruth to Pentecost, Ecclesiastes to the Feast of Tabernacles, Lamentations to the anniversary of the destruction of Jerusalem, and Esther to Purim.

Prior to the events narrated in Ezra and Nehemiah, God had foretold 70 years of captivity for His people because they had persisted, for centuries, in faithlessness to His covenant (see Jer. 25:11-12; 29:10). Jerusalem had suffered minor deportations in 605 and 597 B.C. before Nebuchadnezzar destroyed the city and temple and carried away all the leading families in 586 B.C. Then, in 539 B.C., Cyrus the Persian conquered Babylon, and the Lord began the gracious work of restoring His chosen people to the land of promise. The first full year of Cyrus's reign was 538 B.C. (Ezra 1:1). The Persian emperor instituted a policy of resettling captive peoples in their homelands and promoting native religions in order to gain the favor of every deity everywhere. Cyrus thought he was helping himself, but all the time it was the Lord moving the heart of the Persian emperor to fulfill the restoration promises of Israelite prophets.

NOTES ON THE PRINTED TEXT

In Ezra 3:1, reference is made to the "seventh month" of the Jewish year, namely, Tishri. This month extended from about mid-September to mid-October. Several important sacred observances and customs occurred during Tishri (for example, the Feast of Trumpets, the Day of Atonement, and the Feast of Tabernacles or Booths; see Lev. 23:23-43). The year was not specific. Thus, it might have been during the first year of Cyrus (538 B.C.) or his second year (537 B.C.). Most scholars favor the second option. The returnees had been in their homeland for about three months. During that period, they settled in the cities surrounding Jerusalem. Before any more time passed, however, the Jews wanted to reestablish the proper worship of God. So the pioneers assembled as a group in Jerusalem (Ezra 3:1).

Under the initiative of Jeshua and Zerubbabel as well as their associates, the people gradually built an altar for worshiping the Lord. This task was the first step in their efforts to rebuild the Jerusalem temple. Even as Abraham and Joshua before them, the exiles marked their entrance into the Promised Land with the construction of an altar to the Lord (see Gen. 12:7; Josh. 8:30-31). In Ezra 3:2, Jeshua was mentioned first because this was primarily a religious matter. The group offered sacrifices in accordance with the Mosaic law. They remembered Moses as God's official representative and messenger.

Either a bull, ram, or male bird (for instance, a dove or young pigeon) without any defect could be used for a sacrifice. When offered, it was to be entirely consumed on the altar (see Lev. 1; 6:8-13; 8:18-21; 16:24). The burnt offerings served several purposes: a voluntary act of worship; atonement for unintentional sin in general; and an expression of devotion, commitment, and complete surrender to God. All of the activities associated with the altar reminded God's people that it was necessary to approach the Lord through the provision of an acceptable atoning sacrifice.

In ancient times, altars were constructed of various materials. The oldest altars either were made out of mud brick or were simply mounds of dirt. The Hebrew people generally used uncut stones for their altars, since to place any hewed stone on an altar symbolized defilement (see Exod. 20:24-25; Deut. 27:5). In the court of Solomon's temple was an altar made out of bronze. It measured about 30 feet in length, about 15 feet in height, and had some type of horns at the corners (see 1 Kings 1:50-51; 2:28-29). There was also an altar made out of gold located just outside the Most Holy Place in the temple (see 7:48). Altars were used for the presentation of sacrifices to God (or to pagan deities). These sacrifices were usually animals. In fact, the Hebrew word for "altar" means "place of slaughter." Nevertheless, fruit or grain was also offered for sacrifice at these altars.

The group of returnees succeeded in setting the altar on its base (Ezra 3:3). They did this despite a lingering fear over the presence of non-Jews in the area. Once the altar was finished, God's people sacrificed burnt offerings on it at sunrise and sunset (see Exod. 29:38-42; Num. 28:3-8). This stands as a tribute to the Jews' wholehearted trust in the Lord, despite their apprehensions about living among their pagan neighbors (see Ps. 62:6-8).

The Jews performed every aspect of their worship in strict accordance with God's Word (Ezra 3:4). Perhaps they wanted to avoid bringing the Lord's displeasure through some violation of the law. God's people observed the Feast of Tabernacles (or Booths, Ingathering). This was typically done between September and October, five days after the Day of Atonement. Tabernacles involved a week of celebration for the harvest, as well as living in booths and offering sacrifices.

The festival was intended to commemorate the journey from Egypt to Canaan and to give thanks for the productivity of Canaan. God's people offered the right number of sacrifices for each day of the festival. Through this celebration, the Jews memorialized their successful journey from Mesopotamia to Palestine. This time it was comparable to a second exodus from a second bondage to carve out a home amid hostile neighbors. The returnees gave thanks for God's abundant provision and protection, and they expressed their gratitude for experiencing a safe return.

The Jews also reestablished all the other various sacrifices, sacred seasons, and feasts associated with the temple (vs. 5). This included the new moon festival. This religious holiday occurred at the beginning of each new month. Through the offering of special sacrifices and the blowing of trumpets, the Jews set apart this time of observance. During the festival, all forms of work and activity were discontinued.

Even though we don't offer morning and evening animal sacrifices to the Lord on a stone altar, our heavenly Father expects many "spiritual sacrifices" (1 Pet. 2:5) from us. These include sacrifices of praise, or "the fruit of our lips giving thanks to his name" (Heb. 13:15). The greatest sacrifice we give Him is our lives, a "living sacrifice, holy, acceptable unto God" (Rom. 12:1). In turn, our sacrifices of praise often lead to acts of service. As living sacrifices, we worship God by means of the days we dedicate to doing His will.

For the returned exiles, building the altar was the first action step in constructing the temple Cyrus commissioned at their hands. Fifteen days before the Feast of Tabernacles actually began, the priests had started to sacrifice "burnt offerings" (Ezra 3:6) to God. While the sacrifices and festive seasons of Israel had been restored, the foundation of the Lord's temple had not yet been laid. This was an important matter, for God wanted His people to rebuild the temple. This house of worship would enable them to properly focus their minds and hearts on the Lord. From the preceding information, we can surmise that God's people were sincere and determined to reestablish the proper worship of God in His holy city. They recognized that, while having a sanctuary would have been desirable, it wasn't essential at this point. Be that as it may, the Jews' commitment to rebuilding the temple continued to be strong.

God's people allocated funds to purchase building materials and to pay laborers to construct the temple. Specifically, the Jews hired "masons, and . . . carpenters" (vs. 7). The people also sent grain, wine, and olive oil to the cities of Sidon and Tyre as payment for cedar trees. These logs were bound into oceangoing rafts and floated down the Mediterranean coast from Byblos in Lebanon to Joppa, which served as port for Jerusalem. All this activity was in accordance with Cyrus's decree. This king had inherited the throne of Anshan, a region in eastern Elam, from his father in 559 B.C. It was evident from the beginning of Cyrus's reign that the king was ambitious. One of his first actions was to increase his territory by unifying the Persian people. And then, in 550 B.C., he attacked and conquered the region of Astyages.

Even with a vast area already under his control, Cyrus was still determined to expand his power by conquering other kingdoms. So he made an alliance with

Babylon against Media, a large but weakly ruled kingdom north of Babylon. He succeeded in subjugating Media and then turned his attention west, to Lydia. In 546 B.C. this, too, came under his control. And in the east, Cyrus extended his kingdom to the borders of India. By 539 B.C. Cyrus was ready to deal with the fertile plains of Babylon. His takeover there was relatively peaceful because the Babylonian people were dissatisfied with their own ruler. They welcomed Cyrus as a liberator.

SUGGESTIONS TO TEACHERS

Ezra 3 gives an account of joy, fear, sadness, disappointment, faith, and great emotion. People today who feel rescued sometimes experience the same range of mixed emotions.

1. START SOMEWHERE—NOW! The Jews could have argued about the timing of building an altar when they had not yet laid the foundation for a new temple. Although they did not have everything exactly as they might have hoped, at least they began with what they had. That is an important principle in spiritual life. We cannot wait until everything is perfect before taking steps in our walk with God. Do it now. Begin today.

2. MAKE WORSHIP A PRIORITY. The worship of God through the observance of feast days and offering of sacrifices took priority with the returned Jews. That gives us a clear lesson about worship's importance. It is not an act that can wait until a future day when we think we have more time. Learn to worship God here and now, no matter what else is happening in your life.

3. LIVE IN FAITH, NOT FEAR. The Jews had many enemies around them, and God's people lived in dread of their foes. But that fear did not stop the returnees from living in faith. We sometimes feel overwhelmed by those who are opposed to biblical faith. They may seem more powerful, wealthy, influential, and intellectual. That does not matter. Let us learn to live out of faith, not out of fear.

4. RECOGNIZE THE HAND OF GOD. Only the eyes and ears of faith can detect the Lord at work, stirring the hearts of believers and unbelievers alike. Sometimes He moves the hearts of Christians to risk their security and comfort. Sometimes He motivates them to support others with prayers and gifts.

FOR ADULTS

■ **TOPIC:** Celebrating What Is Meaningful

■ **QUESTIONS:** 1. What set of circumstances led to the Jewish exiles returning to their homeland? 2. What respective roles did the religious and civil leaders play in rebuilding the altar? 3. As the returnees offered sacrifices, why did they think it was important for them to follow the instructions in the Mosaic law? 4. In what ways has God recently shown Himself faithful to you? 5. How might you discern whether the Lord wants you to attempt a new beginning in some area of your life?

Coming to God with the Right Heart. When their church's minister of worship and music resigned, Craig and Jackie agreed to fill in until a new person could be found. "How hard can it be?" Craig told his wife. "We just pick some hymns and choruses that go with the pastor's sermon theme, arrange for soloists, and lead the congregation." However, after the couple's first Sunday as worship leaders, Craig wasn't too sure.

"Did you notice their faces?" Jackie asked after the worship service. Craig nodded. "I did. They didn't look like they were worshiping. It felt like we were just up there going through the motions." "Exactly," Jackie affirmed. "We did everything that the former worship minister did, but the spirit wasn't there." The couple promised themselves that the next week they would go into the worship service with prayerful hearts and a reverent spirit of their own. They also decided not to worry about how all the logistics of the service were going to fall into place.

As we discover from this week's lesson, God doesn't expect His people to be flawless in their praise or even to sing supposedly "perfect" songs. Instead, as the Jews returning from exile in Babylon did, He wants us to come into His presence with the right hearts, that is, hearts fully prepared to follow His will and offer Him meaningful praise (see Ezra 3:4-6).

The Source of Our Strength. A group of once-exiled Jews had succeeded in making the journey back to their homeland (see Ezra 3:1). Despite the challenges they faced, they looked to the Lord for the strength they needed to remain faithful to Him.

Before George Matheson (1842–1906) turned two years old, his parents discovered that an infection in his eyes was causing him to lose his sight. Gradually, his sight deteriorated, until by the time he was ready to graduate from Glasgow University (in Scotland), he was completely blind.

Yet, even in this tragic situation, George turned to God and His resources for strength. George graduated with honors in philosophy, but he felt called to the ministry. In a few years, he became the pastor of one of the largest churches in Edinburgh, Scotland. He was well known for visiting his congregation, as well as for writing articles and 12 books. Through it all, George's faith grew stronger.

Whenever we are tempted to be self-reliant, we would do well to remember what George Matheson and his spiritual predecessors discovered. As God's people, we are blessed with all the supernatural strength of the Lord that works in our behalf, if we will only humble ourselves enough to receive it.

Help from God. Imagine an escape artist performing before a packed auditorium. Handcuffs secure his wrists behind his back. A padlocked chain encircles his ankles. A blindfold covers his eyes. Volunteers from the audience then lift him into a coffin-sized box and nail down the heavy lid. The artist's assistant stands to one side of the stage, where a giant stopwatch is on display. She sets the hands ticking. The artist has 10 minutes to escape, or else he will run out of air.

Now imagine the artist inside the box. The key he had hidden in his mouth has fallen out of his reach. He can hear the audience counting down the time he has left. He knows that unless he gets help soon, he will die. The time ticks down to almost nothing. Finally, the artist cries out for help, and the assistant orders the box to be torn open. In a moment, the volunteers free the dazed artist, and the audience responds with grateful applause.

The main message of the Bible is that we cannot help ourselves, not one bit. Much as we would like to have the key to our own salvation, so we could affect our own rescue, we need to admit to ourselves that we have lost the key and cannot be our own deliverers. But this week's lesson reminds us of some good news. Just as God had the power to free the Jews exiled in Babylon and enable them to resettle the towns of Judah (see Ezra 3:1), so too He has the power to deliver us and become our salvation.

FOR YOUTH

■ **TOPIC:** Let's Get Ready to Celebrate!
■ **QUESTIONS:** 1. How do you think the Jewish exiles felt once they had resettled in Judah? 2. Why did the returnees think it was important for them to rebuild the altar? 3. Why were God's people living in fear of the local residents? 4. What spiritual sacrifice can you offer to the Lord this week? 5. As you worship the Lord, how can you use His Word to make sure you're doing things that are pleasing to Him?

■ **ILLUSTRATIONS:**

Worshiping from the Heart. "If the Lord came to many of our congregations today, He would sadly feel out of place because what we have today in most cases are not churches but 'restaurants,'" contends the writer of *Africans Reaching Africa* newsletter. The menus of churches, he explained, can become heavy on desserts and light on the meat of the Word.

The writer continues, "We may impress the world with our plans and services, but in God's eyes we may be building with wood, hay, and stubble." Later, the writer asks, "On the day of reckoning, will our strategies stand the test of fire—or will we be left with ashes to present to our Lord and Master?"

It's possible for a congregation of believers to stray from its mission of being a worshipful, God-centered house of praise. In contrast would be the Jews who returned to Judah from exile in Babylon. Rather than create an overindulgent smorgasbord of programs, they worshiped the Lord through heartfelt sacrifice and celebration (see Ezra 3:2-4). Likewise, regardless of how young or old we are, the same should be true of the worship we offer to God.

Placing Our Trust in God. At age 19, Darlene Rose went to join her husband on the mission field in New Guinea. But Darlene's missionary ambitions were quickly shattered by the events of World War II. Widowed by age 20, stricken with malaria, accused of espionage by the Japanese, and sentenced to death by beheading, Rose had only her faith on which to stand.

In circumstances such as these, it is amazing that Darlene did not buckle under the pressure or curse God. Thankfully, Darlene looked beyond her circumstances and found strength in the Lord, who loved her. Miraculously, Darlene survived the horrors of war and dedicated much of her time before her death to sharing her testimony with others as a witness of God's faithfulness.

The Jews who returned to Judah from exile in Babylon could affirm from their own experiences that the Lord had been faithful to them. Perhaps at one point, the prospect of ever leaving captivity seemed like an impossible dream. Yet, in God's perfect timing, He made it possible for His chosen people to return to their ancestral homeland and resettle in its towns (see Ezra 3:1).

As we journey with the Lord along the path of life, circumstances may threaten to overcome us. But those situations have no real power over us as God's children, especially when we are trusting in Him. The simple fact is that the safest place we could center our trust is in God.

Are You Self-Reliant? A passage in *Fundamentals of Marxism-Leninism,* a textbook that has been used by members of the Communist Party, says the following: "Materialists do not expect aid from supernatural forces. Their faith is in man, in his ability to transform the world by his own efforts and make it worthy of himself."

We can be sure that the Jews who returned to Judah from exile in Babylon would have shaken their heads in disapproval at such a statement of arrogance and self-reliance. But what about us as believers today? Do we in practice sometimes subscribe to that very belief?

Whenever we fail to recognize our dependence upon God, whenever we try to manipulate circumstances to get what we want, whenever we put our personal priorities above what we know God is asking us to attend to—it is then that we act out this fundamental principle of the materialist's belief system. Just as God did with the returnees from exile, so too He summons us today to a different way. It is a life of complete reliance upon Him, with no trace of trust in ourselves.

TEMPLE RESTORED

BACKGROUND SCRIPTURE: Ezra 3:8-13
DEVOTIONAL READING: Psalm 66:1-12

Key Verse: All the people shouted with a great shout, when they praised the LORD, because the foundation of the house of the LORD was laid. Ezra 3:11.

KING JAMES VERSION

EZRA 3:8 Now in the second year of their coming unto the house of God at Jerusalem, in the second month, began Zerubbabel the son of Shealtiel, and Jeshua the son of Jozadak, and the remnant of their brethren the priests and the Levites, and all they that were come out of the captivity unto Jerusalem; and appointed the Levites, from twenty years old and upward, to set forward the work of the house of the LORD. 9 Then stood Jeshua with his sons and his brethren, Kadmiel and his sons, the sons of Judah, together, to set forward the workmen in the house of God: the sons of Henadad, with their sons and their brethren the Levites. 10 And when the builders laid the foundation of the temple of the LORD, they set the priests in their apparel with trumpets, and the Levites the sons of Asaph with cymbals, to praise the LORD, after the ordinance of David king of Israel. 11 And they sang together by course in praising and giving thanks unto the LORD; because he is good, for his mercy endureth for ever toward Israel. And all the people shouted with a great shout, when they praised the LORD, because the foundation of the house of the LORD was laid. 12 But many of the priests and Levites and chief of the fathers, who were ancient men, that had seen the first house, when the foundation of this house was laid before their eyes, wept with a loud voice; and many shouted aloud for joy: 13 So that the people could not discern the noise of the shout of joy from the noise of the weeping of the people: for the people shouted with a loud shout, and the noise was heard afar off.

NEW REVISED STANDARD VERSION

EZRA 3:8 In the second year after their arrival at the house of God at Jerusalem, in the second month, Zerubbabel son of Shealtiel and Jeshua son of Jozadak made a beginning, together with the rest of their people, the priests and the Levites and all who had come to Jerusalem from the captivity. They appointed the Levites, from twenty years old and upward, to have the oversight of the work on the house of the LORD. 9 And Jeshua with his sons and his kin, and Kadmiel and his sons, Binnui and Hodaviah along with the sons of Henadad, the Levites, their sons and kin, together took charge of the workers in the house of God.

10 When the builders laid the foundation of the temple of the LORD, the priests in their vestments were stationed to praise the LORD with trumpets, and the Levites, the sons of Asaph, with cymbals, according to the directions of King David of Israel; 11 and they sang responsively, praising and giving thanks to the LORD,

"For he is good,
for his steadfast love endures forever toward Israel."
And all the people responded with a great shout when they praised the LORD, because the foundation of the house of the LORD was laid. 12 But many of the priests and Levites and heads of families, old people who had seen the first house on its foundations, wept with a loud voice when they saw this house, though many shouted aloud for joy, 13 so that the people could not distinguish the sound of the joyful shout from the sound of the people's weeping, for the people shouted so loudly that the sound was heard far away.

6

Monday, July 1	2 Chronicles 2:1-9	*A Great and Wonderful House*
Tuesday, July 2	1 Kings 8:14-21	*Building a House for God's Name*
Wednesday, July 3	1 Kings 8:22-30	*My Name Shall Be There*
Thursday, July 4	Matthew 21:10-16	*A House of Prayer*
Friday, July 5	Psalm 66:1-12	*Make a Joyful Noise to God*
Saturday, July 6	Psalm 5	*Lead Me in Your Righteousness*
Sunday, July 7	Ezra 3:8-13	*Tears of Joy*

BACKGROUND

Ancient Jewish and the oldest Christian traditions assigned the authorship of Ezra and Nehemiah to Ezra. Many contemporary scholars continue to support the view that Ezra also wrote the books of Chronicles. Included in the evidence that supports this view is the fact that the last two verses of 2 Chronicles and the first two verses of Ezra are virtually identical. Ezra may have done this to make a smooth chronological flow between the two books. Some scholars have suggested that a "Chronicler," perhaps a disciple of Ezra, brought together the memoirs of Judah's kings, Ezra, and Nehemiah to compose 1 and 2 Chronicles, Ezra, and Nehemiah.

The books of Ezra and Nehemiah present the history of God's people during the years following the destruction of Jerusalem and its temple (586 B.C.). These, together with the prophecies of Haggai and Zechariah (both dated about 520 B.C.), compose the main Hebrew records of those years. We learn from these ancient, inspired documents that the return of the exiles from Babylonian captivity to Palestine came in three separate stages. The first group went to restore the temple (starting around 537 B.C.; see Ezra 1–3). The work that began then was interrupted for some years (see 4:5-7, 23), but was resumed at the encouragement of the prophets Haggai and Zechariah (see 5:1-2) and completed around 516 B.C. The second return took place around 458 B.C. under Ezra, who called for reform and a return to covenant obligations (see Ezra 7–10). Nehemiah led the third group of returnees (444 B.C.) and spearheaded the rebuilding of Jerusalem's walls.

NOTES ON THE PRINTED TEXT

Last week we learned that Cyrus's policies permitted the Jews to return to their homeland from exile in Babylon (see Ezra 1—2). We also found out about the efforts the returnees made to rebuild the altar in Jerusalem (see 3:1-5). While this was a noteworthy achievement, God's people had not yet laid the foundation of His temple (vs. 6). The initial step in dealing with this shortcoming was for the Jews to purchase building materials and to pay laborers to construct the temple (vs. 7).

The next step was to organize the lengthy and complex building operation. Verse 8 reveals that it was under the initiative of Zerubbabel and Jeshua, as well as their associates and fellow Jews, that construction on the temple finally began. This was probably the midspring (that is, about mid-April to mid-May) of 536 B.C. The event corresponded with the timing of Solomon's groundbreaking in 966 B.C., some 430 years earlier (see 2 Chron. 3:1-2). In Ezra 3:8, Zerubbabel was mentioned first because this was initially a civil matter with religious significance.

The leaders gave Levites who were over the age of 20 the responsibility to supervise the rebuilding of the temple (Ezra 3:8). In earlier situations, 30 and 25 (respectively) had been the minimum ages for Levitical activity (see Num. 4:3; 8:24). From this information we see that the exilic band did not include an abundance of Levites. The supervising Levites fell into three groups. The clans of Jeshua and Kadmiel were mentioned in the roster of exiles (see Ezra 2:40). The descendants of Henadad are also included among the Levites in Nehemiah's time who built the wall of Jerusalem and sealed the covenant (3:9; see Neh. 3:18, 24; 10:9).

Evidently, it did not take long for the builders to complete the foundation of the Lord's temple. Next, God's people commemorated the momentous occasion. The priests, who were ceremonially dressed in their robes, got trumpets. Instead of the traditional ram's horn, "trumpets" (Ezra 3:10) refers to clarion-like instruments that were long, straight, and metallic. Also, the Levites (the sons of Asaph) obtained cymbals. After taking their places, they thanked and praised God for His abundant provision.

Every action was done in strict accordance with the pattern of worship established for the Levites by David and the precedent set by Solomon when he dedicated his completed temple (see 1 Chron. 6:31-49; 2 Chron. 5:13). The people worshiped God for who He is (namely, His personal attributes and characteristics) and thanked Him for what He does (namely, His presence, power, provisions, and preservation). These emphases are seen in the responsive chorus. The returnees praised God for His kindness and His unfailing love to them even after 70 years of captivity. The entire assembly was united in applauding God for enabling them to lay the temple foundation (Ezra 3:11).

In the biblical era, there were three orders in the hierarchy of priests: the high priests, priests, and Levites. Whereas the Levites were subordinate sanctuary officials who supervised the minor duties of the temple, the priests were associates of the high priests. Priests were to come from the tribe of Levi and had to be without any physical defect. They were organized into 24 divisions that served the sanctuary in rotation. Each of the divisions ministered for a week, beginning on the Sabbath, except during the annual feasts, at which time all the priests served together.

The ceremony of consecration of the priests was much like that for the high priest, but not as elaborate. The clothing of the priests included a tunic, breeches, and a turban—all of which were made with white linen, as well as a white linen girdle embroidered with blue, purple, and scarlet. The chief duties of the priests were the care of the sanctuary vessels and the sacrifices at the altar. But the priests also taught the law, watched over the physical health of the nation, and administered justice.

The size and grandeur of the rebuilt temple foundation paled in comparison to the one Solomon had built. Many of the older priests, Levites, and family members who were alive prior to the exile were sad and disappointed at the sight of the smaller, less impressive scene (Ezra 3:12). Both Haggai (Hag. 2:3) and Zechariah would find themselves addressing a segment of the population discouraged by "the day of small things" (Zech. 4:10). Be that as it may, the dominant mood among the returned exiles still was great joy. In fact, the combined sounds of joy and weeping were so loud that they could not be distinguished. Ezra 3:13 notes that even people at a great distance could hear the resounding noise of this community of worshipers. They dared to take the Lord at His word and risk everything they had to go to ruined towns and farms. In short, they trusted Him to take a remnant, plant them, and grow a nation.

Unlike those who returned from exile, Solomon had the resources to construct a lavish temple. His shrine was made out of the most precious building materials available in his day, with many of them being imported: cedar (1 Kings 5:6), quarried stone (vss. 15-18), gold (6:20-22), olive wood (vss. 23-28, 31-33), cypress or pine (vs. 34), and bronze (7:13-16, 27, 38-45). The project employed a massive number of people: 30,000 laborers (5:13), 150,000 stonemasons and haulers (vs. 15), and 3,300 supervisors (vs. 16). Moreover, the work continued nonstop for seven years (6:37-38). Solomon's temple was a remarkable work of art, being built for the glory of God (8:12-13). Also, the Lord evidently approved of the king's work, for God blessed the sanctuary with His holy presence (vss. 10-11). Nonetheless, even as the construction went forward, the Lord reminded His builder that what mattered most was not a house made out of cedar and gold, but rather keeping the Mosaic law (6:11-13).

Ezra 4 reveals that those who attempt to do the will of God inevitably meet with resistance from a sinful world. To be specific, when the Jewish exiles returned to Jerusalem from Babylon, they came because God had commanded it. They had a royal decree and a divine mandate to rebuild the temple of the Lord in the city of God. But just as Christians today face spiritual opposition when they set their minds to obey God, so the exiles found themselves surrounded by powerful enemies when they began to rebuild their holy city and shrine.

The writer identified as "adversaries" (vs. 1) those who approached the newly returned exiles and offered to help them build the temple. The reason is implied in the way the exiles viewed the temple. It was "a temple unto the LORD God of Israel." "The LORD," which renders Yahweh in the Hebrew text, was God's covenant name, signifying a unique relationship with those who entered into and kept that covenant. An earlier generation had gone into captivity for persistent covenant violation. Understandably, the present generation was committed to observing that covenant.

God wanted His people to rebuild the Jerusalem temple, and He promised to be with them throughout the project (see Hag. 1:7, 13). The presence of opposition, however, must have initially made the fulfillment of the promise seem impossible to the Jews. When God makes a promise, it shows two aspects of His character. First, we see that He is the sovereign Lord of all. What He declares will come true and nothing can thwart His will. Second, we see that God does not change His mind, rethink His strategy, or apologize for not doing something according to our timetable. He is faithful to His Word and will surely bring it to pass. Ultimately, God's promises are encouragements to faith, for they demonstrate the resolve of the Lord's character. His promises give us the courage to face and deal with difficult circumstances.

SUGGESTIONS TO TEACHERS

Praise and worship are in order for those who recognize the work of God in their lives. The returnees knew it when they were rebuilding the temple. And many of them shouted for joy. There were some older attendees, though, who felt sad over the fact that the new temple would not be as grand as Solomon's sanctuary.

1. REMAIN GENUINELY COMMITTED. The Jews' commitment to rebuilding the temple was evident in their decisions. For instance, despite their tight economic circumstances, they allocated money for hiring skilled workers and channeling additional resources for the purchase of cedar logs. Moreover, the returnees appointed trustworthy individuals to supervise the work. Similarly, our commitment to serving the Lord is demonstrated by the priorities we set and the sacrifices we make.

2. COOPERATE TO SUCCEED. The Jews could not have built the temple without the help of other groups. *Cooperation* is not a bad word. It is necessary to achieve what we believe God intends for us to do. Sometimes we cooperate with other Christian groups, and at other times with secular groups. The point is that if our goals are far reaching, we will need help to achieve them.

3. WORSHIP THE LORD OF TODAY, NOT JUST YESTERDAY. The older Jews were so tied to their past that the sight of the new temple's foundation was disappointing to them. Some wept in bitter disappointment while others shouted for joy. The Lord is the God of yesterday, today, and tomorrow (Heb. 13:8). Let's not get stuck in the past and always think it was better than today or tomorrow. The Lord is still God. Also, everything new is not necessarily bad.

4. CHOOSE TO REJOICE. Encourage your students to be among the believers who choose to rejoice rather than mourn. This should be the case even if the present work of God doesn't seem as wonderful as some of their past experiences. Remind them that God is working in hearts and lives, and that it is worth giving praise to Him.

FOR ADULTS

■ **TOPIC:** Finding Joy in Restoration
■ **QUESTIONS:** 1. Why was it important for God's people to rebuild the temple in Jerusalem? 2. How did the civil and religious leaders organ-

ize God's people to rebuild the temple? 3. What are some ways you can encourage your fellow believers to do the Lord's work in an organized manner? 4. Why did God's people feel compelled to praise Him for His kindness and unfailing love? 5. How can believers maintain a balance between remembering the past and enjoying God's present?

■ ILLUSTRATIONS:

Maintaining a Joyful Witness. God calls us to lay many foundations in our lives. Some of them are for houses, churches, schools, office buildings, and new factories. Others are for the long-term security of our lives—spiritual foundations that begin with our expressions of joyful commitment to the Lord.

As the returnees to Judah demonstrated in rebuilding the Jerusalem temple (see Ezra 3:8-11), secure foundations are built with faith, prayer, praise, Bible study, witness, and service. Whatever happens in our homes, churches, and communities, we can find stability and hope in God, for He is the anchor of our souls.

Sometimes we neglect our spiritual foundations. Erosion sets in because we have not kept the Lord first in our hearts. This calls for renewal and recommitment. We should take the lead in spiritual renewal in our homes and churches. Then our strong faith will be a joyful witness and encouragement to others (see vs. 13).

From Travelers to Tourists. Daniel Boorstin's book *The Image: A Guide to Pseudo-Events in America,* points out that over the past 175 years, people have moved from being travelers to becoming tourists. The Old English noun "travel" was originally the same word as "travail"—trouble, work, and torment. For centuries, to travel was to submit to a certain kind of torture, to do something tough.

That began to change in the middle of the nineteenth century. Some entrepreneur came up with the idea of marketing travel as an adventure. Thus was born the tour. Legend has it that the very first tour took place in 1838. A group of people from Wadebridge, England, traveled by special train to the nearby village of Bodmin. They went there to watch the hanging of two killers. Since the Bodmin gallows was in clear view of the uncovered station, the tourists had their experience without even needing to leave their open railway carriages.

Like the Jews who decided to return to Judah after being exiled in Babylon, we should learn the difference between being a tourist in life and a traveler. A tourist is going only where it's convenient and comfortable. A traveler, however, is someone who determines her or his own way in life and will get there even if it means blazing a new trail.

Living in God's Present. After the foundation of the temple had been laid, there were mixed emotions among God's people. Many shouted for joy over what the Lord had done and for this first step in rebuilding the temple. However, a number of older returnees wept when they looked at the less-than-spectacular structure in its initial stages (see Ezra 3:11-12).

The older we get, the more we may joke about the "good old days." Yet, as things change, we must remember that joy is to be found in every phase of life, regardless of the challenges we encounter. Sometimes, we have to look harder to find joy, but it is there for us to celebrate, because God puts it there.

Consider Maria. When she celebrated her tenth anniversary as a breast cancer survivor, she looked better than ever. At one point, she had thought she would never reach this milestone. Maria and her husband, Michael, had been career missionaries in Asia. Raising five kids on the mission field is not easy. But to Maria this seemed relatively bearable compared to the 18 months following her dreaded talk with the oncologist.

Stage four is not the best time for a woman to learn that she has breast cancer. Yet that was the prognosis of the physician when Maria and Michael sat together one warm spring day. Maria discovered that the chances of survival were small. She immediately began the course of treatment that was presented to her. Chemotherapy and other treatments were just a part of the plan, to be augmented with radical surgeries.

As Maria walked in the beautiful flower gardens of her parents' southern Arizona home, she remembered the days that had brought her so close to death's door. However, today she was alive. And how Maria thanked God for the sound of laughter coming down the garden path. It was the sound of her children growing older, and Maria was there to listen.

FOR YOUTH

■ **TOPIC:** Let the Good Times Roll!

■ **QUESTIONS:** 1. What do you think a rebuilt temple in Jerusalem would have symbolized to God's people? 2. Who were the key individuals involved in supervising the rebuilding of the temple? 3. Who are some church leaders you know who are doing important things to advance God's kingdom? 4. In what way did God's people thank Him for the success of laying the temple's foundation? 5. How should we respond when God does new and different things in our lives?

■ **ILLUSTRATIONS:**

The Essence of Our Spiritual Foundation. Some adolescents tend to separate the Lord's work from His worship. They think worship is what they do on Sunday morning and work (or evangelism) is what they do during the week.

Though not every saved teen actually does evangelism, most seem to feel it is far more important than worship. They think worship is easy—just sit back in the pews and enjoy the emotional excitement generated by the service. But many teens probably feel guilty for not witnessing.

The fact is, we worship God for the very things our witnessing proclaims. And a heartfelt worship of God helps to strengthen the spiritual foundation of our lives. As the Jews sang in Jerusalem, they declared, "He is good, for his mercy endureth for ever toward Israel" (Ezra 3:11). From this we see that God's goodness and mercy are the essence of our spiritual foundation.

The Great Comeback. It wasn't long after the exiles from Babylon returned to Judah that they decided to begin reconstructing the Jerusalem temple. The first step in bringing back this sacred structure was to successfully lay the foundation of the sanctuary (see Ezra 3:10).

In *Our Daily Bread,* Dave Branon describes how in the late 1940s, the Ford Motor Company turned around its fledgling automobile business. Prior to that, the "reluctance" of the "leadership to modernize" nearly wiped out the organization. The situation grew so dire that the "government nearly took over the company" out of fear that its "demise might threaten" the nation's "war effort."

The great comeback for the automobile manufacturer occurred after Henry Ford II was discharged from the military. He took over the reins of the business and enacted desperately needed changes. As a result of his efforts, "Ford became one of the biggest corporations in the world."

Two Hands Are Better Than One. In order for the returnees to successfully lay the foundation of the temple, they had to work together cooperatively (see Ezra 3:8-10). Likewise, in Palatka, Florida, several civic groups joined together to build a playground for the city's children. The project was called "Project Play."

Dozens of volunteers met at the playground site over the course of several weeks. Volunteers would be given a specific assignment such as "cut 6 boards 3 feet long and place them on the walk with 4-inch screws." No one part of the project alone seemed important, but all of the smaller assignments together worked. Board by board, nail by nail, post by post the playground seemed to grow out of the earth and take shape.

The day of its dedication was a joy for the entire community. Volunteers inspected their work and said, "I helped build this swing set," or "I worked on the slide." No one person built the playground. Instead, many people working together made it happen.

People get great satisfaction from participating in something like that playground. Most individuals want to make a contribution to their community and make a difference in someone's life. People working together can bring about changes and improvements that someone working alone cannot accomplish.

DEDICATION OF THE TEMPLE

BACKGROUND SCRIPTURE: Ezra 6
DEVOTIONAL READING: Ezra 5:1-5

Key Verse: The children of Israel, the priests, and the Levites, and the rest of the children of the captivity, kept the dedication of this house of God with joy. Ezra 6:16.

KING JAMES VERSION

EZRA 6:13 Then Tatnai, governor on this side the river, Shetharboznai, and their companions, according to that which Darius the king had sent, so they did speedily. 14 And the elders of the Jews builded, and they prospered through the prophesying of Haggai the prophet and Zechariah the son of Iddo. And they builded, and finished it, according to the commandment of the God of Israel, and according to the commandment of Cyrus, and Darius, and Artaxerxes king of Persia. 15 And this house was finished on the third day of the month Adar, which was in the sixth year of the reign of Darius the king. 16 And the children of Israel, the priests, and the Levites, and the rest of the children of the captivity, kept the dedication of this house of God with joy, 17 And offered at the dedication of this house of God an hundred bullocks, two hundred rams, four hundred lambs; and for a sin offering for all Israel, twelve he goats, according to the number of the tribes of Israel. 18 And they set the priests in their divisions, and the Levites in their courses, for the service of God, which is at Jerusalem; as it is written in the book of Moses. 19 And the children of the captivity kept the passover upon the fourteenth day of the first month. 20 For the priests and the Levites were purified together, all of them were pure, and killed the passover for all the children of the captivity, and for their brethren the priests, and for themselves. 21 And the children of Israel, which were come again out of captivity, and all such as had separated themselves unto them from the filthiness of the heathen of the land, to seek the LORD God of Israel, did eat, 22 And kept the feast of unleavened bread seven days with joy: for the LORD had made them joyful, and turned the heart of the king of Assyria unto them, to strengthen their hands in the work of the house of God, the God of Israel.

NEW REVISED STANDARD VERSION

EZRA 6:13 Then, according to the word sent by King Darius, Tattenai, the governor of the province Beyond the River, Shethar-bozenai, and their associates did with all diligence what King Darius had ordered. 14 So the elders of the Jews built and prospered, through the prophesying of the prophet Haggai and Zechariah son of Iddo. They finished their building by command of the God of Israel and by decree of Cyrus, Darius, and King Artaxerxes of Persia; 15 and this house was finished on the third day of the month of Adar, in the sixth year of the reign of King Darius.

16 The people of Israel, the priests and the Levites, and the rest of the returned exiles, celebrated the dedication of this house of God with joy. 17 They offered at the dedication of this house of God one hundred bulls, two hundred rams, four hundred lambs, and as a sin offering for all Israel, twelve male goats, according to the number of the tribes of Israel. 18 Then they set the priests in their divisions and the Levites in their courses for the service of God at Jerusalem, as it is written in the book of Moses.

19 On the fourteenth day of the first month the returned exiles kept the passover. 20 For both the priests and the Levites had purified themselves; all of them were clean. So they killed the passover lamb for all the returned exiles, for their fellow priests, and for themselves. 21 It was eaten by the people of Israel who had returned from exile, and also by all who had joined them and separated themselves from the pollutions of the nations of the land to worship the LORD, the God of Israel. 22 With joy they celebrated the festival of unleavened bread seven days; for the LORD had made them joyful, and had turned the heart of the king of Assyria to them, so that he aided them in the work on the house of God, the God of Israel.

7

Monday, July 8	Ezra 4:1-5	*Resistance to Rebuilding the Temple*
Tuesday, July 9	Ezra 4:11-16	*Accusations of Sedition*
Wednesday, July 10	Ezra 4:17-24	*Temple Construction Halted*
Thursday, July 11	Ezra 5:1-5	*The Eye of God upon Them*
Friday, July 12	Ezra 5:6-17	*Who Gave You a Decree?*
Saturday, July 13	Ezra 6:1-12	*The Temple's Official Endorsement*
Sunday, July 14	Ezra 6:13-22	*The Temple's Dedication*

BACKGROUND

Last week, we learned how God used the prophets Haggai and Zechariah to get the leaders and people of Judah to resume their work on the temple. When Persian officials heard about what was taking place, they investigated the matter. However, they did not stop the Jews from moving forward with their plans. Instead, the officials sent a letter to King Darius. They explained what was going on and asked him to check the Jews' claim that Cyrus had authorized them to rebuild their temple (see Ezra 5:1-17).

A search for the decree of Cyrus was made, but evidently, the records were not found in Babylon. Instead, an important scroll was found in Ecbatana, the former capital of Media and the summer residence of the Persian kings. The official communication verified Cyrus's original command authorizing the rebuilding of the temple and the restoration of its foundation (see 6:1-2). Verses 3-12 reveal the content of Darius's letter. The king specified the size of the temple and ordered that stolen articles were to be returned. His officials were to permit the Jews to complete their work. In fact, funds from the royal treasury were to be used to pay for building materials and sacrificial animals. Those who opposed the king's edict would be severely punished. He directed that his orders be implemented with care, thoroughness, and diligence.

NOTES ON THE PRINTED TEXT

In Ezra 6:13, we are told that Tattenai (who was governor of the province west of the Euphrates River), Shethar-bozenai (another official of the Persian government), and their colleagues, complied at once with the command of King Darius. Clearly, the prophecies the Lord had made through Haggai and Zechariah were coming to pass. God was giving the Jews success in rebuilding and dedicating their temple. During years of delay, the people had fallen into deep discouragement. They now needed reminders of God's love. The people also needed consistent exhortation because their work was hindered by more than just their enemies. It was also hindered by their selfishness and fear. When they decided to trust and obey the Lord, they prospered and God took care of their enemies. The Lord provided encouragement through the messages delivered by Haggai and Zechariah (Ezra 6:14).

Ezra's report of the completion of the temple takes into account all of the layers of responsibility for it. The "elders of the Jews" were responsible for the laborers at the job site. Haggai and Zechariah provided the spiritual motivation that produced success. And the decrees of three Persian emperors—Cyrus, Darius I, and Artaxerxes I—authorized the project at the level of world politics. This was an unlikely coalition, but God is the prime mover of earthly rulers. In this case, He worked through pagan kings to bring about the restoration of His people and their worship of Him in Jerusalem. "The sixth year of the reign of Darius the king" (vs. 15) occurred long before the time of Artaxerxes I, the third emperor credited with the temple's erection. Artaxerxes I is the one who commissioned Ezra to enhance temple worship and teach the law of Moses (see 7:19-20, 25-26).

Having completed their work, the people and their leaders broke into celebration. This was a significant milestone in the nation's history. After all, "the house of God" (Ezra 6:16) was not just another building to His people. The temple was the place where the Lord manifested His presence. The key to understanding this celebration is the contrast between living in exile in a land saturated with pagan idolatry and being able to worship the one true God in His sanctuary. His people were overcome with joy because they now had the latter opportunity.

The upright remnant had learned the painful lesson of God's judgment for their past idolatries. While in exile in Babylon, they missed so much the opportunity for worship afforded by the Jerusalem temple that they established what later became the synagogue service. This included prayers, Scripture readings, and moral instruction. The completion of the second temple ensured that the worship of the one true God remained a vital part of Jewish national life. His people resumed their daily temple services, their annual feasts and fasts, and their worship.

Having returned from Babylon without much money, the people's sacrifice of 100 bulls, 200 rams, 400 lambs, and 12 goats represented a costly commitment to God (vs. 17). Although the 10 northern tribes of Israel had long since disappeared, they were remembered by the 12 goats, 1 for each tribe. The dedication of God's house required significant sacrifices for two reasons. First, sacrifices proved the people's commitment to the Lord. Second, sacrifices reminded them of their sin and God's holiness. Everyone celebrated the dedication of the new temple with great joy. However, this marvelously joyous celebration was tiny compared to the dedicatory service during the reign of Solomon (see 1 Kings 8:5, 63). Moreover, the number of animals sacrificed by the postexilic Jews was considerably smaller than those offered by Hezekiah (see 2 Chron. 30:24) and Josiah (see 35:7). Undoubtedly, this circumstance reflected the poverty of the returnees compared to earlier days. From this we see that true worship is costly.

After offering sacrifices, the people divided the priests and Levites into their various divisions. They were to serve at the temple of God in Jerusalem in accordance with the instructions "written in the book of Moses" (Ezra 6:18). The highlight of the temple's completion came with the Passover observance. Since the returned exiles finished the sanctuary in the "month of Adar" (vs. 15), it made sense for them to observe Passover at its appropriate time in the following month of Nisan, the "first month" (vs. 19) of the Jewish year. It is difficult for us to imagine how much the renewal of this ancient ritual meant to the Jews in Bible times. They had not kept it for several generations. With the rebuilding and rededication of the temple in Jerusalem, they now had the opportunity. It was on April 21, 516 B.C., that the returned exiles observed Passover, a holy day that was originally intended to commemorate Israel's deliverance from Egypt.

Years before, during the reign of Josiah (640–609 B.C.), Passover had been celebrated after a restoration of the first temple. At that time, the king provided an immense number of animals for the festival to feed all the people. The peasants ate from the bounty of the king and the temple. This suggests that Josiah's Passover was a public feast, celebrated through the generosity of the monarch and the sanctuary aristocracy of the kingdom. The situation was much different for the returned exiles. Most of the society would have been village peasants who lived at a bare subsistence level. Meat was a luxury for the wealthy. In fact, any animals the Jewish peasants might have owned were too valuable to consume. The priests and Levites had gone through the purification ritual and so were ceremonially clean. In accordance with the Mosaic law, they slaughtered the Passover lamb for all the returned exiles, for the other priests, and for themselves (vs. 20).

Keeping the Passover symbolically marked the end of the exile for the returnees. Fellowship was once again restored between God and His chosen people. They were joined by other Jews who had renounced pagan worship (vs. 21). The second group consisted of those who remained in Judah during the exile, but did not participate in the unclean practices of their pagan neighbors. Together, they ate the lamb as a sign that they had repented of their sins and wanted to seek the Lord. Verse 22 notes that the people celebrated the Feast of Unleavened Bread for seven days. This is one of the Old Testament festivals that God established for the Israelites. It involved eating bread made without yeast, holding several assemblies, and making designated offerings. It was designed to commemorate how the Lord rescued His people out of Egypt with rapid speed. This festival was observed at the newly rebuilt temple with the same joy that had marked the sanctuary dedication (see vs. 16).

With some effort, we can imagine how God's people must have felt. It was like returning home after a long absence or being reunited with a loved one. Elderly persons would have had a mixture of grief and joy, especially as they remembered the temple of Solomon that had been destroyed (see 3:12). In contrast, younger people would have loved the color, sights, and sounds of the great spectacle (see vs. 11). All the officiating priests would have been filled with awe, especially as some of their peers stood to make sacrifices in God's presence.

The members of the covenant community, who had been restored to their homeland, had just finished constructing the symbol of their national identity. They also had renewed fellowship with the Lord. How great their exuberance must have been! Through the grace of God, the temple was rebuilt, and sacrifices once again were offered in the land of their ancestors. It's important to note that this jubilant time of celebration was based on what God had done through the Persian monarchs. These kings had conquered territory formerly controlled by the Assyrian Empire, which was one of the kingdoms that had exiled God's people (see Neh. 9:32). Because of the Lord's intervention through the Persian emperors, the Jews were strengthened and encouraged to restore the temple in Jerusalem.

The Persian ruler Darius I is called "the king of Assyria" in Ezra 6:22 for the same reason that Cyrus was called "the king of Babylon" in 5:13. These rulers took over the titles as well as the empires of those they conquered. When the Lord directed the Persians to restore the Jerusalem temple, He reversed a policy of deportation and destruction that reached back to the Assyrians whose realm the Persians had absorbed. And as the pagan kings of Persia yielded to the divine will, the Jews witnessed anew the working of God in history.

SUGGESTIONS TO TEACHERS

The Jews who returned to Jerusalem soon realized they could not afford to waste time. By working together with others, they were able to rededicate the temple. In the process, they learned lessons that help us today. In the work of the church, we learn several important truths.

1. WE CAN'T DO IT ALONE. The people needed to work together, not just among themselves, but with the civil authorities. Sometimes civil government is hostile to the work of the Gospel, but sometimes it is surprisingly open and helpful. If we can, we should make use of it to the best of our ability.

2. WE CAN DO IT WITH GOD'S HELP. The temple dedication affirmed that God was the most important relationship to the Jews. As we establish and care for that relationship today, we can accomplish what God wants us to do.

3. WHEN IN DOUBT, CELEBRATE! The celebration at the temple's dedication was both a civil and a religious event. The people learned how to celebrate as part of their religious dedication. Celebration today can be in a church, of course, but it can also occur as we drive down the road, wash dishes, paint the house, or do a thousand other chores. God is pleased with sincere expressions of joy and thankfulness to Him.

4. "RITUAL" IS NOT AN UNACCEPTABLE WORD. The Passover was reintroduced as part of the Jewish worship. Rituals like that, as part of worship, should not concern us as being too formal. Specific elements of worship help teach us the content of our faith.

■ **TOPIC:** Celebrating with Joy

■ **QUESTIONS:** 1. What prompted the Persian officials to allow the Jews to complete the rebuilding of the temple? 2. How has God used unbelievers in your life to bring about His will for you? 3. What role did Haggai and Zechariah serve in the rebuilding effort? 4. Who participated in the Passover celebration? 5. What are some ways we can celebrate God's goodness in our lives?

■ **ILLUSTRATIONS:**

Celebrating Victories. After the completion of the Jerusalem temple, the people celebrated with great joy (see Ezra 6:16, 19, 22). These were not humdrum rituals or ceremonies, since they marked the Jews' return to their homeland.

More recently, during one American town's annual Fourth of July parade, two or three churches made magnificent floats—so good that often one of them took home first prize. It was their way of informing the public that the worship of God was still a viable option for many people. Then, as time went on, the floats these congregations made gradually disappeared. Why? It's because they required too much work to build and there were not enough people who volunteered to make them.

Making floats, of course, is just one way we can share with others the victory we have in the Lord Jesus. Sometimes we can celebrate with music that has a Christian emphasis. On other occasions we can give praise to the Lord through the performance of skits. Regardless of what we do, our focus should remain on God and not ourselves.

Rescued! Like the Jewish exiles who returned to Judah from Babylon, believers today have many reasons to rejoice. Take, for example, the testimony of an oil rig worker named Darrel Dore. On June 1, 1975, Darrel was working on an offshore platform in the Gulf of Mexico. Suddenly, the huge structure began to wobble. Then it tipped to one side and crashed into the water.

Darrel was horrified to discover that he was trapped inside a room. As the rig sank deeper into the ocean, the lights went out and the room filled with water. Next, Darrel thrashed about in the darkness. Not long after that, he accidentally found a large air bubble that was forming in the corner of the room. Instinctively, he thrust his head inside the pocket of air.

Just then, a terrifying thought sent a shiver down Darrel's spine. "I'm buried alive!" He began to pray out loud, and as he did, something remarkable happened. He later said, "I found myself actually talking to someone. Jesus was there with me. I could sense His comforting presence." For the next 22 hours, Jesus continued to comfort Darrel.

But now the oxygen supply inside the air bubble was giving out. Death seemed inevitable. It was just a matter of time. At that point, Darrel noticed a tiny shaft of light in the pitch-black water. As Darrel squinted his eyes, he could see the light growing brighter. Again, Darrel squinted. He concluded that the light was real. It was coming from a diver's helmet. Someone had found Darrel. His 22-hour ordeal was over. Rescue had come. He was delivered!

This remarkable incident reminds us that our Lord is always present. He is powerful enough to help us and caring enough to comfort us. There is no problem we face in our lives that He cannot handle. For this we can rejoice.

Come Celebrate! Sofia was considering throwing a surprise unemployment party for her husband, Juan. Sounds a bit strange, doesn't it? Maybe it shouldn't.

Well-meaning friends and relatives have expressed concern over Juan's extended period of unemployment. After all, this is the second time and second company from which he was laid off within 7 years. For 18 years prior, Juan's work life had been stable. If anyone had been predictable, it was Sofia's husband.

Recently, the couple's 16-year-old nephew approached Juan, quietly and on the side, to ask with genuine concern, "How will you take care of your family?" No unemployed person particularly likes that sort of question. After all, it can resurrect feelings of inadequacy. Thankfully, God provided Juan with an answer for his nephew. Juan gently replied, "God will take care of us. He has, and He will."

Did Juan have control over the World Trade Center terrorism of 2001 and the resultant downscaling of business that caused him to lose his first job? Did he have control in 2008 over the worst economic crisis to hit the US since the Great Depression, during which his company consolidated out of state and eliminated his second job?

In faith, we can only say, "God will take care of us. He has, and He will." The Jews of Ezra's day could also affirm this truth. Indeed, they celebrated the fact that the Lord worked through a variety of prolonged and difficult circumstances to bring to completion the rebuilding of the Jerusalem temple (see Ezra 6:16, 19, 22).

FOR YOUTH

■ **TOPIC:** Praise in the House

■ **QUESTIONS:** 1. What motivated God's people to continue working on the rebuilding of the temple? 2. What promises in Scripture can God use to change your attitude when you're feeling discouraged? 3. How can you depend on God's presence and love to help you overcome opposition from others to His work? 4. How do you think the returnees felt when the work on the sanctuary was completed? 5. What religious festivals did the Jews observe to commemorate their achievement?

■ **ILLUSTRATIONS:**

Let's Celebrate! How great it is when our favorite sports team wins and we can celebrate the victory. Nothing excites us quite like winning a championship. For a few moments we can be jubilant. But soon the fizz of excitement evaporates, and we have no more zip than old soda pop.

Like the returnees who celebrated the completion of the Jerusalem temple (see Ezra 6:16, 19, 22), as Christians, there are times when we can enter into festivities and special occasions. On other occasions, however, we decide to withdraw because things get out of hand. Knowing when to do so requires discernment.

Our celebrations do not have to be boisterous public displays. We can rejoice in the Lord as we sit by a lake with our Bibles. We can also celebrate with a friend at Bible study or on a retreat. Real celebration takes place in our hearts, not just on the streets or at music concerts.

God Is with You! At one point, prior to the completion of the Jerusalem temple, the returned exiles were so discouraged by their circumstances that they lost sight of the big picture and grew apathetic toward rebuilding the sanctuary. It was through the preaching of the prophets Haggai and Zechariah that the covenant community was able to bring to completion the work it had started on the temple (see Ezra 6:14).

The Hiding Place is a movie that shows how Corrie ten Boom and her sister, Betsie, were sent by the Nazis to a women's work camp for their part in helping to hide Jews in their father's home. In one scene, after Corrie's sister had died, the women of the camp were all standing at roll call on a bitter cold December day. This particular morning, Corrie's name was called, and she was told to step forward, presumably to be taken away and put to death.

But before leaving her place in the lineup, Corrie handed her tiny New Testament to the woman next to her, encouraging her in her newfound faith. Then, as Corrie made her way forward, she turned to the rest of the women, and in a voice husky with emotion, exclaimed, "God is with you!" The Lord, not the Nazis, would prevail in their hearts and lives. God, not the Nazis, held the prisoners' days and hours and months in His hand. And the Lord, not the Nazis, could give them eternal salvation.

The "Yea, God!" Party. Completing the Jerusalem temple was a major milestone in the life of the returnees. It gave God's people cause to celebrate and thank Him for His mercy and love toward them (see Ezra 6:16, 19, 22).

I recently learned about a church that is planning a "Yea, God!" party to celebrate all that the Lord has done for them in the past year. This body of believers recognizes the mighty acts of God that have blessed their existence, and they are excited about giving the Lord credit and praise for these gifts and blessings.

From what I hear, this won't be a small, quiet church service. It is going to be an all-out event. There will be a dynamic presentation highlighting many things God has done, special music, testimonials, singing, and great food. What a wonderful way to celebrate and honor the Lord for His mighty works among His people!

FASTING AND PRAYING

BACKGROUND SCRIPTURE: Ezra 8:15-23
DEVOTIONAL READING: 2 Chronicles 7:12-18

Key Verse: So we fasted and besought our God
for this: and he was intreated of us. Ezra 8:23.

KING JAMES VERSION

EZRA 8:15 And I gathered them together to the river that runneth to Ahava; and there abode we in tents three days: and I viewed the people, and the priests, and found there none of the sons of Levi. 16 Then sent I for Eliezer, for Ariel, for Shemaiah, and for Elnathan, and for Jarib, and for Elnathan, and for Nathan, and for Zechariah, and for Meshullam, chief men; also for Joiarib, and for Elnathan, men of understanding.
17 And I sent them with commandment unto Iddo the chief at the place Casiphia, and I told them what they should say unto Iddo, and to his brethren the Nethinims, at the place Casiphia, that they should bring unto us ministers for the house of our God. 18 And by the good hand of our God upon us they brought us a man of understanding, of the sons of Mahli, the son of Levi, the son of Israel; and Sherebiah, with his sons and his brethren, eighteen; 19 And Hashabiah, and with him Jeshaiah of the sons of Merari, his brethren and their sons, twenty; 20 Also of the Nethinims, whom David and the princes had appointed for the service of the Levites, two hundred and twenty Nethinims: all of them were expressed by name.

21 Then I proclaimed a fast there, at the river of Ahava, that we might afflict ourselves before our God, to seek of him a right way for us, and for our little ones, and for all our substance. 22 For I was ashamed to require of the king a band of soldiers and horsemen to help us against the enemy in the way: because we had spoken unto the king, saying, The hand of our God is upon all them for good that seek him; but his power and his wrath is against all them that forsake him.
23 So we fasted and besought our God for this: and he was intreated of us.

NEW REVISED STANDARD VERSION

EZRA 8:15 I gathered them by the river that runs to Ahava, and there we camped three days. As I reviewed the people and the priests, I found there none of the descendants of Levi. 16 Then I sent for Eliezer, Ariel, Shemaiah, Elnathan, Jarib, Elnathan, Nathan, Zechariah, and Meshullam, who were leaders, and for Joiarib and Elnathan, who were wise, 17 and sent them to Iddo, the leader at the place called Casiphia, telling them what to say to Iddo and his colleagues the temple servants at Casiphia, namely, to send us ministers for the house of our God. 18 Since the gracious hand of our God was upon us, they brought us a man of discretion, of the descendants of Mahli son of Levi son of Israel, namely Sherebiah, with his sons and kin, eighteen; 19 also Hashabiah and with him Jeshaiah of the descendants of Merari, with his kin and their sons, twenty; 20 besides two hundred twenty of the temple servants, whom David and his officials had set apart to attend the Levites. These were all mentioned by name.

21 Then I proclaimed a fast there, at the river Ahava, that we might deny ourselves before our God, to seek from him a safe journey for ourselves, our children, and all our possessions. 22 For I was ashamed to ask the king for a band of soldiers and cavalry to protect us against the enemy on our way, since we had told the king that the hand of our God is gracious to all who seek him, but his power and his wrath are against all who forsake him. 23 So we fasted and petitioned our God for this, and he listened to our entreaty.

BACKGROUND

Ezra finally appears in the seventh chapter of the book that bears his name. After Moses, Ezra was the most important human figure in the shaping of classical Judaism. Moses was considered the giver of the law, while Ezra was considered the teacher of the law. Ezra demonstrated that a godly scholar could do as much as, if not more than, a general or a politician to shape the character and destiny of a nation. Chapters 7 through 9 are taken from the memoirs of the great scribe. The memoirs begin abruptly as though no time had elapsed between the completion of the temple in 516 B.C. and the seventh year of Artaxerxes (458 B.C.).

Ezra referred to the people living in Jerusalem as "Israel" rather than "Judah" (unless Ezra was specifically referring to the Persian province). Clearly, Ezra wasn't interested in religious innovation. Instead, he focused on recapturing the covenant that the Lord had made with His people when the 12 tribes of Israel were united under Moses. Ezra mentioned in passing that he had initiated the contact with Artaxerxes. He asked for authorization to teach the law in Jerusalem, to mobilize a party of priests to strengthen worship at the temple, and to gather contributions for improvements within Jerusalem. Ezra played down the courage it must have required to approach an Eastern despot (see Esth. 4:11). On the other hand, he repeatedly emphasized the role of God's blessing on him and others (Ezra 7:6, 9; see also vs. 28; 8:18, 22, 31).

In this summary of Ezra's venture, which he then expanded in 7:11–8:36, the scribe mentioned that he was accompanied by various spiritual leaders, ranging from highly regarded priests to lowly temple servants (7:7). Again, he credited God's hand for the success of the trek. Ezra also stressed the graciousness of the Lord's travel mercies (vss. 8-9)—which become more obvious when the expanded version of the story reveals the size of the party, the wealth they transported, and their vulnerability to robbery. Throughout this undertaking, the most obvious quality of Ezra's personality was devotion (vs. 10). Not surprisingly, this descendant of the high priestly family of Israel had set his heart on studying "the law of the LORD." Ezra's obedience was not a slavish legalism, but wholehearted devotion to the Lord. Moreover, Ezra did not simply focus on his own personal holiness, but also taught others and motivated them to godly knowledge and living.

In verse 11, Ezra once again noted that he was a priest, a teacher, and an expert in the law of Moses. Then, in verses 12-26 an official letter of Artaxerxes is recorded. The document, which authorized Ezra's mission to Jerusalem, is the other portion of this book written in Aramaic (4:6–6:18 is the first). The use of this international language reminds us that God can work through the unwitting emperors of pagan empires just as readily as He uses believers to fulfill His purposes. The content of Artaxerxes' letter was clear evidence to Ezra of the gracious hand of God on his mission to Jerusalem.

NOTES ON THE PRINTED TEXT

In 8:1-4, Ezra listed the Jewish people who returned with him from Babylon to Jerusalem. He included various priests, descendants of royal heritage, and common Jews. This last category includes a list of 12 families consistently arranged as follows: the family name, the current head of the family, and the total number of men who relocated.

According to 7:9, the journey from Babylon to Jerusalem began on the "first day of the first month," that is, Nisan. This month coincided with March–April of our modern calendar. This would have been April 8, 458 B.C. The decision to travel in the spring was sensible, especially since there would have been an ample supply of water available along the route. Ezra and the Jews he led arrived in Jerusalem "on the first day of the fifth month," that is, Ab. This coincided with July–August of our modern calendar. This would have been August 4, 458 B.C. This means the entire 900-mile journey (which first headed northwest along the Euphrates River) took four months.

When 7:9 is compared with 8:31, it appears there was an initial delay of 11 days. Part of that delay is accounted for in 8:15. It states that Ezra gathered God's people at a canal that flowed toward the district of Ahava, where they camped in tents for 3 days. The exact location of this area remains unclear, though the canal might have flowed into either the Tigris or the Euphrates river. Ezra took this step to organize the caravan for the long journey ahead back to Jerusalem. According to verse 31, the excursion began on the "twelfth day of the first month," that is, Nisan. This means the group first assembled at the Ahava canal on the ninth of Nisan.

When Ezra surveyed the assembly, he found there were no Levitical priests in the group to serve the faith community once it had resettled in the Promised Land (vs. 15). The absence of Levities was a major point of concern, especially given that they performed important routine tasks in the temple and helped with the offering of sacrifices. In response, Ezra sent for nine influential leaders and two teachers known for their insight and discernment (vs. 16). Ezra wanted these individuals to persuade some of the Levites to journey with their fellow Jews back to Jerusalem. Verse 17 mentions one prominent Levite named Iddo, who was living in Casiphia. This town remains unidentified, though some have speculated it was located north of Babylon on the

Tigris River. Ezra directed his representatives to ask Iddo and his relatives to provide God's people with Levites so that they could serve as "ministers" in the temple after the group had arrived in Jerusalem.

Verse 18 reveals that it was due to the gracious intervention of the Lord that a Levite named Sherebiah and his extended family agreed to join the returnees at their river encampment before making the journey to Jerusalem. Sherebiah is described as a person having skill, insight, and prudence. He was a descendant of Mahli, who in turn traced his lineage back to Levi (see Exod. 6:19; Num. 3:20; 1 Chron. 6:19, 29; 23:21; 24:26, 28). Sherebiah was accompanied by his sons and relatives, who numbered 18 men.

Ezra 8:19 mentions two other prominent individuals named Hashabiah and Jeshaiah. Both of them were descendants of Merari. He was the third son of Levi and the father of Mahli (see Gen. 46:11; Exod. 6:16; 1 Chron. 6:16). Along with Hashabiah and Jeshaiah were 20 of the latter's kinsmen and their sons (Ezra 8:19). In addition, there were 220 temple servants (vs. 20), all of whom were listed by name. During the reign of David, their ancestors had been set apart by the king's officials to help the Levites in their work. With only a few days to consider, all the individuals mentioned in verses 18-20 were willing to uproot themselves from life in exile and return to Jerusalem. The providential intervention of God in bringing about this outcome helped to give legitimacy to Ezra's undertaking.

Ezra announced at the Ahava canal that there would be a mandatory fast to seek the Lord's favor. Through this fast the participants would humbly recognize their inability to safeguard their journey from potential dangers. In addition, they would be able to request that God make the trip level and straight (in other words, free from any life-threatening situations). They would ask the Lord to protect their entire group, including their young children and valuable possessions (vs. 21). The priceless items being transported by the group would be an especially tempting target for marauding bandits.

The Hebrew verb translated "ashamed" (vs. 22) refers to the presence of embarrassment or disgrace as a result of an awkward circumstance or adverse turn of events. This is how Ezra would have felt had he requested from Artaxerxes a military escort of foot soldiers and mounted troops to safeguard the Jews' trek back to Jerusalem. Previously, the scribe explained to the Persian king that God had displayed His favor on those who were committed to Him. In contrast, God's wrath was displayed against those who rebelled against Him. In light of these comments, Ezra felt he would have brought humiliation upon the name of the Lord (whom he represented) if he had requested a body of armed men to accompany the returnees. For this reason, God's people fasted and prayed to the Lord for a safe journey. In turn, He graciously answered their petition (vs. 23). In contrast, about 13 years later, Nehemiah would request a military escort when he made the journey to Jerusalem (see Neh. 2:7-9).

Suggestions to Teachers

God moved the heart of Artaxerxes and the hearts of His people to carry out His promise and His will for the covenant community. Against this backdrop, Ezra took the reins of leadership by proclaiming a fast. The intent was that he and his fellow Jews might humble themselves and ask God to give them a safe journey (see Ezra 8:21). And their efforts were not wasted, for the Lord granted their request (see vs. 23).

1. PRAYING TO DO GOD'S WILL. We can imagine the remnant of Jews still in Babylon asking God for release from their captivity. Undoubtedly, they saw their petitions as being in line with God's will for their lives. When we bring our petitions to the Lord, our motive should also be that He will achieve His will in our lives.

2. ASKING GOD TO MOVE HEARTS. Perhaps at first, the wait for the Jews still in exile seemed interminable and their circumstances impossible. Yet, at exactly the right time, God moved in the heart of the Persian king and the hearts of the faith community to carry out His divine purpose. Be sure to encourage the class members to ask God to move hearts to do His will in present circumstances.

3. SEEING GOD DO AMAZING THINGS. Let the students know that as they pray for God's will to be done, He can do amazing things to accomplish His plans and purposes. An example of this would be the way in which the Lord responded to the fasting and petitions made by the returnees in Ezra's day. Also, encourage the class members not to miss out when God speaks to their hearts, especially as remarkable opportunities to join in His work come their way.

4. AFFIRMING GOD'S FAITHFULNESS. Consider ending the teaching time by leading the students together in prayer. God will be honored by their affirmation of His faithfulness and power to do what seems impossible. They can also thank Him for His will, which is right and true and good.

FOR ADULTS	■ TOPIC: Preparing for the Journey

■ **QUESTIONS:** 1. Why did Ezra think it was important for the Levites to be part of the group of returnees? 2. How was Ezra able to convince some Levites to uproot and resettle in Jerusalem? 3. How would you characterize your devotion to God? 4. Why did Ezra proclaim a fast? 5. What can believers do to ensure that they have the right motives for serving God?

■ **ILLUSTRATIONS:**

Thinking about Prayer. As people journey through life, they learn new skills they can use along the way. For instance, people enjoy talking about how they learned to use a new electronic gadget. And they might even laugh about the mistakes they made and how they inadvertently erased some important information. Others share about the refresher courses they took to upgrade their professional skills.

Learning to pray can feel like that, especially because for many of us praying is a new skill. It's not something you fall into. Prayer is also a developed practice. And it takes a considerable level of training and discipline. While we pray, we learn more about it and find new pleasure in it. Yet, it still requires time and commitment from us.

As Ezra and those he led back to Jerusalem prepared for their long journey, they sought the Lord in prayer. Specifically, they petitioned Him to protect them from danger (see Ezra 8:21). Likewise, as we move through our spiritual pilgrimage, we will want to bring all our endeavors to the Lord and ask Him to bless what we do.

Having the Right Motive. Ezra could have drawn attention to himself by arrogantly insisting that he be given a military escort to accompany the returnees making the trek from Babylon to Jerusalem. But the scribe did not do that. Instead, he and his fellow Jews decided to fast. And by doing so, they humbled their hearts before asking the Lord to keep them safe as they began their journey (see Ezra 8:21-22).

As he walked to the church podium with his Bible and notes in hand, the pastor looked a little tired. But before turning to the Scripture passage, he said matter-of-factly, "I'm sorry if I seem a little out of it this morning. Because I've been fasting, I'm feeling a little foggy in the brain. It must be low blood sugar."

The pastor's statement was an offhanded remark. But some members of the congregation picked up on the remark, instead of the well-prepared sermon that followed. The pastor was probably offering a simple explanation for an "off" day he might have had in the pulpit. The last thing he would have wanted to be was a spiritual showoff. Likewise, we are not to do the right things, such as fasting and prayer, to obtain public recognition and glory for ourselves.

Trust God Completely. Undoubtedly, Ezra discerned the risk he was taking in leading a group of his fellow Jews from Babylon to Jerusalem. Instead of fretting over the circumstance, the scribe thought it was better to proclaim a fast and join the remnant in humbly asking God to protect them on their journey. And they were not disappointed by trusting God completely, for He graciously answered their prayer (see Ezra 8:21-23).

When Helen was in her second year of medical school, she wondered how she would ever finish. Her father had died when she was 11, leaving his wife with five young children, but no pension or life insurance. Helen's mother had always encouraged her children to pursue their dreams, but she made it clear that her two jobs could do little more than manage the expenses of their household. The children would have to pay for their own college education.

What Helen's mother could not give in financial help, she more than made up for in spiritual wisdom and direction. She taught her children the importance of giving, long before they entered school. Tithing on babysitting and newspaper route money was a common practice among Helen's brothers and sisters.

Though Helen often wondered how she would pay her way through school, she remembered hearing a quote from John D. Rockefeller, the millionaire tycoon of Standard Oil Company. When asked by a reporter, in his later years, how much money he planned to leave behind at the time of his death, Rockefeller wisely replied, "All of it." This pearl of understanding paralleled the exact course that Helen heard her from her mother her entire life.

God had always provided for Helen—rarely early, but never late. So, He had long since proved to Helen that she need never worry when she sought to live according to His will. His provision would always be sufficient for her needs. Though Helen missed her dad, she knew that her heavenly Father was always nearby to comfort and help her.

 FOR YOUTH

■ **TOPIC:** Preparing for the Journey

■ **QUESTIONS:** 1. Why do you think Ezra and the returnees camped by the Ahava canal for three days? 2. Whom did Ezra ask for help in convincing some Levites to journey to Jerusalem? 3. Why did Ezra decide against requesting a military escort? 4. How well does your life reflect what you know about God's providential care? 5. How have you recently experienced God's gracious hand?

■ **ILLUSTRATIONS:**

Prayer as Conversation. Ezra was about to lead a group of his fellow Jews on a 900-mile journey from Babylon to Jerusalem. But before they began to travel, they remembered to pray to the Lord for safety (see Ezra 8:21).

The concept of prayer as conversation with God has tremendous appeal to teens. We have to take prayer out of the realm of stuffy, pious jargon. We also have to show adolescents that prayer is not limited to people who petition the Lord in public places. Instead, prayer pleases God because it shows that we love Him and His fellowship.

Often, saved teens pray for the first time on retreats, or in small campus and church groups. They touch levels of intimacy in prayer because they are vulnerable to each other, more so than many adults. Therefore, our concern is not with the right words and tone of voice, but with honesty and integrity.

Our goals for youth are to encourage strong daily prayer habits, as well as quality prayer in fellowship groups. Then, as they pray, they can develop the needed fortitude for standing up to the spiritual battles they encounter in life.

Not Just for Show. Built by Louis XIV from 1664 to 1715, the Chateau of Versailles, France, is an incredible collection of massive, ornate buildings, a courtyard that could hold several football fields, and two and a half square miles of well-trimmed shrubbery, intricate flower gardens, and water fountains. Inside, every inch of every room has been gilded, sculpted, hung with rich tapestries, or painted with glorious scenes from mythology. Today, the complex would cost tens of millions of dollars to build.

The palace, however, was not all show and no substance. It was home to more than 20,000 people: nobles, administrative staff, merchants, soldiers, servants, and, of course, the king and his family. But after touring its rooms and gardens, one cannot help thinking that somewhere along the line, someone should have said, "Enough, Louis. You've already impressed everyone."

In this week's lesson, we encounter an entirely different leader. His name was Ezra. His goal was not to impress his fellow Jews. Instead, it was to safely lead a group of them from Babylon to Jerusalem. And Ezra was so concerned about honoring the Lord, that the scribe decided not to ask for a military escort. Instead, Ezra called for a fast, so that he and the other returnees could humbly petition God to protect them on their long journey (see Ezra 8:21).

Learning to Trust God More. Ezra could have worried excessively about the challenging journey that awaited him and his fellow Jews. Instead, he chose to fast and pray to the Lord. And God lovingly responded by giving His people a safe journey from Babylon to Jerusalem (see Ezra 8:21-23).

Janet's dog, Acorn, became a worrier at a young age. There was good reason. When Acorn was a puppy, she had been mishandled by a field trainer whenever he sternly yelled, "Come!" And when Acorn did not respond in the way he wanted, he would exclaim, "She's worthless!"

From that moment onward, the command "come" became a bittersweet experience for Acorn. When called, she would be worried about coming. But whenever she came to Janet, Acorn would be lavished with praise. Even though Acorn has never seen that field trainer again, her humiliating experience affected her outlook for a long time.

Over the years, Acorn has become an energetic and accomplished retriever. Janet has used hand signals—and words other than "come"—whenever possible. Acorn has made steady progress, especially as she has experienced good things when she has responded to Janet's calls.

Sometimes, as people, we act like Acorn. After we have been hurt deeply by someone, we begin to distrust others. We begin to "shut down." Sometimes, in our fear, we don't want to respond to anyone—not even to God. Yet the Lord, the patient Master, kindly and continually calls. He waits for us to make our move.

When we commune with God in prayer, He doesn't scold and reject us. Instead, He lavishes us with His love. And as our relationship deepens, our trust in Him increasingly overshadows any anxiety we once might have felt.

GIFTS FOR THE TEMPLE

BACKGROUND SCRIPTURE: Ezra 8:24-30
DEVOTIONAL READING: Mark 12:38-44

Key Verse: Ye are holy unto the LORD; the vessels are holy also; and the silver and the gold are a freewill offering unto the LORD God of your fathers. Ezra 8:28.

KING JAMES VERSION

EZRA 8:24 Then I separated twelve of the chief of the priests, Sherebiah, Hashabiah, and ten of their brethren with them, 25 And weighed unto them the silver, and the gold, and the vessels, even the offering of the house of our God, which the king, and his counsellors, and his lords, and all Israel there present, had offered: 26 I even weighed unto their hand six hundred and fifty talents of silver, and silver vessels an hundred talents, and of gold an hundred talents; 27 Also twenty basons of gold, of a thousand drams; and two vessels of fine copper, precious as gold. 28 And I said unto them, Ye are holy unto the LORD; the vessels are holy also; and the silver and the gold are a freewill offering unto the LORD God of your fathers. 29 Watch ye, and keep them, until ye weigh them before the chief of the priests and the Levites, and chief of the fathers of Israel, at Jerusalem, in the chambers of the house of the LORD. 30 So took the priests and the Levites the weight of the silver, and the gold, and the vessels, to bring them to Jerusalem unto the house of our God.

NEW REVISED STANDARD VERSION

EZRA 8:24 Then I set apart twelve of the leading priests: Sherebiah, Hashabiah, and ten of their kin with them. 25 And I weighed out to them the silver and the gold and the vessels, the offering for the house of our God that the king, his counselors, his lords, and all Israel there present had offered; 26 I weighed out into their hand six hundred fifty talents of silver, and one hundred silver vessels worth . . . talents, and one hundred talents of gold, 27 twenty gold bowls worth a thousand darics, and two vessels of fine polished bronze as precious as gold. 28 And I said to them, "You are holy to the LORD, and the vessels are holy; and the silver and the gold are a freewill offering to the LORD, the God of your ancestors. 29 Guard them and keep them until you weigh them before the chief priests and the Levites and the heads of families in Israel at Jerusalem, within the chambers of the house of the LORD." 30 So the priests and the Levites took over the silver, the gold, and the vessels as they were weighed out, to bring them to Jerusalem, to the house of our God.

9

HOME BIBLE READINGS

Monday, July 22	Hebrews 10:1-14	*A Single Offering for All Time*
Tuesday, July 23	Exodus 35:20-29	*Stirred Hearts and Willing Spirits*
Wednesday, July 24	Numbers 7:1-6	*Bring Offerings before the Lord*
Thursday, July 25	2 Chronicles 31:2-10	*Contributing Tithes and Offerings*
Friday, July 26	Mark 12:28-34	*More Important Than Offerings and Sacrifices*
Saturday, July 27	Mark 12:38-44	*The Gift of a Poor Widow*
Sunday, July 28	Ezra 8:24-30	*The Offering for God's House*

BACKGROUND

In last week's lesson, we learned that Ezra asked Artaxerxes for permission to return to Jerusalem. He granted Ezra everything he requested because the king was convinced that a strong Jewish population in Judah would foster peace and security as well as result in greater loyalty from his Jewish subjects. Artaxerxes gave Ezra the responsibility of leading about 1,750 men (perhaps a total of 5,000 people) in the second return from Mesopotamia to Jerusalem (see Ezra 7:1-28).

Having obtained this authorization from the Persian monarch, Ezra gathered an impressive group of family leaders and their kin who wanted to go with him back to Jerusalem. Two of the clans were priestly families, and most were following relatives who had returned with Jeshua and Zerubbabel (see 8:1-14). Ezra delayed departure eight days while he found key Levitical families to infuse new vigor into the temple ritual. Also, Ezra would not accept an armed escort for their 900-mile journey. The returnees trusted the Lord to guard them from bandits as they transported tons of precious metals to the temple treasury (see vss. 15-23).

NOTES ON THE PRINTED TEXT

To oversee the safe conveyance of the sacred items to the Jerusalem shrine, Ezra appointed 12 leaders from among the Jewish priests, along with 12 Levites (vs. 24; see vs. 30). Two of the Levites—Sherebiah and Hashabiah—were mentioned in verses 18 and 19, respectively. They were part of the group of Levites who had responded to Ezra's request for "ministers" (vs. 17) to serve in the sanctuary in Jerusalem. Sherebiah and Hashabiah were joined by "ten of their brethren" (vs. 24).

"Brethren" renders a Hebrew noun that can also mean "relatives" or "colleagues." A huge responsibility was being shouldered by the 12 priests and 12 Levites whom Ezra put in charge of the costly items he was transporting to the Jerusalem temple. The catalog of sacred objects included such precious metals as silver and gold (vs. 25). There were also numerous vessels intended to be used in the sanctuary of God. These utensils had been contributed by the Persian monarch, his counselors, his overseers, and wealthy Jewish families living in Mesopotamia at the time.

Verse 26 details the enormous quantities of money as well as instruments that had been dedicated for use in the temple. The Hebrew noun rendered "talents" refers to a weight of circular shape, which could be made out of gold, silver, bronze, or iron. In ancient times, the weight of a talent ranged from 62 to 66 pounds. So, 650 "talents of silver" was about 40,000 to 43,000 pounds. The "silver vessels" weighing 100 talents and the 100 talents of "gold" each varied between 6,200 and 6,600 pounds. Verse 27 refers to 20 gold basins worth 1,000 "drams" (which was about 19 pounds in weight). The dram (or daric) was a highly valued Persian gold coin used at that time. There were also two well-crafted vessels made out of finely polished bronze. These utensils were so exquisitely made that they were considered as valuable as gold.

The importance of the temple for God's people cannot be overstated. To begin, the sanctuary had an indispensable theological function to serve. It was the place where the Lord manifested His holy presence in Israel. It was also the spot where sacrifices were made in response to God's gracious choice of Israel as His people. In the sanctuary, God's people could spend time in prayer. Furthermore, its design, furniture, and customs were object lessons that prepared the people for the Messiah.

Additionally, the temple had important political and economic roles to play in Jewish society. It was the institution that held together the entire covenant community—the past as well as the present and the future. The sanctuary gave political identity to the people. Access to its courts identified who was properly a citizen and who was excluded. From an economic perspective, rooms in the temple functioned as a treasury—in effect, the society's bank. Because of the sanctuary's demands for tithes and offerings, a large portion of the Israelite economy passed through the temple personnel and storehouses. In brief, without the sanctuary, God's people had little opportunity to pull together as a coherent society to face the challenges of the future.

The Hebrew noun rendered "holy" (vs. 28) refers to what has been set apart as sacred or consecrated to the Lord. In this case, Ezra declared that both those serving in the Jerusalem sanctuary and the objects placed within the Holy Place were regarded as being specially designated for the temple service. Ezra also noted that the "silver" and "gold" were a voluntary "offering" that had been made to the Lord, the God of the returnees' ancestors. Because of the sacredness of the temple ministers and items, it was essential that the utmost caution and care were exercised, especially as God's people made the long and dangerous trek back to Jerusalem.

Accordingly, Ezra directed the 12 priests and 12 Levites mentioned in verse 24 to be careful with and protect the sacred items entrusted to their care. Their vigilance was to be maintained until the precious cargo arrived safely at the Jerusalem temple. At that time, the priests and Levites were to put the "vessels" (vs. 28) on scales in the designated storerooms of the sanctuary complex. Moreover, this was to be done in the presence of the chief priests, the Levites, and the family leaders of "Israel" (vs. 29).

In turn, they would verify that whatever had been designated as "holy" (vs. 28) arrived in Jerusalem safely and intact.

Whether it was the tabernacle or temple, both consisted of three sections. First, there was the outer court, and on its eastern side was the entrance. Second, within the courtyard, facing the entrance, was the altar of burnt offerings. Behind it, toward the west, was the laver for the priests' ceremonial washing. Third, in the western portion of the courtyard was the sanctuary proper. This was divided into two chambers by a hanging curtain.

The first of these was the Holy Place, which only the priests could enter. It contained the table of showbread, the lampstand, and the altar of incense. The second of the chambers was called the Holy of Holies or the Most Holy Place. It contained the ark of the covenant (which was called the mercy seat). The high priest entered this area once a year on the Day of Atonement. Precious metals and finely woven colored materials were employed in the construction of the Most Holy Place. Also, only objects made of rare and costly materials were located near the sacred space. The objects placed farther away were made of bronze and ordinary woven cloths (see Heb. 9:1-7).

"The priests and the Levites" (Ezra 8:30) willingly accepted responsibility for the precious metals and consecrated vessels placed under their care. They would ensure that whatever had been weighed out to them was transported safely to the Jerusalem temple. After that, Ezra and the Jews who were with him began the journey from Mesopotamia to Jerusalem. Ezra was convinced that God enabled them to survive the long trek. In fact, the Lord rescued His people from attack and abuse by vandals. After their arrival, they rested and refreshed themselves for three days. Then, on the fourth day, they distributed the money and the items dedicated for use in the temple. Everything was meticulously accounted for (vss. 31-34).

As an expression of worship, the returnees offered various animals to the Lord. They did so because they were thankful for the grace of the Lord in their lives. The sin offering mentioned in verse 35 was an atonement for specific unintentional sins, confession of sins, forgiveness of sins, and cleansing from defilement (see Lev. 4:1–5:13; 6:24-30; 8:14-17; 16:3-22). These temple offerings remind us that it is necessary to approach God through the provision of an acceptable atoning sacrifice. In faithful service to God, the Jewish leaders also delivered the king's directives to his various Persian officials in the Trans-Euphrates region of the empire. In compliance with Artaxerxes' orders, these officials assisted the Jews and their work in the temple (Ezra 8:36).

Achieving a difficult goal after years of effort—such as the successful return of God's people to Jerusalem—is an exhilarating accomplishment. Ask the athlete who endured the pain and loneliness of training to win an Olympic medal. Ask the small-business person who sacrificed vacations and weekends to carve out a niche for his or her service. Ask the missionary who endured hardship and sickness to provide a translation of the New Testament to an indigenous tribe. At times, these people may have thought the struggle would go on forever and the goal would never be reached. But in the end, at least for believers, the attainment of the objective is by God's grace.

SUGGESTIONS TO TEACHERS

In this week's Scripture passage, it's clear that God's people were fully committed to doing His will. For instance, Ezra was able to set apart 12 leading priests and 12 Levites to take charge of the temple offerings and vessels being transported from Mesopotamia to Jerusalem. Moreover, those remaining behind gave generously so that the Jerusalem shrine might be properly furnished. From this we see that believers can find true satisfaction by putting God and His concerns first in their lives.

1. A LIFE TAKEN ONE DAY AT A TIME. In a world full of poverty, disease, and starvation, it is easy for believers to experience feelings of worry and panic. Undoubtedly, this was just as true for God's people in Ezra's day, especially as they embarked on the return to their homeland. Then, as now, we can decide to trust God and act according to His will so that the panic does not overwhelm us.

2. A LIFE FILLED WITH PURPOSE. The keynote of Ezra's life was purposefulness. There is a tendency for adults today to lack a sense of purpose and direction to their lives. Stress to your class that from an eternal perspective, merely living for the moment is foolish. Believers who are truly consecrated seek to serve God throughout their lives. They discover, as Ezra did, that living for the Lord is not a waste of time. Rather, it bears eternal fruit.

3. A LIFE FILLED WITH VALUE. In the hustle of everyday life, adults might lose track of why they are here. They might begin to think that going to work and raising a family are valueless, at least from society's point of view. Relate to your students that regardless of what they do in life, it should be seen as a ministry that is done in the Lord's name. For instance, the work they do at the office is a testimony of their faithfulness to God, and the example they set for their children is a statement of how important it is to be Christlike in one's conduct.

4. A LIFE COMPLETELY DEDICATED TO GOD. Some adults think the teaching of God's Word is the only legitimate ministry being performed in the church. Point out to your students that God wants every aspect of their lives to be completely dedicated to Him. In this regard, even the administration of various church programs and the oversight of congregational expenditures are vital to the smooth operation of the church. Without meticulous care being exercised in the so-called mundane matters of life, the proclamation of the Gospel could be hindered.

returnees? 3. What sort of donations had been made to furnish the Jerusalem temple? 4. What are some ways we can give generously to the Lord and His work? 5. Why is it important for believers to ensure that whatever is given to God is properly used?

■ **ILLUSTRATIONS:**

Dedicated to Serve. The covenant community was blessed by the dedicated service provided by the 12 leading priests and 12 Levites mentioned in Ezra 8:24 and 30. Their sacrificial efforts were like a generous gift made to their fellow returnees.

In his book *A Call to Excellence,* Gary Inrig describes a similar sacrificial mindset. In the late 1800s, a large group of European pastors came to one of D. L. Moody's Northfield Bible Conferences in Massachusetts. Following the European custom of the time, each guest put his shoes outside his room to be cleaned overnight by the hall servants. But since this was America, there were no hall servants.

That night, while Moody walked through the dormitory halls, he saw the shoes and determined not to embarrass his peers. He mentioned the need to some ministerial students who were there, but met with only silence or pious excuses. Moody returned to the dorm, gathered up the shoes, and, alone in his room, the world-renown evangelist began to clean and polish the shoes.

That episode is a vital insight into why God powerfully used D. L. Moody. He was a believer with a servant's heart.

Uncommon Faithfulness. In 458 B.C., Ezra set apart 12 priests and 12 Levites for special service to the Lord. Scripture reveals they accepted and faithfully carried out their God-given assignment (see Ezra 8:24, 30).

"Be thou faithful until death"—that is the command found in Revelation 2:10, and it appears on the card that Pastor Samuel Lamb gave a group of Christians while they were visiting him in his home in Canton, China. He takes that verse literally. Living in a country officially closed to the Gospel, he was imprisoned for 25 years for leading a church, which meets in his home.

Pastor Lamb faithfully speaks about his belief in Christ to everyone he meets, including those who imprisoned him. Threats, prison, and the confiscation of his materials have not silenced him. Officials have taken his hymnbooks, fans, public- address system, televisions, cameras, and computers. Yet his ministry continues, and attendance increases!

It was humbling for visitors to sit with this elderly believer and hear him talk about the joy of serving the Lord. Pastor Lamb's continuous smile and enthusiasm were contagious. God has not called this Christian minister to a huge church that meets in a beautiful facility, or given him a large salary. God has moved his heart to reach the people of Guang Zhou (Canton). Stress?—no question! Faithfulness?—uncommon! Nothing short of death will stop Pastor Lamb.

It's Up to You. Choice seems to define our American culture these days. We can subscribe to cable or satellite television systems offering hundreds of channels, eat at food courts serving a wide variety of cuisines, and shop online businesses offering thousands of products.

Although the number and type of choices have changed dramatically during the past 25 years, one fact about choices has been true for as long as people have walked the earth: Every person must choose whom he or she will serve in life. Will they devote themselves to live for God, or will they give themselves over to something else? While few people today have actual wood or stone gods in their homes, our modern world offers numerous attractions to which we can devote ourselves: a career, material possessions, popularity, entertainment, prestige, wealth, and power (to name a few).

Thousands of years ago, Ezra put the issue of choice before 12 leading priests and 12 Levites. In turn, they accepted the challenge to serve the Lord faithfully (see Ezra 8:24, 30). Today, as in Ezra's time, everyone must decide who or what will be the foremost priority in their lives, including their hearts. It's up to us to dedicate every aspect of our lives in service to the Lord.

■ **TOPIC:** Give It Up!

■ **QUESTIONS:** 1. What did Ezra expect the 12 leading priests to do? 2. In what way had the Persian king and his officials been exceedingly generous to God's people? 3. Why would Ezra declare the 12 leading priests to be consecrated to the Lord? 4. In what sense are believers holy to God? 5. Who are some believers whom you would consider to be faithful servants of the Lord?

■ **ILLUSTRATIONS:**

Called by God to Special Service. The Christian faith is sometimes considered as a one-time-only commitment: You make a decision, take the church membership class, get your name on the church roll, and that's it. But the enemy of our souls never stops trying to subvert that decision. He wants us to avoid the tough moral and ethical requirements of committing every aspect of our lives to the Lord and His service.

The devil is especially delighted when saved teens live just like unbelievers. Indeed, many youth find it easier to follow the crowd than to make their own decisions. However, when they are challenged to follow a better way, some of them respond positively.

Ezra's forthright challenge to the 12 leading priests and 12 Levites is what youth prefer to hear (see Ezra 8:28-29). In contrast, young people do not respond well to exhortations to serve that are blurred by vague statements. Every day adolescents step forward and answer God's call to Christian service. They don't always know exactly what challenges they will face, but they know God, and that is enough for them.

Working Together to Help. Realizing that hospitals aren't much fun for sick children, students from two Pittsburgh-area schools created coloring books for young patients. Fifth-grade students at Sewickley Academy wrote and illustrated *Limericks and Animals of the Rain Forest.* Meanwhile, elementary students at Mt. Lebanon Academy created *Valentine Animals* and *My Happy Book.*

The books target children of various ages and include pictures and limericks. At the end of each book are a few blank pages where the hospital children can draw pictures and write return letters to their new friends. Children at the academies have enjoyed hearing from the boys and girls in the hospital. They had reached out to comfort and encourage the sick. For those in the hospital, help came from an unexpected source: peers who cared.

We should always be ready to accept the opportunities God brings us to serve Him and others. We know from Scripture and life experiences that He works in the most wonderful and unusual ways. For example, after some effort, Ezra found 12 priests and 12 Levites and gave them the opportunity to safeguard many valuable temple offerings and vessels. Thankfully, they did not refuse to accept the task. Instead, they welcomed it and faithfully carried it out (see Ezra 8:24, 30).

Ali Baba Bunny. In 1957, Warner Brothers featured a Bugs Bunny cartoon called "Ali Baba Bunny." It begins with a very muscular looking man named Hasan who is ordered to guard the closed entrance to a cave that is filled with treasure. Right after this, Bugs Bunny and Daffy Duck are seen burrowing past Hasan and under the cave's entrance. When the two finally stop and pop out of the ground, they are dismayed to learn that they're not at Pismo Beach.

It doesn't take long for Daffy Duck to see all the treasure stored in the cave. He becomes so filled with greed that he shoves Bugs Bunny back into the ground and claims all the treasure for himself. Daffy Duck's eyes become enormous as he thinks about all the riches surrounding him. There are endless piles of gold coins, diamonds, and pearl necklaces. He begins rubbing his hands together and declares himself to be "rich," "wealthy," and "comfortably well off."

What a contrast Daffy Duck is to the 12 priests and 12 Levites we learn about in this week's lesson. Ezra gave them an important assignment. They were to make sure that a large amount of gold, silver, and precious utensils made it safely from Mesopotamia to Jerusalem. Instead of greedily hoarding any of these valuable items for themselves, they faithfully carried out the task they were asked to do (see Ezra 8:24-30).

FESTIVAL OF BOOTHS

BACKGROUND SCRIPTURE: Nehemiah 7:73b–8:18
DEVOTIONAL READING: Exodus 23:12-17

Key Verse: All the congregation of them that were come again out of the captivity made booths, and sat under the booths. . . . And there was very great gladness. Nehemiah 8:17.

KING JAMES VERSION

NEHEMIAH 8:13 And on the second day were gathered together the chief of the fathers of all the people, the priests, and the Levites, unto Ezra the scribe, even to understand the words of the law. 14 And they found written in the law which the LORD had commanded by Moses, that the children of Israel should dwell in booths in the feast of the seventh month: 15 And that they should publish and proclaim in all their cities, and in Jerusalem, saying, Go forth unto the mount, and fetch olive branches, and pine branches, and myrtle branches, and palm branches, and branches of thick trees, to make booths, as it is written. 16 So the people went forth, and brought them, and made themselves booths, every one upon the roof of his house, and in their courts, and in the courts of the house of God, and in the street of the water gate, and in the street of the gate of Ephraim. 17 And all the congregation of them that were come again out of the captivity made booths, and sat under the booths: for since the days of Jeshua the son of Nun unto that day had not the children of Israel done so. And there was very great gladness.

NEW REVISED STANDARD VERSION

NEHEMIAH 8:13 On the second day the heads of ancestral houses of all the people, with the priests and the Levites, came together to the scribe Ezra in order to study the words of the law. 14 And they found it written in the law, which the LORD had commanded by Moses, that the people of Israel should live in booths during the festival of the seventh month, 15 and that they should publish and proclaim in all their towns and in Jerusalem as follows, "Go out to the hills and bring branches of olive, wild olive, myrtle, palm, and other leafy trees to make booths, as it is written." 16 So the people went out and brought them, and made booths for themselves, each on the roofs of their houses, and in their courts and in the courts of the house of God, and in the square at the Water Gate and in the square at the Gate of Ephraim. 17 And all the assembly of those who had returned from the captivity made booths and lived in them; for from the days of Jeshua son of Nun to that day the people of Israel had not done so. And there was very great rejoicing.

10

HOME BIBLE READINGS

BACKGROUND

Ezra traveled from Babylon to Jerusalem in 458 B.C. (see Ezra 7:8). Nehemiah arrived in Jerusalem from Susa, one of the Persian capitals, in 445 B.C. (see Neh. 2:1). Both accounts appear to have been written soon after the occurrence of the events they describe. The Book of Ezra may date from about 440 B.C., and the Book of Nehemiah from about 430 B.C. With respect to the latter document, it records Nehemiah's determination to rebuild the walls of Jerusalem and renew the commitment of its people to the Lord. This brisk, forceful book emphasizes the importance of faithfulness to God and perseverance in trials.

Even though the books of Ezra and Nehemiah go together, they make a contrasting pair. On the one hand, both documents narrate events in Jerusalem after a remnant of Judah returned from the Babylonian captivity. On the other hand, while Ezra was a meditative scribe who led reforms by means of teaching and holiness of character, Nehemiah was an official in the Persian government who led reforms by means of bold plans and force of character. The personality differences between these two leaders are significant. For example, when Ezra heard that some of the Jewish men had taken foreign wives, he tore out his own hair. When Nehemiah confronted the same problem, he tore out the hair of the offenders.

NOTES ON THE PRINTED TEXT

Scripture relates that while Ezra was in the capital of Judah, he wept bitterly over the sins of the people (see Ezra 9). In response, many Jews gathered to confess their transgressions and weep alongside their spiritual leader. The people then made a covenant to obey God and to put away the foreign wives who had caused them to abandon the Lord (see 10:1-4). The efforts of Ezra to initiate a spiritual renewal lasted for a short period. But by the time Nehemiah returned, the spiritual fire had fizzled. As a matter of fact, in the 13 years between the end of the Book of Ezra and the beginning of the Book of Nehemiah, the Jewish people once again fell into their sinful ways. They intermarried into families with foreign religions and neglected to support the temple.

Thankfully, God was at work in the hearts of His people. They had seen the Lord's hand on Nehemiah, and they knew that to survive, they needed God's help. They also understood that to receive God's help, they needed to dedicate themselves to obeying His commands. Rather than waiting for Ezra or Nehemiah to start another spiritual revival, the people started it themselves. On October 8, 444 B.C., the Jews assembled in Jerusalem. The event was timed to coincide with the Feast of Trumpets, the New Year's Day of the Jewish civil calendar (later known as Rosh Hashanah; see Neh. 7:73–8:1). This was one of the most noteworthy seasons on Israel's religious calendar (Lev. 23:23-43), and it was celebrated by the blowing of horns or trumpets from morning until evening. After the exile, the festival was observed by the public reading of the Mosaic law and by general rejoicing.

The people gathered in an open plaza in front of the Water Gate, an entryway leading to the Gihon spring (Jerusalem's primary source of water). The gate was located on the eastern side of the city, slightly south of the wall's midsection, and directly opposite the temple. This area was not considered sacred, which meant laypeople could participate with priests in the gathering. Women and children, who did not always attend temple ceremonies, were present in accordance with Moses' instructions in Deuteronomy 31:10-13 (Neh. 8:2; see 2 Chron. 20:13). The occasion for the assembly was Ezra's reading of the "book of the law of Moses" (Neh. 8:1), which the Lord had given Israel to obey.

Ezra faced the open square just inside the Water Gate from early morning until noon and read aloud from the Torah scroll to everyone who could understand. In ancient times, this was the customary practice. All the people, in turn, paid close attention to what they heard (vs. 3). Imagine standing for five or six hours in reverential silence while attentively listening to the Bible being read! From this incident comes the modern Jewish tradition of standing as the Torah scroll is read in the synagogue (a ritual some Christian churches also observe). Everything that was done and the way it was reported points to the deep commitment and devotion of God's people. Ezra the scribe was standing on a high wooden platform that had been built for this occasion. He wasn't alone, either. Standing next to him was Nehemiah, and they were flanked on their right and left by priests, Levites, and other Jewish leaders (vs. 4; see vs. 9). They evidently stood alongside Ezra to assist in the long time that it took to read, translate, and interpret God's Word.

Ezra stood on the elevated platform in full view of the people. When they saw the scribe unroll the Torah scroll, they rose to their feet in unison out of respect for the reading and exposition of God's Word (vs. 5). This spontaneous response from the crowd must have warmed the scribe's heart. Once Ezra and his associates were done, the audience departed to do all that the leaders had said. They ate and drank at a festive meal, shared gifts of food with the disadvantaged, and celebrated the occasion with "great mirth" (vs. 12), for they had both heard and understood the Word of God that had been read and expounded to them. The next day, the leaders of each family along with the priests and Levites assembled to meet with Ezra. His goal was to help them understand the law better (vs. 13).

According to verse 14, in 444 B.C., the religious and civil leaders of the covenant community discovered that the Feast of Booths was celebrated during the fall season five days after the Day of Atonement. The leaders announced in Jerusalem and Judah that the people were to observe the sacred day. This involved going out to the hill country and obtaining a variety of branches—from cultivated and wild olive trees, myrtle trees (evergreen shrubs that gave off a pleasant fragrance), date palms, and other leafy trees—to construct temporary shelters for living outside. This was done in accordance with the Mosaic law (vss. 14-15). The Feast of Booths (also called Tabernacles or Ingathering) was characterized by a week of celebration for the harvest in which God's people lived in booths and offered sacrifices. This observance memorialized the Israelites' journey from Egypt to Canaan (when they lived in tents) and gave them an opportunity to thank the Lord for the productivity of the land (see Exod. 23:16; Lev. 23:33-43; John 7:37).

The people complied with the directive given them by the religious and civil leaders. The people went out, cut branches, and used them to build shelters in every possible location of Jerusalem, that is, on the flat roofs of their houses, in the courtyards of their homes, in the outer and inner courtyards of God's temple, and in the plazas around the Water Gate and the Ephraim Gate (the latter being on the north side of the city and facing toward the territory of Ephraim; Neh. 8:16). The people living in the surrounding villages also built temporary shelters.

This holiday had not been observed in quite this way and with this much joy since the time of Joshua centuries earlier. The people were once again giving thanks to God for His blessings with the same enthusiasm and zeal as the Israelites of Joshua's day had done (vs. 17). As we have learned, the events that transpire in Nehemiah 8 took place during the celebration of two of Israel's sacred days: the Feast of Trumpets (see vs. 2) and the Feast of Booths. Absent in this account is the celebration of a third feast: the Day of Atonement. The people's prior disobedience and lack of attention to God's law may have caused them to neglect this important day.

Understanding of biblical truth is dry without the joy that God produces. Likewise, feasting and joy are meaningless without the firm foundation of God's Word. That is why Ezra read from the Mosaic law each day throughout the entire seven-day period of celebration. On the eighth day, a solemn assembly took place in accordance with the law (vs. 18). The purpose of the reading was not only to preserve the law, but also to encourage every generation to revere and obey God's Word. This public reading led the Jews to renew their commitment to God's covenant and to instruct their children to do the same.

SUGGESTIONS TO TEACHERS

When Ezra read the Mosaic law to God's people, a spiritual revival broke out among them. They immediately praised God, joyfully observed the Feast of Booths, and humbled themselves before the Lord. Even the study of application of Scripture is important to believers. Our Maker gives us instructions in His Book, the Bible, that will help us lead better lives.

1. WE ALL NEED TO KEEP REFRESHING OUR MEMORY OF SCRIPTURE. Even if you've been reading the Bible for years, you need to keep reading it. Read it in a different translation. Study it with the aid of Bible reference works. Do whatever it takes to keep the Bible fresh in your mind. If you approach the Bible with the humble attitude that you can never come to the end of your need for it, God will honor you with new insights and new help for living.

2. COMBINE WORSHIP WITH BIBLE LEARNING. The Bible is not a mere text; it is God speaking to us. It is entirely appropriate, therefore, for us to offer prayers of thanks and praise to God when we approach the Scriptures.

3. TRY TO REALLY UNDERSTAND WHAT YOU'RE READING. Sometimes people never get beyond a devotional reading of Scripture. But there is a time for study—for doing the hard work of trying to understand this ancient, complex, and unique book. Just as God's people listened to Ezra teach them the Word, so we must make sure we understand what Scripture says.

4. DON'T BE DISCOURAGED. The Bible will reveal your shortcomings. Face those shortcomings and realize that they displease the Lord. But never forget the grace of God, which is able to forgive your sin and help you overcome the bad habits you've developed. In obedience is freedom.

FOR ADULTS	■ **TOPIC:** Great Rejoicing

■ **QUESTIONS:** 1. Why did Ezra, along with the leaders of the covenant community, value the study of God's Word? 2. What was the significance of the Feast of Booths? 3. Why did the covenant community in Ezra's day celebrate the Feast of Booths? 4. What connection do you see between the Word of God and celebration? 5. What can you do to renew a commitment to know and do God's will?

■ **ILLUSTRATIONS:**

Responding to God's Law. We all accept the axiom that ignorance is no excuse when we break the law. Yet we tend to tolerate ignorance of God's laws and wonder why our lives and our churches seem to lack spiritual authority, power, and joy.

A researcher in church growth has noted that preaching is essentially useless unless people first confess their sins. But why should they confess when they have no standard by which to measure their behavior? God's laws are that standard. Unless we know those guidelines and respect them, there's not much likelihood for confession to occur.

Just as Ezra did in his day (Neh. 8:13), our task is to make God's Word clear and applicable to all of life. Only then will we see spiritual growth and strong discipleship in our lives and in our churches. Likewise, as with God's people in Ezra's day (see vs. 17), that is when we will experience the overwhelming joy of being freed from the guilt of sin.

The Value of God's Word. In this week's lesson, we discover that the leaders of each Jewish family, along with the priests and Levites, assembled to meet with Ezra. He helped them better understand the Mosaic law (see Neh. 8:13, 18). Ezra's efforts were important, for the Jews did not possess personal copies of the law. Thus, the main way they were able to become familiar with it was by hearing it read and explained.

Several decades ago, tears glided silently down Emily's cheeks as she sat quietly and listened to Beluk read the first four chapters of John's Gospel to his tribe. However, in Emily's heart, she was exuberant. When she graduated from college, she made a commitment to Wycliffe Bible Translators. Emily's continuing education and association with the Summer Institute of Linguistics (SIL) brought her to this equatorial aboriginal group 10 years earlier. Her work, like that of so many Bible translators, began with years of tedious analysis—both of the structure of the culture and its language.

Emily discovered that being accepted into a primitive culture took time, and the hardships she encountered were enormous. For instance, Emily had malaria three times in the first six years. Finally, after becoming part of the social community, she developed an alphabet from the language sounds and wrote a primer. She then spent time teaching key tribal members how to read. After almost eight years, Emily began to work on her translation of John's Gospel. Now, as Beluk publicly read Emily's work, she gazed at the tears appearing on the faces of these eager listeners. They were hearing the precious words of salvation for the first time in their own language!

Road Map. In 1997, the Central American city of Managua, Nicaragua, adopted a program that most cities take for granted. The city named its streets and numbered its buildings. Larry Rohter writes in the *New York Times* that for 25 years, Managua, with a population of 1.8 million, had been without that basic necessity following a devastating 1972 earthquake, which relocated most residents.

During that time, people learned to make do, wandering down the wrong streets, asking strangers where to go, and making one wrong turn after another until they hopefully found their destination. *Illogical* is a good word to describe the system—if you can call it a system. "Formal addresses have come to be defined neither by numbers nor street names," writes Rohter, "but in relation to the nearest landmark, as in: 'From El Carmen Church, a block toward the National Stadium' or 'Across from Los Ranchos Restaurant.'

"That, in turn, has made it necessary to name the points of the compass in giving directions or addressing a letter, an issue that has been resolved in an equally baffling fashion. 'Toward the lake' has come to mean north, 'toward the mountain' means south, 'up' means east and 'down' means west.

"Furthermore, though some of the original guideposts still exist, many others have vanished, leaving all but prequake residents confused. A leading economic research institute, for instance, offers visitors the following address: 'From where the gate of El Retiro Hospital used to be, two blocks toward the lake, one block down.'"

Finding one's way in Managua sounds a lot like trying to spiritually revive one's life without the clear guidance of God's Word. One is dependent on directions from others who may not know the right way. One operates by trial and error. One wanders and feels lost. How much better to have a map! As the members of the covenant community in Ezra's day learned (see Neh. 8:13, 18), Scripture offers us clear direction to live by so we know where we are going—and can tell others how to get there too!

TOPIC: Remembering to Celebrate

QUESTIONS: 1. What prompted the leaders of the covenant community to assemble with Ezra? 2. Why is it important for God's Word to be explained to believers? 3. Why had Moses directed God's people to observe the Feast of Booths? 4. Why do you think God's people were so filled with joy as they celebrated the Feast of Booths? 5. Have you ever been through a phase of your life when you neglected to read the Bible? What effect did it have on you?

ILLUSTRATIONS:

Right Words. All of us use favorite send-off words to encourage our friends, such as the following: "Live strong," "Keep your chin up," and "Hang in there!" Right words do make a difference. The best words to remember are found in the Bible.

"The joy of the LORD is your strength" (Neh. 8:10) is one of those classic biblical promises. It means a lot more when we recall its original setting. When God's people wept for their sins, Nehemiah told them that it was now time for them to experience God's joy. In turn, this truth enabled the covenant community to celebrate the Feast of Booths with great joy (see vs. 17).

Scripture brings us to confession and joy. Divine words of truth are always the right and best ones for us. When we neglect them, it's like neglecting food and drink for our bodies. The Bible helps us to overcome our sins, to find joy, and to give joy to others.

The Treasure of Truth. Have you ever been on a treasure hunt? You look all over for the treasure because you know it is worth finding. And when you find it, you call others over to see!

The Bible, God's Word, is our treasure. It is filled with words of hope, healing, and comfort. Although the Bible was written a long time ago, its truths are still relevant to us today. What a gift to have God's promises to guide our lives. This is certainly how the Jews of Ezra's day must have felt, especially as they attentively listened to him explain to them the meaning of the Mosaic law (see Ezra 8:13, 18),

In the Lord Jesus, we have the treasures of wisdom and knowledge along with the riches of understanding (see 1 Cor. 1:30). That's why we need to know the promises of the Bible, to live by them, and share the Gospel with others. The great thing about this treasure is the more you give away, the more you have yourself!

The Gift. In Ezra's day, God's people did not have individual copies of the entire Bible to read. That is why Ezra took time to teach them what the Mosaic law said (see Neh. 8:13, 18). Contrast this situation with what prevails today in Western society. Many families have several Bibles in their homes and think nothing of it. Of course, in numerous other places around the globe, people still do not have access to a Bible, particularly in their own language.

Many years ago, an American missionary society assigned a young woman from Chicago to live with a tribe in central Africa, where she was to teach English to both the adults and the children of the tribe. She spent many years with them and became quite close to several families. In fact, a number of them trusted in the Lord Jesus as their Savior because of the Christian love displayed to them through this missionary.

After several years, the missionary decided to take a year's sabbatical. She returned to America to visit with family and friends and raise further support. But before she departed, she decided to give her family Bible to her closest friend in the village. Her friend was full of joy at receiving such a precious gift, for she knew that the missionary was giving her something that had been passed down to her from her mother.

The year went quickly for the missionary, and soon she was back in the African village, telling her friends about her trip across the ocean. It was then that she noticed the Bible she had given her friend, who held it in her arms. The Bible was in terrible shape. Many pages had been torn out. At first the missionary didn't know what to say. She couldn't believe her friend seemed to have such little regard for God's holy Word.

Then, as anger began to take hold, the missionary pointedly said to the woman, "What did you do to this Bible? It's all ripped!" The woman was startled but smiled and replied, "The Bible is so priceless to me that I had to give different parts of it to my friends and family, so they too can understand the wonderful message about Jesus, God's Son."

COMMUNITY OF CONFESSION

BACKGROUND SCRIPTURE: Nehemiah 9:1-37
DEVOTIONAL READING: Luke 15:1-10

Key Verse: The seed of Israel separated themselves from all strangers, and stood and confessed their sins, and the iniquities of their fathers. Nehemiah 9:2.

KING JAMES VERSION

NEHEMIAH 9:2 And the seed of Israel separated themselves from all strangers, and stood and confessed their sins, and the iniquities of their fathers. . . . 6 Thou, even thou, art LORD alone; thou hast made heaven, the heaven of heavens, with all their host, the earth, and all things that are therein, the seas, and all that is therein, and thou preservest them all; and the host of heaven worshippeth thee. 7 Thou art the LORD the God, who didst choose Abram, and broughtest him forth out of Ur of the Chaldees, and gavest him the name of Abraham; . . . 9 And didst see the affliction of our fathers in Egypt, and heardest their cry by the Red sea; 10 And shewedst signs and wonders upon Pharaoh, and on all his servants, and on all the people of his land: for thou knewest that they dealt proudly against them. So didst thou get thee a name, as it is this day. . . . 30 Yet many years didst thou forbear them, and testifiedst against them by thy spirit in thy prophets: yet would they not give ear: therefore gavest thou them into the hand of the people of the lands. 31 Nevertheless for thy great mercies' sake thou didst not utterly consume them, nor forsake them; for thou art a gracious and merciful God. 32 Now therefore, our God, the great, the mighty, and the terrible God, who keepest covenant and mercy, let not all the trouble seem little before thee, that hath come upon us, on our kings, on our princes, and on our priests, and on our prophets, and on our fathers, and on all thy people, since the time of the kings of Assyria unto this day. 33 Howbeit thou art just in all that is brought upon us; for thou hast done right, but we have done wickedly: 34 Neither have our kings, our princes, our priests, nor our fathers, kept thy law, nor hearkened unto thy commandments and thy testimonies, wherewith thou didst testify against them. 35 For they have not served thee in their kingdom, and in thy great goodness that thou gavest them, and in the large and fat land which thou gavest before them, neither turned they from their wicked works. 36 Behold, we are servants this day, and for the land that thou gavest unto our fathers to eat the fruit thereof and the good thereof, behold, we are servants in it.

NEW REVISED STANDARD VERSION

NEHEMIAH 9:2 Then those of Israelite descent separated themselves from all foreigners, and stood and confessed their sins and the iniquities of their ancestors. . . .

6 And Ezra said: "You are the LORD, you alone; you have made heaven, the heaven of heavens, with all their host, the earth and all that is on it, the seas and all that is in them. To all of them you give life, and the host of heaven worships you. 7 You are the LORD, the God who chose Abram and brought him out of Ur of the Chaldeans and gave him the name Abraham. . . .

9 "And you saw the distress of our ancestors in Egypt and heard their cry at the Red Sea. 10 You performed signs and wonders against Pharaoh and all his servants and all the people of his land, for you knew that they acted insolently against our ancestors. You made a name for yourself, which remains to this day. . . .

30 "Many years you were patient with them, and warned them by your spirit through your prophets; yet they would not listen. Therefore you handed them over to the peoples of the lands. 31 Nevertheless, in your great mercies you did not make an end of them or forsake them, for you are a gracious and merciful God.

32 "Now therefore, our God—the great and mighty and awesome God, keeping covenant and steadfast love—do not treat lightly all the hardship that has come upon us, upon our kings, our officials, our priests, our prophets, our ancestors, and all your people, since the time of the kings of Assyria until today. 33 You have been just in all that has come upon us, for you have dealt faithfully and we have acted wickedly; 34 our kings, our officials, our priests, and our ancestors have not kept your law or heeded the commandments and the warnings that you gave them. 35 Even in their own kingdom, and in the great goodness you bestowed on them, and in the large and rich land that you set before them, they did not serve you and did not turn from their wicked works. 36 Here we are, slaves to this day—slaves in the land that you gave to our ancestors to enjoy its fruit and its good gifts."

Monday, August 5	Acts 3:17-26	*Repent and Turn to God*
Tuesday, August 6	Matthew 21:28-32	*A Changed Mind*
Wednesday, August 7	Job 42:1-6	*I Repent in Dust and Ashes*
Thursday, August 8	Matthew 5:21-26	*First Be Reconciled*
Friday, August 9	Luke 18:9-14	*God, Be Merciful to Me*
Saturday, August 10	Luke 15:1-10	*Joy in Heaven*
Sunday, August 11	Nehemiah 9:2, 6-7, 9-10, 30-36	*The Community Confesses Together*

BACKGROUND

Two days after the last joyous day of the Feast of Booths, on October 30, 444 B.C., the people of Judah and Jerusalem gathered once again in the holy city (Neh. 9:1). Previously, Ezra and Nehemiah had discouraged mourning over sin during the festival days when the people were to draw spiritual strength from the joy of knowing the Lord (see 8:9-10). Now, they assembled again to explore another aspect of being the people of God through fasting, separation from idolatry, and confession of sin. Rough goat-hair garments and dust-covered heads illustrated the state of mourning the Jews adopted as the proper approach to confession of their sins. Most likely, the sackcloth worn by the confessing Jews was a coarsely woven cloth of goat hair (9:1).

Sackcloth irritated the skin and was too rough for ordinary clothing. Because of its durability, this material was typically used to create bags. The sackcloth worn by people in mourning could have simply been two rectangular pieces sewn together, with holes for the head and arms. Or it could have been nothing more than a loincloth. The physical characteristics of this coarse material served as a powerful symbol of how the wearer felt. Mourners wore sackcloth as a form of self-abasement and to illustrate how their sorrow chafed their spirit. They were prepared to connect their personal sins with the rebelliousness of their ancestors before the captivity.

NOTES ON THE PRINTED TEXT

In this episode, the participants stood for three hours of reading from the Mosaic law and three hours of confession and worship, just as they had stood all morning on the first of the month to hear Ezra read the law (Neh. 9:2-3; see 8:3, 5). The people stood in reverence because the law had come through Moses from "the LORD their God" (9:3). Probably the assembly of Judah gathered for confession before the same platform in the square at the Water Gate, where Ezra had previously read the Mosaic law (see 8:1). Most likely, the steps on which the Levites stood as worship and confession guides were the stairs to the platform. Two groups of eight Levites are named in 9:4-5.

The Levites called on the people to stand for worship (vs. 5). This display of reverence consisted of praise that focused on the covenant relationship between God and His people Israel. Jewish tradition attributes to Ezra the beautiful prayer recorded in verses 5-37. The prayer is structured carefully to guide the worshipers of Judah and Jerusalem in contrasting themselves with the Lord. His glorious name was worthy to be praised, even though no human expression of adoration was great enough (vs. 5). The participants declared that God alone is the Lord who brought all things into existence. This included the "heavens" (vs. 6), the "heaven of heavens," and the vast multitude of stars. Furthermore, the Lord created the earth, along with all the plant and animal life found on the land, within the seas, and in the air. Because every living thing owed its existence to God, the angels of heaven worshiped Him.

Verse 7 recounts the fact that the sovereign Lord chose Abram while he was living in Ur of the Chaldeans (a city on the Euphrates River in what is today southern Iraq) and summoned him to resettle his family in Canaan. Moreover, God changed the patriarch's name from "Abram," which means "[my] father is exalted," to "Abraham," which means "father of a multitude." In this way, the Lord designated the patriarch in a special way as His servant. This is the only Old Testament reference outside Genesis to God renaming Abraham (see Gen. 17:5).

Nehemiah 9:8 notes that the Lord found Abraham to be trustworthy and characterized by integrity. God responded to the patriarch's faithful disposition by establishing a covenant with him. In it, the Lord pledged to give the land of Canaan to Abraham's descendants (see Gen. 15:18-20). Later, God promised to make the patriarch "the father of many nations" (17:4). God fulfilled His pledge, for He is "righteous" (Neh. 9:8). This renders a Hebrew adjective that emphasizes the integrity and uprightness of the Lord in all His dealings with people.

The Jewish assembly next recited God's mighty works of the Exodus. The Lord heeded the anguish of their ancestors in Egypt and at the Red Sea when escape seemed hopeless (vs. 9). God performed awesome acts of power against Egypt's ruler, his officials, and all the inhabitants of the nation. The Lord did so, for He knew how insolently the Egyptians had acted against the ancestors of the Jews. By means of the 10 plagues, God earned a lingering reputation among the nations (vs. 10). Then the Lord opened the barrier of the sea to save Israel and swallow the pursuing Egyptians (vs. 11). The phrase "as a stone into the mighty waters" echoes the victory song of Moses and Miriam sang on the shores of the Red Sea (see Exod. 15:5).

The returnees of Ezra's day acknowledged the justice, righteousness, and goodness of every kind of command their ancestors received from God on Sinai. The Jews expressed special gratitude for the gift of the Sabbath through God's revelation to Moses. The confessing congregation affirmed the physical sustenance that God gave Israel in the desert, along with the spiritual food of the Mosaic law (Neh. 9:15). Furthermore, the Lord gave the Israelites manna from heaven every day, water from the rock in emergency circumstances, and the opportunity to enter Canaan and enjoy its riches (see Exod. 16:4; 17:6; Num. 14:8-9; 20:7-13). At that moment, the Jews confessed that their ancestors had been poised to receive a fulfillment of God's promise to Abraham (Neh. 9:15).

The pronouns "you" and "they" interchange throughout Nehemiah 9:16-38, as the Jews compared and contrasted the deeds of God and their ancestors. Despite their deliverance from bondage in Egypt, the revelation of the Mosaic law at Mount Sinai, the guidance and nourishment the Israelites received in the wilderness, and the clear instructions God gave them on how to enter and possess the Promised Land, the nation stubbornly bowed its neck like an ill-tempered ox and rebelled against the Lord (vs. 16). The people disregarded His revealed will and His gracious miracles of deliverance and decided to go back to Egypt and slavery (vs. 17; see Num. 14:1-4). Only God's graciousness and compassion kept Him from abandoning Israel when they went further and worshiped a golden calf (Neh. 9:18; see Exod. 32:4).

Tragically, in the centuries that followed, the Israelites became progressively more arrogant, stubborn, and stiff necked in their refusal to heed the oracles of God. The Lord knew Israel was becoming impervious to His law, but His Spirit patiently kept sending prophetic warnings (Neh. 9:30). Despite God's displays of kindness, His people paid no attention to Him. Consequently, there was no option but to bring upon them the curses threatened in the law for repeated, persistent disobedience (see Deut. 28:15-68). Even then, the Lord, in His abundant mercy (Neh. 9:31), prevented Israel's annihilation. And, out of God's great compassion, He refused to forsake His chosen people.

Starting in verse 32, the assembled Jews began to focus their prayer of confession to their own time within the Persian Empire. They praised God for being great, mighty, and awesome. The worshipers declared that the Lord remained faithful to His covenant, which was characterized by His steadfast love. In contrast, the returnees bemoaned the distress of their political leaders, spiritual leaders, and tribal structures. They saw a straight line of well-deserved misery starting with the Assyrian conquest of the 10 northern tribes in 722 B.C., through the Babylonian destruction of Jerusalem in 586 B.C., right down to their plight under Persian domination. The people of Judah and Jerusalem asked God not to regard all the adversities they were experiencing as an inconsequential matter.

The assembly of Jews confessed that whenever the Lord punished His people, He remained righteous. He had dealt with them faithfully (vs. 33). In contrast, the ancestors of the returnees were guilty of acting wickedly. Political leaders, spiritual authorities, and tribal heads all had strayed from the Mosaic law and ignored every prophetic warning to repent (vs. 34). Even when they had become a prosperous, independent nation, the covenant community refused to serve the Lord. Moreover, despite the fact that in His "great goodness" (vs. 35), He blessed His chosen people with a "large and fat land," they refused to turn from their wicked practices.

In the end, the assembly of Jews appealed to God's mercy on the basis of their status as "servants" (vs. 36) in their own country, their own cities, and their own homes. Their livelihood was disappearing to pay the crippling taxes that the Persian emperors imposed on all the provinces (vs. 37). The returnees acknowledged that their own sins were adequate reasons for their subjection to foreign rulers. The worshipers reminded "the great, the mighty, and the terrible God" (vs. 32), who keeps His promises because He is righteous, that they—His repentant servants—were "in great distress" (vs. 37). This had been the sort of thing that moved Nehemiah to leave the palace in Susa to help his people rebuild the walls of Jerusalem (see 1:3). The Jews hoped God would be favorably disposed toward them, too. The Old Testament gives several examples of prayers that reason with God on the basis of His Word and previous deeds. No one has any right to tell God what to do, but He looks favorably on those of His spiritual children who root their prayers in the Scriptures and in His promises to them.

SUGGESTIONS TO TEACHERS

About two days after the completion of the Festival of Booths, the Jews assembled. They fasted, put on sackcloth, and covered their heads with dirt. The people, whose ancestors were from Israel, separated themselves from all foreigners. Then, for three hours, the group stood and listened to the law of God being read. Next, for three more hours, they confessed their sins and worshiped the Lord. God is also pleased when we corporately and privately acknowledge our sins.

1. BEING CONFORMED TO GOD'S WORD. Although the Jews had rebuilt the Jerusalem temple and restored the priesthood, they were not keeping the entire Mosaic law. Observing rituals was not enough to please God. Their entire lives needed to conform to God's Word, not to what was convenient or pragmatic for them.

2. MAKING AN EFFORT TO CHANGE. A Christian is also called to be different in important ways from the rest of the world (see Rom. 12:1-2; Eph. 4:21-24). Changing a lifestyle, however, is often a slow process. Like a child learning to walk, when we slip and fall, we ask for God's forgiveness (see 1 John 1:9), dust ourselves off, and try again.

3. RECOGNIZING ENTICEMENTS TO SIN. Temptations to be like the rest of the world are often subtle and pervasive. The students may find themselves involved in non-Christian habits more than they imagined. Encourage the class members to consider these questions: Do I enjoy gossip? Am I in the habit of telling "small" lies to make myself look good? Do I rationalize questionable business practices or cheat on my income taxes by saying, "Everyone else does it"? Do I enjoy telling or hearing off-color jokes?

4. DECIDING TO OBEY GOD. The Jews of Ezra's day admitted their sin and were willing to change. When God's Spirit points out the changes that need to be made in the lives of the students, do they clean up their act, or do they resist the kinds of changes the Lord wants to make? Emphasize to the students that change involves obeying God, rather than doing what they want to do. The Lord always leaves the choice to them.

<table>
<tr><td>FOR
ADULTS</td><td>■ TOPIC: Admitting Shortcomings
■ QUESTIONS: 1. Why did the returnees feel the need to confess the sins their ancestors had committed?</td></tr>
</table>

■ TOPIC: Admitting Shortcomings
■ QUESTIONS: 1. Why did the returnees feel the need to confess the sins their ancestors had committed? 2. Why did God choose to make a covenant with Abraham? 3. What are some difficult circumstances that God has enabled you to endure? 4. How did God remain merciful to His people, despite their rebellion? 5. Why is it important for believers to remain faithful to God?

■ ILLUSTRATIONS:

Getting Back on Course. The presence of sin in the faith community of Ezra's day finds numerous parallels today. The returnees confessed that many, including civic and religious leaders, had violated God's will.

On a more positive note, the assembled Jews discovered the power of remorse, confession, and repentance at work in their lives. And the entire faith community was willing to acknowledge and renounce their sins. Beyond that, they willingly accepted considerable hardship in order to make things right.

Confession, repentance, and restoration—these are the sorts of steps to getting back on course spiritually when we sin. No one is exempt, for everyone has sinned. Perhaps it has not been openly or flagrantly, but we have all broken God's laws and have fallen far short of His glory (see Rom. 3:23). That's why we need courageous spiritual leaders who are willing to identify with sinful people. The Holy Spirit honors these leaders, especially when they confront people with the requirements of God's holiness.

Unquestioning Obedience. We are usually careful about what we commit to. And that can be a good thing. We should not sign on the dotted lines of contracts, credit card applications, loans, and other such documents without first knowing what the "fine print" says. We should not, as the saying goes, "sign our life away" without first knowing the details.

Still, there remain commitments we need to make and keep, regardless of the consequences. This was true of the Jews in Ezra's day. On October 30, 444 B.C., the people of Judah and Jerusalem assembled in the holy city. They affirmed God's faithfulness, confessed their long history as a people of unfaithfulness, and prayed for the Lord's continued blessing in their lives.

Centuries later, in A.D. 249, the emperor Decius ordered the first widespread persecution of Christians across the entire Roman Empire. All citizens were required to publicly offer incense yearly to the pagan gods, declare, "Caesar is Lord," and sometimes curse the Lord Jesus. For that act, they would receive a sheet of paper, a *libellus,* from the local magistrate saying they were loyal Romans. In this way, they would avoid going to prison, performing hard labor, or even being put to death.

Many chose to get the sheet of paper. Others did not—and suffered the consequences. The wholehearted commitment of those who refused to renounce the Savior caused the Greek writer Lucian to say the following: "[They] have convinced themselves that they are going to be immortal and live for all time. Therefore, they despise death and even willingly give themselves into custody." May this assessment be true of us today as followers of the Lord Jesus.

The Touch of the Master's Hand. Pierre Auguste Renoir pioneered impressionist techniques in French painting late in the nineteenth century. As Renoir's fame spread, so did the number of Renoir forgeries. The painter was understandably upset by the proliferation of these fraudulent paintings, but after a time he came to accept their existence.

As a favor to collectors he liked who were stuck with one of these fakes, Renoir occasionally touched up a canvas and signed it so the collector could display or resell it as an original. Angry friends urged him to take legal action against the forgers, but Renoir could see no benefit in the litigation. He preferred repairing paintings to punishing forgers. This was a truly gracious response!

Like Renoir, the Lord finds no joy in bringing judgment on people—whether in Ezra's day or our own. Instead, He prefers to rescue the ruined canvases of sinful lives. Only when all opportunities to repent have been rejected will the unrepentant "forgeries" be exposed for punishment.

 For Youth

■ **Topic:** Fess Up!

■ **Questions:** 1. Why did the assembly of Jews feel the importance of turning away from their transgressions? 2. Why is it important for believers to affirm that God is the Creator? 3. Why did God rescue His people from Egypt? 4. What are some ways God has shown His unfailing love to you? 5. In what sense were the returnees slaves in the land of promise?

■ **Illustrations:**

Faithful Leadership Calls for Obedience. One day, as I was shopping at the grocery store, I heard a mother firmly say the following to her disobedient child: "What did I tell you to do? Are you making a good choice? Remember what we talked about before we came inside the store." The child needed to know that heeding her mother's warning was the wisest decision to make.

In ancient Judah, the Lord's spokepersons kept issuing warnings, but God's people ignored them. Despite many years of hearing the prophets' declarations, the people refused to repent. In the end, they experienced sorrow and loss for their disobedience.

God's warning to us is clear. If we disobey Him, He will discipline us. The good news, of course, is that when we turn away from our sins and seek to obey God, we will be eternally blessed. Just as He did for the Jews who returned to their homeland from exile, so today He also gives us the strength to do His will.

The Need for Radical Change. Zig Ziglar, a longtime popular motivational speaker, once told his audience that "reaching your goal is not near as important as what you become in reaching it." Ziglar meant that success is not always measured by the attainment of something, but by the learning that occurs in the process.

For example, a winning runner receives far more than the temporary honor of his or her victory. Years of training have taught the athlete the value of discipline, patience, sacrifice, determination, and hard work. So, the development of a superior runner often requires rigorous and radical changes in a person's lifestyle to reach desired goals.

In this week's lesson, we see how the people of Judah took the painful but necessary steps to confront their sinful lifestyle. It was only when they confessed their transgressions and decided to follow God that the people could experience His blessings in their lives.

Listen Carefully. Our ears are made so that sound vibrations can pass to the part of our brain that controls hearing. It starts with sound waves causing our eardrums to vibrate. Thousands of individual fibers make this possible. As a result, messages are sent through an auditory nerve to the center of hearing in our brain, which then classifies and interprets the sounds.

We are made to listen carefully, but when it comes to paying attention to God, something else comes into play—not our physical ears, but rather our spiritual hearts. This is why Scripture admonishes us to hear and heed God's Word. The focus isn't on our auditory nerves, but rather on our souls.

To listen to God means to love, honor, worship, and obey Him. We can hear His truth with our ears, but fail to respond with our hearts. In this case, we may hear, but we do not love Him with the totality of our hearts, minds, and wills. Just as in the time of Ezra, we should avoid such faulty listening at all costs.

DEDICATION OF THE WALL

BACKGROUND SCRIPTURE: Nehemiah 12:27-43
DEVOTIONAL READING: Psalm 96

Key Verse: They offered great sacrifices, and rejoiced: for God had made
them rejoice with great joy: the wives also and the children rejoiced:
so that the joy of Jerusalem was heard even afar off. Nehemiah 12:43.

KING JAMES VERSION

NEHEMIAH 12:27 And at the dedication of the wall of Jerusalem they sought the Levites out of all their places, to bring them to Jerusalem, to keep the dedication with gladness, both with thanksgivings, and with singing, with cymbals, psalteries, and with harps.
28 And the sons of the singers gathered themselves together, both out of the plain country round about Jerusalem, and from the villages of Netophathi; 29 Also from the house of Gilgal, and out of the fields of Geba and Azmaveth: for the singers had builded them villages round about Jerusalem. 30 And the priests and the Levites purified themselves, and purified the people, and the gates, and the wall. 31 Then I brought up the princes of Judah upon the wall, and appointed two great companies of them that gave thanks, whereof one went on the right hand upon the wall toward the dung gate: 32 And after them went Hoshaiah, and half of the princes of Judah, 33 And Azariah, Ezra, and Meshullam, 34 Judah, and Benjamin, and Shemaiah, and Jeremiah, 35 And certain of the priests' sons with trumpets; namely, Zechariah the son of Jonathan, the son of Shemaiah, the son of Mattaniah, the son of Michaiah, the son of Zaccur, the son of Asaph: 36 And his brethren, Shemaiah, and Azarael, Milalai, Gilalai, Maai, Nethaneel, and Judah, Hanani, with the musical instruments of David the man of God, and Ezra the scribe before them. . . . 38 And the other company of them that gave thanks went over against them, and I after them, and the half of the people upon the wall, from beyond the tower of the furnaces even unto the broad wall; . . . 43 Also that day they offered great sacrifices, and rejoiced: for God had made them rejoice with great joy: the wives also and the children rejoiced: so that the joy of Jerusalem was heard even afar off.

NEW REVISED STANDARD VERSION

NEHEMIAH 12:27 Now at the dedication of the wall of Jerusalem they sought out the Levites in all their places, to bring them to Jerusalem to celebrate the dedication with rejoicing, with thanksgivings and with singing, with cymbals, harps, and lyres. 28 The companies of the singers gathered together from the circuit around Jerusalem and from the villages of the Netophathites; 29 also from Beth-gilgal and from the region of Geba and Azmaveth; for the singers had built for themselves villages around Jerusalem. 30 And the priests and the Levites purified themselves; and they purified the people and the gates and the wall.
31 Then I brought the leaders of Judah up onto the wall, and appointed two great companies that gave thanks and went in procession. One went to the right on the wall to the Dung Gate; 32 and after them went Hoshaiah and half the officials of Judah, 33 and Azariah, Ezra, Meshullam, 34 Judah, Benjamin, Shemaiah, and Jeremiah, 35 and some of the young priests with trumpets: Zechariah son of Jonathan son of Shemaiah son of Mattaniah son of Micaiah son of Zaccur son of Asaph; 36 and his kindred, Shemaiah, Azarel, Milalai, Gilalai, Maai, Nethanel, Judah, and Hanani, with the musical instruments of David the man of God; and the scribe Ezra went in front of them. . . .
38 The other company of those who gave thanks went to the left, and I followed them with half of the people on the wall, above the Tower of the Ovens, to the Broad Wall, . . . 43 They offered great sacrifices that day and rejoiced, for God had made them rejoice with great joy; the women and children also rejoiced. The joy of Jerusalem was heard far away.

12

Monday, August 12	Psalm 96:1-9	*Celebrating God's Greatness*
Tuesday, August 13	Psalm 96:10-13	*Celebrating the Lord's Coming*
Wednesday, August 14	Deuteronomy 12:2-7	*Celebrating God's Blessings*
Thursday, August 15	Nahum 1:6-15	*Celebrating Freedom from Oppression*
Friday, August 16	Jeremiah 30:18-22	*Celebrating the Restored Nation*
Saturday, August 17	Isaiah 66:10-14	*Celebrating the Restored Jerusalem*
Sunday, August 18	Nehemiah 12:27-36, 38, 43	*Celebrating a Completed Task*

BACKGROUND

This week's lesson focuses on Nehemiah's dedication of the rebuilt wall in Jerusalem (Neh. 12:27). Because access to the city was difficult, it at one time enjoyed a relatively protected location. But when a major regional trade route developed through the city, Jerusalem became commercially and strategically desirable to every subsequent political force that came to power.

Jerusalem's wall provided its best defense against attack. Yet, when the Babylonians demolished the wall in 586 B.C., the city became defenseless against any invading army. In 444 B.C., Nehemiah learned that the condition in Jerusalem was not good. This situation moved him to ask God to intervene on his behalf, especially as he made his request known to Artaxerxes (see Neh. 1). Then, when Nehemiah asked the king for permission to go to Jerusalem and rebuild the city's walls, Artaxerxes agreed (see 2:1-10). While Nehemiah was in his beloved city, he inspected the condition of the wall. He also encouraged the Jews living there to repair and rebuild the demolished stone structure (see vss. 11-20).

In Nehemiah 3, the author listed over 40 Jewish groups that helped rebuild the wall (which was not completed until 6:15). The extent of destruction and repair was not uniform. Some sections of the wall and the buildings would demand more time and attention than other areas. The wall surrounding Jerusalem symbolized the preservation of God and His faithfulness in reestablishing His people. Its successful restoration indicated that the Jews in the heart of their capital would remain safe. God would protect them from attack and abuse by vandals. Moreover, rebuilding the wall would end Jerusalem's humiliating condition (see 1:3). The city would no longer seem like a disgrace to the Jews and their God.

NOTES ON THE PRINTED TEXT

Previously, when Nehemiah inquired about the condition of his homeland, he asked about both the people and the place (see Neh. 1:2). He did not celebrate the physical rebuilding of the Jerusalem walls until the people who would live within them had been spiritually rebuilt as well. From this observation we see that bricks and mortar are never as important as hearts and lives. Even in our churches today, we need to keep in mind, as Nehemiah did, that every facility we build should advance the work of God in human hearts and lives.

Nehemiah's first-person account of the restoration of Jerusalem had broken off after 7:5. It picks up again at 12:27 and continues through the end of the book. When Nehemiah was ready for an official celebration by the renewed people to dedicate the rebuilt walls of the city, he needed to have Levites available to assist in the ceremony. These individuals had the instrumental and vocal musical skills necessary for a mass celebration (for example, leading songs of thanksgiving accompanied by music played on cymbals, harps, and lyres).

Accordingly, Nehemiah had the Levites brought to Jerusalem from wherever they lived in Judah. Furthermore, the Levitical families of singers and musicians were brought together from the regions around Jerusalem and from the outlying villages of Benjamin and Judah where they lived (vss. 28-29). Before the priests and Levites dedicated the recently completed walls, they conducted purification ceremonies (vs. 30). These rituals were not concerned with physical cleanliness, but with spiritual preparation to be in God's presence. The unspecified ceremonies may have involved washings by the priests and Levites and sacrifices for the people, the gates, and the walls (see Exod. 40:30-32; Lev. 14:49-53).

Nehemiah directed all of the community leaders of Judah to ascend the wall for the dedication (Neh. 12:31). He divided the priests and Levitical musicians into two large choirs. The Hebrew text literally says these choirs represented "two thanksgivings." In other words, they embodied what they did. The choirs got in formation atop the wall and marched around the city; the first choir moved in a counterclockwise direction, and the other clockwise.

The starting point was the Dung Gate. This gate (mentioned earlier) was the city exit to the garbage dump in the Valley of Hinnom on the southern tip of the city. Ezra probably led the first procession, followed by singers and instrumentalists (vss. 35-36). The political leaders brought up the rear (vss. 32-34). Old Testament compass points are determined by facing east. So, "on the right hand" (vs. 31) means "to the south." This choir rounded the southern tip of Jerusalem and processed north atop the eastern wall alongside the ancient City of David and his royal residence (vs. 37).

The second choir matched the first in makeup (vs. 38). Nehemiah joined the other civic leaders at the rear. He did not lead this sacred procession because he was not a priest. The people also divided themselves in two masses and followed one or the other choir of thanksgiving around the wall. The second choir marched north atop the western wall, then east atop the northern wall (vs. 39). At the Gate of the Guard (or Prison Gate; see 2 Kings 11:6, 19; Jer. 32:2), in the vicinity of the temple at the northeast corner of Jerusalem, the two choirs of thanksgiving met one another face-to-face and halted. When the Jews dedicated the walls of Jerusalem, purity preceded praise, and praise resulted in faithful service. Today, we praise God best when our lives back up what our lips declare.

After encompassing Jerusalem with a parade that claimed the city as God's gift to His people, the two choirs descended from the walls and assembled "in the house of God" (Neh. 12:40). This refers to the courtyards of the temple—not in the actual Holy Place, where no one went but the ministering priests and Levites in the course of their daily routines. Nehemiah and half the civil leaders joined the choirs and 15 priests (7 of whom blew trumpets) for a choral festival under the direction of Jezrahiah (vss. 41-42). His name meant "The Lord Shines Forth," and he fulfilled his name's significance by directing the gathered multitude in glad adoration of the Lord.

The leaders, priests, Levites, and ordinary citizens worshiped the Lord with numerous sacrifices on the brazen altar before the temple entrance on its east side (vs. 43). Men, women, and children launched into a time of praising God for the joy He had given them and was giving them through His gifts of the city walls and the renewed covenant. Ninety-two years before (that is, 536 B.C.), the exiles who returned under Zerubbabel and Jeshua had made a noise of celebration that could be heard a long way outside the city. They were rejoicing that the foundation of the temple had been laid. As was noted in lesson 6, at that time, sorrow mixed with joy as some old-timers remembered better days (see Ezra 3:10-13). In contrast, as the walls were dedicated in 444 B.C., no sorrow dampened the spirits of the revelers. They had no doubt that God was in their midst and ready to affirm them as His chosen people in His holy city.

Out of the joyous dedication of the walls came a repeated pledge to serve the Lord faithfully and gladly. Stewards were appointed to keep track of the firstfruits and tithes brought to the temple storerooms (Neh. 12:44). At this time, the Jews were pleased with the spiritual labor of the priests and Levites in assisting Ezra in bringing about revival. Moreover, the people were glad to make donations from their fields, orchards, and vineyards to support the work done in the temple. For their part, the priests and Levites were prepared to follow the worship duties spelled out centuries before by kings David and Solomon (vss. 45-46; see 1 Chron. 23–26).

Nehemiah reported that the people of Judah regularly contributed to the support of the priests, Levites, and temple worship all during his governorship and that of his predecessor Zerubbabel (Neh. 12:47). The Levites remembered to give a tithe to the priests from the tithes they received from the people. Regrettably, some of the Jews after the exile did not support their spiritual leaders. Nehemiah and the contemporary prophet Malachi dealt forcefully with those who shirked their responsibilities to worship (see Neh. 13:10-11; Mal. 1:7-8; 3:8-9). From this observation we see that after the flush of enthusiasm that accompanies an exhilarating worship experience, it often takes determination and reliance on the Lord's power to follow through on our spiritual commitments day after day.

SUGGESTIONS TO TEACHERS

At first, the material in this week's lesson might seem irrelevant to the lives of Christians. Yet, the dedication ceremony from thousands of years ago described in the Scripture text teaches us about the importance of worshiping God. Indeed, doing so is the basis for experiencing a joyous relationship with Him.

1. GENUINE WORSHIP. The passages in this week's lesson give us a glimpse into how God's people in Nehemiah's day strove for genuineness in their worship. Until God is the sole object of our adoration and praise, life will be hopelessly chaotic and destructive. Our reverence for Him must not be left to our moods or whims. Rather, we must worship Him "in spirit and in truth" (John 4:24).

2. AUTHENTIC WORSHIP. The Jews refused to be superficial and mechanical in their worship. Instead, they tried to be authentic. One way to ensure this was by every participant being ritually purified (see Neh. 12:30). Ask the class members to think of ways in which they can prepare themselves to worship the Lord in an authentic manner.

3. INDIVIDUAL AND CORPORATE FORMS OF WORSHIP. For many of us, worship has become something we wait to do on Sunday morning as part of a congregation of believers. While our corporate worship among God's people is certainly pleasing to the Lord, it does not need to be the only time we engage in adoring our wonderful, loving God. We can also do so on an individual basis each day, regardless of where we are.

4. CREATIVE WORSHIP. The covenant community could have gone through a perfunctory dedication ceremony. Thankfully, they decided to be creative in their expression of worship. Verses 31-43 reveals that the participants split into two choirs. Then, after circling the Jerusalem wall in opposite directions, they rejoined at the temple to give God praise. Take a few moments to discuss with the students some fresh, creative approaches to worship your church might adopt.

FOR ADULTS

■ TOPIC: Taking Pride in Accomplishment

■ QUESTIONS: 1. What challenges had to be overcome to make the rededication of the rebuilt Jerusalem wall possible? 2. Why was it important to seek out Levites for the rededication ceremony? 3. Why were the two choirs so jubilant in giving thanks to God? 4. What are some ways your church celebrates major milestones it achieves? 5. What key events in your life bring you deep and abiding spiritual joy?

■ ILLUSTRATIONS:

Remembering to Express Thanks. Rebuilding the Jerusalem wall was quite an accomplishment. This is especially so when we consider all the challenges God's people had to overcome. In the end, though, they realized it was the Lord who enabled them to be successful in their endeavor. And this is why, when they dedicated the wall, they gave thanks to the Lord.

None of the students in your class can truthfully claim to have a problem-free existence. For some, there are health issues; for others, there are financial pressures; and still for others, there are relational setbacks. Ultimately, the only way to overcome these challenges is by the grace of God. In turn, He deserves to be thanked for the amazing ways in which He is working in their lives.

God's desire for worship is part of a reciprocal love relationship He wants to establish with the class members. It is a relationship in which they worship Him exclusively in fresh, creative ways. In fact, setting aside special times of worship is one approach to help develop that relationship.

Talk of God's Wondrous Works. In 444 B.C., God's people experienced the fulfillment of a long-held desire. Despite various trials, they succeeded in rebuilding the wall of Jerusalem. And to commemorate the momentous event, they dedicated the stone structure. Everyone was filled with so much gladness that the "joy of Jerusalem was heard even afar off" (Neh. 12:43) by non-Jews.

Recently, a week before Labor Day, Margaret's eight-person department at work got word that one of them would be laid off the week after the holiday. Her coworker Denise was so nervous that she had trouble sleeping. "What would you do if it happened to you?" she asked Margaret. "I don't know," was her response. "But I'm really not worrying about it."

Denise said, "How can you not worry about being laid off?" Margaret explained, "Well, this might sound strange, but I believe that God brought me to this new job for a reason. If I lose my job, I have faith that God has something else in store for me." After a pause, Denise said, "Is that what it means to have faith? Just saying, 'God will take care of it'?"

Margaret had been working side by side with Denise for six months, and they had become friends. But now Margaret was grateful for their current tense work situation. Margaret felt it gave her the opportunity to talk openly about how she had experienced God working wondrously in her life. Much to Margaret's surprise, she learned that telling non-Christian friends about God was not that hard.

How many believers have held back from telling others about God's deeds because of the needless fear that they would say something wrong, start an argument, be embarrassed, or lose friends? It doesn't matter if we don't know all the right theological words. Our unsaved colleagues and friends don't know them either. It also does not really matter if we don't cover the entire plan of salvation. God will use what we do share with others for His glory.

Ultimately, what does matter is our willingness to talk honestly about God's role in our lives. As His good works fill our lives, we should not hesitate to share the blessings we've experienced. In that way, we give sincere witness to God's power and the reality of our faith.

Praise the Lord Anyhow. This was a popular slogan back in the 1970s. Christians who experienced flat tires and job termination could be heard quipping the phrase. I was young then and could not understand why someone would praise God for a disappointment. Wasn't that just pretending you didn't hurt when you really did? Wasn't that pasting on a smile and saying you praised God when really you were upset with Him?

What I have since come to realize is that for believers who truly trust God's goodness and His purpose, praising Him in the middle of a challenge is the sincerest expression of faith. Their "praise the Lord anyhow" attitude flows out of a belief that God is always with them and will help them through every difficulty, just as He did for His people in Nehemiah's day. In their case, the result was an opportunity to rejoice loudly over the fact that because of God's help, the wall of Jerusalem had been successfully rebuilt (see Neh. 12:43).

FOR YOUTH

■ **TOPIC:** Celebration by Dedication

■ **QUESTIONS:** 1. Why did the civil and religious leaders think it was important to rededicate the rebuilt Jerusalem wall? 2. What role did the Levites play in the rededication ceremony? 3. Why was it important for the priests, Levites, and other participants to be ritually purified? 4. What are some ways you can express thanks to God for what He has done in your life? 5. How might you encourage other saved youth to celebrate the ways in which God is working in their lives?

■ **ILLUSTRATIONS:**

Making Worship a Priority. Even saved teens experience times when their feelings don't match up with what they know they should be doing. It's similar to those Monday mornings when they just don't feel like going to school, even though they know they should.

It's not uncommon for adolescents to have similar feelings about church and worship. Whether they are tired from a late Saturday night social event, upset with a sibling or peer, or simply not having a good day, it isn't always easy for them to sing songs of praise and thanksgiving.

This is where making worship a priority comes into view. Despite all the hardships God's people in Nehemiah's day had to overcome, they did not let these challenges prevent them from giving thanks to the Lord in worship. Similarly, encourage your students to consider how they can make the worship of God their primary goal.

Heavenly Minded. Recently, the lottery jackpot in the state where I live reached a record amount. Everywhere I turned, the question loomed: "What would you do with all those millions of dollars?" The front page of one local newspaper featured an article about all the luxury items a person would suddenly be able to afford.

Then I remembered a sermon a pastor I know had just preached. He told about the times during his childhood when he would visit his grandfather, a retired minister. The older man was devout and wise, but the boy noticed occasional moments when the man would "blank out." He would stare into space with a faraway look in his eyes for a minute or two, then suddenly come back to the here and now.

When the grandson got older, he discussed the episodes with his grandfather. The young man asked, "Did you ever see a physician about those? I always worried about you being off in your own world somewhere." His grandfather explained, with a smile, "I wasn't in my world. I was in God's. Sometimes, things would strike a chord in me, and I'd recall a special Bible verse or phrase from a hymn or some miracle God had worked in my life. And I'd have to meditate on it right then and there, and thank God." He chuckled, "I never thought about what that might look like to anyone else!"

When this man daydreamed, he did not waste mental effort wishing for things he did not have or could have done. Instead, he meditated on the Lord's blessings, His Word, and His will. Similarly, God's people in Nehemiah's day did not obsess over adversities, setbacks, and missteps in their lives. Rather, they meditated on what He had done and was doing for them. In turn, this became the basis for them expressing thanks and praise to Him when they dedicated the wall of Jerusalem.

Performing an Act of Praise. In the Disney movie *Pollyanna,* a young girl is sent to live with her strict aunt Polly. Soon the girl learns that the town is a collection of bullied souls who are afraid to stand up to the girl's wealthy and influential aunt. As a result, the entire populace has a chronic case of speaking disparagingly about their situation.

Pollyanna changes that circumstance when she starts telling people about her father's "happy thought" system: No matter what the situation, people are encouraged to look for the good that can arise from it. Her idea catches on, and soon the entire town is transformed by one girl's better way of seeing the world.

This week challenge your students to reflect on the fresh, creative approaches to praising God you've explored in the lesson. Ask them to make an effort to integrate at least one act of praise into every day. This could be as simple as praying a prayer of thanksgiving every morning or night. It might involve singing to the Lord while walking alone or with a few other believers on a scenic trail. Most obvious of all is gathering in corporate worship to praise God. Doing any or all of these things can work wonders for the attitudes of the class members.

SABBATH REFORMS

BACKGROUND SCRIPTURE: Nehemiah 13:4-31
DEVOTIONAL READING: Mark 2:23-27

Key Verse: I commanded the Levites that they should cleanse themselves, and that they should come and keep the gates, to sanctify the sabbath day. Nehemiah 13:22.

KING JAMES VERSION

NEHEMIAH 13:15 In those days saw I in Judah some treading wine presses on the sabbath, and bringing in sheaves, and lading asses; as also wine, grapes, and figs, and all manner of burdens, which they brought into Jerusalem on the sabbath day: and I testified against them in the day wherein they sold victuals. 16 There dwelt men of Tyre also therein, which brought fish, and all manner of ware, and sold on the sabbath unto the children of Judah, and in Jerusalem. 17 Then I contended with the nobles of Judah, and said unto them, What evil thing is this that ye do, and profane the sabbath day? 18 Did not your fathers thus, and did not our God bring all this evil upon us, and upon this city? yet ye bring more wrath upon Israel by profaning the sabbath. 19 And it came to pass, that when the gates of Jerusalem began to be dark before the sabbath, I commanded that the gates should be shut, and charged that they should not be opened till after the sabbath: and some of my servants set I at the gates, that there should no burden be brought in on the sabbath day. 20 So the merchants and sellers of all kind of ware lodged without Jerusalem once or twice. 21 Then I testified against them, and said unto them, Why lodge ye about the wall? if ye do so again, I will lay hands on you. From that time forth came they no more on the sabbath. 22 And I commanded the Levites that they should cleanse themselves, and that they should come and keep the gates, to sanctify the sabbath day. Remember me, O my God, concerning this also, and spare me according to the greatness of thy mercy.

NEW REVISED STANDARD VERSION

NEHEMIAH 13:15 In those days I saw in Judah people treading wine presses on the sabbath, and bringing in heaps of grain and loading them on donkeys; and also wine, grapes, figs, and all kinds of burdens, which they brought into Jerusalem on the sabbath day; and I warned them at that time against selling food. 16 Tyrians also, who lived in the city, brought in fish and all kinds of merchandise and sold them on the sabbath to the people of Judah, and in Jerusalem. 17 Then I remonstrated with the nobles of Judah and said to them, "What is this evil thing that you are doing, profaning the sabbath day? 18 Did not your ancestors act in this way, and did not our God bring all this disaster on us and on this city? Yet you bring more wrath on Israel by profaning the sabbath."

19 When it began to be dark at the gates of Jerusalem before the sabbath, I commanded that the doors should be shut and gave orders that they should not be opened until after the sabbath. And I set some of my servants over the gates, to prevent any burden from being brought in on the sabbath day. 20 Then the merchants and sellers of all kinds of merchandise spent the night outside Jerusalem once or twice. 21 But I warned them and said to them, "Why do you spend the night in front of the wall? If you do so again, I will lay hands on you." From that time on they did not come on the sabbath. 22 And I commanded the Levites that they should purify themselves and come and guard the gates, to keep the sabbath day holy. Remember this also in my favor, O my God, and spare me according to the greatness of your steadfast love.

13

Monday, August 19	Exodus 16:13-26	*A Sabbath to the Lord*
Tuesday, August 20	Exodus 31:12-18	*Keep the Sabbath Holy*
Wednesday, August 21	Isaiah 58:9c-14	*Honoring the Sabbath*
Thursday, August 22	Mark 2:23-27	*The Lord of the Sabbath*
Friday, August 23	Mark 3:1-6	*Doing Good on the Sabbath*
Saturday, August 24	Nehemiah 13:4-14	*Restoring the Sanctity of the Temple*
Sunday, August 25	Nehemiah 13:15-22	*Restoring the Sanctity of the Sabbath*

BACKGROUND

Nehemiah's book ends on a bittersweet note. In 432 B.C., after spending time back in Persia (see 5:14; 13:6), this extraordinary, forceful man returned to Jerusalem for a second term as governor of Judah. Nehemiah's walls still stood firm, but his spiritual reforms were in disarray. He immediately began to take corrective action. Perhaps Nehemiah's prayers of frustration recorded in chapter 13 are a fitting way for this period of Old Testament history to end. After all, the best human efforts to keep God's commandments usually fail—then as now. The final chapter of Nehemiah virtually calls out to God to send the promised Messiah and make things new.

At some point after the dedication of the walls of Jerusalem, the "book of Moses" (vs. 1) was being read at a public assembly. Nehemiah's first reforms began when the law was read during the Feast of Tabernacles (see 7:73–8:18). It was appropriate that the second set of reforms should begin in the same way. When Deuteronomy 23:3-6 was read, the participants discovered that the Mosaic law banned certain foreigners from the assembly of God's people because of how their ancestors had treated Israel when the nation approached Canaan to conquer it (Neh. 13:2). As before, the public reading of Scripture had a powerful practical impact on its hearers. The Jews began expelling unconverted aliens from their communities (vs. 3).

NOTES ON THE PRINTED TEXT

Earlier in the book, Nehemiah had asked God to remember his care for the poor and the wickedness of his opponents (see Neh. 5:19; 6:14). In the governor's prayer recorded in 13:14, he feared all the advances he had made might be lost. He pleaded with God to preserve the new reforms enacted for the temple and its services. Nehemiah recognized how deviations from the stipulations recorded in the Mosaic law could undermine the spiritual and moral vitality of the covenant community. A case in point would be the observance of the Sabbath. Years before, Nehemiah had faced foreign merchants coming to Jerusalem to sell goods on the Sabbath (see 10:31). At that time, the Jews had decided to accept the practice. After all, they weren't the ones running the shops.

In Nehemiah's absence, disregarding Sabbath violations by foreigners had led to Jewish physical labor as well as Jewish commercial activity on the Sabbath. For instance, on that holy day, Nehemiah saw the local residents of Judah treading wine-presses. Others loaded onto their donkeys sacks filled with grain, grapes, figs, and other agricultural products so that these could be brought to Jerusalem and sold in the city. The situation had reached a critical point and Nehemiah decided to take corrective action. Specifically, he directed his fellow Jews to stop selling "victuals" (13:15) on the Sabbath.

"Tyre" (vs. 16) was a port city in Phoenicia on the Mediterranean coast north of Jerusalem. At that time, Tyre was regarded as the commercial capital of the entire region. Nehemiah learned that merchants from the seaport were transporting salted and dried fish, along with a wide variety of other goods, into the city. Then, on the Sabbath, the foreigners sold their merchandise to Jewish residents. Nehemiah dealt with the irreligious Phoenicians by confronting the prominent leaders of Judah. The governor questioned how they could profane the Sabbath day by allowing an evil activity to occur in the holy city (vs. 17). Nehemiah reasoned that the ancestors of the Jewish remnant were guilty of similar transgressions. In turn, these violations of the Mosaic law were the basis for God bringing about the horror of the exile and the destruction of Jerusalem. Nehemiah accused the officials of bringing more of God's "wrath" (vs. 18) down on "Israel" by allowing the Sabbath to be profaned.

After rebuking the nobles of Judah for allowing the Sabbath to be profaned, Nehemiah did not fall into inactivity. Instead, he waited until the next Sabbath, when he ordered the gates of Jerusalem to be closed and barred. He issued the directive as the shadows of late afternoon darkened the recesses of the doorways (vs. 19). The Sabbath officially began at sundown, but the governor shut the gates early and posted his personal guards to emphasize that business hours were done until the following evening. For the first couple of weeks, merchants showed up outside the locked gates of Jerusalem as they had done before (vs. 20). They either had not heard or did not believe the Jews were strictly observing the Sabbath. Nehemiah finally confronted the merchants with the pointed question as to why they were camping out during the night by the city wall. Then the governor sent them away with a threat that he would take decisive action if they showed up again before the start of the Sabbath (vs. 21).

Nehemiah directed the Levities to go through a ritual purification ceremony. Doing so was in keeping with the sacred nature of the Sabbath day. Afterward, they were to stand guard at the Jerusalem gates during the 24-hour period of the Sabbath to ensure that it was not profaned by any sacrilegious commercial activity. Once more, Nehemiah asked God to "remember" (vs. 22) him. In this case, the petition did not just mean to call to mind, for the governor was not afraid that God would forget about him. Rather, in this context, to "remember" means to intervene. Specifically,

Nehemiah asked God to show His servant grace and loving mercy by preserving the work he had done for God's people.

When Nehemiah noticed that the situation was amiss in Judah, he started with a problem in the heart of everything—the integrity of the Jerusalem temple. Then, he attacked the problem of ignoring the Sabbath. Finally, he went after an issue that extended through the whole nation, namely, intermarriage. Nehemiah began in the center and worked out. More than 25 years earlier, Ezra had imposed the drastic measure of sending away foreign wives (see Ezra 9–10). When Nehemiah returned from Persia for his second term as governor, the practice had surfaced again (Neh. 13:23).

In the streets of Jerusalem and other towns or villages of Judah, the governor heard children who spoke the languages of their mothers from the Mediterranean coast or the lands east of the Jordan River (vs. 24). Nehemiah did not approach this problem through the leaders of the people, as he had the previous two problems. Instead, he went directly to the fathers who had arranged these marriages with foreigners, and he did not treat them gently (vs. 25). He scolded the fathers. The governor invoked the curses that accompanied the Mosaic covenant they had made with God (see 10:29). Nehemiah also physically struck some of the offenders and pulled the hair of their beards.

Finally, Nehemiah compelled those who had given their children in marriage to foreigners to swear an oath in God's name that they would not repeat the practice with their younger sons and daughters. The governor preached a short sermon about the dire consequences of King Solomon's prolific intermarriage with foreign women (13:26). Nehemiah reminded his fellow Jews how that national hero—one of Israel's greatest kings, whom God loved—had fallen into grievous sin and led the nation after him to violate the Mosaic law. Nehemiah asked them rhetorically whether they wanted to do the same thing in their generation through their sons and daughters (vs. 27).

The worst incident of intermarriage with a foreigner involved a member of the high priestly family and a daughter of Sanballat—one of Nehemiah's archenemies during the construction of the walls of Jerusalem (vs. 28). The governor would not allow that kind of spiritual corruption so close to the high priesthood. Nehemiah prayed that God would deal in the same way with those who defiled the priesthood (vs. 29). This kind of depravity immediately touched the entire covenant God made with His people and the Levitical community, who stood between the Lord and His people as servants.

Consequently, Nehemiah once again reviewed the organization and practices of the priests and Levites to be sure nothing inappropriate compromised their holiness to the Lord (vs. 30). The governor verified that all the duties connected with the temple and the sacrificial system were properly assigned and carried out. Also, he once again organized the rotating system of responsibility for the temple wood supply (vs. 31). Finally, Nehemiah motivated the general populace to be faithful in bringing its first-fruits to supply the needs of the temple and its servants. The governor's final words capture the energy that restored the walls of Jerusalem and the spiritual integrity of the postexilic Jewish community. "Remember me, O my God, for good," Nehemiah prayed. "For good" virtually reads "with favor." In other words, the governor asked the Lord for His refreshing blessing on His servant's life as a reward for his faithfulness.

SUGGESTIONS TO TEACHERS

The people of Judah in Nehemiah's day had mixed-up priorities. They were supposed to honor Him by keeping the Sabbath holy. Instead, they dishonored Him by allowing commercial activity to occur on that sacred day (see Neh. 13:15-16).

1. KNOW GOD'S PRIORITIES. God wants us to know His priorities and embrace them. Sometimes, however, we get caught up in our own plans and desires. They seem so important that we can see nothing else. As the Lord did with His people through Nehemiah, He might need to intervene and undo our plans to get our attention and turn our focus toward His priorities.

2. LOOK TO GOD'S WORD FOR DISCERNMENT. If we're confused about priorities, God's Word is still the best source for determining what's most important. Some godly priorities we can be certain of include caring for our families (see 1 Tim. 5:8), loving other Christians (see 1 John 4:21), and making disciples (see Matt. 28:19-20).

3. BE ACCOUNTABLE TO OTHERS. Another way of checking our priorities is being accountable to other mature believers who see where we're putting our efforts and energies. Believers who know and care about us can help shift our focus when needed. They can redirect us to what is truly meaningful and eternal, especially if they see us putting too much of our energy into our jobs or material needs.

4. RELY COMPLETELY ON GOD FOR HELP. God does not play hide-and-seek with His priorities. As we discovered in this week's lesson, He has revealed them in His Word. We can be encouraged, knowing that He promises to give us direction and equip as we begin to obey Him.

 FOR ADULTS

■ **TOPIC:** Getting It Right

■ **QUESTIONS:** 1. Why was it important for God's people in the Old Testament to observe the Sabbath? 2. Why did Nehemiah put a stop to foreign merchants conducting business in Jerusalem on the Sabbath? 3. What reason did Nehemiah give to the leaders of Judah to keep the Sabbath holy? 4. What can you do to encourage the leaders in your church to honor the Lord in their ministerial activities? 5. How can you ensure that your faith is strong enough for you to do the right thing, even if you seem to be the only one doing it?

■ ILLUSTRATIONS:

Following the Teachings of God's Word. God wanted His people to observe the Sabbath. This mind-set is different from our modern way of thinking. Supposedly, we can choose which of God's moral principles to keep and forget the rest.

In this cultural climate, it's hard for believers to be unequivocal about the commands of God's Word. On the one hand, they don't want to be considered narrow minded and intolerant by their peers. On the other hand, believers know that what the Lord has revealed in Scripture is best for society as well as their individual lives.

Therefore, we cannot afford to explain away the principles and priorities of God's Word. It's also unwise to tone down or make exceptions to His commands just to gain popular approval. After all, so much of society is at risk, and so many people's lives are messed up. So we must insist, as Nehemiah did in his day, that the only way to improvement lies in following the teachings of God's Word.

The "One Thing." In the classic Billy Crystal movie *City Slickers* three longtime friends face middle age. And in their identity crisis, they find themselves losing their focus and in danger of losing their families. To reignite the fire in their lives, these city slickers sign up as "cowboys." Their job is to help a dude ranch move its herd of cattle from high in the hills down to the lower valley.

A grizzled old cowboy named Curly leads the dudes. He seems to be the toughest, canniest, and wisest person the three have ever met. Billy Crystal asks the usually tight-lipped cowpoke what makes his life seem so strong, centered, and sure. Curly smiles, raises his grubby, gloved index finger, and proclaims, "It is just one thing." Then, without saying another word, he suddenly rides away. Billy's character spends the rest of the movie frantically trying to figure out what Curly meant. What is that mysterious "one thing"?

Experts of all stripes warn us not to expect one person to provide for all our emotional, intellectual, and relational needs. But what might be true for our human connections does not hold true for our deepest spiritual needs. Nehemiah tried to get the people of Judah to recognize that their relationship with God was more important than the prospect of making more money buying and selling goods on the Sabbath. Likewise today, there is only one person who can satisfy our deepest longings, namely, the Lord Jesus.

Different Destinies. Tom lay seriously ill in the intensive care unit of the hospital after having major surgery. Although a good family man, he had not been a faithful, practicing Christian. Did he understand the different destinies that confronted him? He heard the pastor's words about the Father's love and forgiveness in the Son. How hard it was to be sure whether he understood his need to admit his sins and receive the Savior.

Sadly, many people are like Tom. They do not reach out to God early in life, even though they have a religious upbringing. God is not a major factor in their lives. They do not realize that the choice they make in this life will determine their future in the next. Nehemiah made different destinies clear when he warned the leaders of Judah about bringing more "wrath" (Neh. 13:18) on God's people due to their profaning of the "sabbath." How much better it is to turn to God as our loving Father than to receive His just condemnation in the end. Our lives will be filled with His eternal blessings when we choose to live responsibly in the community of faith.

FOR YOUTH

■ **TOPIC:** Profane No Gain!

■ **QUESTIONS:** 1. What was the Sabbath? 2. Why did Nehemiah object to the people of Judah doing work on the Sabbath? 3. How did Nehemiah confront the foreign merchants who kept trying to sell their goods in Jerusalem on the Sabbath? 4. How can you tactfully communicate your commitment to obey God, especially to those who would like you to fudge a little? 5. How can you become more like Nehemiah in your passion for serving God?

■ **ILLUSTRATIONS:**

Following God's Will. In Nehemiah's day, the people of Judah and Jerusalem were conducting business on the Sabbath. Nehemiah warned them not to desecrate that holy day. He noted that their ancestors' violation of the Sabbath had displeased God and led to their long exile from their homeland (see Neh. 13:15-18). The decision to follow God's will in every area of life remains just as imperative for young people today.

Jim's best friend and fellow athlete went for a drive one night. Earl seemed like a good guy who went to church. Despite the fact that they were both under the legal drinking age, Earl took a six-pack of beer in his car and urged Jim to drink a can with him. Jim refused. From then on the two drifted apart, Earl into a rather typical pattern of short-term jobs and drinking and Jim into the ministry.

Of course, that one decision did not determine how the two would live their lives. But it does illustrate the different choices young people have to make, not just about drinking but also about sexual practices, using drugs, cheating in class, and so on. That's why we should teach and demonstrate that Christian ethical values differ sharply from the world's profane moral code.

Profit and Loss. In Nehemiah's second session as governor of Judah, he discovered that God's people placed a higher value on making a profit on the Sabbath than on honoring Him. They decided it was more important for them to obtain as much money as possible buying and selling earthly goods than doing what was right.

More recently, firefighters were stunned by a tragedy that had happened during a four-alarm blaze in a condo development at the edge of some suburbs. The people who lived in these units were middle class, and most of them worked at a nearby tech center. One casualty of the blaze was Jarrod.

Until then, Jarrod seemed like a normal 15-year-old. He loved life and was very popular. He also loved sports—especially collecting sports memorabilia and cards. He had a collection that was worth well into five figures. When the firefighters first arrived at the condos, the place was slowly smoldering. Thankfully, they were able to get everyone out of the units before the fire got out of control. When Jarrod and his brothers came out, their parents and neighbors embraced them.

Then, as the fire began to roar up again, Jarrod demanded, "My card collection! Somebody's got to save my card collection!" The firefighters warned Jarrod that no firefighter would risk her or his life going into the smoky condo for a collection of baseball cards. Suddenly, Jarrod bolted for the front door of his unit. Before anyone could catch him, he was inside. When the firefighters entered with their smoke hoods in place, it was too late. Jarrod had died of smoke inhalation while still clutching a box of card binders. His possessions had cost him his life!

Decisions That Make a Difference. In Nehemiah's day, the people of Judah had made a decision. They would profane the Sabbath by conducting commercial activity in Jerusalem on that holy day. The governor warned them that if they continued to do so, they risked bringing "more wrath upon Israel" (Neh. 13:18).

Even today, our decisions can make a tremendous difference for us. Cheryl's life story is an appropriate example. As she made her way out of the courtroom, Cheryl smirked at the prosecutor. In disgust, the official threw down his notepad. As on previous occasions, a legal technicality had rescued Cheryl, enabling her to be freed from legal custody. It was another loss for justice and another step toward spiritual darkness for Cheryl.

The young woman had been in courtrooms since childhood, first for custody hearings, but soon for a variety of crimes. Cheryl was a "habitual offender" who knew how to play the system, and she was rarely convicted. Among the crowd of unsavory characters she ran with, she was affectionately known as "Cheryl: Princess of Thieves."

Three years later, the same prosecutor again had his grip on Cheryl. She was sentenced to two years in jail. While serving her time, Cheryl was gloriously saved. She said it was the persistent witness of a volunteer chaplain who had made the difference.

When Cheryl got out of jail, she went right back to her old crowd, but with a calling from God to win them for Christ. Cheryl took her responsibility seriously. She shared the Good News with them, and the results were extraordinary. Her unconditional love was her pulpit, and her changed life was her message.

See the
Power *of* God

through the stories of ordinary people facing extraordinary circumstances

This popular digest-sized resource is filled with gripping articles about Christians living out their faith. With a focus on start-up ministries, world missions, and challenging issues, *Power for Living* provides a unique perspective on the power of God in all areas of life.

QUARTERLY EDITIONS FEATURE:

- Thirteen lead articles with a variety of faith-based stories

- *Christian Classics* feature, highlighting perspectives from theologians such as D.L. Moody and Charles Spurgeon

- Daily Bible Readings to encourage daily Bible study

- Coordinates with adult David C Cook curriculums

Great for
personal growth
& evangelism

Power for Living

Holiness
ARE WE PURSUING IT?

300.323.7543   DavidCCook.com

David C Cook®
transforming lives together